DATE DUE

OC 18 '04			
DE 2 3 '04			
NO 17 '04			
AP 15 '05			
NO 5 '04			
NO 2 2 '04			
DE 8 '04			

DEMCO 38-296

THE ORGANIZATION
AND CONTROL
OF AMERICAN SCHOOLS

THE ORGANIZATION AND CONTROL OF AMERICAN SCHOOLS

SIXTH EDITION

Roald F. Campbell
Late of the University of Utah

Luvern L. Cunningham
The Ohio State University

Raphael O. Nystrand
The University of Louisville

Michael D. Usdan
*Institute for Education Leadership
and Fordham University*

Merrill, an imprint of
Macmillan Publishing Company
New York

Collier Macmillan Canada, Inc.
Toronto

Maxwell Macmillan International Publishing Group
New York   Oxford   Singapore   Sydney

Macmillan Publishing Company
866 Third Avenue
New York, NY 10022

This book was set in Garamond.

Administrative Editor: David Faherty
Production Editor: Sharon Rudd
Art Coordinator: Ruth Ann Kimpel
Cover Designer: Brian Deep:

Library of Congress Catalog Card Number: 89-62920
International Standard Book Number: 0-675-21126-3
Printed in the United States of America
    4   5   6   7   8   9—94   93

*W*e dedicate this book to Roald Fay Campbell, lead author of this book through six editions, who died September 17, 1988. Professor Campbell was a giant figure in the field of educational administration over nearly five decades. The first edition was developed under his leadership as he served as director of the Midwest Administrative Center at the University of Chicago in the early 1960s. Later editions were completed while he served as the Novice G. Fawcett Professor of Educational Administration at Ohio State University and as professor emeritus of Educational Administration at the University of Utah. He was a marvelous friend, mentor, and colleague, exhibiting intellectual strength and leadership over the quarter-century of this volume's history. We feel his loss deeply and will be guided by his high standards of scholarship and professionalism always.

Preface

Our main purpose in this book is to examine the nation's schools in terms of the complex milieu in which they are embedded. Understanding American schools requires such an approach, for each state and its educational system stand in a reciprocal relationship with society as a whole. In our democratic society, the school not only exerts influence, but influence in many forms is exerted upon it.

Our perspective for viewing these relationships is that of the open systems theory. From this perspective, control is much more than a legal concept. The variables affecting the school are numerous and complex; they are both obvious and subtle, formal and informal. The better school administrators understand these variables, the more effectively they can perform. Although specific events and actors in educational systems change over time, certain structures and processes persist.

A major change in this edition is a new chapter that explicates important demographic changes in our nation. This discussion in Chapter 2 establishes the context for considering issues and actors in the organization and control of schools and makes clear that the future of our educational system is likely to differ substantially from its past. In systems terms, the schools will be called on to respond to contextual or environmental changes.

The roles of individuals within open systems are emphasized. The roles of school administrators, school board members, teachers, and citizens as they participate in the processes of school governance are described and analyzed. Another new chapter focuses on the role of school principals, in recognition of their strategic importance to educational reform and the growing emphasis on school-based management. Special attention is also given to the superintendency and the importance of this office in the future of American education. The function of the school board and the significance of the school board/superintendent relationship are examined in the context of local control and administration of schools.

During the 1980s, our country witnessed a demonstration of interest in education comparable to, and perhaps even greater than, that which followed the launching of Sputnik by the Soviet Union in the late 1950s. The subsequent emphasis on improving education, particularly in science and mathematics, has been explained as a reaction to a perceived military challenge. The more recent interest is in response to a perceived economic challenge—the need to retool the American economy in order to compete more effectively in world markets and in a highly technological world society. A number of distinguished state and national commissions issued reports that indicted American schools for a range of shortcomings, urged new commitments to excellence, and suggested various means of achieving it. Many of these reports noted the relationship between education and economic development, acknowledged the dramatically changing economy, and called for educational improvements to ensure that our society keeps pace. As America moves into the 1990s, the promulgation of reports and recommendations continues at a vigorous pace, and commentators discuss moving through a second wave of school reform into yet a third. By all accounts, the education issue has occupied the public attention span well beyond the time usually accorded public issues.

This reawakened and continuing public interest in education has intensified activity at all levels of school governance. The action has been particularly intense at the state level, where numerous legislatures have enacted reforms dealing with such matters as requirements for high school graduation; certification, evaluation, and compensation of teachers and administrators; essentials skills testing; and programs for gifted and talented students. Despite some reversion at the federal level, the formal involvement of both federal and state government in schooling continues to be substantial, and much of this involvement has been regulatory. Likewise, court decisions continue to be a prominent influence on school policymaking.

The federal and state presence in school affairs has often come at the behest of citizens groups. Moreover, many of these groups possess considerable political sophisticiation and realize that they can pursue their objectives not only by petitioning school officials but by appealing to public opinion and to various agencies that have some jurisdiction regarding schools. As a consequence, school policy matters are increasingly caught up in interagency conflicts, jurisdictional disputes, and appellate reviews.

In studying the control of education, the administrator is dependent on the social and behavioral sciences. This book draws on concepts and research findings from the disciplines of psychology, sociology, and political science, and economics. The schools are institutions designed to serve particular social purposes. They are part of a larger social system, linked through formal structures of government to a vast array of influences that affect the course of decision making. The many influences exerted by the larger social system are mediated by the subsystem, the schools.

As in past editions, we have tried once again to make predictions about the course of future events. Each chapter closes with a brief overview of coming developments as we see them and a summary of major control factors discussed in the chapter. The final chapter recapitulates and synthesizes these factors in a general discussion of control elements affecting schools.

This book has been written essentially for students of school administration, administrators in public and nonpublic schools, the academic community, and interested lay persons, especially school board members. This volume will also be useful as the source book for any teacher or other professional who wishes to understand the dynamics of school operation. Since this work deals with the stresses and strains present in most local school environments, much of our analysis will be of value to nonschool people responsible for thinking through and acting on school issues.

Our gratitude is extended to the many scholars and practitioners who have helped with this manuscript in various ways, especially those who have offered thoughtful criticisms, among them Philip Kearney (University of Michigan), Glenn Schroeder (University of Northern Colorado), and Lowell Jackson (University of Idaho). We are also grateful to the many researchers and practitioners from whom we have acquired data and new ideas. We are particularly indebted to Roderick F. McPhee, coauthor of the first and second editions, whose contributions continue to be evident in this edition.

Contents

1   **SCHOOLS IN THE AMERICAN SCENE**   1

A Statistical Picture of American Schools   3

Schools as Open Systems   4

     Organization, 7 □ Control, 8 □ Schools, 9

The Development of American Schools   10

     A Brief Overview, 10 □ Some Legal Milestones, 11 □ Persistent
Issues, 15

Plan for the Book   19

2   **CHANGING DEMOGRAPHIC SETTING OF SCHOOLS**   22

The New Demographic Picture   23

Changes in Family Structure   25

Some Characteristics of Students   27

     Numbers, 27 □ Distribution, 28 □ Socioeconomic Composition, 29

Implications for Schools   30

Summary and Future Prospects   36

3   AMERICAN SCHOOLS AND
    THE FEDERAL GOVERNMENT   42

From Dual to National Federalism   43

Dual Governments, 43 □ National Federalism, 44 □ Import for
Education, 45

Early Federal Relations   46

Land Grants, 46 □ Vocational Education, 47 □ Depression
Legislation, 48 □ Other Federal Programs, 49 □ The United States
Office of Education, 49 □ Nature of Early Federal Activities, 50

Rapid Expansion of Federal Influence   50

The GI Bills, 50 □ The National Science Foundation, 51 □ The
Cooperative Research Program, 52 □ The National Defense
Education Act, 53 □ Vocational Education, 53 □ The Elementary
and Secondary Education Act of 1965, 54

Vacillation During the 1970s   55

Reappraisal of Programs, 55 □ The President and Congress, 56 □
National Assessment, 56 □ Reorganization of the Federal Agency, 57
□ Greater Federal Intrusion, 58

The Reagan Reversion: The First Term   60

The Proposals, 61 □ Response to Proposals, 62

The Reagan Second Term   65

The Era of Secretary Bennett   66

Some Implications, 67

Summary and Future Prospects   69

Federal Controls, 69 □ Outlook for the Future, 70

4   AMERICAN SCHOOLS AND STATE GOVERNMENT   76

The Development of a State Structure   76

Early Movements, 76 □ From General to Special Government, 79

The Emerging Role of the States   81

Conditions Stimulating Change, 81 □ New Expressions of the State
Role, 83

Current Organizational Arrangements   85

Responsibilities of the Legislature, 85 □ State Executive
Arrangements, 86 □ Delegation to Local Agencies, 89

Decisions Made at the State Level   91

The Instructional Program, 91 □ Certification of Personnel, 93 □
Facilities Standards, 93 □ Financial Support, 94 □ Nonpublic
Schools, 95

Suggested Functions of the State Education Agency   95

Summary and Future Prospects   99

State Controls, 99 □ Outlook for the Future, 101

5   THE LOCAL SCHOOL DISTRICT   105

The School District in Local Government   105

What a School District Is   106

Origin and Development of School Districts, 110 □ Legal Basis of
School Districts, 111 □ School Districts and Municipalities, 112 □
Fiscal Independence, 114 □ Reorganization of Districts, 115

The Current Scene   121

Summary and Future Prospects   125

6   THE INTERMEDIATE UNIT
    OF SCHOOL ADMINISTRATION   132

Development of the Intermediate Unit   133

The Status of the Intermediate Unit   136

Needed or Not?, 137 □ The Question of Function, 138 □ The
Question of Structure, 141

Socioeconomic Forces Affecting the Intermediate Unit   143

Growth in Technology, 143 □ School District Reorganization, 144 □
Demographic Trends, 144

Summary and Future Prospects   146

7   SCHOOL ATTENDANCE AREAS   153

What an Attendance Area Is   154

Decisions on Boundary Formations   157

Geographical-Organizational Problems, 157 □ Political-Social
Problems, 159

Community Control and Decentralization   164

Three Cases   168

Case A, 168 □ Case B, 169 □ Case C, 170 □ Significance of Cases,
172

Summary and Future Prospects   173

8 THE COURTS   **178**

Structure of the American Judicial System   178

  Some Early History, 179 □ The Federal Court System, 179 □ The
  State Court Systems, 182

Premises and Processes of Judicial Policymaking   185

  Some Basic Premises, 185 □ Judicial Trends in Education, 186 □
  The Basis of Federal Involvement, 186 □ Compliance with Judicial
  Decisions, 189

Examples of Judicial Influence   191

  School Desegregation, 191 □ School Finance Reform, 196

Summary and Future Prospects   198

9 THE BOARD OF EDUCATION   **204**

The Control Function   205

  Mandatory Powers and Obligations, 208 □ Discretionary Powers
  and Obligations, 208 □ Ethical Responsibilities, 209

Selection of School Board Members   211

  Appointive Systems, 211 □ Elective Systems, 213 □ Motives for
  Seeking School Board Posts, 214

Men and Women Who Serve   215

  Their Characteristics, 217 □ Community Ties, 218

Commentary on Research   219

Local Control and Contemporary American Scene   224

Summary and Future Prospects   227

10 THE SUPERINTENDENT OF SCHOOLS   **236**

Kinds and Numbers of Superintendents   236

  Evolution of the Position, 237 □ Legal Definition and Status, 239

Characteristics of Superintendents   241

Concept of the Position   243

  Scientific Management, 243 □ Human Relations, 244 □
  Bureaucracy, 245 □ Open Systems, 246

Professional Development of the Superintendency   247

  Preparation Programs, 248 □ The Superintendency as a Career, 249

The Role of the Superintendent   250

  Place in the Organization, 250 □ What Superintendents Do, 251 □
  Administration and Leadership, 253 □ The Superintendent and the
  Environment, 254

The Influence of the Superintendent   255

    Influence on the Board, 255 □ Influence on the Staff, 257 □
    Influence on the Local Community, 259 □ Influence on the Larger
    Community, 260

Summary and Future Prospects   260

    Influence of the Superintendent, 260 □ Outlook for the Future, 261

11 **SCHOOL PRINCIPALS AND CENTRAL OFFICE STAFF**   269

The Principalship   269

    History of Position, 269 □ Middle Management, 271 □ Principals at
    Work, 272 □ Debate on Principal's Role, 275

Central Office Staff   279

    History of Central Office Positions, 279 □ Major Issues, 281

Some Organizational Problems   282

    Differing Views of Administration, 282 □ Bureaucracy and
    Professionalism, 283 □ Conflicting Environmental Influences, 284
    □ Selection and Evaluation of Administrators, 285 □ Continuing
    Professional Development, 287

Models of Administrative Power   288

    An Early Model, 288 □ The Open Systems View, 289

Summary and Future Prospects   290

    Influence of the Hierarchy, 290 □ Outlook for the Future, 291

12 **THE TEACHERS**   297

The Teacher in America: Past and Present   297

    Professional Criteria, 299

Characteristics of the Teacher Group   301

Teachers Organizations   303

    National Groups, 303 □ State Teacher Organizations, 310 □ Local
    Teacher Organizations, 312

Associations, Unions, and Control   313

    Political Activism, 313 □ The Bargaining Role, 315

Informal Organization   316

    Teachers' Influence, 317

Recent Developments   320

Summary and Future Prospects   323

13 SCHOOL-ORIENTED GROUPS 329

Organizations with State and National Affiliations 329

The National Congress of Parents and Teachers, 329 □ The National
School Boards Association, 333 □ The National Citizens
Commission for the Public Schools, 335 □ The National Committee
for Support of the Public Schools, 337 □ The National Committee
for Citizens in Education, 338 □ The Council for Basic Education,
339

Locally Based Groups 342

Background of the New Participation, 342 □ Objectives of Citizen
Participation, 345

Summary and Future Prospects 347

14 OTHER INTEREST GROUPS 353

Groups Concerned with Ideology 354

Racial Minorities 356

Black Americans, 357 □ Other Minority Groups, 359

The Issue: Equal Educational Opportunity 363

The Approach: Due Process and Direct Action 365

The Feminist Movement and Women's Organizations 367

Business Organizations 375

Interest Groups and the Political Process 378

The Function of Interest Groups, 378

Summary and Future Prospects 380

15 AVAILABILITY OF RESOURCES 386

Differentials in Wealth 386

Among School Districts, 386 □ Among States, 387 □ The Role of
Federal Aid, 388 □ Financial Resources and Control, 390

Differentials in Governmental Access 391

Operating Funds, 391 □ Governmental Access and Control, 393

Differentials in Aspiration 393

Kind of Education Desired, 394 □ Quality of Education Desired,
396 □ Aspirations and Control, 398

Recent Trends 399

Reform of the State School Finance Programs, 399 □ Tax Limitation,
401 □ School Reexamination, 401

Summary and Future Prospects 403

16 COLLEGE INFLUENCES   407

The Historical Relationship   407

The Latin School, 407 □ The Growth of Colleges, 408 □ The
Academies and the Common High Schools, 409 □ New Disciplines,
410 □ The Committee of Ten, 411 □ The Cardinal Principles, 412

College Influences on School Programs   413

The College Entrance Examination Board, 413 □ Testing Programs,
415 □ The Advanced Placement Program, 417 □ Changing
Admissions Standards, 417 □ New Developments in Curriculum, 418
□ Accrediting Agencies, 419 □ Preparation of Teachers and
Administrators, 421

Summary and Future Prospects   423

17 NONPUBLIC SCHOOLS AND OTHER ALTERNATIVES   428

Nonpublic Schools Yesterday and Today   429

Controls on Nonpublic Schools, 430 □ Nonpublic School Statistics,
431

Types of Nonpublic Schools   433

Sectarian Schools, 436 □ Nonsectarian Schools, 440

The Alternative School Movement   442

Status of Alternatives Within Public Schools, 444 □ National Calls
for Reform, 446 □ Vouchers and Tuition Tax Credits, 449 □ Home
Schooling, 450 □ Entrepreneurial Schools, 451

Summary and Future Prospects   452

18 CONTROL ELEMENTS: SUMMARY AND CONCLUSIONS   458

The Control Categories   458

Demographic Control Elements, 459 □ Legal Control Elements, 461
□ Structural Control Elements, 463 □ Ideational Control Elements,
465 □ Knowledge Control Elements, 468 □ Financial Control
Elements, 470 □ Network Control Elements, 472

General Nature of Controls   474

Controls and Open Systems, 476

INDEX   479

1
Schools in the American Scene

On October 17, 1979, President Jimmy Carter signed Public Law 96–88 which established the Department of Education. He commented at the time, "My guess is that the best move for the quality of life in America in the future might very well be this establishment of this new Department of Education, because it will open up for the first time some very substantial benefits for our country."[1] His formal statement noted that the department bill "will increase the Nation's attention to education . . . make Federal education programs more accountable . . . streamline administration of aid to education programs . . . (and) ensure that local communities retain control of their schools and education programs."[2]

Less than two years later, Ronald Reagan replaced Jimmy Carter in the White House and declared his intention to dissolve the new Department of Education. For the next eight years, the Reagan administration sought reductions in federal spending for education and cut back government regulations in some areas. However, the administration soon abandoned its proposal to dissolve the department. Indeed, by 1987, Secretary of Education William Bennett was proposing increases in some federal education programs for fiscal 1989.[3]

These developments will be considered in more detail in Chapter 3. Here it is sufficient to note that they raise questions about the federal presence in education that have continuing relevance. Why was the Department of Education established? What does it do? Why did President Reagan want to terminate it? Why did he not follow through with this? What import does the presence of the Department of Education have for local and state control of education? Answers to these questions suggest that education is a national as well as a state and local concern, as indicated by the following vignettes.

In a speech on January 28, 1983, Governor Lamar Alexander of Tennessee outlined his Better Schools Program, calling it "the most important proposal I will make in my eight years as governor." The cornerstone of his proposal was a Master Teacher Program, which he described as "an incentive pay system that will make teaching a fully professional career, draw our best young people into it, keep our best teachers in it, challenge our best teachers to do even better, and inspire excellence in our classrooms by rewarding excellence in our teachers."[4]

In the same speech, Alexander said he would propose a general tax increase to support the Better Schools Program. The Tennessee Education Association (TEA) responded to the governor's proposal by supporting other elements of the Better Schools Program while stating strong objections to the Master Teacher Program. The governor responded that this was "the heart" of his program and that he would not support a general tax increase without provision for the Master Teacher Program. Thus the battle lines were drawn for a very contentious legislative session.

Both the governor and the teachers took their cases to the general public. The governor campaigned so vigorously for his proposal that he gained national recognition as the country's leading advocate of career ladders. The teachers responded that they were not consulted adequately about the plan; that funding it would necessarily impose quotas on the number of teachers at higher levels; that the proposed evaluation systems were cumbersome, expensive, and of doubtful validity; and that all teachers were deserving of a substantial pay raise.

The TEA lobbied successfully and blocked approval of the plan by the 1983 legislature. The governor reacted by vetoing a TEA-supported insurance bill and an across-the-board pay increase of 3 percent for teachers and other state employees. He also stepped up his public campaign on behalf of his plan. At the same time, the legislature established a Select Committee on Education to develop an educational reform package for consideration in 1984, and an Interim Certification Commission was appointed to develop methods of evaluating teachers.

The Select Committee on Education issued its report in November, calling for a reform package that included a career ladder plan. The governor convened a special session of the legislature in January 1984 to consider the reform legislation and the taxes necessary to fund it. The reform program and the accompanying tax package eventually were enacted with the endorsement of the TEA. Its support was gained by modifying Alexander's original proposal in several ways. These included making participation in the career ladder program optional for teachers employed before 1984, removing the quotas associated with various levels of the program, placing more emphasis on local rather than state evaluations of teachers, and establishing a series of "fast-track" options for teachers with at least three years' experience to move beyond the apprentice level of the ladder.[5]

During the initial year of the program, nearly 39,000 of 41,000 eligible teachers elected to participate.[6] However, the program has remained controversial with teachers because of its evaluation procedures and the relatively small numbers of teachers moving to higher levels on the ladder. Challenges to the program in the 1986 session of the legislature were unsuccessful.

Why would a governor be so outspoken and determined regarding an education issue? What does this case suggest about the relationship between state legislatures and teachers? What are the implications of this case for state and local control of schools? Some other kinds of local issues are suggested by the following vignette.

A suburban board of education voted 4–3 not to renew the contract of the superintendent of schools when it would lapse the following spring. Many community residents were displeased by this action and charged that it was taken primarily because the superintendent had exercised strong leadership toward integrating local schools. Members of the board asserted that their action had nothing to do with integration for they too supported this policy. They contended, however, that they found it difficult to work with the superintendent. An estimated fifteen hundred persons, most of them sympathetic to the superintendent, attended the meeting at which the board voted. Before taking this action the board heard from more than fifty speakers, most of whom praised the superintendent and urged the board to retain him. The audience applauded speakers who supported the superintendent, jeered those who spoke against him, and reacted angrily when the decision of the board was announced. Following this action the superintendent reportedly asserted that he had been "hung in a kangaroo court" and demanded an opportunity to defend himself against written charges in an open hearing.

In the days following the board meeting, supporters of the superintendent held demonstrations, wrote letters to newspapers, held press conferences, distributed buttons and bumper stickers, and collected signatures on petitions urging his retention. Seven black members of the caucus that traditionally screened local board of education candidates resigned, charging that "black representation on the caucus does not serve well the interest of the black community." The local teachers' association criticized the manner in which the board acted, threatened to withhold cooperation from any new superintendent selected by the board, and noted the possibility of action "that might preclude the opening of school in the fall."

Finally, after meeting with the local human relations commission, the board unanimously agreed not to act on the superintendent's contract until after the election in the following spring at which three members (two of whom voted to dismiss the superintendent) would be candidates for reelection.

What are the issues here? Why did the board of education choose not to exercise its legal prerogative by holding to its original decision? How and why was such widespread support for the superintendent mobilized? Will carrying the issue over to the next board election resolve the problem? What will be the impact of these events upon interracial and other group relationships in the community? It is with questions like the ones provoked by these vignettes that the authors of this book are concerned.

A STATISTICAL PICTURE OF AMERICAN SCHOOLS

A statistical picture of American elementary and secondary schools is difficult to develop and becomes obsolete in a short time. Even so, a rough approximation of that picture seems necessary at this point. The United States contains both public and nonpublic schools. The public schools are organized into nearly 16,000 operating school districts or basic administrative units. The number of school districts varies widely among the states. For example, there is only 1 district in Hawaii, 24 in Maryland, and more than 1,000 in California, Illinois, and Texas. In the public school districts of the nation there were in 1983 an estimated 58,000 elementary schools and 22,400 secondary schools.[7] In the same year there were an estimated 13,300 nonpublic elementary schools and 2,200 nonpublic high schools.[8] Nonpublic schools include those organized under church auspices as well as those under other private agencies.

Estimated enrollments in public and nonpublic schools for 1981, 1985, and 1990 are shown in Table 1.1. The figures indicate that enrollments declined in the mid-1980s but are beginning to increase at the elementary level. This increase reverses a trend that dates back to the early 1970s.

The number of teachers in public schools in 1985 was approximately 1,190,000 in elementary schools and 960,000 in secondary schools.[9] Nonpublic schools employed approximately 246,000 teachers in elementary schools and 97,000 teachers in secondary schools.[10] Principals, supervisors, and other administrators totaled approximately 300,000 in public schools, and 80,000 persons held comparable positions in nonpublic schools.[11] These figures are shown in Table 1.2.

Estimates for 1985 indicate that public schools expended $159.3 billion for current operation, capital outlay, and debt service. This was more than three times the 1970 expenditure level. The financing of nonpublic schools at the same time was estimated to be $13.3 billion for the same purposes.[12] When combined with expenditures for higher education, these costs represent approximately 6.5 percent of the gross national product. In contrast, total education expenditures represented approximately 7.5 percent of the gross national product in 1970.

SCHOOLS AS OPEN SYSTEMS

We view the organization and control of schools from the perspective of open systems. This view emphasizes the interdependence between an organization and its environment, and is based upon the work of David Easton, who developed a model

TABLE 1.1
Estimated Enrollments in Public and Nonpublic Schools for 1981, 1985, and 1990

	Public			*Nonpublic*		
	1981	1985	1990	1981	1985	1990
Elementary (1–8)	27,665,000	23,762,000	25,606,000	3,692,000	3,560,000	3,760,000
Secondary	13,319,000	12,430,000	10,944,000	1,357,000	1,400,000	1,200,000

Sources: U.S. Bureau of the Census, *Statistical Abstract of the United States,* 103rd Edition (Washington, D.C.: U.S. Government Printing Office, 1982), 132 and U.S. Department of Education, *Digest of Education Statistics, 1985–86* (Washington, D.C.: U.S. Government Printing Office, 1986), 7.

TABLE 1.2
Estimated Education Staff in Public and Nonpublic Schools for 1985

	Public	Nonpublic
Elementary teachers	1,190,000	246,000
Secondary teachers	960,000	97,000
Principals, supervisors and other administrators	300,000	80,000
Total	2,450,000	423,000

of political systems that is helpful in understanding the organization and control of schools.[13] The key concepts in such a model are *system, environment, response,* and *feedback.* A *system* can be defined as any set of variables (e.g., individuals, agencies, governments) that interrelate. It is a political system if it produces authoritative decisions. The *environment* refers to all other systems outside the boundaries of the system under scrutiny. *Response* refers to the actions a system takes in response to stimuli from other systems in its environment, and *feedback* refers to the effect of the system response upon other environmental systems.

The relationship among these concepts is shown in Figure 1.1. The environment produces inputs to the political system which, in an effort to persist, responds by making decisions or policies that result in outputs. These outputs act as feedback to

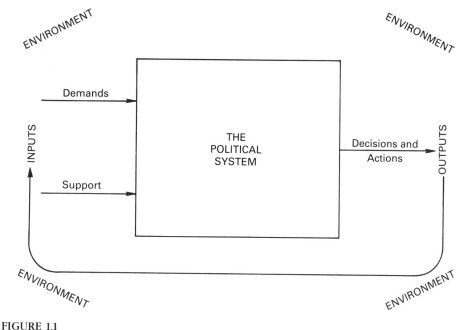

FIGURE 1.1
A Simplified Model of a Political System

Source: David Easton, *A Framework for Political Analysis* (Englewood Cliffs, NJ: Prentice-Hall, Inc., 1965). Used by permission of the author.

environmental systems, which accordingly modify their demands and supports to the political system.

Recall the vignette about the suburban school district that appeared earlier in this chapter. If we regard the school district as a system for analytic purposes, we can say that the board of education's decision not to renew the superintendent's contract produced feedback in the form of demands from the environment that the board reconsider its decision. In the absence of clear, countervailing supports for its decision, the board of education modified its original decision and deferred action on the superintendent's contract.

The open system perspective contrasts with the literature that argues that schools traditionally have been bureaucratic systems that are nonresponsive to their environment.[14] As subsequent chapters will show, administrators, teachers, and others within school systems often have considerable effect upon policy decisions and school activities. But other individuals, groups, and agencies influence these decisions as well. We will explore many facets of this general theme in the following chapters. As we shall see, the model is made more complex by the fact that actors within the system (e.g., teachers) often have affiliations with groups outside the system (e.g., unions and professional associations).

Schools are open systems in another respect that deserves mention at this point. In Karl Weick's terms they are "loosely coupled."[15] Weick says that "coupled events are responsive but . . . each event preserves its own identity and some evidence of its physical or logical separateness."[16] In terms of the organization and control of schools, this suggests that different events in the environment may have different effects for various schools within a single system. For example, parent concerns about textbooks or extracurricular activities at one school will not necessarily affect conditions at other schools. Or, faculty concerns at any given school may differ substantially from those at other schools. Loose coupling also means that it is difficult for the central administration to enforce uniform compliance with many policies across the entire district. Even if desired, it would be very difficult, for example, to ensure that all third-grade teachers across a city district are teaching the same things at the same time and in the same way.

The systems perspective indicates that organizations are mutually interdependent with their environment and must change continuously in order to maintain equilibrium within that environment. However, the systems perspective does not speak to the question of why actors within organizations act in particular ways. The classical view of organizations is that they are goal-oriented and that actors within them make the choices that are most consistent with organizational priorities. In schools, for example, it would be assumed that decisions are always made according to "what is best for the children." However, people who study organizations understand that the goals and priorities of persons who work in and shape policies for organizations may not be identical to those of the organization. Particularly in organizations characterized by ambiguous goals and uncertainty about how to achieve or measure progress toward them, individuals (sometimes acting in groups) may work toward goals that are of more benefit to themselves than to the organization.

Examples are legion. Some state legislators eschew support of school reform initiatives that require additional taxes for fear of jeopardizing their reelection. Board of education members in some communities show more interest in the school budget as a means of hiring their constituents than for educating children. Principals may stress control or "keeping the lid on" particular schools or classes because they know they are judged in the central office primarily by their ability to keep things running smoothly. Some teachers, recognizing they have the protection of tenure and seeing no particular incentive to do exceptional work, just put in their time at school and urge their union to gain as many new benefits as possible for them while they work hard at a second job.

A theoretical approach that accounts for such behavior and is consistent with open systems theory is the perspective of political economy or public choice. This approach "assumes that rational self-interested individuals try to maximize their own welfare (or benefits) within the context of the institutional or organizational reward structure they face." [17] Or, as Michaelson says,

> We may assume that bureaucrats, including schoolmen, seek to survive, to enlarge the scope of their activities, to gain prestige, to avoid conflict, to control the organization and content of their daily round as much as possible. All of these are, as it were, profit in kind. By accepting this theory of motivation, we do not rule out altruism. Administrators and teachers, like entrepreneurs, take pride in their work and strive for excellence. The issue is not whether bureaucrats are altruistic but rather whether there are mechanisms available to harness their self-seeking to the public interest.[18]

The public choice perspective is helpful in considering the behaviors of education and education policymakers at all levels. It seems particularly appropriate for loosely coupled settings in which mechanisms of organizational control are absent or ineffective.

The concept of system is a general one that can be applied to many phenomena at different levels. It is possible to refer to a single school as a system, to a school district as a system, to a state educational system, or to the educational system in the United States. The term will be used in each of these ways throughout this book. Within the context of open systems we will give particular attention to the concepts of organization, control, and schools. The following paragraphs provide explicit meanings for and delimitations to these terms.

Organization

The word *organization* is a broad term. At times in this book it will be used in a formal, legal sense. Thus, we shall speak of the organization of education at the federal, state, and school district levels. We shall also deal with the organization of intermediate units, most often at the county level, and of attendance areas or single schools.

At other times we shall speak of organization in an extralegal or less formal sense. Thus, we shall deal with the organization of the board of education, the administrative structure of a school system, and the formal and informal organizations of teachers. Despite these many uses of the word *organization,* we shall do our best through modifiers and context to clarify our usage of the term.

Perhaps we should share one predilection we have about organization: we see it as a means and not an end. In other words, to speak of how we organize schools for a moment, we think that argument about the merits of 6–3–3 versus an 8–4 organization is largely beside the point. More important to us is what kind of program goes on when schools are organized in these or other ways. Likewise we know of no administrative organization which, per se, we would defend above all other forms of organization. More important than the formal organization chart are the work patterns that chief administrators and their subordinates have been able to establish.

In keeping with our conviction that organization is a means and not an end, we do suggest that organizations can be managed to facilitate or obstruct the achievement of goals. For instance, some students of the problem conclude that it is easier to provide an adequate instructional program in school districts enrolling 10,000 pupils than in those enrolling 1,000 pupils. But organization of larger districts alone will not achieve the end; the resources of the larger units must be used for school purposes. In like manner, the division of a large high school into "houses" may permit, but does not guarantee, more intimate student-personnel arrangements. Again, what is done within the organization is more significant than the organization itself.

Control

Control is also a word of many meanings. We shall speak of both legal and extralegal control. Legal control tends to be more formal, and as the name implies, grows out of the law. In each of the fifty states there is a formidable body of school law—constitutional provisions, statutory enactments, court decisions, and administrative regulations. The law specifies or implies the powers and duties of the legislature, state boards and state departments of education, local boards of education, and other official bodies. Thus a local board of education often has some tax discretion within limits set by state statute. Or, a local board of education may employ teachers, provided they meet certification standards established by the state board of education under power given by state statute.

Legal control also resides at the federal level. While no specific mention of education appears in the United States Constitution, the general welfare clause is sufficiently broad to provide the basis for legislation on the part of Congress. The general welfare clause and the First, Fifth, and Fourteenth Amendments have also supplied the United States Supreme Court with adequate grounds for a number of decisions having to do with education. Administrative regulation on the part of the executive branch of the federal government or federal court decisions also constitute a form of legal control.

But legal control, whether exercised at the local, state, or federal level, is only part of the picture. We shall also consider extralegal control, which some may prefer to call extralegal influence. We do not wish to quibble about words. We are interested in examining how decisions pertaining to American education actually are made and implemented rather than simply how they are formalized. Thus, any force or movement that in the end affects the decision is, in our judgment, an aspect of control and thus within the purview of this book.

Many people do not view control in this broad context and their limited definition of control has led to naive citizenship and inept school management. Equating control with its legal manifestations leads to a rather superficial focus on the formal expression of policy and overlooks the motives and processes that produce that policy. Since we are interested in control as it concerns not only policy decisions but also the implementation of policy, we have chosen to deal with formal structures of school government, with the activities of interest groups, and with any other forces that appear to control the schools.

Schools

We'll use the term *schools* in its customary sense to include institutions established to provide elementary and secondary education. We won't attempt to describe the organization and control of colleges, although to be sure, some of the legal controls pertaining to schools also pertain to colleges, and many of the extralegal controls affect colleges in much the same way they do schools.

The growth of the junior or community college and programs of adult education makes the distinction between school and college less clear-cut. A number of these colleges are established by local school districts as extensions of their programs in elementary and secondary education. In these cases organization and control tend to be even more like that found in elementary and secondary schools but again no explicit treatment of the college will be included. The growing importance of early childhood education also calls our definition of schools into question. While some early childhood programs are offered by local school districts, most are controlled independently.

We'll treat private and parochial as well as public schools. While the book as a whole will deal with public schools more fully than with private and parochial schools, these alternatives to public education will be examined specifically and the relationship between the public and alternative arrangements for schools will be noted at many points.

This choice reflects our conviction that to understand the schools of America one must look at the public *and* the nonpublic schools. The presence of the nonpublic school affects in many ways the organization and control of public schools. Also, events in some public school systems have given impetus to nonpublic alternatives. It is time that as complete a picture as possible of all American schools be drawn because alternatives to traditional public as well as nonpublic school programs are being considered more frequently by educators and lay persons alike.

THE DEVELOPMENT OF AMERICAN SCHOOLS

A Brief Overview

American schools during the seventeenth and eighteenth centuries, despite the passage of the Massachusetts laws of 1642 and 1647, were essentially private or church institutions. Such schools were few in number; attendance was usually selective; and control rested in the hands of individual or church groups. About 1800 there began a growing demand for public education in America. Thomas Jefferson, in Virginia, was among the first to propose a system of free public elementary schools. His proposal was not adopted, but a little later, largely as a result of the work of Horace Mann in Massachusetts and Henry Barnard in Connecticut, the public schools movement of America was launched.

The small community district became the unit in which the public school, usually a one-room elementary school, was established. Early state laws permitted school districts to be formed almost anywhere a half-dozen families wished to establish one. The simplicity of the plan was appealing. A community wishing to establish a school and pay taxes to support it could establish one; a community not desiring a school or not wishing to pay taxes for its support could let matters alone. To be sure, as the nineteenth century progressed, the states became more adamant about the establishment of public schools and tax support for them. The small district pattern of organization, with some modification in the county-unit states of the South and in the cities, remained for that century and even much of the twentieth century the predominant pattern of organization.

The development of control mechanisms for the schools of Massachusetts has been reported in some detail.[19] Using Massachusetts as a prototype, we find that for two hundred years the schools were under the direction of the town meeting and later of the town selectmen or a committee of the selectmen. For this entire period, school government was very much a part of other local government. In 1826 and 1827 the Massachusetts General Court (legislature) established the town school committee (school board) as a separate governmental body. This action was approximated in other states and school government came to be separated from other government at the local level.

During our early history, school management was a function performed by lay citizens. However, with the growth of cities and the merger of school districts within cities, the problems of school administration became too demanding for part-time, lay school board members. This led to the creation of the office of superintendent of schools. The evolution of this office is noted in Chapter 10.

In the cities, one-room schools tended to give way to two-room, four-room, eight-room, and even larger schools. The increase in school size and the grading of pupils provided the need for a head or principal teacher in each school. We find that Cincinnati established a principal-teacher in each school as early as 1838.[20] The Quincy School of Boston reported in 1847 that all departments had been placed under a single principal. St. Louis had placed each of its schools under a single principal by 1859.

Initially, the duties of the principal were essentially clerical in nature, such as the compilation of enrollment and attendance figures. Later, the principal was relieved of teaching so that he or she might give full time to organization and management duties. The classification of pupils by grade levels was not the least of these duties. In recent decades, the principal has tended to become, or is at least thought of as, an instructional officer in the school.

Our early schools, largely under the control of the local communities, seemed to serve a rural, homogeneous society rather well. As noted previously, in the growing cities these small districts were combined, in time, into city school systems. Moreover, for much of the nineteenth and some of the twentieth century secondary education was available, for the most part, only in the academies that remained under private and parochial auspices. Gradually public education came to be viewed as important to the political and economic progress of America. The growth of secularization and of egalitarianism also served to promote the extension of public education.

The schools of today are not only the product of the forces noted above; they also exist in a complex, largely urban, and pluralistic society. Moreover, worldwide ideologies and practices affect today's schools beyond the wildest dreams of the citizens of this nation during the last century.[21] Under these circumstances, the questions of organization and control of American schools have new meanings and require fresh analyses.

Some Legal Milestones

In the development of public education, as we have previously suggested, there have been a number of legal milestones that deserve some mention. The first of these was the establishment of the legal basis for public education in the various states. By 1820 thirteen of the twenty-three states then in existence had constitutional provisions and seventeen had statutory provisions pertaining to public education. All except two of the states had either constitutional or statutory provisions and nine states had both.[22] Today, most states have firm constitutional mandates regarding public education, as is illustrated by the Ohio constitution:

> The General Assembly shall make such provisions, by taxation, or otherwise, as, with the income arising from the school trust fund, will secure a thorough and efficient system of common schools throughout the State; but no religious sect, or sects, shall ever have any exclusive right to, or control of, any part of the school funds of this State.[23]

Provisions for compulsory attendance and tax support for schools as found in the constitutions or the statutes of the various states became particularly important in the establishment of public education. Beginning with Massachusetts in 1852, each of the fifty states enacted compulsory education laws. The question of minimum school attendance for the child was no longer a decision for the parent but for the state.

To begin with, the laws providing tax support for schools were often permissive, and in some cases schools for pauper children were the first schools for which money was mandated. New York in 1812 became the first state to pass a permanent law for the organization of public schools. New Jersey provided for the education of pauper children in 1820 and for all children in 1838. Ohio and Delaware authorized taxation for education in 1821 and Illinois followed in 1825. Cubberley notes that "the battle for the establishment of tax supported schools was a bitter one, but after about 1850 it had been won in every Northern state."[24] Thus, tax support and required attendance became important steps in establishing the public schools of America. Both reflected the growing power of the state over a function once left to individuals and the church.

Fundamental questions of tax support for schools were again brought before the courts in the early 1970s. A series of cases filed in both state and federal courts challenged school funding arrangements based principally upon local property taxation.[25] It was contended that states that promulgated such systems did not guarantee equal educational opportunity to children in the state because this opportunity was a function of the taxable property located within their particular school district. Some state courts found that such systems violated their respective state constitutions. However, the U.S. Supreme Court held that they did not violate the Constitution because education is not a "fundamental" right guaranteed by it.[26] Even so, the Court noted the imperfections in current finance systems and indicated that their reform was a matter for the attention of state legislatures. This issue is discussed in more detail in Chapter 8.

While state laws generally came to require the establishment and support of "common schools," there still remained some doubt that common schools included secondary schools. This question became the heart of the Kalamazoo case.[27] In 1874 the Supreme Court of Michigan said:

> We content ourselves with the statement that neither in our state policy, in our constitution, or in our laws, do we find the primary school districts restricted in the branches of knowledge which their officers may cause to be taught, or the grade of instruction that may be given, if their voters consent in regular form to bear the expense and raise the taxes for the purpose.[28]

This and similar decisions in other states made it clear that local boards of education had powers to establish schools and levels of instruction and to use tax money in support of those schools even though the state laws did not specifically provide for such schools and levels of instruction.

With the growth of public schools it is not surprising that the idea of eliminating all nonpublic schools should have evolved. Major arguments for schools seemed, in many cases, to be arguments against nonpublic schools. This question was ruled on by the U.S. Supreme Court in the now-famous Oregon case.[29] The court held that the statute that required all children to attend only public schools was unconstitutional as being an undue infringement on the rights of parents to control the education of their children. While the state had the right to inspect and reasonably regulate private schools, it did not have the right to abolish them. Since 1925 it has been clear that nonpublic schools may be an acceptable alternative to public schools.

But the question of public versus nonpublic schools was not yet settled. Louisiana passed a law providing free textbooks for children attending public and parochial schools alike. The law was challenged and eventually reached the U.S. Supreme Court. In the Cochran case, the Court declared the Louisiana law constitutional and in so doing created a new doctrine called the "child benefit" theory.[30] This theory has not always been accepted by state courts, and it was vigorously contested in the Everson case in the U.S. Supreme Court.[31] In a 5–4 decision, however, the Court ruled that the New Jersey law permitting boards of education to provide transportation for any school pupil, public or private, was constitutional. Again, a number of state courts have ruled that state constitutions do not permit the expenditure of public money for transportation of pupils to private schools. Despite the division of judicial opinion on this matter, the "child benefit" idea has become a powerful one.

The separation of church and state was the basic issue in the Pierce, Cochran, and Everson cases noted briefly in the preceding paragraphs. A number of other cases have dealt with other aspects of this issue. In 1948 the U.S. Supreme Court ruled, in a split decision in the McCollum case, that the "released time" religious education program being conducted in the Champaign, Illinois, schools was not constitutional.[32] The chief objections to the practice seemed to be the use of the school buildings for the program and the administrative assistance given to the program by the school officials. Justice Black, who wrote the opinion for the majority, contended that these practices were contrary to the First Amendment of the Constitution.

About four years later, the Zorach case in New York State, which again raised the question of released time religious education, reached the U.S. Supreme Court.[33] In this instance, the Court sustained the New York law permitting released time religious instruction. The chief differences between the New York and Illinois practices appeared to be that in New York the religious classes were not held in the school buildings and the school officers exercised less control over the attendance of pupils in the religious program. Again, however, there was a split decision and in this instance Justice Black found himself in the minority.

During the late 1960s and early 1970s, some states enacted legislation that extended aid to nonpublic schools for teachers' salaries and other expenses related to specific "secular" courses. The U.S. Supreme Court held that such aid was unconstitutional because its implementation would foster "excessive entanglement" of government and religion.[34] Subsequent legislation to achieve the same purpose by providing partial reimbursements for tuition expenses to parents of nonpublic school pupils was also declared unconstitutional.[35] However, in 1983, the Supreme Court upheld a Minnesota statute that permits residents to deduct for state income tax purposes "tuition, textbooks, and transportation" expenses of dependent children who attend public or nonpublic elementary or secondary schools.[36] The Court took special note of the fact that *all* parents could claim the deduction and that deductions for materials used in teaching religion would be disallowed.

The issue of relationships between public and nonpublic schools became more intense in the 1980s as a result of federal proposals for tuition tax credits, nondenominational prayer in public schools, and teaching creationism as a theory contrary to evolution. Attention to these relationships was encouraged by public statements of support for tax credits and school prayer by President Reagan. However, the constitutionality of both these issues remained in doubt in the late 1980s, and a Louisiana law that would require the teaching of creationism was held unconstitutional.[37]

These cases and others not cited here suggest that although schools may not require students to participate in religious observances, a degree of cooperation between the public schools and religious groups will be found to be constitutional. Should that cooperation go too far, however, the Court will declare the matter contrary to the principle of separation of church and state.

Perhaps the most notable decisions of the U.S. Supreme Court having to do with education are the Brown case of 1954[38] and the implementing decision one year later.[39] In the initial decision the long-accepted "separate but equal" doctrine was declared inadequate in the field of public education. Forced segregation of black pupils into separate schools was found to be contrary to the equal protection of the law as guaranteed by the Fourteenth Amendment. The Court recognized that many difficulties would arise in implementing the decision and that these problems might vary by location. Hence, in 1955 the enforcement of the decision was remanded to the appropriate federal courts. The lower federal courts were instructed to accept "reasonable progress" toward the ultimate goal of desegregated schools.

Efforts to achieve desegregation concentrated first on those southern states where dual school systems were in existence. Resistance to these efforts was considerable. Each plan of resistance resulted in additional court cases, and in most instances plans that proposed to achieve indirectly what had been forbidden directly were struck down. Probably the most widespread plan in the South was "freedom of choice" in which students were allowed to choose enrollment in schools outside their immediate neighborhood if space were available there. The U.S. Commission on Civil Rights reported that factors such as residential segregation, segregated teaching staffs, administrative judgments as to what constitutes overcrowding, and transportation policies limited the amount of desegregation resulting from such plans.[40] Indeed, the commission found that, in the North and South alike, more blacks attended segregated schools in 1965 than at the time of the 1954 Brown decision.[41]

The Supreme Court subsequently held that more positive action was required to dismantle dual school systems. In October 1969 the Court ruled that a number of school districts in Mississippi could no longer postpone desegregation and called for the immediate termination of dual school systems.[42] In a later decision, *Swann* v. *Charlotte-Mecklenburg Board of Education,* the Court authorized compulsory busing as a method to achieve this purpose.[43] Thus the Court clearly indicated the need for school districts to initiate affirmative remedial action where the law had previously tolerated or encouraged dual systems.[44]

Left unsettled by the Court, as it reviewed desegregation cases emanating from the South and other areas where official efforts were made to segregate schools, was the matter of state responsibility to desegregate school districts where segregation

was a product of residential patterns rather than legal action. Moreover, these instances of *de facto* segregation became more numerous as urban residential patterns
became more segregated. A series of lower court decisions suggested that affirmative
action may be required in this regard also and posed the issue for the Supreme
Court. Among the alternatives considered favorably by lower courts was the possibility of busing students across city district lines in metropolitan areas. However, the
U.S. Supreme Court held that federal courts could not mandate such action unless
the state or one or more of the surrounding districts could be shown to have caused
interdistrict segregation.[45]

Let us summarize these legal milestones as they pertain to the public schools.
In response to social, economic, and political developments in this country, there
was first the establishment of public schools by constitutional and statutory provisions. As time went on, attendance of pupils in school and payment of taxes for school
purposes were required. In the latter half of the nineteenth century the public school
program was extended to include the secondary level. Convictions about the importance of public schools, however, were not sufficient to eliminate the nonpublic
school. While the doctrine of separation of church and state still pertains, it does not
rule out the use of some public money for the benefit of pupils in nonpublic schools,
nor does it prohibit a limited amount of cooperation between schools and religious
bodies. Finally, the obligation of the public school to serve all children without regard
to race or color has been given rigorous interpretation by our highest court.

In these developments it seems quite clear that public schools and schools in
general do not enjoy a protected status. Schools take shape in response to the
ideological and practical demands of the society of which they are a part. In fact, they
have been battlegrounds in the resolution of social conflict. What is meant by separation of church and state may have been clarified more through school decisions
than by any other means. Certainly the extension of civil rights to blacks and other
minorities is being attempted through the schools as much as through any other
realm of activity. With school decisions being part of the mainstream of life, there is
little wonder that school control is a matter of consequence.

Persistent Issues

While a historical perspective helps in understanding the organization and control
of schools, we must also consider issues that face the schools. Issues provide focus
for the behavior of educators and substance for debates and political efforts of
educational policymakers. A few of those issues that are of historical and continuing
importance will be noted here as a preface to more extensive treatment in subsequent
chapters.

The first issue is what the tasks of the schools are. Should the schools emphasize
intellectual, social, personal, or vocational objectives? Thirty years ago, a surprising
amount of agreement was found among educators and lay citizens in their perceptions of the task of the school.[46] All groups considered intellectual tasks to be most

important, but many individuals saw social, personal, or vocational goals as more important.

A 1986 survey suggested that American priorities for education have shifted toward vocational aims. When asked the chief reasons they want their children to receive an education, 47 percent of citizens responded in terms related to jobs and improved finances. In contrast, 23 percent of respondents cited preparation for life, and only 10 percent said to acquire knowledge.[47] The relationship between educational attainment and future job opportunities for Americans has been made known to the public by a series of well-publicized government and foundation reports.[48] These reports, which received strong backing from business leaders, asserted that future economic development in the nation depends upon strengthening the nation's schools. Indeed, this argument became the primary rationale for the educational reform movement of the 1980s.

The United States's economy is in the midst of a change that parallels the industrial revolution in significance.[49] The shift from an economy based principally on manufacturing and hardware to one dominated by services and information development and dissemination has important implications for education. Economic competition with Japan and other countries depends upon technological advances, leading business and government leaders to call for school improvement. They want more than additional vocational training or greater stress on the basics, and the public apparently agrees. A recent survey of the Carnegie Forum on Education and the Economy found that 91 percent of the general population agreed with the proposition that preparation of the future work force must go beyond teaching the "basics" to develop student skills that enable individuals "to work independently and solve complex problems on their own."[50]

The current concern for quality in American education underscores a second persistent issue: the relationship between educational purposes and national social problems. Some argue that contemporary society requires schools that go beyond traditional purposes of intellectual development and preparation for work and citizenship. Along with economic issues, social developments such as changes in family structure, teen pregnancy, the growing number of Spanish-speaking school-age children, and high rates of youth and minority unemployment concern educational policymakers.[51] In addition, questions of what constitutes equal education opportunity in an increasingly heterogeneous society are especially complex.

Moreover, it is increasingly clear that education takes place in many settings outside the school. For example, the media now disseminate much information that traditionally was included within school curricula. The diffusion of educational activities and programs raises a number of questions. What priorities are to be established for the schools? How can agreements regarding these priorities be reached? In what ways should the purposes and programs of schools be related to the purposes and activities of the home, the church, and other community agencies? What alternatives should exist to schools as we presently know them? To what extent should school programs be adapted to local conditions and priorities, and to what extent should national purposes be served?

Actions to resolve the above questions necessarily involve local, state, and federal governments, and other official agencies. What then should be the relationship of local, state, and federal governments regarding school questions? The day of extreme localism is clearly at an end. On the other hand, few people would place actual operation of schools in the hands of federal agencies. During the past decade state involvement in education has become more critical, particularly with regard to finance reform and the expansion of statewide program mandates. Recent years have also made clear the intensifying tensions between different levels and branches of government. For example, local board of education members and state legislators sometimes blame each other for difficulties in financing schools or implementing state-mandated programs. Both local and state officials may resent the regulations federal officials believe necessary to achieve compliance with federal laws.

Before us is the task of determining the most appropriate partnership of local, state, and federal governments for education. How can we achieve a balance between local, state, and national goals in education? How can state responsibility for education be harmonized with national interests and local priorities? To be sure, these questions about education are not unrelated to the provision for and control of other services in our society such as health, welfare, law enforcement, transportation, and communication. Again, the possibility of competition exists between education and these agencies at local, state, and federal levels.

A third issue is the financial support of schools. This issue has several aspects. The first of these pertains to the amount of the school tax bill. As noted earlier, the support of public and private education at elementary, secondary, and college levels requires approximately 6.5 percent of our gross national product (GNP) each year. If all adult education, publicly and privately supported, and all education programs of governmental departments and research grants of those departments to universities and other agencies are included, the total educational share of the GNP is appreciably increased. The question of what part of our resources should be used for education has always been complex and must be addressed at various governmental levels.

A second aspect of the finance issue has to do with the source of funds. Are local funds, largely dependent upon the property taxes, to be the primary source of revenue for schools? Or are state funds, chiefly dependent upon sales and income taxes, to be the main financial support for schools? Or might federal revenues, now about 61 percent of all taxes collected at all levels of government and largely dependent upon personal and corporate income taxes, become a major source of school support?

The 1970s and 1980s witnessed considerable controversy concerning financing arrangements. Extensive litigation, citizen initiatives to repeal tax measures, and refusal to support taxes in public referenda provided evidence of public dissatisfaction with current school funding arrangements. It remains to be seen if these arrangements can be modified in ways that make them both more effective and politically palatable. The Reagan administration reduced both federal taxes and spending for education. The administration asserted that the reduction in federal taxes enabled state and local officials to raise taxes for education if they wished to do so. They also said that the same cuts should increase the likelihood of private gifts to schools. Some states did raise taxes, and a number of school districts established local education foundations to attract such contributions.

A third aspect of the finance issue is that of prudent allocation and effective use of funds. This concern, in combination with growing doubts about the effectiveness of schools and the credibility of school officials, gave rise to the accountability movement. For many years, most school systems experienced steady enrollment increases that provided a strong rationale for increases in school expenditures. When this ceased to be the case, school officials found it increasingly difficult to convince the public to spend more for schools. Moreover, widespread publicity about dropouts and low achievers has made legislators as well as the general public more concerned about forcing schools to be accountable for particular results. This has led to more state mandates, greater emphasis on legislative oversight, increased emphasis on program and performance audits, and minimum competency requirements in many states. While educators may find some comfort in the fact that citizens are also challenging the credibility of and calling for greater accountability from other professionals and government employees, the issue is one that portends changes in the organization and control of schools.

The fourth and last issue we shall present here has to do with the roles of lay citizens and professional educators in determining school purposes and procedures. The concern for accountability has brought increased attention to this issue. The proliferation of citizen advisory committees indicates the possibility of new lay-professional relationships. However, the functioning of most such groups is largely perfunctory and often dissatisfying to both citizens and professionals. The underlying issue here is that of how to share control of an organization between constituents who pay for and benefit from it and professionals who are specially trained and pursue their careers in it.

This is not an easy problem to solve. In a complex, technological society there is always the question of how the specialist and the generalist can work together. Despite the insistence of some special interest groups, there seems to be no way that public policy can be turned over to the specialists—public health to the doctors or foreign affairs to the military, for instance. Yet the generalists, or the public at large, if they are to have a hand in determining public policy, must somehow come to possess much of the specialists' knowledge. There is a great need for generalists who can assess the significance of the knowledge of the specialists, who can convey their assessments to lay citizens, and who can secure a measure of agreement in terms of the commonweal. This need exists in the realm of school operation as truly as it does in other areas.

The brief presentation of these issues suggests the setting for this book. Basic questions of public policy regarding our schools are before us. These policies have to be determined within our organization structures and our control mechanisms. We need to see clearly what the structures and processes are by which basic educational decisions are now made. Neither structures nor processes may be adequate to the demands of the times. Therefore, in addition to analyzing what is, we will suggest what ought to be in light of current developments in the organization and control of American schools.

PLAN FOR THE BOOK

Beginning with the work of Mayo and Roethlisberger, the behavioral scientists have developed some useful concepts about organizations and much empirical work has been done to test these concepts. As a result the in-organization or interpersonal relationships of organizations have been described with considerable accuracy. We shall make use of some of that work when we speak of organization within the school and when we deal with the controls exercised by the organized profession. The major focus of this book, however, is not on internal organization.

Instead, we wish to focus on the out-organization relationships. In Parsons's terms we will deal less with the technical level of the school organization, more with the managerial level, and most of all with the institutional level.[52] In other words, we are less interested in how things are done in schools than we are in the processes through which policies or general directions are established for the schools. Our principal thesis is that the schools are open systems influenced by a broad range of forces, both governmental and nongovernmental, and that school policies are developed through interaction of these forces with school officials. Our purpose is to describe and explain these relationships. The discussion will view school organization and control chiefly in social, political, and economic terms. In short we are attempting to look at the school in its total environment.

In the chapters to follow, we will begin with a description of the demographic setting and the formal structure at federal, state, and local levels. Next the internal and interstitial organization segments, such as board of education, administration, and teachers will be examined. The social matrix within which the school operates will then be analyzed. A picture of nonpublic and alternative schools as an influential part of the American school system will then be presented. Finally, we will summarize the many kinds of controls that affect American schools.

This book will be descriptive, analytical, and interpretative. Where research data are available, we will make use of them. Where research evidence appears skimpy, we'll resort to the best commonsense analyses we can muster. Our arguments will be made on the basis of the research evidence and our experience with the phenomena under study. We hope that this kind of treatment will increase the understanding of school administrators, school practitioners, students of school administration, and others interested in the nation's schools.

NOTES

[1]"Remarks by President Jimmy Carter at the Department of Education Organization Act Bill Signing Ceremony," 17 October 1979, Administration of Jimmy Carter, 1979, 1,956.

[2]Statement on Signing S210 into Law, Administration of Jimmy Carter, 1979, 1,979.

[3]"In an About-Face, Bennett Seeks to Curb Cutbacks," *Chronicle of Higher Education* 33 (10 June 1987): 1.

[4]Quoted in Carol Furtwengler, Joyce McCarty, and George Malo, "The Career Ladder Program in Tennessee," Presentation to the National Conference on Measurement in Education, Chicago, IL, April 1985, 6.

[5]See Furtwengler et al. and Janet R. Handler, "Shaping Tennessee's Career Ladder Program," Report to the American Education Research Association Annual Meeting, San Francisco, 1986.

[6]Furtwengler et al., 13–14.

[7]U.S. Department of Education, *Digest of Education Statistics, 1985–86* (Washington, DC: U.S. Government Printing Office, 1986), 11.

[8]Ibid.

[9]Ibid., 10.

[10]Ibid.

[11]Ibid., 6.

[12]Ibid., 16.

[13]David Easton, *A Framework for Political Analysis* (Englewood Cliffs, NJ: Prentice-Hall, 1965), and David Easton, *A Systems Analysis of Political Life* (New York: John Wiley & Sons, 1965). For another discussion of American schools from this perspective, see Frederick Wirt and Michael Kirst, *Schools in Conflict* (Berkeley: McCutchan, 1982).

[14]See, for example, Marilyn Gittell and T. Edward Hollander, *Six Urban School Districts* (New York: Praeger, 1968).

[15]Karl E. Weick, "Educational Organizations as Loosely Coupled Systems," *Administrative Science Quarterly* 21 (March 1976): 1–19.

[16]Ibid., 3.

[17]William Lowe Boyd, "The Political Economy of Public Schools," *Educational Administration Quarterly* 18 (Summer 1982): 113.

[18]Jacob B. Michaelson, "Revision, Bureaucracy, and School Reform," *School Review* 85 (February 1977): 329, quoted in Boyd, 114.

[19]Henry Suzzallo, *The Rise of Local School Supervision in Massachusetts,* Teachers College Contribution, no. 3 (New York: Columbia University, 1906).

[20]Paul R. Pierce, *The Origin and Development of the Public School Principalship* (Chicago: University of Chicago Press, 1934).

[21]See David Tyack and Elizabeth Hansot, *Managers of Virtue* (New York: Basic, 1982), Diane Ravitch, *The Troubled Crusade* (New York: Basic, 1983), and Roald F. Campbell et al., *A History of Thought and Practice in Educational Administration* (New York: Teachers College Press, 1987).

[22]Lee M. Thurston and William H. Roe, *State School Administration* (New York: Harper & Row, 1957), 59–60.

[23]*Ohio Constitution,* art. VI, sec. 2.

[24]Elwood P. Cubberley, *Public School Administration* (Boston: Houghton Mifflin, 1929), 10.

[25]The best known were *Serrano* v. *Priest,* 96 Cal. Rptr. 601, 487 P 2nd, 1241, 5 Cal 3rd, 584 (1971), *Robinson* v. *Cahill,* 62 N.J. 473 (1973), and *San Antonio Independent District et al.* v. *Rodriguez et al.,* 411 U.S. 1 (1973).

[26]*San Antonio Independent School District et al.* v. *Rodriguez et. al.*

[27]*Stuart* v. *School District No. 1 of Village of Kalamazoo,* 30 Michigan 69 (1874).

[28]Ibid.

[29]*Pierce* v. *Society of the Sisters of the Holy Names of Jesus and Mary,* 268 U.S. 510 (1925).

[30]*Cochran et al.* v. *Louisiana State Board of Education et al.,* 281 U.S. 370 (1930).

[31]*Everson* v. *Board of Education of Ewing Township et al.,* 330 U.S. 1 (1947).

[32]*People of the State of Illinois ex rel. McCollum* v. *Board of Education of School District No. 71, Champaign Co., IL, et al.,* 333 U.S. 203 (1948).

[33]*Zorach* v. *Clauson,* 343 U.S. 306 (1952).

[34]*Lemon* v. *Kurtzman,* 403 U.S. 602 (1971).

[35]*Committee for Public Education* v. *Nyquist,* 413 U.S. 756 (1973) and *Sloan* v. *Lemon,* 413 U.S. 825 (1973).

[36]*Mueller* v. *Allen,* 463 U.S. 388 (1983).

[37]*Edwards* v. *Aguillard,* 107 S.C. 2d 2573 (1987).

[38]*Brown* v. *Board of Education of Topeka,* 347 U.S. 483 (1954).

[39]*Brown* v. *Board of Education of Topeka,* 349 U.S. 294 (1955).

[40]U.S. Commission on Civil Rights. *Racial Isolation in the Public Schools,* vol. 1 (Washington, DC: U.S. Government Printing Office, 1967), 66–70.

[41]Ibid., 2–10.

[42]*Alexander* v. *Holmes County,* 369 U.S. 19 (1969).

[43]*Swann* v. *Charlotte-Mecklenburg Board of Education,* 402 U.S. 1 (1970).

[44]For discussion of this and related decisions, see John C. Hogan, "School Desegregation—North, South, East, West: Trends in Court Decisions, 1849–1973," *Phi Delta Kappan* 55 (September 1973); 58–63.

[45]*Bradley* v. *Milliken,* 345 F Supp 914 (1972), 42 LW 5249 (July 25, 1974). A more extended discussion of litigation pertaining to desegregation will be found in Chapter 8.

[46]Lawrence W. Downey, *The Task of Public Education* (Chicago: Midwest Administration Center, University of Chicago, 1960).

[47]Alec M. Gallup, "The 18th Annual Gallup Poll of the Public's Attitudes Toward the Public Schools," *Phi Delta Kappan* 68 (September 1986): 49.

[48]See, for example, National Commission on Excellence in Education, *A Nation at Risk: The Imperative for Educational Reform* (Washington, DC: U.S. Government Printing Office, 1983), and Task Force on Education for Economic Growth, *Action for Excellence* (Denver: Education Commission of the States, 1983), and Carnegie Forum on Education and the Economy, *A Nation Prepared: Teachers for the 21st Century* (New York: The Forum, 1986).

[49]See John Naisbitt, *Megatrends* (New York: Warner, 1982).

[50]Carnegie Forum on Education and the Economy, *Redesigning American Schools—The Public Speaks* (New York: The Forum, 1986), 58.

[51]See, for example, the argument for the school as broker of community-based resources in Shirley Brice Heath and Milbrey Wallin McLaughlin, "A Child Resource Policy: Moving Beyond Dependence on School and Family," *Phi Delta Kappan* 68 (April 1987): 576–580.

[52]Talcott Parsons, "Some Ingredients of a General Theory of Formal Organization," in *Administrative Theory in Education,* ed. Andrew W. Halpin (Chicago: Midwest Administration Center, University of Chicago, 1958), ch. 3.

2
Changing Demographic Setting of Schools

One of the most time-honored principles of American education is that schools exist to meet the needs and serve the interests of their students. It follows from this proposition that student interests and needs must be represented in the development and implementation of school policies. For the most part, this representation has been indirect in that lay citizens and school personnel have noted the characteristics of students and made decisions on the basis of these traits. Many of these decisions, however, are still predicated on the no-longer-valid assumption that the great majority of students are white, middle-class, and English-speaking. In fact, more than 30 percent of our public school population already is of minority origin, and the proportions of blacks, Hispanics, Asian-Americans, and native Americans continue to grow.

This chapter will focus on the new demographic picture that is reshaping the nature of the student body, their families, and our society at large. We will discuss the implications of these changes in demography and family structure for the governance of American schools. Growing numbers of the school-age population are now of minority origin, non–English-speaking, or economically disadvantaged, and fall under the label of "at-risk" students who need special supportive services. In addition, basic changes in family structure have compounded the problems of children and the schools that serve them as fewer students come from economically secure, two-parent households. There will be discussion of some of the forces that are compelling a reassessment of how our schools are structured, and we will briefly address some promising new educational approaches that are being considered. The point will be emphasized that educational policymakers must look beyond just numbers in ascertaining the special needs of an increasingly heterogenous at-risk student body. We will conclude with a discussion of how these demographic changes may alter how schools are organized and controlled.

THE NEW DEMOGRAPHIC PICTURE

While concern about racial balance in student bodies quite legitimately remains a critically important concern in school districts throughout the country, rapid and far-reaching demographic changes have reshaped much of the debate about desegregation. Indeed, many school districts that recently implemented desegregation plans have become resegregated due to population shifts and differential fertility rates.

Hodgkinson points out that minority birth rates have stayed about the same while that of Caucasians has declined since the postwar baby boom.[1] As a result, the minority proportion of the school-age population is increasing and will reach more than 30 percent for the nation as a whole by 1990. Immigration of Spanish-speaking young people also has had substantial effect on the school-age population in many states. These two factors in combination with the disproportionate attractiveness of nonpublic schools to white students have resulted in increasing minority enrollments in the public schools of many states. For example, in 1980, minority students (blacks, Hispanics, Asian-Americans, and native Americans) constituted 52 percent of the public school enrollment in Mississippi, 43 percent in Louisiana and California, 46 percent in Texas, 33 percent in Florida and Maryland, and 32 percent in New York.[2] The 1990 census will reflect continuing increases in these trends with the proportion of minority students inexorably increasing throughout the country, particularly in large influential states such as California, Florida, Illinois, Ohio, Pennsylvania, Texas, and New York.

Hodgkinson focuses upon the demographic reality that schools will be responsible for educating increasing numbers of the kinds of students they have found most difficult to teach in the past.[3] More children will be entering school from minority and poverty backgrounds, single-parent households, and homes in which the parents are not married. Smaller percentages of these children will have experienced Head Start and similar programs despite the escalating need for such services. There will be more "latch-key" children who do not have adults to watch over them after school because of the growing numbers of working mothers. More children will be raised by poor teenagers with the resulting nutritional and child-development problems.

These changes in socioeconomic backgrounds of students will place unprecedented demands on the schools. Growing numbers of children will require multiple support systems at an early age, and the schools, in collaboration with other social agencies, will have to provide coordinated services that meet the basic child-care as well as educational needs of disadvantaged youngsters.

Indeed, a persuasive case can be made that the future of our democracy and economic system may be predicated upon our ability to accommodate the special needs of an increasingly diverse and heterogeneous student population. The schools are the first major institution confronting this unprecedented demographic pluralism.

We accept the proposition that these demographic trends will be of paramount importance to the organization and control of American schools in the years ahead and thus want to elaborate upon their profound political, social, and economic implications early in the book.

For example, the Hispanic population is the fastest-growing segment of the minority population with approximately two-thirds of the nation's Hispanics being located in only three states (California, Texas, and New York). More than 85 percent of the Hispanic population lives in only nine states (New Jersey, Florida, Colorado, Illinois, New Mexico, and Arizona, in addition to the three states just mentioned). This dramatic skewing of the distribution of the Hispanic population creates a serious problem of demographic illiteracy as most of the country remains ignorant of the full import of the dramatic growth in the number of Hispanics. Indeed, Hispanics are the youngest population group, so additional increases in the Hispanic population are quite predictable.

California, our most populous state, by 2000 will be "majority-minority," meaning that minorities will constitute more than half of the total population. The student bodies in twenty-three of the twenty-five largest school systems already are majority-minority, and unless we improve the quality of the education and life chances of these minority youngsters, the social fabric of our society may well be imperiled as economic polarization escalates between more affluent whites and a more disadvantaged younger minority population.

The demographic phenomenon of "gray power" also will be of increasing significance as the population ages and the number of citizens sixty-five years of age and older rapidly expands. By 1990, the number of youngsters under twenty will fall below 30 percent of the nation's population for the first time in history. In fact, in 1983, there were more people sixty-five years of age or older than teenagers. The implications of these changes are brought forth starkly by an analysis of the ratio of working to retired people. In 1950, 17 citizens worked for every retired person; in 1985 the ratio was 5.3 to 1; and a ratio of 3 to 1 is projected for 1992, with one of the three workers being from a minority.[4] Thus, growing numbers of retired individuals will be dependent upon a younger population, increasingly minority in composition, to sustain the economy in general and to maintain the viability of an already rather vulnerable Social Security system.

Any discussion of the demographic context in which schools will function, given the dramatic increases in minority enrollment, should focus explicit attention on the shocking reality that almost one-half of black teenagers have no jobs and that minority youth unemployment remains higher than 20 percent, persisting at more than twice the unemployment rate for the country at large.

In addition to the traditional, morally compelling arguments for equality or the equalization of educational opportunity, there are now selfish, vested-interest reasons for the population at large to want to improve big-city schools whose student population will be 90 percent minority by 1990. As the demographic data reflect, our population is aging, and shrinking cohorts of young people must generate the revenues necessary to support public services in a changing economy. More of these youngsters will be of minority origin, and they represent valuable human resources that our nation and economy cannot afford to fritter away. Indeed, there will be a 20 percent reduction in the number of sixteen- to twenty-four-year-olds entering the work force through 1990. These numbers indicate that we need to develop the capabilities of all of our youth to their fullest potential. We must substantially improve our 35 to 45 percent high school dropout rate.

Levin explicitly stresses the negative economic consequences of ignoring the growing needs of educationally disadvantaged youngsters in terms of a serious deterioration in the quality of the work force.

> As long as the disadvantaged were a small minority, they could be absorbed by low skill jobs or remain unemployed without intolerable consequences for the economy. But, as they become an increasing share of the labor force, their inadequate educational preparation will be visited on the competitive position of the industries and states in which they work and on our national economic status.
>
> High dropout rates, low test scores, and poor academic performance of a group that will become a larger and larger portion of the school population mean that a larger and larger portion of the future labor force will be undereducated for available jobs. Here we refer not only to managerial, professional and technical jobs, but to even lower level service and assembly work. Clerical workers, cashiers and sales-workers all need basic skills in oral and written communications, acquisition of which is hardly guaranteed in the schooling of the disadvantaged. A U.S. government study in 1976 found that while 13 percent of all 17 year olds were classified as functionally illiterate, the percentages of illiterates among Hispanics and blacks were 56 and 44 percent respectively.[5]

Levin estimates that in 1982, a total of about 12 million or 30 percent of the nation's 40 million students could be classified as being disadvantaged.[6] Demographic patterns clearly indicated that this percentage will continue to grow.

CHANGES IN FAMILY STRUCTURE

Another set of socioeconomic trends that affects the nature of the student body in a school involves changes in family structure. An increasing number of children spend a significant amount of their lives in single-parent homes and of those with two parents at home, an increasing number have mothers in the labor force. The 1980 U.S. Census estimated that of the children born that year, 48 percent would live "a considerable time" with one parent.[7] Also in that year, the mothers of 53 percent of children who lived in two-parent families were in the labor force.[8] These trends have persisted and expanded in the 1980s. There are at the present time literally millions of "latch-key" schoolchildren who let themselves into an empty house at the end of the school day. Schools with large numbers of children from single-parent or two-parent earner families often face different problems. For example, it is much more difficult to close school or send children home early because of snow accumulations. Moreover, there is some evidence that children from single-parent homes do less well in school than their peers.[9] Some schools are responding to changes in family structure by establishing extended-day programs whereby parents can bring their children to school early in the morning and pick them up at the end of their workday. The additional time can be used for supervised study, clubs, music lessons, or sports activities.

The Children's Defense Fund has documented the significant transition the American family has undergone in the past few decades. During the 1970s, for example, the number of youngsters living in a single-parent household increased from 8.4 million to 12.2 million, a dramatic increase from 12 percent of the children in 1970 to 19.7 percent in 1980.[10] Hodgkinson also documents the major changes in family structure, pointing out that in 1955 many households in the country consisted of a working father, a homemaker mother, and two or more school-age children. By 1985, there was an astonishing change with only 7 percent of the households consisting of this traditional family unit pattern.[11] The census indicates that of the children born in 1983, 59 percent will live with only one parent before reaching their eighteenth birthday. Of every 100 children born in 1983:

- □ 12 were born out of wedlock
- □ 40 were born to parents who will divorce before the child is 18
- □ 5 were born to parents who separate
- □ 2 were born to parents of whom one will die before the child is 18
- □ 41 will reach 18 "normally"[12]

This growing problem of "at-risk" children is exacerbated by the fact that our country is confronted with an increase in the number of children born outside marriage. Fifty percent of such children are born to teenage mothers who are more apt to give birth to premature babies, who in turn are more likely to have major health problems. Prematurity leads to low birth weight, which is a good predictor of serious learning problems when the child starts school. This means that approximately "700,000 babies of the annual cohort of around 3.3 million births are almost assured of being either educationally retarded or difficult to teach."[13]

Although experts disagree in their interpretations of the social implications of these data, there can be little doubt that within the past decade or two men and women have been shaping new relationships and that the basic nuclear family with a father working and a mother at home raising the children is less dominant. The women's movement has motivated many women to work for other than economic or material reasons. A national survey by the National Assessment for Educational Progress indicated that only 3 percent of seventeen-year-old females selected "housewife" as their first-choice career. Almost all of these young women assumed they would be working for a living.[14] A number of women feel unfulfilled in traditional housekeeping and maternal roles and thus seek the stimulation of outside work. These feelings, not surprisingly, are manifested particularly by the growing numbers of college-educated women. As a result, new styles of marriages and personal relationships have evolved, as well-educated women defer marriage for careers and opt for smaller families and flexible homemaking arrangements. More and more women are heads of households in families without men. For various reasons, then, women are entering the job market in huge numbers. Eli Ginzburg, a nationally renowned work-force analyst, describes this development as "the single most outstanding phenomena of our century. Its long-term implications are absolutely unchartable, in my opinion. It will affect women, men and children, and the cumulative consequences of that will only be revealed in the 21st and 22nd centuries."[15]

What then are the implications of these developments for public education? Enrollment in nursery schools and kindergartens for three- and four-year-olds has increased significantly within the past two decades from about 10 percent in the mid-1960s to nearly 39 percent in 1985.[16] The major reason for this growth, of course, is the continuing dramatic increase in the number of working mothers with young children. To meet the growing child-care needs of working parents, large numbers of new part-time and full-time day-care centers and nurseries have been established. In addition, more homemakers have availed themselves of such facilities to pursue their interests outside of home. Mothers with higher levels of formal education were more likely to enroll their children in preschool programs than were those mothers with less formal education. For example, "among mothers of 3- and 4-year-olds in nursery school, 27 percent had finished high school, 40 percent had some college and 63 percent were college graduates."[17]

The Children's Defense Fund reported a number of years ago that almost 5 million children between the ages of three and thirteen had mothers who worked full time and also were caregivers. Another 1.8 million children cared for themselves while their mothers worked. While there were 22 million children under age fourteen whose mothers worked, there were only 900,000 children enrolled in the nation's 18,307 day-care centers. In addition, there were only 122,000 center slots for infants under age three and 126,000 for after-school care. The Children's Defense Fund estimated that there were at least 3 million children under age three with working mothers, and another 14.5 million school-age children whose mothers work.[18]

These statistics pertaining to families and children indicate that there is a growing demand for child-care and preschool education, and unique opportunities exist for public schools to extend their programs and make collaborative efforts to meet the special needs of this particular constituency.

SOME CHARACTERISTICS OF STUDENTS

Numbers

The early 1970s marked the crest of a steady increase in school enrollments. However, a larger proportion of American children spends more time in school than ever before. As noted in Chapter 1, student enrollment in both public and private elementary and secondary schools was 44.7 million in October 1985, a decline of 14 percent from 1970 to 1985.[19] Elementary and secondary enrollment declined in the 1970s and early 1980s as the postwar baby boomers moved out of school systems throughout the country. Enrollments increased in the late 1980s as the children of the baby boomers began to enroll in school in larger numbers. However, it is anticipated that enrollments will decline again in the second half of the 1990s.

Distribution

Like the general population, students are not distributed evenly across the nation. Moreover, approximately 20 percent of the population moves annually. This rate is even higher among the school-age population as young families establish new households. It is important therefore that substantial commonality exist among school programs in various parts of the country in order to provide some continuity for mobile students.

Population shifts also mean that some districts face teacher shortages and demands for new classrooms while others dismiss surplus faculty members and close schools. The current decade, for example, is witnessing dramatic population shifts back and forth from the Northeast and Midwest to the Sun Belt. Another population trend is the movement out of major metropolitan centers to small towns and semi-rural areas. These trends result from economic relocations and improved communications and transportation.

The consolidation and decentralization of school districts have done little to equalize district enrollments on a national basis. For example, while there are about 16,000 local school districts in the country, approximately 26 percent of the national public school enrollment is in only 161 of them.[20] Further evidence of this disequilibrium is presented in Table 2.1, which shows that more than 60 percent of public school students are enrolled in 10 percent of the districts in the nation. It also indicates that more than half of the districts in the nation enroll fewer than 1,000

TABLE 2.1
Number of Public Systems, Enrollment, and Schools, by Size of System: United States, Fall 1983

Enrollment size	School Systems		Enrollment[1]		Number of Schools[1]	
	Number	Percent	Number (in thousands)	Percent	Number	Percent
25,000 or more	161	1.0	10,257	26.1	15,346	18.6
10,000 to 24,999	456	2.9	6,743	17.1	11,383	13.8
5,000 to 9,999	970	6.2	6,780	17.2	12,386	15.0
2,500 to 4,999	1,963	12.5	6,845	17.4	13,823	16.7
1,000 to 2,499	3,545	22.5	5,777	14.7	14,448	17.5
600 to 999	1,813	11.5	1,420	3.6	4,824	5.8
300 to 599	2,293	14.6	1,000	2.5	4,794	5.8
1 to 299	4,197	26.7	534	1.4	5,703	6.9
None[2]	349	2.2	———	———	8	———
Total	15,747	100.0	39,355	100.0	82,715	100.0

[1]Data are for fall 1982
[2]Systems not enrolling students
———Indicates data either not reported, not available, or not applicable.
Note: Enrollments and numbers of schools should be regarded as approximations only. These totals differ from those in other tables because this table represents data reported by school systems rather than by states. Because of rounding, details may not add to totals.
Source: National Center for Educational Statistics, *Digest of Educational Statistics, 1985–86* (Washington, DC: U.S. Government Printing Office), 64.

students each. The scope of school programs is often related to the size of schools in which they are found. In other words, school districts with larger enrollments can afford to employ more teaching specialists than can much smaller districts. For example, a high school with an enrollment of 2,000 students is large enough for teachers of five different foreign languages to teach full schedules in their specialties. This would not be possible in a high school of 400 students. Thus, board of education members and administrators who make program decisions for two such schools do so within different sets of constraints established by enrollment figures.

Socioeconomic Composition

The spatial distribution of the population and widespread adherence to neighborhood school policies mean that student bodies are often segregated by socioeconomic characteristics. For example, there are small rural schools in which most students come from farm backgrounds, schools in well-to-do suburban neighborhoods where most students come from professional or managerial families, schools in working-class neighborhoods where most students come from low- or middle-income blue-collar families, and inner-city schools where virtually the entire student body may be eligible for public welfare assistance. Generally speaking, the socioeconomic status of a student body reflects the education, occupation, and income of adults in the community.

The correlation between social class and academic success is well known. Students from middle- and upper-class backgrounds are more likely than lower-class students to do well on achievement tests, graduate from high school, and go on to college. On the other hand, lower-class students are more likely to enter school with severe educational deficiencies, behave in ways that middle-class teachers consider inappropriate, and leave school at an early age.

Probably the best-known decisions based upon socioeconomic characteristics of students are those dealing with Chapter 1 of the Elementary and Secondary Education Act and other compensatory programs. School eligibility for these programs is determined on the basis of student socioeconomic characteristics. Many other programs are also affected. Expensive program options such as summer tours in Europe are offered more often in neighborhood schools where parents can afford them. Similarly, some high schools in high-status neighborhoods offer virtually no vocational preparation because it is assumed that almost all students will go on to college. High schools in poor neighborhoods are less likely to offer advanced courses in mathematics and foreign languages than their suburban counterparts because of expectations based on social class and achievement. There is also long-standing evidence that many city teachers prefer to teach in middle- and upper-class schools.[21] As a consequence, teachers with experience and seniority often transfer from lower-class schools, leaving younger and relatively inexperienced teachers to provide most of the instruction for lower-class children. The Houston Public Schools recently began to offer financial incentives to teachers willing to teach in difficult settings in an attempt to counter such actions.

In addition, the socioeconomic composition of the student body can determine the relative emphasis teachers and administrators give to instruction and pupil control in the school. The fact that many schools are still racially segregated continues to influence decision making in some school systems. Apparently some decisions to assign black teachers, counselors, and administrators to predominantly black schools are still being made on this basis. Also, some school systems hesitate to assign a black principal or "too many" black faculty members to certain all-white schools. By the same token, some teachers are influenced in choosing the school where they prefer to teach by the racial composition of its student body. In terms of the school curriculum, the heritage and contributions of minority groups are more likely to be emphasized in schools where members of those groups are enrolled.

IMPLICATIONS FOR SCHOOLS

Public schools are very logical agencies to become a, if not the, major delivery system for preschool education. As enrollments have declined in some areas of the country, space is available in existing school facilities, and the administrative and teaching staff infrastructure is already in place. Albert Shanker, president of the American Federation of Teachers, and other educational leaders have argued that schools as permanent institutions in every community should be "the prime sponsor for all early childhood and day-care programs" and that such programs should not be subjected to the fragmented efforts and slipshod administration that characterize some inexperienced community groups starting up new programs. Schools are permanent institutions in every community and should be used. If they are not performing well, they should be improved, not bypassed.

On a more pragmatic note, public school leaders in some areas of the country support day-care and preschool programs because such programs provide jobs and a broadening of the base of support for schools in sections where school enrollments are declining. Many public school people, however, are apprehensive about expanding the role of the schools because they regard such programs as a possible drain on already limited budgets. There also is strong ideological opposition as many educators as well as citizens at large believe that the quality of education has been diluted because the schools already have been asked to do too much beyond their fundamental function.

Critics of the public schools have vigorously protested legislation or policy that would make the schools the exclusive or dominant delivery system for preschool programs. These critics, particularly many representatives of minority and civil rights groups, feel that the schools would be too bureaucratized and unresponsive to the special needs of very young children and their families. These families need a comprehensive human-services approach to their problems that will address the health, physical, and socioemotional needs of parents as well as children. There is skepticism as to whether most school systems are prepared either operationally or philosophically to develop the close ties with communities and parents that are so essential to successful preschool programs. Disagreement also exists as to appropriate content and structure of preschool education with some critics warning of the dangers of offering formal learning programs too early in the development of children.[22]

The public schools, regardless of which agency or agencies control preschool education, have an enormous stake in the possible growth of the early childhood enterprise. Public policy and services ultimately will have to respond to the dramatic changes in family life and social mores mentioned earlier. Although the public schools may not become the exclusive delivery system for early childhood services, they are likely to be active, major participants in providing preschool programs.[23] Indeed, many believe that the advocates of enlarged preschool programs under public school auspices have only temporarily relented in their efforts to gain control of the early childhood area. Current fiscal pressures on existing school programs have diverted interest from new activities that might siphon away increasingly scarce resources.

The policy debate about expanding the role of public schools to include early childhood programs also gets caught up in the interests of the growing number of private child-care providers who resist both competition and regulation. There are serious quality problems in many profit-oriented small private preschools, as some of the recent accusations of child abuse have brought to light.

Recent political and economic developments may provide more opportunity for public school advocates and their critics in the child-care community to collaborate more closely to achieve common goals.[24] Cuts in social and education programs by the Reagan administration compelled former foes to coalesce to combat a perceived common adversary. The fact that there are many more black and other minority superintendents and high-ranking administrators in urban school systems and recent improvements in test scores have somewhat reduced or at least mitigated the minority community's alienation towards schools in some districts. In an increasing number of school systems creative partnerships are being forged between the schools and child-care advocates. Such coalitions will become more common because of the interrelated demographic, political, and economic factors we have discussed. The continuing unmet child-care needs of working parents, particularly mothers, will compel the development of more responsive public policy in this neglected area as we shall now discuss.

If the schools are to be successful with preschool children and their families, efforts must be made to develop closer ties with parents and the communities. This is particularly important with low-income and minority families who are often dubious about the depth of the commitment of public school personnel to the well-being of their children. The importance of working cooperatively with parents and supporting families becomes even more significant when there are greater numbers of children coming from single-parent homes or from households where both parents are working. Indeed, if child-care services are to be extensive enough to meet our society's burgeoning needs, the facilities, outreach, and resources of the public schools may be of great importance.

No other institution has comparable social penetration. The possibility of schools becoming comprehensive social and medical, as well as educational, service delivery vehicles for children and families is exciting. The need for such focused community services is as real in affluent suburbia as it is in the most disadvantaged urban area.

Many believe that these social problems and social transformations call for significant changes in educational policy and thought. The presumption no longer holds that the majority of mothers are at home rearing children as they were only a decade or so ago. The policies of school systems as well as other governmental and private agencies and institutions must be altered to better serve students who are growing up in family and community environments that have changed dramatically in recent years.[25] Indeed, many of the major problems of families are due to circumstances beyond their control, such as lack of employment opportunities and the fiscal constraints caused by a changing economy, automation, and other factors. Merely educating parents in areas such as consumerism, child rearing, and nutrition will not suffice. Support systems may be necessary for families and children. No other institution is in a better position to assume responsibility for integrated educational, economic, health, child, and family-care services than the neighborhood schools, and the concept of extended-day programs being offered under the aegis of school systems may well receive increased attention.[26]

The area of educating parents to assist their children in school, in particular, offers unique service possibilities for schools. For example, the entry of women into the work force raises important questions of role definition for some of them. Can they enjoy their status as job-holders and at the same time meet their family obligations? Can they do both well? This ambivalence is very understandable and poses serious problems and choices as family and work priorities and obligations are sorted out. Creative thinking and flexibility are needed. An institutional base of support should be available to help adults and children work through such important problems. With the role of the extended family decreasing in a transient, urban society, neighborhoods and communities must provide the necessary social and cultural infrastructure to offset the anomie that so frequently afflicts both children and parents in an impersonalized mass society.[27] Berger and Neuhaus, for instance, focus on the need to strengthen the "mediating structures" of family, neighborhood, church, voluntary associations, and ethnic and racial subcultures if citizens are to be effectively served in the areas of education, child care, social services, health care, law enforcement, and housing.[28]

If present trends continue, changes in family structure will make traditional, largely at-home child care increasingly unfeasible. Policy must be generated that will meet contemporary conditions by being more responsive to the needs of working parents and the growing number of families requiring dual incomes. The caliber and extent of society's responses to these child-care needs will affect public schools significantly. If, as many child development specialists believe, the plasticity of the first five years of life makes that period crucial in the intellectual and emotional growth of children, then the quality of preschool education is of paramount importance.[29] If youngsters are so malleable in these early years, then their preschool experiences will influence significantly their ultimate performance and behavior when they enter the public schools. Thus, the public schools, even if they are not extensively engaged in preschool programs, should be concerned with the type of experiences preschool youngsters have.

There are encouraging indications that the major national educational organizations representing teachers, administrators, school boards, parents, and other state and local school officials are recognizing the crucial linkage between the effectiveness of schools and the changes in demography and the family that are so dramatically transforming American society. In a recent statement, these mainstream education organizations under the aegis of the Forum of Educational Organization Leaders issued a statement focusing on the special needs of growing numbers of the nation's disadvantaged young.[30]

Other influential leaders and organizations from both the private and public sectors are beginning to address the need to improve the capacity of our existing school structures to meet the multiple needs of an increasingly disadvantaged student population. For example, the Committee for Economic Development (CED), a prestigious business group that has served as an influential forum for policy development on many major and controversial issues since 1942, published two influential reports on schools in the 1980s. In making the case for business involvement and support for additional resources for education, CED stated:

> Human resources determine how the other resources of the nation will be developed and managed. Without a skilled, adaptable, and knowledgeable work force, neither industry nor government can work efficiently or productively. The schools are the central public institution for the development of human resources. Tomorrow's work force is in today's classrooms: the skills that these students develop and the attitudes toward work that they acquire will help determine the performance of our business and the course of our society in the twenty-first century.[31]

We will discuss the growing involvement of the business community in education in some detail in a later chapter. We allude to CED here because this influential private-sector organization also has lent its influential voice in support of early education for at-risk children, expressing the hope that "local school districts, with the encouragement and support of their state governments, would undertake a serious and systematic investment in enriched early childhood education for children from poor families. Such programs should be available to all four year olds from impoverished backgrounds in every school district for one year before they enter kindergarten."[32]

The CED, which usually moves along to other concerns after publishing a report on a particular substantive policy issue, sustained its involvement in education by issuing another significant report in 1987. This widely heralded statement focused on the special needs of disadvantaged children and contended "that reform strategies for the educationally disadvantaged that focus on the school system alone will continue to fail these 'children in need.' We have learned from experience that effective strategies reaching beyond the traditional boundaries of schooling and providing early and sustained intervention in the lives of disadvantaged children can break this vicious cycle of disaffection and despair."[33]

In addition to reaffirming the critical importance of investing in early intervention, the significance of business involvement, and the need for additional resources, the 1987 CED report stressed what it deemed to be the three most important investment strategies for improving the prospects of children in need: prevention through early intervention, restructuring the foundations of education, and retention and reentry.

The CED recommendations, if implemented, would have profound implications for the role and governance structure of schools. The emphasis on early intervention, for example, might well influence how resources are allocated for education as the CED report emphasizes that "in 1986, the nation spent $254 billion on education for children age six or older, while it spent only $1 billion for educating children five years and younger."[34] Other CED recommendations also have important implications for how the schools will be organized, controlled, and financed. Special programs designed to encourage pregnant teenagers and those with babies to stay in school; to provide prenatal and postnatal care for pregnant teens and other high-risk mothers; to provide family health care and developmental screening for children; to offer parenting education and child-care arrangements for teenagers in school and poor working parents; and to provide quality preschool programs for all disadvantaged three- and four-year-olds will all cost considerable sums of money as well as dramatically increase the scope of the school's responsibility.[35]

CED also criticized the basic manner in which our schools currently are organized, contending that they have been unable to ensure that disadvantaged children will develop the necessary academic skills and work habits to succeed. Indeed, CED contended that schools serving disadvantaged students must "undergo fundamental restructuring" that will require them and "their communities to reach beyond the traditional boundaries of education in order to provide the comprehensive services and substantial effort needed by disadvantaged children and youths."[36]

The CED believes that any plan to restructure schools to better serve the disadvantaged should have the following organizational characteristics:

- School-based management that involves principals, teachers, parents, students, and other school personnel in shared decision making and accountability for results.
- Teachers who have made a commitment to working with the disadvantaged and who have expertise in dealing with children with multiple problems. We are concerned with the expected shortage of quality teachers and especially minority teachers.
- Smaller schools and smaller classes that can raise achievement levels and increase interactions with teachers and other adults.
- Support of preschool and child-care programs by the school system where appropriate for the community.
- Up-to-date educational technology integrated into the curriculum to provide new learning opportunities for students and additional pedagogical support for teachers.

- □ Support systems within the schools that include health services, nutritional guidance, and psychological, career, and family counseling.
- □ Increased emphasis on extracurricular activities that help build academic, social, and physical skills.[37]

Other national reports also have focused on the changes that will be necessary in schools if the needs of disadvantaged youngsters are to be met. Funded by a consortium of major foundations—including Ford and the Carnegie Corporation of New York and under the aegis of the National Coalition of Advocates for Students, a grouping of some eighteen regional, state, and national child-advocacy groups—called for significant changes in the manner in which schools were organized, controlled, and financed.[38] This coalition created a Board of Inquiry chaired by Marion Wright Edelman of the Children's Defense Fund and former U.S. Commissioner of Education Harold Howe II, which held hearings throughout the country and heard 285 witnesses who provided more than 100 hours of testimony.[39]

The conclusions reached by the coalition's Board of Inquiry were quite similar to those reached by the CED and other groups that recently have expressed the judgement that the schools are failing to meet the needs of growing numbers of at-risk children. In a series of recommendations that have important governance, programmatic, and financial implications for education, the Board of Inquiry recommended the following strategies to improve the effectiveness and operations of schools:

- □ Continued, rather than diminished, federal, state, and local attention to the rights of the disadvantaged and those discriminated against because of race, language, sex, or handicapping condition.
- □ Greater willingness on the part of those in positions of responsibility to adjust schools to the diverse needs of all students who attend them.
- □ More democratic governance of all schools which assures parents of a significant role in making decisions about the education of their children and teaches students, by example, principles of democratic participation and the exercise of constitutional rights.
- □ Establishment of comprehensive early childhood education, day-care programs, and in-school support services for children and youth as a means of preventing school failure.
- □ Enactment of more equitable and adequate systems for financing schools, so that the quality of education available does not depend upon where a child lives.
- □ More systematic attention to the problems of jobs for youth and dropouts by federal, state, and local education authorities.[40]

Education and public policy analysts, as well as broadly representative national study commissions, are beginning to call for a reassessment of the basic organizational structure of schools to better meet the special needs of increasingly diverse and needy student populations. Heath and McLaughlin, for example, call for the formulation of new child resource policies and a somewhat altered role for schools that more appropriately fits contemporary demographic and family patterns.[41] They stress that academically and emotionally secure and successful youngsters often have the advantage of participating socially in a wide array of community activities such as athletics, Scouting, and work experience. Heath and McLaughlin maintain that community institutions and volunteer agencies can and should provide for the children of working and single-parent families "access to adults with a wide range of talents and perspectives."[42] Such institutions can provide out-of-school educational experiences that not only enrich the growth of disadvantaged youngsters but also motivate them to work harder in school.

Heath and McLaughlin contend that traditional forms of family-school relations are no longer relevant as "family demographics, the demands of the contemporary professional workplace, the wage structure, and the multiplicity of socio-cultural groups have made community organizations necessary and allowed them to persist" despite serious fiscal limitations in recent years.[43]

In other words, the current educational and social problems of many students demand resources that cannot be provided by today's schools and families as they are functioning. The child must be viewed as a participant in a community environment and social networks that are much larger than the school itself and school must be viewed as a nexus of institutions within the environment:

> The societal responsibility for educating children necessitates a changed governance structure and planning across the traditional boundaries of the public and private sectors. The school becomes the nexus for community, business and family collaboration that places academic learning within the nurturant ecosystem of athletic, vocational, and service-oriented agencies and of institutions dedicated to mental and physical health. No longer would school boards and district offices focus on the school as a separate institution and attempt to meet only parental demands. Instead, district and state personnel would bring together representatives of local community agencies, businesses, and athletic groups to decide on shared goals and general strategies for providing coordinated partnership efforts to meet these goals.[44]

Kirst also articulates the case for more comprehensive approaches in the formulation and implementation of policies involving children and youth. Policymakers must begin to analyze and act upon the interrelationships between complex issues such as educational achievement, teen pregnancy, poor nutrition, parental illiteracy, and poverty. In describing the evolution of plans to develop a comprehensive report that describes the condition of children in California, Kirst cites the earlier report on education done by his Policy Analysis for California Education group and the group's growing realization that "we could not look at education without looking at the broader conditions of children."[45]

SUMMARY AND FUTURE PROSPECTS

The fundamental types of changes in the organization and control of schools we have discussed are far from being implemented at this time. We have no illusions about the political difficulties that confront the policymakers, planners, and practitioners who attempt approaches requiring greater coordination among professionals and organizations that have long-established and well-entrenched concepts of their roles and territorial prerogatives. Such changes will require, as Heath and McLaughlin state, "moving from the time-honored (and sometimes serviceable) strategy of making incremental policy adjustments in existing institutions to a radically different conception of the school and its role in preparing the nation's youth for tomorrow's workplace, family and community."[46]

A major objective of this chapter has been to stress that the profound demographic and family changes that have been discussed may compel basic structural and governance changes if public education, as we currently know it, is to succeed. We recognize that the perception of the school as a component of a comprehensive social network and support system for children and their families and not a discrete, insulated, and single-purpose institution is unlikely to gain widespread acceptance in the years immediately ahead.

Demographic and family realities, however, we believe, will compel some changes in how schools are organized and governed, particularly in urban districts in which large and growing segments of the student population require multiple support systems.

The role of schools will have to be broadened to meet the varied needs of their changing student clientele. The growing numbers of older citizens in the population will compel schools to broaden their base of support for political as well as substantive educational reasons. Fewer than 30 percent of the population currently have youngsters enrolled. Educational leaders can no longer assume the public support they could generate, for example, when 60 percent to 70 percent of the population had children in the schools in the rapid growth era after World War II. Schools will have to reach out to cultivate new and broader constituencies and provide expanded programs if they are to acquire the necessary support as older citizens and other groups make increased demands for services in a period of declining resources. Public schools will have to be viewed as a civic responsibility by the majority of the population, which will not have children involved or a direct stake in the educational process. Educators can no longer assume that they have a broadly gauged support base and certainly cannot afford the luxury of pulling the wagons around in a circle and shooting inwardly as has often been the case in the intramural or internecine warfare that has occurred with some frequency over collective bargaining, church-state relationships, funding allocations, desegregation, interlevel responsibilities, and other issues that will be discussed in ensuing chapters of this book.

The demographic imperatives we have discussed in this chapter call for educational leaders to reconfigure and essentially redefine education as constituting more than just traditional schools or formal institutions of learning. Such action would expand the coalition in support of public education to include preschool children, senior citizens, the numerous older workers who will have to be retrained, and others in the society who will require educational and/or training opportunities in a changing economy. This expanded outreach will be a great asset to educators in their efforts to reach out politically not only to buttress and expand their own support base and programs but also as they seek to help fill the escalating education needs of adult groups such as senior citizens, older workers who need retraining, and single and two-career parents with latch-key children.

In closing this chapter, we will use the preschool issue as an illustration of the implications of an expanded educational program on the control of education. Most school-age youngsters in the United States attend school during the state-determined compulsory attendance years, most often from age five through age sixteen. The states of the United States patterned themselves, at least in part, after Great Britain in the establishment and enforcement of school attendance policy. Policy regarding school attendance, a state prerogative, was determined in the nineteenth century. It was fashioned in response to public needs and now, a century later, new issues regarding the education of children in the preschool years are developing.

An expanded educational program raises a number of control issues. For example, should the states develop new legislation regarding the certification of personnel, the licensing and supervision of institutions providing preprimary programs, and the location of administrative and supervisory responsibilities? Currently the states vary in the scope and specificity of policy governing preprimary education. The states' interests in the lives of young children date back to the emergence of kindergartens, many of which were nonpublic. There was concern about the states' responsibilities for their supervision, especially on issues pertaining to the welfare of children and the absence of compulsory attendance laws covering this age group.

The number of children presently enrolled or likely to enroll in preschool is becoming so large that governance and control problems have a new immediacy and urgency. Approximately 2 percent of the nation's total population are presently in attendance in a preprimary setting. The problem is not simply one of numbers but one of substantial philosophical, educational, political, social, and economic dimensions.

An important political and governance issue is involved in the administration and supervision of preprimary programs. Should such responsibilities rest with state education, health, or welfare departments? Or do they belong elsewhere? Or should those responsibilities be shared? Certainly the administrative organizations within each of these areas and the interest groups they attract have preferences regarding the placement of administrative and supervisory responsibilities. Those preferences are based in part on philosophical beliefs about what should be emphasized in the lives of young children and in part on the ever-present pressure to extend and sustain the bureaucracies themselves. The same issues are prominent at the federal level as questions of children's welfare surface within Congress, the executive branch, and the federal courts.

Economic issues also raise policy problems in regard to preprimary school programs as well as other public interventions in the lives of young children. We have referred to the income requirements of single-parent families as well as those where both parents are employed to improve their family's standard of living. These trends appear to be irreversible, given the entrenched belief in the free enterprise system. Another economic issue is institutional ownership. Day-care centers, nursery schools, and other forms of preprimary schooling have become big business in recent years. There are strong private interests striving to keep public institutions from expanding their services to include the preschool age group. Ownership of nursery schools and day-care centers can be profitable. So much so that day-care and nursery school chains are developing.

School districts, it can be argued, are the logical local governments to assume public responsibility for preschool programming. Proposals for incorporating these responsibilities within the public schools, however, are challenged by those who oppose preschool programming itself, resist the expansion of public school control, and fight increased support for the public school system. In addition, private-sector interest groups argue for educational options as well as for benefits to the taxpayer that accrue if such services remain within private-sector management.

The demographic and family changes we have discussed in this chapter will compel our society to attempt to resolve such complex control issues in the years ahead, not only in the area of preschool education but in the provision of other support programs that will be necessary if ever larger numbers of our at-risk young people are to become productive citizens.

NOTES

[1] Harold L. Hodgkinson, "Guess Who's Coming to College: Your Students in 1990" (Washington, DC: National Association of Independent Colleges and Universities, 1983, Mimeographed), 3.

[2] Ibid., 6.

[3] Harold L. Hodgkinson, *All One System: Demographics of Education, Kindergarten through Graduate School* (Washington, DC: Institute for Educational Leadership, 1985), 10.

[4] Ibid., 3.

[5] Henry M. Levin. *The Educationally Disadvantaged: A National Crisis.* Working Paper 6 (Philadelphia, PA: Public Private Ventures, 1985), 9.

[6] Ibid., 8.

[7] B. Frank Brown, "A Study of the School Needs of Children from One-Parent Families," *Phi Delta Kappan* 61 (April 1980): 537–40.

[8] *Characteristics of American Children and Youth: 1980* (Washington, DC: Bureau of the Census, 1982), 1.

[9] Brown, "Study of the School Needs."

[10] Children's Defense Fund, *Employed Parents and Their Children: A Data Book,* (Washington, DC: 1982), 49.

[11] Hodgkinson, *All One System,* 3.

[12] Ibid.

[13] Ibid., 5.

[14] Newsletter, Project on the Status and Education of Women, Association of American Colleges, no. 20 (June 1978): 3.

[15] Robert Lindsey, "Women Entering Job Market at Extraordinary Pace," *New York Times,* 12 September 1976, 1, 49.

[16]Office of Educational Research and Improvement, *Elementary and Secondary Education Indicators In Brief* (Washington, DC: U.S. Department of Education, 1987), 32.

[17]William Dunn, "The Patter of Little Feet Swamps Nursery School," *Detroit News,* 20 February 1978, 16.

[18]Children's Defense Fund, *Employed Parents and Their Children,* 89.

[19]*Elementary and Secondary Education Indicators in Brief,* 30.

[20]National Center for Educational Statistics, *Digest of Educational Statistics, 1985–86* (Washington, DC: U.S. Government Printing Office, 1986), 64.

[21]See Howard S. Becker, "The Career of the Chicago Public School Teacher," *American Journal of Sociology* 52 (March 1952): 470–77 and Robert E. Herriott and Nancy Hoyt St. John, *Social Class and the Urban Schools* (New York: John Wiley & Sons, 1966), 206.

[22]See, for example, Deborah Burnett Strother, "Preschool Children In the Public Schools: Good Investment? Or Bad?," *Phi Delta Kappan* 69 (December 1987): 304–308.

[23]A growing number of states are funding preschool programs designed to assist at-risk youngsters. As of 1987, twenty-five states offered such programs. See "The Governors 1991 Report on Education," *Results in Education: 1987* (Washington, DC: National Governors Association, 1987), 20.

[24]See, for example, James A. Kelly, "Child Care and the Schools," Address delivered at the Conference on Child Care and the Role of the Schools, Spring Hill Center, Wayzata, MN, 10 December 1984, Mimeographed.

[25]*Toward a National Policy for Children and Families* (Washington, DC: National Academy of Sciences, 1977). See also *Barriers to Excellence: Our Children at Risk* (Boston: National Coalition of Advocates for Students, 1985).

[26]Education Commission of the States, *Families and Schools: Implementing Parent Education* report no. 121 (1979). See also James A. Levine, *Day Care and the Public Schools: Profiles of Five Communities* (Newton, MA: Education Development Center, 1978).

[27]David S. Seeley, *Education Through Partnership: Mediating Structures and Education* (Cambridge, MA: Ballinger, 1980).

[28]Peter L. Berger and Richard John Neuhaus, *To Empower People: The Role of Mediating Structures in Public Policy* (Washington, DC: American Enterprise Institute for Public Policy Research, 1977).

[29]Benjamin S. Bloom, *Stability and Change in Human Characteristics* (New York: John Wiley and Sons, 1964).

[30]"Meeting the Needs of Children and Youth At Risk of School Failure: The National Imperative," Statement of the Forum of Educational Organization Leaders, 1 June 1987, Mimeographed.

[31]Committee for Economic Development, *Investing in Our Children: Business and the Public School* (New York: Committee for Economic Development, 1985), 5.

[32]Ibid., 46.

[33]Ibid., 1.

[34]Ibid., 21.

[35]Ibid., 20–37.

[36]Ibid., 39.

[37]Ibid., 38–63.

[38]*Barriers to Excellence: Our Children At Risk.*

[39]Ibid., vii.

[40]Ibid., xii–xiii.

[41]Shirley Brice Heath and Milbrey Wallin McLaughlin, "A Child Resource Policy: Moving Beyond Dependence on School and Family," *Phi Delta Kappan* 68 (April 1987): 576–580.

[42]Ibid., 579.

[43]Ibid.

[44]Ibid., 580.

[45]"Towards a New Youth Agenda: Assessing the Conditions of Children in California," *Youth Policy,* vol. 9, no. 7 (July 1987): 13.

[46]Heath and McLaughlin, 580.

3
American Schools and the Federal Government

The federal Constitution adopted in 1788 contained no mention of public education or public schools. At least two circumstances may explain the absence of any such reference. In the first place, the Constitution created a federal government that was to have delegated to it only certain enumerated powers and those implied by such enumeration. As made clear in the Tenth Amendment, "the powers not delegated to the United States by the Constitution, nor prohibited by it to the States, are reserved to the States respectively, or to the people." The spirit of the time, as well as the official language, made for a carefully limited federal government.

A second condition should also be noted: when the Constitution was being written, the states had not yet established any genuine public school systems. Some beginning steps had been taken, but it was to be fifty to a hundred years before public schools were finally established in the several states. Schools were still very much in the private and parochial domain. Since provisions to place schools in the public domain were as yet either weak or nonexistent in state constitutions, there appeared to be little need to transfer such an incipient matter to the federal government.

Despite the lack of specific mention of public education in the federal Constitution, the critical importance of the schools in preserving its meaning and heritage has been stressed throughout American history. More recently, former Chief Justice Warren E. Burger and others involved in the Commission on the Bicentennial of the U.S. Constitution in 1987–88 stressed the central roles schools were expected to play in perpetuating the values espoused in the Constitution during the bicentennial observances.[1]

Moreover, the federal government has always had a hand in public education. Beginning with the land grant acts, which actually preceded the federal Constitution, and continuing until the last session of Congress, certain provisions for public schools have been enacted. The general welfare clause of the federal Constitution, Article I, Section 8, authorizes Congress "to lay and collect Taxes, Duties, Imports and Excises, and to pay the Debts and provide for the common Defense and the general Welfare of the United States." This clause has been interpreted as giving Congress power to tax for broad social purposes, and this power was upheld by the United States Supreme Court in *Helvering* v. *Davis,* which concerned the Social Security Act.[2]

While there seems to be no case on record involving the power of Congress to tax for public education, the language of other cases makes it clear that the national government may tax and spend in support of schools and school programs. Moreover, our history suggests that the national government may enter into agreements with the states for the mutual support of education and may exercise whatever controls are necessary to accomplish the purposes for which federal funds are provided.

In this chapter we will describe the context within which the federal government has related to schools, note how federal relationships have evolved over our history, indicate the nature of the controls exercised by the federal government, and consider probable future developments in federal relationships.

FROM DUAL TO NATIONAL FEDERALISM

The relations of the federal government to state and local governments for any purpose cannot be understood without recognizing that over the years there has been a shift from dual to national federalism. We use the term *dual federalism* to mean the historical separation of powers between state and national governments. Power, as we shall show, has shifted more and more toward the national government; *national federalism* has come to prevail, despite some recent slowing of this trend.

Dual Governments

Early American government was a very limited one at both state and national levels. Government dealt with civil and political matters, and had little to do with social or economic problems. Jefferson spoke for his generation when he contended that less government was better government. The founding fathers intended to limit government at all levels and to leave much to the individual's discretion.

When the framers of the United States Constitution met in 1787 to revise the Articles of Confederation, with which they had become dissatisfied, they cast aside the old document and wrote a new one. Clearly, they wanted to create a national government and not just a league of separate states.

The Constitution did represent an attempt to separate the powers of government between the states and the nation. To be sure, there was disagreement from the beginning as to just what this attempted separation meant. Hamilton advocated a strong federal government, particularly a strong executive branch. Jefferson tended to emphasize states' rights more than federal responsibility. He was also disposed to place more faith in legislative than in executive action.[3] In terms of today's developments, however, both Hamilton and Jefferson might be seen as exponents of dual federalism.

The economic and political circumstances of the United States in its first decade or so of existence affected the design of American government. The economy was predominantly rural in nature. In the South, particularly, there were large landholders, but the corporate form of business had not yet evolved. While war was seen as a possibility, and indeed became a reality in 1812, armed conflict on a worldwide scale was not imagined. The thought that the new nation would one day devote a major portion of its budget to defense would have seemed preposterous. In other words, dual federalism seemed quite adequate for a nation chiefly concerned with its own domestic problems, the expression of which tended to be somewhat unique to each of the states. Logical as the separation of power between the state and the national governments appeared to our founding fathers, Grodzins has contended that there never was a genuine separation.[4] Instead of comparing federalism to a layer cake—one layer representing local government, the second layer state government, and the third layer national government—Grodzins has used a model of a marble cake. Each function, he contends, is mixed in the American federal system. Each level of government interacts with and influences every other level of government. In fact, Grodzins maintains that federalism is a plan for sharing the functions of government and not a plan for separating them.

In terms of the actual operation of government, he may be correct. His description of shared functions may be even more accurate for today's government than for government two centuries ago. Even so, the original concept of federalism did attempt to delegate to a national government certain necessary but limited functions and to reserve for the states or for the people the remaining functions. This concept, never one upon which there was complete agreement and one still invoked by some politicians, has been subject to many changes, as we shall now see.

National Federalism

A number of circumstances contributed to the demise of dual federalism and to the development of national federalism. Many of these circumstances were social and economic in character. The rural economy of the early nineteenth century gave way to industrialization and urbanization. These developments were national in scope. Communication and transportation increased greatly in volume and efficiency. A great depression and two world wars required action that only the national government was in a position to take. In growing numbers, people were beginning to think of the nation as a single political entity.

Governmental provisions reflected these changes in social and economic circumstances. Following the Civil War, the Fourteenth Amendment was added to the U.S. Constitution. This amendment made citizens of the individual states also citizens of the United States and forbade the states from depriving "any person of life, liberty, or property without due process of law." By the time the U.S. Supreme Court upheld the Social Security legislation of the 1930s, the position of the national government on social as well as civil matters was well established.[5]

Grodzins does not decry this shift from dual to national federalism; he suggests that the national government, instead of doing too much, is actually doing too little.[6] He points out that national deficiencies in education, health, housing, urban development, air pollution, water supply, and mass transportation require additional, not less, attention on the part of the national government. Most of these problems extend beyond the boundaries of local government and in many cases beyond the boundaries of state governments. The extent of the problems, coupled with the fact that most of the tax resources accrue to the federal government, makes it apparent that even with some revenue sharing, national action is required.

Import for Education

The shift from dual to national federalism has had great import for education. Historically, education was seen as one of those matters left to the states. To be sure, the national government never ignored schools and colleges completely, but for the most part, the state legislatures exercised plenary power over education, particularly the public elementary and secondary schools. Many people wanted to retain this state of affairs. As late as 1962 the American Association of School Administrators contended:

> The Executive Committee of AASA reaffirms its believe in the principle long held in the United States that education is a state function, and that the principle works exceedingly well when the responsibility of the state is delegated in large measure to local boards of education who operate with close sensitivity to the needs of developing young people and adults in a given community. Although the record is never perfect, and not even good in some instances, the Executive Committee holds to the concept that on the whole the educational needs of the local community, the state, and, indeed, the nation can best be served when the control of education rests at the state and local levels rather than at the national level.[7]

In more recent years, AASA has been less explicit about local control. For instance, in 1987 the organization adopted a resolution explicitly recognizing the "demonstrated and urgent need" to increase the level of federal financial support to public education through general aid, categorical programs to meet the special educational needs of disadvantaged children, and partnerships with local and state governments "to equalize programs which will guarantee every student maximum opportunities for quality public education."[8]

In spite of the current reappraisal of the federal role in education, national involvement continues. Some of those who resist the growth of national government have devised another argument that is often employed in connection with attempts to secure federal aid for schools. They attack the federal government's reputed wasting of money. Some claim that much of the money sent to Washington is not returned in public services, but instead supports unnecessary government overhead. Wealthy states, to be sure, never receive from Washington services equivalent to the taxes collected by the federal government from those states. Poor states, on the other hand, tend to receive services in excess of federal taxes collected within their borders.

These circumstances provide those who would keep all taxes low with an excellent opportunity to lament the takeover by the national government and to decry the waste of the bureaucrats in Washington. Actually, the national government, more than local and state governments, can collect taxes where the resources are and provide services where they are needed. Thus, if schools or any other service for the entire nation is to be brought up to a minimum standard, some action on the part of the federal government is necessary. Moreover, federal tax collection costs are much lower than state and local tax collection costs.

The issue of general versus categorical aid also figures in the growth of national federalism. If educational policy is seen as the major province of the states, the argument for federal grants of money without stipulation as to purpose seems to make sense. But if educational policy is also seen as the province of the national government, it is clear that categorical aid, not general aid, should be provided by the federal government.

Attempts to secure general aid began in 1870 and have continued with little success in intervening years.[9] On the other hand, Congress has a long record of providing categorical aid to the schools and colleges of the various states. The legislative record provides concrete evidence of the growth of national federalism. The Morrill Act of 1862, the Smith-Hughes Act of 1917, Public Laws 815 and 874 (designed to assist federally impacted areas), the National Defense Education Act of 1958, the Elementary and Secondary Act of 1965, and other congressional actions all reflect a desire on the part of the national government to assist education—but to assist it in particular ways. While categories may be revised or consolidated, reversal of this policy seems unlikely.

This shift from dual to national federalism is unrecognized in some quarters, causes concern in others and strong resistance in still others. The nature and magnitude of the social, economic, political, and technological problems facing the nation have made this shift inevitable. Education has some relationship to all these problems and thus is caught up in the increasing scope of government at the national level.

EARLY FEDERAL RELATIONS

Land Grants

Early federal legislation pertaining to education had to do chiefly with land grants and the establishment of land grant colleges. In the Ordinance of 1785 Congress declared that in the Northwest Territory (later to become the states of Indiana, Illinois, Michigan, Ohio, Wisconsin, and part of Minnesota) "there shall be reserved the lot No. 16 of every township, for the maintenance of public schools, within said township."

The Ordinance of 1787 dealt with the sale of 1½ million acres of land to the Ohio Company and might properly be described as a governmental and not a land act. Nevertheless, one clause of the ordinance was destined to have a salutary effect on education. That clause reads, "Religion, morality and knowledge, being necessary to good government and happiness of mankind, schools and the means of education shall forever be encouraged."

With the admission of California to the Union in 1850, sections sixteen and thirty-six were set aside for school purposes. Fourteen states followed suit when they entered the Union reserving two sections of each township for school purposes. In Utah, Arizona, and New Mexico, where land was cheap, four sections of each township were so reserved. Thus, with the thirteen states that came into statehood earlier, a total of thirty states received grants of some 80 million acres of land.

The Michigan legislature in 1850 petitioned Congress for a grant of public land to establish a college of agriculture. Illinois made a similar request in 1853, and Michigan renewed its request in 1857. Senator Justin Morrill of Vermont introduced a bill in 1857 that granted 20,000 acres of land to each state for each senator and representative in Congress for the purpose of establishing colleges of agriculture. Congress approved the bill, but it was vetoed by President Buchanan. In 1862, however, the Morrill Act passed, and the grant increased to 30,000 acres for each senator and representative. The act provided for the

> endowment, support, and maintenance of at least one college where the leading object shall be, without excluding other scientific and classical studies, and including military tactics, to teach such branches of learning as are related to agriculture and the mechanic arts—in order to promote the liberal and practical education of the industrial classes in the several pursuits and professions of life.

Other legislation pertaining to the land grant colleges included the Hatch Act of 1887, which established the experiment stations; the so-called second Morrill Act of 1890; the Nelson Amendment of 1907, which allowed the training of teachers; and the Bankhead-Jones Act in 1935, which extended some of these functions.

Vocational Education

In 1917, influenced to some extent by World War I, Congress passed the Smith-Hughes Act for the support of vocational education. In its own language, the act was

> for the purpose of cooperating with the states in paying the salaries of teachers, supervisors, and directors of agricultural subjects, and of teachers of trade and industrial subjects, and in the preparation of teachers of agricultural, trade, and industrial, and home economics subjects—and for the purpose of making studies, investigations, and reports to aid in the organization and conduct of vocational education.

The act originally required that the states and the local school districts match federal funds. Public interest in vocational education grew until many high schools in practically every state had vocational agriculture and vocational home economics as established parts of the high school curriculum. A number of trade or vocational high schools were established in large cities, and trade and industry programs were also established in some comprehensive high schools. The initial legislation was later extended by the George-Reed Act of 1929, the George-Ellzey Act of 1934, the George-Deen Act of 1937, and the George-Barden Act of 1946.

Depression Legislation

Spurred by the depression of the 1930s, the national government enacted a great many relief measures, and many of these measures affected school operation. The Civil Works Administration and later the Public Works Administration, for example, set up grants and loans and in some instances supplied materials to help with the construction, alteration, and repair of school buildings. The two relief measures that seemed to have most influence on school programs were the Civilian Conservation Corps and the National Youth Administration.

The CCC was created by an act of Congress in 1933. The act was designed chiefly to relieve unemployment through "the restoration of the country's depleted natural resources and the advancement of an orderly program of useful public works." Young men between the ages of seventeen and twenty-two years, most of them in the larger cities, were sent to camps in remote areas of the country where they made trails, planted trees, built bridges, and performed many other useful tasks. For this service, the men were housed, fed, provided with medical care, and paid a small wage.

Learning opportunities existed in the program from the start, but in 1937 Congress stipulated that "at least ten hours per week may be devoted to general educational and vocational training." In time each camp was provided with an educational adviser appointed by the United States Office of Education. These advisers recruited a staff of part-time teachers from among the personnel of the camp and they also often enlisted the help of teachers in nearby high schools and colleges. More than 3 million young men were enrolled in the CCC program and 2.7 million participated in some kind of organized educational activity during its ten-year history.

The NYA was established by executive order of the president in 1935 and received congressional appropriations until its liquidation in 1944. The purpose of NYA was to provide full-time employment for youths sixteen to twenty-four years of age who were in high school and college. While most of the young people in the program lived at home, a number of states did establish NYA resident centers. In many instances, young people performed useful services in the construction of public buildings, in the performance of clerical tasks, in augmenting services performed by public libraries and museums, in assisting with research projects, and in other ways.

For most of its history, NYA was an independent federal agency and had its own federal, state, and local administrative organization. In 1939 NYA, along with CCC, was placed in the Federal Security Agency, and in 1940 part of its budget was channeled through the U.S. Office of Education. The out-of-school work program reached a peak employment of about 470,000 youths in February 1941. The maximum employment under the student work program was 482,000 in April 1940. Peak appropriations for the program were for the 1940–41 fiscal year and amounted to $157,159,000.[10]

Other Federal Programs

Federal relationships were too numerous to be described in full here, but a few additional federal activities in education will be noted. For example, the federal government has a long history of providing schools in areas under special jurisdiction. Since 1804 Congress has provided for the schools in Washington, DC. The Bureau of Indian Affairs since 1824 has been charged with providing schools for Indians and Eskimos. The schools of the territories have often been administered by federally appointed officials. The federal government has also established and operated schools on reservations where it maintains "forts, magazines, arsenals, dockyards, and other needful buildings." The creation of defense bases around the world has also created a sizable school system under the various military jurisdictions.[11]

Another example of federal activity in education is found in the provisions made for federally impacted areas. Beginning with the Lanham Act in 1941, Congress appropriated money to aid local government in the construction and operation of schools and other facilities where war-related federal activities had created burdens on local government. Many of these provisions were continued with the enactment of Public Laws 815 and 874 in 1950 and with their extensions since that time.

The United States Office of Education

Federal programs for education have been organized in many ways, some under a separate agency, some under other agencies of government such as the Department of the Army or the Navy, and some under the United States Office of Education. The U.S. Office of Education, first known as the Department of Education, was created by act of Congress in 1867. An early report by the commissioner states the department's purpose as follows:

> to collect such statistics and facts as shall show the condition and progress of educa-
> tion in the several States and Territories, [and] to diffuse such information respecting
> the organization and management of schools and school systems, and methods of
> teaching, as shall aid the people of the United States in the establishment and mainte-
> nance of efficient school systems, and otherwise promote the cause of education
> through the country.

For many years, the U.S. Office of Education was in the Department of the Interior. In 1939 the office was transferred to the Federal Security Agency and in 1953 to the Department of Health, Education, and Welfare. The office was headed by a commissioner of education, appointed by the president. Over most of its history, the office exercised a very modest role in American education. In recent years, as will be shown later, the education agency has become the Department of Education and its functions somewhat modified. In no sense, however, has the agency ever been a national ministry of education as that term is understood in many other countries.

Nature of Early Federal Activities

This historical background of federal relations with education might be summarized by brief reference to the findings of two studies completed about 1950. Allen, as a member of the Hoover task force on the reorganization of the federal government, had a unique opportunity to examine the character and extent of federal programs in education. His report suggested that at least twenty federal agencies were engaged in bona fide educational programs, that the annual expenditures for these programs amounted to more than $3 billion, and that only 1 percent of that amount was channeled through the Office of Education.[12]

In 1951 Quattlebaum prepared a report for Congress in which federal activities in education were carefully assessed.[13] His summary of federal allocations for fiscal year 1950 totaled $3.6 billion. Of this amount, 81 percent was for expenditures through the Veterans' Administration. Nineteen other departments or agencies of the federal government were also shown to have funds allocated for education.

Data from both Allen and Quattlebaum permit us to draw a number of conclusions regarding federal activities in education as of 1950. One, these activities were extensive and widespread. Two, the money appropriated for such activities was appreciable. Three, the U.S. Office of Education had meager influence and even less control over this vast program. Four, there was apparently little, if any, coordination of the programs of the several federal agencies.

RAPID EXPANSION OF FEDERAL INFLUENCE

While federal participation and influence in education has been with us since the founding of the nation, the twenty-year period from 1950 to 1970 is particularly noteworthy as a time of rapid growth of federal involvement. The federal courts may have done as much as Congress to create a national policy for education. Their role is discussed in Chapter 8. Now we'll examine some of the major programs established during that period and give some attention to the federal structure created to administer those programs.

The GI Bills

Congressional authorization of educational benefits for veterans has come chiefly through the Vocational Rehabilitation Act of 1943 (Public Law 16), the Servicemen's Readjustment Act of 1944 (Public Law 346), and subsequent legislation written to apply to veterans of the Korean and Vietnam conflicts.

Under Public Law 16, the Veterans' Administration emphasized the need for vocational advisory service to the disabled veteran. This service was given by the regional offices of the Veterans' Administration and also by more than 300 educational institutions under contract with the Veterans' Administration. The policy also provided that, if possible, the veteran would be trained in his or her own community and in existing accredited schools and colleges. By July 1, 1959, 675,000 disabled veterans had taken vocational rehabilitation training.[14]

Under the provisions of Public law 346, practically all veterans were eligible for educational benefits. The veteran was free to elect a course of study, to enter any approved school or college, and to pursue that course for one year plus the number of months he or she was in service (not in excess of forty-eight months).

The federal government made payments directly to the veteran and also to the school or college the veteran attended. In 1955 the 82nd Congress in Public Law 550 simplified the method of payments and required that the veteran be responsible for payments to the educational institution. Increased benefits for Vietnam veterans were provided by the passage of PL 92–540 in 1972. Educational assistance for single veterans enrolled in a full-time program was set at $220 per month. Additional allowances were provided for veterans with dependents.

Altogether the IOUs represented by all of the GI bills have been collected by approximately 30 million men and women. Counting all forms of educational benefits—college, secondary, and on-the-job training—about 48 percent of the World War II veterans claimed benefits, about 42 percent of the Korean veterans claimed benefits, and responses from Vietnam veterans indicate that the percentage claiming benefits may well go beyond that of World War II.[15] By 1956 the education of veterans had cost the federal government $14.5 billion.[16] By now, the total cost is more than double that amount with additional benefits to Vietnam veterans having pushed the total costs much higher.

The full impact of veteran enrollment and federal money on school and college programs cannot be assessed here, but certain facts are noteworthy. The federal government did assume responsibility for interrupting the school or college careers of the young people who served in the war. Approved existing schools and colleges were utilized and subsidized by the federal government. Public and private schools and colleges alike were approved for the veteran programs and hence for federal subsidy. In effect veteran benefits established a far-flung system of federal scholarships at the college and graduate school level. These scholarships tended to go to the academically talented.

The National Science Foundation

The establishment of a National Science Foundation in 1950 was essentially an outgrowth of American experience in World War II; the scientific resources of the nation had been mobilized by the federal government. The foundation was created "to promote the progress of science; to advance the national health, prosperity, and welfare; to secure the national defense; and for other purposes." As such, the act was a response to meet a need described in terms of the national welfare.

Among the eight functions the foundation was authorized and directed to perform, those pertaining to education are:

1. to develop and encourage the pursuit of a national policy for the promotion of basic research and education in sciences;
2. to initiate and support basic and scientific research in the mathematical, physical, medical, biological, engineering, and other sciences; . . .

4. to award . . . scholarships and graduate fellowships in the mathematical, physical, medical, biological, engineering, and other sciences;. . . .

While functions (2) and (4) have specific educational import, it is clear that the broad wording in (1) provides considerable latitude for interpretation. The several kinds of educational programs initiated by the foundation in the past years can be justified on the basis of the discretionary powers granted therein. In 1959 it was expressly the existence of these programs that resulted in the amendment of function (2) to include support for "programs to strengthen scientific research potential . . . by making contracts and other arrangements . . . to support such scientific activities."[17] These changes were viewed by the sponsoring legislators as making "explicit the Foundation's authority to support programs designed to stimulate improved scientific teaching and to encourage the undertaking of careers in science."[18]

Control of the organization was vested in a National Science Board consisting of twenty-four members and the director. Only the board could make policy decisions, and it had to approve all contracts and grants pursuant to the statutory functions of the foundation. Thus, the National Science Foundation, in keeping with the dominant thinking of Congress, was established as a quasi-independent agency in the executive branch of the government. Indeed, its significance has continued to grow because of the nation's need for well-trained scientists in an increasingly competitive world economy.

The Cooperative Research Program

In 1954 the 83rd Congress passed Public Law 531 establishing the cooperative research program. The U.S. Commissioner of Education was authorized to enter into contracts with universities, colleges, and state education agencies for the conduct of research, surveys, and demonstrations in the field of education. There was the further stipulation, however, that these contracts could not be made until the commissioner had obtained the advice of educational research specialists on the merit of the proposals. No money was appropriated for this program until 1956–57.

The Cooperative Research Program was begun in fiscal 1957 with an appropriation of $1 million. By fiscal 1965 the appropriation had reached $16 million. In that year the program was incorporated in Title IV as part of the Elementary and Secondary Education Act. Research support was broadened to include research and development centers, regional laboratories, and the training of researchers, as well as project support. Estimated expenditures for successors to these programs for fiscal 1979, though hard to isolate in the 1979 budget, totaled about $300 million.[19]

A few observations about the cooperative research program are appropriate. First, the program was lodged in the U.S. Office of Education and not established as an independent agency, as was the National Science Foundation. Second, the money, while relatively small in amount as compared to other federally supported research programs, has given great impetus to educational research. Scholars in many basic disciplines, particularly the social sciences, as well as those in education have turned their attention to research problems in education. Third, the project approval procedure and later the approval of research and development centers and regional laboratories have inevitably influenced the nature and course of educational research.

The National Defense Education Act

The National Defense Education Act, Public Law 85–864, provided for loans to college students, fellowships for graduate study, centers for research and study of foreign languages, experimentation with television and related media, and improvement of statistical services in state departments of education.

In many ways NDEA served as a precursor for subsequent legislation. For instance, the student loan program, Title II, was enlarged to include many more students largely on the basis of need; and curriculum improvement, Title III, originally limited to science, mathematics, and foreign languages, was broadened to include many other school subjects. Several titles in NDEA have also been incorporated into more recent legislation. Area vocational education, Title VII, became part of the Vocational Education Act of 1963. Help for statistical services for states, Title X, was merged with the Elementary and Secondary Education Act of 1965. Institutes for teachers and other school personnel, Title XI, was incorporated into the broadened Educational Professions Development Act of 1967. NDEA contributed to local-state-national partnership in education and also set a precedent for assisting nonpublic as well as public schools. In a decade total appropriations for NDEA were about $3 billion.

Vocational Education

The Vocational Education Act of 1963 represented a new emphasis for the federal government in the area of vocational training. The purpose of the legislation, as stated in Section 1 of the act, follows:

> It is the purpose of this part to authorize Federal grants to States to assist them to maintain, extend, and improve existing programs of vocational education, to develop new programs of vocational education, and to provide part-time employment for youths who need the earnings from such employment to continue their vocational training on a full-time basis, so that persons of all ages in all communities of the State—those in high school, those who have completed or discontinued their formal education and are preparing to enter the labor market, those who have already entered the labor market but need to upgrade their skills or learn new ones, and those with special educational handicaps—will have ready access to vocational training or retraining which is of high quality, which is realistic in the light of actual or anticipated opportunities for gainful employment, and which is suited to their needs, interests, and ability to benefit from such training.

Whereas appropriations to the states for vocational education under the Smith-Hughes and George-Barden acts had been about $52 million per year, the new legislation provided $60 million for fiscal 1964, and $225 million for fiscal 1967 and each year thereafter. These provisions take on added significance when they are viewed in connection with the Area Redevelopment and the Manpower Training acts, both of which authorized vocational training programs for the unemployed and for the underemployed.

The Vocational Education Act of 1963 and its subsequent revisions not only provided additional financial support but represented an attempt to broaden and redefine the area of vocational and technical education. Each state was required to submit a plan to the U.S. Commissioner of Education.

The Elementary and Secondary Education Act of 1965

The most sweeping extension of federal involvement in education was provided in the Elementary and Secondary Education Act of 1965. Bailey and Mosher have contended that the act "mandated a series of programs and priorities which involved a massive shift in the locus of policy-making power in American education."[20] The law directed federal attention to local educational agencies for the education of children of low-income families (Title I). It provided a continued federal "impact on poverty" and allocated $1.06 billion for the first year toward a program of assistance. The act also provided for a five-year expenditure of about $100 million for school library resources, textbooks, and other instructional materials (Title II). ESEA called for the establishment of supplementary educational centers and services of a wide variety—academic enrichment, guidance, counseling, health services, and remedial instruction (Title III). Title IV subsumed PL 83–531 and called for the extension of cooperative research programs sponsored by universities and state departments of education; it also authorized research and development centers and regional educational laboratories. Title V was designed to strengthen state departments of education by improving planning, research, and personnel.

After a few years of its operation, Berke and Kirst had this to say of ESEA:

> It is true that the pupil achievement results on Title I are at best unknown and at worst very discouraging. But to evaluate whether a program that reaches nine million children "works" on the single dimension of achievement test scores is to ignore the multitude of other political objectives embedded in Title I: Title I's defenders point to such positive outcomes as the fiscal equalization impact of Title I funds and the concern it has generated among educators all over the nation for the previously neglected disadvantaged child. Others have contended Title I funds were intended to be "a sugar solvent" to help ease acceptance by the South of black children rather than forsake the federal financial windfall. In effect, Title I held out so many different aspirations to so many different constituencies that inevitably several of these aspirations were never met. Perhaps multiple objectives in large-scale federal programs is a formula for insuring that no single objective will be substantially accomplished.[21]

Later studies indicated that ESEA continued to make a difference. Michael Knapp and his colleagues at SRI International examined, in a number of school districts, the impact of federal aid programs from 1965 to 1980 dealing with student populations with special educational needs.[22] Specifically, their study dealt with Title I of ESEA, which discusses the educationally deprived; PL 94–142, which discusses the handicapped; Title VII of ESEA, which discusses limited English proficiency; the 1968 amendments to the Vocational Education Act, which discuss support for handicapped and disadvantaged students; and the civil rights laws—Title VI of the Civil Rights Act of 1964, Title IX of the Education Amendments of 1972, and Section 504 of the Rehabilitation Act of 1973, all of which were designed to prohibit discrimination against students and staff. The general conclusions of the study were as follows:

> Collectively, federal and state policies for special populations have substantially improved and expanded the array of educational services for the intended target students. The policies have increased the structural complexity of schools and districts, which appears to represent a necessary consequence of providing targeted services. Over time, local problem solving, federal and state policy adjustments, and gradual local accommodation have generally reduced to a manageable level the costs associated with special services.[23]

VACILLATION DURING THE 1970s

The rapid increase in the number of federal programs for education began to slow down about 1970. The 1970s became a time of vacillation and even retrenchment on one hand and a time for even more extended federal intrusion on the other. We'll now examine some aspects of this seeming paradox.

Reappraisal of Programs

During the 1950s and the 1960s there seemed to be no deficiency in American life that could not be corrected by education, particularly by federal intervention in education. As might be expected, the time came when questions about the effectiveness of these programs were raised. One of the first of these inquiries was authorized by the Civil Rights Act of 1964, which charged the commissioner of education to conduct a survey "concerning the lack of availability of equal educational opportunities for individuals by reason of race, color, religion, or national origin." It seemed appropriate, ten years after the Brown decision had ordered an end to desegregated schools, to find out what had been accomplished.

The survey became a monumental task. Under the general direction of James S. Coleman, scores of scholars in and out of the U.S. Office of Education were engaged in the effort. The major report was more than 700 pages in length and there was a supplement almost as long.[24] In brief, the great majority of American children were found to attend segregated schools. Moreover, schools serving primarily blacks and other minorities were generally inferior, as measured by accreditation, class size, and teacher background, to schools attended by whites. With the exception of some Oriental Americans, achievement of minority pupils was distinctly below that of whites. However, when characteristics of schools were related to pupil achievement, with the socioeconomic background of students held constant, a small fraction of the differences in pupil achievement appeared to be related to school characteristics. This has been the subject of much controversy and other scholars, employing different methods of analysis, have found school factors somewhat more important.[25]

The President and Congress

The nature of the real and potential conflicts between the president and Congress was clearly revealed in the Nixon administration. The position of the Nixon administration with regard to federal support of elementary and secondary schools was epitomized in the Better Schools Act of 1973. Since earlier attempts at revenue sharing contained no specific provisions for education, the Better Schools Act was seen as a special form of revenue sharing for the schools. In some ways "revenue sharing" was simply new rhetoric for federal aid, but the act did make explicit the position of the administration on certain matters. For instance, the act proposed to consolidate federal assistance to schools into thirty programs. Before the act the U.S. Office of Education had been administering some 100 categorical programs affecting the schools. The broad national purposes to be served by the consolidated program included aid for the disadvantaged, aid for the handicapped, vocational education, assistance for schools in federally affected areas, and supporting services.

The Better Schools Act did not receive approval in Congress for a number of reasons. Consolidation of grants obviously meant that some specific forms of federal aid would no longer be sustained. Also, there seemed to be some uncertainty as to how much control the governors of the states might exercise over the money to be allocated to the states. In addition, there was an initial attempt to sell the formula to Congress without specifying dollar amounts for the program.

National Assessment

Another movement begun in the 1960s, the National Assessment of Educational Progress (NAEP), has been continued. National Assessment was encouraged in 1963 by Francis Keppel, then U.S. Commissioner of Education. The first chairman of the exploratory program was Ralph W. Tyler, then director of the Center for Advanced Study in Behavioral Sciences at Stanford, California. The early funding for national assessment came from the Carnegie Corporation of New York. Funds also were received from the Ford Foundation's Fund for the Advancement of Education. Major funds for national assessment were later provided by grants to the Education Commission of the States from the U.S. Office of Education. Federal funding in the early 1970s shifted from OE to the National Institute of Education. To implement such a program, appropriate achievement tests had to be developed and a testing schedule established. Initially, plans called for 140,000 people to take sections of the tests over a three-year cycle. The procedures used did not make it possible to compare individuals, schools, and school systems. Groups to be tested in the assessment program were classed by region (Northeast, South, Midwest, and Far West), age level nine, thirteen, seventeen, and thirty, community type (rural, urban fringe, medium-sized city, and large city), race, and economic level. Students in public, private, and parochial schools and persons no longer in school were to be tested. The areas to be assessed were reading, writing, science, mathematics, social studies, citizenship, music, literature, vocational education, and art. Assessment techniques were to include paper-and-pencil tests, interviews, and observations.

The program has been implemented: tests have been formulated and administered, the results analyzed, and reports made to the public. On reading tests, for instance, pupils in the Northeast did better than pupils elsewhere, girls did better than boys, whites did better than blacks, surburban pupils did better than inner city pupils, and pupils with educated parents did better than those without. With results such as these in hand, policymakers could ask why something was so and what could be done about it. Assessment was becoming the basis for policy decisions. Indeed, assessment data were widely quoted in *A Nation at Risk* and other national reports on education.[26] It should be noted that in 1983 the contract for the administration of NAEP was shifted from the Education Commission of the States to the Educational Testing Service.

The growing significance of NAEP and the widespread public demand for greater accountability in education will be discussed later in this chapter.

Reorganization of the Federal Agency

What should be the purpose of the U.S. Office of Education had long been debated.[27] With Keppel's interest in reform, the mission and effectiveness of the office became the subject of even more controversy. Developments requiring that the office support and monitor programs in research and development as well as in the operation of schools and colleges contributed to the complexity of the issue. One suggested course of action, growing quite logically out of the development of regional laboratories and research and development centers, was that an institute, or institutes, of education be established. Such an institute, it was thought, might be given the research and development functions, and the distribution of aid to operational programs might be left to the Office of Education. This reorganization of education at the federal level received the support of the president and Congress, and the National Institute of Education was established in 1972. At the same time a new Division of Education was to be created in the Department of Health, Education, and Welfare. The two programs were to be "separate, coequal" units. The reorganization was apparently facilitated by making the Commissioner of Education the assistant secretary for the new division in HEW.

This reorganization was typical of the period. The institute moved ahead on the basis of its new authority. After some delay the president nominated, as provided by law, the members of the National Council on Educational Research, which was to be the general policy body of the new institute. After still more delay council members were approved by Congress. In the meantime most of the research and development programs had been transferred from the office to the institute and the institute found it necessary to move ahead with many of these activities. As a result, the institute became operational even before its policies had been approved by the new council.

In the late 1970s a more significant reorganization of the federal structure in education was considered. President Carter, strongly supported by the National Education Association and some other groups in education, proposed that a cabinet-level department of education be established. Such a department, he said, would be designed to consolidate education functions found in other departments of government. For example, the programs then located in HEW would be transferred to the new department. Proponents of the reorganization contended that educational concerns became lost among other concerns of HEW, such as welfare reform, Social Security, and national health insurance. Supporters believed that the new department would give education first-class status and the full-time attention of cabinet-level policymakers. Rufus Miles made a strong case for the new department.[28] However, not all students of the problem were convinced that a new department would make much difference. Gerald Sroufe, for instance, maintained that members of the president's cabinet have little to do with policymaking.[29]

These considerations aside, a Department of Education was approved by Congress and the president in 1979. The proposal passed the House by only four votes but was approved in the Senate by a vote of seventy-two to twenty-one. The reorganization bill was signed by the president and became effective early in 1980. By July of that year, the first Secretary of Education, Shirley Hufstedler, was appointed. Since Hufstedler was a California jurist and largely unknown to the education world, the appointment came as something of a shock to some educators. Even so, many education groups, including the National Education Association and the American Association of School Administrators, saw merit in the appointment and voiced their support for the new secretary.

Initially, the new department was to be responsible for 152 programs in education, the employment of approximately 17,000 personnel, and a $14 billion budget. The department's personnel structure would include six assistant secretaries—one each for elementary and secondary education, post-secondary education, vocational and adult education, educational research and improvement, special education and rehabilitative services, and civil rights. In addition, there was to be an administrator for overseas education and an office for bilingual education and minority affairs.

The election of 1980 had severe repercussions on the new department. President Reagan pledged to eliminate the department. By January 1981, Terrell H. Bell was the new Secretary of Education, and a program of reversion, described later, was begun.

Greater Federal Intrusion

We have discussed reappraisal and retrenchment aspects of this vacillation in the preceding sections. We turn now to the phenomenon of even greater federal intrusion. Brief treatments of Title IX and Public Law 94–142 will be offered as illustrations.

Title IX (PL 92–318) was but one part of a legislative explosion in the 92nd Congress (1971–72) designed to end sex discrimination in schools and colleges.[30] For instance, Title VII of the Civil Rights Act of 1964 was amended to cover employment in all institutions whether or not they received federal funds. Also the U.S. Commission on Civil Rights was given jurisdiction over sexual discrimination. Finally, Title IX of the Education Amendments of 1972 forbidding sex discrimination against students and employees in federally assisted education programs was passed. Title IX covered only about two pages in the U.S. Code and was little noticed at the time of enactment.

A major provision in Title IX read: "No person in the United States shall, on the basis of sex, be excluded from participation in, or be denied the benefits of, or be subjected to discrimination under any educational program or activity receiving federal financial assistance." In other sections of the act, virtually all programs affecting students were covered, including classes once designed for one sex only and participation in athletic programs. No longer could girls be kept out of a shop program, nor could the sports program for boys dominate use of the gymnasium.

Whereas the initial legislation was relatively brief, the rules and regulations governing Title IX, which appeared June 23, 1974, were extensive. They occupied twenty-seven three-column pages in the *Federal Register* and covered in great detail what schools and colleges had to do to prevent sex discrimination.

In some ways Public Law 94–142, passed in 1975, extended federal control over schools even further than Title IX or legislation on vocational education. The law itself was long and detailed, requiring twenty-three pages in the U.S. Code. The purpose of the law was comprehensive: "to assure that all handicapped children have available to them . . . a free appropriate public education which emphasizes special education and related services designed to meet their unique needs. . . . " The meaning of the terms used in the statement of purpose was not left to the conjecture of school officials or OE rule-makers; they were specified. For example, *special education* meant "specially designed instruction, at no cost to parents or guardians, to meet the unique needs of a handicapped child, including classroom instruction, instruction in physical education, home instruction, and instruction in hospitals and institutions." *Related services* meant "transportation, and such developmental, corrective, and other supportive services (including speech pathology and audiology, psychological services, physical and occupational therapy, recreation, and medical and counseling services, except that such medical services shall be for diagnostic and evaluation purposes only) as may be required to assist a handicapped child. . . . "

A notable part of PL 94–142 was the detail specified for the state plan, which had to be submitted to the U.S. Commissioner of Education for the state to qualify for federal assistance. For instance, the plan had to include: a statement of the goal of providing full educational opportunity to all handicapped children, a detailed timetable for accomplishing such a goal, and a description of the facilities, personnel, and services necessary to achieve the program. The plan also had to give assurance that the state education agency was responsible for seeing that all educational programs for handicapped children, including those provided by any local agency, met the education standards of the state education agency. Indeed, the state agency was required to prescribe rules and regulations for local agencies and to oversee compliance with these rules.

Five columns in the rules were devoted to the requirements for local school districts. The specified procedures to be used to identify the handicapped; facilities, personnel, and services to be used in the program; provisions for participation of and consultation with parents; the nature of records to be kept on the handicapped; and the contents of reports to be made to the state agency.

The rules spoke not only to the nature of identification and evaluation procedures but also to the nature of the school environment in which instruction was to
be offered. The term used was *least restrictive environment* and two specific requirements were set forth. The first requirement was "that to the maximum extent appropriate, handicapped children . . . are educated with children who are not
handicapped . . . " The second was "that special classes, separate schooling, or other
removal of handicapped children from the regular educational environment occurs
only when the nature or severity of the handicap is such that education in regular
classes . . . cannot be achieved satisfactorily."

As prescriptive as the language of PL 94–142 was, the real "teeth" of the law
was in Section 504 of the Rehabilitation Act as amended in 1974. The section read as
follows: "No otherwise qualified handicapped individual in the United States . . . shall
solely be reason of his handicap, be excluded from participation in, be denied the
benefits of, or be subjected to discrimination under any program receiving federal
assistance."

The rules set up for the administration of this brief section required twenty-
seven three-column pages in the *Federal Register* on May 4, 1977. Obviously these
rules had broad application to both education and employment, but subpart D had
specific references to preschool, elementary, and secondary education. These provisions were explicitly coordinated with those of PL 94–142. Some of the specific
language follows:

> While the Department does not intend to review individual placement decisions, it
> does intend to insure that testing and evaluation required by the regulations are car-
> ried out, and that school systems provide an adequate opportunity for parents to chal-
> lenge and seek review of these critical decisions. And the Department will place a
> high priority on pursuing cases in which a pattern or practice of discriminatory place-
> ment may be involved.

Much of the strength of Section 504 derived from the fact that it was related to
the Civil Rights Act. In the language of that section, "the procedural provisions
applicable to Title VI of the Civil Rights Act of 1965 apply to this part." School practices
concerning handicapped students were specified in great detail. According to Section
504, departure from those practices would constitute discrimination. Schools or
persons guilty of such discrimination could, if the case went to court, be found guilty
of denying the civil rights of a student. The sanctions for discrimination against the
handicapped, when placed within the civil rights context, were very powerful.

In recent years, the U.S. Department of Education, in keeping with the Reagan
administration policy of decentralization and deregulation, proposed changes governing the operation of Public Law 94–142. Those interested in the handicapped,
such as the Council for Exceptional Children, mounted public pressure against such
changes and as of this writing, none of those proposals has been implemented.

THE REAGAN REVERSION: THE FIRST TERM

Over our history, the nature of the federal influence on American education can be
characterized as follows: a long period of modest influence, a rapid expansion of

influence during the 1960s, a vacillation between retrenchment and even greater intrusion during the 1970s, and then the Reagan reversion. Reagan described his program as "new federalism" although he was actually advocating a return to dual federalism. We now turn to this last period. We'll examine the major proposals set forth by President Reagan, report legislative action and other responses to his proposals, and suggest some implications related to these changes for the Bush administration.

The Proposals

As a candidate and later as president, Ronald Reagan made it clear that he intended to restructure the federal government. He believed social and human services, including education, should be delegated to state and local governments rather than undertaken at the federal level. One observer noted that as a candidate, "Reagan had reacted negatively to the formation of the Department of Education, stating that he thought it ought to be abolished. He stood strongly for 'deregulating' education, and, more radical yet, favored tuition tax credits."[31]

Thomas has provided even more detail with respect to the Reagan position on education:

> President Reagan's definition of the federal role in education has been manifested in such developments as: (1) sharp reductions, on the order of 20% to 25% in spending for elementary and secondary education programs and college student aid; (2) support for antibusing legislation and reduced willingness of the Justice Department to bring or aid in desegregation suits; (3) a proposal, as part of President Reagan's New Federalism, to consolidate all federal aid to education into two block grants that would be disbursed by the states and would not be subject to federal requirements or standards; (4) proposed regulations that put "reasonable limits" on rights of handicapped students and on the services that schools must provide to them; (5) Reagan's strong personal endorsement of tuition tax credits for parents of children attending private schools; and (6) the proposal to abolish the Department of Education.[32]

President Reagan himself made his proposals quite clear. For instance, as part of his "A Program for Economic Recovery" dated February 18, 1981, he made specific recommendations to the Congress regarding several education programs. The then-current budget authority and proposed budget authority for these programs, taken from the message, are shown in Table 3.1. The proposed reductions are dramatic.

After interviewing members of the new administration and examining many pertinent documents, Clark and Amiot said that the hallmarks of the administration's efforts to disassemble the federal educational establishment were:

> Diminution—to reduce the size and scope of federal expenditures in education;

> Deregulation—to reduce federal control and monitoring in the field of education;

> Decentralization—to accomplish a transfer of responsibility for education from the federal to the state and local levels;

Disestablishment—to eliminate the bureaucratic structure for education at the federal level, that is, the Department of Education; and

Deemphasis—to remove educational policy from a position of priority on the federal agenda.[33]

While some might demure about the nature and magnitude of Reagan's proposals, it seems clear to us that a policy shift was being advocated.[34] In some ways, it is remarkable that a new administration could make proposals plausible to Congress and others that countered decades of federal interest and involvement. Thomas has suggested that the restructuring of national educational policy was a product of several factors. These are paraphrased as follows: (1) the ideological convictions and persuasive talents of Reagan himself, (2) a recognition by elite groups that education alone could not solve social problems, (3) a substantial decline in the power of education interest groups, and (4) an appeal to popular feelings regarding race, religion, and federal control.[35] We would add one other factor. The federal intrusion, particularly with respect to Title IX, Public Law 94–142, and Public Law 94–482, having to do with vocational education, did seem excessive. The laws themselves were long and detailed and the regulations were even more extensive. Compliance had become a complex and time-consuming task on the part of state and local educational agencies.

Response to Proposals

Despite opposition from some quarters, the Reagan reversion succeeded remarkably well. Let us examine a few of the specifics. Chapter 2 of the Educational Consolidation and Improvement Act (ECIA) did consolidate some twenty-eight federal programs in elementary and secondary education. Also, state and local agencies were given some authority to determine just how the federal funds for these programs were to be expended.

The Chapter 2 consolidation and movement toward block grants, of course, raised some basic questions about which policy strategies are most effective in achieving federal goals in education. The Reagan consolidation policies reduced the control of federal officials and provided state and local education agencies with greater discretion. This represented a significant change in direction from more narrow, carefully regulated categorical grants designed to achieve specific federal policy objectives.

There was also an actual reduction in the dollar amounts for many of the programs in the early years of Reagan's first term. As Table 3.1 illustrates, expenditures for the major programs in elementary and secondary education were, over a two-year period, reduced by almost 30 percent. It is appropriate to note that Congress followed the lead of the president in authorizing these reductions.

In addition to persuading Congress to accept his program, President Reagan also made use of his appointment powers. For instance, in 1982, he replaced ten members of the fifteen-member National Council on Education Research (NCER),

TABLE 3.1

Federal Expenditures for Certain Programs in the Department of Education, 1981 and 1983

Program	*Expenditures in Millions of Dollars*	
	1981	1983
Vocational education	682	500
Impacted aid	682	287
Disadvantaged	3,104	1,942
Bilingual education	158	95
Handicapped	1,025	846
Other programs	216	407
State block grants	538	433
TOTAL	6,405	4,510

Adapted from Paul E. Peterson and B.G. Rabe, "The Role of Interest Groups in the Formation of Educational Policy:
Past Practice and Future Trends," *Teachers College Record* 84 (Spring 1983): 715.

the policymaking arm of the National Institute of Education (NIE), even though terms of many of the incumbents had not yet expired. Observers reported that the president had given NCER a "conservative cast with the naming of George Roche as chairman" and by appointing Onalee McGraw as a member of the council.[36] Roche was president of a private college that had refused to accept federal funds. McGraw was an outspoken critic of federal social research and on the staff of the conservative Heritage Foundation. President Reagan made an additional change in council membership by appointing a new director of NIE. These changes were apparently made on ideological grounds and without counsel from the research community in education.

On two matters, strongly recommended by Reagan, there was not favorable action. Bell, Secretary of Education in Reagan's first term, as directed by the president, did, as early as October 1981, develop four possible replacement arrangements for the department. He made it known that he favored converting the department to a foundation, somewhat like the National Science Foundation, to preside over the federal role in education.[37] Congress took no action on this proposal, which, in essence, was never viable politically. Reagan's proposals for tuition tax credits likewise failed.

One development in the Department of Education seemed to provide a surprising plus for the administration in its first term. In August 1981, Secretary Bell created the National Commission on Excellence in Education and directed it to present a report to him and the American people by April 1983. A distinguished group of educators and lay citizens was appointed to the commission. David P. Gardner, then president of the University of Utah, was selected chairman. The commission was given several specific charges, including: the assessment of the quality of teaching and learning in the nation's schools and colleges, a comparison of American schools and colleges with those of other advanced nations, and a definition of the problems that must be overcome if the nation is to pursue a course of excellence in education. While the charge was broad, the commission focused its attention on the high school. The commission held a number of hearings across the country, commissioned papers from experts on schools and colleges, used the assistance of a competent staff, and then published a succinct report, *A Nation at Risk,* subtitled *The Imperative for Educational Reform.*[38] The language of the report was, in some instances, dramatic, as the following excerpt illustrates:

> If an unfriendly foreign power had attempted to impose on America the mediocre educational performance that exists today, we might well have viewed it as an act of war. As it stands, we have allowed this to happen to ourselves. We even squandered the gains in student achievement made in the wake of the Sputnik challenge. Moreover, we have dismantled essential support systems which helped make those gains possible. We have, in effect, been committing an act of unthinking, unilateral educational disarmament.[39]

Whether it was the nature of the report or the tenor of the times, or both, the report provoked widespread attention and response. Several other major reports on education, sponsored by authoritative bodies, also appeared in 1983. Education became a major national concern. In general, there was widespread support for the recommendations set forth in *A Nation at Risk.* The media and citizens generally agreed that something should be done to rescue the nation from "a rising tide of mediocrity." Scores of state legislatures and hundreds of school boards prepared their own responses on excellence in schools.

There were a few more discerning voices. For instance, Meg Greenfield in *Newsweek* had this to say:

> You give a child nothing, I think, when you give him this joyless, driven concept of learning. But alas, there are plenty among us who think this is just fine. Following the great cackles of the political antipermissiveness crowd when this report was released, I was struck again by how much such people, who claim to be champions of education, implicitly view education as a disagreeable thing.[40]

In a thoughtful commentary on reform studies on education, Harold Howe made the following point:

> It is important to add, however, that we must settle one issue soon: the role of the federal government in education. The recent studies and reports, including that of the National Commission on Excellence, generally agree that the federal government should play a strong role in identifying national priorities in education, in doing something about them through legislation and appropriations, in supporting research on education, and, particularly, in dealing with issues of equity and equal opportunity. Right now we face a major political division on these matters. Both houses of Congress lean in the direction that the reports suggest, but the President tilts in the other direction.[41]

Even though *A Nation at Risk* and other reports failed to mention Reagan's own agenda for education—such matters as school prayer and tuition tax credits—the president soon saw that education was a politically viable issue. He responded to Bell's invitation to appear at several regional meetings where implementation of the report's recommendations was considered. Public acceptance of *A Nation at Risk* apparently provided the president with an opportunity to appear a champion of education.

While Ronald Reagan did not fully achieve his education agenda in his first term, both his philosophy and successful program initiatives (buttressed in no small measure by his personal popularity) did earn him somewhat paradoxically, in one observer's view, the "rarely bestowed mantle of Education President."[42]

THE REAGAN SECOND TERM

When President Reagan won a landslide victory over Democratic candidate Walter Mondale in 1984, commentators speculated on the permanence of the Reagan reversion, as we have labeled the diminishment of the federal role in education. Although Ronald Reagan lost some congressional support in 1984 and the Democrats regained control of the Senate in the off-year elections in 1986, the president's continuing popularity and ability to communicate effectively with the American people made many educators and their supporters apprehensive about the future of federal aid and fearful of even deeper cuts in national support. Indeed, the growing federal budget deficit in the mid and late 1980s exacerbated these concerns and made the education budget seemingly more vulnerable. But Congress resisted further reductions in federal education funding despite substantial reductions in executive branch budget proposals.

Not surprisingly, commentators differed in their assessment of the permanence and significance of the changes in federal education policy during the Reagan era. Jennings, for example, argued at the beginning of Reagan's second term that there had been little enduring change in the federal role in education and that "the smoke of debate should not obscure the reality that the prospects for the survival of federally funded education programs are greater today than at any time since Reagan took office."[43] Other analysts such as Doyle and Hartle agreed with Jennings's premise, contending that "in basic outline the federal role in education looks very much as it did under Presidents Nixon, Ford, and Carter."[44]

Clark and Astuto, however, in discussing Reagan's second term, contended that their 1983 assessment, discussed earlier in this chapter, continued to be valid. They argued that a major redirection of educational policy transpired during the Reagan presidency and that the federal role had been changed in fundamental ways. They saw a new bipartisan consensus supporting a different and redirected federal role rather than the programs of the 1960s and 1970s. Indeed, Clark and Astuto predicted that "the scope of the redirection will be broadened over the next 5–15 years, and many of the changes will become institutionalized in a new era of federal educational policy."[45]

Clark and Astuto in elaborating on their thesis that the most consequential policy shift in education was not the reduction of financial support for education but the delegation of authority back to the states, said:

> The consequence of devolution for federal policy and programs in education is the maintenance of a visible presence without operational responsibilities by offering advice, counsel, support, encouragement, and exhortation to those who have operational responsibility—parents, local communities, and state governments.[46]

Clark and Astuto maintain that the Reagan administration's educational policy preferences were very unlike those of earlier periods. They cite the differences in the Reagan era's "lexicon" from the language of the pre-Reagan period shown in Table 3.2, in illustrating their point about the extent of the changes.

The Era of Secretary Bennett

The political spear carrier for the Reagan educational agenda in the second term was William J. Bennett, who was appointed Secretary of Education early in 1985. Bennett, educated in philosophy and law, had served as director of the National Endowment of the Humanities during Reagan's first term.

Bennett was a blunt, outspoken critic of the quality of the public schools. His rather limited background in elementary and secondary education and harsh criticisms of the enterprise quickly alienated many educators who were much more comfortable with the personality, style, and more traditional background of his predecessor. Bell, while certainly not immune to sharp criticism by educators during Reagan's first term, was still widely respected and trusted within education circles as a dedicated and understanding educator who did the best he could under difficult circumstances to combat the tide of "anti-education," or ideological conservatism, during the early years of the Reagan era.[47]

Bennett, on the other hand, quickly became a favorite of the New Right and traditional conservatives as he emphasized his three C's of character, content, and choice; stressed the need for discipline and rigor in schools; and chastised the educational establishment for low standards, apathy, and ineffectual leadership. Bennett's articulation of the central role that parents must play in the education of their children and the need for schools to convey values as well as "book knowledge" struck responsive chords not only with conservatives but also among large segments of the general public that shared his judgment that schools were too permissive and not sufficiently demanding intellectually.[48]

TABLE 3.2
Terms That Characterize the Federal Educational Policy Stance Before and After 1980

Pre-1980 Term	Post-1980 Equivalent
1. Equity	1a. Excellence; standards of performance
2. Needs and access	2a. Ability; selectivity; minimum standards
3. Social and welfare concerns	3a. Economic and productivity concerns
4. Common school	4a. Parental choice; institutional competition
5. Regulations, enforcement	5a. Deregulation
6. Federal interventions	6a. State and local initiatives
7. Diffusion of innovations	7a. Exhortation; information sharing

Source: David L. Clark and Terry A. Astuto, *The Implications for Educational Research of a Changing Federal Educational Policy,* Occasional Paper no. 4 (Charlottesville, VA: Policy Studies Center of the University Council for Educational Administration, 1987), 3.

Bennett's aggressive rhetoric was aimed at higher education as well as the elementary and secondary schools. His strident criticism of students who were exploiting student aid—illustrated by his provocative call for "stereo divestiture"—coupled with his criticisms of the declining quality of colleges and universities antagonized the higher education community. Indeed, the secretary was not timid at all about taking on many of education's "scared cows," which traditionally had been supported by both Republicans and Democrats. His advocacy, for example, of having religion play a more prominent role in schools, more options for bilingual education programs, and tuition tax credits generated almost constant controversy between the secretary and the major national education associations and their affiliates and allies throughout the country.

It was widely acknowledged by both supporters and detractors that Bennett was remarkably successful in raising a cabinet position of relatively low status to great public visibility in the debates that raged around the Reagan program and ideology. In fact, Bennett's adroit use of the media as the administration's national spokesperson on education issues enabled him to articulate and set the agenda, the intellectual context, and the nature of the national debate over basic education issues. In other words, Bennett successfully used his unique "bully pulpit" to project his ideas and philosophy to the forefront of public discourse not only on education issues but also as a powerful advocate for the entire Reagan program and approach to government.[49] In brief, both the Reagan and Bennett message was that in education, as well as in other public-sector areas, the problem was not necessarily the need for more money but for incentives, and greater productivity and accountability.

Bennett's critics accused him of being too ambitious and politically motivated and of using his cabinet status as a platform to run for national office. They charged that the secretary was a "headline hunter," a "bull in a china shop" who politicized educational issues in dysfunctional and simplistic ways and betrayed the constituencies he had been appointed to represent.[50]

Both supporters and detractors alike agreed that William Bennett reshaped the role of the nation's chief education officer. Despite the inherent limitations of his office, Bennett, through his pronouncements and reports, exercised great influence on the national debate on education issues.[51] Paradoxically, liberals who for years had advocated extensive federal intervention on education issues observed to their dismay how the office of the Secretary of Education could be used effectively to promote an antithetical agenda. Conversely, conservatives began to fear as the Reagan era drew to a close that if power reverted to those who advocated a stronger federal role, the office could be filled by a forceful individual of very different political and ideological persuasion, an individual who could use the "bully pulpit" as effectively as Bill Bennett.[52]

Some Implications

While at this writing it is too early to assess the full impact of the Reagan policies on education, some implications growing out of recent federal action and current debate can be suggested.

First, federal action can make a difference. We already have cited Michael Knapp and his associates, who concluded that "despite the vagaries of state and local handling of specific program provisions, the overall effects of federal involvement in the education of target students have been relatively clear and consistent."[53]

In other words, the presence of federal programs, even though they required modifications in local school organizations, were found to be compatible to these organizations. In short, it was demonstrated in the Knapp study that federal aid can achieve national goals and, at the same time, not abridge or destroy local initiative.

As a second implication, recent federal legislation appears to have reduced the equity provisions of federal programs. Two studies support such a conclusion. The American Association of School Administrators surveyed a random sample of 2,500 large, medium-sized, and small school districts with respect to the impact of block grants (money from Chapter 2, passed by Congress in 1981) on school district operation.[54] Responses from these districts led to two conclusions. First, Chapter 2 funds were being used to help districts move into the high-technology era. Second, the block grant system was creating a serious equity problem. While the block grants program meant federal funds were being dispersed to a larger number of school districts, small districts received an increase in federal funds while large districts received a decrease. Larger districts with average grants of $941,299 before block grants received grants of $105,463 after block grants. This decrease had crippled desegregation and other equity projects. The problem was further exacerbated by a decrease in total appropriations.

While block grants may have simplified administrative procedures in the Department of Education and possibly have permitted more state and local discretion, they seem to be wanting in terms of equity provisions. If equity is still a national concern, Chapter 2 apparently should be revised.

As a third implication, and contrary to Reagan's initial proposals, there is a federal role in education. As we've noted, Howe, after examining *A Nation at Risk* and other recent reports on education, was convinced that the elements of a federal role in education must be confronted. Anne Lewis also found that all of the reports on school reform, despite their differences in practicality and tone, emphasized a federal role in education.[55] Moreover, Lewis found that the reports supported the type of federal involvement that has been shaped over the past several years with a focus on equity and a recognition of other national interests. She contended that recommendations from the several reports require an increase, not a decrease, in federal funding.

In view of these conclusions and the essential link that will have to be forged between education and economic development, as discussed in Chapter 2, it is not surprising that Congress and selected officials from both parties are deeply concerned with school issues. At this writing Congress was considering the Education for a Competitive America Act, which would be linked with a trade bill and "reauthorize grant programs designed to improve mathematics and science instruction; extend the Chapter I program aiding disadvantaged students; and create initiatives in foreign-language instruction, vocational training, adult literacy, and school-business partnerships."[56]

SUMMARY AND FUTURE PROSPECTS

Let us summarize the kinds of federal controls now being exercised and suggest the probable nature of future federal relationships. Federal control or influence is frequently denied. Indeed, many of the bills enacted by Congress contain a specific stipulation that nothing in the act should be construed as giving the federal agency control over local and state education agencies. And at least until recently, local and state agencies presumably were free to turn down federal money. But the matter is not that simple. Controls are of many kinds and include those suggested below:

Federal Controls

1. *Law.* Congress can and does enact a great many laws having to do with education. Title IX on sex discrimination in education and PL 94–142 on education of the handicapped are two examples. Not only must schools cope with statues enacted by Congress, schools must also follow the regulations prepared by the U.S. Department of Education or other federal agencies. When law and regulation are further fortified by civil rights enforcement, as is true particularly under Title IX and PL 94–142, control at the federal level is enhanced.
2. *The Courts.* The federal courts exercise great and growing control over the operation of schools and state education agencies. In particular, the courts exercise jurisdiction in matters pertaining to civil rights in areas such as desegregation and sex discrimination.
3. *Money.* For the most part federal dollars are for categorical purposes such as aid to the disadvantaged and funds for vocational education. The very nature of these subventions constitutes control; in no way can local or state agencies use the money for other than the specified purpose.
4. *State Federal Offices.* Federal control is also exercised through the establishment of specific offices and divisions with federal support in state departments of education. Thus, state education agencies have divisions devoted to vocational education, disadvantaged pupils, sex discrimination, the education of the handicapped, and for other federally funded programs. While these divisions are nominally under the direction of the state board of education and the chief state school officer, their existence, their operation, and their funding hinges on federal initiative and support. Such units are established to "help" local districts comply with federal directives.
5. *Regional Resource Centers.* Regional resource centers designed specifically to promote federal programs at state and local levels also foster federal control. In the case of education for the handicapped, regional centers

were established, well staffed and quite active. Any local or state education agency that wishes to keep current will see that teachers and administrators participate in the workshops and other activities of these centers.

6. *Teacher Training.* Some federal legislation contains specific provisions having to do with the preservice or in-service training of teachers. The special requirements such as those found in vocational education are intended to help provide the understanding and skills needed in special fields of teaching but these experiences also do much to socialize teachers into the norms of the particular field in question.

7. *Professional Interest Groups.* Still another aspect of federal control is the use of federal money to foster the growth of specialized professional groups. This form of control has long been present in vocational education: teachers in that field have part of their salaries paid from federal money; much of their training is provided with the aid of federal money; in each state agency for education there are special supervisors and directors, largely supported from federal money; and these state officers are frequently convened in special workshops and conferences sponsored by the National Center for Vocational Education, which awards sizable federal grants. Communication among persons at local, state, and national levels is frequent and continuous. All of this builds a powerful group of professionals ready to support vocational education at all levels of government. Similar arrangements are found in other areas of major federal involvement.

8. *Special Interest Groups.* Perhaps even more significant than the building of special interest groups in the profession is the building of special interest groups among citizens. Federal programs have frequently identified citizens with special interests, made those interests legitimate, and utilized such interests in promoting federal programs. This process is frequently fostered by the establishment of citizens' advisory committees made up almost entirely of citizens who have special interests and is clearly exemplified in the law on education for the handicapped. Federal legislation often specifies powers for these advisory committees that tend to make them much more than advisory. Indeed, these advisory bodies often determine the decisions officially enacted by the boards of state and local agencies.

Outlook for the Future

The above controls represent pervasive federal influence. What about the future? The following predictions are offered as highly likely. First, despite the Reagan reversion, the federal presence in education will continue. Federal influence of one kind or another has been with us for a long time; it is part of our tradition. Also there are great disparities among the states and within the states in the economic ability of states and school districts to support programs of education. Although current programs designed to alleviate these disparities have not always been effective,[57] such programs will continue to appear. Certain problems in education of national import, such as education of the disadvantaged, will continue. Many policymakers will support federal action to alleviate what appear to be national deficiencies. Within the federal system bucking problems to the next level of government is a common strategy of interest groups. When minority groups, for instance, find that they do not get redress at the local level, they may buck the problem to the state or even the national level.

Second, with other demands on the federal budget and reduced allocations for education already in place, increased money for education will be hard to come by. For the most part, money that is made available for education will probably go to meet national needs or to effect reforms in current practices. In both cases the federal aid will be for specific categorical purposes, and this specificity acts as a control mechanism. Indeed, the unprecedented budget deficits run up in the Reagan era may have a most lasting effect on federal education policy. The magnitude of the deficits, concerns about the economy, and the trauma of the stock market collapse late in 1987 have assured that deficit reduction will be the primary issue for the foreseeable future. The funding of education programs as well as all other governmental services will be affected significantly as the Gramm-Rudman legislation and other efforts to curb federal spending receive greater political support. The nation's continuing fiscal crisis is reflected in recent political impasses that have caused federal budgets to be enacted only through makeshift procedures rather than established legislative processes. The likelihood is that financial constraints on the federal budget will severely curtail new or increased funding for education and other domestic programs. In fact, education may well be fortunate if it is able to sustain its current levels of funding. Although federal aid to elementary and secondary education increased 35 percent from 1980, in real terms (adjusted for inflation) funding was reduced by approximately 12 percent during the Reagan era.[58]

Third, many actors will continue to participate in policymaking at the federal level. The president and Congress, of course, are major policy actors. In addition, the federal bureaucracy, particularly the Office of Management and Budget, has emerged as a very powerful determiner of federal policy. The courts, too, have become more and more influential. No single policy decision has affected schools as much as the Brown decision in 1954. The pervasive influence of the courts in many areas will probably continue. These formal actors, we are convinced, will continue to be joined by a host of informal actors or interest groups who wish to affect federal decisions.

Fourth, federal agencies have taken a reform stance with respect to education. This reform objective is reflected in much of the legislation passed by Congress, in the federal guidelines developed by the department, in the evaluation procedures required of support programs, and even in the decisions of the judiciary. The push for reform as exemplified by Title IX and PL 94–142 is likely to continue, but some reduction in regulations, begun by the Reagan administration, may also continue.

Fifth, federal agencies exert influence through evaluation and assessment. The federal role, as we discussed earlier, will very likely expand in the growing movement to assess student achievement more comprehensively both on a national and state-by-state basis. The ever-increasing demand for public scrutiny and accountability in education has exerted powerful pressure to expand the federally funded, congressionally mandated National Assessment of Educational Progress program. There is little question but that there will be growing emphasis on documenting educational outcomes and quality in the years ahead and that federal resources will be provided to support the expansion of NAEP to incorporate "state-by-state comparisons and more detailed information on academic accomplishment in a wider variety of subjects including science, history, geography, civics and writing skills."[59]

Federal influence is also sustained through the allocation of federal money to state education agencies. Most of these agencies now receive about half of their operating funds from federal sources. Much of this money is allocated for the "improvement" of state departments of education in the areas of planning, research, and evaluation. In part, this is an attempt to implement the evaluation requirements made a part of all federal grants. This increased emphasis on evaluation implies a conviction that there ought to be greater correspondence between costs and benefits. We suspect that the emphasis on costs and benefits will continue to motivate federal policymakers.

While federal intrusion has been somewhat reduced, for the most part, the statutory language for most federal programs remains unchanged. Thus, federal influence will continue. Moreover, the long-term shift from dual to national federalism, while slowed, will likely continue. The influential studies of education and projections of future policymaking patterns, including *A Nation at Risk*, all identify a significant role in education for the federal government.[60] Indeed, Secretary Bennett in the waning months of the Reagan administration urged his fellow Republicans to "recognize that there is a proper, though limited federal role in improving American education" and that they "ought to set forth a distinctive tough-minded and positive education agenda" that includes explicit attention to improving the education of the disadvantaged.[61]

NOTES

[1]Warren E. Burger, "Supporting Constitution Bicentennial Efforts," *The School Administrator* 44 (May 1987): 20–21.

[2]*Helvering* v. *Davis,* 301 U.S. 619 (1937).

[3]Leonard D. White, *The Federalists* (New York: The Macmillan Company, 1948), 512.

[4]Morton Grodzins, "The Federal System," in *Goals for Americans,* Report of the President's Commission on National Goals (Englewood Cliffs, NJ: Prentice-Hall, 1960).

[5]*Helvering* v. *Davis,* 301 U.S. 619 (1937); also *Stewart Machine Co.* v. *Davis,* 301 U.S. 548 (1936).

[6]Grodzins, "The Federal System," 282.

[7]*The School Administrator* 20 (November 1962): 3.

[8]*The 1987 Handbook of the American Association of School Administrators,* (Washington, DC: AASA, 1987), 7–8.

[9]Frank J. Munger and Richard F. Fenno, Jr., *National Politics and Federal Aid to Education* (Syracuse, NY: Syracuse University Press, 1962).

[10]Hollis P. Allen, *The Federal Government and Education* (New York: McGraw-Hill Book Company, 1950), 94–97.

[11]See "List of Accredited Schools by States and Overseas," *North Central Association Quarterly* 57 (Fall 1982): 298–305.

[12]Allen, *Federal Government and Education.*

[13]Charles A. Quattlebaum, *Federal Educational Activities and Educational Issues Before Congress,* 3 vols. (Washington, DC: U.S. Government Printing Office, 1951).

[14]Charles A. Quattlebaum, *Federal Educational Policies, Programs and Proposals,* Part 2 (Washington, DC: U.S. Government Printing Office, 1960), 221.

[15]Story Moorefield, "The Remarkable GI Bill," *American Education* 10 (August–September 1974): 25.

[16]"World War II G.I. Bill Expires," *Higher Education* 13 (September 1956).

[17]"An Act to Amend the National Science Foundation Act of 1950," *U.S. Statutes at Large* (Washington, DC, 1959), LXXIII, 467.

[18]"Amendments to NSF Act—HR 8282, Sectional Analysis of Bill," *U.S. Code Congressional Service* (86th Congress, 1st Session, 1959), II, 2245.

[19]*Special Analyses, Budget of the US, FY 1979* (Washington, DC: U.S. Government Printing Office, 1978), 220.

[20]Stephen K. Bailey and Edith K. Mosher, *ESEA—The Office of Education Administers a Law* (Syracuse, NY: Syracuse University Press, 1968), 3.

[21]Joel S. Berke and Michael W. Kirst, *Federal Aid to Education—Who Benefits, Who Governs?* (Lexington, MA: D.C. Heath, 1972), 392.

[22]Michael Knapp et al., *Cumulative Effects of Federal Policies on Schools and Districts,* SRI Project 3590 (Menlo Park, CA: SRI International, January 1983).

[23]Ibid., 159.

[24]James S. Coleman et al., U.S. Department of HEW, Office of Education, *Equality of Educational Opportunity* (Washington, DC: U.S. Government Printing Office, 1966).

[25]See Samuel Bowles and Henry M. Levin, "The Determinants of Scholastic Achievement—An Appraisal of Some Recent Evidence," *Journal of Human Resources* 3 (Winter 1968): 3–24.

[26]National Commission on Excellence in Education, *A Nation at Risk* (Washington, DC: U.S. Department of Education, 1983).

[27]For instance, see Donald R. Warren, *To Enforce Education* (Detroit, MI: Wayne State University Press, 1974).

[28]Rufus E. Miles, Jr., *A Cabinet Department of Education: Analysis and Proposal* (Washington, DC: American Council on Education, 1976).

[29]Gerald E. Sroufe, "The Case Against the Department of Education," *Phi Delta Kappan* 58 (April 1977): 597–600.

[30]See Bernice Sandler, "Title IX: Antisexism's Big Legal Stick," *American Education* (May 1977): 6–9.

[31]James W. Guthrie, "The Future of Federal Educational Policy," *Teachers College Record* 84 (Spring 1983): 683.

[32]Norman C. Thomas, "The Development of Federal Activism in Education," *Education and Urban Society* 15 (May 1983): 284–85.

33David L. Clark and Mary Anne Amiot, "The Disassembly of the Federal Educational Role," *Education and Urban Society* 15 (May 1983): 368–69.

34See Chester E. Finn, Jr., "Reflections on the Disssassembly of the Federal Role," *Education and Urban Society* 15 (May 1983): 389–96.

35Thomas, *Development of Federal Activism,* 285.

36"President Names Conservatives to Policymaking Education Research Panel," *Education Times,* 7 June 1982.

37Martha Snyder, "Federal Dateline," *The School Administrator* (October 1981): 25.

38National Commission on Excellence in Education, *A Nation at Risk* (Washington, DC: Department of Education, April 1983).

39Ibid., 5.

40Meg Greenfield, "Creating a Learning Society," *Newsweek,* 16 May 1983, 100.

41Harold Howe II, "Education Moves to Center Stage: An Overview of Recent Studies," *Phi Delta Kappan* 65 (November 1983): 169–170.

42For an interesting and critical analysis of presidential attitudes and influence on education, see George R. Kaplan, "Hail to a Chief or Two: The Indifferent Presidential Record in Education," *Phi Delta Kappan* 66 (September 1984): 7–12.

43Jack Jennings, "Will Carl Perkins' Legacy Survive Ronald Reagan's Policies," *Phi Delta Kappan* 66 (April 1985): 565–567.

44Denis Doyle and Terry Hartle, "Ideology, Pragmatic Politics, and the Education Budget," *Maintaining the Safety Net: Income Redistribution Programs in the Reagan Administration* (Washington, DC: American Enterprise Institute for Public Policy Research, 1985), 149.

45David L. Clark and Terry A. Astuto, "The Significance and Permanence of Changes in Federal Education Policy," *Educational Researcher* (October 1986): 4.

46David L. Clark and Terry A. Astuto, *The Implications for Educational Research of a Changing Federal Educational Policy,* Occasional Paper no. 4 (Charlottesville, VA: Policy Studies Center of the University Council for Educational Administration, 1987), 1.

47For a candid, highly personalized exposition of Bell's internal struggles with right-wing ideologues within the Reagan administration, see Terrell H. Bell, *The Thirteenth Man* (New York: Free Press, 1988).

48Secretary Bennett's contention that the quality of American education had been diluted at all levels was buttressed by several widely read books critical of schools and colleges. See for example, E.D. Hirsch, Jr., *Cultural Literacy: What Every American Needs to Know* (Boston, MA: Houghton Mifflin Company, 1987), and Allan Bloom, *The Closing of the American Mind* (New York: Simon and Schuster, 1987).

49Edward B. Fiske, "Education Chief: Using Bully Pulpit," *New York Times,* 4 September 1986, B13.

50For a rather critical assessment of Secretary Bennett, see John B. Judis, "Mister Ed," *The New Republic,* 27 April 1987, 16–19.

51See, for example, William J. Bennett, *First Lessons: A Report on Elementary Education in America* (Washington, DC: U.S. Department of Education, 1986).

52Edward B. Fiske, "Reagan's Man for Education," *New York Times Magazine,* 22 December 1986, 68.

[53]Knapp et al., *Cumulative Effects of Federal Policies,* 162.

[54]*The Impact of Chapter 2 of the Education Consolidation and Improvement Act on Local Education Agencies* (Washington, DC: American Association of School Administrators, 1983).

[55]Anne C. Lewis, "Washington Report," *Phi Delta Kappan* 65 (November 1983): 163–166.

[56]Julie A. Miller, "Senate Panel Approves $1-Billion Package of Education Initiatives," *Education Week,* vol. VI, no. 37 (10 June 1987).

[57]See Berke and Kirst, *Federal Aid to Education.*

[58]Deborah A. Verstegen, *Fiscal Policy for Education in the Reagan Administration.* Occasional Paper no. 5 (Charlottesville, VA: Policy Studies Center of the University Council for Educational Administration, 1988), 78.

[59]"U.S. Proposes Expanded Testing of Student Skills," *New York Times,* 28 August 1987, A16.

[60]See, for example, David L. Clark and Terry A. Astuto, *Education Policy After Reagan—What Next?,* Occasional Paper no. 6, (Charlottesville, VA: Policy Studies Center of the University Council for Educational Administration, 1988).

[61]William J. Bennett, "Education Reform and the 1988 Election," Address at the National Press Club, Washington, DC, 8 September 1987, Mimeographed, 15.

4

American Schools and State Government

Although the Constitution of the United States contains no direct reference to education, most state constitutions have specific provisions that make education a legal responsibility of the state. Moreover, the statutes of most states stipulate in considerable detail how schools are to be governed. Much of this control is delegated to district boards of education and to other bodies, all of which become a part of the state system of education. In a sense, then, we have fifty systems of education in America, but in many respects these various systems are similiar. In this chapter we will review how a state structure for education developed, note the emerging shift of power to the state level, examine current organizational arrangements for schools found in the states, consider the types of decisions made by state school agencies, indicate the major functions of state school agencies, and suggest the types of controls states exercise over schools.

THE DEVELOPMENT OF A STATE STRUCTURE

Early Movements

Education in colonial America was closely allied with religion. This alliance took different forms in the various colonies. In most of New England early government was a theocracy. In these church-states it was thought necessary that all children learn to read the Bible and the laws of the colony. Compulsory education laws, such as the famous acts of 1642 and 1647 in Massachusetts, were passed by all New England colonies except Rhode Island.

While compulsory school laws were passed, compulsory attendance laws were not. In effect these Puritan commonwealths required that parents and masters assume responsibility for the education of their children. This was a reflection of the colonists' English background, in which education was conceived as a private and not a public matter. Only in later years did New England towns begin to contribute to the support of schools.

The middle colonies presented another picture. Instead of the relative homogeneity of the Puritans, there were Dutch, French, Irish, Scotch, Germans, and many other national groups. Religious sects included Presbyterians, Jews, Lutherans, Catholics, Quakers, Mennonites, and Moravians. Some of these colonies also passed early laws requiring that parents and masters instruct their children in reading and writing for religious and governmental reasons. Examples were the "Great Law" in Pennsylvania in 1682 and the Public School Act in New York in 1732.

Unlike New England, however, the middle colonies lacked singleness of purpose, and little seems to have been done to enforce such laws. As time went on, primary education became essentially a church or parochial responsibility and secondary education became a private matter. In neither case was educational opportunity widespread.

Conditions were different still in the southern colonies. Whereas many groups in New England and the middle colonies were motivated by the Reformation, leaders in the southern colonies were for the most part adherents of the Anglican Church and were willing to support it as long as it did not interfere with their way of life. The well-to-do believed education to be a private matter. Virginia did pass legislation in 1642 providing for the education of orphans, but it was at least a century later before the opportunity to learn to read and write was provided for dependent children and children of pauper parents.

The Society for the Propagation of the Gospel in Foreign Parts, an auxiliary of the Anglican Church, began sending missionaries to America in 1702. These missionaries numbered in the hundreds; most of them settled in the middle and southern colonies. Their purpose was to establish and revive the Anglican Church, but they also organized schools as a means of training children in religious worship.

While these colonial activities with regard to schools may seem meager by today's standards, Thurston and Roe suggest that some important concepts were beginning to emerge.[1] Among these were the belief in the worth of the individual regardless of wealth or lineage, the realization that education is necessary for successful government, the notion of education as a state function, and the recognition that church and state are not one.

Following the colonial period, it took at least two generations before the outlines of state school administration, as we know it today, began to emerge. The leaders of the first generation included Thomas Jefferson, Alexander Hamilton, George Washington, and Benjamin Franklin. They helped established the United States as a nation and were also deeply interested in education.

Jefferson offered the most definitive plan for a state school system. In 1779 he and Wythe reported to the Virginia assembly "A Bill for the More General Diffusion of Knowledge." Under the plan each county was to be divided into "hundreds" of such size that all children living in these subdivisions could conveniently attend the school that was to be established in each. All free children, girls as well as boys, were to attend school for three years without paying tuition and for longer than that at private expense if their parents, guardians, or friends thought proper.

The Jefferson plan also provided for a statewide system of secondary schools. Twenty districts, each composed of two to seven counties, were to be organized and a grammar school was to be established in each. Promising boys who had finished the "hundred" schools were to have an opportunity to attend the grammar school tuition-free. The best scholars in the grammar schools were to be selected and sent to William and Mary College for three years at the expense of the state.

One notable feature of Jefferson's plan was the provision that all free children attend the primary school for three years at public expense. But the plan was ahead of the times; the bill did not pass in 1779. A somewhat similar measure, again drafted by Jefferson and presented to the Virginia assembly in 1817, also failed to pass. The colonies were not yet ready for universal education, but the concept by no means died.

The work of Jefferson, Washington, and other leaders of the Revolutionary period was carried on by Horace Mann of Massachusetts, Henry Barnard of Connecticut, John D. Pierce of Michigan, Calvin H. Wiley of North Carolina, Caleb Mills of Indiana, and John Swett of California. Each of these men marshaled the forces in his state behind a plan to develop schools open to all children and paid for out of the public treasury. Each of these leaders deserves recognition, but the work of Horace Mann set a precedent for others.

Mann was trained as an attorney and served for ten years in the Massachusetts legislature. In 1837 he was made secretary of the newly formed State Board of Education in Massachusetts. For the next twelve years he attempted to inform and unify the people regarding public education. He held many meetings for teachers, head masters, and the public at large. His annual reports still stand today as distinguished documents on education. He also founded and edited for many years the *Common School Journal*.

Mann had to contend with indifference, conservatism, political opposition, and sectarian bigotry. To his task he brought considerable ability and great dedication. Not content with existing knowledge about education, he studied educational programs in Europe. Perhaps most important for this work, he made the state board of education and the state superintendency respected and necessary agencies for education and for government.

Some revisionist historians question the motives of the early public school founders. For instance, Katz says, "What they did not admit . . . was that the bureaucratic structure, apparently so equitable and favorable to the poor, would in fact give differential advantage to the affluent and their children, thereby reinforcing rather than altering existing patterns of social structure."[2] We believe, however, that the early champions of the public schools were motivated by a genuine desire to extend educational opportunity.

From General to Special Government

Early school laws passed by the colonies suggested that education in the beginning was controlled by general government. The general assembly made regulations for education as it saw fit. There were no state boards of education, no chief state school officers. When towns, upon direction from the general assembly, began to take some responsibility for schools, the town selectmen dealt directly with educational matters. There were no separate boards of education for the first 200 years of our history.

The basis for state control over education was pretty well established as early as 1820 by constitutional and statutory provisions of the states. As can be seen in Table 4.1, thirteen of the twenty-three states had constitutional provisions for education, seventeen had statutory provisions, nine had both constitutional and statutory

TABLE 4.1
Statutory and Constitutional Provisions for Public Education in States Prior to 1820

State	Date Admitted to Union	Statutory Provisions for Education	Constitutional Provisions for Education
Delaware		Yes	Yes—Direct establishment
Pennsylvania		Yes	Yes—Direct establishment
New Jersey		Yes	No
Georgia		Yes	Yes—Direct establishment
Connecticut		Yes	No
Massachusetts	Original	Yes	Yes—Protect and encourage
Maryland	States	Yes	No
South Carolina		Yes	No
New Hampshire		Yes	Yes—Protect and encourage
Virginia		Yes	No
New York		Yes	No
North Carolina		No	Yes—Direct establishment
Rhode Island		No	No
Vermont	1791	Yes	Yes—Protect and encourage
Kentucky	1792	No	Yes—Direct establishment
Tennessee	1796	No	No
Ohio	1803	Yes	Yes—Protect and encourage
Louisiana	1812	Yes	No
Indiana	1816	Yes	Yes—Protect and encourage
Mississippi	1817	No	Yes—Encourage schools
Illinois	1818	Yes	No
Alabama	1819	No	Yes—Protect and encourage
Maine	1820	Yes	Yes—Protect and encourage

Source: Ellwood P. Cubberley and Edward C. Elliott, *State and County School Administration* (Macmillan Company, 1915), 12–17, and from a study of early state statutes, as prepared by Thurston and Roe, *State School Administration,* 59.

provisions, and only two states—Rhode Island and Tennessee—had neither constitutional nor statutory provisions for education.

Lack of special government for education probably stemmed from two conditions. First, government was just beginning to recognize that it had a direct role to play in providing schools. Though many of the constitutional provisions indicated that government was to "protect and encourage" schools, the concept of establishing and supporting schools was not as yet well developed. Second, schools for the most part were still simple institutions. Their purposes were straightforward, enrollments were small, each teaching staff was composed of one or just a few persons, and no great specialization of subject matter or pedagogy had as yet developed. Thus, members of the general assembly and the town selectmen felt equal to any educational governing required of them.

But special government for education was soon to emerge, first in the form of a chief state school officer, often called a state superintendent of public instruction, and later in a state board of education. The first state superintendency was established in New York in 1812. Shortly thereafter, however, the office was abolished and was not reestablished until 1854. Maryland went through a similar experience: the office was established in 1826, then abolished, and reestablished in 1864. Michigan, Kentucky, and Massachusetts established the state superintendency in 1836 or 1837, and the office has been maintained in those states since that time. By 1870, thirty-six of the states had created such a position; by 1900 all states admitted to the Union—forty-four in number—had chief state school officers; and all states since admitted to the Union also have such officials.

Mann, Barnard, Pierce, Wiley, Mills, and Swett were all chief state school officers in their respective states. Their careers illustrate that such officials can be very effective in marshaling public opinion for a program of public education, in convincing a state legislature that schools should be organized and supported, in establishing teacher training facilities, and in providing professional leadership to teachers and school administrators.

Many chief state school officers who have followed the pioneers in this office, however, have not had the vision or influence of their predecessors. In fact, as will be shown later, one of the problems surrounding the office at present is that of attracting able people to it. Although this state of affairs has changed recently in a growing number of states, some local superintendencies are still accorded more prestige than the office of the chief state school officer.

Almost coordinate with the development of the state superintendency for education was the evolution of the state board of education as a second expression of special government for education at the state level. New York is usually credited as the first state to establish this agency, which it did in 1784.[3] Actually, the legislature created the Board of Regents of the State of New York and gave it some jurisdiction over the academies and colleges of the state. It was not until 1904 that the board was given control over the public schools of the state.

North Carolina created a state board in 1825 under the name of President and Directors of the Literary Fund, and Vermont and Missouri soon after established state boards of education. However, the main impetus for this movement was the action of Massachusetts in 1837 and the demonstration in that state, under Mann's leadership, of the efficacy of a state board of education. By 1900, thirty-four states had state boards of education, and by 1960, forty-six states had state boards exercising general supervision over elementary and secondary schools. Today, only Wisconsin has no such body.[4] In Wisconsin, powers ordinarily lodged with the state board of education are given to the state superintendent of public instruction. In Hawaii, also somewhat of an exception, the state board of education is a district board of education; the schools in Hawaii are operated much as they are in a single city school district.

In the beginning, membership on most state boards of education was *ex officio* and often included the governor, the attorney general, and the state superintendent of public instruction. Gradually this changed and board members were appointed by the governor or elected by the people. In 1982 board members in thirty-four states were appointed by the governor; in twelve states they were elected by the people; and in three states they acquired office in other ways.[5] Since that time Texas has changed from an elected to a governor-appointed board, and the elected board in New Mexico has been expanded to include five members appointed by the governor.

To recapitulate, during the past century forms of government designed specifically to cope with education have developed in every state. In nearly all states a state board of education composed of lay citizens, most often appointed by the governor but in a number of cases elected, has come into being. All states have a chief state school officer. In more than half of the states the chief state school officer is selected by the state board of education and serves as its executive officer, while in the remaining states the relationship of the chief officer to the state board of education is less well defined.

But the development of this special government has not taken education away from general government. The state legislature retains plenary power for education. The legislature may create special machinery, may charge state boards and state superintendents with particular functions, as it has done, but it may also alter the machinery and call back the functions. Moreover, the governor's budget is still a most persuasive instrument with most legislatures. State boards and state superintendents must recommend to the governor a budget for the schools of the state, but neither the governor nor the legislature is required to accept their recommendations. Special government for education, then, supplements but does not replace general government.

THE EMERGING ROLE OF THE STATES

In recent years the state's role in education has received increasing attention. This shift runs counter to our long tradition of local control and represents an interesting turn of events since the 1960s when great emphasis was placed on the federal role in education. We'll note some of the conditions that seem to have contributed to the emerging importance of the states and some of the ways through which increasing state influence is now being expressed.

Conditions Stimulating Change

A number of trends in recent years seem to have converged to require that the state exercise a more definitive role in the governance of education. The first of these is a matter of money. School expenditures have increased much faster than the gross national product. Census figures show that for the period from 1960 to 1985 school expenditures for the nation as a whole went up 874 percent whereas the gross national product increased 774 percent.[6] With expenses increasing faster than income, most school districts have found that local revenue resources are inadequate and that more money must be secured from state sources.

As states have been pressed to provide more money for school purposes, they have found that state finance programs are often inadequate. In some cases state revenues were meager and new funding plans, often requiring use of an income tax, had to be devised. Equally inadequate have been state plans for the allocation of funds to school districts. While most states have had so-called equalization programs designed to provide more money to poor districts and less to wealthy districts, many of these programs were of doubtful merit in the first place and often, like the federal tax structure, they have been subjected to continuing amendments until they no longer serve an equalizing function.

The shortcomings of state school finance programs have been dramatically demonstrated in the state and federal courts. Many of these decisions, such as *Serrano* in California, *Rodriguez* in Texas, and *Cahill* in New Jersey, have now provided household words. Some important principles have emerged from the litigation. For instance, it now seems clear that the wealth of the state, not the wealth of a school district, determines the resources behind a pupil's education. While the U.S. Supreme Court did not see education as a "fundamental interest," the Court did suggest that school finance reform was an appropriate activity for state legislatures. The New Jersey Supreme Court, in *Cahill,* placed the task in perspective. If the mandate of the state constitution that there be a "thorough and efficient system of free public schools" were not observed for any reason, the matter was to be rectified by the state legislature.[7] In a sequel to the Cahill decision, the state supreme court found it necessary to close all public schools in 1976 in order to force the legislature to act. As a result, a graduated income tax, designed to meet constitutional requirements, was enacted.[8]

Still another concern of the state is the increasing demand for accountability in education. This demand has been heightened by the rash of "educational excellence reports" heralding the weaknesses of public education released in the mid-1980s. In state after state elected officials reacted by initiating reforms designed to improve teaching and learning. Some states, including Kentucky and New Jersey, enacted "academic bankruptcy" laws. These statutes provide for intervention by state officials in local district management when districts fail to meet state minimums for academic performance. As Siegel has noted, "By taking matters into their own hands, governors and legislators strove to make state education systems more responsive to their needs for information, more accountable to their demands for improvement."[9] While some states may move more rapidly than seems warranted in terms of our knowledge and technology, the fact remains that people are insisting that states require school districts to give attention to the outputs and not merely to the inputs of school programs.

Teacher power also leads to more state jurisdiction. Teachers' organizations often find that the coffers of many school districts are quickly emptied. If more money is to be had for increased salaries and other benefits, it must be secured at the state level. Little wonder that Aufderheide found that teachers' organizations in many states were the most powerful education interest group.[10] On the political front teachers' organizations employed two resources: votes and money for campaign purposes. Leaders of teachers' organizations were quick to acknowledge that they wished to influence the legislature because "that is where the action is." While some legislators were not sympathetic with the efforts of teachers to shape legislation, few denied their influence with the state legislative body.

Teachers have also been moving forward on another front. For the sake of controlling their own profession, teachers' organizations in state after state have pushed hard for the establishment of a professional practices board composed chiefly of teachers. A recent survey reports that forty-seven of the fifty states have some type of professional practices board or commission.[11] Only Connecticut, North Carolina, and South Dakota have no such boards, and the first two of those states are considering establishing them. In forty-four of the forty-seven states with boards, these bodies serve in an advisory capacity to the state education agency. In three states—California, Minnesota, and Oregon—the professional practices boards have been given authority for some governmental functions, such as establishing certification standards and approving preparation programs. Whether the professional practices board, the established state board of education, or the legislature is currently responsible, control has shifted to the state level.

Both the Nixon and Carter administrations suggested a decreased federal role in education and stressed the need for a more prominent state role. While these expressions supported the emergence of the state as an important partner in education, it remained for the Reagan administration to insist upon a decreased role on the part of the federal government.

New Expressions of the State Role

The augmented role of the state in education is expressed in many ways. In 1983 alone, several states, including California, Florida, Illinois, and Mississippi, passed major reform legislation. Doyle and Hartle document the growing role of the states in their analysis of the reform movement in the early 1980s. They discuss the growing proportion of money the states were spending relative to declining local and federal shares and the increases in state oversight and controls, which are exercised by legislatures, governors, and state agencies.[12]

Even more dramatic has been recent action of the National Governors Association depicted in its 1987 report, *Results in Education.* The report assessed what had been done by each state in the educational arena during 1986 and laid plans for a five-year attack on educational problems. Seven major issues, requiring continuous attention of governors and other state education policy leaders, were set forth:

1. Creating a more highly professional teaching force;
2. Strengthening school leadership and management;
3. Promoting greater parent involvement and choice . . . ;
4. Helping at risk children and youth meet higher education standards;
5. Making . . . more effective use of new technologies . . . ;
6. Making better use of resources invested in school facilities; and
7. Strengthening the mission and effectiveness of colleges and universities.[13]

School finance and tax reform obviously require legislative action, so legislators are always involved in education. While the involvement of legislators and governors in the area of finance is necessary, the nature of that involvement represents a departure from past decades. Governors and legislators are not merely reacting to what is presented by others—they are taking the initiative in school finance reform. Moreover, issues other than finance have prompted legislative action. As noted above, almost half of the state legislatures have taken some kind of action in the accountability area. Frequently, this action was taken despite the opposition of educators.

As a wider range of actors began to play important roles in state policymaking for education, government offices added to their staffs persons who could supply them with information basic to policy decisions. Whereas governors and legislators once relied on interest group organizations, chiefly teacher groups and state departments of education, for information, they now turn increasingly to their own staffs.

Another sign of the emergence of state governance in education is the disappearance of most of the state coalitions in education. Bailey noted that in the 1950s and 1960s in the northeastern states where school finance reform was achieved, the influence of an effective education coalition was always present. This coalition ordinarily included the education interest groups—teachers, administrators, school board members, representatives of citizen groups (particularly the Parent Teacher Association), and representatives of the state education agency. The coalition frequently had easy access to legislative leaders and to the governor.

By the early 1970s most of these arrangements no longer existed. Of the twelve states in the Governance Project, educational coalitions retained some degree of their former power in only Colorado and Tennessee.

While the labor-management split between teachers' organizations and organizations representing school boards and school administrators will not be easy to heal, there is now some evidence, particularly in Pennsylvania, that new economic pressures and turbulent environments have forced educational interest groups to reconsider the matter.[14]

In their study of *Legislative Education Leadership in the States,* Rosenthal and Fuhrman note that the governance of education changed in the 1970s: " . . . by the end of the decade legislatures were in the thick of policy making in education. Many had wrested the initiative from state departments and interest groups; and most had started to exercise control over the design, funding, implementation, and assessment of education in their states."[15]

The most dramatic change in this direction was the establishment in the early 1970s of the office of secretary of education in at least four states.[16] The most complete reorganization took place in Pennsylvania, but the transition was partially achieved in Massachusetts, South Dakota, and Virginia. In recent years Massachusetts has dispensed with the office of secretary and New Mexico has added it. In each case the secretary was appointed by and responsible to the governor. The secretary was usually a member of the governor's cabinet and thus the formal structure required that educational concerns be considered in a total state context.

Not all states moved education as far into general governance as those noted above. Under Illinois' recent reorganization, for instance, the state board of education members are appointed by the governor with the consent of the senate. The board has jurisdiction over a number of matters, specifically those delegated by the legislature. The board selects and employs its own executive officer. But even in states where the structure of the government has not been changed, it seems doubtful that the autonomy once ascribed to the state agency for education will continue.

CURRENT ORGANIZATIONAL ARRANGEMENTS

Responsibilities of the Legislature

Most state constitutions contain language charging the state legislature with the responsibility of establishing and maintaining a system of free public schools. In the Utah constitution, for instance, the provision reads as follows: "The Legislature shall provide for the establishment and maintenance of a uniform system of public schools, which shall be open to all children of the State, and free from sectarian control" (Article X, Section 1). The courts of the several states have consistently interpreted such language as ascribing plenary power to the legislature. In a Florida case in which the jurisdiction of school districts was in question, the plenary power of the legislature was reiterated:

> County school boards are part of machinery of government operating at local level as agency of state in performance of public functions, and character of their functions and extent and duration of their power rest exclusively in the legislative discretion. Power of county school boards may be enlarged, diminished, modified or revoked, and their powers rest exclusively in the legislative discretion.[17]

This plenary power does not mean that there are no restrictions on the legislature. To begin with, the legislature cannot take action contrary to the state constitution or the U.S. Constitution. The courts also have consistently ruled that the legislature cannot exercise its power in an unreasonable manner, nor can the legislature delegate its plenary power to other governmental agencies.

Constitutional and statutory language, court interpretations, and long practice make it clear that the legislature of each state is the "big school board." The dismay with which many state legislatures view the school bills of each legislative session is, in a sense, inevitable; the basic decisions regarding education cannot be made anywhere else. To be sure, state boards of education and appropriate state commissions can do much to screen and improve the proposed legislation, but only the legislature can decide basic policy questions regarding the schools.

Another development in many legislatures is the desire to exercise legislative oversight. The oversight function is often implemented with the help of legislative staffs and in some states interim committees of the legislature. Legislative oversight was demonstrated dramatically in Florida, where the legislature was particularly concerned about the implementation of three of its policy enactments: management at the school site level, the establishment of citizens advisory councils for each school, and the effects of the Florida school finance program. Rather than depend entirely upon reports from the state department of education and from school district officers regarding these matters, the legislature decided to employ a group of consultants to help determine the extent and nature of the impact of these legislative actions. The legislature also sought recommendations about how to improve its general oversight procedures for educational legislation. The consultants did provide the legislature with a comprehensive report of their findings and recommendations.[18]

The work of legislatures is done through committees, and the finance and education committees of the senate and the house are crucial bodies in regard to legislation affecting schools. But these committees do not sit and deliberate in an aseptic environment. Every special interest group in the state interested in education or in expenditures, and some beyond the state, attempt to influence the education and finance committees.

In a study of the role of education interest groups in state policymaking for education, Aufderheide found that teacher associations were the most effective interest groups, particularly in terms of influence on the legislature.[19] Only in three of the twelve states studied did school board associations appear to come near to matching the influence of teacher groups. Generally, school administrator associations were found to have still less influence in policymaking. Moreover, in most states noneducation interest groups did not match teachers in terms of influencing the legislators, although when educational issues also became tax issues, business, labor, and agricultural groups exerted more influence than normal.

The state legislature, then, has plenary power in making basic policy decisions regarding the schools. This power is exercised amid the welter of forces that constitute American society. In a sense, the legislature is the arena within which these forces make the best case they can and marshal all the influence they can muster. Any realistic appraisal of controls imposed on American schools must consider not only the arena but all of the actors who contend for influence within that arena.

State Executive Arrangements

Control over education is also exercised by the executive branch of state government. The governor, the chief state school officer, the state board of education, the staff of the state department of education, and other state agencies all participate in school government.

The governor exerts influence in several ways. Because the governor is head of a political party at the state level, his or her position on educational questions is crucial, particularly if the governor's party controls the state legislature. The governor's viewpoint on education is usually set forth in the messages submitted to the legislature. Provisions for education in the budget the governor recommends to the legislature are often the most fateful expression of the governor's control over education. The governor also has the power to veto education legislation. Finally, in a majority of the states the governor appoints, often with the approval of the senate, the members of the state board of education. In recent years more and more governors have insisted on an increased role in educational matters.

In 1982, eighteen of the chief state school officers were elected by popular ballot, twenty-seven appointed by state boards of education, and five appointed by the governor.[20] Since then, Minnesota and Iowa have changed from board-appointed to governor-appointed chiefs, and Louisiana has changed from an elected to a board-appointed chief. In the case of those appointed by the governor and those elected by popular ballot, the chief state school officer is legally an officer of the state and as such exercises the sovereignty of the state. Most chief state school officers appointed by state boards of education are legally employees and not officers of the state. In these cases, the sovereignty of the state has usually been lodged with the state board of education.

In practice all chief state school officers can exercise considerable influence over education in their states. In many cases the chief state school officer influences state policy for education by giving public expression to educational needs, by enlisting grassroots support, by recommending action to the state board of education, and by influencing the legislature and the governor as they consider educational problems. Moreover, this official is usually charged by statute or state board of education regulation to exercise general supervision over the schools of the state, to organize a staff of professionals in the state department of education, and to actually direct the operation of certain special schools, such as those for the deaf and the blind, which may be under state jurisdiction.

We have noted that forty-nine states have a state board of education charged with the general supervision of elementary and secondary schools within the state. In those states where the chief state school officer is elected by popular ballot, there is often confusion between the basic responsibility of the state board of education and that of the state superintendent of public instruction. In states where the state board of education selects its own chief executive, this confusion does not ordinarily exist.

Most state boards of education are composed largely of lay citizens rather than professional educators. In a majority of the states, these members are appointed by the governor. A number of states have provided for the election of state board members by popular ballot. In most cases state board members serve without salary, although a per diem and expenses for attending meetings may be allowed. Ordinarily, state boards of education meet at least once every three months.

In one sense, state boards of education are administrative agencies, usually charged with exercising general control over the elementary and secondary schools of the state. In a few cases they are also given some jurisdiction over higher education. State boards are also seen as having a policymaking function, specifically in those areas delegated to them by the legislature, and also in terms of supporting policy positions to the governor and the legislature. Based on a study of the state governance of education the policymaking role of most state boards is more fiction than fact.[21] For the most part, state boards of education tended to legitimize the policy recommendations of the chief state school officer and exercised little policy initiative on their own.

The governance study also supported Sroufe's earlier conclusions that state board members were much alike whether appointed or elected.[22] He thought this might be due to the low visibility of the board in most states, which makes it unlikely that the governor will appoint candidates who might be controversial. The governor tends to rely on selected advisers or representatives of educational professions for assistance. In states where board members are elected, the voters, like the governor, find it impossible to make choices among candidates who seem to have no positions on substantive issues, and must rely on educational reputation and general status. These are the only criteria available to the governor or to the electorate and explain why board composition is so predictable.

The state department of education is the professional arm of the chief state school officer and the state board of education. In recent years, new and expanded functions of state departments have required an increase in professional personnel. This growth in staff has been facilitated by the expansion of federal assistance for state departments that began in the 1960s.

In 1982, the average number of full-time professionals on staff in the headquarters of state departments of education was 273.[23] The highest number of staff members was 1,233 in California and the lowest was 34 in North Dakota. Ten years earlier, the average number of staff members in state departments of education was 191. Ordinarily, these people are organized into divisions such as administration and finance, teacher certification, instructional services, junior colleges, vocational and adult education, and vocational rehabilitation. These divisions suggest the areas in which members of the professional staff give supervision to the schools of the state.

In many cases state department personnel are required to enforce the regulations of the state imposed either by statute or by state board action. Sometimes enforcement duties are thrust upon state boards of education but the boards are given no supporting budget to carry out such responsibilities. In recent years most state departments have tried to increase emphasis on the leadership role of the department. While state departments appear to have been strengthened in recent years, many are still too overburdened with regulatory duties to exert much leadership.

In terms of enforcing minimum standards upon the schools of the state, however, state departments of education are rather effective. These standards may apply to such practices as the adoption of textbooks, the certification of teachers, and the distribution of state money. In all instances state department personnel are charged with following statutory provisions or state board of education regulations.

Ordinarily, a number of other state agencies has some control over the schools. These agencies may have jurisdiction over certain aspects of the health and safety of pupils, the auditing of school funds, the employment of minors, and other matters. In Illinois, for example, these agencies include the following: the auditor of public accounts, who apportions state school funds; the attorney general, who may give legal opinions on educational questions; the State Teachers Certification Board, which administers the teacher certification function; the Department of Labor, which exercises some control over the employment of minors; the Board of Trustees of the Retirement Fund, which administers the teachers' retirement program; the Scholarship Commission, which awards scholarships to high school graduates; and the School Building Commission, which allocates state funds to "needy" school districts for school building purposes. While these agencies have only those powers granted to them by the legislature, the exercise of these powers inevitably requires some discretion and thus represents a measure of control.

In summary, the execution of educational government at the state level is performed by the governor, a chief state school officer, a state board of education, a state department largely composed of professionals in education, and a number of other state agencies to which certain kinds of educational functions have been delegated by the legislature. In some cases, these officers and agencies seem to understand rather clearly what their respective duties are and they perform these duties satisfactorily. In other cases, neither perception nor performance appear to be adequate. Emphasis upon local government of education, even among state officials, has undoubtedly weakened state government of education, a condition now undergoing some change but still demanding attention.

Delegation to Local Agencies

While the legislature and certain executive agencies have much to do with the government of education, responsibility for the actual operation of most of our schools has been delegated to district boards of education. The nature of these boards' powers has been set forth in Chapter 9. In brief, the duties of school board members include the right to establish schools, to build school houses, to employ a superintendent, to establish necessary rules to manage and govern the schools, and to raise and expend money. The courts have consistently held that such delegations by the state legislature to district boards of education are appropriate. An excerpt from a New Jersey case follows:

> Recent years have witnessed an increasing liberality in the approach of our courts toward the construction of legislative delegations of power. The keynote was struck in *Ward v. Scott,* 11 N.J. 117, 123–4, A 2nd 385 (1952), where Justice Jacobs observed that "the exigencies of modern government have increasingly dictated the use of general rather than minutely detailed standards in regulatory enactments under the police power."[24]

This extensive delegation to district boards of education is always within the framework established by the state legislature. While local boards of education may, for instance, raise and expend money, they do this within the limits prescribed by law.

Often the ceiling on the local tax rate is set by law. Nearly always, expenditures for capital outlay must be approved by a referendum in the district. Nearly all other operational powers of school boards are circumscribed in similar fashion.

Many states establish an additional agency to assist with educational government. As noted in Chapter 6, more than half the states have organized intermediate units of school administration. The intermediate units may be represented in the office of the county superintendent of schools, in the county board of education, or in both. While the function of the intermediate unit is not always clear, the county superintendent or the county board is usually charged with preparing information and making reports to the state department of education, assisting in the reorganization of school districts, registering teachers' certificates, assisting in the supervision of rural schools, assisting with the in-service education of teachers, and providing some special services in weak districts. The stipulation of the functions of these intermediate units is another clear example of the delegation of power by the state legislature to agencies nearer the scene where the school is in actual operation. The county superintendent throughout most of U.S. history has been charged with seeing that school districts, particularly those in rural areas, operate schools as the legislature intended.

States, then, have delegated powers—within stipulated limits—to district boards of education to operate schools. In many states, particularly those with numerous rural districts, the state has established an inspection office to see that schools are operated according to the law. Both legislative and executive branches of state government play a part in the control of the schools. The judicial branch of state government, too, particularly through decisions rendered by state courts, affects school operation. The nature of our state and federal courts, and the role the courts play in school matters are treated at length in Chapter 8.

At this point it seems appropriate to ask if the structure of state government, including the state education agency, has a bearing on that agency's capacity to conceptualize and implement its functions. In 1976 Campbell and Mazzoni dealt extensively with that question and we will refer briefly to that discussion.[25] They explicated three possible models for state governance of education: the centralized executive model, the separate agency model, and some combination of the two. Each of the three models stressed particular values in governance. The centralized executive model, for example, emphasized the role of the governor as the chief executive of the state, in education as in other state functions. While no state employed a complete centralized model, some states, such as Massachusetts and Pennsylvania, had moved in that direction. Whereas the centralized executive model would make education a part of general governance, the separate agency model emphasized considerable independence of educational governance. This independence was to be achieved through separate educational arrangements: a state board of education and a chief state school officer. Many states employed some variation of this model with New York, where education was almost a fourth branch of government, having the most independent arrangement. At the other extreme, found in several states, was the elected-chief model where the chief state school officer was publicly elected.

Several variations of the combination model were also discussed. One of these variations, also found in several states, was the governor-appointed authoritative board with the board selecting the chief state school officer.

After analyzing these various models and considering the preferences of persons knowledgeable about state structures for education, Campbell and Mazzoni came to the following conclusion:

> We reiterate our two major concerns: *(1) formal structure must be seen as one of many variables in any plan for the reorganization of state governance for education, but undue reliance cannot be placed on structure alone, and (2) at the same time there should be a recognition that structure can make some difference.* It is quite clear that how people choose to work within a structure makes a difference. It also seems that formal structure may permit, may actually encourage, certain kinds of behavior on the part of policy makers. Even if changing structure does not guarantee desirable changes in behavior, the fact that it might encourage such changes seems to be sufficient inducement to consider structural arrangements.[26]

It seemed quite clear, for instance, that an elected chief state school officer and a governor-appointed state board of education could often invoke political and jurisdictional issues in place of dealing with the substantive functions of the state education agency.

DECISIONS MADE AT THE STATE LEVEL

We have touched on a number of the types of educational decisions made at the state level. We will now take a closer look at these decisions. While states vary somewhat in their practices, a number of decisions are rather common among the states.

The Instructional Program

Most states make a number of decisions having to do with the instructional program. They usually determine the scope or the extent of the program. The common school for which states take responsibility now refers to both the elementary and the secondary school. In some states the kindergarten is recognized as part of the state program, but in many states the kindergarten is optional and its organization is left to the discretion of local districts. A number of states now have permissive junior college legislation, including some state financial support, but most states have not yet included the junior college as part of the public school program. The extent to which vocational education, education for the handicapped, preschool education, and adult education are given attention is often dependent upon decisions made at the state level. Prescriptive federal programs, as noted in Chapter 3, have come near to forcing states to take action in vocational education and in education for the handicapped.

In addition to determining or at least influencing the scope of the instructional program, most states exercise some authority in establishing standards for the program. A few states actually write these standards into the statutes. A more common practice is for the legislature to delegate the establishment of standards to the state board of education or to the office of the chief state school officer. In Ohio, for instance, the state board of education is given specific authority to formulate and prescribe minimum standards for elementary and secondary schools. These standards pertain to the curriculum, instructional materials, pupil admission and promotion, and graduation requirements. Formulation of standards under such authority makes these standards a part of the administrative law under which the schools of the state operate. The recent reform movement has prompted many states to raise academic standards, increase graduation requirements, and require more testing of students.

All states have passed laws requiring all children, except those who are physically or mentally incapable, to attend school. While the period of compulsory attendance varies somewhat among the states, and as part of the integration struggle the provisions were modified in Mississippi, South Carolina, and Virginia, a common required attendance period is from age eight to age sixteen or graduation from the eighth grade. Most states also prescribe the minimum school term, usually nine months or about 180 school days. Many states also define a minimum school day.

Some states require their state boards to specify a course of study for the schools to follow. The state board of education in North Carolina, for instance, is required to adopt a standard course of study upon the recommendation of the state superintendent of public instruction. To meet a requirement such as this, most state boards appoint a committee of professional school workers to prepare the course, or courses, of study. The materials prepared by these groups would then be approved by the state board of education and made available to the schools.

In some states the course of study provided by the state is binding only on rural school districts; city school districts may have authority to prepare their own courses of study. In other states the county superintendent's office is charged with specifying a course of study for all rural districts. In most states, however, the statutes affect the course of study in some way. A common stipulation is the requirement of United States history and government for graduation from high school.

Many states also have requirements governing the selection and use of textbooks. For example, the Texas Education Agency is required to purchase and distribute textbooks. The agency appoints a state textbook committee and charges it with examining and recommending books to be used. Ordinarily, the agency accepts the recommendations of the committee. A few states still have single textbook adoptions for elementary schools, but a number of states adopt multiple lists from which school districts may select books. Some states leave selection of books to local school districts or to the county office, but they do require that each selection be reported to the state education authority.

State decisions concerning the instructional program may deal with the scope of the program, the establishment of standards, the requirement of a course of study, or the approval of books to be used. Some of these decisions are specified in the statutes, but more often they emanate from the state board of education or the office of the chief state officer in keeping with statutory authority. The financial support program of the state may, in effect, also control the program. For instance, many districts would find it difficult to provide kindergarten and junior college programs unless they were included in state aid provisions.

Certification of Personnel

More definitive than program decisions are state regulations having to do with the certification of teachers. Haberman and Stinnett report that all states have set up controls governing teacher certification and administer these regulations directly.[27] In recent years the testing of prospective teachers has become a major element in certification programs. Rudner reports that as of April 1987, "24 states tested applicants to teacher education programs, 26 states tested individuals as a requirement for initial teacher certification, three states tested veteran teachers, and seven states used a formal observation instrument to assess the performance of beginning teachers."[28] Several additional states were planning to implement testing programs in the near future.

Another practice among states is the approval of institutions and programs for teacher education and the certification of graduates from such programs without further individual appraisal. This practice requires that the state department of education have staff members who can examine teacher education programs, make judgments about them, and ultimately recommend to the appropriate state authority what programs be accepted or rejected. Recently, in some states there has been political pressure to "open up" some certification requirements. This pressure has frequently been stimulated by the shortage of math and science teachers and the need to recruit as teachers, even on a part-time basis, persons with math and science backgrounds who have difficulty meeting rigid certification requirements.

Another development is the growth of reciprocity of certification among the states. About three-fifths of the states grant certificates to teachers of other states provided they have graduated from institutions accredited by the National Council for the Accreditation of Teacher Education. NCATE is a voluntary organization composed chiefly of persons representing organizations of teachers' colleges, teachers' associations, administrators' associations, and school board groups. Its influence is an example of how private groups can exercise as much or more control than public government. Responding to criticism of its membership and procedure, NCATE in 1986 completed a reorganization designed to achieve more reliable accreditation decisions, improve articulation between NCATE and state approval of teacher education programs, and reduce duplication of effect between state and national accreditation agencies.[29]

Facilities Standards

Almost all states exercise some control over school facilities. Such control may include the establishment of school plant standards, approval of school sites, and the approval of plans and specifications for new buildings. The school plant standards may actually appear in the statutes, but more commonly an administrative body has the authority to establish standards. This body in many cases is the state board of education; in other cases it is the industrial commission or some similar agency in the state. In New York the education and public works departments collaborate on some aspects of this function.

In some states grants or loans from the state for school plant outlays are available to school districts under some circumstances. Often these districts have to appear needy to qualify for state aid. Moreover, school districts in these circumstances are often required to accept an austerity building. Since these districts are often the ones with rapidly expanding school enrollments and depleted local funds, they ordinarily have no recourse but to accept the conditions stipulated by the state agency. Thus a more severe form of control sometimes follows the dollar. A number of states have established special agencies to administer these special grants for school plants.

Financial Support

State control over education is often the strongest in matters of money for school operation and capital outlay. In some states, particularly in New England, and in some large cities school districts are fiscally dependent upon some other agency, such as the city council, for the approval of their budgets. In a majority of school districts, however, boards of education need not submit their budgets to another agency; hence they are considered fiscally independent.

Even in fiscally independent school districts, however, numerous state controls are imposed. Boards of education may have the power to determine their own budgets, but the tax rate used to generate revenue must ordinarily fall within limits set by the state. Sometimes, by means of a referendum, these limits may be extended, but even then the upper limit for the operating levy is usually set by the state legislature. Sometimes special levies are permitted for supplementary purposes, such as transportation.

Most states not only set a ceiling on school district taxes, but they also stipulate how the school budget is to be prepared, what budget breakdowns must be shown, and how budget approval must be sought. Often the board of education is required to advertise the budget and hold a hearing on it.

Crucial to the financial operation of the school districts are the assessment practices applied to real estate and other property. As with other taxing jurisdictions, state government and often county government determine the nature of these practices. Some states have established strong equalization boards that influence the local assessment practices and that apply corrections among counties designed to equalize assessments. Most local school districts are very dependent upon these equalization boards.

The state exerts control over capital outlay funds as well as operating funds. Nearly every state limits the borrowing capacity of school districts for capital outlay purposes. Michigan and Virginia do not appear to impose debt limits on certain types of districts. There is usually a limit, often expressed in percentage of assessed valuation, beyond which bonds may not be floated even by vote of the people. In Illinois, for instance, this limit was 5 percent of the assessed valuation of the school district. In most states, the percentage must be approved by a simple majority of qualified electors voting; in other states, a two-thirds majority of electors is required. In some states, electors must also be property holders to vote in a bond election, and in a few states a two-thirds majority of property holders is required to pass the bond referendum.

In most states, financial controls imposed upon school districts are stipulated in detail in the statutes. An administrative board, often the state board of education, may be required to allocate the money among the school districts of the state, but ordinarily these bodies can exercise little, if any, discretion.

Nonpublic Schools

Most of the state-level decisions mentioned thus far apply specifically to public elementary and secondary schools of the state. The role of the state in regulating nonpublic schools is not as plain. Opinions on this issue are varied: some would make such schools illegal while others would have states take a "hands-off" policy. The U.S. Supreme Court made it clear in the Oregon case that states could not require all pupils to attend the public schools. An excerpt follows:

> No question is raised concerning the power of the State reasonably to regulate all schools, to inspect, supervise and examine them, their teachers and pupils; to require that all children of proper age attend *some* [italics added] school, that teachers shall be of good moral character and patriotic disposition, that certain studies plainly essential to good citizenship must be taught and that nothing be taught which is manifestly inimical to the public welfare.[30]

Following the decision of the Court, it seems clear that the compulsory education laws of states can also be observed by attendance at nonpublic schools. For many, it seems equally clear that states are obligated to see that nonpublic schools meet appropriate standards. McCarthy found, however, that "many questions remain unanswered in connection with the states' regulatory authority over religious schools."[31] Court decisions vary among states but overall the courts have not yet clarified whether government interests in monitoring private schools should override parental interest in directing the religious upbringing of children. Should Congress enact any form of tuition tax credit for nonpublic schools, as advocated by the Reagan administration, the need for state regulation of nonpublic schools would become even greater.

This discussion has not covered all types of state-level decisions for education. Enough has been said, however, to indicate the nature of state school decisions for education. We shall next turn to some broad functions of the state education agency.

SUGGESTED FUNCTIONS OF THE STATE EDUCATION AGENCY

As we have seen, many decisions for schools are made at the state level. Governors, legislators, the state education agency, and other actors participate in this decision-making process. We will look now at the functions assigned specifically to the state education agency. In so doing, we are defining the state agency to include the state board of education, the chief state school officer, and the professional staff of the department. Our description of these elements is based on actual practice in some of our more advanced states as well as what practice needs to be in all of our states. In a sense we are suggesting that, if schools are to be conducted in keeping with American values and in the American scheme of government, state education agencies have a unique and crucial function to perform.

State departments of education, as we have shown, have a regulatory function. Minimum standards are an important area of regulation. Personnel in the state department of education should have a hand in developing such standards. The formulation of these standards should take into account professional knowledge in the area, whether that knowledge is gained from looking at educational practice in other states or from relevant research.

Ordinarily the process of arriving at a statement of the minimums should be a cooperative one. In attempting to develop a state program on teacher certification, for instance, teachers, administrators, school board members, and professors in teacher education institutions should be consulted. Also the views of people who will be affected by the state program should be ascertained and any special insights these people have should be noted.

Once standards have been established, they should be enforced. Ordinarily this will be done through explanation and persuasion. The emphasis should be on achieving excellence rather than merely conforming to the minimum standards. When state minimum standards are clearly ignored, however, the state should have legal recourse to require compliance. This may be done through such measures as denying approval of schools, withholding state funds, and, if necessary, by means of mandamus action and recourse to the courts. State departments represent the people of the state and, in terms of minimum standards, the state, not the locality, is sovereign.

A second function of state departments of education is direct operation of schools. In the past a number of states have been charged with operating special schools for the blind and deaf. Sometimes special vocational or technical schools and junior colleges have been set up under the immediate control of the state board of education. In recent years, however, there has been a tendency to distribute these special school functions among existing school districts or to create special school districts for such functions. For example, many city school districts now conduct their own classes for the blind and hearing impaired. It is not unusual either to find special districts of combinations of districts organized for slow learners. Special junior college or technical institute districts are also common in some states.

State departments of education, we believe, should give up the direct operation of schools wherever they can find or establish a local agency to take over such a function. Direct operation of schools is inconsistent with the other functions a state department is called upon to perform. For instance, states operating schools for the deaf might be more reluctant to examine alternative programs for such people than states that do not have such vested interests.

Most state education agencies try to help the schools of the state improve their operation. Thus, service is a third function of these agencies. In the past, this service was extended more frequently to rural than to urban districts but that condition is changing. One of the first services provided by many state agencies was the preparation and distribution of instructional materials. Some of the early visual aids libraries and testing centers, for instance, were located in state departments of education. Most state agencies have also prepared, usually with the assistance of teachers and administrators from the schools of the state, courses of study and teaching guides for the use of the schools.

A recurring question is how a supervisory agency can be helpful to an operating agency, particularly when the supervisory agency also has regulatory duties to perform. In an attempt to solve this problem most state education agencies have made staff available to consult with teachers and administrators on an individual basis. State agencies may anticipate the need to provide consultation on new programs or new demands being made on the schools. For instance, in the area of computer education, a state agency might have one or two very knowledgeable people on call for advice throughout the state.

Obviously, in populous states the one-to-one approach to consultation is not sufficient to serve thousands of school people. Therefore, state agency staff members have set up in-service education workshops for groups of teachers and administrators or for key personnel in local school systems, who would carry the message to others in their own districts.

Planning, research, and evaluation are a fourth responsibility of state departments of education. Each state department of education should have a strong division of planning and research responsible for the collection and analysis of relevant statistics on the operation of the schools. This unit would investigate numerous questions such as how many high school graduates took advanced placement courses, how many school districts have introduced the mathematics study materials, and how many teachers are teaching in their major fields.

State education departments should not stop with status research; evaluative research should also be done. Objectives for experimental programs should be set, then evidence should be gathered to ascertain how well the objectives had been achieved. For instance, a number of school districts with year-round schools might cooperate with the state department in determining to what extent the objectives for such a plan were accomplished.

A few state departments may also find it possible to do basic studies that ascertain relationships among variables. However, most basic research will probably still be done on university campuses or in special research organizations. In many ways this separation of research functions is desirable, for it permits both universities and state departments to do the type of research for which they are best fitted and in which the members of the respective organizations have the most interest.

While funds are not as plentiful as they once were, some money for research and evaluation is available from the U.S. Department of Education and from other agencies. State departments should also seek state funds for such purposes. In addition to actually doing research, state departments should encourage and give leadership to research and evaluation activities among the school districts of the state. Unfortunately, very few school districts have either the staff or the budget for such purposes. Moreover, professional workers in these districts are confused about the meaning of research, about how to apply the results of research, and about what research can and cannot do. State departments should provide education on these matters at the local level.

Perhaps the most important aspect of the research function in the state department of education is the communication of research. Research personnel should not only be informed about the studies done in their own department, but they should know what is going on in important research agencies across the nation. Ways of summarizing this knowledge and transmitting it to all state department personnel and to many school and college workers in the state should be developed. This information could be used by the state board of education and the legislature as they consider basic educational problems.

If state departments expanded their role in planning, research, and evaluation and left operation to the schools themselves, the state departments would become more useful in the government of education. Such a shift in emphasis would give substance to the leadership departments provide to the schools. Leadership is the fifth function of state education departments. Major problems confront us: How can schools be made more effective? How does the management style of principals affect learning? How can the teacher workplace be made more attractive? How can schools be more adequately financed? How can schools be appropriately desegregated? To answer these and many more questions, we need additional research knowledge, but even more we need the judgment of competent people who know what the facts are, who ask the right questions, who are sensitive to probable consequences, who reflect the basic values of our culture, and who can point to a course of action designed to improve our lot. Hopefully, some of this vision will come from the membership of the state board of education, some from the chief state school officer, some from professionals within the state department, and some from other lay citizens and professional school workers over the state. The state agency should have a means of utilizing the contributions from these sources to develop goals and directions for education in the state.

State departments of education should lead not only by helping people to do better what they are now doing but also by helping them to see new and important things to do. This means that long-range planning should be an important task of the state department; it means that the best brains among lay people and professionals in the state should be involved in this long-range planning. It means that consultants outside the state may be sought to stimulate thinking about goals and programs to be undertaken. Finally, it means that state agencies—boards, chief state school officers, and departmental specialists—should play a part in policymaking for education.

The question arises, What is the appropriate balance among these five functions for a state education agency? Or, if the operation of schools is eliminated, what is the appropriate balance among the four remaining functions? That very question was raised by the State Board of Education in Delaware.[32] In Delaware the effort devoted to regulation, service, and leadership was under review. While measurement was difficult, there seemed to be evidence to suggest that, in terms of staff time expressed in person-weeks, 48 percent of the department's effort went to regulatory activities, 14 percent to leadership activities, and 38 percent to service activities. There are no magic formulas for computing what these percentages ought to be, but the consultants did suggest that the effort going into leadership was less than it should be. The effort going into regulation confirmed the reality of that obligation for state education agencies. Delaware, perhaps more than many other states, emphasized the service function and that effort was met with widespread approval among the teachers and administrators in the schools.

This effort to map out directions cannot be dominated by a small group. Goals must make sense to lay citizens and to professional school workers. Ultimately, if the programs proposed to meet these goals are to be implemented, they, or rather the money to support them, must be approved by the legislature. The marshaling of positive public opinion so necessary to legislative action is a prime leadership task of the state education agency.

SUMMARY AND FUTURE PROSPECTS

State controls over the schools take numerous forms. Many of these controls are implemented by the state education agency, but some may be exercised directly by the governor, the legislature, the attorney general, the state auditor, or by other state agencies, such as those that consider new buildings or establish health standards. The major state controls operating in most states are summarized below.

State Controls

1. *Control of Information.* The state education agency, and to a lesser extent other state agencies, require school reports and conduct studies of school practices and in the process build data banks about the schools of the state. For the most part, these agencies determine what data are to be collected, what uses are to be made of such data, and to what extent reports of data analyses are to be made public. At times, state legislatures require specific studies and federal agencies often require specific reports.
2. *Technical Services.* The state education agency determines, in large part, what technical services are to be made available to the schools of the state. Decisions on services influence the staffing required in state departments of education and the establishment of relationships with local school districts. Whatever that staffing, whether in reading, evaluation, or computer education, the influence of the state department is tipped in that direction.
3. *Regulation of Standards.* By constitution and statute legislatures are required to set certain standards for the schools of the state. Legislatures

then generally require that the state agencies, most often the education agency, check up on the implementation of those standards. Thus, the state agencies may be required to check on such matters as school attendance, the use of books and other instructional materials, and the keeping of certain fiscal records. In each case, school districts are required to obey the law.

4. *Allocation of Money.* The state education agency is usually required to allocate state funds to the schools. While the allocation formula is usually found in the law, the state education agency must often interpret the law, and sometimes some portion of the state appropriation is left to the discretion of the chief state school officer or to the state agency to meet emergency needs in the state. The allocation of money is a sanction of some importance.

5. *Certification of Personnel.* All states have now taken over the function of certifying persons who may teach or administer in the schools of the state. Some states delegate most of this function to the teacher education institutions of the state, but in many states education agencies determine the nature of preservice preparation programs for the teachers and administrators and the requirements for the renewal of certificates. State agency control is frequently challenged by the universities and also by teacher organizations, but in most states the right to determine those who enter and those who stay in the profession is a state prerogative.

6. *Coalitions.* Many state agencies have solidified their influence through the maintenance of coalitions with educators and related groups in the state. In the past, these coalitions often included teacher organizations, school administrator organizations, the state school board association, the parent teacher association, and other groups. With the advent of collective bargaining by teachers, many of these coalitions were dismantled but there is some evidence that they are now being reestablished. In any case, most chief state school officers still find that their strength with the legislature and governor is enhanced through alliance with some of the education interest groups.

7. *Legislative Oversight.* The determination of legislatures to see that their enactments are implemented represents another increasingly important aspect of state control. As noted earlier, the Florida legislature went so far as to employ consultants from outside the state to determine to what extent three legislative mandates were being implemented. In many states the legislature depends upon its agencies or a staff employed by the legislature itself to conduct these implementation studies.

8. *The Courts.* In the many relationships between officials at the state level and those at the school level, it is quite normal that differences in interpretation and judgment would emerge. Frequently, these differences have been carried into court; while those cases based on the federal Constitution, such as school desegregation, have gone to federal courts, many state

issues have ended up in the state courts. These issues may include compulsory attendance, teacher fitness, and the use of public money. The courts often must say what the law is and insist that it be obeyed.

9. *The State as Federal Proxy.* States are frequently asked to allocate federal funds to the school districts and to enforce the federal regulations pertaining to those allocations. To achieve these ends, one-half to two-thirds of the staff members of many state departments of education are paid from federal funds. These staff members are found in the administration of funds for such programs as those pertaining to the disadvantaged, the handicapped, planning and evaluation, and vocational education. In the process, the state is helping to establish special interest groups among professionals and also among lay people. These special interest groups in turn are becoming strong and influential advocates for their own narrow concerns.

Outlook for the Future

Let us now shift to some consideration of future prospects at the state level. Control of schools at the state level will probably grow. Several considerations lead us to this conclusion. First, by constitutional and statutory provisions, education is a state and not a local function. School districts have delegated, not plenary, power. The growing interest of state legislatures in the operation of schools, particularly in legislative oversight, is another expression of the plenary power of the legislature.

Another factor leading to more state control is the increasing demand for more money from state sources. When current state funding programs are found to be unconstitutional, states are ordinarily required to provide additional revenues to equalize educational opportunities throughout the state. While money and control do not stand in a one-to-one relationship, it is difficult to envision added state funding without some increase in state control.

Still another condition leading to more state control rests in the program of the Reagan administration to shift some educational decisions from the federal to the state level. While that attempt met with uneven success, it further enhanced the role of the state. With increased presence of the state in education, we suggest that in many states structural arrangements for the governance of education need examination.

But the enhancement of the state role in education has a somber side. In terms of money, many states will find it most difficult to meet the additional responsibilities thrust upon them. The Education Commission of the States, after examination of funding prospects of the states through the year 2000, came to a conclusion that "the fiscal condition of the states is, on the whole, bad."[33] A recent study of problems confronting state legislatures revealed that funding was the number one issue. Indeed, funding elementary, secondary, and higher education was named the "top education issue in all but five legislatures in 1986 and is expected to repeat as a priority in all but six states in 1987."[34] Thus, our second prediction is that resources for education in many states will be limited and their procurement will require hard choices, well-supported requests, and capable management on the part of state officials.

In spite of this bleak outlook, a third prediction for the future is that state education agencies will not be able to escape their regulatory function. The demands for more regulation are probably on the increase. For instance, many state legislatures have mandated competency standards for promotion or for high school graduation and require that the state education agency implement such standards. As to service, most state education agencies will continue to provide technical assistance to the schools and school districts of the state. State agencies may become selective in the nature of these services and in the strategies employed, but the service function will continue.

As the state is called upon to exercise a greater role in regulation, service, and leadership, it will be very difficult to meet those demands without a more extensive knowledge base, which requires more planning, more research, and more evaluation. Thus planning, research, and evaluation as a state agency function will grow in importance. States will be required to provide more leadership. Some traditional service functions will probably have to be reduced in order that more attention can be given to planning, research, and evaluation.

To meet the challenges facing states, state education agencies could justify the use of more personnel, but the money for increased staff seems unlikely. So our fourth projection is the more careful selection of personnel and a more rigorous allocation of their time.

With more prudent regulation, more extensive planning and evaluation, and more discerning leadership in state agencies, many chief state school officers, members of state boards of education, and even legislators and governors will see the need for competent personnel. Moreover, the chief clients of the state agency, the schools and school districts of the state, will demand competence. While the state agency was once relevant to the rural districts and largely ignored by the urban districts, that day is passing. Districts with competent leadership will be able to expect the same from the state education agency.

NOTES

[1]Lee M. Thurston and William H. Roe, *State School Administration* (New York: Harper & Row, 1947), ch. 2.

[2]Michael B. Katz, *Class, Bureaucracy, and Schools!* (New York: Praeger, 1975), xxi.

[3]W. W. Keisecker, *State Boards of Education and Chief State School Officers,* Office of Education Bulletin 1950, no. 12 (Washington, DC: U.S. Government Printing Office, 1950).

[4]Council of Chief State School Officers, *Educational Governance in the States* (Washington, DC: U.S. Department of Education, 1983).

[5]Ibid.

[6]*Statistical Abstract of the United States* (Washington, DC: U.S. Government Printing Office, 1987) 115, 416.

[7]See Arthur E. Wise, "Legal Challenges to Public School Finance," *School Review* 82 (November 1973): 1–27.

[8]Allan Odden et al., *School Finance Reform in the United States: 1976–1977* (Denver, CO: Education Finance Center, Education Commission of the States, December 1976), 4.

[9]Peggy M. Siegel, "Rethinking State Educational Governance," Report to National Conference of State Legislatures, February 1987, 1.

[10]J. Alan Aufderheide in Roald F. Campbell and Tim L. Mazzoni, Jr., *State Policy Making for the Public Schools* (Berkeley: McCutchan, 1976), ch. 5.

[11]American Association of Colleges for Teacher Education, *Teacher Education in the States: 50-State Survey of Legislative and Administrative Actions* (Washington, DC: AACTE, June 1987) vii–x.

[12]Dennis P. Doyle and Terry W. Hartle, *Excellence in Education: The States Take Charge* (Washington, DC: American Enterprise Institute, 1985).

[13]National Governors Association, *Results in Education* (Washington, DC: NGA, 1987).

[14]William L. Boyd, "Interest Groups and the Changing Educational Environment of State Policy-making: Developments in Pennsylvania," Paper presented at American Educational Research Association, 23 April 1987.

[15]Alan Rosenthal and Susan Fuhrman, *Legislative Education Leadership in the States* (Washington, DC: Institute for Educational Leadership, 1981), 1.

[16]See Roald F. Campbell and Tim L. Mazzoni, Jr., *State Policy Making for the Public Schools* (Berkeley: McCutchan, 1976), ch. 10.

[17]*Buck* v. *McLean,* 115 So. (2d) 764 (FL 1959).

[18]Luvern L. Cunningham et al., *Improving Education in Florida: A Reassessment* (Tallahassee: Select Joint Committee on Public Schools of the Florida Legislature, February 1978).

[19]J. Alan Aufderheide, "The Place of Educational Interest Groups in State Educational Policy-Making Systems" (Ph.D. diss., Ohio State University, 1973).

[20]Council of Chief State School Officers, *Educational Governance in the States,* 23–25.

[21]Campbell and Mazzoni, *State Policy Making for the Public Schools,* ch. 2.

[22]Gerald E. Sroufe, "Selection Procedures and Self-role Expectations of State School Board Members: An Exploratory Description and Analysis" (Ph.D. diss., University of Chicago, 1970).

[23]Council of Chief State School Officers, *Educational Governance in the States.*

[24]*Schinck* v. *Board of Education of Westwood Consolidated School District,* 159 A. (2d) 396 (N.J. 1960).

[25]Campbell and Mazzoni, *State Policy Making for the Public Schools,* ch. 10.

[26]Campbell and Mazzoni, *State Policy Making for the Public Schools,* 433.

[27]Martin Haberman and T. M. Stinnet, *Teacher Education and the New Profession of Teaching* (Berkeley: McCutchan, 1973), 18.

[28]Lawrence M. Rudner, *What's Happening in Teacher Testing: An Analysis of State Teacher Testing Practices* (Washington, DC: Office of Educational Research and Improvement, U.S. Government Printing Office, 1987), 3.

[29]Donna M. Gollnick and Richard C. Kunkel, "The Reform of National Accreditation," *Phi Delta Kappan* 68 (December 1986): 310–314.

[30]*Pierce* v. *Society of Sisters,* 268 U.S. 510 (1925).

[31]Martha M. McCarthy, *The Delicate Balance: Church, State, and the Schools* (Bloomington, IN: Phi Delta Kappan Educational Foundation, 1983), 160.

[32]Henry M. Brickell and Roald F. Campbell, *An Evaluation of the Delaware Department of Public Instruction* (Denver, CO: Education Commission of the States, 1978).

[33]Allan Odden et al., *School Finance Reform in the States: 1983* (Denver, CO: Education Commission of the States, 1983), 5.

[34]Peggy M. Siegel, "State Education Reforms and Emerging Issues," Report to National Conference of State Legislatures, February, 1987.

5
The Local School District

The local school district is the basic administrative unit in school organization. In this chapter we will examine local school government through the perspective of history; we will review the current status of school districts and school district reorganization; we will contemplate the future of local school districts in keeping with contemporary as well as what appear to be emerging developments in local government in the United States; and we will suggest, at least by implication, ways district structure may affect the control of American schools.

THE SCHOOL DISTRICT IN LOCAL GOVERNMENT

Local school government in the United States is not a historical accident. Our founders' deep belief in freedom, as well as the exigencies of a rigorous environment, led quite naturally to a reliance on local government. As Dewey said, describing the newcomers to this continent, "The imagination of the founders did not travel beyond what could be accomplished and understood in a congeries of self-governing communities."[1] Local government today is undoubtedly a grotesque representation of the image of government held by the framers of our federal and state constitutions. In the past two centuries we have witnessed a steady movement away from the sharp separation of powers among the three levels of government. The oft-cited changes in our way of life, including rising expectations for governmental services, have contributed to a new national federalism. Some activities of government, once essentially local, are now blended with strong state and federal interest; some revenue sources, once the property of only one level, are now shared.

Because of the interdependence of the levels of government as well as the complex mixing of local units, it is difficult to understand local units without comprehending the intricacies of intergovernmental affairs. The function of local governments in the total mosaic of governments is expressed aptly in the quotation that follows:

> A study of intergovernmental relations without adequate attention to local government would be as invalid as a physical examination by a doctor who examined only the exterior of the body and the limbs and assumed that the tissues and the muscles had no bearing on the body as a whole. Local governments are to total government what basic tissues are to the human body. Without them, government would have no vitality. The counties, cities, towns, villages, and boroughs serve as training schools for the leaders of government, and in the affairs of local government are tried those who aspire to State and National office. More important still is the use of local government to soften the impact of arbitrary State and National laws and regulations and to modify them to fit a population quite diverse in its cultural, economic, geographic, and political elements.[2]

The Advisory Commission on Intergovernmental Relationships, thirty-three years later, maintains a similar posture on local government:

> For decades, local government analysts have searched for a seemingly ideal pattern of local organization—consolidated metropolitan government, two-tier systems, or any arrangement that would reduce the governmental complexity ordinarily found in metropolitan areas. This report suggests that there is no ideal pattern suitable for all local communities and regions. Rather, local citizens and officials need to be empowered to create optimal patterns of order for themselves. Perfection will continue to be elusive. Different communities will make different trade-offs, and every community can learn from these natural experiments.[3]

The commission, for the most part, leaves out school districts in its local and intergovernmental analyses. This is somewhat ironic since school districts are the most numerous of local units (more than 15,000) and are the recipients of large amounts of tax resources. Nevertheless, school districts are very much a part of local government and thus are affected markedly by other layers and units of government, including the courts. As a government unit unto itself, however, the school district does have some distinguishing characteristics.

WHAT A SCHOOL DISTRICT IS

A school district is the basic governmental unit through which the exercise of local control of schools is effected. It is a unit of government, possessing quasi-corporate powers, created and empowered by state law to administer a public school or a public school system. A school district is controlled by a governing board; it has taxing power, the right to make contracts, and the right to sue and be sued. It may or may not employ a superintendent; thousands of common school districts, the one-room rural schools, do not have superintendents.

Local districts are at once the most common and the most diverse of all local jurisdictions. They range from districts comprising great cities such as New York, Los Angeles, Chicago, and Detroit to nonoperating districts that number in the hundreds and include a conglomeration of sizes, classes, and types in between. Their diversity illustrates the tenaciousness with which Americans hold to these remnants of localism and grassroots expression of the public will.

Education is a legally constituted responsibility of each state and is subject to the direction and sometimes the vagaries of state government. Local school districts are the instruments through which education is overseen and managed; they are extensions of state governments. Any state, within its unique constitutional and statutory framework, can destroy, modify, or proliferate these units. It is remarkable, however, how unwilling legislatures have been to change school district structure. Modifications that are made are most often the result of long, arduous, and carefully organized efforts of special interest groups working for school district reor-ganization.

School districts, along with townships, municipalities, fire districts, sanitary districts, park districts, and a number of other local governments, are considered by most Americans to be essential units in the effective administration of public services. Through school districts, local decisions on the management and operation of the schools are reached. Likewise, through these districts the policy of the state is implemented. The local district is expected to be a servant of the public interest, and in this case the public interest is as broad as the state itself.

The municipal character of the school district's responsibility is discussed in detail later in this chapter. The school district has many characteristics of the munic-ipality and at times is expected to observe laws that pertain to municipal government. The autonomy enjoyed by school districts differs among the states and frequently among classes of districts within states. The statutes provide the framework and the specifications to govern the formal relationships among local units of government. But independent of the formal relationships there exists a strong set of informal liaisons among units of local government irrespective of the special purposes for which they were created and designed.[4]

Important connections exist between local districts and the federal government. In the 1960s and 1970s local school districts were often involved directly or indirectly with federal agencies. Affirmative action directives, mainstreaming requirements for the handicapped, mandatory citizen involvement, and guidelines involving acquisition and expenditure of federal monies are illustrations. The economic policies and decentralization philosophy of the Reagan administration altered past practice in intergovernmental relationships. As a result, more of the responsibility for education and attendance control shifted to the states and local districts. Ironically, this is where responsibility and control rest constitutionally. Since the new federalism affected all local governments similarly, new competition for local and state revenue sources altered relationships between and among local units of government.[5]

In the public mind, school districts have been set apart from other govern-mental bodies. They have enjoyed this distinction primarily out of public reluctance to associate anything as fundamental as education with the supposed muck and mire of practical politics. Corruption, graft, and cynicism are assumed to be trademarks of politics at all levels, and while they are tolerated in some arenas of public concern, they are much less acceptable when attached to the shaping and training of the immature minds of the public's progeny. For this reason school districts in the majority of cases enjoy considerable autonomy in the management and control of their fiscal affairs and in retaining nonpartisanship in the selection of citizens to serve on local school boards. This separation has been perpetuated and reinforced by professional educators.

Peterson believes that local governments (including school districts) have limited ability as individual units to achieve equity in the distribution of benefits and services.[6] Even with the aid of federal and state policy interventions, achieving genuine and far-reaching equity is doubtful. National politics, Peterson observes, has produced a range of welfare-state policies, including low-income housing, compensatory education, food stamps, and unemployment compensation. As appealing as these concepts and their accompanying programs are in theory, they fail in practice to assure fairness and non-discrimination in the availability of public services such as education. Given the disparities in the quality of educational programs that exist between and among school districts, the question of what can be done to achieve equity becomes singularly important.

The Advisory Commission on Intergovernmental Relations has identified metropolitan area revenue sharing as one way to mitigate local fiscal disparities. The responsibility of achieving equity need not be left exclusively to state and national governments. Creative ways to reduce the fiscal inequality between have and have-not school districts may rest with metropolitan area revenue-sharing authorities, such as the one created for Minneapolis–St. Paul, Minnesota. A 1971 Minnesota statute provided that municipalities in the Minneapolis–St. Paul metropolitan area would share 40 percent of the area's future growth in commercial-industrial property assessments. This form of revenue sharing addresses the generic tension between equity on the one hand and control on the other.

Admittedly some of the control of public schools that once resided with local district officials has been shifted to other levels of government or is being shared to some extent with agencies and interests outside of government. Some years ago Campbell suggested that local control was more folklore than fact:

> It is quite clear that the public schools of this country have always operated within a framework established by the various states and that federal influences of some kind have always been prevalent. In recent decades, state controls over schools have been strengthened and federal activities in education, widely dispersed among many agencies, have multiplied. Federal influence has been piecemeal, haphazard, perhaps even surreptitious and often clothed in pious affirmation of state and local control. But inevitably the national stake in education and the growing social and economic interdependence of the nation have required congressional action and United States Supreme Court interpretation on educational questions. The time seems ripe for a realistic view of circumstances as they are and the forging of an honest local-state-federal partnership in education.[7]

Two particularly interesting examples of intrusion on local control occurred in 1988, one involving the state and the other a major university with the approval of the state. New Jersey state education officials "took over" the Jersey City school system following a fifteen-month investigation. The investigators cited financial irregularities, political patronage, cronyism, union pressure on personnel decisions, and school climate not conducive to learning. These and other problems led to the take-over decision, the first under new legislation outlining policies and procedures that allow the New Jersey Department of Education to exercise the state's plenary power over education.[8] In Massachusetts, a local school committee in a 5–1 decision invited Boston University to co-manage the Chelsea Public Schools. The president of Boston University in 1985 had offered to manage the Boston Public Schools, but the offer was rejected by the Boston School Committee. Chelsea saw merit in the offer, leading to its invitation. State authorities in Massachusetts had to provide enabling legislation since local and state control was being abridged.[9]

Despite interference in local control by outside forces, the citizens for the most part appear to value the local district and the opportunity to participate in educational decisions that have significance for the welfare of the people of their community. Some have attributed this to the reluctance of citizen-taxpayers to relinquish one of the few remaining opportunities to affect directly the expenditures of public funds and thus control the tax rate. No doubt this is true; many citizens are rightly concerned about mounting educational costs. On the other hand, many citizens value local control because it permits some local discretion, permits the local district to be responsive to local needs, allows local districts to exceed minimum standards established by the state; and allows large numbers of citizens to participate in the consideration of the objectives and directions of local schools.

Public sentiments regarding local control ebb and flow. In the 1950s there was substantial resistance to federal aid on the grounds of encroachment. A surge of interest in "community control" took place within large urban districts in the early 1960s. Deeply embedded in this movement was the realization that, for whatever reason, thousands of inner-city residents were not having an adequate say in how their schools were performing. Statewide ground swells of support for local control occurred in several states in the late 1970s. Revisions in the Florida Constitution reflected a strong "home rule" theme. California passed the much-publicized Jarvis-Gant Amendment to the California Constitution in June of 1978, which substantially reduced the property tax and was in large measure a populist revolt against big and centralized state government. In 1981, voters in Massachusetts, through initiative, passed Proposition 2 1/2, which limited total local property tax levies to 2.5 percent of full and fair cash value of a municipality's taxable property. This statewide initiative had a severe impact upon local school districts, many of which suffered drastic budget cuts. Furthermore, Proposition 2 1/2 introduced intense strain among local governments. The Massachusetts example illustrates how one form of grassroots control, the initiative, can serve to constrain local governments. Considerable control was exercised over school districts, themselves instruments designed to reflect the preferences of local citizens.[10]

Origin and Development of School Districts

The school district, as a unit of school government, was created in Massachusetts, but it existed for nearly a century and a half before it was legally recognized. Dexter explains how the school district began:

> As each little settlement extended its boundaries, it became convenient for families so far removed from the centre of population as to make it difficult for them to send their children to the town school, to form a separate nucleus of educational interests and establish a separate school. The region contributing to the separate school formed the school district. In Massachusetts it arose without legal recognition, for the General Court Act of 1647 established the schools upon a town basis; but as the district plan worked well under colonial conditions, it was fully legalized by the act of 1789, and continued to be the dominant school power within the state until well into the nineteenth century, and was not legally abolished until 1882.[11]

The celebrated Act of Massachusetts General Court in 1647 required towns to establish schools. This legislation was important not only because it provided for the formal education of colonial children but because it enunciated the principle of state authority in the control of schools.[12] This principle was adopted in all of New England and ultimately spread throughout the United States. In Massachusetts, the town was the local unit of government responsible for schools. This arrangement was satisfactory for those who lived in the town itself or near enough to walk to school each day. But it failed to meet the demands of the rural residents, and it was out of their needs that the districts emerged. The districts were actually subdivisions of the towns; the town in New England contained the "town," or population center, as well as a considerable farming area on the periphery. These areas were carved into smaller units, and provisions were made to provide schooling in each of the new "districts." Various schemes were devised to carry on instruction in the districts; the "moving school" and the "divided school" were common in New England.[13] The control of the schools remained with the towns under these arrangements; likewise, the responsibility for supporting the schools rested with the towns. It was not until the end of the eighteenth century that the districts were granted power to conduct and control their own schools. Horace Mann described the Massachusetts Act of 1789, which granted legal rights to school districts, as the most unfortunate legislation on common schools enacted in Massachusetts. The act provided for the appointment of school committees within the districts and was followed by legislation in 1801 granting the local districts the power to raise money through taxation for the support of district schools. Until then, this privilege had resided only with the towns.

Horace Mann's concern was founded not on opposition to the principle of local control per se but was based on the demonstrated inability as well as unwillingness of these very small units to provide adequate schools. Dexter writes about the situation in Massachusetts:

> The really disastrous legislation came, however, in 1801, granting the district the power to raise moneys by taxation, a right which had heretofore been vested in the larger social unit, the town. In actual practice, the district proved too small to be entrusted

with final legislation in money matters, in many cases the sentiment among the limited number of voters within a single district being the opposite of generous toward the schools or the district too poor to do much; and although the acts of 1789 and 1801, and similar laws passed in the neighboring states a little later, gave to New England the "little red schoolhouse" in great numbers, they were frequently not very red for want of paint, nor was the teaching within their walls of a very high order. Yet it cannot be denied that much good came from them.[14]

Either because the district system worked reasonably well in New England or because the conditions that spawned the system were present in other places, it was adopted and adapted in other parts of the United States. As the country developed and populations migrated westward, the district system seemed to move west too. Except in the South, the New England pattern ultimately spread across the land, partially because the nation, until the twentieth century, was a rural nation dependent upon agriculture economically. Even though the responsibility for and control of schooling was with the states, the creation of subdivisions within the states was necessary for them to fulfill their responsibilities for education. The Midwest, Far West, and Northwest were marked by the early proliferation of local districts, a condition many states have modified through school district reorganization and consolidation legislation.

In the South the basic unit of school government became the county. The principal reason for the difference between the New England affinity for a town and district system and the South's proclivity for a county system stems from a fairly fundamental difference in church-state relationships in the colonies of New England and the colonies of the South. The Church of England, predominant in the South, assumed authority over education in the southern colonies; this pattern was transferred to those colonies directly from England, where the authority and control of public and private schools had been placed in the hands of the bishops by the Canons of the Church of England in 1603.[15] As a consequence, church affairs and school affairs in southern colonies were closely related. The parish and its officials and the county and its officials became the administrative arms of the Church of England as well as of the colonial government. Teaching was often the responsibility of the clergy, and, as in England, importance was placed on educating or training orphans, indigents, and other unfortunates. The responsibility for schooling was centralized, and this feature of school organization has persisted through the years. The influence of the church was marked in the South; although the church and the state were separated by the ratification of the federal Constitution, the centralization that prevailed in the colonial period still characterizes the South today. The county unit has persisted and been adopted in other parts of the country, notably Utah and Nevada.

Legal Basis of School Districts

School districts are arms of state government created to implement the mandates of the state and to ensure the rights and privileges of a free education to the people. School districts are the instruments through which the state can fulfill its constitutional obligations; they are the legally established and authorized subdivisions of government constructed for the purpose of maintaining a system of public schools. As noted in Chapter 4 legislatures of the states, within constitutional limitations, have plenary power over school district organization; they can create, modify, consolidate, reorganize, or destroy school districts; they can make these subdivisions autonomous, independent fiscal units, or they can make them dependent units, subject to fiscal control by other subdivisions of government.

Legislatures can classify districts, even charter districts under special circumstances, and can differentiate duties, obligations, or amount of discretion among the classes of districts they create. If state legislative bodies are so disposed, they may actually require counties, cities, towns, or townships to assume the responsibility locally for providing schools; or the legislatures may simply constitute the geographical area of some subdivision as a school district and vest it with independence. Legislatures may also establish separate school districts covering the same geographical area but for different purposes. For example, in California and Illinois separate elementary and secondary districts frequently serve the same area.

The supremacy of the legislature has been well established.[16] Unless the constitutions of the various states stipulate to the contrary, the legislatures can establish or alter school districts without the consent of the people. As will be noted later, the legislatures have been reluctant to change school district arrangements in the face of widespread public opposition, but they do possess the power to do so. In the same way, they possess the power to delegate authority to establish school districts; this delegation could be to a special committee or to another governmental subdivision or to an official. The specific statutes that have created school districts are numerous. The laws providing for one class of school district, the community unit district in Illinois for example, at one time covered eighteen pages in the code book of that state.[17]

School Districts and Municipalities

Because of the peculiar nature of the public service they render, school districts are commonly called quasi-corporations, and in some cases, the courts have determined them to be municipal corporations. The corporate status of school districts is not uniform among the various states, although there are similarities. The many distinctions between consideration of a school district as a quasi-corporation and a municipal corporation are important, and each school administrator needs to know the interpretation of the courts of his or her state.

Considerable confusion has arisen because school districts and other governmental units often comprise the same geographical area but are autonomous subdivisions. Cities, townships, towns, and counties have been determined by legislatures to be fit and convenient geographical entities within which school systems can be organized, and thus school districts have been created to serve these same subdivisions. Cities and incorporated towns are municipal corporations established for the purpose of local self-government, and the statutes of the state pertaining to municipal corporations apply to these subdivisions. The school districts serving the same areas are quasi-corporations, created for administrative purposes to enable the state to fulfill its constitutional responsibility for education. As a quasi-corporation, the school district, and its governing board, is limited to the exercise of powers specifically granted in the law plus such discretionary powers designated by the law or determined necessary to meet reasonably the state's obligation to provide an educational system.

Only a few municipal corporations have responsibilities for providing or managing schools. Only those municipal corporations that have been delegated responsibilities for education by state legislatures have these obligations. In other words, there is nothing inherent in the municipal corporation that requires this subdivision to provide and manage a system of public schools. At the same time there is no prohibition against legislatures fixing responsibility for schools upon municipal corporations.

Some school districts and municipalities provide services to one another, such as purchasing, warehousing, libraries, recreation facilities, personnel administration, levying and collecting taxes. On occasion conflicts and misunderstandings have occurred. For example, the San Francisco Unified School District was established in 1917. Prior to 1917 the administration of education was the responsibility of the city of San Francisco. When the new district was established, however, the city retained responsibilities such as purchasing, warehousing, legal services, and health services. Over the years, tensions related to these services grew and in the 1970s led to the complete or partial transfer of many of those responsibilities to the San Francisco Unified School District. In addition, there was controversy over the ownership of school sites since clear title to school sites had not been transferred in 1917. Eventually such property titles will be clarified by the courts since the value of land is appreciating and is sought for other private and public purposes.[18]

The courts in the several states have been called upon to clarify the corporate nature of local school districts. Disputes have arisen involving the police power of municipalities when exercised against school boards, the local financing of schools, the control of school buildings, the interpretation of home rule charters, and the relationships between school and municipal officials. The numerous cases involving the determination of the municipalities' rights, privileges, and obligations and the school districts' rights, privileges, and obligations have failed to provide clarification because the court decisions lack consistency and uniformity. For example, controversies have been generated by attempts of municipalities to apply their building codes to school structures over the objections of school district officials. In some instances, the courts have ruled that municipalities have the right and indeed the obligation to apply building codes to school facilities. In other cases, the courts have decided that school districts, as extensions of the state, are immune from municipal codes and regulations, unless the statutes have stipulated that local school districts are to abide by municipal building standards. When the laws are explicit and the relationships between these subdivisions are stated, the courts have only to adjudicate in terms of the statutes. In the absence of clear positions, the courts are forced to decide on other bases, such as precedent or the supremacy of the state in educational matters. It is in this area of budget approval and control that an important distinction between two types of school districts must be made.

Fiscal Independence

The independent or dependent nature of school districts continues to be subject to extensive debate. On the one hand, there are the professional educators, supported by a substantial number of lay leaders, who believe strongly that school districts should be independent or autonomous; that is, they should maintain control over their budgets, they should have taxing authority, and they should have board members selected by the citizens of the districts they serve.

On the other hand, there are some political scientists, and citizens sympathetic to their general position, who believe that there is no justification for autonomous school districts. They argue that provisions for schools should be managed in the same way and within the same governmental structure as other public services; they hold that there should be some unity in local government and that much of the proliferation of local subdivisions is accounted for in local school districts; they maintain that separation of school fiscal policy from other local governmental fiscal policy leads to waste and inefficiency. They believe further that the independence of local school districts, coupled with the increasing professionalizing of school administration, has given unwarranted advantage to local school districts in the competition for local fiscal resources.

Proponents of independence contend that school affairs should not become political affairs; that the special nature of schooling sets it apart from other governmental services; that the fundamental importance of schools justifies a special structure that places school affairs close to the citizenry; that the run-of-the-mill municipal official is not prepared to make important policy decisions for schools, and that the fixing of responsibility may be elusive under dependent arrangements.

It is most interesting to note that, while most school professionals support independence and rely heavily on the unwholesome manifestations of some political activities as the basis of their argument, these same professionals depend on political activity in the administration of schools. Some years ago Bailey made the point that the success of school people in eight northeastern states in acquiring state aid had been directly related to the sophistication of their understanding of the political instruments available to them.[19] These same political skills are necessary at the district level.

One of the most fundamental points upon which decisions about independence or dependence should turn is whether or not one structure permits demonstrably better schools than the other. And it is on this point that we are woefully short of evidence. If one is in fact better than the other, it is not obvious on the basis of superficial analyses. James and his colleagues at Stanford University found that fiscally independent or dependent districts did not differ greatly in their patterns of expenditure.[20]

Another strong argument for independence is noted by the Advisory Commission on Intergovernmental Relations. School districts by virtue of their independence and single-purpose function are removed from annexations and other territorial or jurisdictional changes experienced by general governments. A move to a metropolitan form of government would not affect independent school districts unless special provisions were made to include them in a consolidation.[21]

The Stanford group challenged the traditional definitions of dependence and independence and proposed some useful comparative analyses of local school governments. They contend that there are actually very few, if any, independent local school governments. There are instead, these educators believe, various types of dependent school districts, more reasonably conceived of as falling along a continuum of more dependence to less dependence.

Ninety percent of all school districts in the United States are fiscally independent, as defined by the Bureau of the Census. Four states—Hawaii, Maryland, North Carolina, and Virginia—have only dependent units. Hawaii, in fact, has one school district that covers the entire state; the schools of Hawaii are administered through a department of state government. In twenty-three states there are only independent districts, and the remainder of the states have both types.

Reorganization of Districts

Legislators have generally been reluctant to act arbitrarily in altering existing units or establishing new districts. The existence of hundreds of small, inefficient districts is testimony to the fact that legislators have been slow, in many states at least, to reorganize their districts. It is significant, however, that the number of school districts in the United States was reduced by nearly 79,000 in the thirty-five year period of 1947–1981 (see Table 5.1). Since 1967 the reduction has slowed tremendously, to the point where some stabilization seems to have occurred.

Some legislatures have taken action. The decrease in these numbers is all the more important when examined in the light of the severe political wrestling that normally surrounds most changes in the statutes governing district organization. It would be erroneous to imply that gross reductions in numbers automatically result in better district organization. Obviously this is not true; many consolidations of small, poor, inefficient districts have resulted in larger, poor, inefficient districts. And as those who have worked hard for reorganization of districts know, the second try for reorganization is much more difficult than the first.

Legislation to encourage or realize school district reorganization is usually classed as permissive, semipermissive, or mandatory. Permissive legislation simply permits districts to merge, to consolidate, or to reorganize. There are no prescriptions, no real teeth in the laws of this kind; districts are given the opportunity to rearrange themselves and the ground rules to guide these changes. In many states, laws permitting changes have been on the books for years; as one would suspect, relatively few significant reorganizations have grown out of permissive legislation. Too many barriers and too few incentives were present; large-scale satisfaction with the status quo, fear of the loss of local control, transportation problems, and general conservatism have worked against purely voluntary reorganization.

TABLE 5.1
Numbers of Local School Districts in the U.S., 1947–48 through 1980–81

Year*	Number of Districts**
1947–48	94,926
1951–52	71,094
1955–56	54,859
1959–60	40,520
1963–64	31,705
1967–68	19,977
1971–72	16,838
1975–76	16,376
1979–80	15,929
1980–81	15,912

Source: Data are drawn from official publications of the National Center for Educational Statistics, U.S. Office of Education.
*These are the most recent data available.
**Totals include both operating and nonoperating districts with the exception of 1967–68 and 1971–72, which include only operating districts.

Some states, in efforts to accelerate district reorganization, passed laws that were semipermissive. Local districts were to reorganize within limits incorporated in the law, and reorganization acceptable to the state had to be proposed within a specified number of years. The initiative for reorganizing was taken from the local districts; the states became the initiators but the residents of local districts were free to express their voice in the reorganizations. Many of these laws were not effective because they included many checkpoints where proposed reorganization could be defeated. Failures of early semipermissive legislation led to strengthening of reorganization statutes and to the incorporation of financial incentives for reorganization. Financial incentives for creating more efficient districts stimulated some reorganization, but even laws of this type did not generate rapid changes.

Mandatory reorganization laws characterized post-World War II reorganization legislation. These acts combined the formation of local committees, usually at the county level; specific time schedules for the submission of reorganization proposals to state agencies for review, recommendations, and appraisal, and for the vote of citizens; financial incentives for reorganization; and financial penalties to be exacted against small, inefficient units that failed to reorganize. Much of the legislation enacted since World War II has been patterned after the recommendations of the National Commission on School District Reorganization.[22] Laws that forced reorganization usually had some safeguards built into them to avoid poor or ill-advised rearrangements. The opportunity for local participation was provided and sufficient checks were incorporated to ensure the approval of the citizenry. There was, however, one important proviso: if the machinery for some reason broke down, if citizens failed to agree or if they submitted what were determined to be weak proposals for reorganization, the state would step in and arbitrarily effect reorganization. Such action was considered drastic in most cases, but it could be done and was done. The reorganization in those instances was decided by a state agency authorized by the legislature to make such decisions.

School districts were markedly affected during the period of rapid post-World War II population growth, including the large-scale rural to urban migrations. School administrators and school board members were growth-conscious in that period and took great pains to project enrollment trends accurately. Now the demographic picture is less clear overall and there are important trend differences within and between regions of the United States as well as within and between metropolitan and nonmetropolitan areas. The implications of such changes are not clear nor are they likely to be the same in all parts of the United States. We can say, however, that these changes do exist and have meaning for those responsible for educational planning at all levels.

Desegregation may also be linked to school district reorganization. In Kentucky, where the Louisville and Jefferson County school districts were involved in a school desegregation lawsuit, the Louisville school board voted to dissolve the Louisville school district and merge with the county district, forming a single county district. A desegregation plan then involved children from the entire county, in fact most of the metropolitan area, because Jefferson County includes most of the Standard Metropolitan Area. In contrast, the courts forged a new school district in Delaware, the New Castle County district. It covered one-third of the state, had the former Wilmington district at its center, and inherited simultaneously the desegregation of schools and the reorganization of what formerly were eleven independent school districts. The New Castle County district was again reorganized in 1980 into four districts, each of which contains part of the city of Wilmington. District structures may be altered in other metropolitan areas where school desegregation litigation involving suburban districts and city districts is still in the federal courts. St. Louis and nearby suburban districts have been ordered to cooperate, short of district reorganization, in ways specified by the court to achieve desegregation.[23] The case of *Jenkins v. Missouri,* came to trial in 1983 to achieve a similar objective in Kansas City.

Despite the magnitude of the assignment, the question of reforming educational government has been placed directly before the people in several metropolitan areas.[24] A few changes were effected in the 1960s. Nashville-Davidson County, Tennessee, is one example of how city and county districts were consolidated through a voting process. Another federation was established in Detroit during the 1970s and early 1980s, involving eight subdistricts each with its own school board. Those districts and their boards were discontinued in 1982. (See Chapter 9.)

Recent history of school district reorganization in Illinois, 1983–84 through 1988–89, illustrates the status of efforts to continue reducing the number of school districts in one of the states with large numbers of districts. There are several ways the number of districts in Illinois can be changed: consolidation, annexation, conversion, detachment, deactivation, or in some combination. The reorganization by type of school district over this period is illustrated in Table 5.2. The number and forms of reorganization are summarized in Table 5.3.

The total number of districts was reduced by thirty-five through thirty-six school district reorganization actions. Reorganization activity was stimulated by the Illinois Commission on the Improvement of Elementary and Secondary Education, established in 1983. Its 1985 report, *Excellence in the Making,* included recommendations for school district reorganization that stimulated intense statewide discussions. Each of Illinois's fifty-nine regions (intermediate units) were directed to form reorganization study committees and to produce reorganization proposals. Many of the post-1985 district changes grew out of these proposals with more to come in the future.[25]

California, another state with a large number of school districts, has had no change in number between 1975 and 1985. There are 1,026 districts with enrollments ranging from six to 589,099. Its three classifications of districts, elementary (K–8), high school (9–12), and unified (K–12) have not changed since 1935.[26].

TABLE 5.2
School District Reorganization in Illinois 1983–84 through 1988–89, By Type of District*

	1983–84	1988–89	± Change
Elementary	435	422	− 13
Secondary	125	117	− 8
Unit	447	443	− 14
DOC**	1	1	0
Total	1008	973	− 35

* Excludes Special Education and other special districts
** Department of Corrections
Source: Illinois State Board of Education, 1988.

TABLE 5.3
Numbers and Forms of Illinois School District Reorganizations, 1983–84 through 1988–89

Form	Numbers by Year						
	1983–84	1984–85	1985–86	1986–87	1987–88	1988–89	Total
Consolidation	1	1	4	1	6	1	14
Annexation	1		1	3	4	8	17
Annexation/Conversion					1	1	2
Annexation/Detachment						1	1
Deactivation					2		2
Total	2	1	5	4	13	11	36

Source: Illinois State Board of Education, 1988.

Problems of district organization in rural areas are different from those in urban areas. In analyzing school district reorganization in terms of a rural-urban dichotomy, one is guilty to some degree of establishing an unrealistic, if not false, division. It may be more defensible to conceive of an urban to rural continuum along which one could place communities or areas according to criteria of urbanism or ruralism. Obviously the rapidly increasing areas of rural-urban fringe are difficult to classify as either urban or rural. We believe, however, that the extremely rural and the extremely urban are unlike enough to warrant independent discussion.

Reorganizing Districts in Rural Areas

The small districts, those that often have few pupils enrolled and inadequate financial resources, are usually in rural areas. They may be one-room rural school districts, offering elementary education only; they may be districts that attempt to provide secondary education only; or they may be unit districts offering both elementary and secondary school programs. Four states—California, Illinois, Nebraska, and Texas—accounted for more than 25 percent of the school districts in the nation in 1980–81.[27] Each of these states had more than 1,000 local school districts. Despite the elimination of thousands of districts in recent years, many reorganized districts fall short of meeting reasonable criteria of adequacy.

Among the barriers to reorganizing districts in rural areas have been the persistence of the idea of home rule; resistance to tax increase for any public service; the fact that many people simply do not realize that the quality of the educational program in their districts is inferior; and, as Kammeyer reported, the degree of heterogeneity reflected in rural populations.[28] Kammeyer studied 110 small Iowa communities that had reorganization involving secondary schools between 1956 and 1959. Ethnically homogeneous communities displayed less opposition to the loss of their high schools than did heterogeneous communities. It is extremely difficult to pinpoint reasons why citizens in any given area resist changes in local districts. Undoubtedly a range of factors influences decisions about reorganization, not the least of which are sentiment or strong feelings about the "old school" and the nature of the people themselves. In rural sections where population movement in and out of school districts, at least among community leaders, is not so pronounced, traditions are maintained, and the feelings of identification with a given institution are strong.

Substantial improvements in educational opportunity have been realized in many rural areas. Fine new schools have been constructed, school programs have been strengthened, and the level of preparation of professional personnel has been increased. But the job is far from complete. (See Chapter 6.)

Reorganizing Districts in Urban Areas

As impressive as the need for reorganizing rural districts is, the problems may be even more critical in urban areas. The urbanization process has introduced innumerable demands for public services that government is often inadequately prepared to provide. It is an immense undertaking in areas undergoing urbanization to meet needs for such things as police and fire protection, parks and recreation facilities, libraries, sanitation and water supply, roads, and schools.

Growth rates during the 1970s were lowest in the largest metropolitan areas. The New York metropolitan area, the largest of all, experienced a loss of more than 900,000 persons between 1970 and 1980. Of the six other metropolitan areas with a 1970 population of more than 3 million, Philadelphia, Detroit, and Boston had small losses, while Chicago had a small gain. Only the Los Angeles and San Francisco metropolitan areas grew significantly during the period (15.2 and 11.9 percent, respectively). Together these seven very large areas had a net growth of only 1.1 million (2.1 percent) in the 1970s, compared with 7.1 million (15.5 percent) for the same areas in the 1960s.[29] These changes reflect the "Sun Belt" growth patterns as well as the decline of the older cities of the East, South, and Midwest. The phenomenon of relatively uncontrolled growth on the peripheries of central cities is continuing, and in many places land will be used indiscriminately, overburdening the existing local governmental structures. Mushrooming subdivisions, irregular location of industry, businesses, and residences, destruction of natural drainage systems, speculation in land values—all characteristic of urbanization—will continue. *Urban sprawl* is the term attached to this kind of growth; in most cases there are no controls to guide land use on the urban fringes. In the few places where planning bodies exist, they have notable records of ineffectiveness in regulating the growth and development of areas over which they ostensibly have jurisdiction.

Existing districts on the outskirts of our central cities are studies in extremes.[30] The haves and the have-nots can be found side by side. The haves possess taxable wealth in the form of industrial property, business property, or residences owned by upper-class families with sufficiently high personal incomes to afford generous local levies for schools as well as other local services. The have-nots usually have little industrial or business valuation; the taxes for local purposes must be assessed against middle- or lower-income family residences owned by families that more often than not are struggling to meet payments on their houses, automobiles, home furnishings, and other obligations. The have districts, often serving mostly upper-middle- and upper-class citizens, normally have high expectations for their schools. The people who live in the have-not districts also have expectations for their schools but these may be of a different order. Whereas affluent suburbanites may prefer emphasis on aesthetic and intellectual goals for their schools, the blue-collar citizen may want applied arts such as home economics and vocational education stressed.[31] Between these extremes are districts of modest wealth, differential states of development, and mixed expectations for schools that reflect the heterogeneous character of the citizens who live there. The variety of circumstances defies adequate description. There are districts with exceptional concentrations of industrial wealth and few school-age children; the tax valuation behind each youngster of school age is sizable. At the same time, the residents of these districts may have relatively modest expectations for their schools. Close by may be districts with middle- and upper-middle-class families, most of whom are caught up in the upward mobility patterns characteristic of business and professional people, and who hold expectations for schools that are extraordinarily high with respect to the districts' abilities to finance schools.

The district structure in suburban areas is something to behold. The range of variables to be considered in suggesting improved district organization for urban America is almost incomprehensible. For example, these factors must be considered: aspirations of the public, including its many subpublics, for schools; present and potential capacity to finance local government including schools; tax assessment practices; present and potential provisions for planning; role of the state and federal governments in school support; present and potential relationships among local units of government; locations of transportation routes such as superhighways or commuter railroads; and the social stratification of urban residents.

One criterion for organizing school districts that has received acclaim has been the plan of arranging school district boundaries around "natural" communities. Districts in suburban areas and in the rural-urban fringes frequently overlap several municipalities or population centers. The "natural" community, if it exists at all, is at best hard to discover. The expectation that school district or attendance area boundaries can somehow accommodate communities or neighborhoods has been sharply debated. The issues in attendance area decisions are examined in Chapter 7.

The problem of defining criteria of school district adequacy is troublesome. To date, universally acceptable criteria or universally applicable criteria are not available. It is clear that adequate districts in sparsely populated sections of rural America will differ from what should be defined as adequate districts in urban areas. The American Association of School Administrators' Commission on School District Reorganization in 1958 listed nine points to be examined in determining the effectiveness of existing school districts. They are educational program, pupil population, financial resources, educational leadership provisions, instructional personnel, use of personnel, school plant provisions, framework for operation, and provisions for community participation.[32] The 1958 AASA commission statement is the most recent available despite the continuing importance of achieving sound, defensible local units.

THE CURRENT SCENE

The elimination of a vast number of school districts has contributed little to reducing the kinds, classifications, or types of districts. In fact, new classes have been created. The array of district types has caused confusion among those who wish to understand better the arrangements of districts in the states. Each state classifies its own districts. In Nebraska, for example, there are six classes that are differentiated in a number of ways, such as school census enumeration, scope of program to be offered, number of school board members, and amount of discretion permitted school officials. Other states have similar systems with some having but one legal class, as in Nevada.

Two other useful ways of categorizing districts were used by the AASA Commission on School District Reorganization.[33] One scheme was to describe districts in terms of the scope of school program they provide; the other method was to classify districts in terms of their geographical or territorial characteristics. There were five types within each of these two categories. When districts are regarded in terms of the scope of the program they provide, one of the most familiar is the elementary unit. In 1977 there were approximately 4,121 elementary districts variously classified as K–6, 1–6, K–8, or 1–8, K–9, 1–9.[34] Although most of these districts are of the one-room rural school variety, there are many elementary districts in metropolitan areas. Most of the elementary pupils in Cook County, Illinois, (outside the Chicago School District) are enrolled in elementary districts. Likewise, there are numerous elementary units in Arizona and California. The extremes in quality of education are exemplified in this category. On one end of the continuum are the thousands of rural districts with small enrollments, frequently with less well-trained teachers, narrow programs, and in some cases weak financing; at the other extremity are the historically prominent, widely known elementary districts such as Winnetka and Glencoe, Illinois. Reorganization in rural areas is reducing the number of elementary districts rapidly in many states, but considerable work remains to be done.

There were 608 school systems that offered only secondary education programs in 1977.[35] Such high school districts overlay elementary districts and receive their students from one or more of these "feeder" units. They are most numerous in California, Illinois, and Montana. Some of the high schools, many of which are located in the suburbs of our metropolitan areas, reflect the finest in secondary education to be found in the United States. At the other end of the scale there are high school districts that enroll fewer than 100 pupils, offering grossly inadequate programs, costing more than they are worth, and persisting despite efforts to reorganize them into more desirable districts. The distributions of enrollments among district types in Illinois are summarized in Table 5.4.

TABLE 5.4
Number of Illinois School Districts by Type and Enrollment, Fall of 1977 and 1986

Enrollment	Elementary Districts		Secondary Districts		Unit Districts		Total*	
	1977	1986	1977	1986	1977	1986	1977	1986
25,000 or Over	0	0	0	0	3	3	3	3
24,999 to 10,000	2	1	4	2	12	9	18	12
9,999 to 5,000	10	7	14	9	23	19	47	35
4,999 to 2,500	43	29	16	19	35	30	94	78
2,499 to 1,000	102	97	36	32	133	119	271	248
999 to 600	55	65	15	17	121	99	191	181
599 to 300	77	72	10	13	114	128	201	213
Less than 300	152	157	30	29	7	36	189	222
Total	441	428	125	121	448	443	1,014	992

*In 1977, five non-operating districts and one Department of Corrections District increased the total number of organized districts from 1,014 to 1,020. In 1986, one non-operating district, one Department of Corrections District, and four state-operated school districts increased the total number of organized districts from 992 to 998.
Source: Illinois State Board of Education, Annual Report, 1987, 25.

Most of America's pupils attend schools in unified districts—those that provide both elementary and secondary education and, in a few cases, junior college programs as well. In 1977 there were approximately 10,897 unified districts, more than two-thirds of all school districts.[36] The large number of pupils attending is explained by the fact that most of our large cities such as Chicago, New York, Detroit, Cleveland, and Baltimore are unified districts. In every state at least one unified district exists; all districts are unified in nine states; and in several others, almost all districts are unified.

The number of small, unified districts in some states is further illustration of the need for continuing district reorganization. The AASA Commission on School District Reorganization has contended: "The unified, or 12-grade, school district which is adequate in size has proven to be the best system of school government devised by the American people."[37] The success of this unit is premised upon sufficiently large enrollments as well as sufficiently generous local resources. Both of these are currently lacking in thousands of unified districts. In some places the landscape is dotted with numerous inefficient unified districts that could be reorganized into much more efficient units that could provide correspondingly more effective programs.

Districts offering junior college or community college programs, special education, and vocational-technical education have been established in many states. Each year the number of such districts increases. Justification for these special units is based on the inability of many other districts to provide post-high school, special, or vocational-technical programs. Often larger areas can reasonably support such offerings and serve an important public need. In rural areas, the special district is often the only way local government can provide such educational opportunities.

One of the little-known types, described in terms of scope of program, is the non-operating district. These are bona fide governmental subdivisions, and they provide no program at all. In 1981 there were 311 of these districts.[38] They have school boards that meet in accordance with the law, but they do not operate schools. In some of these districts in rural areas there may be no children of school age; or there may be so few pupils that it is more economical to contract with neighboring districts for the schooling of these youngsters; or it may be that most or all of the school-age pupils are enrolled in nonpublic schools. Some states have succeeded in doing away with these units, but where they continue to exist there is usually strong opposition to their elimination. The non-operating district serves to protect the tax interests of its residents. It is much less expensive to contract for the education of a very few pupils than to maintain a school for them. At the same time it is advantageous to keep property out of reorganized districts that provide comprehensive and more expensive educational programs. Any attempt to reorganize non-operating units or to consolidate them with neighboring districts is automatically viewed as a threat to the tax advantage non-operating districts enjoy. These units are anachronisms, and in due time, they will be eliminated.

Districts classed by geographical or area characteristics[39] are usually treated as follows: (1) community districts—those organized around "natural" communities and labeled as such in the law, (2) city districts—those coterminous with city boundaries, (3) county districts—the county is designated as the basic unit of school government, (4) towns or townships—hundreds of districts are coterminous with towns or townships; township high school districts are a good example, and (5) common school districts—there are thousands of these found in twenty-seven states, and they include the remaining one-room rural schools. A large portion of the elementary districts described in the scope of program classification are also common school districts, in many cases identified as "common schools" in the laws of the states.

The financial circumstances of districts affect the scope and quality of educational programs. Thus wealth, either its presence or absence, helps define the limits of schooling and is a controlling or determining factor in district-level decision making. Similarly, the characteristics of the population that resides within the districts are limiting factors. Bainbridge found a high percentage of the population over twenty-five years of age with less than five years of formal education, a low birth rate, and large numbers of middle-income families in Ohio school districts that were voting down millage rate increases or bond issues for new construction.[40] Population characteristics likewise determine the eligibility of districts for federal and state funds that often make it possible to meet the specific needs of large numbers of children. From another perspective, the characteristics of the student population are frequently reflected in special demands made of school officials, through, for example, multicultural, bilingual, vocational-technical, and academically talented education programs.

We've referred to the extremes present in existing district structures. Some districts serve no pupils at all (non-operating units) or just a very few, while others serve hundreds of thousands. For example, two districts in Nevada—Elko and Nye—both cover an area over 18,000 square miles, yet Elko County serves about 3,900 and Nye enrolls about 1,100. There are in other states extremely small districts covering only one, two, or three square miles; some enroll very few pupils, but others equally small may serve large concentrations of population and thus large numbers of students. San Francisco City Unified School District in California, for example, covers but forty-five square miles yet has an enrollment of more than 60,000 pupils.

Districts vary too in their capacities to finance schools and in the quality of their programs, as noted in the scope of educational needs provided for, in the training, experience, and performance of teachers and school administrators employed. These variations are notable within states and even within counties. Quality differences are so important that many people select their residences in terms of what local districts provide or fail to provide. These contrasts have existed for decades; it will take decades more to reduce these differences and to construct more adequate local units.

Our concern thus far has been essentially structural and not operational. Although some generalizations have been made about the relative performance of different types of districts, these were introduced to make the structural descriptions more meaningful. Obviously the decisions made by public officials who serve in these units of government are political decisions. It is apparent to the professionals in education and to thoughtful lay people that the attainment of educational objectives depends upon the successful operation of our political system. The future of local school districts appears to be caught up in the question of whether or not our political system, functioning through the mechanisms of local districts, can carry its burdens. Banfield has offered a basis for judging the "effectiveness" of a political system:

> In judging how a political system will work over time, increases and decreases in the burdens upon it are obviously extremely relevant. They are not all that must be considered, however. Changes in the "capability" of a system, that is, in its ability to manage conflict and to impose settlements, are equally relevant. The "effectiveness" of a political system is a ratio between burdens and capability. Even though the burdens upon it increase, the effectiveness of a system will also increase if there is a sufficient accompanying increase in its capability. Similarly, even though there is an increase in capability, the effectiveness of a system will decrease if there is more than commensurate increase in burdens.[41]

SUMMARY AND FUTURE PROSPECTS

What are the burdens that local districts must carry in the years ahead? We believe the most crucial burden will be informed decision making; it is at this point that local districts seem most vulnerable. As indicated in Chapter 9, we believe that improved processes and approaches to decision making can be adopted that respect the limits of local discretion and at the same time maximize the opportunities for the exercise of local control.[42] Dror argues that the quality of policy can be improved in the public sector if public officials will use policymaking knowledge and allocate resources to that end.[43]

Knowledge about policymaking can profitably be applied in our judgment to questions of local control or the allocation of responsibilities to levels of government. Lieberman charged thirty years ago that "local control of education has clearly outlived its usefulness on the American scene. Practically, it must give way to a system of educational controls in which local communities play ceremonial rather than policymaking roles: *Intellectually,* it is already a corpse."[44]

Furthermore, he argued that the mobility and interdependence of our society undermined the idea that local communities should have a free hand in educating their children; that national survival required policies and programs not subject to local vote; that local control in practice could not be reconciled with the ideals of a democratic society; and that local control was the major cause of "the dull parochialism and attenuated totalitarianism that characterizes public education in operation."[45] This was not an idle charge nor a passing, whimsical allegation; Lieberman believed that local control was passé.

This posture stands in sharp contrast to the plaintive cries for community control from ghettoes in most large cities. Parents and other neighborhood leaders genuinely desire a larger role in educational decision making. Many ghetto residents want in on the act, at home, in the neighborhood, not in state houses or in Washington. Implicit in Lieberman's reasoning was the assumption that another type of structure may be more efficient as well as more effective—and of course the alternative to local control was some kind of centralization: state, regional, or national. Following Banfield's notion of "capability," Lieberman's call for centralization rested upon the assumption that central control is able "to manage conflict and to impose settlements"—or to utilize maximum intelligence in decision making.

At the moment there is little evidence that our political system produces more rational or more beneficial decisions about education at the state or federal level than at the local level. Granted that the effects of a good state decision are pervasive, it is also true that the repercussions of a bad state decision are far-reaching. Decisions at all levels of government depend on the capacities, values, and interests of the decision makers involved. Therefore, it serves little purpose to debate the quality of decisions at different levels in the absence of policy output criteria.[46]

The problem appears to be one of searching out the responsive publics, the people and the groups in society, broadly conceived, who are most capable of charting the course for public schools and then creating the means for converting their expressions into public decisions. The converting process is a governmental process. Dewey has given almost poetic description to the problem:

> An inchoate public is capable of organization only when indirect consequences are perceived, and when it is possible to project agencies which order their occurrence. At present, many consequences are felt rather than perceived; they are suffered, but they cannot be said to be known, for they are not, by those who experience them, referred to their origins. It goes, then, without saying that agencies are not established which canalize the streams of social action and thereby regulate them. Hence the publics are amorphous and unarticulated.[47]

As indicated earlier, the ultimate choice of local versus nonlocal control may well rest upon whether substantive quality in decisions on local problems can be attained. It is doubtful that a public inarticulate at the local level will be more articulate at the state level. Transfer of core decisions to the state or national government means that the responsibility for policy in education may be shifted to professional educators and administrators—not by design necessarily, but by public default. Professionals keep schools going; they are always around; they know the problems, they are consulted immediately by official policymakers, the school board members; they cannot but affect policymaking. The canalization of the public will at higher levels of policy formulation may be as illusive as it is at the local level. Again Dewey is insightful when he suggests that the ramifications of the issues before the public are so comprehensive and delicate, the technical matters so specialized, the details so many and so elusive that "the public cannot for any length of time identify and hold itself." He continues:

> It is not that there is no public, no large body of persons having a common interest in the consequences of social transactions. There is too much public, a public too diffused and scattered and too intricate in composition.[48]

The structure of governance for schools cannot be considered in isolation. The future of the local unit of school organization seems to hinge upon what the body politic decides to do about local government affairs in general. The scope and complexity of problems facing local units of government are staggering, particularly in the urban setting. Those problems worsened to some extent as a consequence of President Reagan's new federalism. Reductions in federal support for human services programs, including education, linked with the allocation of increased responsibilities to state and local authorities for meeting "social" problems intensified competitiveness for local resources, especially the property tax. In the past, bargaining to receive federal resources for local services was essentially a vertical process. Under the new federalism, bargaining became a horizontal process between and among local units of government.[49]

One alternative to such intergovernmental competitiveness is some kind of consolidation of disparate authorities, some kind of powerful central control over cities, metropolitan areas, even regions, that would be able to effect a patterned, planned sequence of development. But such centralization seems to be almost impossible: the job is too big; the conflicting interests are too strategic and powerful; the fear of centralization resident in the citizenry is too pervasive; and the capacity of our political system to focus adequate intelligence upon the job of creating a "super" local government is too limited. The prospect of such centralization seems remote, at least in the near future.

A contrasting option is collaboration. Finding ways for institutions, public and private, to work together may be more easily achieved, even more effective, than attempts to reorganize school districts and other human services agencies. Metropolitan area tax sharing, cited earlier, is based on a willingness to distribute resources in the spirit of the common good.

The theory of governance prominent in federated proposals (see Chapter 6) calls for a structure that will accommodate the advantages of both bigness and smallness.[50] The design is expected to meet the general need for efficiency that large-scale enterprise provides; at the same time it allows for extended opportunities for political access. Theoretically, it opens up the political system; practically, it remains to be seen whether or not interested citizens would participate more actively in school affairs given such structural change.

The rural scene is quite another matter. Farmers are relatively self-sufficient with respect to provisions for water, sanitation, and other utilities. Their local governments provide roads, schools, modest police and fire protection, and some other special services. Villages and towns provide more services of course, but these needs have been met in most instances without undue hardship or even delay. The school districts in many places, as we have described them earlier, are archaic and need examination. But the dimensions and complexity of local government problems in rural areas do not approach those of the urban environment. It does not follow that these units of government are any less important or that they can be ignored. Wherever inadequacies in district structure exist they are reflected in inadequacies of educational program; the shortcomings in program manifest themselves immediately in less than satisfactory educational opportunity.

In the past concern for school district reorganization has been focused on reducing the number of districts in rural America. We maintain that, although further progress of this nature is warranted, the focus must be shifted to improving district organization in the urban areas as well as in the expanding rural-urban fringes around our metropolitan centers. The remaking of district structures should include evaluation of the place of intermediate units in the total milieu of educational government.

The 1970s and early 1980s were marked by paradox. Many school districts, accustomed to rapid and sustained growth since World War II, faced decline for the first time. Increasing enrollments, new facilities, and program extensions gave way to retrenchment, reductions in force, and program cutbacks. The pronounced nature of these changes coupled with school finance uncertainties and the impact of the courts on the schools placed new stresses on the governance and management of education. The future of local school districts appears to be caught up in the question of whether or not our political system, functioning through the mechanisms of local districts, states, and federal centers of responsibility can carry its burdens.

Thus we see four fundamental challenges confronting local school districts in the years ahead. The most basic is operational responsibility for the conduct of instruction. The state and federal centers of responsibility are structurally remote from the day-to-day activities of teaching and learning. Thus they essentially set directions and follow through by facilitating and supporting programs to meet stated objectives. Because local districts carry the principal responsibility for school effectiveness, the pressures for instructional accountability from parents, students, and the citizenry in general are likely to affect local district officials even more severely in the future than in the past. Consequently, the existing patterns of school districts may be examined in light of the public's assessment of their effectiveness.

A second challenge, therefore, is the specification of comprehensive criteria to use in the appraisal of school district effectiveness. Organizations of professional educators, school board groups, interested lay people, and researchers will need to address the criteria problem. It will be difficult to identify useful indications of effectiveness. This is not a new problem but we are hopeful that neither its complexity nor its political nature will deter concerted efforts to identify such indications of effectiveness. Educational government should never become so rigid that it fails to respond to the needs confronting society.

A third challenge is the integration of diverse community interests and resources into educational policies. It is likely that mediating public structures, such as the Twin Cities Metropolitan Council of Minneapolis and St. Paul, and planning organizations, such as the Citizens' League of Minneapolis and St. Paul, will have a growing impact upon local governments, including school districts. In fact there is evidence that new bonds are being developed between the public and private sectors as well as between citizens organizations and both sectors.[51] Cleveland notes that the reactive mode of modern government requires that most new ideas originate outside in "nongovernments." Nongovernments involve thinkers, nongovernmental experts, and advocates linked with government officials and legislators.[52] Such bridging mechanisms may increase the amount and improve the quality of information upon which many critical school district decisions will be based.[53]

A fourth challenge is for local district leaders to join in or take initiatives in the study of educational structure and governance for the future. The structural and governance forms of American public education have been relatively stable through periods of intense change. Anticipating the year 2000, it may be time to inspect the viability of our governmental arrangements generally but with a special focus on education. *New York Governance in the 21st Century—A Public-Private Partnership* may be a model to follow. It is a joint initiative of the State Academy for Public Administration and the Nelson A. Rockefeller Institute of Government. Four task forces have been commissioned to examine: (1) alternative structural organization, (2) financing the cost of government, (3) the public service of the future, and (4) preventive policies, based on the belief that broad collaboration involving the public, private, and voluntary sectors will be essential in the future.[54]

The locus of school control in the future must depend upon the structure of government that can most successfully translate the informed public will into effective public policy. Our concern is not with state or federal or local control per se; rather, we are interested in perfecting our public capacity to select the most appropriate level for focusing our collective intelligence on public educational problems.

NOTES

[1]John Dewey, *The Public and Its Problems* (Denver, CO: Alan Swallow, 1957), 111.

[2]"An Advisory Committee Report on Local Government," (Washington, DC: Commission on Intergovernmental Relations by the Advisory Committee on Local Government, June 1955), 9.

[3]*The Organization of Local Political Economies* (Washington, DC: Advisory Committee on Intergovernmental Relations, 1987), 3.

[4]A persuasive case for integrating local governments, formally and informally, is made in Roscoe C. Martin, *Government and the Suburban School* (Syracuse, NY: Syracuse University Press, 1963), 102–5.

[5]For a useful analysis of intergovernmental relationships see Donald Phares, "Federalism, State-Local Sector, and Education: A Look to the 1980s." *Issues in Education* (1983): 31–55.

[6]Paul E. Peterson, *City Limits* (Chicago: The University of Chicago Press, 1981), ch. 11.

[7]Roald F. Campbell, "The Folklore of Local School Control," *The School Review* 68 (Spring 1959): 15.

[8]*School Board News* 8 (8 June 1988): 1, 5.

[9]*School Board News* 8 (7 August 1988): 6.

[10]Lawrence Susskind and Cynthia Horan, "Proposition 2 1/2: The Response to Tax Restrictions in Massachusetts," *The Property Tax and Local Finance,* Proceedings of the Academy of Political Science, vol. 35, (1983): 158–171.

[11]Edwin Grant Dexter, *A History of Education in the United States* (New York: Macmillan, 1922), 183.

[12]R. Freeman Butts and Lawrence A. Cremin, *A History of Education in American Culture* (New York: Holt, Rinehart and Winston, 1953), 103.

[13]Ibid., 100–108.

[14]Dexter, *A History of Education in the United States,* 184.

[15]Butts and Cremin, *A History of Education in American Culture,* 104–107.

[16]For further elaboration see Newton Edwards, *The Courts and the Public Schools* (Chicago: University of Chicago Press, 1955), 63.

[17]*School Code of Illinois,* Art. 11, Secs. 6–10.

[18]San Francisco Public Schools Commission, *School District: City and County of San Francisco, An Analysis of Relationships* (San Francisco: San Francisco Public Schools Commission, 1976), 25.

[19]Stephen K. Bailey et al. *Schoolmen and Politics: A Study of State Aid to Education in the Northeast* (Syracuse, NY: Syracuse University Press, 1962), 104.

[20]H. Thomas James, J. Alan Thomas, and Harold J. Dyck, *Wealth, Expenditure and Decisionmaking for Education* (Stanford, CA: School of Education, Stanford University, 1963), 99.

[21]*The Organization of Local Political Economies,* 24–25.

[22]*Your School District* (Washington, DC: Department of Rural Education, 1948).

[23]*Craton Liddell et al., v. The Board of Education of the City of St. Louis,* no. 72-100C (3) (E.D. Mo. July 5, 1983).

[24]The theory of a federated structure is elaborated in Raphael O. Nystrand and Luvern L. Cunningham, "Federated Urban School Systems: Compromising the Centralization-Decentralization Issue" in *Toward Improved Urban Education,* ed. Frank Lutz (Worthington, OH: Charles A. Jones, 1970).

[25]*Excellence in the Making—Revisited* (Springfield, IL: Illinois Commission on the Improvement of Elementary and Secondary Education in Illinois, June 1988), 21–23.

[26]*Conditions of Education in California* (Berkeley, CA: Policy Analysis for California Education, 1988), 49–50.

[27]*Digest of Education Statistics, 1982* (Washington, DC: Office of Educational Research and Improvement, 1982), 59.

[28]Kenneth C. W. Kammeyer, "Community Homogeneity and Decision Making," *Rural Sociology* 28 (September 1963): 238–45.

[29]U.S. Bureau of the Census, Current Population Reports, series P-20, no. 374, *Population Profile of the United States: 1981* (Washington, DC: U.S. Government Printing Office, 1982).

[30]For a thoughtful analysis of the equality of educational opportunity problem as it relates to district structure see Arthur E. Wise, *Rich Schools, Poor Schools* (Chicago: University of Chicago Press, 1968).

[31]Lawrence W. Downey, *The Task of Public Education* (Chicago: Midwest Administration Center, University of Chicago, 1960).

[32]American Association of School Administrators, *School District Organization,* Report of the AASA Commission for School District Reorganization (Washington, DC: AASA, 1958), 122.

[33]Ibid., 88–103.

[34]National Center for Educational Statistics, U.S. Department of Health, Education, and Welfare, *Education Directory 1977–78 Public School Systems* (Washington, DC: U.S. Government Printing Office, 1978).

[35]Ibid.

[36]Ibid.

[37]AASA, *School District Organization,* 92.

[38]*Digest of Education Statistics, 1982,* 59.

[39]Approximately 80 percent of all school districts have areas differing from those of other units of local government.

[40]William L. Bainbridge, "An Analysis of the Relationship Between Selected Economic, Social, Demographic, and Election Variables and Voter Behavior in Outer City School District Property Tax Elections" (Ph.D. diss., Ohio State University, 1979).

[41]Edward C. Banfield, "The Political Implications of Metropolitan Growth," *Daedalus* 9 (Winter 1961): 61.

[42]Luvern L. Cunningham, "Policy About Policy: Some Thoughts and Projections" *Executive Review* 1 (November 1980).

[43]Yehezkel Dror, *Policymaking Under Adversity* (New Brunswick: Transaction Books, 1986), 281–284.

[44]Myron Lieberman, *The Future of Public Education* (Chicago: University of Chicago Press, 1960), 34. (Italics in original.)

[45]Ibid.

[46]For a useful review of the function of criteria in policy appraisal see Yehezkel Dror, *Public Policymaking Reexamined* (San Francisco: Chandler, 1968).

[47]Dewey, *The Public and Its Problems,* 131.

[48]Ibid., 137.

[49]See Richard P. Nathan, "State and Local Governments under Federal Grants," *Political Science Quarterly,* 98 (Spring 1983): 56–57.

[50]Peterson defines federalism as a system of government in which powers are divided between higher and lower levels of government in such a way that all levels have substantial responsibilities for their constituencies. Peterson, *City Limits,* 67.

[51]Judith Getzels, Peter Elliott, and Frank Beal, *Private Planning for the Public Interest* (Chicago: American Society of Planning Officials, 1975). See also, Jeanne Oakes, *Improving Inner-City Schools: Current Directions in Urban District Reform* (Washington, DC: Center for Policy Research in Education, 1987), 50–58.

[52]Harlan Cleveland, "People Lead Their Leaders in an Information Society," in *Communications and the Future,* Howard F. Didsbury, Jr. (Bethesda, MD: World Future Society, 1982), 173.

[53]For a detailed account of third party mediating structures in education see Luvern L. Cunningham, "Third Parties As Problem Solvers," in *Communities and Their Schools,* Don Davies (New York: McGraw-Hill, 1981), ch. 5.

[54]*New York Governance in the 21st Century* (Albany, NY: Rockefeller Institute, 1987), 8.

6
The Intermediate Unit
of School Administration

H istorically, the term *intermediate unit of school administration* referred to the office or agency in an intermediate position between the state department of education and local school districts. Within the past decade or two, intermediate units in many states have undergone substantial change. Initially, their primary function was regulation and control as instruments of state educational agencies. A major objective was to ensure that state policies and programs were administered in local districts. In more recent times, however, as we shall discuss, the paramount purpose of intermediate units has evolved to be that of providing needed educational services to districts too small to provide them.[1] The importance of these units will likely increase as demands for greater efficiency in the public sector intensify in the face of inflation and increased competition for resources. Within the immediate future these somewhat "invisible" units may become centers of attention as educators are compelled to develop more efficient delivery systems and structures.[2]

Thirty-nine states have some form of intermediate unit. In most states, mainly in the Midwest and West, the intermediate unit of school administration has the same boundaries as the county. In New York the Board of Cooperative Educational Services serves essentially as an intermediate unit, and this organization is not coterminous with county boundaries. The remaining eleven states have no intermediate unit of school administration; many of them have operating school districts that for the most part are county-wide.

The supervisory unions found in the New England states have often been treated as intermediate units of school administration. Actually, these supervisory unions serve chiefly as a way of promoting cooperative action among the boards of the local districts (towns). The union is composed of board members who, in many unions, meet to select a superintendent of schools and attend to other joint business. The superintendent tends to work with each district board instead of in an intermediate district capacity.

In some of the literature on intermediate units the county school district is treated as one type of intermediate unit. Such a concept is erroneous, for in some states the county district is the basic operating unit of school government and does not stand in an intermediate position. The literature also refers to regional subdistricts of large cities as intermediate units. We do not include these organizational arrangements here for they are variations effected within basic operating school districts and not intermediate between the state and local districts.

DEVELOPMENT OF THE INTERMEDIATE UNIT

Each of the thirty-nine states with intermediate units of school administration has a somewhat unique history of the unit's development. Louisiana, Montana, Virginia, Indiana, and Minnesota are among the states that have created intermediate units relatively recently. Obviously, this is not the place for detailed state-by-state discussion. Instead, we will note the development of the office in two states and make a few generalizations that seem to characterize the growth of the office generally. Michigan is one of the states in which the intermediate unit has been coterminous with the county until recently, and the history of the intermediate unit in Michigan can be used as an illustrative case for this group of states.

In Michigan the territorial laws of 1827 and 1829 provided for township officials who would have some jurisdiction over schools and who were required to divide the township into school districts. Thus, the township became the first intermediate unit in Michigan. The Michigan constitution of 1835 provided only for local officials to supervise the schools but the law of 1837 created school inspectors for each of the townships. In 1867 Michigan provided for an elective office of county superintendent of schools. This plan was repealed in 1875 and the plan of township inspectors was reestablished. It was 1891 before the plan of having a chief county school officer was reinstated under the title of the county school commissioner. For fifty years, 1841 to 1891, there was a constant tug-of-war to determine whether the county or the township would become the intermediate unit of school administration in Michigan.[3]

During this period there was constant criticism of township officials as politicians attempted to deal with such problems as certification, supervision, and reporting to the state school office. At the same time, the township was reluctant to relinquish any control to the county. This controversy finally ended in Wayne County (Detroit area) in 1937 when board members of local school districts were authorized to select a county board of education and that board in turn was to select a county superintendent of schools. The county board became the creature of local boards of education and the county board operation was limited to those functions favored by local school districts. This plan was made uniform for the state in 1947. In 1962 the Michigan legislature strengthened the intermediate school district financially and administratively and provided a means whereby as many as three counties might be combined into one unit.

Since 1962 the Michigan legislature has repeatedly strengthened the intermediate district. In 1976, fifty-eight of Michigan's eighty-three counties had intermediate districts, which included all of the operating local school districts of the state. The boundaries of the intermediate districts were no longer determined by county lines but by the boundaries of the constituent local districts. By the 1970s there were fifteen multi-county intermediate school districts; nine served two counties, four served three counties, one served four counties, and one served a five-county region. In consolidated intermediate districts, board members were elected at large while in regular intermediate districts they were elected by representatives of local boards of education. In all cases the intermediate superintendent was appointed by the intermediate district board.

In recent times the Michigan intermediate districts have taken statewide initiatives to achieve school improvements. They have exerted substantial political influence on state educational policy. In 1985–87 for example, through the leadership of a small coterie of intermediate district superintendents, a comprehensive analysis of high technology was completed and a report issued that identified policy proposals about technology to be considered by the state, local districts, and the intermediate units themselves.[4]

The intermediate unit in New York is not coterminous with the county. In New York State as early as 1795 the law established a body known as the town commission that was to apportion state school money among the several school districts of the town, confer with district trustees about the qualifications of teachers, and exercise a modicum of supervision over the course of study. This early provision was strengthened in 1812, and two years later the town commissioners served as a sort of board and the inspectors actually did more of the school visitation.

This arrangement continued until 1841 when legislation created a deputy superintendent, apparently deputy to the state superintendent, who was to be appointed by the county board of supervisors. Half of the deputy superintendent's salary was to be paid from state funds, an arrangement that smacked of state control. In 1843 town commissioners and town inspectors were eliminated and a town superintendent was created. For a time both the town superintendent and the deputy superintendent, operating at the county level, served intermediate functions. Shortly, however, the deputy superintendent was eliminated. This left the town superintendent to represent the intermediate unit until 1856. In that year the town superintendency was eliminated and an elected county superintendency was provided. Almost all duties of the town superintendent were transferred to the new office, which remained in effect for more than fifty years.

In 1910 the elected county superintendency was abolished and supervisory districts, each comprising a number of towns, were established. All territory outside cities of 4,500 or more in population was to be included in supervisory districts. Initially, there were 208 such districts and each had a district board of school directors that selected the superintendent of schools. Even so, the superintendent appeared to be responsible directly to the state commissioner of education.

After extended study an intermediate unit law was passed in 1948. As an interim step, provision was made for boards of cooperative services to be composed of representatives of local district boards. These boards selected their own superintendent of schools and had general supervision over the services to be provided to component districts. Within two years after this permissive legislation there were ninety boards of cooperative school services and about 1,200 professional workers providing services in some twenty-five categories to many thousands of pupils in New York. As of 1973 the supervisory districts had been reduced to forty-six, boards of school directors had been abolished, and each of the districts was governed by a Board of Cooperative Educational Services (BOCES). Each of these boards selected a district superintendent. The district superintendent, while responsible to the state commissioner of education, also served as executive officer of the Board of Cooperative Educational Services. The forty-four BOCES's in New York now serve all but 21 of the state's 740 school districts.

New York, like Michigan, has a long history of intermediate unit expressions, beginning in 1795 and continuing until 1948, when the present arrangement emerged. Much of this controversy centered on whether the town or the county should be the intermediate unit. Finally, groups of towns were formed into supervisory districts and became, in effect, the intermediate units. The creation of the deputy superintendent in 1841, however, sparked another controversy that continues today. The question is whether the intermediate office stands midway between the local school districts and the state department of education or whether the intermediate office actually represents the state department of education.

Cooper and Fitzwater some years ago examined the evolution of the intermediate district over 150 years of American history,[5] and their conclusions suggest these trends:

1. There has been a growing recognition of education as a state function and the need for a workable number of intermediate offices to facilitate communication between the state and a great number of local school districts.
2. In the early stages the intermediate unit was seen essentially as an extension of the arm of the state department of education.
3. Over the years there has been a gradual transfer of the functions of the intermediate office from a lay board to a professional or semiprofessional officer.
4. Progress toward making the intermediate office more than a perfunctory one has been slow because people resisted any encroachments upon their exercise of control of education at the local district level.
5. In recent years the intermediate unit has come to be viewed by many people as an agency to provide to small local school districts services which they cannot ordinarily provide for themselves.

There is considerable variety in the organizational arrangements of the intermediate unit of school administration in the thirty-nine states. In nineteen states there are only two levels of school government: the state and the basic operating school district. Hawaii stands alone and actually operates as one large centralized school district.

In most cases, local boards of education are the governing body of the intermediate unit. In some states the traditional practice of reposing legal responsibility in the county superintendent of schools alone has been retained. For the most part, these board members are elected at large by popular vote. In Iowa and Washington they are elected from wards. In New York and Pennsylvania the members of the intermediate boards are elected by representatives of the local boards of education. In Pennsylvania intermediate board members must be serving on local boards at the time of election. In a number of states superintendents of intermediate districts are appointed, in most cases by the intermediate boards and in New Jersey by the state commissioner. However, intermediate superintendents are elected by popular vote in many states. In a number of these states intermediate boards of education are also elected by popular vote. Presumably, these superintendents are supposed to serve as administrators for these intermediate boards, but it is clear that the boards have no ways of holding the superintendents responsible.

A look at the intermediate unit of school administration raises a number of questions. What should be the structure and function of the intermediate unit? If eleven states have managed without recognized intermediate units, can the other states do likewise? If an intermediate unit is needed, what can we learn from the wide variety of practices that now exists? Is it possible that functions that were necessary in a rural America of a century ago are no longer needed? We'll now turn to these questions.

THE STATUS OF THE INTERMEDIATE UNIT

In the past decade or so, substantial changes have been made in more than twenty states in the organization of intermediate units. In Kansas, the county as an intermediate unit was eliminated entirely. In other cases the number of intermediate units was reduced either by elimination or by combining counties for intermediate purposes. In Nebraska, even though the county superintendency was retained, nineteen service units were created. Texas, in a sweeping reorganization, created a statewide network of twenty educational service centers for its 254 counties. Iowa created Joint County School Systems, Georgia established a statewide network of Cooperative Educational Service Agencies, and West Virginia in 1972 established multi-county Regional Educational Service Agencies. In 1975 Montana mandated the creation of five Special Education Regional Services and Virginia enacted legislation to create voluntary Regional Education Service Agencies. In 1976 Indiana passed enabling legislation for the creation of Educational Centers, and Minnesota established ten Educational Cooperative Service Units.

These and other actual and pending changes receiving serious study in numerous other states suggest that the intermediate unit is on trial. Possibly the intermediate unit of school administration has always been evolving. It may be that any unit that attempts to find a place between the legally fixed responsibility for education at the state level and the jealously guarded operation of schools at the local district level is inevitably in flux. In any case this is an issue that needs to be examined closely.

Needed or Not?

The first consideration revolves around the question of whether the intermediate unit is or is not needed. Those who favor the intermediate unit point out that in most states we have hundreds and even thousands of local school districts, the majority of which are too small or too poor to offer complete educational programs; therefore, some intermediate office must provide a number of services, such as supervision and guidance, or else rural children will be deprived of adequate educational opportunity. To those who suggest that districts should reorganize into larger and more efficient units, the supporters of the intermediate unit reply that such arrangements decrease local control and local identification, and that rural citizens are opposed to such arrangements.

Those who favor abolition of the intermediate unit say there are better solutions. They say local districts can be reorganized into adequate units of school administration wherever possible, with pupil enrollments in grades 1 through 12 of no less than 10,000 or 12,000, and such units can provide, in most cases, adequate elementary and secondary school programs. They also point out that with proper leadership reorganizations have been effected and that after a few years in the reorganized districts, most people do not favor a return to the old plan.

A second alternative, if districts are to remain small and there is to be no intermediate unit, is a plan of cooperation among districts. One or more cooperative plans might be established. For instance, an audiovisual center might be established through the voluntary cooperation of several districts and the cost prorated among the districts. Or, small districts might contract with a larger district to provide some service, such as classes for the mentally handicapped, which small districts find impractical to establish on their own. Actually, some county superintendents, who do not have service staffs of their own, are facilitating agreements among districts in order to provide some of these services on a cooperative basis. One wonders, however, if many cooperative plans will be fostered without the vision and encouragement of professional persons not ordinarily found in small rural districts.

Local problems sometimes cause school districts to join forces formally to deal with difficult issues. In Franklin County, Ohio, vexing problems of taxable wealth and the residential locations of pupils growing out of a three-decade pattern of property annexation by the city of Columbus were not being solved. Those annexations included territory within a number of suburban school districts, townships, and villages. Skyrocketing land values and pockets of students walled off within their own districts by highways and natural barriers created difficult situations for the Columbus city district and a number of suburban districts in Franklin County. After lengthy discussions a consortium was created and titled the Franklin County Council of School Districts. Through the council tedious negotiations involving numerous special interests were pursued. Those discussions led to the successful redrafting of a few district and attendance area boundaries and a more equitable distribution of property values. It is a unique but nevertheless effective instrument for resolving difficulties outside the county and state educational authority systems.

The third possible solution is the decentralization of the state department of education. It is conceivable that, in place of establishing an intermediate layer of school government with more boards, administrators, and staff, the state department might establish a number of regional offices throughout the state and equip each office with personnel who could provide consultative services to local district board members, administrators, and teachers.[6]

Decentralized regional offices established by the state department of education would be a new arrangement, and these offices could probably be established where needed, not necessarily in every county. Much recent thinking about the intermediate school district has suggested that in sparsely settled areas such districts might embrace more than one county. Whether an intermediate service is provided by a reorganized intermediate district or by a decentralized state department of education, it seems clear that it should not be tied inevitably to county lines. Parenthetically, we might add that county lines are obsolete for a number of other governmental services as well.

The Question of Function

The discussion above suggests that the general question of providing or not providing an intermediate unit of some type is by no means settled. The function of such a unit is also debated. Traditionally, proponents of the intermediate unit have suggested that the chief functions of such a unit are: general educational leadership, specialized educational services, and certain management and purchasing services for small districts.

The school codes of most intermediate unit states are replete with references to the duties of county boards of education and the duties of the superintendents who serve such areas. These seemingly are broad grants of power and responsibility, but actual practice suggests that they tend to be pious affirmations, little more. This may be accounted for in several ways. The wording of such injunctions tends to be so general that each person can interpret them as he or she sees fit, at least as long as the incumbent county or district superintendent does not take the provisions too seriously. By contrast, state legislatures have given local boards of education very specific powers and duties having to do with school operation, and there is a body of case law making it clear that most operating decisions rest with local boards. While local boards may listen to the advice of the county or district superintendent, they are more apt to seek the advice of their own employee, the local superintendent of schools.

The superintendents of intermediate school districts were included in a 1982 American Association of School Administrators survey of the American school superintendency. David A. Nicholls, using AASA survey data, drew comparisons between intermediate unit administrators and local school district superintendents.[7] There were many similarities among the two groups but also some noteworthy differences. The intermediate district superintendents saw special education, public support for nonpublic schools, and consolidation of small districts, for example, as much more important than did local district superintendents. Local superintendents ranked such issues as negotiations, staff recruitment and selection, and student discipline much higher than their intermediate counterparts. These comparisons reflect the distinctions between intermediate and local districts. Intermediate officials, removed from the day-to-day problems of dealing directly with children, see questions such as the consolidation of local districts to be more germane to the intermediate role. Local officials are in the trenches and focus on issues such as discipline and staff recruitment that relate directly to operating schools and accountability to parents.

To be sure, county or district superintendents do perform certain legal functions, but often these have to do with recordkeeping and reporting required by the state department of education. In the rural school districts of some states, the power of the county superintendent may extend to the recommendation of all teaching and administrative personnel. The exercise of this function is often *pro forma* in nature, ignored altogether, or dispensed with by a majority vote of the local board. It's clear why county boards of education and their superintendents feel frustrated about the roles they are to perform.

Despite the general confusion regarding the traditional function of the intermediate unit, increasing numbers of intermediate organizations, usually those in metropolitan settings, have forged ahead with new and expanded programs. New York's BOCES in Southern Westchester County, for example, had a 1983–84 budget of $24.7 million to service the needs of twenty-nine component districts, six non-component districts, and school districts in several other BOCES areas. The Southern Westchester BOCES provides a wide variety of occupational education, special education, computer education, teacher and administrator training, and other instructional and related services.[8]

Ohio's eighty-seven county offices of education provide supervisory, special education, administrative, and other services to 793,000 students and 40,000 educators in the state's 381 local school districts.[9] The Cuyahoga County Board of Education in the Cleveland area, for example, offers a wide variety of services and programs and in 1988–89 had a staff of 373 with a budget of approximately $12 million.[10]

In Table 6.1, data about four intermediate districts in four states are summarized. These districts are similar as well as different. Each provides a range of services; some services are offered directly to local districts in the service area, others through contract to districts outside the service area. Enrollment data are not included, but obviously large numbers of students are affected through intermediate district programs and services.

Cuyahoga County, Ohio, is, in some respects, an anomaly. It is the largest county in the state in terms of population yet it provides direct services to only three local school districts enrolling 2,058 students in 1987–88. Cleveland and a large number of suburban districts make up the balance of Cuyahoga County school systems. County (intermediate) districts in Ohio can serve directly only districts that are labeled "locals" in the state's district classifications. They can provide contract services to other units, however. Wayne County Intermediate District, west of Detroit, overlays districts that have a range of ethnically, racially, and socioeconomically different students. Its services are highly regarded by the systems in the county and have earned a reputation of excellence across Michigan. Santa Clara County, California, and Southwestern Westchester, New York, likewise are well regarded, offering a broad range of services to districts in their service areas. As indicated by Table 6.1, their budgets, number of employees, and districts served vary substantially.

More and more states have accepted the service function of the intermediate unit and have provided, over time, state funds to the unit for services. By combining federal, state, and county funds with school district funds through contractual arrangements, many California county departments of education, for example, have been able to finance a wide range of services for local school districts. Thus, an increasingly influential movement that clearly perceives service, not regulation and control, as the primary function of the intermediate or middle-echelon unit of school administration is already under way. Numerous models of these recently rejuvenated units can be cited. Although their names and structures vary considerably among states and even within states, entities such as Michigan's Regional Dissemination Centers, New Jersey's Educational Improvement Centers, and Connecticut's Educational Service Centers are becoming more vital mechanisms within the educational infrastructure.[11] Advocates of these regional service centers cite the following to illustrate the benefits they provide:

1. They can facilitate the provision to local districts of easily accessible and definite self-determined supplemental and supportive services of high quality.
2. They can facilitate the development and/or provision of required programs and services to local districts in the event the local unit is unable to do so.
3. They can contribute substantially to the equalization of educational opportunities for all children by minimizing the accident of geography and neutralizing artificial barriers as important determinants of the kind of educational programs available.

TABLE 6.1
Budgets, Employees, and Districts Served by Four Geographically Dispersed Intermediate School Districts

| | | | Number of Districts Served | |
Intermediate Districts	Budgets	Number of Professional Employees	Directly	Through Contracts
Santa Clara County, CA	$ 7,935,417		37	0
Wayne County, MI	$75,000,000	550	34	0
Southwestern Westchester, NY	$35,000,000	450	35	65
Cuyahoga County, OH	$12,000,000	373	3	63

4. They can promote the better utilization of known applications and force a systematic search for new applications of cost-benefit/cost-effectiveness principles in the delivery of educational programs and services within the state school system.
5. They can contribute to the healthy interface between urban, suburban, and rural interests in the search for solutions to areawide educational and educationally related issues.
6. They can contribute significantly to the development of a statewide research, development, evaluation, and dissemination network in the state and promote the concentration of and best use of resources to foster the network once it is in place.
7. They can contribute significantly to the establishment of a statewide network of resident change agents possessing both authenticity in the eyes of their principal constituencies and legal mandates, where necessary; they can also more readily implement the staffing and resources necessary to effect fundamental change in the workings of the state school system on a regular and planned basis.
8. They can substantially promote meaningful local school district involvement in statewide and regional planning and decision-making processes:[12]

While this discussion of function could be extended, enough has been said to illustrate that the purposes of the intermediate unit vary from state to state. This confusion seems to reside in a few general areas. There is first the area of direct service to small local districts aimed at strengthening the total educational program. Thus, for example, film libraries, counseling services, and supervisory services were provided, where budgets permitted, by the intermediate unit and made available to local school districts. Now many local districts have grown to the point where their own film libraries, counselors, and supervisors are superior to those available in the county or intermediate office. What does this suggest about direct service for the future?

A second area of confusion is often referred to as the leadership role of the intermediate unit. At one time, and possibly in many places still, the county superintendent or members of his or her staff if there were a staff, might provide useful advice to rural school boards and administrators. Again, with the reorganization and increased size of school districts, and possibly, too, with the increased specialization of education, county superintendents often find they have little advice to give or that local boards and local superintendents do not seek such advice. What should be the leadership role of the intermediate unit in the future?

The Question of Structure

Just as basic questions are being raised about the functions of the intermediate unit, basic questions are also being raised about the organization and financing of such units.[13] We've already referred to the question of the geographical area to be contained in the intermediate unit. In most cases the intermediate unit covers one entire county. While there are some conveniences in having the county as the intermediate unit, in terms of having a unit large enough and with resources enough to perform many functions, the county, at least in sparsely settled areas, will not suffice.

A tendency to reject the county as the appropriate geographic area for the intermediate unit may be noted in legislation in Iowa and Wisconsin, where two or more counties were permitted to join units; several such combinations have been made. Legislation in Michigan requires that counties be joined to form intermediate units if any single county has a population of less than 5,000. The actual and proposed structural changes represented by these and other states have a long tradition to overcome, but the question does appear to be a live one.

Whether the intermediate unit should have a board and, if so, how that board should be selected, are also major questions at this time. Several states have no county board of education even though they have county superintendents of schools who perform some intermediate unit services. Should the intermediate unit become more significant as a part of the educational structure of these states, intermediate boards will probably be established.

In states that have intermediate unit boards of education, board members are selected in a number of ways. In some states, members are elected from the intermediate unit at large. In a few states board members are elected from areas or wards within the intermediate unit. In other states intermediate board members are elected by local board members or by representatives of local board members. Recent legislation in Michigan altered this arrangement somewhat and in New York the plan was initially seen as an interim arrangement. In any case these and other practices suggest that the manner of selecting intermediate unit board members still varies widely.

The structure of the intermediate unit office must also take into account the professional staff provided by such an office. Near one end of the scale, we find that San Diego County, California, employs many professionals, including administrators, coordinators, and special teachers. Somewhere in the middle of this continuum, largely due to legislation passed during the last decade or so, is Ohio, where every county school district now has at least one professional person in addition to the county superintendent of schools; many county school districts have a rather diversified staff of professional workers. On the other end of the scale, however, some county school superintendents are pleased to have just a secretary. Indeed, the county superintendent may even look upon the job as part-time employment. In some states the lack of professional staff may signify quite clearly the tenuous position of the intermediate unit.

Financial support for the intermediate unit includes state appropriations, a tax levied by or at the behest of the intermediate unit, and contracts with local school districts. In California all three plans are in operation. One concern of school people in California is that county school funds are under the control of the county supervisors, thus making the intermediate unit dependent fiscally for at least the county share of its budget. In Iowa, on the other hand, legislation has conferred taxing power and thus fiscal independence on the intermediate unit. The intermediate unit in Washington, however, and in a number of other states has no tax-levying authority. In both Washington and California the intermediate unit may enter into contracts with local school districts for services to be provided. In any state where the intermediate unit is taken seriously, its financing becomes an important problem.

SOCIOECONOMIC FORCES AFFECTING THE INTERMEDIATE UNIT

To understand more fully what has been happening to the intermediate unit of school administration over the last several decades, it is necessary to examine some of the socioeconomic forces operating in our society. Certainly a plan for the future must take into account such forces. A brief discussion of some of these influences and their possible implications for the intermediate unit follows.

Growth in Technology

The growth of technology in America affected rural as well as urban life. With increased farm mechanization, each farm owner attempted to get more acres to cultivate, displacing some farm laborers and increasing the size of farms. Thus, in the past half century or so farm population decreased even though total population increased. In 1920 farm population was 30 percent of total population while sixty years later it was less than 5 percent.

Along with farm mechanization came improved transportation and communication. Aided by the Rural Electrification Administration in the 1930s, farms received electricity and, with the advent of satellite dishes and VCRs, farm children now have access to the same movies and TV programs as city children. With improvements in roads, many farmers got jobs in industrial plants and often drive thirty to fifty miles to such plants, thus becoming part-time farmers. Good roads also have enabled city dwellers to move to the suburbs and retain their jobs in the city. In short it is becoming more and more difficult to draw a line between rural and urban areas. Indeed, recent demographic analyses indicate, as we'll see shortly, that the massive migration to urban areas is being reversed and a perceptible population shift to rural and smaller communities has been under way for some time.[14]

Population migration affects schools and school organization. Notably, people who make their living on farms are fewer in number. But in some rural areas where agriculture is marginal, population overall is growing. Nuclear families are re-aggregating. Children and grandchildren are returning home, sometimes increasing enrollments at local schools, and otherwise placing heavier burdens on other human services agencies. There is often little or no employment for those who return or the returnees compete for the few jobs available, making it more difficult for those who never left. The children of the unemployed sometimes have more learning difficulties or other problems calling for special services usually available only through county or other intermediate units.

Rural people traditionally have resisted school district reorganization. Controversy over reorganization or consolidation lingers long after the change has taken place. Emotion around such changes equals or surpasses that generated by desegregation. Even when the need is apparent and educational and economic advantages are clear, voters resist reorganization. Bus transportation makes it possible; local sentiment stands in the way. Local school district reorganization is at best difficult; often intermediate units can assert leadership in achieving consolidations, mergers, or other forms of reorganization.

School District Reorganization

School district reorganization over the last four decades has affected the nature and function of the intermediate unit. The intermediate unit, up until the end of World War II, particularly as reflected in the office of the county superintendent, was a product of rural America. Many counties in the Midwest contained 75 to 100 small school districts, most of which operated a one-room, eight-grade school. Each district had a board of trustees or directors who knew little about schools, and each district had a teacher who had completed the eighth grade and passed the county teacher's examination in the school subjects. The county superintendent acted as the arm of the state in seeing that minimum legal requirements were met, in distributing small amounts of state funds usually derived from school lands, and in supplying simple statistics to the state superintendent of public instruction. He or she visited the schools, the teachers, and the board members no less than once a year, usually as stipulated in the law.

With improved roads, the one-room school, often located within walking distance for all pupils, made less sense. With the growth of high schools, it was clear that not every district could support a high school. These circumstances led in some states to reorganization of school districts even in the early decades of this century. Many of these reorganizations resulted in the establishment of elementary schools of 100 to 200 pupils and of high schools of 50 to 100 pupils. Often these schools were located in villages adjacent to the farm areas. As some of the villages grew into towns and cities, school enrollments increased. Other villages and the open country actually decreased in population, and this created the need for a new round of district reorganization.

This movement received genuine impetus in the years following World War II. As noted in Chapter 5, school districts have been reduced from more than 100,000 to about 15,000. Some people have suggested that this process should be continued until there are no more than 10,000 school districts in the nation. Even attaining this goal would leave us with many school districts enrolling as few as 2,000 pupils.

A district of 2,000 pupils would not be, in our judgment, self-sufficient. While it could support elementary and secondary schools, it could probably provide only limited programs for gifted pupils, slow learners, the vocationally oriented, and the physically handicapped. Total pupil enrollments of at least 10,000 are necessary if complete educational programs are to be provided.[15] In rural areas, even if school districts are created to serve 10,000 pupils, some intermediate level of organization will be necessary if a comprehensive educational program is to be made available.

Demographic Trends

Until relatively recently, only demographic changes in rural areas were considered. More recently, the growth of urban areas, and implications for educational organization, has been recognized. In the past few decades, while the total population has been increasing, many of the central cities have been declining in population. The population in the suburban areas surrounding these cities grew as core cities lost residents. The 1980 census indicated that most of the central cities were continuing to lose population. Indeed, in the mid-1960s American society reached a demographic watershed when the suburban population for the first time surpassed the central city population. (See Chapter 2 for a comprehensive overview of demographic trends.)

More recent demographic trends reflect changing population patterns that will have significant ramifications for educational governance, particularly for intermediate districts. In the 1970s the nation's largest metropolitan areas experienced a marked decline in the rate of their population growth, a development without precedent since the first census was compiled in 1790. Moreover, the nation's large metropolitan centers—New York, Los Angeles, Chicago, Philadelphia, and Detroit—showed net population losses during the 1970s while many small towns in many less populous areas experienced considerable growth. These trends, of course, reflect the widely acknowledged shift of population away from the Northeast and North Central regions to the "Sun Belt" areas of the South and West.[16]

These trends, not foreseen even a few years ago, reflect a series of private, personal, and business decisions that are significantly different and have profound implications for educational governance. Economic diversification also has been a vital factor in reducing rural poverty and altering the realities of country life. While rural poverty still abounds in our society, the massive migration of the less affluent to the industrial centers of the North has substantially altered the geographical distribution of the nation's poor.

Another salient point is that racial, social, and economic segregation is pronounced in most metropolitan areas, frequently along school district lines. Bluntly stated, the cities are increasingly black and the suburbs are white.[17] City schools are becoming pauper schools for poor and often minority children.[18] Although progress was made in the 1960s to close the gap between black and white city workers with similar educational backgrounds, blacks today still earn only approximately 65 percent as much as their white counterparts. These are some of the reasons reformers are urging closer suburb-city or "metro" relationships in education. Of course, other problems, such as transportation, housing, air and water pollution, energy conservation, and airport congestion, are also regional in nature and are becoming more acute.

Although suburban communities are predominantly white, they are no longer exclusive residences for upper- and upper-middle-class people. After World War II lower- and middle-class people also fled to the suburbs. The desire to have more living space, combined with the decentralization of industry and improved expressways into the cities, led to this influx to the suburbs. Many of the suburban communities for working-class people, however, were poorly planned and often short on public services; the result has been the random and irregular growth known as urban sprawl.

The changing composition of large central cities, the migration to the suburbs, and incipient rural growth have many implications for school government and organization.[19] School systems in central cities, often cumbersome, bureaucratic, and impersonal organizations, are beset with very serious problems. Some suburban school districts have grown so much that intermediate units are no longer appropriate. Rural districts, on the other hand, traditionally understaffed and poor in programs, may well be on the threshold of an exciting new era of enrichment and growth if these demographic trends persist. Such developments may create enlarged roles and responsibilities for intermediate units of school administration.

SUMMARY AND FUTURE PROSPECTS

We have reviewed briefly the development of the intermediate unit of school administration in its various forms; we have made some assessment of its current operation; and we have noted the socioeconomic forces that may bring about a new role for the intermediate unit. We'll now suggest some alternative solutions and some directions for the future.

While there are notable exceptions, by and large the intermediate unit still is not performing a vital role in American education, and we believe it should either be eliminated or reconceived. If the intermediate unit were eliminated, a massive reorganization of school districts, far beyond anything now contemplated, would be required. If a minimum student enrollment of 10,000 is needed to support a comprehensive educational program, sparsely populated states would suffer under such an arrangement. In Wyoming, for instance, it would mean dividing the state into four or five school districts. The closest approximation of this arrangement we have is in Alaska where, except for a few city school districts, everything is included in District #1.

Another alternative for eliminating the intermediate level might be a decentralization of the state department of education into regional offices. New Jersey already has moved in this direction. The county superintendent is considered a member of the state department of education staff and is appointed by, paid by, and responsible to the state board of education. More than a decade ago the New Jersey legislature provided for area service programs including state funds to help finance such programs. These centers now exist in nearly all of the state's twenty-one counties, and the great majority of New Jersey's school districts receive their services.

For a small, highly industrialized state like New Jersey, this plan seems to have many advantages. One level of government is eliminated, services complementary to those provided by local school districts are available, and coordination with the state department of education appears complete. Whether or not our larger and more diversified states are ready for such a plan is still a question. If people in these states resist centralization of government at the state level, movement in this direction could be very slow. To make the New Jersey plan work in populous states such as California and Illinois would require a very large number of professionals on the staff of the state department of education and hence a generous state department budget. The decentralized state department plan does not seem to be the best solution for many states.

There are very tangible signs that the intermediate unit movement is already well on the way to being reconceived and revitalized. There appears to be a new dynamism inherent in the movement as administrative entities once known as intermediate units are being restructured and renamed "regional educational service agencies." The change in terminology reflects the belief that these units are now "essentially organizations intended to serve constituent local school districts (rather than agencies designed primarily to perform administrative and regulatory functions for the state education agency as was true of the dominant historical middle-echelon unit—the county school system)."[20]

The concept of regional educational service agencies has grown considerably since the mid-1960s and the fact that approximately one-half of the states have recently reorganized their former middle-echelon units along these lines is ample testimony to their potential and viability. A study of emerging regional educational service agencies in a dozen states (Colorado, Georgia, Iowa, Michigan, Nebraska, New York, Oregon, Pennsylvania, Texas, Washington, West Virginia, and Wisconsin) reports that elements such as the following are found in these units:

1. Comprehensive programs and services for exceptional children in virtually all the states
2. Comprehensive educational media programs and services in virtually all the units
3. Curriculum subject matter consultant services in a majority of the units
4. Comprehensive data processing services in many of the units
5. Staff development activities in a majority of the units
6. Vocational-technical programs and services[21]

This growing grassroots restructuring of middle-echelon administrative units triggered the creation of an organization in Washington, DC to represent the interests of the nation's educational service agencies. In February 1977 the American Association of Educational Service Agencies was created at the national convention of the American Association of School Administrators (AASA). This organization, a contract agency of AASA with a membership of 193 contracted educational service agencies, established a national office and publishes a newsletter, conducts regional workshops on career education for small school districts through the resources of educational service agencies, represents the agencies in Congress and the executive branch, and disseminates information about the regional service agencies through research and publications.[22]

These developments are impressive. This exciting reconceptualization of traditional intermediate units augurs well for their future, but even the most ardent advocates of the movement recognize that such progress has been spotty and that most units are still in an embryonic stage with respect to services provided and students reached. In the rural setting, especially, many districts will continue to depend upon the traditional intermediate unit for certain services. Such rural intermediate units should continue to meet the following criteria:

1. The major functions of the intermediate unit should be: planning for local district reorganization; determining the location of school plants; providing supplemental financing designed to further equalize educational opportunity; offering specialized instructional programs such as technical and junior college programs; providing specialized educational services

such as psychiatric help to pupils in local districts; and providing educational leadership to local school districts.

2. Whenever possible, there should be a minimum enrollment of 10,000 pupils in the public schools of the areas included in an intermediate unit. An enrollment of 20,000 to 30,000 pupils would be even better.

3. The boundaries of the intermediate unit should be coterminous with the outer boundaries of a logical combination of the local school districts that the intermediate unit is to serve. There should be no required relationship between the boundaries of the intermediate unit and the boundaries of the counties.

4. Each intermediate unit should be under the direct control of a board of education elected at large by the residents of the intermediate area. The board should appoint the intermediate superintendent and determine salary and tenure for that position. The board should adopt policies to govern the operation of the intermediate unit, employ the necessary personnel upon recommendation of the superintendent, and appraise the effectiveness of the policies as they are carried out by the employed personnel. An advisory committee to the intermediate unit board should be elected from the membership of the local district boards of education.

5. The intermediate board of education should be fiscally independent; it should have independent taxing power and the authority to determine its own budget. State funds should also be made available to intermediate units. The intermediate-unit board should also have power to contract with local district boards to provide certain services.

6. The intermediate superintendent should be a person with the qualifications and competence to earn and deserve high professional recognition by administrators in all types of local school districts. In order to obtain a superintendent of such quality, an intermediate board of education should not be limited in its choice of a superintendent by residence requirements.

7. Both in structure and functions the intermediate unit should be sufficiently flexible to adapt to changing educational conditions and needs. There should be legal provisions for the reorganization of intermediate units similar to those presently applicable to local districts. As local districts become capable of providing more of their own services, it should be possible for an intermediate unit to discontinue a function no longer needed and to assume another that changing conditions indicate to be desirable.

As we contemplate the future of urban areas, it seems clear that the fates of the central cities and their suburban fringes are closely related. Integrated planning for the inside and outside of these metropolitan areas is a clear necessity. It also becomes very plain that planning for education must be coordinated with planning for housing, parks, fire and police protection, transportation, water and sewage disposal, and other services. Moreover, the well-being of more than two-thirds of our people is affected by what is done in these metropolitan areas.

The general issue of metropolitanism has been raised frequently throughout the country in recent years and is discussed in some detail in Chapter 5, but metropolitan governance of education has rarely been achieved: Nashville in Tennessee's Davidson County and Louisville in Kentucky's Jefferson County are the outstanding examples. "Metro" solutions are proposed, but they are vary rarely adopted. Why is metropolitanism less popular with voters and politicians than it is with planners, social scientists, and "ivory tower" professors? There are a number of reasons that can be briefly cited. As the more affluent and largely white population has moved to suburbia and as the minority and lower-income classes have stayed in the cities, there has been a growing racial and economic polarity. Metropolitanism would mean a basic redistribution of resources with suburbanites being taxed more heavily. Social class factors, of course, are also significant. The move to suburbia often means "we have made it." The fear of tax increases is pervasive. Thus the future of metropolitan government is not particularly bright politically—we will never have many examples of metropolitan government unless there are massive financial incentives for this specific purpose.

Many may think of regionalism and metropolitanism as additional examples of the disturbing trend towards centralization. A more realistic view might be to see the regional approach as perhaps the only means through which we can now create workable and responsive governmental entities of reasonable size in the United States. If we do not develop imaginative regional approaches, major decisions will necessarily be made at the state and federal levels. We have seen some manifestations of suburb-city cooperation, such as Operation Exodus in Boston, in which ghetto children have been bused to schools in the suburbs, and Project Wingspread in Chicago, where there have been suburban-urban exchanges. We have seen cities, such as Hartford, Connecticut, involved in suburban-city pupil exchanges. But these few tiny programs affect only a handful of youngsters.

In the 1970s, the desegregation thrust lost much momentum, and many of the integration initiatives have either disappeared or remain rather limited. The volatile issue of busing and the concomitant racial and social-class tensions make it unlikely that metropolitan area approaches to school governance will have political viability. Indeed, metropolitanism probably will stay dormant, for the short run at least, unless the courts act, as they have in decisions involving Wilmington, Delaware; St. Louis, Missouri; and Louisville, Kentucky. The sustaining of lower court decisions compelling the merger of predominantly black city school systems with largely white suburban districts, for example, probably offers the best, and perhaps only, opportunity for meaningful metropolitanism to occur in the next decade or so. The U.S. Supreme Court's 5–4 decision in the summer of 1974 rejecting a metropolitan school desegregation approach in Detroit, will serve, of course, as a major deterrent to similar efforts to create such regional districts.

While the formation of viable intermediate units in rural areas will often involve combining all or parts of two or more counties, the problem is quite different in urban areas. In our central cities, particularly those with populations of more than 200,000, we may need to break the city school district into several legally autonomous school districts. Each of these districts might contain one or more high schools and several elementary schools, represent a recognized division within the city, and contain a population of 100,000 to 200,000 people or 20,000 to 40,000 pupils in elementary and secondary schools. Thus, a city of 1 million people might be divided into five to ten autonomous school districts.

We are convinced that some such division, coupled with plans to rehabilitate central cities and make them once more habitable for all classes of people, will go far toward eliminating the bureaucratic outlook among the professionals and restoring a feeling of local responsibility among lay citizens. It seems clear that early attempts to decentralize huge school districts into subdistricts, as in New York and Chicago, achieved neither of these ends. One must acknowledge, however, that these attempts did not have the benefit of overall city planning and rehabilitation.

The breakup of large city school districts is necessary to the organization of the most effective intermediate unit in the urban setting. Once this is done, the phenomenon of a single giant district in the center surrounded by scores of smaller districts is gone. In many respects school districts in the city and outside the city will be on a somewhat equal footing. Moreover, if both central city and suburban areas have been made habitable for all classes of people, the way for cooperation among all districts in a metropolitan area will be cleared. Thus, each metropolitan area should establish an intermediate unit to include all school districts in the entire area.[23]

This intermediate unit might correspond in area to other metropolitan authorities established to provide water, police protection, highways, and other services. The intermediate unit in the urban setting should meet many of the criteria suggested above for the intermediate unit in the rural setting. The intermediate school district should have independent taxing power and authority to determine its own budget. State funds should also be made available to intermediate units. The way should also be open for the intermediate board to contract with local school districts to supply certain services.

The major functions of the urban unit would be similar to those of the rural unit, except that fewer specialized services to local districts would probably be necessary. There would be no problem with minimum enrollments in the intermediate unit. Boundaries would not be too difficult to determine. With respect to the controlling board, professional staff, and flexibility of organization, the two plans would be quite similar.

Variations of the intermediate district both in urban and rural settings may well become more vital forces within the educational governance structure. In many ways this middle tier of administration represents a logical compromise between fragmented local districts, which are too small to provide quality educational programs in an increasingly complex social, economic, and political environment, and overly centralized city, state, or federal systems, which are cumbersome and unresponsive to local needs.

Escalating demands for greater efficiency in the delivery systems that provide educational and other public services might serve to buttress and enlarge the role of intermediate, or regional, educational service agencies in the difficult years ahead. Education, its problems exacerbated by financing problems is a singularly labor-intensive enterprise. Regional approaches are a rational means for reducing school costs; the political and economic reasons for strengthening intermediate units may become compelling.[24]

The impact of technology and computers is increasingly reflected in the programs being offered by intermediate or regional units. The Oakland County Intermediate District in Michigan offers data processing services for a number of local districts in Michigan, as well as districts in other states. The Twin Cities Metropolitan Study Council provides leadership by reviewing educational software and data processing equipment. Growing numbers of intermediate units, such as the Board of Cooperative Educational Services of Nassau County in New York State, are providing programs that prepare individuals for the changing job market in a fluid, technological economy.[25] Growing numbers of regional service units are offering services similar to those provided by the Merrimack Education Center Technology Lighthouse Project, which serves as a clearinghouse in computer technology for twenty-two school districts in northeastern Massachusetts.[26]

These technological changes and the other economic and demographic factors discussed in this chapter have significant implications for the influence and the nature of control exercised by the intermediate district. Although legal, ideational, structural and, to a great extent, financial control elements continue to place intermediate units in a relatively invisible and ostensibly uninfluential role, basic changes in the economic and social needs of the society will in all likelihood increase substantially the types of control these districts will exercise in the years ahead. In other words, intermediate districts will be uniquely and increasingly positioned not only to manifest more voluntary forms of leadership but also to exercise their control more directly because of the society's profound need for more coherent, economical, and effective means of networking knowledge and allocating scarce resources.

A particularly important development that could portend more control and influence for intermediate districts is the fact that the rapid technological changes and economic challenges confronting American society have helped rekindle the interest of business and industry in schools, training, and employment issues. There is a growing recognition that all segments of the society have a collective stake in developing educational delivery systems that foster collaborative or bridging efforts between and among the various sectors. Regional service centers and intermediate units are uniquely positioned to provide the more flexible programs that will be needed if we are to thrive economically in the face of strong foreign competition.

NOTES

[1]Harold S. Davis, *Educational Service Centers in the U.S.A.,* (Hartford, CT: Connecticut State Department of Education, 1976), 72.

[2]Rae M. Levis, *The Education Service Agency—Where Next?* (Washington, DC: American Association of School Administrators, 1983).

[3]Harlan D. Beem and H. Thomas James, *Report of the Michigan Committee for the Study of the Intermediate Unit of School Administration* (Chicago: Midwest Administration Center, University of Chicago, 1956).

[4]For a review of those policy recommendations see Luvern L. Cunningham and Lila N. Carol, *The Policy Forum Report* (Plymouth, MI: Wayne County Intermediate School District, 1986), 85.

[5]Shirley Cooper and Charles O. Fitzwater, *County School Administration* (New York: Harper & Row, 1954), 108–9.

[6]Stephens Associates, *Education Service Agencies: Status and Trends* (Burtonsville, MD: Stephens Associates, 1979), 2.

[7]David A. Nicholls, "Comparative Profiles of Three Types of Intermediate District Superintendents" (Ph.D. diss., Ohio State University, 1983), ch. V.

[8]*1983–84 Estimated Budget: BOCES Southern Westchester* (Port Chester, NY: BOCES Southern Westchester, 1983).

[9]*The County Office of Education: Ohio's Vital Learning Link* (Columbus, OH: Ohio County Superintendents Association, 1978), 1.

[10]*Annual Report of the Cuyahoga County Board of Education 1988–89* (Bedford Heights, OH: Cuyahoga County Board of Education, 1989).

[11]See, for example, Frank R. Yulo, *Educational Service Centers in Connecticut* (Hartford, CT: Connecticut State Department of Education, 1977).

[12]E. Robert Stephens, *Regional Educational Service Agencies* (Arlington, VA: Educational Research Service, Inc., 1975), 57–58.

[13]Stephens Associates, *Education Service Agencies,* 88–125.

[14]Calvin L. Beale, *Where Are All the People Going—Demographic Trends* (Washington, DC: Rural Housing Alliance and Rural America, Inc., 1975).

[15]A minimum of 30,000 pupils is recommended in E. Robert Stephens et al., *The Multi-County Regional Educational Service Agency in Iowa* (Iowa City, IA: Iowa Center for Research in School Administration, College of Education, University of Iowa, 1967).

[16]Harold L. Hodgkinson, *All One System* (Washington, DC: The Institute for Educational Leadership, 1985), 7, 8.

[17]Ibid.

[18]For an analysis of minority population in Ohio see Harold L. Hodgkinson, *The State and Its Educational System* (Washington, DC: The Institute for Educational Leadership, 1987), 7.

[19]See, for example, Vincent Ostrom, Robert Bish, and Elinor Ostrom, *Local Government in the United States* (San Francisco: ICS Press, 1988), ch. 9.

[20]Stephens, *Regional Educational Service Agencies,* 1.

[21]Ibid.

[22]*American Association of Educational Service Agencies, Annual Report, 1982–83* (Washington, DC: 1983, Mimeographed).

[23]Stephens Associates, *The Role of Education Service Agencies in Metropolitan Areas* (Burtonsville, MD: Stephens Associates, 1980).

[24]"Regionalism: Help in Cutting School Costs," *The School Administrator* 34 (November 1977): 6.

[25]Board of Cooperative Educational Services of Nassau, *The 1982–1983 Skills for Success Planner* (Westbury, NY: BOCES of Nassau, 1982).

[26]"A Lighthouse on Computers," *AAESA Report: Perspectives on Service* 1 (March–April 1983): 2.

7

School Attendance Areas

The early 1990s promise some of the excitement of the 1960s as interest in parental control of schools regains momentum. Parental control, if widely practiced, may shift power and authority away from school boards and state officials, lodging it with attendance area councils made up of a parent majority, teachers, the principal, and other citizens.

Determining the attendance area for a particular school seems to be a rather straightforward administrative problem—one that could be resolved with dispatch, permitting school leaders to move ahead with important matters of teaching and learning. But such is not the case, at least not today. Few school problems have elicited such continued public outcry as those associated with school attendance areas. The word *busing* alone has created large scale community turmoil and intense debate in state legislatures and the U.S. Congress. School closings, often necessary as enrollments decline, produce similar responses.

The issues related to the social, racial, and ethnic fabric of a school's population that were once thought to be simple administrative matters, subject to professional judgments of school administrators, are now policy matters and demand resolution at the level of the board of education and even the courts. The segregation of pupils on a racial basis violates the federal Constitution, but the action of the U.S. Supreme Court in 1954 has not resolved the thousands of attendance area problems across the land. In fact, the reverse is true. The action of the courts and the spirited drive of minority groups seeking their civil rights have catapulted the attendance area question into one of national interest and importance.

WHAT AN ATTENDANCE AREA IS

There are two main problems of definition regarding attendance areas. One is essentially geographical or territorial; the other is administrative and political. In this chapter we will acknowledge both and highlight some of the recurring attendance area problems facing school officials and their communities.

An attendance area or attendance district, as it is sometimes called, is that portion of a school district in which pupils are required to attend a particular school as designated by the local school board. In a more general sense, an attendance area could be defined as the geographical area from which a school's population is drawn. Within an operating school district there is always at least one attendance area, and in large districts there are many attendance areas. If we said that for every school building there is an attendance area, we would be right most of the time but not always, for in some instances there may be different attendance areas for different grade levels within a single building. Attendance areas are far from uniform, and defining them is not a simple matter.

There is a tendency, particularly on the part of lay people, to confuse an attendance area with a school district. Many people believe the area served by a given school building is a school district and fail to understand the difference between the two units of school organization. Citizen naiveté about this distinction is often revealed in discussions of community control. Prominent issues in citizen participation debates turn on legal differences between the prerogatives of professionals and citizens located at the district and the attendance area levels. The school district is the total area under the jurisdiction of the school board whereas the attendance area is ordinarily the territory served by a particular school building.

A rural school district, the typical one-room rural school at least, has the entire geographical area of the district as its attendance area. Every youngster wishing to attend a public school is expected to attend the school within that district. But even here exceptions are made where geographical barriers such as rivers or mountains or dangerous highways and railroads intervene. In these cases young people may be permitted to attend other schools in other districts on a reciprocal exchange or a tuition-payment basis. For the most part, however, the attendance area boundaries and rural school district boundaries are coterminous. Similar circumstances prevail in thousands of small town districts that may have but one public elementary school and one public secondary school. The boundaries of the district are also the attendance area boundaries for each of the two schools.

The number of public schools in the United States has decreased substantially since 1929–30, while the number of nonpublic schools increased. The attendance area concept does not apply to the nonpublic school in the same sense as to the public school, but the shifts in numbers of schools are still noteworthy. If each public school is considered to have a single attendance area, there were 82,039 attendance areas in 1982–83 in the United States.[1] (This total is at best an approximation, however, because, as was explained earlier, a single school may have more than one attendance area.) In 1931–32, there were 312,812 public schools. The elimination of

168,007 schools by 1975–76 was due primarily to school district reorganization throughout the nation. The decline came for the most part in one-teacher schools; in 1975–76 only 1,166 of these remained, whereas there were 143,000 in 1931–32.[2]

When districts are large enough to warrant more than one building at a given level, attendance boundaries within a district must be established—unless a district chooses to try an open enrollment policy, permitting students to attend any school they choose within the district.

Boundaries for attendance areas in the nation's large districts can be confusing to citizens. A family might reside in a different attendance area for each school level. In other words the attendance areas for an elementary school, a junior high school, a senior high school, and possibly a junior college would not be identical. A family might even have second- and fifth-grade children in one school and third- or fourth-grade children in another school. For elementary school purposes alone, this family would be living in two attendance areas.

Attendance areas are important, and professional educators as well as interested lay people are increasingly concerned about how they are established. The decisions about where to draw the lines among schools are difficult, and the consequences of such decisions are far-reaching. The nature of a given school population frequently is determined by where attendance lines fall. In many school districts in recent years controversies over racial balance often have focused on whether plans to redraw attendance lines increase or decrease integration.

The right of school boards to establish attendance areas is implicit in their authority to require attendance at a given school. A school board can designate which schools pupils will attend as long as it acts reasonably and does not abuse its discretion, especially as such discretion applies to the constitutional rights of children.[3]

The authority of school boards to establish attendance boundaries or to assign pupils to schools has been challenged frequently in recent years. Much of the litigation has grown out of school district reorganization. Following reorganization, pupils, and in some cases whole classes, have been transferred to other schools. In some instances students have been transferred from small town and village schools to schools in rural areas. Parents, fearful that their children so transferred might be deprived of educational advantages, have contested such school board decisions. Other cases involve parents who demand that their children be transferred to another school.[4] In a case in Mississippi, parents requested that their daughter be transferred because she was reported to have headaches brought on by the butane gas heat at the school to which she had been recently asssigned. Furthermore, the girl had purchased a class ring, helped raise funds for a senior class trip, and had been elected to the yearbook staff in the school she had attended the year before as a junior. The court held that these were not sufficient reasons for the girl to be transferred back to her former school and that the assignment by the school board would stand.[5]

The 1954 decision in *Brown* v. *Board of Education of Topeka* denied the use of race as a criterion for the assignment of pupils to the public schools. This historic decision found segregation on the basis of race to be in violation of the Fourteenth Amendment. The court ruled that children so segregated were deprived of equal educational opportunity and that the doctrine of "separate but equal" had no place in American public education. As a consequence, the question of attendance areas has become one of the most significant and controversial issues in American education in this century. The black American in 1954 regarded the decision as a second Emancipation Proclamation although the battle of segregated schools was far from over. The spirited optimism of blacks and other minorities turned to cynicism in many sections of the United States as communities complied with great reluctance to court-ordered desegregation orders and to directives from the U.S. Department of Health, Education, and Welfare. Although desegregation has been implemented grudgingly and the effects are still under appraisal, conservative scholars such as Thomas Sowell believe that there are many objective indicators that " . . . ethnicity is changing in a changing America" and for the better.[6]

Derrick Bell, a prominent black civil rights legal authority, is less sanguine. Bell argues that "merely integrating schools, in a society still committed to white dominance, does not insure black parents and their children equal educational opportunity."[7]

During President Nixon's and President Ford's terms in office, the national posture on school desegregation remained confused. Nixon showed ambivalence and inconsistency on the desegregation issue. While the executive branch openly opposed busing as a means of forcing racial desegregation, a number of the federal courts actively sought to eliminate deliberate attempts to segregate school pupils on the basis of race.[8] Ambivalence marked the early history of the Carter administration too, but it was of a different order. The executive branch supported school desegregation including busing while the U.S. Supreme Court, reflecting the sentiments of its several Nixon appointees, remanded cases for reconsideration to the lower courts in several instances (Dayton, Omaha, Milwaukee) where large numbers of students were to be bused.[9]

The Nixon and Ford administrations failed to support affirmative legislative or executive branch initiatives that would actively require racial desegregation. Their postures generated widespread public antibusing feeling that turned school desegregation into a political football. Violence erupted most dramatically in Boston and Louisville. The early and mid-1970s were difficult especially in Northern school districts. The backlash against actions to desegregate, court-ordered or otherwise, contributed to the uneasiness of many already troubled school districts, some of which were trying in their own way to achieve better racial balance in their attendance areas.

President Reagan, openly hostile to busing as a remedy, supported proposals within Congress that would restrict "forced" busing as a means to achieve school desegregation. The nation received contradictory messages from the White House; although Reagan claimed to support justice and equality, he consistently opposed measures such as busing that would make desegregation possible.

Several bills have been introduced designed to limit the authority of the federal courts in cases involving desegregation. Such legislation, supported by President Reagan, provoked the Citizens Commission on Civil Rights to issue a strong protest arguing that such legislation reflected a critical misunderstanding of the role of the courts and would eliminate vital protections against government abuse of the rights of citizens.[10] Despite the reluctance of the president's office to locate and support means to ensure equality of educational opportunity, the federal district courts continued to endorse remedy plans requiring busing. The St. Louis, Columbus, San Franscisco, Indianapolis, Omaha, and Cleveland remedy plans during the late 1970s and early 1980s involved extensive transportation to achieve desegregation. Large numbers of school closings also occurred in those school districts engendering attendance area problems resulting from declining enrollments.

Cases pertaining to desegregation are discussed in greater detail in Chapter 8, which focuses on the importance of the courts in determining educational policy.

DECISIONS ON BOUNDARY FORMATIONS

Two types of issues must be considered in the determination of attendance areas: geographical-organizational and political-social. The more mechanical and less troublesome decisions pertain to geographical-organizational issues; the difficult decisions usually grow out of political-social issues.

Geographical-Organizational Problems

One set of decisions relates to size—the size of enrollment to be accommodated in a building and the size of the geographical area to be served. The actual dimensions, measured in square miles or square blocks, are functions of population density and the availability of transportation. Size, however, is not the only consideration; it is one of several factors. Since 1954, for example, racial and ethnic criteria have become particularly significant. Attempts were made to define optimum unit sizes in terms of preferred total enrollments and distances from school. These ideal conditions proved to be extremely difficult to achieve, and usually the recommendations in regard to size ended up as very general statements based on ease of transportation for students, suitability of the school facility as a community center, and the attendance area's capacity to provide an adequate staff and a flexible program.

A major attendance area problem of the 1970s and 1980s was school closings and the resulting redrafting of attendance boundaries. The decline in public elementary and secondary enrollment between 1973 and 1983 was not uniform across the states. The changes in enrollment ranged all the way from increases of 24 percent in Utah and 18.2 percent in Wyoming to decreases of 31.2 percent in Delaware and 34.7 percent in the District of Columbia. In most states that had significant enrollment declines, the number of schools also declined.[11]

The decline in the number of schools during the 1970s was primarily in the number of very small and very large schools. The number of schools with fewer than fifty students and with fifty to ninety-nine students dropped by 13 and 16 percent, respectively. Schools with 1,000 to 1,999 students and those with 2,000 students or more declined in number by 11 and 5 percent, respectively. At the same time, schools with 250 to 499 students increased by 16 percent. By type of school, the changes in number reflected both enrollment changes and changes in policy. The number of elementary schools dropped by more than 5 percent, reflecting the severe declines in enrollment at that level. The number of schools in the "other" category, which consists primarily of combined elementary/secondary schools, dropped by more than 27 percent. This decline was a result of the movement toward separate schools for younger and older age groups, and a recognition of the need for such specialized facilities as laboratories and gymnasiums for secondary school students. Schools not classified by grade level include those serving special education and handicapped students. These more than doubled in number during the 1970s as policies supporting the need to educate all children took effect,[12] particularly passage of Public Law 94–142, The Education for All Handicapped legislation.

In cities, enrollment decline combined with school desegregation requirements intensified the geographical-organizational issues and created new social and political dimensions in school attendance area decisions. In Omaha, Nebraska (1983), and Columbus, Ohio (1982), for example, lawsuits were filed in opposition to the closing of high schools based upon the argument that those schools were naturally integrated historically. School officials in both cities maintained that although the enrollments were integrated racially, enrollment decline and costs required the closing of secondary schools. The buildings chosen for closing were losing enrollments and too expensive to maintain. The courts upheld local school officials in both districts.[13]

In some circumstances, geographical characteristics in the district may force school officials to abandon optimum unit size and to determine attendance areas almost totally on the basis of geography. The existence of barriers, natural as well as artificial, cannot be ignored. Small enclaves in large cities or rural environs may be hemmed in by railroads, superhighways, rivers, lakes, industrial concentrations, business districts, or airports. Such barriers may preclude the application of more desirable guidelines for attendance area determination.

If a district is able to transport students or if district policy includes transporting students outside of an established radius of its schools, such conditions affect decisions regarding attendance areas. Of course, transportation decisions and attendance area decisions can hardly be separated in practice. The substantial cost of transportation cannot be ignored in determining school size and the geographic area to be served. Moreover, the national energy shortage made transportation costs a much more visible and important factor. On the other hand, distances and numbers to be transported should not, by themselves, dictate school size and location.

Finally, there is a relationship between school level and attendance area size. Elementary school attendance areas, in large city districts at least, are usually smaller than junior or senior high school attendance areas. In some dense population sections it is not uncommon to find entire elementary school enrollments coming from two or three large apartment buildings. Elementary units, even though they include more grades as a rule than do junior or senior high schools, are most often smaller in total enrollments. Secondary schools must draw their population from a more extensive area because of larger capacities and the decreases in attendance caused by dropouts.

Attendance areas and *neighborhood schools* are terms often thought to be synonymous. The neighborhood school essentially refers to a geographical area rather than an administrative designation. Its significance is primarily psychological; it is cherished by many parents and other citizens and does satisfy many of the criteria for attendance area formation. Recently, the neighborhood school concept has received renewed interest and support from unexpected quarters, namely parents who resist school closings, especially their neighborhood schools.

Political-Social Problems

Segregation is most often thought of in relation to blacks and other racial minorities, but segregation occurs when any minority group is set apart from a majority group, whether the minority is defined in terms of race, national origin, creed, intellectual skill, economic status, personal capacity, physical handicap, or some other differentiating characteristic.

We are speaking of "imposed" segregation in contrast to "self-imposed" segregation. If we extend the application of the segregation concept beyond its racial usage, segregation becomes significant in relation to a wide range of school board and administrative decision making. The point has been made frequently that school boards and school officials make few preparations for problems growing out of segregation and are not able to comprehend some of the unanticipated consequences of their acts. Usually this criticism has been leveled when racial issues have arisen, but the lack of preparation for other types of desegregation should be acknowledged too. The segregation of gifted children or any other group for "special" education purposes—that is, imposed segregation—carries with it important social and psychological consequences for the segregated group as well as for the majority group. Bettelheim has cautioned educators to be aware of what they are doing when they segregate the intellectually capable from the less capable.[14] Segregated youngsters learn of their minority status and observe the fact that they are kept apart from others who may be treated with either more or less respect than they are. They may react with feelings of superiority or inferiority, a sense of exhilaration or humiliation, an attitude of acceptance or rejection.

As important as these other segregation issues are, the most compelling problem is racial segregation. The numbers of pupils involved and the social-political implications of the racial issue outstrip all others. The problem is extraordinarily complex and is interwoven with other contemporary social issues. Unquestionably, many honorable men and women facing the racial question at the local school district level have made very bad decisions with the feeling that they were doing the right thing. Few people possess the comprehensive intelligence necessary to consider all the relevant factors at once. Furthermore, decisions about segregation are made in fluid circumstances: each judgment affects subsequent judgments, and decision making continuously alters the landscape for decision.[15]

The opponents of racial segregation and the proponents of integration, for the most part the same people, object to segregation of any kind—*de jure* or *de facto*. The perpetuation of the concept of the neighborhood school, it is argued, is antithetical to the interests of the individual student when such attendance area determinations ensure segregated schools.

Powder-keg situations arose throughout the United States in the 1960s. Numerous urban school districts were faced with protests against *de facto* segregation and discriminatory employment practice. Emotionalism spread in schools in most large cities and led to attacks on teachers in classrooms, walkouts, boycotts, and outbursts of violence. As Isaacs contended, blacks throughout the world were caught up in a profound and massive change in their concept of their place in the world, and, most important of all, were being compelled to change their concept of themselves.[16] Isaacs argued further that whites too must develop a new self-concept. The system of western white supremacy no longer exists; it has fallen, he maintains, as white supremacy fell in Asia and Africa: "We are all participating in this great intercontinental rearrangement of power and relationships; whites are being compelled to abandon the habits of mastery, and non-whites the habits of subjection."[17]

Numerous court decisions, social science studies, and community confrontations kept the attendance boundaries of schools in the vortex of the racial turmoil in the late 1960s and the 1970s. The courts, as well as political leaders, continued to push into the public limelight the issue of racial school segregation.[18]

Let us now look briefly at some examples.

The Supreme Judicial Court of Massachusetts unanimously upheld a statute requiring local school districts to submit plans to eliminate racial imbalance when it existed in a public school; *racial imbalance* was defined as "a ratio between non-white and other students in public schools which is sharply out of balance with the racial composition of the society in which non-white children study, serve and work."[19] The Supreme Court of Illinois in a 4–3 decision voted to uphold a similar statute that required local boards of education to consider the prevention of segregation in determining attendance units.[20]

The power of state-level educational authorities to attempt to eliminate *de facto* segregation has also been accepted by the courts and has been viewed as a reasonable educational policy and thus a policy that can be enforced on local school districts. The Commissioner of Education in New York, for example, ordered specific actions to further integration in a number of local districts and his authority to make such public policy has been upheld by the state's highest court.[21] The Supreme Court of New Jersey likewise affirmed the power of the Commissioner of Education to require local school systems to accept particular plans to eliminate racial imbalance and thereby provide greater equality of educational opportunities.[22]

Local boards of education also were deemed by the courts to have been within their powers in correcting *de facto* segregation on their own initiative. Michigan's Court of Appeals sustained the Flint Board of Education in its use of racial balance as one of four criteria in establishing high school attendance districts.[23]

A federal district court in Connecticut upheld the initiative of the Norwalk school board in busing black and Puerto Rican youngsters out of their neighborhoods to correct racial imbalance.[24] Interestingly, the plaintiffs in this case were civil rights adherents who reflected in their action the growing dissatisfaction among minority groups with the one-way busing of only black students and other desegregation efforts. This dissatisfaction was, of course, a major cause of the minority group separatist thrust that began to emerge dramatically in the late 1960s.

The 1970s saw no abatement of judicial decisions that potentially have profound implications for how school attendance areas are determined. Cases such as *Swann* v. *Charlotte-Mecklenburg Board of Education,*[25] *Bradley* v. *School Board of the City of Richmond, Virginia,*[26] *Bradley* v. *Milliken,*[27] and *Keyes* v. *School District No. 1, Denver, Colorado,*[28] which are discussed elsewhere in this volume, can dramatically influence districting patterns in school systems. For example, the cases establishing the affirmative duty of school boards to dismantle "dual school systems" (*Swann*), the state's obligation to include predominantly white suburban districts in the desegregation of predominantly black metropolitan school districts to remedy discriminatory practices (*Bradley*), and the school board's responsibility to prove the absence of segregative intent throughout the system if intentional segregation has been proven in a substantial portion of the district (*Keyes*) can alter radically the manner in which school attendance areas are determined throughout the United States.

In the late 1970s the U.S. Supreme Court introduced the concept of "incremental segregative effect" when it remanded a proposed district-wide desegregation plan in Dayton, Ohio, to the U.S. District Court for further hearings.

> The duty of both the District court and of the Court of Appeals in a case such as this, where mandatory segregation by law of the races in the schools has long since ceased, is to first determine whether there was any action in the conduct of the business of the school board which was intended to, and did in fact, discriminate against minority pupils, teachers or staff. *Washington* v. *Davis, supra.* All parties should be free to introduce such additional testimony and other evidence as the District Court may deem appropriate. If such violations are found, the District Court in the first instance, subject to review by the Court of Appeals, must determine how much incremental segregative effect these violations had on the racial distribution of the Dayton school population as presently constituted, when that distribution is compared to what it would have been in the absence of such constitutional violations. The remedy must be designed to redress that difference, and only if there has been a systemwide impact may there be a systemwide remedy. *Keyes, supra.* at 213.[29]

Justice William Rehnquist, who authored the Dayton decision, later issued a stay in the implementation of a system-wide remedy plan in Columbus, Ohio, in part because in his judgment the Sixth Circuit Court of Appeals, in upholding the decisions of the federal district court, failed to consider properly the meaning of incremental segregative effect.[30] The U.S. Supreme Court in a 7–2 decision on July 2, 1979, denied an appeal by the Columbus defendants, lifted the stay, and ordered implementation of a district-wide remedy plan, thus laying to rest the concept of incremental segregative effect.

Various studies and reports also have kept the issue of school desegregation visible and controversial. The findings of the historic Coleman report continue to receive extensive attention as have some modifications in Coleman's earlier perspectives on the implications of school desegregation. Professor Coleman has expressed concerns more recently regarding the circumstances of school attendance that follow court-ordered desegregation. The movement of pupils to achieve racial balance removes the constraints that have been imposed on account of race. Such actions, however, produce additional constraints embedded in hostility and negative feelings toward the different schools to which pupils are assigned.[31]

Sociologist David Armor challenged the purported benefits of school desegregation, claiming that busing had neither improved race relations nor raised the academic achievements, aspirations, or self-esteem of black young people.[32] Armor's analysis, based on studies of busing programs in Boston, Massachusetts; White Plains, New York; Ann Arbor, Michigan; Riverside, California; and the Connecticut cities of Hartford and New Haven, tended to buttress the view that academic achievement is not likely to be raised simply by changing attendance areas to achieve desegregation.

Professor Thomas Pettigrew and his colleagues claimed in rebuttal that Armor's research was distorted and incomplete and that school desegregation was not a static but a dynamic process.[33] Armor, they contended, ignored the critical distinction between desegregation (achieved simply by ending physical segregation) and integration involving the quality of interracial interaction. Armor retorted that Pettigrew and his associates furthered the prevailing ambiguities and confusions in the field of race relations by not observing the essential distinction "among the findings of science, the results of policy, and the dictates of law or morality."[34] This exchange among prominent social scientists indicates how controversial the sociological and psychological data are on the effects of desegregation and illustrate the issue's intense volatility and pervasive political ramifications. It thus seems safe to predict that the manner in which school attendance areas are drawn will remain a very visible and significant public policy issue in part because of the incontrovertible historical record of racial discrimination in America.[35]

In the late 1970s there were some important new contours in the desegregation terrain that were not formed through the actions of the courts. Andrew Greeley presented two basic options for school desegregation in the future.[36] One is to extend our most recent history of " . . . judicial decision and bureaucratic rule, fashioned and enforced by elites."[37] The other option is to build on growing public acceptance of the need for racial integration in schools, and in the society as well, and the public's increasing willingness to do something about it. Greeley favors the second option based on his analysis of longitudinal data on public attitudes toward desegregation amassed by the National Opinion Research Center. The number of persons who favor integration has been growing steadily since the early 1960s. Many support integration and reject busing. Greeley believes that within a climate of acceptance it is possible to achieve substantial integration without imposing involuntary pupil assignments and transfers. His is a rather sharp departure from the diehard view that the nation must stamp out racism, prejudice, and discrimination through " . . . a desperate fight for the soul of America," including the use of the school bus to achieve that objective.[38] This view is represented by David L. Kirp and others.[39]

There is a substantial minority sentiment in favor of voluntary approaches to school desegregation, rather than busing, linked with an emphasis on and genuine concern for quality education.[40] Persons with this view are not separatists; rather they hold tenaciously to the tenets of the Constitution and oppose racism, discrimination, and injustice in all their forms. They believe that the benefits of American society can most effectively be attained by concentrating on quality education accessible to everyone.[41]

Education alternatives within the public schools, such as magnet schools and schools of special emphasis, have support from many parents, including some minority parents. The shifting sentiments of some minority leaders regarding school desegregation and the growing acceptance of integration by whites may affect attendance area decision making. Local districts may be able to implement more approaches to school desegregation that do not require massive busing. Magnet schools may grow in significance though in the past they have often been viewed with skepticism as desegregation remedies. Such organizational alternatives, initiated simultaneously, have been created in many public school districts. Alternative schools usually develop programs of special emphasis such as mathematics, science, or the arts, and they often attract students from throughout the district. Many advocates of desegregation-integration may find fresh philosophical meanings within a public school setting that provides free choice, quality education, subsidized free-choice transportation, and quotas reflecting district-wide enrollment patterns.

The most far-reaching school desegregation development of the early 1980s occurred in St. Louis. After eleven years of litigation (*Craton Liddell et al.* v. *The Board of Education of the City of St. Louis, State of Missouri et al.*), an interdistrict "settlement plan" was negotiated involving twenty-three St. Louis county suburban school districts and the city of St. Louis school district.

The initial St. Louis school desegregation lawsuit was filed in 1972. From that date through 1980, the litigation involved only one district. Beginning in 1980, the lawsuit expanded to include fifteen St. Louis county school districts and the St. Louis city school district. Three years later (July 1983), twenty-three suburban districts and the St. Louis city school district were ordered by the federal district court to become parties to an interdistrict desegregation remedy entitled the Settlement Plan. The plan was essentially a negotiated agreement among the parties.

Key provisions of the Settlement Plan call for: (1) voluntary interdistrict transfers of students, with specified ratios and goals for racial balance of student populations in participating districts; (2) a hiring and transfer program, with specified goals for the racial balance of administration and teaching staff of the participating districts; (3) the state of Missouri to bear a major share of the costs involved; (4) the establishment of specialized educational programs, including: programs focused on the all-black schools remaining within the city of St. Louis; magnet schools; part-time programs; cooperative programs with paired schools and with local cultural, civic, and business institutions; and (5) an administrative body to coordinate and review implementation of the programs.[42] The agreement has extraordinary significance in regard to pupil assignment, attendance areas, school finance, and interdistrict administrative and coordinative authority.

COMMUNITY CONTROL AND DECENTRALIZATION

In the late 1960s the related issues of community control and decentralization surfaced dramatically to further compound the problem of determining school attendance areas in large urban districts. Although a number of small cities did
desegregate their school systems, these success stories had little relevance for major
cities where increasingly a majority, or a large percentage, of the school population
was nonwhite and where the sheer number of students, extensive residential segregation, and geographical distance made desegregation efforts logistically and politically very difficult. Minority group members, as we mentioned earlier, became
increasingly disenchanted with abortive efforts to achieve widespread or meaningful
desegregation. Frustrated by these efforts and spurred by escalating separatist sentiment, growing numbers of urban nonwhites demanded community control and
decentralization of big city school systems. Both of these concepts obviously can
affect in a profound manner the establishment of school attendance areas.

It is important to clarify at the outset of this discussion the differences between
decentralization and community control, two ideas that are often blurred in the
public mind. The two concepts, although related, are not the same. Decentralization
usually means internal administrative reorganization with very few concessions offered to those who wish to change the locus of educational control. Community
control, on the other hand, entails a basic restructuring of governance, with major
alterations in the distribution of power and authority. National attention was focused
on the issue by the bitter and protracted struggle in New York City that pitted the
powerful teachers union against large segments of the black community. This highly
publicized and harsh decentralization struggle illuminates the complexities of the
issue in urban schools throughout the country.

New York's decentralization law, which was passed in 1969 after an acrimonious
legislative debate, divided the city into thirty-one community school boards with a
substantial measure of operating control over elementary, intermediate, and junior
high schools. Each of the nine-member elected boards had the right to select its own
community superintendent and was empowered to hire employees, submit budget
requests to the system's central office, select instructional materials from those
sanctioned by the chancellor, operate community centers and school cafeterias, and
submit proposals for new schools and the repair of existing schools. The central
board, however, maintained control of the high schools and key personnel prerogatives. While the community boards did not have the independence to warrant calling
them examples of true community control, they did tend to decentralize and bring
somewhat closer to the people some facets of a school system that for years had been
criticized for being remote, inefficient, and unresponsive.[43]

The city of Detroit and the state of Michigan, like New York City and New York
State, were enmeshed in controversy over decentralization.[44] In 1969 the Michigan
legislature, upon urging from a Citizens Committee, enacted a school decentralization bill. The Detroit Board of Education shortly thereafter developed attendance
boundaries that would have dramatically increased racial desegregation. A massive

backlash set in and the board's authority to create district lines was nullified. The desegregationist board was subsequently recalled as 60 percent of the voters favored its removal from office. New decentralized attendance areas that perpetuated existing segregated patterns were then established by a gubernatorial commission.

When new elections were held for membership on the reconstituted central board and the eight regional boards, the conservative nonintegrationist elements clearly dominated and blacks gained a majority on only two of the eight regional bodies, although there was a majority of black students in six of the eight local districts or regions. Observers attributed these results not only to obvious black-white polarization but also to the damaging split within Detroit's black community between moderates who still advocated desegregation and separatists. Detroit's public schools were beset with a critical financial crisis as well as the strife generated by its decentralization struggle.

Parents and other citizens of Detroit as well as public officials in Lansing criticized the two-tier system. The system was charged with inefficiency, ineffectiveness, poor pupil achievement, over-bureaucratization, and excessive cost. A special citizens committee named by Governor Milliken in 1977 neither affirmed nor denied the allegations. The committee urged that the decentralization system be continued with some modifications. After nearly fourteen years of trying to make the two-tier system of decentralization work in Detroit, however, it was dropped in 1982. The district returned to a central board of education, a pattern of governance that once again centralized all attendance area decisions.[45]

There are few hard data on the impact of school decentralization or community control on student achievement although adherents of these concepts would argue that the process of participation alone improves the attitudes of both parents and students. Involvement in the institution, in other words, breeds familiarity, mitigates alienation, and thus helps to generate a better learning environment. One of the few systematic studies of local control was undertaken by Professor Marilyn Gittell and several of her associates at the Institute of Community Studies at Queens College.[46] This study funded by the Ford Foundation analyzed the three decentralized demonstration districts in New York City. These three districts—Ocean Hill–Brownsville, IS 201, and Two Bridges—figured prominently in the 1968 teacher strike and were absorbed into larger districts under the 1969 decentralization legislation. The major findings were that the three experimental districts recruited different types of community school board members. Experimental district boards were usually composed of members who were black, public school parents, female, and high school graduates with experience as poverty workers.[47] Conversely, most other members of community school boards were typically college-educated, middle-class professionals who were white, male, and had children in parochial schools. The boards in the three demonstration districts purportedly were more participative, change oriented and reform minded. These districts ostensibly made special efforts to employ minority supervisory personnel. Ocean Hill–Brownsville's attempts to transfer teachers precipitated the showdown with the teachers union that led to the strike and the ultimate demise of all three demonstration districts. According to the Gittell study these three experimental districts were more innovative than other local boards in generating new programs and in creating a more conducive learning environment in which student educational achievement improved despite declines elsewhere in the city. Gittell and her colleagues considered the three demonstration projects to be relatively successful politically and educationally and felt that the "long-run cumulative impact of the districts" may be "more significant than the immediate results."[48]

It seems clear that in conjunction with Office of Economic Opportunity, Head Start, model cities, and other social programs of the 1960s, the decentralization thrust helped to facilitate greater public participation in the governance of their institutions. Important to the decentralization and community control issue also is the emergence of federal- and state-mandated citizen participation, especially at the building level. Most federal legislation enacted in the early 1970s required citizen consulting and advisory mechanisms. The number of federally mandated advisory councils was staggering: there were approximately 14,000 district-wide Title I Parent Advisory Committees and 44,000 building-level committees with a total of nearly 900,000 members; another 150,000 persons served on Head Start, Follow Through, and other district and building-level groups.[49]

The movement to have communities participate more actively in the life of their schools has been reinforced by the recommendations of several prestigious statewide commissions. The Fleishmann Report in New York, for example, recommended the creation of Parent Advisory Councils in every public school "in order to foster and facilitate citizen involvement in the educational process."[50] In Florida, the Governor's Citizens Committee on Education recommended that the legislature "should mandate local school boards to establish School Advisory Councils at each school" that were "broadly representative of the community served by the school, including parents, teachers, administrators and students, where practicable."[51] These councils were also to assist in the preparation of an "annual report of school progress," which would include "school population data, fiscal data, results of assessment programs, attitudes toward the school as well as plans and programs for school improvement." These recommendations, along with site-based management, were mandated by the Florida legislature in 1973.[52]

In the early 1980s decentralization of schools and citizen involvement in educational decision making appeared to slow in the United States just when participation seemed to be generating momentum in other parts of the world.[53] Mandated citizen involvement seemed to run out of steam. Ironically, John Naisbitt identified decentralization of decision making as a major future trend based on the experience of business and industry in Japan, Europe, and the United States.[54]

Naisbitt may be right. In the late 1980s, the attendance area became the level of school organization where two important issues of structure and governance joined. One issue is the right of parents to determine where their children will attend public school as opposed to the local board of education's right to assign pupils to schools. The other issue is formalizing parent involvement in the governance and management of schools within the attendance area where their children are enrolled. The 1986 report of the National Governors Association titled *Time for Results* contained strong arguments for public choice and involvement, as well as specific recommendations to states and local districts regarding measures to be taken to achieve choice and parental involvement in attendance area governance.[55] There is an important difference between *vouchers* and *choice*. Mary Anne Raywid, a strong advocate for public choice, defines a voucher as an arrangement where individuals are in effect handed public funds to purchase schooling outside the public sector. Public choice is the deliberate differentiation of public schools, permitting students and their families to select the type of school each youngster will attend.[56]

Choice and parental involvement in attendance area governance have the potential, advocates argue, for improving education at the attendance area level substantially. Councils at the building level with strong parental membership, such as those mandated in South Carolina or proposed in 1988 for the Chicago Public Schools, promise to shift some aspects of control away from the school board to the attendance area level. Choice introduces competition and adjusts the attitudes of principals and teachers toward their clients. Enrollments are no longer guaranteed, but determined by how parents feel about the quality of the professionals' work.

The 1980s will be known for attempts to reform teaching and teacher education, including more involvement by teachers in decisions at the building level. The Holmes Group and the Carnegie Forum on Education and the Economy produced analyses of what is needed to improve the quality of teaching in U.S. schools. Both argued for more teacher involvement in grassroots educational decision making as well as substantial improvements in the professional workplace. The Carnegie Forum urged that " . . . teachers should be provided with the discretion and autonomy that are the hallmarks of professional work."[57] Furthermore, districts should foster collegial styles of decision making and employ "lead teachers" who are to play central leadership roles at the building level. The Holmes Group noted that "the existing structure of schools, the current working conditions of teachers, and the current division of authority between administrators and teachers are all seriously out of step with the requirements of the new profession."[58] Reports by these two groups have led to substantial debate over the meaning of freshly empowered teachers joining parents in governing the schools of the future. If these trends continue there will be more educational ferment than ever at the attendance area level.

Two initiatives from President Reagan in the early 1980s have significance for educational control and policy at the building level. The first was the establishment in December 1981 of the President's Task Force on Private Sector Initiatives. Its mission was to encourage the private sector to take a more active role in solving community problems, including those in education.[59] The second was the report *A Nation at Risk* issued by the National Commission on Excellence in Education in April of 1983. The commission was created by Secretary of Education T. H. Bell.[60] The formation of these citizen groups had unexpected symbolic meaning for education as well as practical significance at the grassroots. New emphasis was placed on developing partnerships with businesses and industries at the attendance area level, especially in urban school districts. Boston seemed to be leading the way with the Boston Compact, which emphasized the partnership concept along with incentive programs to encourage students to stay in school, excel, and enter college.[61]

THREE CASES

Three school districts attendance area cases have been selected to illustrate a number of attendance area issues facing American school districts. Case A describes a rapidly growing rural district in an agricultural state. Case B depicts how a metropolitan school board approached the increasingly common problem of declining enrollments and surplus teachers and classrooms. Case C involves an extended period of desegregation litigation with consequences for attendance area decision making.

Case A

This example reflects not only typical patterns of rapid school district growth but also the special problems of school districts that have private schools in fiscal difficulty within their attendance areas. The situation in Case A is not yet critical, but it illustrates how a decline in nonpublic school enrollment can influence a public school's attendance area boundaries.

The school district is located in a burgeoning rural area of a "farm-belt" state. The system was organized in 1960 when fifty-one small rural school districts were consolidated. The district, which covers 555 square miles, includes five different counties and has a population of 22,000 citizens. The largest town in this farm area has a population of 3,500.

The student population growth in the district can be attributed largely to the closing of a number of Catholic schools. The district originally had only two small high schools and sixteen elementary units, many of which were one-room rural schools. In 1960 the Catholic school system consisted of twenty-six schools, seven of which were high schools. The Catholic enrollment of 5,100 students far exceeded the 711 students attending the public schools. Of the twenty-six schools in the Catholic system, only thirteen remain open and seven of these have shared-time arrangements with the public schools where students split their day between a parochial and a public school. Almost one-third of the students in the district enroll on a shared-time basis.

The public school district's major problem is finding adequate classroom space despite having built in recent years nine schools or additions, including a junior high school, five elementary schools, and a senior high school. This building program, however, was not adequate to meet the system's escalating space requirements. The district still is compelled to lease thirty-one portable classrooms and three former parochial school buildings.

The uncertainty of the continued existence of the remaining parochial schools hampers efforts to devise long-range space utilization plans or districting patterns that would solve or at least mitigate the district's perpetual space problems. Under existing state law private school youngsters may enroll in public schools in a shared-time arrangement. Although relationships have always been excellent between the public and the parochial school systems, long-range planning has been impossible.

Shared time is accepted as a fact of life in the district and there is little overt community conflict over the issue. Requests by private school students have never been refused and mutual cooperation and respect between the two systems prevail.

Despite these amicable arrangements, neither system is pleased with the existing situation. The private schools, where massive financial problems have caused attrition, look grimly to the future and feel that only massive state or federal assistance can make them viable. The public school district is disturbed by the administrative problems and the mixed student loyalties caused by shared time. Public school officials, however, would be more concerned if all the parochial schools were compelled to close and the public schools forced to accommodate their students.

School attendance area patterns are complicated because of the relatively large number of students enrolled in parochial schools and the prevalence of shared time. In the school district's largest town, for example, a kindergarten center is the only public school. The largest Catholic high school, with an enrollment of more than 800 students is located in this town. The public high school students are bused to the district's single high school. The complexity of the situation is illustrated by what happened to some of this town's fourth-graders after the parochial school found that it did not have either the space or resources to accommodate this group. The public school system leased classroom space in a former parochial school and hired a teacher to accommodate these fourth-graders. Similar mixed attendance arrangements exist in other areas of the school district with youngsters shifting between the parochial and public schools.

A district covering such a huge geographical area, needless to say, has major busing problems. Indeed, the second largest item in its budget (instruction is first) is to maintain and operate its fleet of fifty-four buses. Special attempts are made to enroll the younger children in school attendance areas as close to their homes as possible. Both attendance area and transportation policies are affected by the extensive shared-time arrangements and the classroom leasing practices found in the district.

Case B

The district in Case B is in a large metropolitan area. It is affluent, with expenditures of $8,300 per child. The school system's eight schools enroll only 7,100 students, down from a peak enrollment of 11,178 in 1972. Less than 2 percent of these students are from minority groups. About 10 percent of the school-age population attends nonpublic schools, some church related, some high tuition prep schools. More than 90 percent of those graduating from the public schools enter post-secondary education. The same holds for those in nonpublic schools. There is no prospect for enrollment growth since the villages in the first-ring suburbs are built up tight. This contrasts with neighboring second- and third-ring suburbs, which are growing rapidly, opening new schools as fast as taxpayers approve bond issues for their construction.

School officials are struggling to close Adams, an elementary school. Adams is an old building, a landmark actually, with bad heating and plumbing, a very small playground, and little room for parking. Enrollment has shrunk to 110 pupils. It is the logical school to be closed. But logic does not always prevail. To accommodate the closing several attendance areas would have to be adjusted with Adams children going to three other elementary schools. Some children would be bused. Some parents in the receiving schools fear overcrowding.

Closing Adams would save substantial operating costs, plus return funds to the district when the building was sold. These savings, and a small new capital funding levy, would allow all buildings in the district to be repaired and modernized. Also a series of high-technology projects, requiring capital funds, could be added.

Feelings are running high. Adams parents have packed board meetings objecting to the closing. The PTA leadership is divided. Two members of the seven-member board have asked for a reconsideration of the decision after having supported it earlier. Metropolitan newspapers and television stations ordinarily disinterested in suburban educational politics are covering board and community meetings. There are rumblings about the superintendent and her role in proposing the closing. A small number of influential Adams area parents have threatened recall of the board.

In April, voters turned a capital levy down three to one. A local newspaper voter survey following the election indicated that parents liked the schools the way they were. Adams parents thought another school should have been closed. Some objected to technology. A small number objected to the increase in taxes.

The school board faces new decisions after the election. Should it resubmit the same proposal to voters in November? Should it keep Adams open even though the enrollment will drop below 100? Should the board close Adams risking recall? Should it ask the voters only for funds to repair and modernize buildings, omitting the high-technology item? Lively times lie ahead.

Case C

Like many Northern school districts, this district (along with the state) was found liable for many discrete racially discriminatory acts. Some were recent, others occurred many years ago. The cumulative pattern of isolated discriminatory actions, many of which were attendance area decisions, was sufficient in the judgment of the court to require a system-wide remedy. The Denver (*Keyes*) case was the principal legal precedent.

The school district at the time of the liability findings had 33 percent minority enrollment and 67 percent white enrollment. The court determined that minority enrollments in each school must fall within a range of 15 percent of the 33 percent district-wide minority enrollment. For example, a school that had 90 percent white and 10 percent minority enrollment would not meet the court's criterion of racial representations. A school that was 83 percent white and 17 percent minority would meet the criterion.

More than 160 school buildings were operating prior to the desegregation order. The primary basis for determining attendance areas for elementary purposes was proximity. Junior and senior high school attendance was based essentially on feeder patterns. There were several schools that served the entire district for special education, career education, adult education, or alternative schools purposes. A voluntary desegregation plan in operation was aimed at reducing racial isolation but only about 8 percent (mostly white) of the enrollment was involved. A white school board majority strongly defended the neighborhood school attendance area concepts and resisted the imposition of a system-wide remedy.

The federal district court placed with local school officials the responsibility for preparing a system-wide remedy. Eventually a remedy plan was developed that was satisfactory to the court. That plan included contiguous and noncontiguous pairings and clusterings as well as several school closings. Each attendance area in the school district was affected. More than 42,000 students were to be transported for desegregation purposes. More than 200 new buses were purchased; additional storage and maintenance facilities were acquired, and new drivers were employed and trained.

The remedy plan also required detailed preparation for implementation. School officials (local and state) had one year to make pupil reassignments, acquire transportation, alter programs, and prepare students, parents, personnel, and the community. The local board of education met every deadline and fulfilled each requirement of the courts. At the same time the school board availed itself of every available avenue of appeal, even the U.S. Supreme Court.

The U.S. Supreme Court granted a stay of implementation less than thirty days prior to implementation. The school board ordered an immediate dismantling of the remedy plan and reestablished all previous attendance areas, reassigned pupils to their former schools, and ended all other preparations.

Parents and other citizens registered their feelings in many ways during the litigation that led to the stay. Opposition to desegregation was reflected in the defeat of tax-rate increases, for example. Conservative, antibusing persons were returned to the school board. Pro-neighborhood schools and antibusing groups sprang up. Groups formed to fight school closings. Celebrations were held when the announcement of the stay of implementation came. At the same time neutral or supportive sentiments were in evidence. New as well as established community organizations provided leadership in preparing for a responsible, law-abiding implementation. The mayor, business leaders, and the media publicly endorsed peaceful implementation although many privately resented the need to bus thousands of students.

School administrators encountered a spate of political, logistical, technical, planning, financial, and other problems. Among the most severe political problems were those engendered by school closings. Groups of parents descended en masse upon board meetings and administrators' offices. *Ad hoc* "save-our-school" committees held public meetings, letter-writing campaigns, and press conferences. The resentment surrounding school closings was based only partially on school desegregation. Most parents objected to the closing of "their schools" but not others. The school board majority tried unsuccessfully to pass the responsibility for school closings to the federal district court. When the stay of implementation was granted, all closed schools were reopened with pupils, principals, and staff assigned, even though less than a month remained before schools were to open in the fall. Decisions to reopen the schools and to reestablish attendance areas were made in spite of declining enrollments and severe financial pressures.

The future of this school system and its attendance areas rested with the courts. The Supreme Court, after one year, lifted the stay of implementation and remanded the case back to the federal district court. The federal district court immediately ordered implementation of a system-wide desegregation remedy plan.

When schools opened in the autumn of 1979, parents and students found that a new set of attendance areas were in place, reflecting not only the requirement of a system-wide desegregation effort but a number of school closings as well.

The school system, especially its school administrators, encountered many new problems of school-community relations as the system-wide remedy was implemented. Old patterns of parent involvement had to be modified and new ones developed. Daily schedules for employees were altered. New and different faces filled classrooms, many with educational needs unlike those of prior students. Disequilibrium was present for a while. In 1983, after four years of desegregation, every graduating senior had experienced four years of desegregated education. Remarkable progress had been made in the district despite a complete realignment and redrafting of school attendance areas.

Two years later the federal district court declared the school district unitary and withdrew its supervision, returning full responsibility to the school board for maintaining a desegregated system. There were immediate pressures on the board to drop its busing plan and return to pre-desegregation attendance areas. In 1988, under the leadership of a new superintendent, all attendance areas were reviewed in an attempt to reduce the number of children bused for desegregation purposes and adjust some attendance boundaries.

Significance of Cases

In Case A school officials in a rapidly growing rural area face attendance area problems that are difficult to handle because of uncertainty about the continuation of nonpublic schools that enroll a very substantial proportion of the district's school-age population. External factors over which public school officials have virtually no control frustrate efforts to plan rationally. Political realities dictate the widespread continuation of the administratively cumbersome, if not chaotic, shared-time arrangements. The district's entire structure and operations as well as the determination of its school attendance areas are inextricably linked to the rather tenuous financial condition of the parochial school system.

In Case B a board of education faces an uncertain future. Board members and their superintendents are public stewards charged with the prudent use of district funds. Closing a school seems the prudent thing to do even in a wealthy suburb. The case is devoid of the racial or ethnic overtones so often factors in other attendance area decisions. And there are apparently high levels of satisfaction with the schools. Students are succeeding at least in terms of entrance to college. What should this board do? Are there options that may have been overlooked? Could the board propose renting Adams to a nearby rapidly growing district, for example? There is less drama in this district's case, but nevertheless it is similar to a large number of districts with school closing problems.

In Case C a school district successfully turned to judicial appeal. The U.S. Supreme Court, however, upheld the findings of both the district and the appellate courts, returning the responsibility for overseeing implementation of the district-wide remedy plan to the court of original jurisdiction. Every attendance area in the district was changed as a consequence. This case illustrates the prominence of school attendance area decisions in the history of this district as well as the power of the courts in their regard.

These cases highlight a point made at the beginning of this chapter. Attendance area decisions were once rather straightforward administrative decisions. Now, because of widespread social, political, economic, and demographic changes in our society, attendance area decisions are political decisions and demand resolution at the several policy levels.

SUMMARY AND FUTURE PROSPECTS

Attendance area boundaries, as indicated, are currently much less stable and enduring than school district boundaries. Consequently, changes in attendance boundaries are likely to lay bare the issues of control more often than boundary changes at district levels.

There are several areas of existing or prospective change that have implications for attendance areas.

1. Education returned to the public agenda in the 1980s, stimulated initially by the work of the National Commission on Excellence in Education and later by dozens of other local, state, and national public-sector reports urging reform. In the mid-1980s private-sector reports and individual statements by influential business leaders strengthened a growing national concern about education. That concern was so severe that the platforms of both political parties in the 1988 presidential election contained strong language about the importance of education to the nation's general well-being. Strong sentiments emerged favoring choice and parental involvement in governance at the school level. Education is likely to remain high on the national agenda in the 1990s and as a part of the continuing desire for quality, the companion issues of choice and governance will attract increasing attention.

2. School desegregation, although an exceedingly important public problem, will likely enter into a new phase. This phase will reflect the large demographic shifts in the U.S. population and a strengthened commitment to quality education rather than racial balance. The growth of the Spanish population particularly could shift the concern about equality of educational opportunity away from essentially a black-white focus to a multicultural, multi-ethnic focus.[62] Simultaneously, several influential black leaders are emphasizing quality education and non-busing alternatives to achieving school desegregation, especially in large school districts. The 1983 Settlement Plan for St. Louis and St. Louis county suburban districts may become a precedent for a small number of other metropolitan areas.

Should this occur there will be new implications for interdistrict coordination and control. With fewer intradistrict remedy plans in the offing, desegregation may have less meaning for attendance area decisions in the future.

3. Building-level advisory councils and school site management promises to continue to stimulate new debates regarding local control. The traditional tensions of local control center on the power and authority of local school boards with respect to state and federal governments. Many who have been apprehensive about the erosion of authority and responsibility from above may become concerned about erosion from below. As school site management and citizen participation become effective, new strength will be added to a district's governance and management system. School officials at the district level need not perceive these developments as a threat. One distinct area for development is collective bargaining vis-à-vis the rights and obligations of attendance area representatives to participate. School site management and citizen participation at the building level are concepts with wide application. They are as germane in rural settings as they are in metropolitan areas.

4. The administrative and policy decentralization movement may be stabilizing. Feelings about the effectiveness of school district decentralizations are mixed, ranging from advocacy to skepticism to rejection. The meaning of decentralization for attendance area decision making is still not clear. Energy has been invested in specifying the policymaking prerogatives of central and subdistrict offices. Not enough attention has been given to such clarification at the building level. Adoption of site management philosophy and practice will force such clarification and produce improved understanding of the dimension of control that should reside at each level.

5. The expansion of magnet schools, schools of emphasis, and other educational alternatives will likely continue. These require school officials to reevaluate traditional attendance areas. Alternative schools can introduce a healthy competitiveness and stimulate education improvements in conventional attendance areas, but if there are only a few alternative schools and they are highly specialized, negative consequences can result. Often the best students opt for the alternative programs, draining local schools of high-ability young people.

6. Changes in the teaching profession may affect the control of schools, especially at the building level. The spate of 1980s reforms includes several aimed at strengthening the preparation of teachers as well as altering teaching conditions. *Empowerment of teachers* is a term used in ever-widening circles, implying that teachers should have more influence in curriculum decisions, more control over how buildings are run, and generally more power to control their own professional lives. This move to empower teachers coincides with the proposals to extend parental involvement in the governance of individual schools and promises to raise new issues of performance appraisal and accountability.

7. Controversies surrounding school closings, which often occur because of attendance area changes, create severe political problems for local school officials. So do school openings. In those districts where enrollments are growing, sites for new schools have to be located, often becoming decisions of significance for property owners, city planners, and investors as well as parents. Given the patterns of enrollment change, decline in some districts and growth in others, large numbers of attendance area decisions lie ahead. Local school officials will need to be as skillful as possible in making these decisions, thus leading to less controversy and bitterness within local communities.

NOTES

[1]*Digest of Education Statistics 1985–86* (Washington, DC: Office of Educational Research and Improvement, 1986), 11.

[2]*The Condition of Education, 1983 Edition, A Statistical Report* (Washington, DC: National Center for Education Statistics, 1983), 27.

[3]Newton Edwards, *The Courts and the Public Schools* (Chicago: University of Chicago Press, 1955), 540.

[4]For a discussion of the authority of school boards to assign pupils see E. Edmund Reutter, Jr. and Robert R. Hamilton, *The Law of Public Education* (Mineola, NY: Foundation Press, 1970), 117–120. A more recent statement on the establishment of attendance areas and assignment of pupils can be found in Leroy J. Peterson, Richard A. Rossmiller, and Martin W. Volz, *The Law and Public School Operation,* (New York: Harper & Row, 1978), 289–290.

[5]Ibid., 45.

[6]Thomas Sowell, "Ethnicity in a Changing America," *Daedalus* (Winter 1978): 215–237.

[7]Derrick Bell, "Learning from Our Losses: Is School Desegregation Still Feasible in the 1980s?" *Phi Delta Kappan* 64 (April 1983): 575.

[8]For a discussion of changes in the desegregation situation that occurred in the Nixon administration and the impact of the courts on educational policy, see Donna E. Shalala and James A. Kelly, "Politics, the Courts, and Educational Policy," *The Teachers College Record* 75 (December 1973): 225–226.

[9]Arthur S. Miller, "The Politics of the American Judiciary," *The Political Quarterly* 49, (April–June 1978): 200–207.

[10]*"There is no Liberty. . . " A Report on Congressional Efforts to Curb the Federal Courts and to Undermine the Brown Decision* (Washington, DC: Citizens Commission on Civil Rights, 1982).

[11]*Digest of Education Statistics 1985–86,* 32.

[12]Ibid.

[13]For summaries of some school districts' responses to school closings see *Surplus School Space—The Problem and the Possibilities* (Columbus OH: Council of Educational Facility Planners, International, 1978).

[14]Bruno Bettelheim, "Segregation: New Style," *The School Review* 66 (Autumn 1958): 251–272.

[15]For a thorough review of the policy dimensions of school desegregation see Thomas F. Pettigrew, "Racial Change and Social Policy," *Annals* 441 (January 1979): 114–131.

[16]Harold R. Isaacs, "The Changing Identity of the Negro American" in *The Urban Condition,* ed. Leonard J. Duhl (New York: Basic, 1963), 276–77.

[17]Ibid.

[18]For an analysis of these cases see Karl E. Taeuber, "Housing, Schools, and Incremental Segregative Effects," *Annals* 441 (January 1979): 157–67.

[19]*School Committee of Boston* v. *Board of Education,* 352 Mass 693, 227 NE (2d) 729 (1967).

[20]*Tometz* v. *Board of Education* 39 Ill (2d) 593, 237 NE (2d) 498 (1968).

[21]*Vetere* v. *Allen,* 15 NY (2d) 259, 206 NE (2d) 174 (1965).

[22]*Booker* v. *Board of Education,* 45 N.J. 161, 212 A(2d) 1 (1965).

[23]*Mason* v. *Flint Board of Education,* 6 Mich. App 364, 149 NW (2d) 239 (1967).

[24]*Norwalk CORE* v. *Norwalk Board of Education,* 298 F Supp 213 (D Conn 1969).

[25]*Swann* v. *Charlotte-Mecklenburg Board of Education,* 402 U.S. 1, 15 (1971).

[26]*Bradley* v. *School Board of City of Richmond, Virginia,* 462 F. 2d, 1058, 1060 (1972).

[27]*Bradley* v. *Milliken,* 345 F. Supp. 914 (1972).

[28]*Keyes* v. *School District No. 1, Denver, Colorado* 413 U.S. 189 (1973).

[29]*Dayton* v. *Brinkman,* 433 U.S. 406 (1977).

[30]*Columbus* v. *Penick,* A-134 U.S. (1978).

[31]James S. Coleman, "Choice in American Education," in *Parents, Teachers, and Children* (San Francisco: Institute for Contemporary Studies, 1977), 1–12.

[32]David J. Armor, "The Evidence on Busing," *The Public Interest* 28 (Summer 1972): 90–126.

[33]Thomas F. Pettigrew et al., "Busing: A Review of the Evidence," *The Public Interest* 30 (Winter 1973): 88–118.

[34]David J. Armor, "The Double Double Standard: A Reply," *The Public Interest* 30 (Winter 1973): 119. For an excellent anthology of differing views on the interrelated issues of school desegregation and busing see Nicolaus Mills, ed., *The Great School Bus Controversy* (New York: Teachers College Press, 1973).

[35]John Hope Franklin, *Racial Equality in America* (Chicago: University of Chicago Press, 1976).

[36]Andrew M. Greeley, "Freedom of Choice: Our Commitment to Integration" in *Parents, Teachers, and Children: Prospects for Choice in American Education* (San Francisco: Institute for Contemporary Studies, 1977), 183–205.

[37]Ibid., 185.

[38]Ibid.

[39]David L. Kirp, "School Desegregation and the Limits of Legalism," *The Public Interest* 47 (Spring 1977): 101–28.

[40]Ronald R. Edmonds, "Desegregation and Equity: Community Perspectives," *Harvard Graduate School of Education Bulletin* (Winter 1974–75). See also Ray C. Rist, "Race and Schooling: Key Policy Issues," *Educational Forum* 50 (May 1976): 522.

[41]Derrick Bell, "Non-Separation Based Educational Inequalities and the *Brown* Decision." Paper prepared for the San Francisco Public Schools Commission, May 1976, 15, 572–75. See also Mary Anne Raywid, "Schools of Choice: Their Current Nature and Prospects," *Phi Delta Kappan* (June 1983): 684–88.

[42]*Craton Liddell et al., v. The Board of Education of the City of St. Louis,* No. 72-100C(3) (E.D. Mo. Jul. 5, 1983).

[43]For observations on decentralization and the status of education in New York City see E. Babette Edwards, "Why a Harlem Parents Union?" in *Parents, Teachers, & Children,* 59–65.

[44]William R. Grant, "Community Control vs. Integration: The Case of Detroit," *The Public Interest* 24 (Summer 1971): 62–79.

[45]See "Schools," in *Michigan Legislative Bulletin* 79–1003 (1982): 204.

[46]Marilyn Gittell and Associates, *Demonstration for Social Change: An Experiment in Local Control* (New York: Institute for Community Studies, Queens College, 1971).

[47]Ibid., 15.

[48]Ibid., 137.

[49]A comprehensive overview of the status of mandated citizen participation can be found in Luvern L. Cunningham et al., *Improving Education in Florida: A Reassessment* (Tallahassee, FL: Select Joint Committee on Public Schools, 1978), 215–95. For further help in understanding the development of local building councils see Jim Stanton, Bobbi Whittaker, and Ross Zerchykov, *Resource Guide and Bibliography on School Councils* (Boston: Institute for Responsive Education, 1978).

[50]*The Fleishmann Report on the Quality, Cost, and Financing of Elementary and Secondary Education in New York State,* vol. 4. (New York: Viking Press, 1973), 7.

[51]*Improving Education in Florida: A Report by the Governor's Citizens Committee on Education* (Tallahassee, FL: The Governor's Citizens Committee on Education, 1973), 11.

[52]Ibid.

[53]George Baron, ed. *The Politics of School Government* (Oxford, England: Pergamon, 1981): ch. 1, 10.

[54]John Naisbitt, *Megatrends* (New York: Warren, 1982), ch. 5.

[55]*Time for Results* (Washington, DC: National Governors Association, 1986), 171.

[56]Mary Anne Raywid, "Public Choice Yes; Vouchers No!" *Phi Delta Kappan* 68 (June 1987): 762–69.

[57]*A Nation Prepared: Teachers for the 21st Century* (New York: Carnegie Forum on Education and the Economy, 1986), 56.

[58]*Tomorrow's Teachers* (East Lansing, MI: The Holmes Group, Inc., 1986), 67.

[59]The President's Task Force on Private Sector Initiatives, *Building Partnerships* (Washington, DC: The Task Force, 1982).

[60]National Commission on Excellence in Education, *A Nation at Risk* (Washington, DC: U.S. Department of Education, 1983).

[61]See Jeannie Oakes, *Improving Inner-City Schools: Current Directions in Urban District Reform* (Washington, DC: The Rand Corporation, October 1987), 22–25.

[62]Gary Orfield. *Change and Desegregation in Large School Districts* (Alexandria, VA: National School Boards Association, 1988).

8
The Courts

The role of the federal and state courts in shaping school policies is significant. Virtually every school district relies on legal counsel for assistance of some kind, and an increasing number of districts employ one or more attorneys on a full-time basis. It is not uncommon for school districts to be sued and administrators often are named personally as defendants. One administrator remarked recently that he had lost track of the number of lawsuits in which he was named as a defendant. Litigation is both time-consuming and expensive in that attorney's fees are sometimes more than $200 per hour. Everywhere legal issues have become a prominent topic of discussion at meetings of administrators. The courts have had long-standing influence on schools and this influence is noticeable in a number of areas.

This chapter is not intended to be a primer on school law nor a substitute for detailed material or counsel in any particular area. Instead, it provides an overview of the American court structure and its dynamics as they relate to education and covers the structure of the American judicial system, the premises and the processes of judicial policymaking, some examples of judicial influence, and the outlook for the future.

STRUCTURE OF THE AMERICAN JUDICIAL SYSTEM

A fundamental characteristic of the American judicial system is that it is actually composed of overlapping systems. Each of the states has its own court system, as does the federal government. Some questions are a matter of state jurisdiction, others are initiated in the federal system, and still others can be initiated in state courts and reviewed by the U.S. Supreme Court. Moreover, both the state and federal systems have tiered court structures that allow for the appeal of judicial decisions from one level to another.

Some Early History

The origins of the American legal system are found in the British common law.[1] American colonists were expected to be guided by the common law, and the colonies followed the English precedent of making the legislature (in England, the House of Lords) the highest court. However, geographical separation and colonial initiative combined to produce a number of deviations from the English system. Because of a shortage of trained lawyers and judges in the colonies, it was not uncommon for citizens rather than lawyers to be appointed to the bench. The colonists, however, favored this arrangement; they preferred that their neighbors, rather than appointees of the royal crown, serve as judges. In fact, among the criticisms of George III in the Declaration of Independence was that "he has made judges dependent on his will alone, for the tenure of their offices and the amount and payment of their salaries." Thus it was not surprising that postrevolutionary judicial reforms included the legislative election of judges and the expansion of the role of juries to decide questions of law as well as fact.

The colonists had reservations about strong courts and these were manifested in the debates of the Constitutional Convention. While the delegates agreed there was a need for a single national, or supreme court, many lodged strong reservations about establishing a federal court system. They feared that such a system would intrude upon the jurisdictions of the respective state courts. Some argued that state courts could serve as lower tribunals to the supreme court. Unable to resolve the issue, the convention deferred it by providing for "one Supreme Court, and . . . such inferior Courts as the Congress may from time to time ordain and establish."[2]

The matter of the federal court structure was considered by the first Congress. The Judiciary Act of 1789 established the Supreme Court with a chief justice and six associates. It also established three circuit courts and thirteen district courts at the bottom of the federal judicial hierarchy. Furthermore, this act established the procedure through which the federal courts could review and, if appropriate, declare void state laws and court decisions that conflicted with federal powers established by the Constitution.[3]

The Federal Court System

Congressional actions since the Judiciary Act of 1789 have expanded the federal court system substantially. The Supreme Court now includes a chief justice and eight associates. There are also twelve circuit courts of appeals and ninety-four district courts. Each state has at least one federal district court and New York and Texas each have four. Most of the district courts and all of the appeals courts have several judges.

Most scholarly work has focused on the Supreme Court because it is at this level that decisions have their most general application. However, most federal cases are actually heard and decided at lower levels in the system. The so-called inferior courts are the courts of first jurisdiction for all but a very few federal cases. Until the Judiciary Act of 1875, however, these courts served little national purpose. This legislation extended the jurisdiction of these courts to most federal questions and thereby helped these courts become "powerful instruments for the centralizing and unifying tendencies of a national law."[4] These courts are able to promote compliance with Supreme Court doctrines.[5] They also serve a shaping and testing function where new legal positions can be formulated for review by the Supreme Court.

Cases brought under a federal question are first heard in a U.S. District Court. The most frequent federal questions concerning education are alleged violations of First or Fourteenth Amendment rights. More will be said about this later in this chapter. Most cases that enter the district court are resolved at that level although either party has the right of appeal to the court of appeals. In 1985, nearly 279,000 civil cases were filed in U.S. District Courts. This represented an increase of 7 percent over the number of cases filed in the preceding year. Most of these did not go to trial; however, in the same year, approximately 34,000 cases were forwarded to one of the Courts of Appeals, and approximately 5,200 cases were on the docket of the Supreme Court.[6] The Court disposes of most of these without a hearing and issues approximately 150 decisions a year. The caseload of the Supreme Court has increased so dramatically in recent years that former Chief Justice Burger called for creation of a new federal court to reduce the high court's workload.[7]

The Supreme Court has original jurisdiction in disputes between the states and in a few other technical matters. Most of its work involves reviewing cases that come to it on appeal. Such cases may come from lower federal courts or from the state supreme courts in the case of state laws that are alleged to be unconstitutional. The Supreme Court has virtually complete discretion to decide which cases it will and will not hear. More than 90 percent of the cases heard by the Court come before it through the process of certiorari. According to this procedure, persons wishing to appeal a case to the Supreme Court submit a petition asking the Court to order the lower court to forward its decision for review. At least four justices must agree to such an order before it is issued. Certain other cases can be appealed to the Court apart from the certiorari procedure, but these too can be declined if the Court holds that they do not present, "a substantial federal question." The power of the Supreme Court to choose which cases it will hear means that it can wait to let a body of law on a subject develop in the lower courts, providing a broad or closely reasoned context in which to render a decision. This power also allows the court to time its decisions according to public interests.

Judicial decision making and public interests also intersect in the selection and appointment of judges. Federal judges are appointed to lifetime terms, and such an appointment is generally considered a high honor. While it is always difficult to assess criteria for such appointments, it can be safely stated that factors other than excellence in jurisprudence are often considered. The actual procedure for the appointment of federal judges is for the president to make them subject to the "advice and consent" of two-thirds of the Senate. In recent years at least, the president has been obliged, as a senatorial courtesy, to first clear proposed appointees with the senators of their home state. As the procedure suggests, there is opportunity for the partisan or personal ideological perspectives of the president and the Senate to have some effect. History shows that this has sometimes been the case. In 1801, when the Federalists were about to surrender the presidency to the Republicans, President Adams appointed several Federalists to newly created judgeships. Adams was the last Federalist president, but his newly appointed chief justice (John Marshall) presided over the Supreme Court for more than thirty years.[8]

Lifetime appointments to the federal judiciary have created ideological tensions between the judicial branch on the one hand and Congress and the president on the other. It has not been uncommon in our history for the Court to reflect a conservative bias at a time when the rest of the government showed more liberal tendencies and vice versa. Thus, as newly elected officials come into office, they may find the Court that awaits them an impediment to their programs. The most dramatic example occurred during the New Deal period of the 1930s when a holdover Court declared unconstitutional some of the emergency legislation promulgated to fight the Depression. President Roosevelt responded by proposing a judicial reform bill that would have allowed the appointment of additional justices to the Supreme Court. This so-called court-packing bill, which was not enacted, aroused great controversy and cost Roosevelt some public prestige. At about the same time, however, one judge retired, enabling Roosevelt to appoint the liberal Hugo Black, and another justice began to cast more liberal votes. Thus the Court began to swing to the liberal posture that characterized it into the 1970s. Most observers believe the Court has become more conservative as a result of appointments during the Nixon and Reagan administrations. The composition of the Court is likely to be determined for many years to come by appointments made in the middle and late 1980s.

The Supreme Court in the past fifty years has had an important impact on American social and political life. First the "new" Roosevelt court upheld efforts to extend the government's role in economic life, thereby allowing for the introduction of new regulations on private enterprise. Subsequently the Court under the leadership of Earl Warren issued a series of landmark decisions in the areas of racial equality, electoral equality, and criminal procedure. These decisions and the response to them by the president, the Congress, and the public have made it clear that the courts are an integral part of the American political process.[9]

As Richard Nixon campaigned for the presidency in 1968 he was critical of the Supreme Court for being unfamiliar with criminal law and procedure and for having " 'gone too far' in imputing its own 'social and economic views' to the rule of decision."[10] He immediately had an opportunity to appoint a new chief justice and selected Warren Burger, who was confirmed to this post. Given the opportunity to make another appointment in 1969, the president declared his intention to appoint a southerner, thereby perhaps appealing to those concerned that the courts had been too aggressive in school desegregation. His efforts to appoint first Clement Haynsworth and then Harold Carswell to this post provoked furious controversy in the Senate, which failed to confirm either candidate. Senate liberals, smarting some from the forced resignation of Justice Fortas, mounted a strong campaign against both men. Nixon subsequently appointed Lewis Powell, James Blackmun, and William Rehnquist to the Court. Neither President Ford nor President Carter had the opportunity to appoint a Supreme Court Justice, and President Reagan selected Sandra Day O'Connor to be the first woman on the court.

When Burger retired, Reagan named Rehnquist as Chief Justice and added Antonin Scalia to the Court. Powell's retirement in 1987 was widely regarded as pivotal because Powell had been the Court's most ideologically centrist member. A former school board member from Richmond, Virginia, Powell was conservative on criminal issues but liberal regarding most social and civil rights matters. His had been the deciding vote in several cases.[11] Thus, by nominating another conservative, Reagan could assure a conservative majority on the Court. His nomination of Judge Robert Bork, an experienced and widely published jurist who had expressed conservative views on privacy, family, and civil rights issues, was vigorously opposed by liberals in general and civil rights and women's groups in particular. Bork's confirmation hearing engendered bitter debate in the Senate. Although a number of Republicans joined with Democrats in rejecting the Bork nomination, the administration charged that Bork was a victim of partisan politics. Following one more abortive attempt to nominate a staunch conservative, the president won Senate approval for the nomination of Anthony Kennedy, who was recognized for his strong career as a jurist and was believed to be relatively moderate in his views. The election of George Bush to the presidency probably will provide the Republicans with further opportunity to alter the ideological balance on the Court.

The importance of partisanship in federal judicial appointments has been clearly documented. Schmandt reports that more than 90 percent of all appointees to the federal courts were members of the president's own party.[12] For example, Eisenhower appointed 190 Republicans and 13 Democrats and Kennedy appointed 141 Democrats and 13 Republicans. More recently, Nixon appointed 198 Republicans and 15 Democrats, and Carter appointed 182 Democrats, 9 Republicans, and 9 independents.

While it is clear that politics and ideological perspectives can influence the nature of appointments to the Court, it is sometimes difficult to predict how a judge will behave once appointed. For example, Hugo Black was once a member of the Ku Klux Klan and Earl Warren supported wartime detention camps for Japanese Americans, yet both became strong advocates for the rights of racial minorities.[13]

The State Court Systems

There are great differences among the states in the way they have organized their court systems.[14] However, they generally follow the hierarchical pattern of the federal system. All states have a court of final jurisdiction that serves as the court of final appeal for state matters. Twenty-three states have intermediate courts of appeals. All states have trial courts of general jurisdiction where cases are initially heard. In addition, all states have one or more trial courts with special jurisdiction, such as probate courts, juvenile courts, and courts of small claims.

Consider the state of Illinois. Excluding the special courts, the lowest or general trial level court in Illinois is the circuit court. There are twenty-one circuit court districts in Illinois, and they have general and original jurisdiction over criminal and civil cases, including those pertaining to schools. At the second level there are five appellate courts. These courts have no original jurisdiction, but they do hear appeals on the basis of the evidence presented in the lower courts. At the apex of the judicial system is the state supreme court. Ordinarily this body, too, acts in an appellate and not in an original capacity. Crucial questions pertaining to schools, particularly those having to do with the constitutionality of certain legislative actions, often progress through all three levels of the state court system.

The state courts are very concerned with interpreting legislative will or intent. The courts recognize the authority of the legislature, and they are loath to substitute their own judgment for legislative intent. There are cases, however, in which the statutes are contradictory or ambiguous and, when required to do so, the courts will rule in such cases. Then, too, when litigation involves disputes between two or more parties, the courts are required to render judgment. The courts also, when called upon, will rule on the constitutionality of statutory provisions.

Court procedures reveal a relationship between the lower and the higher courts. For instance, the court of original jurisdiction ordinarily has more to do with the credibility of witnesses since in lower courts witnesses are examined firsthand. Courts tend to examine only the issues before them, though they may comment *obiter dictum* on others. If the issue is one of procedure, the substantive nature of the problem will not be considered. Higher courts will not reverse decisions of lower courts unless it is clear that there has been an abuse of discretion. A state court of one state may take cognizance of decisions rendered by the higher courts of other states, but it is not bound to follow them. On the other hand, state courts are subservient to decisions of the United States Supreme Court. This was illustrated in a decision of the Supreme Court of Arkansas as indicated in the following language:

> While we deeply deplore the fact that the Supreme Court of the United States did not follow the clear legal precedents announced in *Plessy v. Ferguson,* 163 U.S. 537, 16 S. Ct. 1138, 41 L. Ed. 256, in *Gong Lum v. Rice,* 275 U.S. 78, 48 St. Ct. 91, 72 L. Ed. 172, and in numerous other decisions over a period of fifty years, instead of a long list of nonlegal authorities, yet this court will be subservient to the decision it did reach.[15]

When considering educational issues, the courts have consistently declared board of education members to be state and not local officers. The court of appeals in Kentucky put it this way:

> We have said that the members of a county board of education and its officers are "state officers," although they are elected locally and function in a local capacity, because education is a state function.[16]

Moreover, the courts traditionally have been reluctant to substitute their judgment for that of the board of education. This principle has been enunciated many times and the language from a United States Court of Appeals case as shown below is but an example:

The school board, in the operation of the public schools, acts in much the same manner as an administrative agency exercising its accumulated technical expertise in formulating policy after balancing all legitimate conflicting interests. If that policy is one conceived without bias and administered uniformly to all who fall within its jurisdiction, the courts should be extremely wary of imposing their own judgment on those who have the technical knowledge and operating responsibility for the school system.[17]

On the other hand, there are indications that the courts may now take a harder look at the judgment of school officials and overrule them, particularly as school rules affect individual rights. For example, the Supreme Court held that local school officials legally could not prevent students from wearing black armbands in peaceful protest of U.S. involvement in Vietnam. Part of the opinion delivered by Fortas stated:

The record does not demonstrate any facts which might reasonably have led school officials to forecast substantial disruption of or material interference with school activities, and no disturbances or disorders on the school premises in fact occurred . . . They [the students] neither interrupted school activities nor sought to intrude in the school affairs or the lives of others. They caused discussion outside of the classrooms, but no interference with work and no disorder. In the circumstances, our Constitution does not permit officials of the state to deny their form of expression.[18]

The jurisdiction of state courts extends to any matter except federal statutes and those matters outside their territorial prerogatives brought before them at the trial court level. In the case of issues involving a federal constitutional question, plaintiffs have a choice of initiating their action in state or federal courts. If brought before a federal court, cases involving the constitutionality of state statutes are heard by a three-judge federal district panel with direct appeal to the Supreme Court. Cases involving federal statutes are filed in federal courts. Recent years have seen a growing tendency on the part of individuals and agencies to take matters of dispute to court. As a consequence, court dockets have become very crowded and trials often suffer long delays in the state as well as in federal courts.

The rulings of state supreme courts establish guidelines for their respective states but are not controlling for other states. Similarly the decisions of lower state courts are binding upon the particular litigants involved but do not constitute precedents that necessarily will be adhered to by other courts in the state. Thus at the trial court level it is not uncommon to see a series of cases about the same kind of issue (e.g., locker searches) decided in different ways.

State judges are selected in a variety of ways and serve terms of varying lengths. Some are appointed by the governor, some elected by the state legislature, some elected on a partisan ballot, some elected on a nonpartisan ballot, and some selected through a combination of these means.[19] Virtually all of these procedures lead to the appointment of persons who have local ties to the areas they serve. Thus it is not unusual for a judge to reflect local values and priorities on the bench. Local preferences may influence the judge's interpretation of statutory enactments and higher court rulings. For example, Schmandt has noted:

Many examples of this situation [local court decisions influenced by local values] exist in the handling of civil rights cases by the local judiciary in those Southern cities that have achieved national notoriety in recent years by their open defiance of integration measures. In many situations, the courts have acted in a distinctly political fashion, showing acute sensitivity and even servility to local feelings and pressures. As a result of this type of differential treatment by the local judiciary, acts considered constitutionally protected in one community are regarded as illegal and punishable in another.[20]

In a sense, the courts stand as a last resort in educational government as they do in general government. They determine, when necessary, the constitutionality of legislative action. They interpret the meaning of statutes, being careful to ascertain legislative intent. The structure of the court system permits appeal for judicial review to the higher courts from the lower court where mercy or human frailty may have crowded out justice. While the courts are subject to human foibles, the judges who preside over them do, for the most part, reflect not only the word but the spirit of the law.

PREMISES AND PROCESSES OF JUDICIAL POLICYMAKING

A policy is an authoritative decision that guides other decisions. For example, a school district policy that states that all teachers in the district must hold a degree from an accredited college or university offers some guidance to those who recruit teachers. Similarly, a federal policy of making aid available to school districts in federally impacted areas provides guidance to school officials in those districts and to Department of Education officials. In the first example, policy is enacted by a school board resolution and in the second by federal statute. Court decisions also can provide guidance to other decision makers. Some of the best-known decisions of this type in education were discussed in Chapter 1. While courts do not make laws, their interpretations of laws often have the impact of significant policy decisions. In this section we will explore the process through which the courts exert such influence.

Some Basic Premises

Basic civics books explain that the function of the courts is not to enact laws but to interpret them. In so doing, the courts can act only on the basis of the facts presented to them. Thus, the essence of a court proceeding, be it civil or criminal, is first to ascertain the facts of the case at hand and second to apply the law to those facts. An important resource of the court as it seeks to apply the law is the body of cases on similar matters decided in the past. The doctrine of *stare decisis* (let the decision stand) is an important legal principle. It means that the court will take into account previous rulings on similar issues as it rules on any particular case. This means that the evolution of judicial policy in any particular area is likely to be incremental as it builds upon previous decisions in related areas. It also means that review of past decisions is an important step in determining whether or not to pursue a case in the courts and in assessing its possible outcomes. However, this body of case law is extremely comprehensive and, as a consequence, the courts are often called upon to mediate among conflicting claims of rights and interests when rendering a verdict.

A civil case is usually initiated when one party (the plaintiff) files a formal complaint against another party (the defendant). The defendant files a response to the complaint that either denies that all or part of it is true or admits to the allegations but submits legal justification for his or her behavior. At this point the case is ready for trial although it may be settled by out-of-court negotiations between the parties. While trial may be delayed some time for procedural reasons, a date is ultimately set for a hearing. The court hears evidence about the case and renders a decision. If one or both of the parties are not satisfied with this decision, they may appeal. Testimony is not heard at the appellate level. Rather, the appellate court reviews the record of the trial proceedings as a basis for upholding or reversing the lower court decision or remanding it for further testimony.

Judicial Trends in Education

A number of years ago, Hogan reviewed the history of court actions in education and identified five discernible stages.[21] He identified the first period, prior to 1850, as one of "strict judicial laissez faire" in which education was viewed primarily as a local matter and even state courts were reluctant to intervene. The second period, from 1850 to 1950, was identified as the "stage of state control" during which few cases reached the U.S. Supreme Court and "a body of case law developed at the state level which permitted, if not actually sanctioned, educational policies and practices that failed to meet federal constitutional standards and requirements."[22] This period was followed by a third period, a "reformation stage," that continued into the 1970s and was characterized by federal decisions that brought state-sanctioned policies and practices into conformity with constitutional provisions. Hogan noted that a fourth period, partly concurrent with the third, was one of "education under supervision of the courts" in which the federal courts took on enforcement responsibilities to ascertain that the minimum reform standards for school administration and programs were implemented. Finally, he suggested that the Supreme Court decision in the *Rodriguez*[23] case marked a fifth, new stage of "strict construction."

A clear example of court policymaking in stages three and four is seen in decisions pertaining to school desegregation. The *Brown* decision and several subsequent decisions set forth the principle of school desegregation and called upon school districts to implement it. The dilatory tactics of many of these districts provoked further litigation in which the courts began to mandate specific desegregation plans for particular districts. For example, court orders have been issued requiring districts to implement complex plans, to reassign staff members and students, and, in some cases, to employ or reemploy minority group personnel.

The Basis of Federal Involvement

Policy formation in education often follows a kind of sequence: basic social forces lead to antecedent movements; these movements in turn lead to political action that may culminate in formal policy enactments. This sequence helps to explain the growing involvement of the federal courts in education since the mid-twentieth century. Probably the most important basic force has been the historic pursuit of equality by black Americans. Various civil rights groups have employed diverse tactics in quest of this goal, but one of the most persistent and effective over time has been the legal efforts of the National Association for the Advancement of Colored People (NAACP). The NAACP Legal Defense Fund led in pressing school desegregation cases up to and including *Brown* v. *Board of Education*.[24] Since the *Brown* decision, the fund has continued to provide financial and technical assistance in support of desegregation litigation.

The press of the civil rights movement has also produced legislation that has strengthened the courts' hands in the area of desegregation. The Civil Rights Act of 1964 made it easier to file suits alleging discrimination, forbade the use of federal funds for discriminatory programs, and empowered the Justice Department to side with plaintiffs in desegregation suits.[25] These developments encouraged civil rights advocates to file additional cases, which led the courts to a series of decisions on desegregation.

Other advocate groups have also sought changes in public policy through the courts. A number of Community Action Agencies initially funded under the Economic Opportunity Act of 1964 included legal aid services to the poor. Attorneys for such agencies filed numerous suits on behalf of children and their parents against school districts. Other organizations have emerged as advocates of children's rights; they have helped interpret these rights to young people and have initiated legal actions. Shannon identified nine areas in which legal service agencies had challenged local school districts.[26] They included: (1) student discipline, (2) use of federal funds by local public schools, (3) school bus transportation, (4) racial integration of pupils, (5) school district organization and management, (6) school tuition, (7) application of one man-one vote principle, (8) state aid to local public schools, and (9) educational activities about the law. Moreover, as the courts have acted to broaden the rights of juveniles and students, they have opened the possibility for further litigation. The result has been a great increase in the number of education cases heard in the federal courts and consequently rapidly evolving case law.

The constitutional basis for federal involvement in education derives from a limited number of provisions. Those that have been most important are Article I, Section 10, which forbids the impairment of contractual obligations, and the First, Fifth, and Fourteenth Amendments.[27]

The First Amendment guarantees freedom of speech, religion, the press, assembly, and the right of petition. Its importance in education was noted first in a series of cases dealing with religion and the public schools. First Amendment protections regarding speech, the press, assembly, and petition in relation to student, teacher, and citizen rights have also become matters for litigation.

The Fifth Amendment provides protection against self-incrimination and has been the basis for cases dealing with loyalty oaths and testimony of teachers.

The Fourteenth Amendment states in part that "No state shall make or enforce any law which shall abridge the privileges or immunities of citizens of the United States; nor shall any state deprive any person of life, liberty, or property, without due process of law; nor deny to any person within its jurisdiction the equal protection of the laws." This amendment was proposed and ratified during the post-Civil War period and some argue that it was intended only to protect the rights of freedmen in a white society. Conversely others have argued that Congress intended for it to apply more generally. Particularly in recent decades the courts have been inclined toward a liberal interpretation. It remains to be seen if this interpretation will continue as the composition of the court shifts.

The due process and equal protection clauses of the Fourteenth Amendment have become the two most important means used by the federal courts to invalidate state laws and overturn state decisions.[28] Examples of decisions in education where the Supreme Court has used the Fourteenth Amendment in this way include a declaration that a state law prohibiting foreign language instruction below the ninth grade was unconstitutional,[29] a declaration that a state could not infringe upon freedom of religion through compulsory attendance laws,[30] and a ruling that dual school systems for the purpose of segregation were unconstitutional.[31]

At the heart of Supreme Court policymaking behavior is the concept of judicial review. This refers to the authority of the Court to review the actions of other governmental bodies, namely the state and federal courts and legislatures. The Constitution did not provide this right explicitly although most scholars argue that it was intended. The concept has developed principally through the actions of the courts. Chief Justice Marshall is given credit for much of the initiative in this area, beginning with his decision in *Marbury* v. *Madison* (1803), which said that a provision of the Judiciary Act of 1789 was unconstitutional.

While the precedent of judicial review has been firmly established over the past 150 years, controversy persists over the manner and extent to which it should be used. For example, President Nixon's statement that he would appoint "strict constructionists" to the Supreme Court was evidence of his belief that the concept had been overextended in recent years. Schmandt has categorized views about judicial review as being of three types: restraint, activism, and neutralism.

> The first argues that judges must recognize the primacy of the legislative and executive branches in policy making and must avoid injecting their own socioeconomic preferences into the judicial process. The second approach maintains that courts are policy makers and, as such, should consciously exercise their judicial power to influence the social system in the interest of justice. The third, while showing far less deference for the legislative and executive wills than the advocates of judicial restraint, holds that constitutional judgments may not be based on the court's sympathy toward litigants or their cause but on fundamental and disinterested principles of law.[32]

These terms, of course, are somewhat ambiguous and do more to point up the philosophical issues that grip the Court than to demarcate absolute positions. The historical trend seems to have been toward a more active judiciary. As Kurland[33] points out, however, judicial activism can be conservative as well as liberal; under judicial activism the Court may impose its judgments upon other governmental branches, but the question of whether those judgments should favor the wealthy or the poor, the powerful or the oppressed, the majority or the minorities is left open. One possible consequence of an activist posture of the Court is an opposition stance and efforts to change it by the executive and legislative branches.[34]

Even when the Court has tended toward activism, the nature of the judicial system itself, as set forth earlier in this chapter, imposes certain restraints on court action. It sometimes exercises restraint in determining the grounds on which a case will be decided. For example, the Court was once asked to decide if a law school admissions policy that accepts minority group applicants with lower test scores than white applicants constitutes reverse discrimination.[35] The Court noted that the individual who filed the case had since been admitted to law school and declared the case moot rather than issue an opinion on the principles involved. The Court subsequently considered a similar case involving a white male who was refused admission to medical school. The Court ruled in his favor in a divided decision which demonstrated the tendency to decide cases on narrow grounds.[36] The Court has imposed certain conditions upon itself regarding judicial review. They include the following:

1. The Court will not pass upon the constitutionality of legislation in a friendly non-adversary proceeding, declining because to decide such questions is legitimate only in the last resort, and as a necessity in the determination of real, earnest, and vital controversy between individuals.
2. The Court will not anticipate a question of constitutional law in advance of the necessity of deciding it . . . It is not the habit of the Court to decide questions of a constitutional nature unless absolutely necessary to a decision of the case.
3. The Court will not formulate a rule of constitutional law broader than is required by the precise facts to which it is to be applied.
4. The Court will not pass upon a constitutional question although properly presented by the record, if there is also present some other ground upon which the case may be disposed of.
5. The Court will not pass upon the validity of a statute upon complaint of one who fails to show that he is injured by its operation.
6. The Court will not pass upon the constitutionality of a statute at the instance of one who has availed himself of its benefits.[37]

The point to be emphasized is that as the Court exercises its review function it does so within a context bounded by public values and interests, the positions of other governmental branches, and procedural guidelines that have evolved over time.

Compliance with Judicial Decisions

One school of thought regarding policy analysis holds that it is important to look beyond the making of an authoritative decision to see whether or not anything happens as a consequence of the decision. Thus the question of whether a school district has a policy of individualizing instruction is answered better by observing classrooms than by reviewing the policy manual. The same test can be applied to court-initiated policies by asking to what extent citizens comply with court decisions. History has recorded some spectacular examples of noncompliance. For example, President Andrew Jackson reportedly responded to a Supreme Court decision sympathetic to Indian claims by saying, "John Marshall has made his decision; now let him enforce it!"

The courts depend heavily upon assistance from the legislative and executive branches of government as well as general public support to promote compliance with their decisions. Where such assistance and support is lacking, decisions may go unheeded. The most dramatic example in education is in the area of school desegregation. Thirty-five years after the *Brown* decision, school desegregation remains an issue in the nation. Indeed, for a decade following the decision very little progress was made in desegregating the dual systems of the deep South. Not until passage of the Civil Rights Act of 1964 and the subsequent involvement of the Department of Justice was substantial progress made. However, the Nixon administration then slowed the desegregation litigation filed by the Justice Department and pushed school busing into the limelight as a public issue.[38] Thus pressure mounted once again to slow the desegregation process, particularly in the North.

Despite the slow pace with which school desegregation has gone forward, the Supreme Court has spoken infrequently on this subject since 1954. Wirt and Kirst attribute this to the patience of the Court in waiting for the rest of the nation to accept the principle it enunciated and steadfastly maintained.[39] While acknowledging the political sensitivity of the Court in this regard, they also rightly credit the Court with establishing the principle that over time was to have major impact upon the nation.

The compliance problem is apparent in other areas of school litigation. For example, Dolbeare and Hammond studied five towns and found that in each of them school prayers, Bible readings, and other religious observances continued five years after the Supreme Court decision declared them unconstitutional.[40] In their words, "Local leaders are not deliberately defying the Court; they have simply found it congenial and possible to continue established local practice without regard to the Court's decisions."[41]

Even though compliance with court rulings may be problematic in some instances, the courts are nonetheless influential policymakers. They do establish directions on a number of important matters, and parties aggrieved with regard to any of them have the right to seek a trial and appeal the decision if they wish. Moreover, the decision of the trial court establishes policy in at least a particular instance regardless of the quality of that decision. At the very least such decisions should serve as guides for school officials who realize that departure from such principles may bring another court case. Equally important, the directions established by the courts through the process of judicial review serve to limit the policymaking prerogatives of other governmental bodies.

EXAMPLES OF JUDICIAL INFLUENCE

In Chapter 1 we observed that the Supreme Court exerted important influence on education through a series of milestone decisions. At this point, we will examine the way court influence has evolved in two areas—school desegregation and school finance reform. In the first case, the position of the court has been clarified and its role enlarged as it forced school districts to desegregate their facilities and programs. In the second case, a broadly written Supreme Court decision slowed a movement toward reform that had gained considerable momentum in state and lower federal courts. We have quoted at some length from a number of decisions to illustrate how the courts seek facts, how they reason, and how they build upon precedent.

School Desegregation

The views of the courts regarding school desegregation have evolved slowly since the landmark *Brown* decision and they have been implemented even more slowly. Resistance to implementing the *Brown* decision and the continual refocusing of the issue according to particular geographical or legal bases have led the courts to become increasingly specific about what constitutes unlawful segregation.

The 1954 *Brown* decision was based on cases from Kansas, South Carolina, Virginia, and Delaware in which plaintiffs sought to end enforcement of state constitutional and statutory provisions that permitted or required the segregation of black and white children in the public schools. Taking note of the psychological aspects of learning and prejudice, the Supreme Court said:

> We conclude that in the field of public education, the doctrine of "separate but equal" has no place. Separate educational facilities are inherently unequal. Therefore, we hold that the plaintiffs and others similarly situated for whom the acts have been brought are, by reason of the segregation complained of, deprived of the equal protection of the laws guaranteed by the Fourteenth Amendment.[42]

In a subsequent decision setting forth bases for implementing the first *Brown* decision, the Supreme Court remanded the cases to the district courts to monitor progress toward desegregation and rendered the well-known guideline of "with all deliberate speed." The Court also said:

> The courts will require that the defendants make a prompt and reasonable start toward full compliance with our May 17, 1954 ruling. Once such a start has been made, the courts may find that additional time is required to carry out the ruling in an effective manner. The burden rests upon the defendants to establish that such time is necessary in the public interest and is consistent with good faith compliance at the earliest practicable date. To that end, the courts may consider problems related to administration, arising from the physical condition of the school plant, the school transportation system, personnel, revision of school districts and attendance areas into compact units to achieve a system of determining admission to the public schools on a nonracial basis and revision of local laws and regulations which may be necessary

in solving the foregoing problems. They will also consider the adequacy of any plans the defendants may propose to meet these problems and to effectuate a transition to a racially nondiscriminatory school system.[43]

The next decade was characterized by southern resistance to dismantling dual school systems. For the most part, the Supreme Court was silent as litigation continued at lower levels, although it did uphold lower court enforcement of the *Brown* decisions.[44] In widely noted rulings, the Court held that state legislative, executive, or judicial authorities could not nullify the constitutional rights declared in *Brown*,[45] and that a county could not close its public schools to avoid desegregation.[46]

One procedure employed by school districts to desegregate dual systems was the "freedom of choice" plan. The essence of this plan was that each child would be allowed to attend the school of his or her choosing. In the early stages of the desegregation effort, the court refused to overturn such plans. As time passed, however, it became apparent that "freedom of choice" did not always produce desegregated schools. Against this background, the U.S. Supreme Court accepted a case for review in which freedom of choice had not ended school segregation. The court ruled against the plan in this instance and put the matter in historical perspective:

> For the time immediately after *Brown II* the concern was with making an initial break in a long established pattern of excluding Negro children from schools attended by white children. The principal focus was on obtaining for those Negro children courageous enough to break with tradition a place in the "white" schools. See e.g., *Cooper v. Aaron 358, US 1.* Under *Brown II* that immediate goal was only the first step, however. The transition to a unitary, nonracial system of public education was and is the ultimate end to be brought about; it was because of the "complexities arising from the transition to a system of public education freed of racial discrimination" that we provided for "all deliberate speed" in the implementation of the principles of *Brown I* . . . The burden on a school board today is to come forward with a plan that promises realistically to work and promises realistically to work *now* . . . Where it [freedom of choice] offers real promise of aiding a desegregation program to effectuate conversion of a state-imposed dual system to a unitary, nonracial system there might be no objection to allowing such a device to prove itself in operation. On the other hand, if there are reasonably available other ways, such for illustration as zoning, promising speedier and more effective conversion to a unitary, nonracial school system, "freedom of choice" must be held unacceptable.[47]

A year later the Supreme Court refused to accept further delay in implementing desegregation plans for thirty Mississippi school districts. The Court extended the position it had taken in the *Green* case and ruled that "all deliberate speed" was "no longer constitutionally permissible. Under explicit holdings of this Court, the obligation of every school district is to terminate dual school systems at once and to operate now and hereafter only unitary schools."[48]

The Court was to speak further about the affirmative responsibilities of a school district in bringing about desegregation. The most far-reaching ruling of this type came in *Swann et al.* v. *Charlotte-Mecklenburg Board of Education et al.*[49] The Court spoke to several points. It stated the obligation of school authorities to "eliminate invidious racial distinctions" and "produce schools of like quality, facilities, and staff." The Court affirmed the power of district courts to order the "assignment of teachers to achieve a particular degree of faculty desegregation." The Court also held that district courts could use their authority to oversee future school construction and abandonment so that they "do not serve to perpetuate or reestablish the dual system."

The central issue in the *Swann* case, however, dealt with pupil assignment. The Court held that it was within the district courts' discretion to establish very limited and flexible ratios for pupil assignment among buildings, that "the existence of some small number of one-race or virtually one-race schools within a district is not in and of itself the mark of a system which still practices segregation by law" but that school officials have the "burden of showing that such school assignments are genuinely nondiscriminatory." It also held that the district court can alter attendance zones, that "the pairing and grouping of non-contiguous school zones is a permissible tool," and that it was within the power of the district court to order busing as a remedy. On busing, the court noted that no child would ride a bus for longer than thirty-five minutes under the proposed plan and that "an objection to transportation of students may have validity when the time or distance of travel is so great as to risk either the health of the children or significantly impinge on the educational process."

In *Swann* the Supreme Court moved from enunciating a general principle in the first *Brown* case to stating specifics applicable to the dismantling of dual school systems. At the time the courts were considering these cases, they were also dealing with a number of actions filed against northern school districts. Here school officials and others have maintained that segregated schools were not a result of state action and thus segregated *de jure* but were instead the product of segregated housing patterns and hence *de facto*. Thus the questions before the courts in the North have been somewhat different than those associated with dual systems in the South.

The New Rochelle, New York, schools were the first in the North to be found in violation of the *Brown* provisions. In the 1961 case the federal district court found that the district had deliberately gerrymandered school boundaries to perpetuate segregation. Other early northern cases, however, were decided otherwise. The rationale for such decisions was set forth in *Bell v. School City of Gary*.[50] In a ruling affirmed by the court of appeals, the district court held that

> The problem of Gary is not one of segregated schools but rather of segregated housing. Either by choice or by design, the Negro population of Gary is concentrated in the so-called central area, and as a result the schools in that area are populated by Negro students . . . The Court finds no support for the plaintiff's position that the defendant has an affirmative duty to balance the races in the various schools under its jurisdiction, regardless of the residence of students involved.[51]

Similar reasoning was expressed in a case dealing with *de facto* segregation in Cincinnati. Part of the appeal court decision held,

> We hold that there is no constitutional duty on the part of the Board to bus Negro or white children out of their neighborhoods or to transfer classes for the sole purpose

of alleviating racial imbalance that it did not cause, nor is there a like duty to select new school sites solely in furtherance of such a purpose . . . the crucial fact to be found is whether the racial imbalance was intentionally caused by gerrymandering or by other alleged discriminatory practices on the part of the Board.[52]

More recently, however, the courts have demonstrated a tendency to rule against northern school segregation. Kirp and Yudof note that this has been done "not by repudiating the *de jure/de facto* distinction, but by expanding the scope of *de jure* segregation."[53] They cite *Kelly* v. *Guinn*[54] as an example of this practice. Here the Court noted that the Clark County, Nevada, schools had recently built four new elementary schools within a predominantly black area, closed two other predominantly white schools on the fringe of this area, and also built a new elementary school in a more distant white area. The Court also noted that most of the teachers in the black area were black. The court of appeals concluded "that there was ample evidence to support the district court's finding that the Clark County School District used its power to aggravate segregation in elementary schools in violation of the Constitution." This finding was in the face of the district's defense that it was "simply adhering to a neighborhood school policy" and that "whatever imbalance exists stems not from any official action of the school district, but rather from the racial composition of the Westside population, which is almost completely black."

A subsequent and more far-reaching decision of this type was set forth by the Supreme Court in a case involving the Denver Public Schools. In *Keyes* v. *School District No. 1 Denver, Colorado,*[55] the high court held that if it could be shown that "school authorities have carried out a systematic program of segregation affecting a substantial portion of the students, schools, teachers, and facilities within the school system, it is only common sense to conclude that there exists a predicate for a finding of the existence of a dual school system." The case was remanded to the district court for hearing on this point with the stipulation that if a dual school system was found to exist, then the Board of Education would have the obligation to desegregate the entire school system.

In this case, the Court noted that the Denver schools had never been a dual system under constitutional or statutory provision but maintained its distinction between *de facto* and *de jure* segregation, saying that the "differentiating factor" was *"purpose or intent* to segregate." However, the ruling in this case substantially broadens the grounds on which northern school districts may be required to take affirmative action to desegregate. Moreover, Justice Powell in a separate opinion suggested that the *de facto/de jure* distinction was no longer useful and should be discarded. He wrote:

> I concur in the Court's position that the public school authorities are the responsible agency of the state, and that if the affirmative duty doctrine is sound Constitutional law for Charlotte, it is equally so for Denver. I would not, however, perpetuate the *de jure/de facto* distinction nor would I leave to petitioners the initial tortuous effort of identifying "segregative acts" and deducing "segregated intent." I would hold quite simply that where segregated public schools exist within a school district to a substantial degree, there is a prima facie case that the duly constituted public authorities . . . are

sufficiently responsible to warrant imposing upon them a nationally applicable burden to demonstrate they nevertheless are operating a genuinely integrated school system.[56]

Powell, however, also let it be known that he believed there might be some limitations on the responsibility of school officials to desegregate. Recalling *Swann,* which he said was the "controlling case" in this instance, he wrote:

> To the extent that *Swann* may be thought to *require* large scale or long distance transportation of students in our metropolitan school districts, I record my profound misgivings. Nothing in our Constitution commands or encourages any such court-compelled disruption of public education. It may be more accurate to view *Swann* as having laid down a broad rule of reason under which desegregation remedies must remain flexible and other values and interests be considered.[57]

In subsequent cases, the Court has spoken further about the limits of official responsibility to desegregate. In a case involving the Pasadena, California, schools, the Court ruled that once a school district had implemented a suitable plan to remedy earlier segregative behavior, the district could not be required to revise the plan regularly in order to account for natural population shifts in the district.[58] Thus the Court held out the possibility that school districts that had implemented desegregation plans under judicial oversight could escape this supervision in time.[59] In other decisions, the Court indicated that the test of whether or not a district acted with segregative intent must include evidence that speaks to the purpose as well as the effects of these actions.[60] Moreover, the Court ruled that a finding of liability for segregation against a district does not necessarily require a district-wide desegregation plan. Instead, the scope of the remedy is to be determined by the extent of the impact of the wrongful acts.[61]

As the focus on desegregation litigation has moved to the North and the courts have expanded the doctrine of affirmative duty to northern cities, another important question dealing with jurisdiction has been raised. It deals with the responsibility of the state to require cross-district efforts at desegregation in metropolitan areas where suburbs have remained white as core cities become increasingly black. The most important case was Detroit. A federal district court had ordered a metropolitan plan for desegregating the Detroit schools that would have involved cross-district busing, and this plan was upheld by the court of appeals.[62] However, the Supreme Court struck down this plan by a vote of 5–4. In doing so, the Court reaffirmed the tradition of local school control, determined that there was no proof of segregative action by the surrounding eighty-five suburban school districts, and ruled that it would not be appropriate to impose interdistrict remedies for segregation unless it could be shown that such segregation was the result of interdistrict actions.[63] In a vigorous dissenting opinion written by Justice Marshall, the minority argued that the state of Michigan was responsible for the educational system provided in Detroit and that there was "no basis either in law or in the practicalities of the situation justifying the state's interposition of school district boundaries as absolute barriers to the implementation of an effective desegregation remedy."[64] Despite this division, the impact of the decision was to further clarify the responsibility of local school districts regarding desegregation and to deter similar cases being advanced in other metropolitan areas. However, a metropolitan remedy has been upheld where it was shown that state or suburban action contributed to city school segregation.[65]

School Finance Reform

In 1965 Arthur Wise, then a graduate student at the University of Chicago, wrote an article in which he argued that the Fourteenth Amendment could be used as a vehicle for declaring state school finance plans unconstitutional.[66] He contended, later, in a book that amplified his position, that education was a right that must be provided equally and that the existing variations among school districts' expenditures precluded this.[67] His argument provided the theoretical underpinnings for scholars interested in greater equity in school finance and was the basis for some early court cases. Important among these were a case filed by the Detroit city school board but subsequently dropped and a case in Illinois.[68] Both cases argued that the state had a responsibility to meet the "educational needs" of students. In *McInnis* the court held " . . . (1) the Fourteenth Amendment does not require that public school expenditures be made only on the basis of pupil's educational needs, and (2) the lack of judicially manageable standards makes this controversy non-judiciable."[69]

The Wise position was modified somewhat by John E. Coons, William Clune, and Stephen Sugarman.[70] They argued that the basic constitutional problem with state finance programs was that they allowed wealthy school districts to spend more than others. Shifting from the educational need argument advanced by Wise, they contended that the equal protection clause of the Fourteenth Amendment required states to adopt a position of fiscal "neutrality," that is, one that did not make it easier for wealthier districts to provide more educational opportunities than a less wealthy district. This theory of "power equalizing" provided the basis for the landmark California case, *Serrano* v. *Priest,*[71] and a series of similar cases in states throughout the country.

At the crux of the *Serrano* case were the plaintiff's contentions that the California school financing system violated the equal protection clause because it favored a "suspect classification" (i.e., those who lived in wealthy school districts) and that education was a "fundamental interest" of California citizens. If these conditions could be established as true, then constitutional law required the state finance plan to be declared unconstitutional unless it could be shown "(1) that the state has a 'compelling interest' that justifies the law, and (2) that the particular manner in which the law treats people differently is *necessary* to further the law's valid purposes."[72] The California Supreme Court found that "the school financing system discriminates on the basis of the wealth of a district and its residents." The court also held that education is a "fundamental interest," and rejected the arguments of local and state officials that the present law was necessary. In remanding the case for further hearings the court observed " . . . that if, after further proceedings, that court [the trial court] should enter final judgment determining that the existing system of public school financing is unconstitutional and invalidating said system in whole or in part, it may properly provide for the enforcement of the judgment in such a way as to permit an orderly transition from an unconstitutional to a constitutional system of financing."[73]

Similar cases dealing with other states proceeded through state and lower federal courts. Within a short time after the *Serrano* decision, "roughly comparable" decisions were rendered in Minnesota, Texas, Kansas, Arizona, New Jersey, and Michigan.[74] It appeared that a substantial reform movement was under way. However, an attorney in the Texas case decided to pursue his case before a three-judge federal district court. In late 1971 this court held that the Texas school finance law did not guarantee equal protection, a decision the state of Texas appealed directly to the U.S. Supreme Court.

The decision of the high court in *San Antonio Independent School District* v. *Rodriguez*[75] was a severe disappointment to those who hoped the court would add its support to the reform effort. By a 5–4 decision, the court overturned the district court holding. The Court did so not on narrow technical grounds but on the basic constitutional questions posed in *Serrano* and subsequent cases. In the majority opinion, Powell set forth the task of the court as follows:

> We must decide, first, whether the Texas system of financing public education operates to the disadvantage of some suspect class or impinges upon a fundamental right explicitly or unexplicitly protected by the Constitution, thereby requiring strict judicial scrutiny. If so, the judgment of the District Court should be affirmed. If not, the Texas scheme must still be examined to determine whether it rationally furthers some legitimate, articulated state purpose and therefore does not constitute an invidious discrimination in violation of the Equal Protection Clause of the Fourteenth Amendment.[76]

The Court held that the plan "does not operate to the peculiar disadvantage of any suspect class" and that the system was not "so irrational as to be invidiously discriminatory." Perhaps most significant, the Court addressed the question of education as a fundamental interest. Noting the historic dedication of the Court to public education and its importance to society, Powell nevertheless wrote:

> But the importance of a service performed by the State does not determine whether it must be regarded as fundamental for purposes of examination under the Equal Protection Clause . . . It is not the province of this Court to create substantive constitutional rights in the name of guaranteeing equal protection of the laws. Thus the key to discovering whether education is "fundamental" is not to be found in comparisons of the relative societal significance of education as opposed to subsistence or housing . . . Rather the answer lies in assessing whether there is a right to education explicitly or implicitly guaranteed by the Constitution. . . .
>
> Education, of course, is not among the rights afforded explicit protection under our Federal Constitution. Nor do we find any basis for saying it is implicitly so protected. . . . [77]

The decision had the effect of closing the federal courts at least temporarily to those who sought redress of inequities in state school finance plans. But it did not destroy their recourse altogether. Powell concluded the *Rodriguez* opinion by writing:

We hardly need add that this Court's action today is not to be viewed as placing its judicial imprimatur on the status quo. The need is apparent for reform in tax systems which may well have relied too long and too heavily on the local property tax. And certainly innovative new thinking as to public education, its methods, and its funding, is necessary to assure both a higher level of quality and greater uniformity of opportunity. These matters merit the continued attention of the scholars who already have contributed much by their challenges. But the ultimate solutions must come from the lawmakers and from the democratic pressures of those who elect them.[78]

Moreover, it is a final commentary on the complexity of our court systems that judicial remedies are still possible as well. The fact that the decision was by a 5–4 vote suggests that the Supreme Court might change its mind later. In the meanwhile, state courts offer a potential source of judicial remedy in many instances. In contrast to the federal Constitution, forty-eight state constitutions mention education as a fundamental interest.[79] Moreover, the education clause in some state constitutions may itself be basis for state litigation holding the finance program unconstitutional. This was the finding of the New Jersey Supreme Court in a decision rendered shortly after *Rodriguez*.[80] This court affirmed a lower court ruling that New Jersey statutes that allowed considerable variation in per-pupil expenditures according to local tax patterns did not fulfill the state constitutional requirement to provide "a thorough and efficient system of free public schools." The Los Angeles Superior Court in a follow-up to the *Serrano* decision held that California must promulgate a school finance plan that will reduce differences among districts in basic per-pupil expenditures to less than $100 per pupil within six years. Differences among districts in tax rates are to be reduced to "nonsubstantial variations" within the same period. The legislatures in New Jersey and California enacted new school finance laws in response to their respective courts. Since *Rodriquez,* cases involving the constitutionality of financing arrangements for schools have reached the supreme courts of several states. In some of these states (New Jersey, California, Connecticut, West Virginia, Kentucky, Arkansas, Washington, and Wyoming), the courts have held the existing system unconstitutional. The present system has been upheld in other states largely because of judicial concern over the "fundamental interest" issue and reluctance to override the state interest in preserving local control of schools.[81] Similar cases are pending in other states, such as Texas. Despite the action in some states, it would appear that the Supreme Court decision did have the effect of slowing the momentum that had been building for state school finance reform.

SUMMARY AND FUTURE PROSPECTS

Recent decades have been extremely busy ones for court activity in education. In addition to the important cases we've discussed, the courts have also rendered significant decisions in the areas of student rights, church-state relationships, and teacher rights and responsibilities. Such cases have involved the courts in matters of day-to-day importance to school administrators, and court involvement is likely to continue. Thus it is important that education officials be informed not only about the substance of the law but about the nature of judicial proceedings as well.

The influence of the courts is rooted in the law and the respect of the American population for it. By constitution and tradition the judicial process is regarded as the ultimate authority for resolving conflicts and redressing injustices. Judicial influence is not without its limits, however. Court decisions must be consistent with constitutional provisions, relevant statutes, and, in the case of lower courts, superior court rulings. They also are guided by past decisions in similar cases. Moreover, the courts may only rule on issues that are brought before them. Despite these limitations, court rulings have had a substantial impact on schools. This impact has been conservative from one perspective because it represents an effort to bring schools into compliance with existing constitutional and statutory provisions.[82] In their efforts to understand facts and apply the most appropriate laws in an increasingly complex environment, the courts rely not only on the adversarial pleadings of the parties, their counsel, and expert witnesses, but more and more on their own court-appointed experts, special masters, and advisory bodies.

A review of cases pending before the courts suggests some areas in which future decisions are likely. Certainly there will be further decisions dealing with metropolitan school desegregation and state school finance reform. Another set of finance questions of concern to the courts deals with state aid to nonpublic schools. The 1983 decision of the Supreme Court upholding tuition tax credits for nonpublic school students in Minnesota will likely be followed by legislation and litigation in other states.[83] An apparently critical feature of the Minnesota law is that it allows deductions for education expenses incurred by parents of students in public as well as private schools. The right of states to regulate nonpublic schools is another topic on which further court action is likely.

A major emphasis of litigation in the 1990s will be to extend and clarify the principles established by the courts in the past decades with respect to such issues as student rights, the rights of the handicapped, affirmative action, and fair dismissal of employees.[84] The departure of Justice Powell could portend a shift in the Court's posture on these issues. It also appears likely that the Court will be asked to decide the conditions under which a school district can terminate a court-ordered busing plan.[85] In addition, the value clashes of disparate groups in heterogeneous school settings will continue to present the courts with cases that deal with issues such as textbook selection, religious observances, and the teaching of creationism. At the same time, new trends in society will bring new issues to the courts. One current example is the controversy regarding the applicability and enforcement of copyright laws to high technology and curriculum products such as software and videodiscs. Another set of questions to be litigated will deal with validity and due process considerations associated with competency testing for students and teachers. It is also likely that schools will be affected as the courts consider issues rising from other settings, such as drug testing for employees, the responsibility of public agencies in child abuse cases, and the validity of minority enterprise ordinances.[86]

One can only conclude from such developments that the courts will continue to be active in education and that the law will change as a result. It could be, however, that it will change in ways to limit the considerable use of the equal protection clause. Kurland has suggested this and also that the Supreme Court may choose to place more emphasis on another clause in the Fourteenth Amendment that says, "No state shall make or enforce any law which shall abridge the privileges or immunities of citizens of the United States." This remains to be seen, but appears likely in view of the changing composition of the Court. Likewise, we must wait to see if the courts become more conservative in other respects. However, the growing involvement of the courts in education suggests that educators will need to find efficient ways of keeping abreast of legal developments at all court levels.

NOTES

[1]For an early history of the courts see Francis R. Aumann, *The Changing American Legal System* (Columbus, OH: Ohio State University Press, 1940). See also Robert A. Koenig, "The Law and Education in Historical Perspective," in *The Courts and Education,* Seventy-seventh Yearbook of the National Society for the Study of Education, Part 1. (Chicago: University of Chicago Press, 1978), 1–26.

[2]*United States Constitution,* Article III, Section I. The history of the Constitutional Convention is discussed in Catherine Drinker Bowen, *Miracle at Philadelphia* (Boston: Little, Brown, 1966).

[3]Richard Hofstadter, William Miller, and Daniel Aaron, *The United States* (Englewood Cliffs, NJ: Prentice-Hall, 1957), 142.

[4]Carl McGowan, *The Organization of Judicial Power in the United States* (Evanston, IL: Northwestern University Press, 1969), 30.

[5]Ibid., 16–17.

[6]Administrative Office of the U.S. Courts, *Federal Judicial Workload Statistics* (Washington, DC: U.S. Government Printing Office, 1986), 10 and U.S. Department of Commerce, Bureau of Census, *Statistical Abstract of the United States* 107th edition (Washington, DC: U.S. Government Printing Office, 1986).

[7]Linda Greenhouse, "Burger Proposes New Panel to Cut High Court's Load," *New York Times,* 7 February 1983, 1.

[8]Hofstadter, Miller, and Aaron, *The United States,* 155.

[9]For discussion of this view see William F. Swindler, "The Supreme Court, the President, and the Congress," *The International and Comparative Law Quarterly* 19 (1970): 671–92.

[10]Ibid., 680.

[11]David G. Savage, "Watching a Changing Court: Will the Center Hold?" *Phi Delta Kappan* 69 (October 1987): 135–37.

[12]Henry J. Schmandt, *Courts in the American Political System* (Belmont, CA: Dickenson, 1969), 34.

[13]Thomas Halper, "Senate Rejection of Supreme Court Nominees," *Drake Law Review* 22 (September 1972): 107.

[14]See Henry Robert Glick and Kenneth N. Vines, *State Court Systems* (Englewood Cliffs, NJ: Prentice-Hall, 1973).

[15]*Garrett* v. *Faubus,* 323 SW (2d) 877, 880 (Ark. 1959).

[16]*Hogan* v. *Glasscock,* 324 SW (2d) 815, 816 (Ky. 1959).

[17]*Deal* v. *Cincinnati Board of Education,* 369 F. 2d 55, 61 (6th Cir. 1966).

[18]*Tinker* v. *Des Moines Independent Community School District,* 393 U.S. 503, 514 (1969).

[19]Glick and Vines, *State Court Systems,* 39.

[20]Schmandt, *Courts in the American Political System,* 14.

[21]Reprinted by permission of the publisher, from *The Schools, the Courts, and the Public Interest* by John C. Hogan (Lexington, MA: D.C. Heath, 1974), 5–14.

[22]Ibid., 5.

[23]*San Antonio Independent School District* v. *Rodriguez,* 411 U.S. 1 (1973).

[24]*Brown* v. *Board of Education of Topeka,* 347 U.S. 483 (1954).

[25]For discussion of these developments see Donna E. Shalala and James A. Kelly, "Politics, the Courts, and Educational Policy," *Teachers College Record* 75 (December 1973): 223–37.

[26]Address by Thomas A. Shannon, 15th Annual Convention of NOLPE, Cleveland, Ohio, November, 1969, reported in Susanne Martinez, "Poor People in Public Education in America: Issues and Problems," in *Current Trends in School Law* (Topeka, KS: National Organization on Legal Problems in Education, 1974), 296–97.

[27]E. Edmund Reutter, Jr. and Robert R. Hamilton, *The Law of Public Education,* 2d ed. (Mineola, NY: Foundation Press, 1976), 2–5.

[28]Philip B. Kurland, "The New Supreme Court," *The University of Chicago Magazine* 66 (July–August 1973): 8.

[29]*Meyer* v. *Nebraska,* 262 U.S. 390 (1923).

[30]*Wisconsin* v. *Yoder et al.,* 406 U.S. 205 (1972).

[31]*Brown* v. *Board of Education,* 347 U.S. 483 (1954).

[32]Schmandt, *Courts in the American Political System,* 43.

[33]Kurland, "The New Supreme Court," 5.

[34]See Swindler, "The Supreme Court, the President, and the Congress."

[35]*De Funis* v. *Odegaard,* 42 US LW 4578 (1974).

[36]*Bakke* v. *Board of Regents,* 438 U.S. 265 (1978). While five justices ruled that Bakke must be admitted, five also held that race may be used as a factor in admissions decisions. Four of the five who favored Bakke's admission based their decision on their conclusion that the admissions process in question violated the Civil Rights Act of 1964 rather than the *Constitution.*

[37]*Ashwander* v. *Tennessee Valley Authority,* 297 U.S. 288, 346–48 (1936), quoted in Edward C. Bolmeier, *Landmark Supreme Court Decisions on Educational Issues* (Charlottesville, VA: Michie, 1973), 5.

[38]Shalala and Kelly, "Politics, the Courts, and Educational Policy," 225–26. See also Michael B. Wise, "School Desegregation: The Court, the Congress, and the President," *School Review* 82 (February 1974): 159–82.

[39]Frederick M. Wirt and Michael W. Kirst, *Schools in Conflict* (Berkeley, CA: McCutchan, 1982).

[40]Kenneth M. Dolbeare and Phillip E. Hammond, *The School Prayer Decisions* (Chicago: University of Chicago Press, 1971).

[41]Ibid., 5.

[42]*Brown* v. *Board of Education,* 347 U.S. 483, 495 (1954). A useful source on school desegregation that includes most of the cases cited here (as well as others) and related analytical material is David L. Kirp and Mark G. Yudof, *Educational Policy and the Law: Cases and Materials* (Berkeley, CA: McCutchan, 1974), ch. 4. Also see Betsy Levin, *The Courts as Educational Policymakers and Their Impact on Federal Programs* (Santa Monica, CA: The Rand Corporation, 1977).

[43]*Brown* v. *Board of Education,* 349 U.S. 294, 300–1 (1955).

[44]Frederick M. Wirt and Michael W. Kirst, *The Political Web of American Schools,* (Boston: Little, Brown and Co., 1972), 180.

[45]*Cooper* v. *Aaron,* 358 U.S. 1 (1958).

[46]*Griffin* v. *County School Board of Prince Edward County,* 377 U.S. 218 (1964).

[47]*Green* v. *County School Board,* 391 U.S. 430, 435–36, 439, 440–41 (1968).

[48]*Alexander* v. *Holmes County Board of Education,* 396 U.S. 19, 20 (1969).

[49]402 U.S. 1 (1970).

[50]*Bell* v. *School City of Gary,* 324 F. 2d 209 (7th Cir 1963) cert. denied 377 U.S. 924 (1964). Cf. *Taylor* v. *Board of Education of New Rochelle,* 294 F. 2d 36 (2d Cir 1961), cert. denied 368 U.S. 940 (1961).

[51]*Bell* v. *School City of Gary,* 213 F. Supp 819, 827–31 (N.D. Indiana 1963). Our analysis of this and the Cincinnati case was aided by an unpublished paper by Roger D. Anderson, "The Constitution and De Facto School Segregation."

[52]*Deal* v. *Cincinnati Board of Education,* 369 F. 2d 55, 61, 64 (6th Cir. 1966) cert. denied 389 U.S. 847.

[53]Kirp and Yudof, *Educational Policy and the Law,* 401.

[54]*Kelly* v. *Guinn,* 456 F. 2d 100 (9th Cir 1972).

[55]*Keyes* v. *School District No. 1 Denver, Colorado,* 413 U.S. 189 (1973). For an excellent discussion of this case see Thomas A. Shannon, "The Denver Decision: Death Knell for Defacto Segregation?" *Phi Delta Kappan* 55 (September 1973): 6–9.

[56]*Keyes* v. *School District No. 1 Denver, Colorado,* 413 U.S. 189, 224 (1973).

[57]Ibid., 238.

[58]*Pasadena City Board of Education* v. *Spangler,* 427 U.S. 424 (1976).

[59]Clifford P. Hooker, "Issues in School Desegregation" in *The Courts and Education,* 112.

[60]*Austin Independent School District* v. *United States,* 429 U.S. 990 (1976), and *Dayton Board of Education* v. *Brinkman,* 431 U.S. 902 (1977).

[61]*Dayton* v. *Brinkman,* 431 U.S. 902 (1977). But also see *Dayton* v. *Brinkman,* 443 U.S. 526 (1979) where the Court subsequently held that the facts in Dayton warranted a system-wide remedy. A similar decision was rendered in the case of Columbus, Ohio. See *Board of Education* v. *Penick,* 443 U.S. 449 (1979).

[62]*Bradley* v. *Milliken,* 345 F. Supp. 914 (E. D. Michigan S.D. 1972).

[63]*Bradley* v. *Milliken,* 418 U.S. 717 (1974).

[64]Ibid., 783.

[65]For example, *Evans* v. *Buchanan,* 423 U.S. 963 (1976), and *Morrilton School District No. 32* v. *U.S.* 606 F. 2d 222 (8th Cir. 1979). cert. denied 100 S. Ct. 1015 (1982). Also see *U.S.* v. *Board of School Commissioners of the City of Indianapolis,* 637 F. 2d 1101 (7th Cir. 1980) cert denied 101 S. Ct. 114 (1980). For discussion of interdistrict remedies, see "School Desegregation: Results and Prospects, A Special Report," *Metropolitan Education* no. 4 (Spring 1987): 43–128.

[66]Arthur E. Wise, "Is Denial of Equal Educational Opportunity Constitutional?" *Administrator's Notebook* 13 (February 1965).

[67]Arthur E. Wise, *Rich Schools-Poor Schools* (Chicago: University of Chicago Press, 1969).

[68]*McInnis* v. *Shapiro,* 293 F. Supp. 327 (N.D. Ill. 1968) affirmed. *McInnis* v. *Ogilvie,* 394 US 322 (1969).

[69]Quoted in Joseph A. Williams, Harold W. Gentry, and Michael W. LaMorte, "The Attack on Educational Finance Programs—An Overview," NOLPE *School Law Journal* 2 (Fall 1972): 6.

[70]See their book, *Private Wealth and Public Education* (Cambridge, MA: Harvard University Press, 1970). In presenting this historical account, we have relied heavily upon Joel S. Berke, "Recent Adventures of State School Finance: A Saga of Rocket Ships and Glider Planes," *School Review* 82 (February 1974): 183–206 and Williams, Gentry, and LaMorte, "The Attack on Educational Finance Programs—An Overview."

[71]*Serrano* v. *Priest,* 5 Cal. 3d 584, 96 Cal. Rptr, 601, 487 p. 2d 1241 (1971).

[72]Thomas A. Shannon, "Chief Justice Wright, The California Supreme Court, and School Finance: Has the Fourteenth Done It Again?" (Washington, DC: American Association of School Administrators, n.d.)

[73]Ibid.

[74]Berke, "Recent Adventures of State School Finance."

[75]*San Antonio Independent School District et al.* v. *Rodriguez et al.,* 411 U.S. 1 (1973).

[76]Ibid., 17.

[77]Ibid., 30–35.

[78]Ibid., 58–59.

[79]Berke, "Recent Adventures of State School Finance," 173.

[80]*Robinson* v. *Cahill,* 62 N.J. 473 (1973).

[81]For examples and discussion, see David C. Long, "*Rodriguez:* the State Courts Respond," *Phi Delta Kappan* 64 (March 1983): 481–84, and Michael W. LaMorte and Jeffrey D. Williams, "Court Decisions and School Finance Reform," *Educational Administration Quarterly* 21 (Spring 1985): 59–89.

[82]See Raphael O. Nystrand and W. Frederick Staub, "The Courts as Educational Policy-Makers" in *The Courts and Education.*

[83]*Mueller* v. *Allen,* 103 U.S. 3062 (1983).

[84]See Ralph D. Stern, "The Law and Public Education, Projections for the 1980's," *Education and Urban Society* 14 (February 1982): 211–34; M. A. McGhehey, ed., *School Law in Changing Times* (Topeka, KS: National Organization on Legal Problems of Education, 1982); and Philip K. Piele, ed., *The Yearbook of School Law 1983* (Topeka, KS: National Organization on Legal Problems of Education, 1983).

[85]Savage, "Watching a Changing Court," 137.

[86]Gwendolyn Gregory, "High Court to Hear School-Related Cases," *School Board News* 8 (12 October 1988): 4.

9

The Board of Education

Boards of education are policymaking bodies by tradition and legal interpretation. Educational policymaking is a political activity conducted within complex political environments. Some communities possess unique political cultures that must be understood if one is to comprehend the policymaking and the decision making that occurs within them. In this chapter we will focus on policymakers and the political context within which they perform their public services. We will describe the functions of boards of education and their members in relation to the growing complexity of the environment of local school district governance.

In the United States, lay control of public institutions, especially schools, has had a profound impact on society and the nation. We will point out, however, that there are opportunities to strengthen the quality of local control and to direct school boards to spend more time on fundamental issues of educational policy and less time on trivia.

The significance of lay governance must not be underestimated. Cremin credits the lodging of the governance of education with ordinary citizens as a critical feature of the revolution in education during the early colonial period. Cremin notes further that, "The laicizing of the sponsorship and the control of education was paralleled by a significant broadening of clientele."[1] This was the beginning of universal free public education. Lay participation was essential in its origins; it is equally critical to its extension and improvement.

Several pages in this chapter are devoted to the origins of boards of education and to their responsibilities. We have done this for several reasons. First, citizens and professionals today are not well informed about boards of education, their functions, and their responsibilities. Second, Americans in recent years have been inclined to turn their backs on the past and ignore its richness. Consequently history no longer acts as a lens for looking at the future. Third, the examination of the history of lay control of education, blended with an analysis of contemporary governance issues, can form the basis for projecting refinements and improvements in the governance of education.

The United States's experience with, and commitment to, lay boards of education is the most far-reaching in the world. Canada, England, and Wales have had a somewhat parallel experience with local control, although their histories of lay participation through school boards have been quite different from that of the United States. Many nations, as matters of national policy, are urging more active citizen involvement in education through several participatory forms, especially local councils. Local councils, by and large, have very limited power and authority, and are therefore usually only advisory.[2]

There are approximately 90,000 American citizens serving on school boards in the United States. These people make decisions that affect the educational welfare of the millions of school children in public schools; they give countless hours of their time to this public service. Some are wealthy, some are poor; some are well educated, some have little formal schooling; some are self-seeking, some are genuinely interested in rendering useful public service. Thousands of board members, men and women, exercise a significant measure of control over American public schools.

THE CONTROL FUNCTION

School districts, as described in Chapter 5, are extensions of the states, subject to the will of the legislatures. School board members are agents of the state, chosen locally in accordance with constitutional or statutory provisions, and derive their authority from the state. The relation of the board member to the state has not always been well understood. The courts have been called on to clarify the relationship of board members in the state, and the decisions of the courts have repeatedly acknowledged that these local officials are agents of the state.

Boards fulfill their control obligations locally in two general ways. First, they are the official link with the public. Boards are to reflect the public will in what they do. Second, boards have crucial internal management responsibilities, such as the selection of top administrative leadership, allocation of fiscal resources, and examination of the system's products. Obviously the external and internal faces of responsibility are related. Public policy bodies such as school boards cannot concentrate on internal affairs at the expense of responding to citizen interest. They must effectively mediate the public will.

Thus school boards are controlling bodies, acting in the interests of the local districts they represent, within statutory and constitutional boundaries existing in their states. The local control tradition has a historical precedent. Yet there is substantial evidence that the scope of local discretion is being increasingly circumscribed. The current status of local control will be described later in the chapter.

Local governments of any type are legal fictions unless power and authority are expressly delegated to specific bodies at that level. The famed Massachusetts School Ordinance of 1642 was quite specific in delegating the responsibility for education to the "townsmen." In the words of the ordinance:

> This court, taking into consideration the great neglect of many parents and masters in training up their children in learning and labor, . . . do hereupon order and decree that in every town the chosen men appointed for managing the prudential affairs of the same shall henceforth stand charged with the care of the redress of this evil, so as they shall be sufficiently punished by fines for the neglect thereof upon presentment of the grand jury, or any other information or complaint in any court within this jurisdiction; and for this end they, or the greater number of them, shall have the power to take account from time to time of all parents and masters, and of their children, concerning their calling and employment of their children, especially of their ability to read and understand the principles of religion and the capital laws of this country.[3]

The words are clear. Not only is the state supreme but the delegation to local citizens is specific and binding. The pattern thus established was reinforced in the Massachusetts School Ordinance of 1647 and in amendments to the 1647 ordinance passed in 1671 and 1683. Note, however, that in the 1642 ordinance, control was placed in the "townsmen," persons who also had other local governmental responsibilities. The control of education was not separated from other local regulatory and service functions of the townsmen; the townsmen were both legislative and administrative officials. They made "policies" either as townsmen or through the mechanism of the town meeting at which other citizens could be heard. Reeves credits the townsmen (or selectmen, as they are sometimes called) with deciding such things as the levy of the town taxes, the selection of teachers and the determination of their wages, the length of the school year, and provisions for housing the schools.[4]

Ordinances passed by the General Court of Massachusetts became the models for other colonial legislatures. In 1677 Plymouth Colony passed an act similar to the Massachusetts Ordinance of 1647. The Plymouth Colony law not only called for the establishment of schools but provided state aid to the local community to be collected from assessments against profits arising from Cape Cod fishing. The Connecticut Laws of 1650 likewise followed the Massachusetts pattern but were considerably more specific and detailed in describing the duties and responsibilities of the selectmen, the nature of the education and apprenticeships to be provided, and the ways and means of supporting local colonial schools. For example, two people were to be appointed in each town of the colony and were empowered to demand that every family give support to the school and to see that the gifts were brought to some central location each March. The responsibility of these two people for this service was to continue until relieved by the local selectmen.

The Connecticut Laws were much stronger than the Massachusetts Ordinances. The language was sharp and the consequences for failure to observe the intent of the law were prescribed. When selectmen found parents or apprentice masters negligent in observing the laws, they were directed to take children from their parents or apprentices from masters and place them with acceptable masters until the age of twenty-one for boys and eighteen for girls. The justifications for such arbitrary actions were implied in the act itself: an educated citizenry is imperative if representative government is to survive.

The New England Colonies set the standard for other colonies and subsequently for the states. The control of schools vested in the selectmen continued for nearly two centuries until the task of governing schools became so great that it was separated from the other affairs of local government. With the appointment of the first permanent school visiting committee in 1721 in Boston, the practice of separating school governing bodies from other local governing bodies began. The Boston visiting committee was a subcommittee of selectmen with a specific assignment. The members of the visiting committee were to visit schools and report their observations to the selectmen. This led quite naturally to the delegation of other school responsibilities to this committee until the subcommittee of selectmen was given full legal status and recognized as the governing committee for the schools. Thus the term "school committee" arose and was applied to other local educational control bodies in other colonies and eventually in the states. Now, of course, local school governing bodies are known under many titles: for example, this body is called the school committee in Massachusetts, the school trustees in Indiana, the board of school directors in Oregon, the school board in Nebraska, and the board of education, board of school commissioners, or board of school inspectors in other places. Regardless of what they are titled there are many marked similarities in what they can do.

Today the statutes of the fifty states provide the boundaries within which school boards function and prescribe rather explicitly the frameworks for selecting members and guiding their behavior. Such matters as the size of the board, length of term of members, procedures for filling vacancies on the board, place and time of regular meetings and special meetings, and the duties and responsibilities of board members are described in the laws of the states.

As agents of the state, local school board members must fulfill the mandates of the state; at the same time, local board members express the will of local citizens and interpret public interest. Legally, board members owe their allegiance to the state and must abide by and carry out the state's mandate. Practically, board members are either elected or appointed locally and must be responsive to their constituencies.

The board, as a governmental body, is created to perform specified functions. It exists apart from its membership.[5] In other words, the powers and duties of the board must be exercised by the board as a whole. Its members come and go, but the board remains the control center for the school district. The courts have been called on repeatedly to clarify the authority of local boards of education. The powers of local boards as agreed on by the courts are: (1) those expressly granted by statute; (2) those fairly and necessarily implied in the powers expressly granted; and (3) those essential to the accomplishments of the objects of the corporation.[6]

Although the laws frequently specify in some detail the powers as well as the responsibilities of boards, questions of interpretation continue to arise. Whether a power is "necessarily implied" or is "essential" has had to be settled repeatedly in the state courts. The actions of local boards have been classified by the courts as well as by special analysts of school law as acts that are mandatory and as acts that are discretionary. The day-to-day exercise of local control can be examined in terms of these two classes of board action, although, as will be discussed later, classifying an action is sometimes difficult.[7]

Mandatory Powers and Obligations

With specific powers to act go obligations and responsibilities. Not only do boards have the power to build school buildings, to staff them with teachers, and to determine which students will be enrolled at which building; they also have the obligation to meet building construction codes, to employ legally certified teachers, and to abide by court decisions. Not only do local boards possess the power to enforce compulsory education laws, but they must also provide an education for all the children of their districts. Not only do school boards possess the power to transport children to school, they must also observe the safety precautions written into state and local pupil transportation codes.

The laws are both general and specific. The statutes may empower the local board to make general provisions for educating the mentally handicapped but require every student to pass an examination on the federal Constitution before graduating from high school.

Boards cannot delegate to their administrative officers or to committees of their own members the authority to carry out acts that boards alone are empowered to perform. A classic example is the power to employ teachers; boards cannot delegate this power under any circumstances.[8] The board can request its administrators to make recommendations for employment and then act on those recommendations, but it cannot legally authorize a superintendent to employ teachers.

As the word *mandate* indicates, the board has no choice but to comply with the statutes of the state. When the intent of the law is clear, the board must act in accordance with it. For example, the board cannot refuse to allocate funds to support a local district's financial obligation in a state retirement system. Boards can, however, work through established legislative channels to have statutes amended or abolished.

Discretionary Powers and Obligations

Reeves defines discretionary acts of boards as "those involving the use of judgment in promoting the legal objectives of the board."[9] He goes on to say that many actions require quasi-judicial decisions on the part of boards and that probably most of the activities of school boards are discretionary rather than mandatory; the acts are "desirable" rather than prescribed by the law. A board exercises discretion when it chooses to participate in programs financed under federal auspices, when it elects to surpass minimum curriculum standards, when it votes to employ teachers who are more highly qualified than state certification standards require, or when it decides to add a new member to the district's central office staff.

School boards involved in school desegregation litigation exercise discretionary authority when they choose to appeal rulings of the courts. Despite the relatively small number of school desegregation cases where the findings of liability or scope of remedy have been overturned, local boards generally avail themselves of every appellate opportunity. They do so most often within a prevailing climate of public support. School boards can take alternative discretionary action through a consent decree. Hooker advocates the increased use of this option, which would reduce costs to local districts and remove the cloud of protracted litigation from the community.[10]

Many mandatory actions taken by boards allow for discretionary choices in their compliance with the law. For example, a board may be required by law to keep the schools open and in session 180 days each year but have the right to determine when the schools are to open and close as well as in some instances which days of the year are to be observed as school holidays. Similarly, the law directs most local boards to employ only certified teachers, but the board controls the assignment of teachers within the district. The board can assign its best teachers to the "toughest" schools in the district, or it can assign its weakest teachers to the problem schools. It cannot, however, choose to employ noncertified teachers in defiance of the law.

Ethical Responsibilities

School board members do not live in political or social vacuums. As citizens of local communities, board members assume substantial obligations to act in the best interests of their local constituencies. In each school district modes of acceptable school board behavior develop, and each new school board member more or less fits into these patterns. Moreover, there are well-developed patterns of board member socialization often involving superintendents of schools, incumbent board members, and school board associations.[11]

Sometimes the public schools become the political arena for reconciling many social differences. Browder has described the behavior of a suburban superintendent who tried to influence the outcomes of a school board election.[12] Commuterville (a fictional community) was a harshly factionalized community. When the progressive leadership of the board was threatened by a conservative group, the superintendent decided to intervene. The behavior of individuals and groups before and after this election displays the sweep of community sentiment regarding school affairs. The progressive majority grew comfortable in its control of the board. It proposed a 20 percent increase in the annual budget, which aroused the passions of conservatives. A painful battle ensued with the progressives managing to save two of three contested school board seats.

While readers may debate the propriety of a superintendent's political activity, the events in Commuterville reflect the value structures of hundreds of similar American communities. The travail surrounding this school board reveals the depth of feeling that school board members and candidates bring to school board service.

There are numerous situations in which school boards have been replaced due to widespread reactions of citizens. Some cases have resulted in recall elections and reappointments. In 1961 the New York City Board of Education was replaced. The governor and the legislature of the state of New York removed the entire board and asked the mayor of New York City to appoint a new one. The freshly appointed board assumed its responsibilities and was confronted almost immediately with serious problems on several fronts. The civil rights issues, teacher strikes, and eventually decentralization questions led to further membership changes in the board in 1969. Citizens have registered their dissatisfaction in smaller districts too. In 1977 the seven-member La Crosse, Wisconsin, school board was recalled primarily because of public concern about permissiveness and lack of discipline in the schools.[13]

There are local, regional, state, and national associations for school board members. Most of these have codes of ethics board members tend to observe. To the extent that these are accepted as guides to board member actions, the codes tend to standardize the behaviors of board members. Thus the codes serve as sanctions. The state associations frequently develop handbooks that include the codes and also provide useful information about schools, school laws, and the duties and responsibilities of board members; they are designed to help board members learn and perform their jobs.[14] The codes as a rule address the following topics: relationships with other board members, relationships with the superintendent and members of the school staff, responsibilities of board members to their communities, and the board members' sense of responsibility to children.[15]

The constitutions and statutes of the various states, the expectations of local communities for school board member performance, and shared standards of "good" performance as exhibited in codes of ethics of the school board associations help determine what board members do. Obviously though, these are only a few of the forces that influence what board members do.

The essence of all government is decision making; the decisions made by school boards are the fiber of local school governments. From the standpoint of public interest, the public must be concerned with maximizing "good" decisions and minimizing "bad" decisions. Board members are powerful because they can apply sanctions that will have consequences for future generations as well as the present one: they exercise enormous influence through their discretionary powers, as the following case illustrates.

In 1974 the Detroit Central Board of Education established a residency policy for professional employees. The decision affected nearly 4,000 persons. The action required teachers, administrators, and other professional employees to live within the boundaries of the Detroit Public School District. The policy was patterned after Detroit Common Council residency requirements for police officers and firefighters. The school board policy was immediately challenged by the Detroit Federation of Teachers. The Michigan Supreme Court determined that residency was a "negotiable item," returning the ultimate decision to the public employee bargaining table. Thus, the discretionary power of the Detroit Central Board of Education was exercised in regard to where employees live and pay their taxes. The arguments advanced in support of the residency ruling were that professional employees should live in the environment where they work in order to understand fully the problems of children and youth there. Similarly, it was argued that teachers should live in the district so that their tax dollars would benefit Detroit children. Opponents argued that a residency requirement was an infringement on individual rights.

Board members have been cajoled, threatened, harassed, and sometimes applauded for their stances on emotion-laden issues. Public sentiment has often been strong enough to threaten recall elections, mobilize opposition slates, or otherwise affect the outcome of school board elections. Busing, school closings, tuition tax credits, sex education programs, prayer in the school, reading methods, textbook content, and pupil safety are some of the issues capable of arousing widespread interest in who school board members are and how they have been chosen.

SELECTION OF SCHOOL BOARD MEMBERS

Appointive Systems

People now serving on boards are either appointed or elected. A 1986 study of school boards by the Institute for Educational Leadership, Inc. revealed that 5 percent of the 1,350 board members surveyed are appointed to their boards.[16] There are some regional differences, however. Appointive systems are more common in the South than in the Northeast, North Central region, and West.

In 1961 when the New York City board was removed, the governor and legislature of the state of New York took an active part in the removal. The governor called a special one-day session of the New York legislature to consider mounting unrest and dissatisfaction with the New York City public schools and school board. The legislature forced the removal of the New York board and instructed the mayor to appoint a new nine-member board from a slate of eighteen names selected by a special eleven-member committee appointed by the legislature itself.[17] The New York board is still appointed by the mayor.

Chicago also has an appointed school board. The present system of selecting board members in Chicago emerged from conditions not unlike those in New York City in 1961. Chicago's school board was under fire in the early 1940s, and the mayor of Chicago asked a committee of the presidents of several Chicago colleges and universities to recommend a better system of school board control for the city. The special committee rejected an elective system in favor of continuing the appointive system with some marked changes. To rid the existing system of blatant political overtones, the committee recommended that the mayor appoint members to the board of education from a list of names compiled by a special commission. The special commission was to be created by the mayor and be composed of representatives of organizations reflecting the disparate social interests of the city. The representatives to the commission were not to exceed fifteen in number and were to be selected by the organizations themselves. Labor, the professions, welfare, education, business, and parents were to be represented through organizational representatives. The system was adopted. Each year the commission presents names, usually twice as many names as there are vacancies, to the mayor, who in turn makes appointments from this list.

Among the nation's larger school districts various appointment schemes operate. In 1986 the National School Boards Association surveyed the seventy-two largest districts on school board composition and practices. Of the sixty-one districts responding to the survey, eight had appointed school boards. Appointments were made in five cases by the city council, in one case by the mayor and city council, in one case by the mayor, and in one case by the mayor and judge of the circuit court.[18] Appointment is often used to fill school board vacancies even where board members are regularly elected. In Detroit, San Francisco, St. Louis, and Boston, for example, mayors make such appointments and as a consequence exercise substantial influence over school affairs.

Citizens, concerned with educational programs, have shifted attention in recent years to the structure of educational government in many large cities. The method of selecting board members was the subject of debate among *ad hoc,* as well as established, local citizen groups. Methods were also reviewed within state legislative chambers. New York City's shift to an appointed board is one example of action taken following a study of selection methods. Kansas City remodeled its methods of electing school board members in 1969, allowing for at-large election of a few members and territorial or area representation for others. Seattle, Omaha, Milwaukee, Boston, and Oakland are other city districts where changes in the size and/or methods of selection of boards have occurred in recent years.

The Michigan legislature mandated several changes in Detroit in 1969, including an enlarged Central Board of Education, decentralization of the district, and the establishment of new regional boards. But in 1982 the eight regional boards were discarded in favor of a single central board of eleven members, four of whom are elected at large and seven of whom represent voting districts.[19]

These changes (reduction in size and movement toward regional representation) contradict an earlier trend. Studying the histories of boards in large cities, Tyack documented a trend toward smaller size and away from ward membership from 1893 through 1923 and concluded, "The campaign to centralize control of urban schools in small boards succeeded for the most part."[20]

The changes in Detroit and Seattle were made by state legislatures. In San Francisco, on the other hand, a change in the method of choosing board members was made through a public initiative. A small citizens group obtained more than 45,000 signatures on a petition requesting that a vote on the appointive system be brought before the people. Voters were asked to vote simultaneously on two propositions in 1969. The first was a test of an elected board system that left details of at-large or area representation to the San Francisco Board of Supervisors. The second called for an elected board and area representation with the areas designated in the call for the vote. Voters approved the first proposal by a narrow margin and soundly defeated the second. The outcome demonstrated how emotional the question of boundary designations had become as well as the difficulty encountered when such proposals are brought to a vote of the people.

There are variations in selection procedures within states just as there are differences among states. While most boards in New York are elected, they are appointed in Buffalo and New York City. In Indiana more board members were appointed than elected until Indiana's extensive school district reorganization took place in the 1960s. Now all board members are elected.

Elective Systems

In some states all board members are elected and in others only some board members are elected. The percentage of elected school boards in the United States has remained rather constant over the years. Of the elected members, 86 percent are selected through nonpartisan elections.[21] Further school district reorganizations could lead to a decrease in the proportion of board members chosen through elective systems. However, in some states with large numbers of school districts, the elective system still seems to be the most popular method.

The election laws certainly are not uniform among the states. Within states there are specific provisions under which elections are held, and in some cases the statutes are very precise about the selection of candidates and election procedures. Primarily, board members are elected at large, by wards, or at town meetings.

As significant as the legal selection machinery is, the systems of nominating candidates are of equal importance. The sorting of persons that precedes the actual voting has become a highly developed procedure in many districts, less so in others. To qualify, candidates must observe legal prescriptions for getting their names on the ballot. Some candidates actively seek membership on boards, circulate petitions to have their names placed on the ballots, and campaign for the positions. Other persons are less active and must be sought out and persuaded to run for election. In these instances other people frequently carry petitions, see that the "letter of the law" is observed, and campaign for the candidates of their choice. In some communities caucus systems are used. Caucuses attempt to seek out the best possible persons in the community to serve on school boards with the hope of achieving school programs of the highest quality.

Some caucuses were called for by statute. Formerly Class II districts in Nebraska held nonpartisan caucuses for the purpose of nominating two candidates for each school board position to be filled each year. But that requirement has been abandoned.[22]

Muns defined the caucus committee as "a body of representatives of a school district chosen for the purpose of canvassing, screening, and nominating the best available candidates for school board membership."[23] Muns concluded, in his study of selected counties in Illinois, that superintendents, school board members, and caucus officers considered the caucus committees to be effective and fulfilling their purposes.[24] Most school board candidates nominated by caucus procedures were eventually elected, and frequently highly qualified citizens who would not otherwise consider candidacy for school board positions were secured through the caucus committee procedures. Indeed, the quality of school board members seemed to be enhanced by the caucus system. Political party participation in school board elections appeared to be limited, but about one-sixth of the committees appeared to be controlled by a few organizations or by a few individuals in the district. Board presidents and superintendents in districts where there were no caucus committees were concerned about the political implications of the caucus system.

The caucus system has had both critics and advocates. It has been most frequently attacked on grounds of elitism. It has been most often defended because it is said to choose individuals with ability who are dedicated to schools and the welfare of young people. There appears to be an ebb and flow of interest in the caucus practice. In the 1950s there was a growing interest in caucuses. The viability of the concept seemed to diminish in the 1960s and 1970s in the wake of an expanding commitment to openness and participation. In the 1980s the use of caucuses continued in several parts of the country. It may be revived in other areas through the involvement of larger segments of the community in caucus procedures.

Motives for Seeking School Board Posts

Those who agree to have their names placed on the ballot, whether they accepted an invitation to run or nominated themselves, have various reasons for wanting to be board members.

McCarty investigated the motives of fifty-two board members in seeking school board membership—the relationships of motives to the type of community; the relationships of motives to variables such as age, sex, economic level, occupation, religion, and education; and the effects of these motives on the operation of the board.[25] The board members were from seven communities in Illinois and Wisconsin. Fifty-four percent of the board members expressed self-oriented motivations for seeking office; they were interested in achieving personal goals or in representing special interest groups. Forty-six percent had community-oriented motives; they were interested in advancing the objectives of the school system to benefit the community generally. Within each of these two broad classes of motivations, more specific motives were discerned. Some saw board membership as desirable because it would lead to political advancement, offer personal prestige, or provide a means to plead the causes of special interests or to voice disapproval of the way schools were operated. Others saw school board service as an opportunity to contribute to better education, to become more knowledgeable about schools, or as a professional challenge. Boards composed of a majority of self-oriented board members were found to evidence high friction in the everyday conduct of school board business. On the other hand, boards with a majority of community-oriented members displayed low friction in their operations.

Similar conclusions were reached by Gross who analyzed superintendents' descriptions of board member motivations.[26] Approximately 50 percent of the superintendents in Massachusetts described motives of their board members for the study. Gross classified board members according to three motives: to perform a civic duty, to represent some group, and to gain political experience. As one would suspect, the higher the proportion of board members motivated by civic duty, the more likely the board would be to agree on matters confronting it. Similarly, when boards were made up of members predominantly representing interest groups or out to gain political experience, there was substantially less consensus. Likewise, Gross found that the composition of boards bore a direct relationship to a measure labeled "adherence to professional standards."[27] Professional standards refer to such things as boards appointing only those teachers nominated by the superintendent, helping to sell "good" education to the community, taking full responsibility for decisions, and having a clear statement of the policies under which the school system should be operated. Boards whose members were predominantly motivated by civic duty adhered more directly to these professional standards than did boards composed mostly of members with other motives.

It should be noted that McCarty analyzed the statements of board members themselves and Gross summarized interviews with superintendents. The conclusions in large part agree and together contradict the general image of American school board members as altruistic public servants. McCarty concluded, "The school board, even though it is a voluntary association with presumed magnanimous purposes, attracts some people whose motives for this type of service may well be questioned."[28] Reeves, on the other hand, while admitting that some members have selfish motives, stated that "there can be no doubt that most school board members have assumed the duties of their office because of a sincere desire to render an important public service."[29]

Hentges analyzed large city district board members' preferences for either a trustee or representative orientation to school board service. He found, contrary to expectation, that more than 30 percent of those board members preferred to be viewed as trustees (serving the district at large) rather than representatives of either regions or constituencies.[30] From data collected two years later, however, Carol and colleagues concluded that "board members increasingly are perceived as representing special interests, and the trusteeship notion of service in which board members represent the entire community has been less prominent in recent years."[31]

Most board members receive little or no compensation for their services. Those who do generally indicate that it is not a factor in seeking board membership. Doughty found, however, that black board members felt they must be economically self-sufficient in order to have the necessary time to be effective.[32] In large cities especially, where poor people of diverse racial backgrounds are serving on school boards in larger number, per diem pay and stipends are important. Wage earners and some salaried people cannot afford to take work time for school business. Thus, compensation for serving on school boards makes it possible for broader segments of the population to participate. The National School Boards Association reported in 1986 that of the sixty-one urban school boards it surveyed, only one did not compensate or reimburse expenses to its members. Thirty-one of those districts provided salaries and/or stipends on a per-meeting basis.[33]

MEN AND WOMEN WHO SERVE

Men continue to dominate board membership, but that pattern is changing. In 1927 Counts found only 10.2 percent of all board members were female.[34] The proportion rose to 12 percent in 1962 and 32.8 percent in 1981. After a drop to 28.2 percent in 1982, the percentage of women serving on boards grew to approximately one-third in 1983, and maintained that level through 1986. Nonetheless, the typical American school board member in 1986 was profiled as a forty-one- to fifty-year-old married, white male with children in school. He is a college graduate, holds a professional or managerial position, has a family income of $40,000–$49,000, is Republican, has conservative views on education, has a one- to four-year board tenure, and serves in a small town or rural system of 1,000 to 4,999.[35]

When a comparison is made between 1985 and 1986, the percentage of Hispanics decreased slightly from 1.2 to 1.1 percent; black school board members dropped from 3.0 to 2.4 percent; American Indians increased slightly from .8 to .9 percent; and Orientals dropped from .3 to .1 percent.[36] Authors of the Ninth Annual Survey of School Board Members asserted in 1986 that, "If the U.S. school board is primarily a male preserve, it's an overwhelmingly white one, and getting more so. Again this year, our survey has turned up a slight decline in the number of minority school board members (with the exception of American Indians). The result: school boards nationwide are now 95.2 percent white, compared to 93.5 percent in 1985 and a low of 90.4 percent in 1984."[37]

A 1972 survey of female board members conducted by the *American School Board Journal* confirmed some earlier findings regarding female board members and yielded some new results. Most female board members are between thirty-five and fifty-five, serve at least five years, and are elected. Very few women are appointed. They are almost always a minority on the board, usually a minority of one. According to the survey, women are often motivated to run for boards out of a conviction that governing bodies need a female point of view. Women cite the preoccupation of male members with finance and construction and their disinterest in educational programs and humanistic problems. The survey found that women display coolness under fire, confront tough decisions, and often devote considerable time to their board responsibilities. It also reported that some women have felt discrimination and most reflect a keen awareness of the sentiments of their constituencies.[38]

In 1973 the National School Boards Association established a Commission on the Role of Women in Education Governance.[39] The charge to this commission included a request for recommendations whereby the talents and abilities of larger numbers of women may be drawn upon and utilized more effectively in local lay control of public education. In the commission's initial report, issued early in 1974, three major points were made: (1) the talents of women are grossly underutilized in school governance; (2) attitudes widely held by both men and women are a major impediment to increasing the participation of women; and (3) women currently serving exhibit personal qualities of service comparable to, and sometimes superior to, those of men currently serving. The commission argued that the population of men and women on school boards is grossly out of balance and that steps should be taken immediately to encourage more women to seek membership on school boards. Those findings were supported by a *Survey of Public Education in the Nation's Big City School Districts* during 1973–1974, which included forty-nine of America's largest cities. Of the 398 board members in the fifty-two largest school districts, 120 (30 percent) were women.[40] There is also evidence that women are taking on roles as chairpersons and as leaders of state school boards associations.[41]

In a 1986 article entitled, "How men and women board members match up," Underwood and colleagues reported that although two-thirds of all board members have a four-year college degree, more male board members have advanced degrees.

Further, men report a higher average family income; more men (66.5 percent) than women (36.4 percent) work in professional or managerial careers; and 40.5 percent of the women (and no men) list their occupation as "homemaker." Women board members were also cited as being more involved in the schools than their male counterparts; women board members are more likely to belong to curriculum, public relations, and textbook committees, while men board members are more likely to belong to budget, transportation, and facilities committees.[42]

Their Characteristics

The social characteristics of school board members described by Counts held true for some thirty years after his study.[43] White reported that in 1958–59 occupations of board members had not changed a great deal since Counts's study. White's work indicated that two broad occupational categories accounted for more than three-fifths of the school board members in his sample.[44] One category including business owners, officials, and managers made up 34.5 percent of the board, and a second category consisting of professionals and technical service people made up 27.4 percent. Farmers ranked third, accounting for 12.4 percent of the total membership, and housewives were fourth with 7.3 percent.

Although White's and Counts's classifications are not identical, they are enough alike to permit comparisons.[45] In Counts's accounting there were more farmers on school boards than any other occupational class. White's study shows farmers in third place. The shift is undoubtedly due in part to the consolidation of rural districts and the resulting abolition of hundreds of rural boards, rather than a result of an abrupt shift away from selecting farmers as school board members. Counts found persons engaged in professional service in second place, ahead of proprietors; White's findings placed the proprietor group (business owners, managers, and officials) in first place ahead of professionals. This change may in part be accounted for by the heightened interest of Chambers of Commerce and businesspeople of the time in school district operation, particularly with respect to the tax rate and school finance.

White's data included responses from 4,072 districts, in contrast to 1,654 districts in Counts's earlier study.[46] Nearly half the board members, 48 percent, in White's study were college graduates; the percentage of college graduates for appointed and elected members was about the same. More than three-fourths of the boards had no one with less than a high school diploma on the board. Larger districts had more members with higher levels of education than did smaller districts. Counts collected data on educational level from county, city, state, college, and university boards but omitted local district boards.[47] He found that 61 percent of the members of these four types of boards had education beyond high school; and 19 percent of the members had only elementary school educations. Although school board members have long reflected high levels of educational attainment, the levels appear to be increasing. College graduates, for example, were six times as prevalent among school board members as in the general population.[48]

In the 1982 American School Board Journal-Virginia Tech Survey, Underwood and his associates reported that 63.3 percent of board members have completed four or more years of college. The largest occupational category is professional or managerial occupations (66.6 percent), followed by homemakers (15 percent), clerical sales (6.2 percent), retirees (5.8 percent), and skilled workers (4.3 percent).[49]

Community Ties

What about the relative freedom of board members to act independently? To what extent are board members captives of or beholden to individuals or organizations in the community? The autonomy of board members has been of considerable interest to observers of school board functioning. Some favor boards composed of free agents—well-educated, intelligent, unselfish, community oriented, farsighted individuals—who would act rationally in solving the problems and formulating the policies for local districts. Others recommended having school boards composed of representatives from a broad range of community interests.

Zeigler has emphasized the historical and continuing middle-class representation on boards.[50] He argues that middle-class bias in public service is not unique. What is unique is the political isolation of middle-class board members. They are relatively free of encumbrances to other political systems. As a consequence board members fall prey to the superintendent's claim to expert knowledge and become dependent on the superintendent's leadership.

The behavior of large city boards tends to support Zeigler's contention.[51] Superintendents and board members were unprepared for citizen demonstrations at board meetings, for example. They found it difficult to communicate and understand the sentiments of the poor and underprivileged. Some admitted, in interviews, their anxiety during such encounters. They expressed support for citizen participation publicly but were privately terrified of it; this was especially true for board members from the middle class. Community-oriented representatives on boards were able to communicate easily and sympathize with their constituents. Such board members often became heroes and were visibly inspired by the presence of delegations in attendance. The ease of such board members in their associations with "the people" compounded the uneasiness of middle-class board members who found such associations difficult.

The presence of poor people on school boards in larger numbers has produced another sort of problem, in the short run at least. The 1986 Institute for Educational Leadership study on school boards addressed this particular issue, stating, "Boards, particularly in urban areas, have become more representative of the diversity in their communities and often include indigenous leaders from disparate constituencies within the larger community. This is positive in terms of diverse populations gaining access to board service. However, when board members are not from the traditional community leadership and power structures, they lack easy and influential access to civic, political, and economic decision-makers."[52]

The absence of external ties to other sources of community power was recognized in Detroit in 1972. A new type of broadly representative citizens task force was formed to aid the Detroit Public Schools in problem solving.[53] Its membership included persons from diverse centers of political, social, and economic power. The task force served as a proxy for diverse centers of public interest and tied the school decision system more fundamentally to influential elements and the grassroots. It was connected directly with neighborhood groups and business and industrial leaders, with the mayor's office and the governor of Michigan, and with the state legislature and the superintendent of public instruction. It became a powerful third party and was able to assist in solving serious financial, management, and learning problems. And it served at the behest of the Detroit central board.

As individuals, few school board members appear in the upper echelons of power in their communities. The studies of power structure reveal few school officials, superintendents, or school board members who possess reputations for unusual political influence. There are exceptions of course, mostly in small towns and rural areas. For a small number of persons, school board membership may be a form of public service that will provide entry into the community power system. For others, such as former mayors Richard Lugar of Indianapolis and Joseph Alioto of San Francisco, current mayor Marion Barry of Washington, DC, and former governor James Rhodes of Ohio, it has been the launching point for an active political career. For most board members, however, school board membership marks the zenith of their political and public service careers.

In summary, school board members typically have higher than average income and education. They serve on boards that usually have from three to seven members. The term of office is likely to be three, four, or six years. They are usually nominated through the petition method and elected popularly in nonpartisan, separate elections. They must be qualified voters in order to hold office and most often represent the districts at large rather than geographical subdivisions of districts. They may receive some compensation in the form of reimbursable expenses but seldom receive a salary for services. They may be motivated to serve on a board for various reasons, but they are not always public-service oriented. Personal motives often stimulate desire to be on a board.

COMMENTARY ON RESEARCH

In the past the literature about school boards was filled with descriptions of what good school board members are like and what good school board members should do. Much of what was written reflected an idealism that probably contributed to improved education. On the other hand there was less interest in or recognition of the political nature of school board service until Charters challenged social scientists several years ago to inquire into how school boards reach decisions.

Educational research has given us few useful descriptions—much less explanations—of how school board members reach decisions. Such descriptions must necessarily include reference to the person-to-person relationships underlying the deliberations and actions of board members, since board decisions are products of an essentially social enterprise. One aspect of the decision process that could bear intensive investigation is the matter of social influence. Certain members of a school board, we commonly observe, are more effective than other members in shaping and guiding the formulation of school policy. We know very little about these key people—how they attain their influence, whether or not they are aware of it, and how it affects the process of arriving at decisions. Of critical importance, also, is the question of the school administrator's influence on board members. The board-administrator relationship may turn out to be the crux of understanding school board action.[54] During the thirty-five years since Charters issued his challenge, a few important studies of school boards have been made. Much of the recent research has been done by political scientists, most of whom have witnessed educational politics for a relatively brief period. Their observations of school boards have occurred during an era of extreme turbulence. They see school districts as essentially closed political systems. Tyack notes that many political scientists would like to politicize local school districts to increase their responsiveness, but warns of the possible detrimental effects of such action on education.[55] Wirt and Kirst argue that a broader conceptual framework is needed for understanding boards as small political systems, one that provides for longitudinal analysis and historical perspectives.[56]

Public and professional interest in the control of local education policy and decision making is mounting. One concern is the locus of control—whether at the local, state, or federal level. Another concern is who controls—professionals or lay people. Still another is the characteristics of policymakers—race, sex, wealth, ethnicity. For example, there are almost no minority persons in key administrative decision-making roles regarding finance. Most fiscal officers, comptrollers, and business managers, are white males. The preponderance of school board chairpersons, chief state school officers, superintendents of schools, union officials, state treasurers, and chairpersons of key legislative committees who participate in resource decisions are white and male. These circumstances brought criticism from women, racial and ethnic minorities, and others concerned about who participates in critical decision areas. There has been an awakening to those realities and a mobilization of effort to do something about them. Such events, recent and powerful, are having an impact on school district decision making at all levels.

Vidich and Bensman dealt with school politics as part of an extensive analysis of one small, rural community called Springdale.[57] They focused on the school board and the local school principal, who in this instance also served as the district's chief administrator. The school board was credited as being the source of some of the community's most important decisions—decisions that were perceived to have far-reaching consequences in the community at large. The school had the largest budget in the community, which made the school the community's biggest industry.

The major contribution of the study was the demonstration of how community coordination was achieved through leadership. As the authors pointed out, the overlapping, duplication, and interlocking of leadership roles tended to concentrate community policy into a few hands and provided a high degree of community organization. A wide range of community activities was carried out successfully simply because a small number of individuals occupied a wide range of leadership positions.[58] Four Springdale leaders appeared in several contexts, and together they occupied a great many of the available leadership positions in Springdale.

Only a few studies have been made of power and influence within school districts. Several investigators included educational issues in their analyses of community decision making, but they examined these in the same way as other public issues. Almost all students of community power have failed to differentiate the formal organizational structures within which school decisions must be made from those in which questions such as fluoridation of the water supply, building a new airport, or changing to a city-manager form of government must be settled.

A study of school politics was made by Goldhammer in the early 1950s.[59] A small Oregon school district was the subject for his study. He observed a board of education over a period of time, noting the formal and informal behavior of board members. He was particularly interested in how school board members were integrated into or excluded from the broader community power structure. He found that school board membership was of prime concern to the community's power clique. The school board was to a large extent self-perpetuating, but its capacity to perpetuate itself was contingent upon the acceptability of school board candidates to the dominant community power structure, the general apathy of the voters to school district politics, and the ability of the power structure to sustain its supremacy in the face of challenge. The findings of Vidich and Bensman and those of Goldhammer are similar. Each study reflects the way in which school political affairs become intertwined with other community matters.

Kimbrough and his colleagues at the University of Florida produced much of the investigative work on power structures within school districts. They reported their analyses of two Florida districts in 1964, and labeled the districts River County and Beach County.[60] Identical methodologies were adopted in the study of power structures in the two districts. Common instruments were employed and the teams of interviewers were jointly coordinated. Quite different power structures were found in the two districts: River County had a complex, competitive power structure whereas Beach County had a monopolistic power structure.

A more ambitious research effort involving 122 districts in four states (Florida, Georgia, Kentucky, and Illinois) was completed in 1968 at the University of Florida. Johns and Kimbrough analyzed fiscal policy in districts above 20,000 total population in relation to ability to support education and elasticity in demand for education.[61] They also identified factors associated with change in fiscal policy in school districts, and assessed the power system in each district to ascertain the relationship of selected behavioral and socioeconomic elements of power and financial effort to support education.[62] Their research is unique in the sense that they related power systems to the other significant variables, such as records of support for education. Their work was a substantial step forward in the domain of power analysis.

Crain and several associates from the National Opinion Research Center at the University of Chicago chose school desegregation decision processes as the subject of inquiry in the mid-1960s. They focused on structure, process, and product. Desegregation was an issue of unusual public interest, thus their findings and conclusions have substantive as well as methodological importance. Their work represented an attempt to understand more clearly how large city school boards have responded to external pressures. They examined too the relationship between characteristics of boards and the policies they produced. Symbolic and real outputs were described: for example, a racial policy that will partially satisfy civil rights leaders without actually making a large impact on the school system is a symbolic, not a real, output. They related the policies enacted by boards to the larger political culture of the cities and concluded that the school board is relatively autonomous in its decision-making procedure, yet the tendency to acquiesce to community demands is determined by the overall political structure of the city.[63]

Minar approached his interests in suburban political life through the analysis of decision making within school districts. [64] A comparative study of four suburban districts was stimulated by his earlier work on school system elections and referenda.[65] The four-case comparison was based on Easton's framework for analyzing political systems.[66] Context, political process, and policy were accepted as the three component parts of a political system. More specifically, Minar was interested in (1) the conditioning effect of social structure on the political system; (2) testing an "input-output" model of political process; (3) assuming a pluralistic rather than an elitist view of what is likely to be found in local community life; and (4) utilizing several techniques and concepts in the study of school district politics.[67] The precise focus was on variations in the style and content of the decision-making process and in the division of authority to be found among school systems whose social-structural contexts differ. He distinguished between high- and low-conflict districts for example and associated this distinction with variations in administrators' policymaking roles.

There were many specific findings of interest (for example, the relationship between level of urbanism and decision-making style) but possibly its most useful product was a set of nine propositions that should be tested further. Three of these are particularly worthy of investigation: (1) a principal factor that differentiates systems appears to be the degree to which organizational skills are applied to the political process at both the demand-aggregating and decision-making levels; (2) low-conflict systems appear to have more "orderly," more managed, and more issue-related modes of demand aggregation and presentation; and (3) low-conflict systems grant wider decision latitude to technical-administrative personnel.[68]

The University of Oregon has a long tradition of research focused on school boards, educational decision making, and intraorganizational problems. Much of the recent school board research has been directed by L. Harmon Zeigler. He and his colleagues interviewed respondents from a national sample of school districts. School board members, superintendents, and citizens were included.[69] Zeigler drew an important distinction between schools as service institutions and schools as commonweal institutions, and concluded that the record of schools is better in the service area than in the commonweal.[70] In other words, schools serve the individual interests of children and youth by providing career preparation, entry to higher education, and better lifetime earnings, better than they serve "the public good" by providing equal educational opportunity and ensuring equal access to learning resources in the school district.

Understanding the service-commonweal distinction is necessary for school board effectiveness. Affirmative action, desegregation, equity in educational finance, and suspensions and expulsions are commonweal considerations. Had a commonweal perspective been more dominant in the post-World War II years, American public education may have fulfilled its commonweal and service obligations more effectively.

Zeigler and his colleagues have published their findings widely. They have observed a gradual reduction in distance between schools and the public, the continuing importance of constructive school board-superintendent relationships, and the need for broad representation among those who participate in educational decision making.[71] School politics, they emphasize, still are not democratically governed. In the area of school board selections, for example, "competition is limited, sponsorship and preemptive appointments common. Challenges to the status quo are infrequent; incumbents are but rarely challenged and more rarely defeated."[72] They add that often there are no issue differences at all in an election, and when there are, they seldom concern the educational program per se. They note too that the apolitical myth that has traditionally characterized discussions of decisions in education remains.[73]

An important case study of the Chicago Board of Education appeared in 1976.[74] Peterson focused upon three major issues confronting the Chicago Board of Education in the late 1960s: desegregation, collective bargaining, and political decentralization.[75] His analysis, though emphasizing the school board, addresses the political factors that help shape Chicago educational policy. Peterson applied both bargaining and unitary decision models to case study data and discovered that each had explanatory value.[76] The behavior of the Chicago board reflected Chicago's political history and its attendant political culture. The board was composed of reform-minded and machine-oriented factions, each devoted to ideological perspectives that controlled their positions on Chicago's educational issues. The single sentiment that allowed the factions to coexist was a shared devotion to the central city.

The reform-minded board members were devoted to rational decision-making processes and citizen involvement. They believed, too, in collective bargaining and felt that school integration would in the long run serve Chicago best. The machine-oriented faction preferred a balanced budget to collective bargaining, favored present neighborhood configurations over desegregation, and supported invoking police power to keep black extremists in line. Each faction defended its perspectives by arguing that their positions were in the best interest of the city.[77]

There are many policy scientists who subscribe to the bargaining model. They hold that public policy is formulated through negotiations among a plurality of individuals, groups, agencies, and interests. Peterson distinguished between pluralist and ideological bargaining. Pluralist bargaining was said to occur when dominant policymakers combined an interest in maximizing votes with an interest in compromising among group demands. Ideological bargaining occurred when the dominant policymakers perceived the issues as major questions of race, social class, or regime interests.[78]

Studies of community decision making with special reference to education seldom specify with precision the linkage between external centers of power and influence upon boards of education. Peterson's work is exceptionally thorough in that regard, especially his discussion of the role of the mayor. The mayor was characterized as a pluralist bargainer exercising influence over schools through the political machine as well as through his appointments to the school board and citizens commissions charged with the study and analysis of school problems.[79]

In the late 1960s a comparative analysis was made of the Columbus, Ohio, Board of Education and the Columbus, Ohio, City Council. These are two independent local governments serving essentially the same geographical area, although not exactly. Board members are nonpartisan, serve four year terms, and are elected at large. Both bodies are the same size. School board members serve without pay; council members are paid a modest salary. Board members have longer tenure and more council members aspire to higher political office than do board members.[80]

These two policy bodies behave in quite different ways. Council members put in considerably more time than do school board members. School board members meet less often than council members and rely more heavily on administrative leadership. Board members were more reluctant than council members to substitute their own judgment for that of the chief executive. Not only were board members more accepting of administrative direction, they were less critical of one another and persons in their employ.

Council members were found to be more open than board members. They made themselves available more frequently to their constituencies and provided more regular, publicly announced opportunities for citizens to present their grievances. Council meetings were much less formal and more given to debate than were school board meetings.

The most recent major analysis of school boards appeared in 1986.[81] The Institute for Educational Leadership, Inc. published findings from nine case studies of selected large city school boards, as well as a survey of school board chairpersons from the other districts in the metropolitan areas in which the nine large district boards were located. The studies focused on the perceptions of citizens and board members in respect to the role and function of boards, board-superintendent relationships, board member ideologies, and board development. The results of this work were disseminated broadly and were the subject of discussion at school board conventions, local board retreats, and within other forums from coast to coast.

It is worth noting that the amount of research focused on school boards fell short of the need in the 1980s, given the importance of their function in American society.

LOCAL CONTROL AND THE CONTEMPORARY AMERICAN SCENE

Local control no longer reflects the pure localism and relative autonomy that school boards enjoyed or were thought to enjoy in the past. Moreover, local discretion is likely to become even more circumscribed in the years ahead. Still, every effort should be made to resist unnecessary centralization. Citizens must have the opportunity to participate in decisions that affect the welfare of their children.

Opponents of local boards of education recite a long list of failures as justification for discontinuing local control. They point to the unequal educational opportunity of have and have-not school districts, to high dropout rates in some areas, to rejections from military service because of inability to read and write adequately, to poor job performance of high school graduates, to "soft" curriculums, to shoddy teaching, and to shabby college performance. People who oppose local boards frequently feel these bodies are composed of persons who are unable to make sound decisions and who are dominated by the superintendent of schools. They lack faith in the system and see centralized control as the essence of good school government. Frequently opponents claim that local control is a luxury and cite reasons a centralized system would be more efficient.

Debate about whether school boards will or should continue arises from time to time. Callahan, in reviewing the history of school boards, documents the periodic challenges to the existence of school boards and notes their sources of public and professional support.[82] Superintendents, Callahan says, have politely contended with board members for power and influence, but in the end the concept of lay authority has been sustained. Currently the most powerful contenders for a share in control are the teachers organizations, which Callahan believes have a strong case.[83] Others would agree that lay control is not in jeopardy even though there are ideological and political bases for change.[84] Usdan believes that the viability of school boards is in doubt but maintains that " . . . the local school board will survive in some manner, shape, or form although its basic responsibilities and capabilities must be assessed more realistically."[85] He argues that if school boards were to disappear we would soon set about the task of constructing something similar to replace them. Usdan contends, "Citizen or lay participation of one form or another in local school affairs is simply too important a part of the 'warp and woof' of America's political and educational traditions to disappear."[86]

The authors of the 1986 IEL school board study firmly corroborated this view, citing as one of their major findings that, "There is strong support for maintaining the basic institutional role and structure of the school board."[87] They went on to suggest, however, that school boards are in trouble. While there is strong support among community leaders, parents, local citizens, and educators for preserving school boards to keep schools close to the people, there also is widespread public ignorance of the boards' established roles and functions. Such civic ignorance bodes even greater trouble for school boards in the future, requiring systematic efforts to promote greater understanding of the important role of school boards in communities throughout the country.

Those who believe in local boards and local control argue that the nation could ill afford to centralize educational decisions. They grant that local boards sometimes make bad decisions but hasten to add that they often make extraordinarily good decisions and that one poor centralized policy can be much more debilitating than a number of isolated poor policies. Others argue that centralized control is antithetical to the American tradition and that America's educational process to date is founded on locally controlled school systems. Proponents cite the importance of citizen interest in education and maintain that central control will dampen that interest. They also point out that centralized decision making is vulnerable to political machinations in high places.

School board members and administrators have limited experience in many emerging policy and administrative areas. To succeed they will need expert staff help, much of it from legal counsel. The spillover from court actions affects programs, supervision, personnel, pupil information systems, finance, maintenance, and school construction. Local boards will have to become disciplined in the fulfillment of their duties, and the performance of administrators will require extensive knowledge about the policy and administrative decision areas affected by the actions of the courts.[88]

The emergence of collective bargaining in education in the early 1960s produced interesting initial responses. Administrators, especially superintendents, were threatened by it, as were many board members. Principals were often overlooked in the process, while teachers gradually came to accept it as an avenue to better salaries and other benefits. Board members and professionals reluctantly accepted the concept and showed themselves to be clumsy, even if successful, negotiators. A consequence of bargaining has been the concentration of power in the hands of teachers organizations. Bargaining has crystallized perspectives and rigidified positions on issues and in many cases has immobilized school boards. Many labor disputes, some of which developed into strikes, have occurred. More disputes can be anticipated as resources decrease, exaggerating the difficulties involved. At the same time, more and more issues are being placed on the bargaining table to the extent that increasing concern is expressed about protecting the public interest on basic questions of teaching and learning.

Bargaining has become a private, sheltered, almost clandestine activity. Issues on the table become the decision province of a restricted few, essentially the union and the board representatives. The bargaining process is incredibly difficult and energy-draining. The product of bargaining that eventually emerges is often accepted without extensive board scrutiny and participation. With more and more issues on the table and growing difficulties in achieving resolutions, it is inevitable that more and more educational policy will be decided by a very few persons. A bargained agreement becomes almost sacrosanct when produced. It is the result of intensive work behind closed doors, essentially uninformed by public opinion. Citizens are seldom well informed about what issues are being bargained and what progress is being made. And the eventual agreement becomes unassailable as far as many clients of the school are concerned. Board members, school administrators, and labor leaders need to examine negotiating practices and procedures with a view toward making them as public as possible. One approach may be to include a third party in the process.[89] Teachers and other professionals, as Moskow and McLennan point out, in the past had the support of many community groups in their requests for improved salaries and benefits. With the arrival of "teacher power," teachers now often find community groups against them.[90]

The schools are either the beneficiaries or the victims, depending on one's perspective, of advancing internal and external pluralism. For example, teachers went out on strike in St. Louis in the autumn of 1983 but returned after four days. Extreme community pressure arose when the strike threatened to stall desegregation. The board, with community support, voted to fire every teacher who failed to return to duty. In school systems with strong professional unions or associations there are at least two contending and often contentious authority systems. One is the formal, legal, hierarchial system. It is constitutional and statutory in its origins, reasonably well-known, and provides the framework within which school board members and administrators conduct their affairs. The second is the union or association authority system headed by visible, powerful individuals. Sandra Feldman in New York City and John Elliott in Detroit are heads of locals of the American Federation of Teachers. Each is at least as well-known as the superintendents of schools in those cities. Teachers in those and similar systems divide their loyalties between the union heads and the superintendents. Important educational changes can occur only if supported by both authority systems.

SUMMARY AND FUTURE PROSPECTS

As indicated in the 1982 AASA survey of the superintendency, tensions between school boards and superintendents are likely to escalate.[91] The seriousness of these tensions was reaffirmed in the 1986 IEL study.[92] The demands upon boards and their chief executives will grow as a consequence of strengthened interest in education. Conflict is probable, especially in regard to educational purposes and priorities. The relationships between superintendents and school boards deserve continued attention in both research and practice. The tension between lay and professional concerns is most visible at the school board level, where expectations of citizens blend with professional judgments. Differences about the goals, objectives, and theories of education must be reconciled. The ideological and pluralistic bargaining that Peterson has described manifests itself in these exchanges as well as within boards themselves. It is there that the difficult financial and managerial questions must be resolved.[93]

Until these questions are resolved, school board service will continue to be marked by stress and discord. Successful performance of the board member role will be more difficult in the future due to the increasing complexity of the policy problems that will be encountered as well as the diversity of local community interests. Policy issues will require more study and analysis on the part of school board members and superintendents. In fact, boards may need to develop clear policies to govern their own policy development. Stated differently, board members and administrators need to probe the basic dilemmas of their governance and management practices and locate more effective ways to approach policy problems in the future.

Board members and administrators will continue to face unusually difficult policy problems. They will have to focus on the present and future simultaneously.

Day-to-day leadership has become so demanding that little time or energy is left for looking ahead. A promising method for blending current leadership needs with the intelligent appraisal of future issues is the "decision seminar."[94] The seminar is a device for dispassionate, intensive examination of difficult present and emerging issues confronting school systems. It is designed to combine broad sources of data relevant to issues in a specially designed decision environment. The seminar permits within-system data to be examined along with significant nonsystem data. It allows administrators or board members to examine transcendent problems that have implications for individual sectors of administrative or policy responsibility. It is, as well, a remarkable tool for board development, a need highlighted in the 1986 IEL report.[95] As noted in this important study, board members are not automatically effective. New board members are thrust into decision-making roles in areas where they have little knowledge or direct experience, and many are surprised to discover that having statutory authority does not make them leaders in the eyes of the public.

Board members will be occupied increasingly with issues that are only remotely related to classrooms. These issues are often adult issues, not issues concerning children and youth. In Detroit and Cincinnati boards of education invested hundreds of hours in debate over employee "residency." Philadelphia debated limousines for board members. In dozens of other districts energy was consumed in fighting over inconsequential philosophical differences among board members. The choice of board chairperson or president frequently produces turmoil. That issue is obviously important, since the outcome may determine the future course of board policy. Boards would be well advised to examine their own performance and employ reasoned criteria to ensure that the interests of their clients are properly served.

Boyd has argued that the record of governance and management of local school districts has been relatively strong.[96] Nevertheless, stronger board and administrative leadership will be necessary as society and its institutions move into the post-industrial era. Paige, following a comprehensive analysis of American political leadership, argues that policymakers and administrative personnel require intensive, planned political leadership experiences.[97] Such experiences should reflect five basic principles: (1) the need for broad, general understanding; (2) value clarification; (3) an understanding of people; (4) development of the capacity for innovation; and (5) engagement in practical problem-solving efforts.[98] "Transforming leadership," is a concept described in detail by James MacGregor Burns.[99] Burns emphasizes the leader's need to enable followers to transcend daily affairs, to free themselves from a preoccupation with power, and to build upon man's need for meaning. Peters and Waterman note that leadership transformation is present in successful companies and has equal merit within other forms of enterprise.[100] Paige's five basic principles and Burns's concept of transforming leadership provide a sound basis for school board and administrator leadership development.

Leadership transformation has merit within the community as well. Yankelovich has identified four requirements for creating an informed public that blend well with transforming leadership philosophy. Those requirements are: (1) credible signals to inform the public of existing problems; (2) an incentive for paying attention;

(3) analysis of issues so that leaders can understand the relationship between the technical and the moral aspects of a problem; and (4) time for people to work through their decisions. School board members and administrators can benefit from reflecting on this philosophy of leadership and its relationship to creating an informed public.[101]

School boards and superintendents comprise school district governance and management systems. Board members and their chief executives need to understand the flow of legislative-executive activity that is the heart of governance and management responsibility. Often the work of school boards and superintendents has been too simply dichotomized into policy and administration. However, there is some value in preserving the general distinction between the policy responsibility for board members and administration for the professionals.

To assist in appraising the governance and management capabilities of local districts, fifteen indicators of school board effectiveness were identified by the 1986 Institute for Educational Leadership research team. An effective board

- addresses most of its time and energy to education and educational outcomes
- believes that advocacy for the educational interests of children and youth is its primary responsibility
- concentrates on goals and uses strategic planning to accomplish its purposes
- works to ensure an adequate flow of resources and achieves equity in their distribution
- harnesses the strengths in diversity, integrates special needs and interests into the goals of the system and fosters both assertiveness and cooperation
- deals openly and straightforwardly with controversy
- leads the community in matters of public education, seeking and responding to many forms of participation by the community
- exercises continuing oversight of education programs and their management, draws information for this purpose from many sources and knows enough to ask the right questions
- in consultation with the superintendent, works out and periodically reaffirms the separate areas of administrative and policy responsibilities and how these separations will be maintained
- if it uses committees, determines the mission and agenda of each, ensuring coherence and coordination of policy and oversight functions
- establishes policy to govern its own policymaking and policy oversight responsibilities, including explicit budget provisions to support those activities
- invests in its own development, using diverse approaches that address the needs of individual board members and the board as a whole
- establishes procedures for selecting and evaluating the superintendent, and for evaluating itself
- collaborates with other boards through its statewide school boards association and other appropriate groups to influence state policy and the way state leadership meets the needs of local schools
- understands the role of the media and its influence on public perceptions, develops procedures with the school administration for media contact and avoids manipulating media attention for personal gains[102]

Belief in hierarchical distributions of power, in which a small number of people at the top of a power pyramid possesses extraordinary power and influence, is now being challenged. Boulding defines decentralization as the antidote to institutional helplessness.[103] She adds that "decentralism and the associated problems of how to increase the number of decision points in the lower reaches of any system and how to increase local involvement in decision making are now important issues." Philosophies of decentralism applied to internal decision making do not fit well with philosophies of centralism applied to external decision making. School systems must cope with the spirit as well as the facts of decentralization. There may be serious practical problems for administrators if they act on the belief that an important community power elite exists as they simultaneously endorse grassroots citizen involvement and the extension of decision points at the school attendance area and classroom levels. To whom do they listen? And how do they reconcile mixed messages when they appear?

The American debate about education and its control will continue. Some issues are new, but many are perennial, such as the balance between lay and professional influence in educational policy. National concern about education as reflected in *A Nation at Risk* ensures sustained attention to both the substance and process of education. The National Commission on Excellence in Education reaffirmed the importance of education to the nation's well-being and specified the roles and responsibilities of school boards in achieving education reforms.[104] The consequence of this reaffirmation of belief in education will continue to be elevated expectations and attendant accountability for boards of education.

In the 1980s voices everywhere, including President Reagan's, were speaking out on educational issues. The result of such widespread and diverse concerns was a cacophony of voices, each determined to have a say in how the schools are run. Recent issues such as desegregation, finance, school closings, and teacher contracts are likely to be replaced by the issues of computer literacy, compulsory lifelong learning, facility in the use of two or more languages, health-related matters such as AIDS, and global economics.

Even as this book is being written, forces are in motion to strengthen local school boards. Statewide school board development proposals are under consideration that emphasize the improvement of school board members as individuals, as well as school boards collectively. School boards are likely to remain as the nation's form of local school government sustaining the United States's commitment to public education.

NOTES

[1] Lawrence A. Cremin, *American Education: The Colonial Experience 1607–1783* (New York: Harper & Row, 1970), 170. For a brief, insightful history of school boards see Raymond E. Callahan, "The American Board of Education, 1789–1960," in *Understanding School Boards,* ed. Peter J. Cistone, (Lexington, MA: Lexington, 1975), 19–46.

[2] For a comparative view of national and local structures for citizen participation including school councils see George Baron, ed., *The Politics of School Government* (Oxford, England: Pergamon, 1981).

[3]Edwin Grant Dexter, *A History of Education in the United States* (New York: Macmillan, 1922), 584.

[4]Charles Everand Reeves, *School Boards, Their Status, Functions, and Activities* (Englewood Cliffs, NJ: Prentice-Hall, 1954), 17.

[5]Robert R. Hamilton and E. Edmund Reutter, Jr., *Legal Aspects of School Board Operation* (New York: Bureau of Publications, Teachers College, Columbia University, 1958), ch. 1.

[6]Newton Edwards, *The Courts and the Public Schools* (Chicago: University of Chicago Press, 1955), 146. See also E. Gordon Gee and David J. Sperry, *Education Law and the Public Schools* (Boston: Allyn and Bacon, 1978), section B–1.

[7]Ibid., 147.

[8]Hamilton and Reutter, *Legal Aspects,* ch. 4.

[9]Reeves, *School Boards,* 77.

[10]For an insightful discussion of the consent decree see Clifford P. Hooker, "Issues in School Desegregation Litigation" in *The Courts and Education,* Seventy-seventh Yearbook of the National Society for the Study of Education, Part 1, ed. Clifford P. Hooker (Chicago: University of Chicago Press, 1978), 114–15.

[11]For a recent analysis of school board member socialization see Luvern L. Cunningham and Joseph T. Hentges, *The American School Superintendency: A Summary Report 1982,* (Artlington, VA: American Association of School Administrators, 1982), 59–61.

[12]Lesley H. Browder, Jr., "A Suburban School Superintendent Plays Politics," in *The Politics of Education,* ed. Michael W. Kirst (Berkeley, CA: McCutchan, 1970), 191–212.

[13]Barbara Parker, "This School Board Learned Seven Lessons in Community Relations—After It Got Sacked," *The American School Board Journal* 165 (July 1978): 30–32.

[14]For a recent handbook see Craig Gifford, *Boardsmanship* (Columbus, OH: Ohio School Boards Association, 1978). For other discussions of board member skills see Thomas A. Shannon, "Look Here for the Skills You Need to Survive as a School Board Member," *American School Board Journal* 169 (April 1982): 35, 40, and George Donoian, "Recognize and Acquire These Attributes of a Good School Board Member," *American School Board Journal* 168 (February 1981): 34.

[15]The codes are expected to assist with board member socialization, although much socialization into the role apparently occurs well in advance of incumbency. Peter J. Cistone, "The Socialization of School Board Members," *Educational Administration Quarterly* 13 (Spring 1977): 19–33. For more on school board ideology read Raphael O. Nystrand and Luvern L. Cunningham, *The Dynamics of Local School Control* (ERIC Document Reproduction Service, 1974).

[16]Lila N. Carol, Luvern L. Cunningham, Jacqueline P. Danzberger, Michael W. Kirst, Barbara A. McCloud, and Michael D. Usdan, *School Boards: Strengthening Grassroots Leadership* (Washington, DC: The Institute for Educational Leadership, Inc., 1986), 8.

[17]Terry Ferrer, "Commissioner Allen of the Empire State," *Saturday Review,* 16 (September 1961): 66–67.

[18]*A Survey of Public Education in the Nation's Urban School Districts* (Alexandria, VA: National School Boards Association, 1986), 75.

[19]Senate Bill No. 635, 75th Legislature, State of Michigan, Regular Session, 1969.

[20]David B. Tyack, "Governance and Goals: Historical Perspectives on Public Education," in *Communities and Their Schools,* Don Davies, ed. (New York: McGraw-Hill, 1981), 20.

[21]Suzanne P. Stemnock, "Local Boards of Education: Structures and Status," *Educational Research Circular* no. 5 (Washington, DC: National Education Association Research Division, August 1972), 2.

[22]*Reissue Revised Statutes of 1943,* (Lincoln, NE: Revisor of Statutes, 1981), 196.

[23]Arthur C. Muns, "A Study of Caucus Committee Procedure for Nominating Candidates for Board of Education in Cook, DuPage, and Lake Counties, Illinois" (Ed.D. diss., Northwestern University, 1961), 2.

[24]Ibid., 72.

[25]Donald J. McCarty, "Motives for Seeking School Board Membership" (Ph.D. diss., University of Chicago, 1959). For a brief description of this study and a report of major findings and conclusions, see his "School Board Membership: Why Do Citizens Serve?" *Administrator's Notebook* 8 (September 1959): no. 1.

[26]Neal Gross, *Who Runs Our Schools?* (New York: John Wiley and Sons, 1958), ch. 7.

[27]Ibid., 87.

[28]McCarty, "Motives for Seeking School Board Membership," 163.

[29]Reeves, *School Boards,* 106–8.

[30]Joseph T. Hentges, "The Politics of Superintendent-School Board Linkages: A Study of Power, Participation and Control" (Ph.D. diss., Ohio State University, 1984).

[31]Carol et al., *Strengthening Grass Roots Leadership,* 10.

[32]James J. Doughty, "Black School Board Members and Desegregation," *Theory into Practice* 17(February 1978): 36–37.

[33]*A Survey of Public Education in the Nation's Urban School Districts,* 75.

[34]George S. Counts, *The Social Composition of Boards of Education,* Supplementary Educational Monographs, no. 33 (Chicago: University of Chicago Press, July 1927).

[35]Kenneth Underwood et al., "Ninth Annual Board Member Survey," *The American School Board Journal* (January 1987): 26.

[36]Ibid., 41.

[37]Ibid.

[38]Carolyn Mullins, "The Plight of the Boardwomen," *The American School Board Journal* 159 (February 1972): 27–32.

[39]Marian Thompson, Commission Chairperson, Memorandum submitted to the National School Boards Association Board of Directors, 29 March 1974.

[40]*Survey of Public Education in the Nation's Big City School Districts* (Washington, DC: National School Boards Association), 12.

[41]Laura T. Doing, "Women on School Boards: Nine Winners Tell How They Play," *The American School Board Journal* 160 (March 1973): 34–40.

[42]Underwood et al., "Ninth Annual Survey," 26.

[43]Counts, *Social Composition of Boards of Education,* 52.

[44]Alpheus L. White, *Local School Boards: Organization and Practices* (Washington, DC: U.S. Office of Education, Department of Health, Education and Welfare, U.S. Government Printing Office, 1962), 24.

[45]White studied boards in districts with more than 1,200 pupils enrolled. Counts included districts of all sizes; more than half of his sample was made up of rural districts, hence the prominence of farmers as an occupational group in Counts's study.

[46]White, *Local School Boards,* 18–19.

[47]Counts, *Social Composition of Boards of Education,* 47.

[48]White, *Local School Boards,* 18.

[49]Kenneth Underwood et al., "Fifth Annual Survey of School Board Members," *The American School Board Journal* 170: 22–26.

[50]Harmon Zeigler, "Creating Responsive Schools," *Urban Review* 6 (1973): 40.

[51]Studies of boards of education in Boston, Chicago, Columbus, New York, and Los Angeles were conducted during 1967–70. This research was supported through grants from the Danforth Foundation and was conducted by teams of researchers at New York University, University of Chicago, Claremont Graduate School, Harvard University, and Ohio State University. See, for example, Paul E. Peterson, *School Politics Chicago Style* (Chicago: University of Chicago Press, 1976).

[52]Carol et al., *Strengthening Grass Roots Leadership,* 10.

[53]Luvern L. Cunningham, "Third Parties As Problem Solvers," in *Communities and Their Schools,* ed. Don Davies (New York: McGraw-Hill, 1981), ch. 5.

[54]W. W. Charters, Jr., "Beyond the Survey in School Board Research," *Educational Administration and Supervision* 41 (December 1955): 449–52.

[55]Tyack, "Governance and Goals: Historical Perspectives on Public Education," 20.

[56]Frederick M. Wirt and Michael W. Kirst, *Schools in Conflict* (Berkeley, CA: McCutchan, 1981), 130–31.

[57]Arthur J. Vidich and Joseph Bensman, *Small Town in Mass Society* (Garden City, NY: Doubleday, 1958). For a review of the value of community studies to the practitioner see Luvern L. Cunningham, "Community Power: Implications for Education," in *The Politics of Education,* eds. Robert S. Cahill and Stephen P. Hencley (Danville, IL: Interstate, 1964), ch. 2.

[58]Ibid., 263.

[59]Keith Goldhammer, "Community Power Structure and School Board Membership," *American School Board Journal* 130 (March 1955): 23–25.

[60]Ralph B. Kimbrough, *Informal County Leadership Structure and Controls Affecting Educational Policymaking,* Cooperative Research Project no. 1324 (Washington, DC: Office of Education, 1964).

[61]Roe L. Johns and Ralph B. Kimbrough, *The Relationship of Socio-economic Factors, Educational Leadership Patterns and Elements of Community Power Structures to Local School Fiscal Policy* OE–5–10–146 (Washington DC: Office of Education, 1968).

[62]Ibid., xiii and xiv.

[63]For a brief account of Crain's desegregation decision-making research as well as other large city organizational studies see Robert L. Crain and David Street, "School Desegregation and School Decision-Making," *Governing Education: A Reader on Politics, Power, and Public School Policy,* ed. Alan Rosenthal (Garden City, NY: Doubleday, 1969), 342–62.

[64]David W. Minar, *Educational Decision-Making in Suburban Communities,* Cooperative Research Project no. 2440 (Washington, DC: U.S. Office of Education, 1966) 136–39.

[65]David W. Minar, "Community Characteristics, Conflict, and Power Structures," in *The Politics of Education,* ed. Cahill and Hencley, 125–43.

[66]David Easton, *A Framework for Political Analysis* (Englewood Cliffs, NJ: Prentice-Hall, 1965).

[67]Minar, *Educational Decision-Making,* 3–4.

[68]Ibid., 133.

[69]L. Harmon Zeigler and M. Kent Jennings with the assistance of G. Wayne Peak, *Governing American Schools* (North Scituate, MA: Duxburg, 1974), 269.

[70]Ibid., 243–46.

[71]Ibid., 242–55.

[72]Ibid., 244–45.

[73]Harvey J. Tucker and L. Harmon Zeigler, "Responsiveness in Public School Districts: A Comparative Analysis of Boards of Education," *Legislative Studies Quarterly* 3, (May, 1978): 213–37. See also L. Harmon Zeigler and Harvey J. Tucker, "Who Governs American Education: One More Time," in *Communities and Their Schools,* ch. 2.

[74]Peterson, *School Politics Chicago Style.*

[75]Ibid., ch. 7, 8, and 9.

[76]Ibid., ch. 1–6, and 13.

[77]Ibid., 251–56.

[78]Ibid., 254.

[79]Ibid., ch. 4.

[80]These are unpublished data.

[81]Carol et al., *Strengthening Grass Roots Leadership.*

[82]Callahan, "The American Board of Education" in *Understanding School Boards,* 19–46.

[83]Ibid., 42.

[84]Nystrand and Cunningham, *The Dynamics of Local School Control.*

[85]Michael D. Usdan, "The Future Viability of School Boards" in *Understanding School Boards,* 265–76.

[86]Ibid., 271.

[87]Carol et al., *Strengthening Grass Roots Leadership,* 10.

[88]Raphael O. Nystrand and W. Frederick Staub, "The Courts as Educational Policy Makers" in *The Courts and Education.* See also Luvern L. Cunningham, "Judicial Mandate and Educational Policy," *Cross Reference* (January-February 1978): 40–55.

[89]Harry H. Wellington and Ralph K. Winter, Jr., *The Unions and the Cities* (Washington, DC: The Brookings Institution, 1971), 150–53. See also Sumner M. Roson, "Public Service Unions and Public Service" in *Improving the Quality of Urban Management,* eds. Willis D. Hawley and David Rogers (Beverly Hills, CA: Sage 1974), 580–81.

[90]Michael H. Moskow and Kenneth McLennan, "Teacher Negotiations and Decentralization," in *Community Control of Schools,* ed. Henry M. Levin (Washington, DC: The Brookings Institution, 1970), 215.

[91]Cunningham and Hentges, *The American School Superintendency.*

[92]Carol et al., *Strengthening Grass Roots Leadership.*

[93]Peterson, *School Politics Chicago Style.*

[94]For a concise summary of the decision seminar concept see Philip M. Burgess and Larry L. Slonaker, *The Decision Seminar: A Strategy for Problem-solving* (Columbus, OH: Mer-

shon Center of the Ohio State University, 1978). A comprehensive description is available in Harold D. Lasswell, *A Pre-View of Policy Sciences* (New York: American Elsevier, 1971), 144–59.

[95]Carol et al., *Strengthening Grass Roots Leadership.*

[96]William L. Boyd, "The Public, The Professionals, and Educational Policy Making: Who Governs?" *Teachers College Record* 77 (May 1976): 539–77.

[97]Glenn D. Paige, *The Scientific Study of Political Leadership* (New York: Free Press, 1977), 189–207.

[98]Ibid., 198–99.

[99]James MacGregor Burns, *Leadership* (New York: Harper & Row, 1978).

[100]Thomas J. Peters and Robert H. Waterman, Jr., *In Search of Excellence* (New York: Harper & Row, 1982), 81–85.

[101]Daniel Yankelovich, "Information, Judgment, and Consensus," *Kettering Review* (Summer 1983): 30–31.

[102]Carol et al., *Strengthening Grass Roots Leadership.*

[103]Elise Boulding, "Learning to Make New Futures" in *Educational Reform for a Changing Society,* ed. Louis Rubin (Boston: Allyn and Bacon, 1978), 57–74.

[104]National Commission on Excellence in Education, *A Nation at Risk: The Imperative for Educational Reform* (Washington, DC: U.S. Government Printing Office, 1983).

10
The Superintendent of Schools

In most of the 15,000 operating school districts in the United States, the program is large enough to have prompted the board of education to employ a chief executive officer, usually called the superintendent of schools. This chapter focuses on the kinds, numbers, and characteristics of superintendents; the function and professional development of the position; and the role and influence of the superintendent.

KINDS AND NUMBERS OF SUPERINTENDENTS

While the term *superintendent,* or *superintendent of schools,* is sometimes applied to the chief state school officer, it usually denotes the chief executive officer of a board of education in an operating school district. In most states, when the term *superintendent of schools* is used without the prefix of state or county, it refers to the local school official.

This designation reflects the nature of school organization in the United States. Legally, education has been conceived chiefly as a function of each of the fifty states. Operationally, the legislature of each state, except Hawaii, has divided the state into school districts and created boards of education as the administrative agencies for these districts. These boards, except in those districts where small elementary schools of one or a few rooms are in operation, have employed a chief executive and delegated to that person many of the administrative functions legally assigned to the board itself.

Evolution of the Position

Two movements appear to have created the need for a superintendent of schools. The first was the reorganization of school districts. As long as school districts were organized in the early New England pattern, each district containing a single one-room school, administrative duties could be handled quite adequately by the board of education. However, when many of these districts were combined into a city-wide school district, as was done in numerous cities during the first half of the nineteenth century, management of the entire enterprise became too demanding for a board of education made up of citizens who were volunteering just part of their time to public service.[1]

This problem was accentuated by the growth of cities. Soon the one-room schools located in each ward or section of the city grew into schools of four, eight, or even sixteen rooms each. The work of administering several schools in a single city needed to be coordinated. Moreover, the financial resources of the city-wide school district had to be allocated among the various schools of the city. Again, lay board members were beset with problems and demands that caused them to seek assistance.

Initiative in establishing the new office of superintendent was often taken by the city council. The Buffalo common council appointed a superintendent of common schools on June 9, 1837.[2] On July 31, 1837, the first agent of the public schools of Louisville was elected by the mayor and aldermen.[3] As time went on, boards of education in some states were given statutory authority to appoint superintendents; in other states, the boards proceeded to make such appointments without specific legislative authorization. By 1860 twenty-seven cities or city school districts had established the office of superintendent of schools.[4] Springfield, Philadelphia, Cleveland, Baltimore, and Detroit had to establish the position a second time before it remained, but the new position in city school districts was generally accepted.

Establishment of the local superintendency in noncity areas did not occur until the twentieth century. For years noncity schools were rural schools, and as had been true earlier in the cities, each school district generally had a one-room, eight-grade school. Moreover, a structural plan for giving some supervision to these schools had evolved in the creation of the county superintendency.

In time, however, the movement to combine rural school districts into larger administrative units took hold. Utah was one of the early states to move toward large, consolidated school districts. The Utah legislature passed an optional reorganization law in 1905, and in 1915 mandated the so-called county unit plan of school district organization. Actually, there were five city school districts and thirty-five county school districts, and these forty school districts are still the operating school units in Utah. Bateman attributes this early action on school district organization to the need for high school facilities and to the quality of leadership the state was able to marshall.[5]

Two movements appeared to affect the organization of school districts outside the major cities. The first of these, already alluded to, was the acceptance of the high school as part of the common school system. This was given legal expression by the

Michigan Supreme Court in 1874 in the now-famous Kalamazoo case.[6] Within the next five or six decades, not only city school districts but rural areas as well began to consider ways and means by which high school opportunity could be made available to all youth.

A still more recent development affecting school districts outside (and inside) the central cities has been the growth of suburbia since World War II. In many instances, the possibility of securing "good" schools for their children has been a major motivation for people moving to these suburban communities. Scarsdale, New York; Edina, Minnesota; Shaker Heights, Ohio; and New Trier, Illinois are four such communities with outstanding school systems.

In rural, consolidated school districts and in most suburban school districts, the board of education found it desirable to employ a local superintendent of schools. The concept of the position in these more recent organizations has been influenced by the concepts that first developed in the city superintendency.

Four stages can be identified in the development of the superintendency. To begin with, the office was essentially a clerical one; board members needed someone to relieve them of minor details. Frequently, the first superintendents were not trained in the field of education. As educational programs became more complex, board members began to rely more on their superintendents for assistance with educational problems. Thus, in the second stage the superintendent was chiefly an educator, often a scholar of some reputation. Tyack suggests that "superintendents in the nineteenth century conceived of this task in part as an evangelical enterprise" and that this conception "left behind a legacy of millenial optimism and an ideal of heroic leadership."[7]

With the continued growth of the educational enterprise, boards of education often felt it necessary to employ a superintendent of business as well as a superintendent of education. This frequently led to a dual administrative organization—an executive for business and an executive for education, both reporting directly to the board. Dissatisfaction with this plan plus the influence of a business culture led to the third stage, in which the superintendent became a business manager.[8] At this time, superintendents were budget builders, managers of property, school plant specialists, and directors of elections to pass tax levies and bond issues. They demonstrated business acumen, but they tended to neglect educational purposes and instructional procedures.

The emphasis on business tended to establish unitary control in most school districts. The superintendent became the chief executive for the board of education. But clearly this was not enough; the board needed professional advice on the purposes and procedures of education itself. Thus, the fourth stage, perhaps still evolving, made the superintendent the chief executive and the chief professional adviser in the school system. In the 1980s expectations for this office were elevated everywhere, especially in regard to rising public demands for improvements in instructional programs and student achievement. This concept of the superintendency will be explored further later in this chapter.[9]

Legal Definition and Status

Cunningham and Hentges identified more than 14,000 superintendencies in the United States.[10] In some states the legal definition and the common usage of the term correspond. In Illinois, for instance, any school board employing four or more teachers may employ a superintendent of schools. About 1,000 of the 1,050 districts in the state have employed such an official. Thus, in Illinois there are legally and in common parlance about 1,000 superintendents.

In other states legal definition and common usage of the term are at considerable variance. Until recently in Ohio, for example, legally the term *superintendent* was reserved for the chief executive officer in city and village school districts, of which there were more than 200. Only recently was the so-called executive head of the "local" school district given the legal title *superintendent*. This change in the law confirmed actual practice and thus increased the number of superintendents in Ohio to more than 600.

Other titles are still used in some states. For instance, in New York and Wisconsin, the chief executive of some types of school districts bears the title *supervising principal*. In these and other cases where the officer in question serves as the chief executive for a board of education, we shall apply the more general designation, superintendent of schools.

Figures from the American Association of School Administrators (see Table 10.1) suggest that only about 8,200 of the superintendents and deputies were members of the AASA. An additional 7,000 superintendents, chiefly in districts with small enrollments, were not members of AASA.[11]

TABLE 10.1
Membership of the American Association of School Administrators

The American Association of School Administrators reported the composition of its membership, as of December 31, 1987, as follows:

Superintendents and Deputies	8,190	44.13%
Assistant Superintendents	1,595	8.60%
Directors and Central Office Staff	1,955	10.53%
School Level Staff and Principals	1,476	7.95%
State Personnel	148	.80%
College Personnel	619	3.33%
Association Personnel	164	.88%
Federal Personnel	12	.07%
Others[1]	3,134	16.89%
Institutions[2]	1,266	6.82%
Total	18,559	100.00%

[1]Includes 2,621 retired persons
[2]Includes 135 School Board Services memberships which represent 894 school board members.

Legally, the superintendent of schools seems to have an ambiguous role. There is, to begin with, the question of whether the superintendent is an officer or an employee. An officer, in the reasoning of the courts, usually meets a number of the following criteria: has an official designation, receives salary fixed by law, is usually elected, has duties of a continuing nature, serves in a position created by constitutional or statutory authority; the incumbent is required to take an oath or give a bond, and the position carries with it independence of a superior power other than the law.

Criteria such as these, as applied to the superintendent of schools, have been interpreted differently by the courts of the various states. Gee and Sperry examined the legal status of the superintendent and came to the following conclusion:

> The only generalization that we can reach after careful study of many state laws is that the statutory protection of the job tends to be minimal, with employment conditions dictated primarily by contractual agreement negotiated between the board and the superintendent. Thus, the superintendent who by law may have the right to exercise a good deal of initiative may in fact not be able to survive if the board is determined to restrict or scrutinize his/her every move. Conversely, the superintendent who has little or no statutory authority ascribed to his/her position directly may exercise great liberty and initiative if the board is willing to place faith and trust in the superintendent's judgment and give sustained approval to the administrator's ideas, suggestions, and actions.[12]

The Supreme Court of Kentucky dealt with the same issue and declared that the superintendent was an employee and not an officer. Part of the language of the court appears below:

> The difficulties experienced in defining "officers" are attributable to the court's determination to extend the term beyond the officers named in the constitution. The misgivings expressed in 1896 by Judge Guffy's dissenting opinion in the City of Louisville v. Wilson, supra, proved to be well founded. The term became a creature of the court, not of the constitution itself, resulting in an era of ambiguity and evasion. In the circumstances, a re-examination and reconsideration of the subject are well within the legitimate scope of the judicial process, and we have concluded that the meaning of the word "officers" as it is used in the constitution, Paragraphs 161, 235, and 246 should be restricted to the officers directly named and designated in the text of the constitution.[13]

We are inclined to agree with the Supreme Court of Kentucky that the superintendent is logically an employee, but not all state supreme courts have as yet made such a reassessment.

Another major question having to do with the legal status of the position pertains to the superintendent's official relationship with the board of education. The statutes of almost half the states declare that the superintendent of schools is the executive officer of the board of education. In Illinois, for example, the board of education has power

> . . . to employ a superintendent who shall have charge of the administration of the schools under the direction of the board of education. In addition to the administra-

tive duties, the superintendent shall make recommendations to the board concerning the budget, building plans, the location of sites, the selection of teachers and other employees, the selection of textbooks, instructional material, and courses of study. The superintendent shall keep or cause to be kept the records and accounts as directed and required by the board, aid in making reports required by the board, and perform such other duties as the board may delegate to him.[14]

The fact that school codes in only about half of the states contain language defining the relationship between the board of education and the superintendent is further evidence of the ambiguity of the position. To be sure, individual boards in some of these states have established their own policies and procedures in which the role of the superintendent is clarified, but there is still considerable indeterminacy about the legal status of the office.

We have restricted our discussion of the superintendent of schools to the executive employed by a board of education in an operating school district. The evolution of the position in something over a century has been noted. We found considerable variation in titles applied to the position and great variation in the size of school systems employing superintendents. Despite the general acceptance of the position and its professional development, we saw that there remains considerable legal ambiguity pertaining to it.

CHARACTERISTICS OF SUPERINTENDENTS

In 1960 Griffiths completed a study for the American Association of School Administrators in which he described the superintendents as of that time.[15] Superintendents in school districts of 2,500 and above in total population were nearly all men; there was a wide range in age when they assumed their first superintendency with the median age being 35; their average tenure in position was about eight years; salaries varied greatly by population of district, but the average was about $12,000. At the undergraduate level superintendents had strong backgrounds in liberal arts, while at the graduate level their preparation was concentrated in education and educational administration. Most commonly, superintendents had experience as teachers and principals. As districts increased in population, experience as a staff member in the central office also became common.

More recently, Cunningham and Hentges directed a study, again for AASA, of the school superintendency, and their findings are shown in Table 10.2. They found that the total population of superintendents was 14,260. They divided the population into four categories according to pupils enrolled in the districts where superintendents were employed and sampled each of these categories. Responses from superintendents varied somewhat in terms of size of school districts. Overall, 57.1 percent of all superintendents sampled responded. A national weighted profile, which took into account statistically the differences in sample size of the four enrollment categories and the percentage of respondents from each category, was computed from these responses. Data reported in Table 10.2 are from the national weighted profile.[16]

The superintendent of schools is typically the executive officer of a relatively small school system; over two-thirds of the superintendents in Groups A, B, and C

TABLE 10.2
Summary of Selected Characteristics of the American School Superintendent, 1982

Characteristic	Weighted Mean
I. Age factors	
1. Chronological age	48.0
2. Entry age-first education position	23.9
3. Entry age-first administrative position	30.4
4. Entry age-first superintendency	35.2
II. Professional experience	
5. Years as classroom teacher only	8.8
6. Years as principal only	5.8
7. Years central office only	1.1
8. Years teacher and principal	37.2
9. Years teacher, principal, and central office	30.2
III. Professional preparation	
10. Percentage bachelor's degree only	1.1
11. Percentage masters degree only	48.0
12. Percentage specialist only, 6th year	17.1
13. Percentage doctorate or more	33.4

Source: Luvern L. Cunningham and Joseph T. Hentges, *The American School Superintendency, 1982: A Summary Report* (Arlington, VA: American Association of School Administrators, 1982).

combined are located in school districts that enroll 300 to 2,999 pupils. If these figures are translated into total population, we find that most school systems are in communities with total populations of 1,500 to 15,000 persons. The study also showed that most superintendents were white, male, from a rural or small town background, dedicated to the job, and middle-aged. The weighted mean age was forty-eight years. Female and minority superintendents, according to more recent data, account for only a small percentage of the nation's superintendencies. Females make up about 2 percent and minorities about 3 percent.[17]

Many of the responses in Table 10.3 reveal the relentless day-to-day demands of the superintendency. At least one issue, the greater visibility of the superintendent, ranked eleventh, reveals the concern of superintendents with their own status. This concern is understandable when one considers the criticism currently directed at schools and school officials.

Judythe A. Hummel, one of the Ohio State University staff involved in the 1982 AASA study, completed research on gender differences between male and female superintendents. She found that males and females agreed on what the role of the superintendent is really like and on leadership expectations for occupants of the position. The biggest difference between males and females was their perspectives on issues of equity confronting superintendents.

TABLE 10.3
Superintendents' Ranking of Issues and Challenges Facing the Superintendency, 1982

Type of Issue or Challenge	National Weighted Profile
Financing schools	1
Planning and goal setting	2
Assessing educational outcomes	3
Accountability/credibility	4
Staff and administrator evaluation	5
Administrator/board relations	6
Special education/Public Law 94-142	7
Obtaining timely and accurate information	8
Issues such as negotiations, strikes	9
Rapidly decreasing/increasing enrollments	10
Greater visibility of the superintendent	11
Personal time management	12

Source: Cunningham and Hentges, *The American School Superintendency, 1982.*

Women seem to be more conscious and sensitive about these issues. Female superintendents saw equity as a much more important problem than their male counterparts. Moreover the females felt that initiatives should be taken to ensure equity. Hummel writes:

> Women, it would seem, through organizational socialization have learned acceptable and conforming behaviors to reach the top post, the superintendency. In fact, they appear to view aspects of leadership and the position from a perspective similar to that of their male peers. The areas of distinction become blurred with the exception of issues centering on equity especially perceptions about discriminatory practices in the work place.[18]

CONCEPT OF THE POSITION

While the superintendency in American education began in the nineteenth century, attempts to professionalize the position have been most prevalent during the twentieth century. At least four movements have had major impact on the central concept of the position.

Scientific Management

The first of these influences was that of scientific management. A major contributor to this movement was Frederick W. Taylor, who published *The Principles of Scientific Management* in 1911.[19] Taylor was trained as an engineer, and he worked for the Midvale Steel Company in a wide variety of positions from laborer to chief engineer.

He was convinced that there was much waste and inefficiency in industry, and this conviction led him to formulate his principles of management. This formulation included the time-study principle, the price-rate principle, the separation-of-planning-from-performance principle, and the scientific-methods-of-work principle.

Taylor's ideas influenced the superintendency through the work of Franklin Bobbitt. In 1913 Bobbitt published an article in a yearbook of the National Society for the Study of Education under the title of "Some General Principles of Management Applied to the Problems of City-School Systems."[20] Bobbitt very deliberately applied Taylor's principles to the schools. He said:

> In any organization, the directive and supervisory members must clearly define the ends toward which the organization strives. They must co-ordinate the labors of all so as to attain those ends. They must find the best methods of work, and they must enforce the use of these methods on the part of the workers. They must determine the qualifications necessary for the workers and see that each rises to the standard qualifications, if it is possible and when impossible, see that he is separated from the organization. This requires direct or indirect responsibility for the preliminary training of the workers before service, and for keeping them up to standard qualifications during service. Directors and supervisors must keep the workers supplied with detailed instructions as to the work to be done, the standards to be reached, the methods to be employed, the materials and appliances to be used. They must supply the workers with the necessary materials and appliances. . . . They must place incentives before the worker in order to stimulate desirable effort. Whatever the nature or purpose of the organization if it is an effective one, these are always the directive and supervisory tasks.[21]

Callahan has analyzed with some care the impact of the scientific management movement on the theory and practice of educational administration between 1910 and 1929.[22] He doubts that superintendents of schools could have resisted the movement since the efficiency ideology was adopted wholeheartedly by school boards, the press, and the general public. Even university leaders such as Bobbitt, Cubberley, and Strayer yielded to the tide. Callahan's observations led him to suggest a thesis of the vulnerability of public school administrators.

Human Relations

The second major influence upon the superintendency evolved in some ways in response to the first. The 1930s and 1940s might be characterized as the human relations period in administration. Again there were major contributors in the larger society, and their influence was soon felt in education. The first exponent of the human relations view was Mary Parker Follett.[23] In her book *Creative Experience,* published in 1924, she reflected upon her experience with industry, government, and education and contended that the fundamental problem of any organization was the building and maintenance of dynamic, yet harmonious, human relationships.

Supplementing the philosophical position espoused by Mary Parker Follett was the empirical work of Elton Mayo and his colleagues of the Harvard Business School. From 1923 to 1932 they performed the now-famous experiments at the Hawthorne plant of the Western Electric Company. That work was described in a volume by Roethlisberger and Dickson.[24] To the surprise of the investigators, the long-held assumption that wages and physical working conditions were the chief factors in employee motivation and productivity did not hold.

This finding led to more careful study. The experimenters selected six female employees and studied the factors related to their work patterns and productivity. Again, the findings were surprising. Whenever factors were changed—rest period, length of day, method of payment—even when change meant return to the original condition, productivity increased. Roethlisberger and Dickson state their major findings as follows:

> It became clear to the investigators that the limits of human collaboration are determined far more by the informal than by the formal organization of the plant. Collaboration is not wholly a matter of logical organization. It presupposes social codes, conventions, traditions, and routine or customary ways of responding to situations. Without such basic codes or conventions, effective work relations are not possible.[25]

Thomas Fleming[26] has shown that administration in education was influenced not only by the human relations movement in industry, but by a second progenitor as well: the "democratic" administration movement. John Dewey was an early proponent for this position[27] and the democratic view of administration became a major theme from about 1930 until well into the 1950s.

One prominent book of this period bore the title *Democracy in School Administration*. The authors of this work referred to the Western Electric experiments and to Dewey as they developed their thesis.[28] They suggested that the basic principles of democratic administration were as follows:

1. To facilitate the continuous growth of individual and social personalities by providing all persons with opportunities to participate actively in all enterprises that concern them.
2. To recognize that leadership is a function of every individual, and to encourage the exercise of leadership by each person in accordance with his interests, needs, and abilities.
3. To provide means by which persons can plan together, share their experiences, and cooperatively evaluate their achievements.
4. To place the responsibility for making decisions that affect the individuals.
5. To achieve flexibility of organization to the end that necessary total enterprise with the group rather than with one or a few adjustments can readily be made.[29]

Bureaucracy

A third major influence on the American superintendency, largely a product of the 1950s and 1960s, was the concept of bureaucracy. Perhaps the excesses of some human relations disciples gave rise to a more structured view of organizations. An important contributor to this view, though his work was done in Germany from about 1890 to 1920, was Max Weber. Due to translation problems, Weber's ideas had little impact on English-speaking scholars or practitioners for several decades. For Weber bureaucracy's distinctive characteristics included the following: (1) a clear cut division of labor to permit specialization, (2) positions organized into a hierarchical authority structure, (3) a formally established system of rules and regulations, (4) an impersonal orientation on the part of officials, and (5) career employment in the organization.[30]

March and Simon also contributed to a more structured view of administration. While both men were trained in political science, March at Yale and Simon at Chicago, they approached organizations as behavioral scientists and set forth essentially a social-psychological model. Their concepts were contained in two books, *Administrative Behavior* by Simon[31] and *Organizations*[32] by both authors. March and Simon saw organizational behavior as different from individual behavior. Human beings, they believed, were "intendedly rational" but limited by their capacities and their knowledge. As such, people in organizations when making decisions make a limited search for alternatives, and they tend to select the first satisfactory alternative that comes along. Thus, organizations do not continue to search for optimal decisions; they settle instead for "satisficing" decisions.

March and Simon also contended that the superior in an organization has the power and the tools to structure the conditions and the perceptions of subordinates. While March and Simon acknowledged the importance of rules, they suggested that most behavior in organizations is dependent more on habit, training, routine, and socialization than on rules. These men did extend the Weberian concept of organizations but in doing so regarded organizations essentially as closed systems; they paid little attention to the environment in which organizations existed.

Most people who have dealt with superintendents and school systems over the past couple of decades will realize that these organizations and their chief administrators have been deeply influenced, knowingly or unknowingly, by the concepts of bureaucracy. The superintendent is at the top of a formal hierarchy. Statements of policies and operating procedures become important documents. Some attempts toward specialization of staff are made. When possible, the problems of employees and patrons are placed in a universalistic context. For the most part, great autonomy for the organization, with little interference from the community, is sought. But we need not rely entirely on impressions; Anderson has supplied us with empirical data in which he found the schools of the 1960s to be organized essentially around bureaucratic concepts.[33]

Open Systems

Within the past two decades a fourth view of administration, the open systems concept, has emerged.[34] This view stresses the interdependence between an organization and its environment. Whereas structuralism focuses largely on internal organizational arrangements, open systems recognizes the interaction through input and output between an organization and its milieu. Open systems can be viewed two ways: as political systems, as set forth by Easton, and as loosely coupled systems, as explicated by Weick.

As noted in Chapter 1, Easton suggested a model for political systems.[35] While Easton probably intended his model to describe the political system at the governance level, it can also help to explain political action at the organization level, including schools and school districts, which continually interact with their environments.

Another approach to open systems (also noted in Chapter 1), as set forth by Weick, is to consider them as loosely coupled organizations.[36] Weick states:

> Organizations as loosely coupled systems may not have been seen before because nobody believed in them or could afford to believe in them. It is conceivable that preoccupation with rationalized, tidy, efficient, coordinated structures has blinded many practitioners as well as researchers to some of the attractive and unexpected properties of less rationalized and less tightly related clusters of events.[37]

Such an organization would appear to permit intrusion by forces in the environment more easily than a tightly structured organization.

While the open systems concept may not yet be fully developed, only such a view can fully describe the interaction between an organization and its environment. To be sure, the environment may be difficult to determine when elements in the organization—labor unions, for instance—combine with elements outside the organization to affect the organization.

We suspect that more superintendents still cling to a structural view of administration than an open systems view. McPherson, Crowson, and Pitner illustrate vividly what administrative life is like in contemporary school organizations.[38] The realities of administration, such as interest group demands and governmental intrusions, more and more suggest that administrative behavior can be better understood through an open systems perspective than through a structural perspective. In fact, for many the concept of structuralism makes the superintendency seem untenable.

While the four views affecting the superintendency have been presented in roughly chronological order, none of these views has disappeared. Concepts springing from scientific management, human relations, and bureaucracy are still with us even though open systems is now affecting thought and practice. Indeed, it may be that each view has some usefulness depending on the problem at hand. Also, while for the most part the four views originated outside of education, they quickly permeated administrative thought and practice in education. To be sure, education did have some scholars who contributed directly to administrative thought. These included J. W. Getzels, who developed a social process model of administration, and Andrew W. Halpin, who set forth a leadership theory of administration.[39] The work of these and other scholars is evidence of the growth of knowledge in the field of educational administration over the last few decades.

PROFESSIONAL DEVELOPMENT OF THE SUPERINTENDENCY

A profession can be defined as an occupational group that meets the following characteristics: renders a vital social service, possesses an esoteric body of knowledge, requires rigorous intellectual preparation, possesses considerable autonomy in its practice, and is governed by a high sense of ethics.[40] To be sure, as Becker pointed out, this is an idealized concept of a profession to which no group, in reality, quite corresponds. Even so, the growth of the superintendency toward professional status might be examined in terms of such criteria.

Preparation Programs

A major question concerning the growing professionalism of the superintendency is: have requirements for entrance to administrative programs been made more rigorous? At major universities the answer to this question appears to be yes. The work begun by the Kellogg centers in the 1950s has continued with the organization of the University Council of Educational Administration, to which some fifty universities now belong. These institutions singly and in collaboration tend to set the pattern for admission to and preparation for the superintendency. A majority of the doctorates given in educational administration are given by these universities. UCEA has also devoted considerable effort to the promotion of research and improved preparation programs in educational administration.[41]

UCEA has made a number of attempts to professionalize the field, including organizing career seminars for professors of educational administration. In 1976, for example, such a seminar, co-sponsored by the University of Virginia and UCEA, dealt with the study and practice of politics in education. These deliberations later appeared in a book edited by Mosher and Wagoner.[42] In 1977 the University of Rochester and UCEA sponsored a similar seminar devoted to the topic of "Problem Finding in Educational Administration." These deliberations were also published, under the editorship of Immegart and Boyd.[43] At both seminars participants included representatives from the basic disciplines and practicing administrators as well as professors of educational administration. Participants projected new research frameworks and considered changes in preparation programs for administrators. More recently UCEA designated Ohio State University as a center for the study of the superintendency and school boards. The center opened in 1987 with a national research agenda directed toward issues confronting superintendents and school boards, emphasizing their interdependence and the professionalization of the chief executive role.

Another attempt to professionalize educational administration was the establishment of a scholarly journal in 1963 and an abstracting service shortly thereafter. The first issue of *Educational Administration Quarterly* appeared in 1965 and has been published continuously since that time. *Educational Administration Abstracts* has been published since 1967.

In 1955 the American Association of School Administrators, assisted by a grant from the W. K. Kellogg Foundation, established a Committee for the Advancement of School Administration. This committee, or CASA as it was generally called, took as its first task the examination of the materials that had been developed in the various CPEA centers and attempted to interpret them for the superintendents. In *Studies in School Administration* Moore listed some 300 studies with a brief description of each.[44] CASA also prepared *Something to Steer By* in which thirty-five goals for the profession were set forth.[45] These goals dealt with standards of preparation, programs of in-service education, school board procedures for selecting superintendents, and some broad outlines for needed research. In 1960 a special AASA committee under the chairmanship of Hollis A. Moore, Jr., executive secretary of CASA, prepared a yearbook entitled, *Professional Administrators for America's Schools.*[46] Major sections of the yearbook dealt with the selection, preparation, and in-service education of superintendents.

After these early efforts, AASA took a further step to professionalize educational administration by creating in 1969 the National Academy for School Executives. NASE is guided by a fifteen-member board of directors and a relatively small headquarters staff. Since its inception, more than 47,000 school administrators have participated in 1,175 NASE programs.[47]

The Superintendency as a Career

March and March have provided a sobering note about the superintendency as a career.[48] In a carefully designed study of the school superintendency in Wisconsin over a thirty-two-year period the authors examined 1,528 superintendents in all districts having high schools. Of these persons, only four served in a superintendency for the entire period of the study. The data included 2,516 matches or superintendencies during the period, of which only 353 existed continuously over the thirty-two years. In these 353 positions there were from 2 to 11 matches with a mean of 4.5 matches. The median match or term of a superintendent in one position was four years and the median length of career in the superintendency was about seven years. Using a chance model in the analysis of their data, the authors found that superintendency careers are almost random. Two factors appeared to keep the career from being completely random: up to age fifty-eight the promotion rate of the superintendent decreased slightly with increasing age, and school districts with larger enrollments had longer matches. Two of the conclusions drawn by the authors follow:

> . . . most of the time most superintendents are organizationally nearly indistinguishable in their behaviors, performances, abilities, and values. This is partly a consequence of the filters by which they come to the role, partly a consequence of the ambiguity of inference in educational settings, partly a consequence of the long-run stability of educational activities and organization, partly a consequence of a lifetime spent in educational institutions.[49]

> . . . the same behaviors, abilities, and values that produce successful careers at the top will, on the average, produce unsuccessful ones also; that little can be learned about how to administer schools by studying successful high-level administrators that could not be learned by studying unsuccessful ones; and that the stories we tell each other about success and failure in top management, like the stories we tell about success and failure in gambling, are in large part fictions intended to reassure us about justice and encourage the young.[50]

March and March have given us a rather accurate picture of the Wisconsin superintendency over the thirty-two years covered by the study. Wisconsin over much of that time, however, was a rural state with many small schools. Therefore, with respect to size, the data may be skewed. The mean enrollment in Wisconsin was

862, and 78 percent of the districts had enrollments below the mean. The results might have been somewhat different had the study been conducted in Ohio, Illinois, California, or some other state with a larger number of school districts with sizable enrollments.

Carlson's picture of the superintendency is not quite so gloomy. While Carlson did not use the term *almost random,* he did characterize the superintendency as an *open elite,* meaning that superintendents come and go with some ease. Carlson also divided superintendents into two categories: career-bound and place-bound. Using Seeman's data,[51] he found that the average term of office was 4.6 years for the career-bound and 8.3 years for the place-bound. He also found that the mean years in office for his own sample of superintendents was 7.9.[52] Carlson also noted an AASA study of 859 superintendents where the mean time in office was 9.1 years.[53] In 1982, Cunningham and Hentges found that the superintendents in their sample remained in the superintendency a median of 7.6 years.[54]

Even with these possible modifications in term of office, the Wisconsin study still challenges us. While it does not represent a national sample, there are nevertheless many states with a large number of small schools. The Wisconsin data strongly suggest that selection procedures for superintendents, at the time of employment and also at the time of admission to graduate study, should be more rigorous. In addition, preparation programs for the superintendency may require considerable revision if they are to help superintendents acquire distinctive knowledge and skill.[55]

THE ROLE OF THE SUPERINTENDENT

Place in the Organization

In most school districts the superintendent of schools is the formally recognized chief executive. He is the most visible, most vulnerable, and potentially most influential member of the organization. There are still a few city school districts where the superintendent is coordinate with a business manager or superintendent of business, and there are still some rural districts where the school clerk, in practice if not in name, exercises a role coordinate with that of the superintendent. But for the most part the superintendent is the chief executive.

In sparsely populated school districts, as noted earlier, the superintendent may also double as high school principal and even as part-time teacher. In middle-range school districts the superintendent will ordinarily work directly with school principals and a few central office personnel. In large city school districts the superintendent may have scores and even hundreds of central office, regional, and individual school administrative subordinates. Despite these differences in size and complexity, the superintendent stands at the top of the hierarchy of the organization.

With respect to the board of education, the superintendent of schools is usually recognized as the chief executive officer. In some instances the board may turn to a business manager or a clerk as a coordinate executive in the realm of business management. But business decisions in an educational organization are finally related to the educational program, which is the realm of the superintendent even in dual organizations. Hence, the superintendency in these organizations, as well as in unit organizations, is pivotal.

Much of the writing on board-superintendent relationships suggests that the differentiation of function between the board and the superintendent is a very simple one: the board is to formulate policy, the superintendent is to administer it. This formulation has a certain gross usefulness, but upon examination it becomes apparent that most superintendents influence policy and that most boards have some voice in administration. Houle has suggested that the board and the superintendent are partners in the management of the enterprise, each with distinctive contributions to make.[56] This concept is generally more useful than strict ascription of policymaking to the board and administration to the superintendent.

Expectations of boards for their superintendents are often clarified through an evaluation process. Sonedecker found growing interest in formal evaluation of superintendents. His work, reported in 1984, indicated movement toward more systematic superintendent evaluation, especially in suburban and large city districts. He noted too, that the form of the evaluation and a calendar were often written into the superintendent's contract. Thoughtful and consistent attention to evaluation can not only clarify expectations but lead to a closer correspondence between the goals of the district and how the chief executive's performance is related to those goals.[57]

What Superintendents Do

Most accounts of what superintendents do are based on self-reports. There are, however, an increasing number of studies based on the actual observation of superintendents at work.

Pitner studied the everyday activities of three suburban superintendents.[58] Focusing chiefly on the superintendent as a manager of information, she raised questions about how superintendents spend their time; their role behavior as they deal with different groups; the comparability of their behaviors, abilities, and values; and the rules, strategies, and tactics they employ. Her data came from direct observation, five days for each superintendent, and from interviews with them. She found that superintendents spend about 80 percent of their time talking with others. Five types of information were processed: technical information, legal rules and regulations, past activities of the district, preferences of persons in and outside the school system, and probable reactions of different constituencies to decisions and conditions. Superintendents did differentiate their behavior with different groups, and they appeared to have considerable influence in making policy. Superintendents' activities proved to be largely desk work, phone calls, and scheduled and unscheduled meetings. In terms of tactics, superintendents were seen as interpreters of organization history, interpreters of contemporary events, managers of meaning, and managers of organizational myths or sagas.

In another study, Feilders examined in depth the activities of one urban superintendent, Robert Alioto of San Francisco.[59] Consideration was given to where he spent his time, with whom, at whose initiative, at what time, for how long, and what medium prevailed. The study focused not only on the superintendent's manifest behavior, but on his thoughts, feelings, and intentions. Drawing on techniques used by some ethnographers, Feilders shadowed the superintendent for three days per week over a ten-week period. He recorded his observations and interviews in a journal and made a time study of his activities similar to the one made by Mintzberg.[60]

Some of the explicit features of the job that Feilders discovered were: the work week of the superintendent was long; he spent most of his time in the office meeting with staff members for brief periods; he initiated less than half of his activities; face-to-face communication was the main medium; the discussion usually centered on issues related to personnel; the main purpose of his activities was to process information; and the superintendent's dominant role was that of spokesperson for the administration. Feilders noted some methodological limitations in his study, but his extended description and interpretation of the superintendent's activities are very revealing.

Also influenced by Mintzberg, Duignan did a structured observation study of eight superintendents in the province of Alberta.[61] He supplemented his observation notes with data collected through interviews and information provided by each superintendent on the pattern of his activities for the week prior to the observation period. He found that the superintendents averaged 8.2 hours of working time each day. This time was divided into thirty-eight different activities, each lasting an average of about thirteen minutes. Approximately one-quarter of a superintendent's daily working time was spent in unscheduled meetings and another one-quarter in scheduled meetings. The remainder of his time was spent at desk work, telephone calls, travel, evening meetings, and visits to the schools. A superintendent averaged twenty-six verbal contacts each day and these contacts represented about 70 percent of his working time.

Cunningham and McCloud recently capsulated the work life of a large city superintendent, Lee McMurrin of Milwaukee, Wisconsin, from self-report data aggregated over a period of years.

> McMurrin's recordings of his work are categorized under several headings. Those headings and the days, all or in part, included these entries in 1984: office hours and appointments (203); court, et al. (17); holidays (10); vacation days (16); meetings with local, state and federal officials (59); conferences, conventions and seminars (25); school visits and school related programs and meetings (98); board meetings (48); speaking engagements and evening meetings (81); and sick days (0). He was on school business fifty evenings in 1984. Considerable work occurred on weekends. Obviously stamina was an important attribute for McMurrin's work.[62]

To summarize, major studies of superintendents have concentrated on different aspects of the position. Pitner concerned herself with the nature of the information processed by the superintendents. Feilders concentrated on descriptions of manifest behavior and also attempted to get at the thoughts and feelings of the superintendent. Duignan gave particular attention to the superintendent's need to control his or her time, to the ways others participated in the decision making of the superintendent, and to the relatively little time the superintendent gives to items strictly categorized as instruction.

Also suggested by these studies is the beleaguered nature of the superintendent's day. It is interesting to note that Willower and Fraser, after interviewing fifty superintendents, came to the conclusion that superintendents deal with a wide range of problems, are irked by the paperwork demands of state and federal agencies, regret not being closer to the classroom, and feel the pressures of the job but are ready to do it over again.[63] Willower and Fraser also concluded "that school superintendents are not quite as beleaguered as is sometimes claimed and when they are, they appear to have come to grips with it rather well, often with good humor."[64] Perhaps the term *beleaguering* is, at least in part, in the observer's eye.

In a quite different study of what superintendents do, Cuban made historical case studies of three prominent urban superintendents, Benjamin Willis of Chicago, Carl Hansen of Washington, DC, and Harold Spears of San Francisco, all of whom served during the late 1950s and for most of the 1960s.[65] In analyzing his data, Cuban developed four concepts of the superintendency: the teacher-scholar, the negotiator-statesman, the corporate administrator, and the rational school chief. In characterizing the three superintendents, Cuban saw Willis as a rational school chief and corporate administrator, Hansen as a rational school chief and teacher-scholar, and Spears as a rational school chief and negotiator-statesman. Common to all three superintendents was the designation rational school chief, but each person combined with that approach a unique approach of his own. Cuban then offered three factors for why his superintendents exhibited the approaches described: a historical residue of beliefs and practices, shared by the three men; individual socialization within the school enterprise as a teacher and administrator, also shared by the three men; and conflicting organizational role demands, again largely shared by the three men. It also is significant to note that the role common to all three superintendents, the rational school chief, was very much a reflection of the bureaucratic approach to administration, characteristic of both administrative thought and practice during the time of tenure of these superintendents.

Administration and Leadership

Another significant area of study concerns the extent to which the superintendent attempts to maintain the organization or to change it. Lipham contends that in this distinction lies the difference between administration and leadership.[66] To keep an organization moving in its customary direction, he suggests, is administration; to change the goals or procedures in the organization is leadership. This distinction does not prohibit the administrator from being a leader, but it does suggest that, for the most part, administrators attempt to maintain their organizations.

The role of the administrator in maintaining the organization is given further support in the Hemphill study.[67] The principals who were strong in analyzing situations received negative ratings from their superintendents and teachers. One gets the impression from these data that superintendents and teachers cherish principals who "keep the lid on," who do not have too many "fool notions," and who keep things running smoothly.

It might seem that most organizations cannot stand up under frequent and extensive attempts to change goals or procedures. At the same time, there are periods in the life of organizations when new goals and new procedures are direly needed. Thus, when organizations become ripe for change an administrator who is also a leader should be sought. After a period of innovation, an administrator who is strong on consolidation and short on innovation may then be needed.

The Superintendent and the Environment

Superintendents work not only with their organizations; they must also relate their organizations to the larger society. Legitimization of the organization must come from the larger society and, in the case of a public service such as education, financial support of the organization clearly rests with the larger society. In the relationships of the organization to its environment, the distinction between maintaining and changing an organization can be further elaborated. The administrator might accept the decision of society with respect to resources, or he or she might bargain, manipulate, and fight to obtain greater resources for the organization. Accepting the resources society offers cannot be called leadership; maneuvering to get additional resources would be considered leadership.

Many superintendents are greatly occupied with manipulating the environment to win support for education. In many city school districts where there is great diversity among people with respect to occupation, income, origin, race, and religion, the superintendent lives a life of constant struggle. Different groups of city school patrons may want better education for the gifted, more opportunity for the handicapped, extended preschool education in impoverished neighborhoods, more vocational education, the establishment of junior colleges, and many other diverse programs. At the same time, taxpayer leagues, some business groups, and real estate associations may insist that school taxes are already exorbitant. Blacks may argue that integration of the schools is not moving along or that it should be abandoned. It is in a welter of such demands that the superintendent must strive for wide public support.

The problem takes a slightly different form in the upper-middle-class suburb. The population is often much more homogeneous, most adults have a college education, and professional or managerial occupations are common. But these circumstances make every resident his or her own educational expert. Adults read the literature on basic education. Admission of their children to prestige colleges becomes paramount. The results of College Board examinations and the percentage of National Merit Scholarship winners are accepted as convenient yardsticks for measuring the quality of high schools. Teachers find that high living costs force them to reside outside the community in which they teach. For a superintendent to marshal support for public education from a population of this kind is no easy task.

Even the rural center presents many problems for the superintendent. Here schools have small enrollments, and enrollments continue to go down. Combinations of schools, particularly at the high school level, are obviously needed, but residents fear that losing the local high school may mean the end of their community identity— for example, they would no longer have their own basketball team. Many farm residents and small-town merchants have little interest in college preparatory programs; hence, they see no great need to improve teaching in science, mathematics, or foreign languages. The employment of local teachers, even though they are less well prepared for their posts, may be seen as a way of keeping the community intact, particularly if they are willing to work for slightly less than teachers from outside the community. Superintendents may feel that to accept this situation is cheating the younger generation with whose tutelage they are charged.

The social and educational changes of the last few decades as well as the political, social, demographic, and economic forecasts of the future require a new set of management skills for the superintendent. He or she must be a social analyst, an organizational diagnostician, a planner, and a mediator, all rolled into one. The first two of these roles are conceptual and analytical; the last two are also conceptual, but the action components are generally more apparent. As a planner, the superintendent must be a logical analyst; as a mediator, the superintendent must be a skilled power broker. Administrators, particularly at the top of the hierarchy, must do much thinking before acting.[68]

Obviously, the superintendent has a political role, but it is a political role with educational underpinnings. As long as education remains as decentralized as it is in the United States, there is no alternative. If the superintendents of schools do not make the case for public education and wage the fight for community support, there will be a serious void in many communities. This is not to suggest that the superintendent is without allies. Cultivating lay leadership for education in the community can be a major part of the superintendent's job. Board members and other lay citizens may become community spokespeople for education, but behind them a catalytic agent is needed and for that role the spotlight is on the superintendent.

If adequate educational programs are to be developed and supported, superintendents must attempt to manipulate the environment. Such a course of action is not easy. Many superintendents, despairing of the rigorous professional life, will simply follow the will of the community. Even that course is not without hardship and conflict, however, for in time some will lose patience with the status quo.

As chief executive of the school system, the superintendent interacts with a variety of people on school matters both inside and outside the school organization. Most of the superintendent's time and energy is spent maintaining the organization, but at times he or she may be compelled to exert leadership to change the goals or procedures of the organization. Superintendents are confronted with the question of accepting the resources society offers to support the organization or working within the environment to win a greater share of the resources. They also will have to continue to demonstrate considerable political acumen in order to foster in the larger society the conditions necessary to support viable educational programs.

THE INFLUENCE OF THE SUPERINTENDENT

Influence on the Board

As the chief executive officer of the board of education, the superintendent seems initially to have a position of power. Indeed, many superintendents speak of a honeymoon period early in their tenure when the board grants almost every request. But honeymoons end, and superintendents soon find their boards less tractable. To be sure, boards vary a great deal in this respect. Some boards become completely dependent on the superintendents and in a sense become little more than a rubber stamp. Other boards regard the superintendent as a hired hand. One extreme is as undesirable as the other.

Several studies help to explain the influence superintendents may have with boards. To begin with, we need to recognize that the superintendency is not the same everywhere. Many factors can alter, to some extent, the context within which the superintendent operates. For instance, McCarty and Ramsey, on the basis of their research, posited four types of communities that produce four types of school boards, and they suggested four corresponding roles for the superintendent. These roles include the functionary, the political strategist, the professional advisor, and the decision maker.[69] Carlson has also dealt extensively with career-bound and place-bound superintendents and the effect each type has on the school organization. For instance, the career-bound superintendent seems to have a mandate for change whereas the place-bound superintendent is expected to keep things pretty much as they are. Carlson's findings were confirmed in Dusek's replication in 1982.[70]

The nature of the influence superintendents have with boards was the focus of considerable research by Zeigler and his associates.[71] In essence, Zeigler found that most boards of education rely on their superintendents for policy recommendations. Boards, rather than governing the schools, legitimatize the programs of their superintendents. Zeigler puts the matter as follows:

> Board members, lacking a meaningful relationship to an external political constituency, fall easy prey to the superintendent's claim for "expertise." The recruitment process—looking to the civic-business world for the pool of eligibles, *virtually guarantees that the notion of lay control will be subverted.* We do not have lay control because, among other reasons, school board members do not want to control educational policy. Their background and experience compels them to look toward the superintendent's office for leadership. As the ideological descendant of the nineteenth century reformers, today's school board member is doing a good job: he is leaving the governance of the schools to the experts.[72]

Zeigler's work and a number of related studies have been carefully reviewed by Boyd.[73] He finds the matter much more complex than might be inferred from the conclusions set forth by Zeigler. Boyd summarizes his main contention in the following statement:

> I have argued that if schools are not merely the "mirror images" of the communities they serve, neither are they almost completely insulated bastions dominated by unresponsive and self-serving professional educators. Instead, I have proposed that while educators tend to dominate local educational policy making, they usually operate within significant and generally neglected or underestimated constraints imposed by the *local* community and school board—not to mention those imposed by state and national forces. These constraints (or, put another way, the influence of the community and the board) are likely to vary primarily with the type of school district and the type

of policy issue that is faced. The local citizenry and the board will tend to have more influence in *external, redistributive,* and *strategic* policy decisions, and in *smaller* and more *homogeneous* communities where the professionals tend to anticipate or reflect (especially in middle and upper middle class communities) community demands. The professionals, on the other hand, will tend to have more influence in *internal* and *routine* policy decisions, and in *larger* and more *heterogeneous* communities.[74]

Superintendents in many school districts have considerable influence on their boards of education, and this influence is a product of the person who occupies the superintendency as well as the settings within which the superintendent and board operate. Hentges found, however, that there is considerable variation in the amount of influence on specific issues. Superintendents were able to exercise considerable control over issues essentially internal to the system, such as the educational program, personnel evaluation, and testing practices. Boards exercise control over, even resist superintendents' leadership on, issues involving finance, school construction, school closings, desegregation, and other civil rights matters. Some superintendents, Hentges reported, are able to dominate their boards on all issues but they are in the minority. The balance between professional expertise and lay judgment may not be tipped as far to the professional side as some have maintained.[75]

INFLUENCE ON THE STAFF

The superintendent of schools may influence the staff by exercising the prerogatives of the office and developing prestige with the staff. Office is conferred, but prestige must be earned. These concepts will be discussed more fully in Chapter 11, but let us see now what they may mean for the superintendent.

The superintendent usually selects subordinate personnel in the central office. In large organizations the superintendents will, of course, select only their major subordinates, but in small organizations their preferences will probably determine selections of all personnel. This prerogative means that the superintendent has great influence in defining job expectations, in seeking people who can meet such expectations, and in clarifying the assignments made to such personnel after they join the organization. To be sure, most administrators inherit part of their personnel, but even so, the opportunity to build an organization in whole or in part with people of his or her own choice gives an administrator, initially, great potential influence.

Ordinarily, too, the administrator has some control over salaries and promotions. While formal salary schedules lessen this control, administrators often can channel additional pay to those in their organizations who, in their judgment, deserve it. Promotions to supervisory and administrative posts in the organization, like selection, are often at the discretion of the administrator.

As a further official prerogative, superintendents have some control over the allocation of material resources. They often determine which buildings, which departments, and in smaller school systems which teachers, receive more books, more supplies, more equipment. To be sure, if these decisions become completely idiosyncratic there are ways, both formal and informal, in which an organization can seek redress. However, within limits the superintendent can, by the allocation of resources, determine which areas of the curriculum and which student activities will be promoted and which deemphasized.

But the power of office is hollow unless the superintendent has earned the respect of members of the organization. Prestige might come through the superintendent's ability to clarify purpose and direction for the school system both inside and outside the organization. Prestige might come when the superintendent shows insight on program requirements to meet certain purposes. Prestige might be earned if the superintendent were able to provide appropriate participation for the staff on questions of importance to them. The superintendent might also acquire prestige with staff members if they become convinced that he or she influences the larger society favorably toward the school system. This influence could take tangible expression in the willingness of the community to provide money for school operation. But just as important is the way the superintendent stands behind the staff when representing them to the community. Unless the superintendent acquires some of the power of prestige, the power of the office will begin to erode.

According to the concept of authority suggested by Simon, the superintendent has authority only when subordinates permit their behavior to be guided by the superintendent's decision without independently examining the merits of that decision.[76] This concept should help superintendents recognize that the sanction of office, powerful though it is, must be supplemented by earned prestige and influence. With the increase in teacher militancy, earning prestige and influence will be more difficult, and indeed in some school systems this effort has been abandoned altogether.

The superintendent's influence either through sanction of office or earned prestige can be considerable, but the school system is a loosely coupled system. A loosely coupled system, as Weick has suggested, allows more room for self-determination on the part of the actors.[77] Thus, staff members may or may not be impressed with the power of the superintendent's office and they may vary appreciably in their willingness to be guided by the superintendent's decisions.

The size of the school system can affect how a superintendent exercises the influence of office and of prestige. In large school systems the superintendent's influence on selection of personnel, salaries, and promotion would affect most directly the central office staff and school principals while in small school systems that influence would affect teachers as well. In a large school system the superintendent's capacity to clarify purposes and comprehend programs would perhaps be most apparent to his immediate staff. The details of relationships with the community would also tend to be known only by his immediate staff.

But steps can be taken to make the superintendent visible and influential outside the central staff. This is largely a matter of communication. A willingness on the part of the superintendent to conduct an open school system and to keep staff, board, media, and total community informed about problems, needs, successes, and failures would be a sound platform on which to operate. Obviously media relationships play a major role in these respects.[78]

Influence on the Local Community

Earlier in this chapter we noted that the superintendent is cast in a political role. Unless willing merely to accept what the community provides for school support, the superintendent must manipulate the environment to increase the resources for the schools. Most communities, however, possess certain limiting characteristics the superintendent cannot change. James and his colleagues have suggested that these limits are found in the expectations of the people for education, in the wealth of the school district most often expressed in assessed valuation, and in the government arrangements controlling access to money for schools.[79]

In open systems such as schools, expectations for education are subject to some change. Wealth, however, barring some fortuitous circumstance such as the establishment of new industry, is not subject to change. Limited wealth can ordinarily be offset only by state or federal financial assistance of some kind. Obviously, state restrictions on tax levies, voting requirements, and other access arrangements can only be changed by the state legislature. Thus, at any time each superintendent works within a set of limitations in the community.

Within these limitations, however, there is ordinarily some leeway. The superintendent must find ways to exploit that leeway and in the long run must give attention to ways of reducing the limitations. Since the board of education is officially the intermediate body between the school organization and the community, the superintendent must begin with the board. Frequently board members become emissaries for carrying the school message to the community, but to be effective emissaries board members must understand the purposes behind school programs and something about the nature of the programs themselves. Inevitably, the superintendent becomes the chief agent for providing board members with such information.

In many communities the superintendent must work not only with the board of education but with other lay leaders. These people may be found in business, the professions, labor groups, ethnic societies, civic organizations, and other places. Ways must be found to acquaint these people with school needs. If needs seem important to interest-group leaders, they may be able to help marshal community support for programs to meet those needs. Leadership appears to be dispersed in terms of both people and issues.[80] Nevertheless, certain people in a community do influence the thinking of others, and they must be reached and enlisted in the support of school programs if those programs are to be adequately supported.

As an outgrowth of the civil rights revolution, most city superintendents in recent years have had difficulty interpreting the will of communities made up largely of blacks or other minority groups. At times minority group leaders insist that the schools be desegregated. At other times they accept segregated schools and demand that they have more control over them. When more community control is sought, white teachers and white principals are often not acceptable. Superintendents must develop ways of working with leaders of minority communities just as they do with leaders of other community groups. As noted earlier, not all superintendents now are white; a few blacks and other minority group members have been selected for the position. These numbers are much too small, however, and efforts must be made to appoint more minorities, including women, to superintendencies.

To influence the community, it seems quite clear that the superintendent must have a program, must be aware of the limitations within which he or she is working; must build understanding and support with the board of education; must enlist, with the help of board members if possible, the support of lay leaders in the community; and must utilize mass media and other means to inform the community about school programs, desirable directions, and necessary resources.

Influence on the Larger Community

No school district exists in a vacuum. Actually, as noted in Chapter 5, the district exists as an instrument of the state legislature to carry out certain state purposes. Even the federal government controls much of what schools can do (Chapter 3). Every district, however, is also subject to many extralegal influences. Agencies such as the accrediting associations and the College Entrance Examination Board are examples of influential bodies. No school district is required legally to comply with these programs, but accreditation is important to most communities. College board scores are now demanded by hundreds of colleges as part of the entrance requirements for students. Thus, every local community is part of a larger state, regional, national, even world community.

It may be that the folklore of local school control has blinded some people, superintendents included, to the realities of the world in which they work. At the same time, many superintendents find that in order to assure adequate resources locally they must join in statewide efforts to augment school support. Most superintendents have also come to realize that they must be vigorous in seeking federal aid. In the future, superintendents of schools will be required to operate in the state and national as well as the local arena.[81]

SUMMARY AND FUTURE PROSPECTS

Influence of the Superintendent

Legally most states confer few prerogatives on superintendents. For the most part their legal powers are derived from those ascribed to the board of education. Despite this lack of legal status, traditions in each situation and the personal characteristics of the officeholder combine in some fashion to affect the influence of the superintendent. Also, it may be appropriate to apply here the injunction offered by Cohen and March that college presidents should not take themselves too seriously.[82] But recognizing these limits should not suggest that superintendents have no influence. While most superintendents can no longer dominate school systems, they can in most places influence them in the following ways:

1. *The power of office.* The top administrative official can ordinarily exercise sanctions by way of appointments, assignments, promotions, and levels of

salary. Perhaps even more important is the confidence people have in the holder of the top position in the organization. Unless this confidence is seriously abused, it is assumed that organizational decisions will emanate from that office.

2. *Information.* The capacity to develop, control, and use information is a second source of influence. The top administrator can largely determine what problems need study, can recruit and direct a staff for the studies deemed necessary, and can use or not use the data derived from the studies as he or she sees fit. Only the person at the top of the hierarchy can bring together into a coherent whole the results of formal inquiry with experience and intuition.

3. *Analysis.* The superintendent is an analyst of the school's social milieu and the school organization itself. Analysis obviously goes beyond mere information gathering and arrives at the meanings of the facts through interpretation. To be sure, the superintendents will need help from persons inside and outside the school organization for these analyses, but the capacity of superintendents to recognize and use such help to determine meaning for their organization enhances their influence.

4. *Strategic planning.* In a sense, strategic planning is the logical application of the analyses noted above. Strategic thinking, strategic planning, and strategic management are important ways to frame responsibilities both intellectually and pragmatically. Working strategically allows superintendents to set an agenda and simultaneously overcome, even focus, the predictable buffeting caused by events, the media, and special interests.[83]

5. *Mediation.* While planning is a very rational activity, mediation, or acting as a power broker, is clearly a political activity. The superintendent is continually called upon to exercise political skills within the organization and within the environment in which the organization exists. Frequently, the question is, what is possible under current conditions and what kinds of coalitions can be formed to support the possible? To achieve working agreements, compromise is frequently necessary. The influence of superintendents is determined by their skill in fostering successful negotiations (often with the help of others).

Outlook for the Future

Fewer Superintendents

While the rate of change has slowed, the combination and reorganization of rural school districts will probably continue. In addition, some new school districts may be formed around each of the major cities, areas where major population increase is projected. Also some school districts in our largest cities may need to be subdivided.

These developments portend a modest decrease in the number of school districts and in the number of superintendents. Most of the superintendents in school districts with less than forty or fifty staff members are likely to disappear. This could mean that nearly all of the part-time superintendents—positions combined with high school principalships and with part-time teaching—will no longer exist.

With the reduction in the number of superintendents, there may be an increase in the number of subordinate administrators, particularly directors or assistant superintendents who serve in the central office. In suburban school districts particularly, the number of schools will also probably increase, hence there may be some increase in number of principals, at least full-time principals. The route to the superintendency will continue to be through one or more of these subordinate positions with central office experience being seen as a stepping stone, but better training programs may modify this career route.

Better Selection Procedures
The selection of the superintendent occurs at two major points: when the university admits a candidate to the preparation program and when a board of education actually names a superintendent. Both of these processes will probably become more rigorous.

With fewer superintendents to be prepared and with preparation programs more definitive, as will be discussed next, it seems likely that fewer universities will offer preparation programs for the superintendency. This could mean an increase in the number of collaborative arrangements among universities so that programs for the principalship in many universities would be tied to fully developed programs for the superintendency at just a few universities. In any case, with fewer superintendencies to fill and with their preparation consolidated in fewer universities, selection procedures can become more rigorous and more manageable.

Fortunately, studies on the role of the superintendent, the relationship between personal characteristics and the performance of that role, and the development of procedures for identifying appropriate candidates provide universities with some help in the selection process. These studies will continue and their usefulness to university selection committees will grow. As part of the selection process, universities must rely to a considerable extent on practicing superintendents for the nomination of candidates. Programs for identifying promising candidates among teachers and subordinate administrators will probably be more highly developed and more commonly used. In addition, the pool from which superintendents are drawn may be enlarged to include persons in law, government, and business, as well as those in education.

With fewer school districts as most rural districts combine into larger units, boards of education will be composed of better qualified lay people. Moreover, with the reduction in the number of school districts, more prestige will probably be attached to board membership. Under these circumstances, boards of education, more universally than now, can be expected to be more scrupulous in the selection of superintendents. The practice of a board enlisting the aid of professional consultants to establish criteria for the position, set up selection procedures, and actually screen candidates will probably increase. In any case, it seems probable that boards of education will increasingly seek superintendents with professional strengths.

Improved Preparation Programs

Trends toward improved preparation programs for superintendents seem to be clearly established. Major universities, such as those affiliated with the University Council for Educational Administration, have taken the obligation seriously and are actively engaged in strengthening their programs.

The UCEA-sponsored National Commission on Excellence in Educational Administration, reporting in 1987, urged presidents and academic vice presidents of universities to examine their institutions' educational administration preparation programs. Unless those programs measure up to high standards of excellence they should be discontinued. The commission called for intellectual rigor, high standards of practice, and challenging faculties who are themselves active scholars, valued consultants, and exciting mentors. A quality program would have at least five full-time faculty members, first-rate instructional materials, sophisticated technologies, and a cohort of highly qualified full-time students.[84]

In the more traditional settings as well as in the experimental programs, certain emphases are emerging. There will probably be considerable reliance on the basic disciplines, but these disciplines will not be taken in undigested chunks. Rather, harder questions will be asked about the relevance of the concepts the disciplines provide. The theory movement is an expression of this trend: school experts are realizing that many theories of human behavior may be useful in evaluating the role of the school administrator. In large part, these applications are still undeveloped. A parallel emphasis, and in many cases the dominant emphasis, will be on making greater use of field experience in training programs. Field experience may take several forms, varying from brief periods of observation and participation to long periods of internship. At least one other notion is receiving considerable attention—perhaps it is an old notion with new emphasis—the idea of defining carefully the competencies required of administrators and building a training program around those competencies. Care must be taken, however, that this movement not promote a narrow or mechanistic definition of competence.

Realistic Role Definition

Projecting the future role of the superintendent is an extremely difficult task. Some maintain that current demands on the position make it completely untenable. Others insist that the present generation of superintendents is a failure and what we need is a new breed. The setting in which superintendents of the future will operate will be a difficult one. Many of the problems confronting the larger society will find expression in that setting. These problems emanate from our pluralistic culture in which there is often little agreement on basic values; blacks and other minorities are searching for ways to participate fully in our society, and many feel the conflict between a desire for self-determination and the push of our culture toward uniformity.

In a somewhat different vein, March has noted that education is a declining industry.[85] He suggested that in a declining industry management tends to age, there is some loss of *joie de vivre,* and there is an oversupply of administrators. Perhaps even more significantly, March contends that as it becomes clear that schools can make only a limited contribution to the solution of our social problems, social pressure on schools and school administrators will actually give way to indifference. Current developments may provide more optimism than is found in the March position. Recent studies of education, including *A Nation at Risk,*[86] all reflect a renewed attention to the significance of schooling. This seeming change in attitude coupled with a willingness of the private sector to invest more in education may do much to make education, once again, a growth industry.[87]

Whatever view one takes of the future, there remain a number of dilemmas for the superintendent. Some maintain that the leadership of the superintendent is more vital than ever; others, because of increasing teacher and community power, assign much less importance to the superintendent's leadership. Many superintendents believe that their occupation must be further professionalized through training and certification procedures while many lay persons would like to dispense with professional requirements and open the occupation to able persons generally. There are movements afoot that would make the superintendent's job much more rational through the application of cost-benefit and similar analyses; at the same time some voices insist that the great need is for humanizing the schools and the people who run them.

From one point of view, it seems clear that the superintendent of the future must give more attention to the external or community factors in school operation. Indeed, in the AASA study of the superintendency,[88] one of the challenges of the future dealt with the civic responsibility of the superintendent. Civic leadership was seen as a way of providing a broader view of how schools fit into community life. Moreover, it would also provide an opportunity for the superintendent to deal with the ever-broadening constituencies found in the community.

At the same time, teacher activism and demands for better teaching suggest that the internal aspects of school operation must have priority. The need for superintendents who can use sophisticated techniques, particularly in seeking resources at state and national levels, is clear, but at the same time local problems demand constant attention. As a professional person the superintendent feels the need for considerable autonomy, but by the nature of the job, there is pressure to become a pawn of community and faculty.

These and other dilemmas document the complex task of the superintendent in the future. In the larger social context, as Tyack and Hansot have noted, "the political and ideological disarray of the 1980s suggest that the major task today is to secure a new common ground for the common school."[89] Clearly, the superintendent has a role to play in that demanding task. Some of the best talent of the nation must be attracted to the position. Problem analysis and courageous action, not the application of ready-made solutions, will be necessary. We are encouraged that Cunningham and his colleagues found "vitality" in the American public school superintendency. We look to the future with some optimism.

NOTES

[1]Thomas M. Gilland, *The Origin and Development of the Powers and Duties of the City-School Superintendent* (Chicago: University of Chicago Press, 1935), ch. 2.

[2]Theodore L. Reller, *The Development of the City Superintendency of Schools in the United States* (Philadelphia: The Author, 1935), 82.

[3]Ibid.

[4]Ibid.

[5]E. A. Bateman, *Development of the County-Unit School District in Utah* (New York: Bureau of Publications, Teachers College, Columbia University, 1940), 92.

[6]*Stuart v. School District No. 1 of Kalamazoo,* 30 Michigan 69 (1874).

[7]David B. Tyack, "Pilgrim's Progress Toward a Social History of the School Superintendency, 1860–1960," *History of Education Quarterly* 16 (Fall 1976): 258. See also David B. Tyack and Elizabeth Hansot, *Managers of Virtue* (New York: Basic Books, 1982).

[8]For elaboration of this point see Raymond E. Callahan, *Education and the Cult of Efficiency* (Chicago: University of Chicago Press, 1962), 250.

[9]For a more complete treatment of the evolution of the superintendency see Daniel E. Griffiths, *The School Superintendent* (New York: Center for Applied Research in Education, 1966).

[10]Luvern L. Cunningham and Joseph T. Hentges, *The American School Superintendency, 1982: A Summary Report* (Arlington, VA: American Association of School Administrators, 1982).

[11]"AASA, Membership Composition," *The School Administrator* (March 1988).

[12]E. Gordon Gee and David J. Sperry, *Education Law and the Public Schools: A Compendium* (Boston: Allyn and Bacon, 1978), A-19 and A-20.

[13]*Board of Education v. DeWeese,* 343 S.W. (2d) 598 (Ky. 1961).

[14]*Illinois School Code,* 10–21.4.

[15]American Association of School Administrators, *Profile of the School Superintendent* (Washington, DC: AASA, 1960).

[16]Cunningham and Hentges, *The American School Superintendency, 1982,* 13.

[17]Effe H. Jones and Xenia Montenegro, *Women and Minorities in School Administration* (Arlington, VA: American Association of School Administrators, 1985).

[18]Judythe A. Hummel, "Gender Differences of School Superintendents" (Ph.D. diss., Ohio State University, 1988), 223.

[19]This and other works by Taylor are collected in *Scientific Management* (New York: Harper & Row, 1947).

[20]Franklin Bobbitt, "Some General Principles of Management Applied to the Problems of City-School Systems," in *The Supervision of City Schools,* Twelfth Yearbook of the National Society for the Study of Education, part 1 (Chicago: University of Chicago Press, 1913), 7–96.

[21]Ibid., 7–8.

[22]Callahan, *Education and the Cult of Efficiency,* 246.

[23]Mary Parker Follett, *Creative Experience* (New York: Longmans, Green & Co., 1924), xiii–xiv.

[24]F. J. Roethlisberger and William J. Dickson, *Management and the Worker* (Cambridge, MA: Harvard University Press, 1941).

[25]Ibid., 568.

[26]Thomas Fleming, "Management by Consensus: Democratic Administration and Human Relations" (Ph.D. diss., University of Oregon, 1982).

[27]John Dewey, *Democracy and Education* (New York: Macmillan, 1916).

[28]G. Robert Koopman, Alice Miel, and Paul J. Misner, *Democracy in School Administration* (New York: Appleton-Century-Crofts, 1943), 107.

[29]Ibid., 3–4.

[30]See H. N. Gerth and C. Wright Mills, eds. and trans., *From Max Weber: Essays in Sociology* (New York: Oxford University Press, 1946), 196–204.

[31]Herbert A. Simon, *Administrative Behavior,* 2d ed. (New York: Macmillan, 1957).

[32]James G. March and H. A. Simon, *Organizations* (New York: Wiley, 1958).

[33]James G. Anderson, *Bureaucracy in Education* (Baltimore: Johns Hopkins University Press, 1968).

[34]Roald F. Campbell et al., *A History of Thought and Practice in Educational Administration* (New York: Teachers College Press, 1987).

[35]David Easton, *A Framework for Political Analysis* (Englewood Cliffs, NJ: Prentice-Hall, 1965).

[36]Karl E. Weick, "Educational Organizations as Loosely Coupled Systems," *Administrative Science Quarterly* 21 (March 1976): 1–19.

[37]Ibid., 3.

[38]R. Bruce McPherson, Robert L. Crowson, and Nancy J. Pitner, *Managing Uncertainty* (Columbus, OH: Merrill, 1986).

[39]See Jacob W. Getzels et al., *Educational Administration as a Social Process* (New York: Harper and Row, 1968) and Andrew W. Halpin, *Theory and Research in Administration* (New York: Macmillan, 1966).

[40]Howard S. Becker, "The Nature of a Profession," in *Education for the Professions,* Sixty-first Yearbook, National Society for the Study of Education, part 2 (Chicago: University of Chicago Press, 1962), ch. 2.

[41]Jack Culbertson et al., eds., *Social Science Content for Preparing Educational Leaders* (Columbus, OH: Charles E. Merrill, 1973), and Jack Culbertson et al., *Preparing Educational Leaders for the Seventies,* report prepared by University Council for Educational Administration for U.S. Office of Education, #8–0230, 1969.

[42]Edith K. Mosher and Jennings L. Wagoner, Jr., eds., *The Changing Politics of Education* (Berkeley, CA: McCutchan, 1978).

[43]Glenn L. Immegart and William L. Boyd, *Problem Finding in Educational Administration* (Lexington, MA: D. C. Heath, 1979).

[44]Hollis A. Moore, Jr., *Studies in School Administration* (Washington, DC: American Association of School Administrators, 1957).

[45]*Something to Steer By* (Washington, DC: American Association of School Administrators, 1958).

[46]*Professional Administration for America's Schools* (Washington, DC: American Association of School Administrators, 1960).

[47]American Association of School Administrators, "Annual Report, 1988," *The School Administrator* (March 1988).

[48]James C. March and James G. March, "Almost Random Careers: The Wisconsin School Superintendency, 1940–1972," *Administrative Science Quarterly* 22 (September 1977): 377–409.

[49]Ibid., 405.

[50]Ibid., 408.

[51]Melvin Seeman, "Social Mobility and Administrative Behavior," *American Sociological Review* 23 (December 1958): 642.

[52]Richard O. Carlson, *School Superintendents: Careers and Performance* (Columbus, OH: Charles E. Merrill, 1971), 140–41.

[53]Ibid., 153.

[54]Cunningham and Hentges, *The American School Superintendency, 1982,* 23.

[55]Daniel E. Griffiths, Robert T. Stout, and Patrick B. Forsyth, *Leaders for America's Schools* (Berkeley, CA: McCutchan Publishing, 1988) 251–426.

[56]Cyril O. Houle, *Governing Boards: Their Nature and Nurture* (San Francisco: Jossey-Bass Publishers, 1989).

[57]John Sonedecker, "Evaluation of the American Public School Superintendent," (Ph.D. diss., Ohio State University, 1984), ch. VI.

[58]Nancy J. Pitner, "Descriptive Study of the Everyday Activities of Suburban School Superintendents" (Ph.D. diss., Ohio State University, 1978).

[59]John F. Feilders, "Action and Reaction: The Job of an Urban Superintendent" (Ph.D. diss., Stanford University, 1978).

[60]Henry Mintzberg, *The Nature of Administrative Work* (New York: Harper & Row, 1973).

[61]Patrick Duignan, "Administrative Behavior of School Superintendents: A Descriptive Study," *Journal of Educational Administration* 18 (July 1980): 5–26.

[62]Luvern L. Cunningham and Barbara McCloud, "The School Superintendency: An Impossible Job." Unpublished manuscript, 1988.

[63]Donald J. Willower and Hugh W. Fraser, "School Superintendents and Their Work," *Administrator's Notebook* 28 (1979–80): no. 5.

[64]Ibid. See also Arthur Bloomberg, *The School Superintendent, Living with Conflict* (New York: Teachers College, Columbia University, 1985).

[65]Larry Cuban, *Urban School Chiefs Under Fire* (Chicago: University of Chicago Press, 1976).

[66]James M. Lipham, "Leadership and Administration," in National Society for the Study of Education, *Behavioral Science and Educational Administration,* Sixty-third Yearbook, part 2 (Chicago: University of Chicago Press, 1964), ch. 6.

[67]John K. Hemphill, Daniel E. Griffiths, and Norman Fredericksen, *Administrative Performance and Personality* (New York: Bureau of Publications, Teachers College, Columbia University, 1962).

[68]See Roald F. Campbell, "Time for Vigorous Leadership," in *Bad Times, Good Schools,* ed. Jack Frynier, Kappa Delta Pi Monograph, 1983.

[69]Donald J. McCarty and Charles E. Ramsey, *The School Managers* (Westport, CT: Glenwood, 1971).

[70]Carlson, *School Superintendents.* See also Clayton Dusek, "A Reexamination of the Differences between Career Bound and Place Bound Superintendents" (Ph.D. diss., Ohio State University, 1982).

[71]For instance, see L. Harmon Zeigler and M. Kent Jennings with the assistance of G. Wayne Peak, *The Governing of American Schools* (North Scituate, MA: Duxbury, 1974).

[72]L. Harmon Zeigler, "Creating Responsive Schools," *Urban Review* 6 (1973): 40.

[73]William L. Boyd, "The Public, the Professionals, and Educational Policy Making: Who Governs?" *Teachers College Record* 77 (May 1976): 539–77.

[74]Ibid., 572–73.

[75]Joseph T. Hentges, "The Politics of Superintendent-School Board Linkages: A Study of Power, Participation, and Control," (Ph.D. diss., Ohio State University, 1984), ch. VI. For an important review of superintendent-school board relationships see Lila N. Carol et al., *School Boards: Strengthening Grass Roots Leadership* (Washington, DC: Institute for Educational Leadership, 1986).

[76]Simon, *Administrative Behavior.*

[77]Weick, "Educational Organizations as Loosely Coupled Systems."

[78]Cunningham and McCloud, "An Impossible Job."

[79]H. Thomas James, J. Alan Thomas, and Harold J. Dyck, *Wealth, Expenditure and Decision-Making for Education,* Cooperative Research Project 1241 (Stanford, CA: School of Education, Stanford University, 1963).

[80]Robert A. Dahl, *Who Governs?* (New Haven, CT: Yale University Press, 1961).

[81]Roald F. Campbell and Tim L. Mazzoni, Jr., *State Policy Making for the Public Schools* (Berkeley, CA: McCutchan, 1976).

[82]Michael Cohen and James G. March, *Leadership and Ambiguity* (New York: McGraw-Hill, 1974).

[83]Susan Walter and Pat Choate, *Thinking Strategically* (Washington, DC: The Council of State Planning Agencies, 1984), 50.

[84]National Commission on Excellence on Educational Administration, *Leaders for Tomorrow's Schools* (Tempe, AZ: University Council for Educational Administration, 1987), 23–24. See also National Policy Board for Educational Administration, *Improving the Preparation of School Administrators: An Agenda for Reform.* (Charlottesville, VA: University of Virginia, May 1989), which calls for vigorous program standards, fewer universities preparing administrators, and extensive recruitment of capable students, especially racial minorities and women.

[85]James G. March, "Analytical Skills and the University Training of Educational Administrators," *The Journal of Educational Administration* 12 (May 1974): 17–48.

[86]National Commission on Excellence in Education, *A Nation at Risk* (Washington, DC: U. S. Department of Education, 1983).

[87]See David T. Kearns and Denis P. Doyle, *Winning the Brain Race: A Bold Plan to Make Our Schools Competitive* (San Francisco, CA: ICS Press, 1988).

[88]Cunningham et al., *The American School Superintendency, 1982,* ch. 9.

[89]Tyack and Hansot, *Managers of Virtue,* 217.

11

School Principals and Central Office Staff

S chool systems, particularly as they increase in size, employ not only a superinten-dent but also numerous subordinate administrators—school principals and cen-tral office staff. This chapter discusses the kinds and numbers of principals and central office staff, the major issues and problems growing out of the development of such work groups, and the nature of power exercised by these administrators.

THE PRINCIPALSHIP

There are in the United States approximately 100,000 school principals, 81,000 in public schools and 19,000 in private schools. Divided another way, some 70,000 principals serve in elementary schools, 25,000 in secondary schools, and 5,000 in combined elementary and secondary schools.[1] In recent years, the spotlight has become more focused on this sizable work force. Here we will examine briefly the history of the position, note the nature of the principalship, and consider the current debate about the role of the principal.

History of Position

During the early part of the nineteenth century most elementary schools had few pupils and required only one or two teachers. Under these conditions there was little, if any, need for a school principal. Early high schools were also small. Pierce reported that enrollment in the St. Louis High School during its first year was seventy-two pupils.[2] Pierce has also noted that the two major factors leading to the development of the principalship were the growth of cities, with the corresponding increased size of schools, and the need to grade or classify students.[3] With the development of larger schools, the position of head teacher, principal teacher, and finally principal was established.

By the early part of this century, school principals had developed a sense of self identity and need for a national professional organization. The National Association of Secondary School Principals was organized in 1916. Five years later elementary principals followed with the organization of the National Association of Elementary School Principals. Both of these organizations became departments in the National Education Association, which at that time was an umbrella organization for many groups in education. The seventh yearbook of the NAESP, published in 1928, focused on the position of the elementary school principalship and gave some attention to the evolutionary sequence of the position: one teacher, head teacher, teaching principal (part-time), building principal (full-time), and supervising principal (full-time).[4]

Pierce in his study noted that a common early designation for the position was *principal teacher.* He found first mention of the single term *principal* in the Common School Report of Cincinnati in 1838. Pierce credits the Quincy School in Boston in 1847 as "the first school to have all departments united under a single principal." He also found that St. Louis in 1859 adopted the policy of "one principal in each building, all other teachers being assistants".[5]

In terms of duties, Pierce found that early part-time principals performed largely clerical duties, most frequently the preparation of reports on pupils for the central office. Later, particularly as schools became larger, there was a shift from records and reports to organization and general management, including stabilization of the teaching staff and the division of pupils into instructional groups, often in terms of ability or to meet the needs of atypical children. Since 1920, Pierce observed, principals had taken on many supervisory functions:

> Principals have become skilled in conducting experiments involving classroom methods and materials. They apply the methods of case study to solve the difficulties of maladjusted pupils; they diagnose teaching and learning difficulties; and they classify pupils on scientific bases. Best of all, principals now tend to be critical of their own practices and to apply the methods of science to bring about improvement.[6]

One might well ask what has happened to the principalship in the half century and more since the Pierce study. Most notable seems to be the change in conditions surrounding schools. A largely rural nation has become a largely urban one. In this process many central cities have lost population to suburban communities. Even most of the remaining rural areas, with the help of better transportation, have consolidated schools and school districts in order to become, as Tyack has observed, part of "the one best system."[7]

Also, the character of the school population, particularly at the high school level, has changed. Early in the century a minority of the high-school-age group went to high school. Now, in part due to compulsory education, nearly all youth of high school age enroll in high school. Nationally, about 75 percent of those who enroll graduate. With essentially all youth enrolled in high school for at least two to three years, the school population is much more diverse than was once the case. The question of what curricula and what instructional procedures can best serve this diverse group is a burning one. The issue has become still more critical with the deterioration of many central cities and the resulting concentration of poverty-ridden blacks, Hispanics, and other minority groups as well as poor whites.

City schools remain large as well as diverse, and full-time principals seem necessary. The argument for full-time principals is as compelling for most of rural America as it is for urban America. This argument is complicated with another issue: should the principal be a manager or an instructional leader? After some consideration of the nature of middle management and an assessment of what principals actually do, we will examine the current debate over the role of the principal.

Middle Management

The school principal is clearly a middle manager. Some consideration of the nature of middle management may help illuminate the role of the principal. To begin with and in keeping with a hierarchical arrangement characteristic of most school systems, the principal is a line officer. He or she, most often, is held responsible for the operation of a single school within the school district. School districts, of course, vary greatly in terms of student population. Some districts have few students, one attendance area, and hence one school. In some of these cases the superintendent also serves as the principal. In most school districts, however, there are two or more schools and a principal is in charge of each such school. In many city and suburban districts there are scores and even hundreds of schools with a principal assigned to each.

As a line officer the principal is the representative of the superintendent of schools and responsible to him or her. In populous districts the superintendent usually has a central office staff and the principal may be responsible to the superintendent through one or more members of that staff. Indeed, one of the problems confronting principals in many school districts is that of clarifying to whom to report.

In any case, the principal is very much in the middle of at least four competing forces. First, there is, as noted above, the superintendent and his or her staff with their expectations and demands. Second, there are the teachers at the building site with their expectations and demands. Third, the students, too, have expectations for the principal. Finally, parents and other adults in the community hold expectations for the principal. For parents these expectations are often related to the well-being or progress of their offspring. Other adults may represent varied interests of the community such as emphasis on some activity, whether football, band, or something else; or interest in some element of the curriculum, such as an open or traditional classroom or provision for the gifted or the handicapped; or, indeed, some adults may represent groups that wish to provide either additional or decreased revenues for school programs. In short, parents and other adults in the school community

speak not with one but with many voices. The principal, then, must seek to understand these four-way expectations and do his or her best to mediate among them.

To complicate further the middle management role, there is always the question
of how much autonomy the superintendent and his or her staff are willing to delegate
to the principal or the school site. To what extent does the principal and his or her
associates help build and manage the budget? To what extent does the principal and
his or her associates help select and retain teachers? To what extent does the principal
and his or her associates determine the curriculum and instructional procedures? In
short, does the school system operate with little or much school-site management?
An answer to this question will determine whether the principal as middle manager
is essentially a messenger boy for the central office or a responsible leader and
manager in his or her own right.

Principals at Work

Concern about effective schools over the past decade or so has established a renewed
emphasis on the importance of the principalship. Indeed, the increased attention on
the principalship has been so intense that the U. S. Department of Education, ironically an agency that for most of its life has been committed to deemphasizing the
federal role in education, has recently published a *Principal Selection Guide*.[8] That
guide begins with the following paragraph:

> Amidst the current clamor for school reform, parents, teachers, and legislators often
> ask, "If you could do only one thing to improve schools today, what would it be?" I
> would hire the best principal I could find and then give that person ample authority
> and heavy responsibility. A great school almost always boasts a crackerjack principal.
> Leadership is among the crucial elements in educational success.[9]

We suspect that the creation of a great school is not as simple as this prescription
may suggest, but we agree that an effective principal is a key ingredient of what is
required for a good school. It seems important, then, to examine just what principals
do. One approach to that inquiry is to make use of reports from principals. For
instance, in 1978, the National Association of Secondary School Principals completed
a three-volume study of *The Senior High School Principalship*. From a population of
1,600 principals, 60 "effective" ones were identified and interviewed by members of
the research team. Among other things, principals were asked to indicate how they
planned to spend their time and how they actually spent it over a two-week period.
As noted in Table 11.1, principals planned to spend most time in program development. Actually, they spent most time in personnel, and program development came
third.

These and other rankings, useful as they are, have two limitations. First, as is
true with all categories, many tasks or activities can be masked under the major
headings. In this case the problem has been alleviated to some extent by parenthetical
explanations. The second limitation concerns rankings themselves: we do not know
how much time is represented by each. For instance, we cannot tell whether time

TABLE 11.1
Principals' Priority of Planned Time and Time Spent

Area of Activity	Time Planned (biweekly)	Time Spent (biweekly)
Program Development (curriculum, instructional leadership)	1	3
Personnel (evaluation, advising, conferencing, recruiting)	2	1
School Management (weekly calendar, office, budget, correspondence, memos, etc.)	3	2
Student Activities (meetings, supervision, planning)	4	4
District Office (meetings, task forces, reports, etc.)	5	5
Community (PTA, advisory groups, parent conferences)	6	6
Planning (annual, long range)	7	7
Professional Development (reading, conferences, etc.)	8	8
Student Behavior (discipline, attendance, meetings)	9	9

Source: R. A. Gorton and K. E. McIntyre, *The Effective Principal*, vol. 2 of *The Senior High School Principalship* (Reston, VA: National Association of Secondary School Principals, 1978). Used by permission of the NASSP.

spent on personnel activities was twenty hours or sixty hours for the two-week period. Even with these limitations, however, the data give us some indication of what effective senior high school principals actually do.

A second approach for determining what principals do is that of actual observation. This is a time-consuming and thus an expensive procedure, so few such studies have been done. Perhaps still the most notable is the study done some time ago by Wolcott, who spent a year in one elementary school in the Northwest. He observed the daily life of the principal, Ed Bell, and his interactions with professionals in the school system and with parents and others in the community. Wolcott, a former teacher, also made use of many bulletins and other documents generated by and for the school, and interviewed and received questionnaire responses from many of those who worked with the principal. Wolcott divided what the principal did into formal encounters and informal encounters. In terms of formal encounters, Ed Bell's "average" school day broke down into these types of activity:

Prearranged meetings and conferences 26%
Deliberate but no prearranged meetings and conferences 25%
Casual or chance encounters 15%
Telephoning 9%
Talking on intercom 1%
Alone in office 15%
Alone and en route 9%

These data take on more meaning when broken down another way:

Time spent alone 25%
Time spent with others without verbal interaction 6%
Time spent listening to others 35%
Time spent talking to others (giving information, asking questions, giving directions)
                                                                        36%

The data clearly indicate that the predominant activity of this school principal is his interaction with others. The nature of these interactions is shown more specifically in Table 11.2. Studies such as these reveal that principals engage in a wide range of behaviors, that most of that behavior has to do with interaction between the principal and others, that relatively little of the principal's time is devoted directly to

TABLE 11.2
Interactions of Principal Bell During an Average School Day

Category	Number of Instances When Interaction Was Recorded (6-second intervals)	Percent of Total Time Spent Interacting With Each Category
Teachers, individually	187	16.3
Teachers, collectively		
(Subtotal, all interactions with teachers, 22.1%)	67	5.8
Counsellor	146	12.7
Other professional staff	81	7.1
Secretary	49	4.3
Other non-professional staff		
(Subtotal, interactions with teachers plus all other staff, 50.4%)	48	4.2
Pupils, individually	160	14.0
Pupils, small groups	46	4.0
Pupils, entire class or school		
(Subtotal, all interactions with pupils, 19.3%)	15	1.3
Student teachers and cadet teachers	12	1.0
Other principals	89	7.8
Central Office (superintendents or assistant superintendent)	2	.2
Central Office Personnel (other than superintendent or assistant superintendent)	70	6.1
Parents	97	8.5
Other adults in community	15	1.3
Others	63	5.5
Total Instances Recorded	1147	100.1

Source: Harry F. Wolcott, *The Man in the Principal's Office: An Ethnography* (New York: Holt, Rinehart & Winston, 1973).

the improvement of instruction, and that so-called managerial duties consume much of the principal's time. These findings, for some, suggest that the principal does little to improve teaching and learning, which is after all the primary purpose of the school.

We agree that principals should be centrally concerned about the improvement of instruction. In many cases, we suspect that principals should alter their schedules to give more attention to instructional improvement. But we offer two caveats. First, the principal's role in instructional improvement may be both direct and indirect. Direct might include a visit to a classroom and a subsequent teacher conference or interaction in a conference with a concerned parent. Concern with direct involvement of the principal in the instructional arena should not permit neglect of the indirect or long-term activities of the principal that may ultimately enhance teaching and learning. Both are essential.

Our second reservation about the overemphasis on the principal's role as instructional leader is its unreality. For instance, few, if any, principals can be as effective in directing improvement of first-grade reading as the best reading teachers. In short, the principal's role is one of recognizing where help is needed in the instructional program and then doing his or her best to make such help available. The principal can do much to enhance the recent emphasis on teacher leaders, particularly through such arrangements as career ladder programs, as a way of providing resources to improve instruction.

Debate on Principal's Role

At this point, we would like to examine more carefully the current debate about the role of the principal. Much of the literature on this subject is exhortation: the principal should be an instructional leader, the principal should be a school manager, or the principal should be both. Some of the literature, however, reveals more productive approaches to the problem, as can be seen in the examples to follow.

In the early 1980s, Bossert and others at the Far West Laboratory began their study of the Instructional Management Program, with particular emphasis on the role of the principal.[10] After an extended review of the literature, a framework for examining instructional management was developed and is shown in Figure 11.1.[11]

Bossert and his colleagues described this framework in the following language:

> [This figure] presents our view of the relationship between leadership and organization. It shows that a principal's instructional management behavior affects two basic features of the school's social organization: climate and instructional organization. These are the contexts in which various social relationships are formed which, in turn, shape teachers' behaviors and students' experiences that produce student learning. At the same time, the principal's own management behavior is shaped by a number of factors external to the school.[12]

With their design in hand, Bossert and his colleagues "shadowed" five principals during three full work days over an eight-week period. Principals were later interviewed and asked to clarify their actions. In addition to observations and inter-

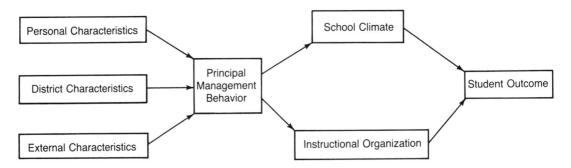

FIGURE 11.1

A Framework for Examining Instructional Management

Source: Steven T. Bossert et al., *Instructional Management Program—Five Principals in Action: Perspectives on Instructional Management* (San Francisco: Far West Laboratory, March 1983), 3.

views, researchers spent twenty to thirty hours in each school observing classes, recesses, and lunch periods, and talking informally with teachers and students. They also collected critical documents such as school plans, test reports, and evaluation forms. Analysis included generated definitions and categories and a search for patterns in each setting. They then developed narrative case studies and checked with each principal to assess their accuracy. These narratives were modified, extended, or verified and then further abstracted to mask the identity of each principal.

The researchers drew a number of interesting conclusions from this preliminary study, some of which are summarized here:

1. These studies suggest, that with slight modification, this framework is useful in studying principal's management behavior.
2. Principals are "comfortable" when their management behavior is consistent with their own personalities and beliefs.
3. The impact of the community was found to be a powerful influence on the principal's behavior.
4. Management behavior was highly personal and varied, ranging from direct and authoritative to indirect and catalytic.
5. The two principals who appeared to be least obtrusive in instructional matters were in schools composed largely of veteran teachers. The principals who intervened more directly were in schools with less mature teachers and with more teacher turnover.
6. While the concept of climate is vague, principals spoke of its importance for positive student outcomes and saw climate essentially as a product of student perception, an area deserving greater study.
7. In all cases principals had a working theory that guided their actions.

Clearly, this study reveals that no simple list of characteristics for effective principals will suffice for describing the many differences found among schools and school districts.

In the mid-1980s the Carnegie Forum on Education and the Economy established a task force on teaching as a profession. The task force, under the chairmanship of Lewis M. Bronscomb, chief scientist and vice president of International Business Machines Corporation, had an additional membership of thirteen other prominent national leaders. A report by the task force, *A Nation Prepared: Teachers for the 21st Century,* was released in 1986. While the report focused on the professionalization of teachers, it also had implications for the principalship. A key paragraph from the report follows:

> No organization can function well without strong and effective leadership and schools are no exception. But the single model for leadership found in most schools is better suited to business or government than to the function of education. The model of a non-teaching principal as head of the school can work in support of the collegial style of schooling we propose, but there are many other models that should be tried. Among them are schools headed by the Lead Teachers acting as a committee, one of whom acts like a managing partner in a professional partnership. In such schools, the teachers might hire the administrators, rather than the other way around. Once the fundamental idea that the primary source of expertise for improving schools lies within them, many ways to organize for leadership are possible.[13]

In this paragraph, the differentiation between the managerial and leadership roles, often ascribed to the principal, goes one step further. Leadership is presumed to reside with the teachers and they, it suggests, might employ their own manager. Few schools, we suspect, are yet ready for such a departure. However, it is clear that alternative roles for the principal are under consideration. Moreover, the report emphasizes that ways must be found to permit teachers to become true professionals with more voice over what they do and how they do it.

In quite a different approach to the problem, Rallis and Highsmith, both experienced observers of principals, have dealt with what they call "The Myth of the Great Principal."[14] They contend that "the first realistic step in school improvement is to recognize that school management and instructional leadership are two different tasks that cannot be performed well by a single individual."[15] They recognize the importance of school management in orchestrating all the loosely coupled structures of the building, such as supervising custodians, scheduling students, seeing that heat and electricity are working, and communicating with parents and the district office. They ascribe to this maintenance management such characteristics as oversight, use of proven methods, orderliness, and daily attention.

Developmental leadership of teachers, on the other hand, requires vision, a willingness to experiment, a capacity to tolerate messiness, an ability to take the long-term view, and a willingness to revise systems. This kind of leadership, the authors maintain, must come from the ranks of teachers. By way of distinction, they suggest,

> The effective principal creates an environment in which procedural obstacles to innovation are removed, an environment in which teachers are treated as professionals who can themselves improve instruction. Creating such a safe and professional climate is the first step that must be taken in order to bring forward the instructional leaders—the master teachers—who are already present in our schools.[16]

Many leaders in and out of education have become concerned about the role of the principal. This kind of concern led the New Jersey State Department of Education, under the leadership of State Commissioner Saul Cooperman, to undertake an extensive study of the matter. In its 100-page report the department reviewed the literature on the subject and then set forth a straightforward description of the role of the principal.[17] Key sentences from that description are:

Clearly then, the principal must function as a SCHOOL EXECUTIVE rather than either a clerical administrator or a teaching expert.

Principals, like other executives, are skilled in analyzing problems systematically by seeking out and organizing relevant information.

Like all executives, principals are skilled leaders of people who recognize when individuals or groups need direction and guidance. . . .

Principals are competent communicators who can express themselves clearly, both orally and in writing, to a range of audiences on a range of topics. . . .

Particularly because principals lead organizations of professionals, they exercise their executive responsibilities, not by making decisions in isolation based upon their own technical expertise. Instead, the school executive is one who is skilled in working collaboratively with the school staff and in leading their participation in the making of professional decisions. . . .

Like executives in other organizations, the principal maintains a vision for the school and leads the participation of teachers and other staff in setting organizational goals. . . .

The principal, like other executives, is responsible for identifying important constituencies of the organization he/she leads. He/she establishes the means for effective two-way communication between the school staff and its external communities, particularly parents. . . .

The principal provides direction and leadership with respect to the support services of the school organization. . . .

The principal functioning as an executive leads the participation of the school staff in the formulation of district policies and budgets which reflect the vision, goals and priorities of the school. . . .

The principal serves as a liaison between the school staff and the central office in the formulation of policies which govern the operation of the district. . . .

The principal, like other executives, has broad responsiblity for personnel matters as they pertain to administrative, clerical, teaching and other professional staff of the organization. . . .[18]

We find much in the New Jersey report that is commendable. To be sure, the principal is responsible for both managerial functions and instructional leadership. But he or she is not caught up in this role conflict. Instead, as the executive officer of the school, the principal is expected to see that these two sides of responsibility are joined; he or she may indeed make good use of others, including skilled teachers, in that process.

CENTRAL OFFICE STAFF

In addition to superintendents and school principals, many school districts also have a central office staff. These staff members represent an extension of the superintendent's office. In larger districts it soon became apparent that the superintendent alone could not meet the demands of the office. With the example of big business ever at hand, this situation led to the appointment of assistant superintendents, supervisors, directors, and others in the central office.

History of Central Office Positions

A history of central office positions can be viewed from two perspectives. One can look at the matter from the viewpoint of school superintendents, school boards, professors of education, and others who were confronted with the problem of how to organize and control education in the growing cities. Or, one can view the problem from the standpoint of historians and other scholars who have been concerned with the growth of bureaucracy in large school systems.

An example of the first perspective is found in *The Portland Survey,* a study of the Portland, Oregon, school system, directed by E. P. Cubberley of Stanford University in 1915.[19] This report was a volume in the School Efficiency Series edited by Paul H. Hanus of Harvard University. Cubberley and his survey team found a growing city and a growing school system with more than 30,000 students enrolled in eleven elementary schools and three high schools. They also found a lay board of school directors (school board) and two departments—the school clerk and the superintendent—reporting directly to the school directors. The school clerk had a staff of twenty-six people to look after finance and physical property matters. The superintendent had a central office staff of nine people to look after educational matters. The survey noted that the lay board attempted to handle "too many things" and the superintendent too few. Moreover, the survey recommended that "the two departments ought to be replaced by centralization into one . . .with subdepartments. . . ."[20]

The survey contained thirteen recommendations on supervision, some of which are summarized below:

1. That the power and responsibilities of the superintendent be greatly enlarged by the withdrawal of the school directors from such work.
2. That the superintendent add to the staff a well-trained administrative assistant, an additional assistant superintendent for the primary grades, and an additional assistant superintendent "to act as a critical educational expert

for the system." Such a person was thought to "prove of great value in measuring, testing, and directing."[21]

In short, the survey staff found that the central office needed reorganization beginning with the lay board, which was trying to take over professional responsibilities. They recommended that business and educational functions be consolidated under the superintendent. With added responsibilities the superintendent was to be provided with additional staff so that those responsibilities could be met. The Portland experience illustrates the process by which central offices in city school districts across the country were staffed.

The second perspective, that of a growing bureaucracy, has been well illustrated in the work of Michael Katz.[22] Using Boston as an example, Katz noted that, "Between 1850 and 1876 the Boston school system became a full-scale bureaucracy."[23] Katz ascribed six elements to bureaucracy: centralized control and supervision, differentiation of administrative duties, qualification for office, expertise in performance, precision and consistency, and administrative discretion. All of these elements were found in the administrative organization of the Boston schools.

Katz recognized the problem of growing urban school systems during the last century:

> Perhaps the most fundamental problem facing school systems was the increasing complexity of the task of administering urban education. For example, in 1855 the city of Boston had only a superintendent and a school committee of seventy-six part-time lay members to supervise and coordinate more than 160 primary schools, which fed nearly fifty grammar schools that led, in turn, to the two high schools. As a part-time pursuit of busy people, the school committee could not oversee the work of individual schools with any care. Under the recently abolished primary school committee, at least someone had been responsible for each school. In some cases this undoubtedly led to close if paternalistic supervision. Now, however, the schools, taught by largely untrained young girls chosen by haphazard methods, were left without guidance. The superintendent, for all his remarkable energy, certainly could not regularly visit and advise more than 200 schools.[24]

Despite the apparent need for augmenting the superintendency by building up a central office staff, the resulting increase in bureaucracy did have some deleterious effects. Again, from Katz:

> One consequence of bureaucratization . . . is the separation of consumption, those who are served by an organization, from control, those who direct it. This distinction points up a significant aspect of the bureaucratization of American urban education: the altered relation of the school to the community. As the organization of urban education became more complex, schools were increasingly divorced from the communities they served, and laymen had progressively less power to influence school policy. In turn, schoolmen themselves gained augmented power to run the schools as they saw fit, with little or no reference to the actual requirements of the community.[25]

The history of the growth of the central office, while not depicted in detail, has been viewed from the standpoint of the practitioner and the historian. Necessary and useful as such staffing often was, the temptation for the professionals to divorce themselves from the clients of the schools and respond to their own professional drummers was and is always present.

Major Issues

In staffing any central office other issues emerge. The first of these has to do with centralization and decentralization. A consideration of this matter involves the relationship of the central office to each of the school sites. Should school sites be given much or little autonomy? Should help needed by teachers be placed in the central office or become a staffing arrangement at each school site? There is also the question of which functions should be centralized and which decentralized. For instance, there may be more justification for centralizing business functions than instructional functions. Another consideration involves the competence of principals and teachers at the building sites. Competent staff at the sites require less supervision from the central office. Our judgment is that most large districts could and should move toward decentralization, providing they also move toward competent teachers and principals at the school sites.

Closely related to the centralization-decentralization problem is the line and staff issue. Is central office staff to serve in a directing or a helping role? Part of this consideration is the matter of specialization on the part of central office staff. If, for instance, the supervisor of special education is highly skilled in the recognition and treatment of handicapped students, it would seem relatively easy for such a supervisor to be helpful to both principals and teachers in the recognition and treatment of such students. On the other hand, in some school systems the supervisor of special education might be responsible for recommending who should be employed as special education teachers, providing them with guidelines to their instruction, checking to see that they conform to the guidelines, and if they do not, recommending that they be discharged. In this instance the helping relationship has moved into the directing relationship, a move we would ordinarily question.

Still another issue is that of whether staffing should conform with the environment of the school system. This contingency theory was perhaps most clearly set forth by Lawrence and Lorsch.[26] For instance, if the state agency has recently set up rather rigorous standards for school plant occupancy that affect receipt of state revenue, it probably becomes necessary to have a director of plant occupancy in the central office. Such a person might report directly to the superintendent of buildings and grounds and undertake the task of keeping records on plant occupancy and preparing reports for submission to the state agency. Or, if student achievement in mathematics is much below recognized norms, it may be advisable for the school system to seek out and employ a mathematics specialist who can help diagnose the problem and work with teachers and principals to improve instruction in mathematics. In short, the central office should be staffed to meet identified problems.

This kind of thinking suggests still another issue regarding central office staffing. Should the staff be permanent or temporary? It may be, to use the example suggested above, that a highly skilled mathematics supervisor, over a five-year period, could be so effective in teaching principals and teachers about mathematics instruction that he or she is no longer needed. If such an appointment was temporary, say one to five years, at the end of that period the contract agreement would have been met and separation should be amicable on both sides. On the other hand, with no such arrangement in mind, both sides might assume that employment of a mathematics supervisor must go on forever. We suspect that many central offices should be staffed by a combination of long-term and short-term members.

Finally, there is the question of how the central office staff should be organized. The simplest arrangement, once the district is large enough to justify it, is to have an assistant superintendent or director for curriculum and instruction and another assistant superintendent or director for support services, both reporting directly to the superintendent. Such a plan would permit the superintendent to devote much of his or her time to the board of education and to interaction with community groups. If a supervisor of mathematics were needed that person would report to the assistant superintendent for instruction. If a director of transportation were needed, that person would report to the assistant superintendent of support services. Clearly, each of the issues mentioned above would have implications for organizing the central office.

SOME ORGANIZATIONAL PROBLEMS

Organizational decisions having to do with principals and central office staff, in addition to dealing with the issues just noted, must also confront other problems, some of which are discussed here.

Differing Views of Administration

Over most of this century four basic views of administration have prevailed.[27] Those four views affect how one perceives the administrative hierarchy. The idea of hierarchy is a key concept in the *bureaucratic view* of administration and the idea of a chain of command permeates most school organizations. While the *scientific management view* of administration dealt chiefly with the shop level of industrial organizations, the concept of hierarchy and the separation of those who labor from those who supervise was always present. The *human relations approach* to administration provided a new challenge to the hierarchy: the superordinates were no longer simply to direct or command; they were to stimulate and inspire. The *open systems view* brought still another challenge to the hierarchy. All previous views of administration had assumed that the organization was essentially a closed system. With the open systems approach the interdependence of the organization and its environment was clearly recognized. The political forces in the environment, for almost the first time, were seen as legitimate and not aberrant factors.

A popular treatment of management, *In Search of Excellence,* reported lessons from America's best-run companies.[28] In one sense, the book might be seen as a revival of the human relations movement in administration but the book is more than that. It showed that managers in the best-run companies do indeed treat employees as human beings, but those managers can also be tough as nails in seeing that the central values or purposes of their companies are understood and in guiding the behavior of employees at all levels in the organization. Instead of relying on hierarchy to sustain their leadership, these managers work to command respect. They are patient coalition builders, altering agendas so that new priorities get attention. Peters and Waterman said of such managers, "like good parents, they cared a lot—and they expected a lot."[29]

Bureaucracy and Professionalism

Another problem has to do with how bureaucracy and professionalism can be reconciled. While school organizations often mediate and modify bureaucracy, it seems improbable that all elements of bureaucracy can or will be eliminated. At the same time, there are many calls for an increase in the professionalism of teachers.[30] These two concepts are not completely at odds. Blau and Scott have noted that the professional and the bureaucratic forms of organizational life have a number of things in common.[31] They state that professionalism is characterized by universalistic standards, by special skill and experience, by effective neutrality in client relationships, and by emphasis on client, not practitioner, needs.

It is mainly in the control structure that the two orientations differ. Control in bureaucracies is characterized by direct relationships to superiors. But professionals typically organize themselves into voluntary associations for the purpose of self-control. Each professional, as a result of a long period of training, is expected to have acquired a body of knowledge and to have internalized a code of ethics that governs his or her conduct. This self-control is subject to the surveillance of one's peers as the only group assumed to be qualified to make professional judgments. At least in the ideal, professionals in a given field constitute a group of colleagues, each with equal status.

Despite some criticism of schools that questions the effectiveness of teachers, there is a movement toward the professionalism of teachers. Teachers are now expected to acquire a larger body of knowledge than they were in the past.[32] The need for in-service education in order to keep abreast of new knowledge is more generally recognized. The call for the empowerment of teachers is stronger. Obviously, some teachers in our best schools have acquired a specialized body of knowledge and skill.

Teachers are seeking to exercise more control over decisions that affect them. Most teachers believe they should participate in decisions pertaining to their job conditions, duties, and prerogatives. In the recent report of the Carnegie Corporation this movement received strong support, as can be seen in the following excerpts:

> Create a National Board for Professional Teaching Standards, organized with a regional and state membership structure, to establish high standards for what teachers need to know and be able to do, and to certify teachers who meet that standard.

> Restructure schools to provide a professional environment for teachers, freeing them to decide how best to meet state and local goals for children while holding them accountable for student progress.

Restructure the teaching force, and introduce a new category of Lead Teachers with the proven ability to provide active leadership in the redesign of the schools and in helping their colleagues to uphold high standards of learning and teaching.[33]

While teaching is moving toward a more professional status, certain factors are hampering this movement. Despite some recent gains, pay scales are so low in many of our school systems that many teachers have found it necessary to supplement their income through part-time jobs. Moreover, the low salaries mean that teachers (and would-be teachers) are often attracted to other fields. To make matters worse, there is some evidence that the more able teachers are the first to move into other fields.[34]

An important question for administrators and boards of education concerning teacher professionalism is, how can the source of discipline be shifted from the administrative hierarchy to the colleague group? This shift cannot occur until teachers are professionally ready for it, but teachers may never become professionally ready until they feel obliged to accept greater responsibility for the control of teaching. Some give-and-take on the part of teachers and administrators will be necessary to achieve some movement on this issue. Still somewhat uncertain is the role teachers unions and other organizations will play in helping teachers assume more professional responsibility.

It seems likely that teachers and special service personnel will become more and more responsible for decisions having to do with the technical aspects of their practice. Actually, in many school systems this procedure is rather well developed. Many principals, for instance, seek the advice of teachers, school psychologists, guidance personnel, and even social workers on decisions having to do with the placement of and programs for students. As another example, many superintendents have found it desirable to have teachers in their own system examine the curricula developed nationally or at the state level.

Despite these developments, teachers have relatively little to say about who will enter teaching, what the composition of the program will be, and what the conditions of employment will be. Interestingly, school administrators do not have control over many of these matters either. Decisions on some of these questions are made by the larger society. In the years ahead, however, society and the administrators will have to concede greater control over teaching to the teachers themselves.

Conflicting Environmental Influences

A third problem for administrators is the impingement of the environment on the organization. No administrator at any level of the hierarchy can escape environmental influences. External forces include other levels of government, such as state and federal governments, as they impinge on local school districts. These external influences may emanate from administrative agencies or from the state or federal courts. Or, the external forces may represent one or more interest groups that have a stake in school operation in areas ranging from citizenship training to the use of local vendors for the purchase of school equipment.

The concepts of open systems and loosely coupled organizations go hand in hand. Thus, not only do external forces impinge on the organization, but since the organization itself is not tightly structured, some parts of the organization may give covert, or even overt, support to the external forces. Teachers unions, partly inside and partly outside the organization, illustrate this play of influences.

Conflicting environmental influences are at the heart of many of the problems facing the school principal. On one hand, an alert group of parents may insist that the law for the education of the handicapped be strictly enforced and that an individualized program be developed for each handicapped student. On the other hand, teachers may not be fully prepared or willing to implement such a plan. To complicate matters further, budget limitations set by the central office may make complete individualization of student programs fiscally impossible. In short, parents say yes; teachers say no, unless the teaching staff can be increased; and the central office, which can offer only minor support from federal sources, says few if any additional teachers can be provided. There is no way the principal can completely satisfy all three groups. The principal must become a mediator. Parents as part of the environment must be taken into account. To what extent can their demands be altered? Teachers and teachers organizations are loosely coupled to the principal. To what extent can their position be moderated? Finally, to what extent can the central office increase its budget? If public funds are not available, are private funds possible? If money cannot be found for additional staff, can volunteers be used to supplement the regular staff? Questions such as these become legitimate when the principal sees himself or herself as a mediator and not merely the executor of central office policy.

Selection and Evaluation of Administrators

In 1987, the National Governors Association issued a second report on education, *Time for Results: The Governors' 1991 Report on Education.* The report highlighted seven major issues, one of which was the need to strengthen school leadership and management. This response to the times was, in a sense, matched by the profession. A twenty-seven-member commission, composed of leaders within and outside of education, was asked by the University Council for Educational Administration "to examine the quality of educational leadership in the country." The commission, under the chairmanship of Daniel Griffiths, found a number of "troubling aspects throughout the field."[35] After much deliberation, the commission set forth its recommendations:

Educational leadership should be redefined.

A National Policy Board on Educational Administration should be established.

Administrator preparation programs should be modeled after those in other professional schools.

At least 300 universities and colleges should cease preparing educational administrators.

Programs for recruitment and placement of ethnic minorities and women should be initiated by universities, school boards, state and federal governments, and the private sector.

The public schools should become full partners in the preparation of school administrators.

Professional development activities should be an integral component of the careers of professors of educational administration and practicing administrators.

Licensure programs should be substantially reformed.[36]

Several of these recommendations bear directly or indirectly on the recruitment, selection, preparation, and evaluation of school administrators.

In light of such a document, the long-standing axiom that the most important single task of a board of education is the selection of the superintendent takes on even more significance. As well, the selection of principals and central office staff, also essential leaders in the educational enterprise, become matters of first importance. There are no foolproof guides to the selection process. A classic study of some years ago helped debunk some of the folklore surrounding this process.[37] The researchers found, for instance, that there was no evidence that men made better principals than women, nor was there any evidence that long experience in teaching was a crucial factor in the success of the principal. Clearly success in the principalship was largely dependent on the expectations held for the position.

In our view, persons with at least moderate intelligence, good interpersonal skills, and knowledge about the educative process should meet the basic qualifications. In addition, we think it essential that role expectations be defined and that the situational factors characteristic of particular schools be taken into account when principals and central office staff are selected and assigned. The nature of the faculty does much to determine what behavior on the part of the principal is appropriate.

Just as the selection of principals and central office staff is essentially a home-grown process, so is the evaluation of these officials. In the Granite (Utah) School District, for instance, a procedure for mid-year and year-end evaluation of principals has been developed. This procedure began with the development of a form, with the participation of principals and teachers, upon which the various categories of the principal's job are listed. These include: staff management, supervision and observations; curriculum; school goals; school climate; community awareness; and others. Principals are asked to supply certain facts, describe briefly their own behavior, and where appropriate provide a self-rating. The next step in the process is a conference, using the evaluation form as a basis for discussion, between a central office representative and the principal. A continuous program of this kind can do much to establish common expectations; provide at least some evidence regarding the competence of the principal; and suggest whether a principal should be retained, discharged, transferred, or promoted.

If, as suggested by the Carnegie report, the Holmes Group,[38] and others, teachers are to be given a much greater voice in both instruction and management, there are direct implications for the selection and evaluation of principals. Again, agreement on role expectations becomes crucial. Principals and central office staff also must become more adept at participatory management than many now are. In addition, if more teacher empowerment also means more autonomy at the site level, as many now advocate, again there are direct implications for principals and for the central office. The leadership role of the principal, particularly with the community will be enhanced. Central office staff will be cast, even more than now, into a helping role.

Continuing Professional Development

Still another organizational problem has to do with the continuing professional development of central office staff and principals. Persons who have occupied an administrative post frequently remark that they were not prepared for such responsibility. This should come as no great surprise since no two administrative positions are identical. They may vary, for instance, in terms of the nature of the work group, scope of responsibility, expectations for the position by superordinates and subordinates in the system, and expectations of groups outside the system. All of this suggests that for most people learning on the job is a necessity. This, then, is the first reason for continuing professional development.

Change of position is another reason for continuing professional development. For example, a science supervisor in the central office may become a school principal, moving essentially from a staff to a line assignment. This supervisor moves from working with many principals and teachers to working with fewer people but much more intensively. He or she also moves from reference groups made up essentially of professionals to reference groups of both professionals and lay people, parents to be more specific. The consequences of these changes would seem to demand some reorientation in both thought and practice.

Then there is the fact that the knowledge base in education is expanding. Research in both instruction and management continues. New findings should be examined. Frequently such findings need to be tested in real situations. In this process administrators and teachers can often participate with researchers in thinking about and testing what they do.

Still another need for continuing professional development is present when a change of position places the administrator in a very different environment. For instance, a principal on one side of a city may have many teachers with little experience and parents who tend to be lackadaisical about school operation. If that principal is transferred to the other side of the city he or she may have many experienced teachers and parents who insist on having a voice in school operation. Some orientation to this change in environment might be attained through an in-service program.

These justifications for continuing professional development tend to be job-oriented and quite specific in nature. There is still an additional reason. Administrators, like other people, need refreshment, just plain doses of liberal education. Be it music, art, science, or social thought, administrators should continue to be learners and to be excited about learning.

Continuing professional development should be largely an individual responsibility. Each administrator can reach out to colleagues and to the outside world for information and inspiration. Indeed, membership in one or more professional networks seems indispensable. In addition to these individual efforts, school districts, often in collaboration with universities and other agencies, should plan, in collaboration with their administrators, in-service programs of a more formal nature.

MODELS OF ADMINISTRATIVE POWER

Greater understanding of the organizational problems of administration can be achieved by placing them in a theoretical context. Let us consider two models, one largely of historical interest and the other reflecting the open systems view, both of which help clarify organizational behavior.

An Early Model

An early model, reflecting largely the human relations and the bureaucratic views of administration, was formulated by Guba in 1960 and is shown in Figure 11.2.[39] Note that power was defined as the actuating force of the administrator in the organization,

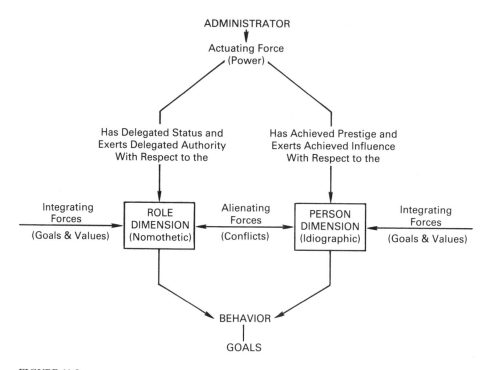

FIGURE 11.2

A Model of Internal Administrative Relationships

Source: Egon G. Guba, "Research in Internal Administration—What Do We Know?" in *Administrative Theory as a Guide to Action,* ed. Roald F. Campbell and J. M. Lipham (Chicago: Midwest Administration Center, University of Chicago, 1960), ch. 7.

and power had two major dimensions or expressions. The first had to do with role or office. Power of this kind resides in status and legal authority. Thus, in a school system, administrators have positions of power. Certain powers are considered inherent in these offices, regardless of who the occupants are. This kind of power is most often considered by those who detect great conflict between administrative and colleague control.

The second source of power had to do with the person of the administrator. In this case the power is not conferred by office; it must be earned. This power is most often referred to as prestige or influence. Clearly some administrators have little prestige and influence, others have a great deal. Administrators who have little influence may find it necessary to invoke status and authority frequently; those who have much influence seldom resort to such formal expressions of power.

Administrators cannot hide the fact that they occupy a formal office and that the office itself represents power. An administrator who ignores status and authority would be only half-powerful. Likewise the administrator who ignores prestige and influence is also only half-powerful. A recognition that at least a portion of administrative power is conferred or withheld by the work group may mitigate, in part, concern for the power of administrative hierarchy.

The model suggested further that conflicts between the role expectations of an organization and the personal needs and dispositions of the people in the organization constitute alienating forces. Indeed, if organizational demands and personal dispositions become too disparate, the organization will cease to be productive or the members will leave the organization. Countering these alienating forces are integrating forces in the form of shared goals and values. If the administrator and members of his or her work group can agree on goals and if they hold certain values in common, organizational demands may be seen in a different context and organizational procedures may be more acceptable.

Finally, the model suggested that if administrative power is composed of both status and prestige, and if agreement on goals and values exceeds conflicts between role expectations and personal dispositions, the members' behavior will help the organization achieve its goals. Obviously, agreement on goals and values implies a great deal of communication and participation within the organization.[40] Guba's model had a number of implications for administrators and organizations in 1960 and many of those implications are still pertinent today.

The Open Systems View

Guba's model is very useful, but it does not deal with the external environment of the organization. It is this limitation that the open systems view addresses. The open systems view is based on the idea that an organization and its environment are in constant interaction. The open systems view, as set forth by Easton, fits neatly with the concept of loosely coupled systems, as set forth by Weick. The notions of interdependence between organization and environment and loose coupling within the organization itself extend and in some instances modify the understandings gleaned from the Guba model.

The power of the administrator is not merely a combination of his or her status and prestige in the organization; that power is also a function of the political forces in the environment and, indeed, in the organization itself. Consider the Bossert model shown earlier. There, at least three variables were seen as contributing to the management behavior of the principal: personal characteristics, district (and one might add school) characteristics, and external characteristics. The addition of external characteristics is important, a clear recognition that a school and a principal exist in an environment that can and does influence what a principal and a school can do. For example, as noted earlier, in some school environments parents expect, even insist on being consulted regarding school operations. In other school environments parents may be quite passive about school operation.

SUMMARY AND FUTURE PROSPECTS

Influence of the Hierarchy

In many respects, what has been said about the power and influence of each member of the hierarchy corresponds to what was said about the power and influence of the superintendent; that is, power is based on the office, information, analytical capacity, planning know-how, and political skills in mediation. But there are some differences between the power of the superintendent and that of the subordinate hierarchy.

1. *Power of office.* While there is only one superintendent, there may be several supervisors and principals, no one of which serves as chief administrator. Furthermore, in the hierarchy there are both line and staff officers. Line officers, generally principals, head at least a subunit in the organization and hence may have considerable power of office. Staff officers, often supervisors, provide information and counsel to the total organization but usually have no subunit of the organization for which they are responsible.

2. *Information.* Different administrators have access to different kinds of information. For example, principals and supervisors may be only partially informed about plans for and operation of the total system and hence less influential than the superintendent. Another distinction may exist between the superintendent and the specialists, supervisors, and staff in the central office. In many instances, the specialist may have more complete information about a particular field, be it reading instruction or long-range planning, than the superintendent. In these cases, the specialist has more influence.

3. *Analysis and planning.* The power accruing from analytical capacity and planning know-how generally favors the superintendent, who must deal with the system as a whole, over principals and supervisors, who are frequently expected to deal with only part of the system. Again, however, if the superintendent has specialists working in these areas, such as in a research division, their influence, though not always apparent, may exceed that of the superintendent.

4. *Mediation.* In the realm of mediation skill, principals and supervisors often have less influence than the superintendent. Once more, the degree of building autonomy may affect this generalization. In some cases, a principal's influence may be welcomed by the superintendent, but in other cases the superintendent may feel such influence threatens his or her position and may take steps, such as transfer or promotion, to reduce the influence of the principal.

The variation in the influence among administrators is evidence that schools tend to be loosely coupled organizations. Subordinate members of the hierarchy exert power and influence in many of the ways exercised by the top administrator, but the extent of the power and influence is contingent on other factors. In tightly structured organizations the power and influence of subordinate administrators tend to be reduced. In organizations that exhibit loose coupling the power and influence of subordinate administrators may be increased.

Outlook for the Future

Focus on Instruction
There is an increasing demand, within and outside of the profession, that administrators at all levels of school organizations focus attention on improving instructional outcomes. Within educational administration itself, it has long been recognized that school administrators engage in many activities that appear to have little relevance to the instructional program. In part, this may be written off as a narrow perception of what it takes to manage a school effectively. But, as Boyan has suggested, there is also a "renewed determination to extract, compile and synthesize data about what actually happens in and around schools. . . . "[41] This new resolve includes an attempt to see what administrative behaviors are related to instructional outcomes.

Outside of educational administration, there is also the call for more effective schools, illustrated by the report of the National Commission on Excellence in Education and subsequent reports by the Carnegie Corporation and the National Governors Association, as noted. In these reports, growing societal concerns about lagging student achievement are clearly set forth, and principals and superintendents are charged with playing crucial roles in developing school and community support for the academic reforms proposed.

Increased Specialization
In the years ahead there may be further consolidation of school districts and thus some reduction in the number of school superintendents. At the same time, as districts become larger, there may be some increase in assistant superintendents and other central office personnel.

More significant than the number of administrators is the growing differentiation of the administrative staff. The need for generalists in the positions of superintendent and principal will remain. But increasingly those line officers will attempt to surround themselves with a specialized staff. This specialization will probably take three forms. The first development, and one already under way in larger school districts, is specialization in terms of the operating areas or functions of administration. There will be more assistant superintendents and directors in charge of instruction, business affairs, staff personnel, and student personnel. As staffs become specialized and schools take on new functions, positions such as directors of school-community coordination, early childhood education, technical education, education of the handicapped, and adult education may take on increased importance.

A second development in the specialization of the administrative staff is the addition of people trained in disciplines relevant to school operation. Thus, persons with strong backgrounds in psychology, social psychology, political science, economics, and other disciplines may be hired to provide additional insight on school operation. In all probability, staff members with competence in such fields of study as planning, research, and evaluation will also be sought.

A third form of administrative staff specialization may develop in curriculum subjects. Schools that can attract few highly trained teachers in various subjects may find it necessary to provide directors, supervisors, or coordinators who have special competence in science, social science, or the humanities. Schools which can attract and retain competent teachers may meet many of these needs for specialization through the use of teacher leaders.

Role Clarification

As school organizations become larger and more complex, there will be a need for greater diversity among administrative personnel, teaching personnel, and nonteaching personnel. In other words, there will be an increase in the number of roles found in school organizations. A consultant in mathematics, for instance, represents a new role for most school systems. An instructorship in Russian is a new role for most high schools, just as a nursery school teaching position is for most elementary schools.

This development will be necessary to school organizations of the future as they take on new and more diverse functions. There is, for example, a growing need for people in school systems who really understand the labor market. Many city high schools will need instructors who can work with students of low academic potential in work-study programs. As noted in Chapter 2, schools may need to sponsor many more preschool programs. The schools of the future cannot meet diverse aims without enlisting people of diverse interests, preparation, and competence.

With more diversity among school positions, it should be possible to attract to these positions people of diverse talent. Also, it is more likely that school workers will be able to find roles that are compatible with their own needs and dispositions. For some, teaching adults may be more satisfying than teaching young people. For others, social work may be more rewarding than teaching. Schools of the future should be able to match the individual to the job more effectively than they have in the past.

As roles become more diverse, the need for role understanding and clarification will be intensified. Ways must be found to help all who work in a school system understand something about the work of others in the system. This will require more effective communication than in the past. It will also require ingenious organization of faculties and small work groups so that role understanding can grow through face-to-face contacts. These sorts of changes will call for astute administration. In addition, administrators themselves will have to define roles much more carefully than they do now.

There is a genuine danger in such advances, however. Formal organizations could, with a dull or lethargic administrator, take the place of a working organization. Or, intermediate functionaries could become merely makers of paperwork or builders of small empires, and contribute little to the achievement of major objectives. Thus, the line administrator must not only define roles, but also appraise the performance of people in those roles.

Not only will administrators of the future find the job of role definition for members of their staff more demanding, they will also find it more difficult to delineate their own roles in the administrative hierarchy. Superintendents and principals will find it increasingly necessary to rely on staff expertise in their decision making. In fact, in professional organizations the line-staff relationships may even reverse. As the science of administration develops, those who can analyze situations and predict with some accuracy the outcomes of administrative decisions will be increasingly needed as members of the administrative group.

Improved Selection and Preparation
The administrators of the future will be more carefully selected and more adequately prepared. As we've seen, selection occurs at two major points: when a candidate is admitted to the preparation program of a university and when he or she is actually hired in an administrative capacity by a school district. Both of these entry points are being scrutinized and steps taken to improve present practices. Universities are no longer accepting for administrative preparation every candidate who appears in the doorway. Moreover, universities are beginning to recruit candidates for administrative training from fields such as law, business, and government instead of limiting themselves to candidates with experience in education.

School districts, too, are building programs to control the entry of candidates into administrative posts. For example, the Cincinnati public schools have for years looked upon the assistant principalship as the point of entry to administrative posts in the school system. Consequently, all candidates for assistant principalships have been carefully appraised. The Chicago schools consider the principalship as the major point of entry, and they have developed a system of examination procedures designed to help identify the best candidates for the principalship.

Fortunately, research on administration has shed light on screening procedures, whether done by a university or a school district. One program designed to improve selection is sponsored by the National Association of Secondary School Principals. Beginning in 1975, with assistance from the American Psychological Association, NASSP established a number of assessment centers throughout the country to identify persons with high potential for success in school administration.[42]

Preparation programs for school administrators are also being strengthened. The *Leaders for America's Schools* report from the University Council for Educational Administration should help in this endeavor. The components of these evolving programs were suggested in Chapter 10. When the entire administrative hierarchy, not just superintendents, is considered, it becomes even clearer that the resources of the entire university are necessary to provide adequate preparation programs in administration. Administration itself is now a recognized part of the study of political science, psychology, sociology, and other disciplines. With further specialization in administration, many other areas of human knowledge become pertinent. The school of education of the future will find one of its main tasks that of coordinating resources of the entire university into the preparation programs for administrators.

Improved Political Skills
Members of the school hierarchy will become more astute as political actors. In part, this will be a matter of survival. Schools are on the defensive. Many citizens are ready to join in movements against taxes and against government. Also, the case for alternatives to the public schools is being made more frequently and more persuasively.[43] These conditions are forcing school people to play political roles. Acceptance of the open systems view of administration will also contribute to more political action as administrators seek to improve their understanding of behavior in organizations and of relationships between organizations and their environments.

Individual schools within each school system are becoming more and more autonomous. Thus superintendents and school boards will have to become more active politically, in large districts especially. As more people in the school environment insist on having a part of the action, demands on the central office for the entire system will become unmanageable. Only as individual schools begin to respond to those demands will school-community interaction become effective.

NOTES

[1]Center for Education Statistics, *Digest of Education Statistics* (Washington, DC: Office of Research and Improvement, U. S. Department of Education, 1987), 11.

[2]Paul P. Pierce, *The Origin and Development of the Public School Principalship* (Chicago: The University of Chicago Press, 1935), 2.

[3]Ibid., 7.

[4]Department of Elementary School Principals, *The Elementary School Principalship,* Seventh Yearbook, Bulletin of the Department (Washington, DC: National Education Association, 1928), 160.

[5]Pierce, *Origin and Development,* 9.

[6]Ibid., 215.

[7]David B. Tyack, *The One Best System* (Cambridge, MA: Harvard University Press, 1974).

[8]Office of Educational Research and Improvement, *Principal Selection Guide* (Washington, DC: U.S. Department of Education, 1987).

[9]Ibid., 1.

[10]Steven T. Bossert et al., *Instructional Management Program—Five Principals in Action: Perspectives on Instructional Management* (San Francisco: Far West Laboratory, March 1983).

[11]Ibid., 3.

[12]Ibid., 2.

[13]Task Force on Teaching as a Profession, *A Nation Prepared: Teachers for the 21st Century* (New York: Carnegie Forum on Education and The Economy, 1986), 61.

[14]Sharon E. Rallis and Martha C. Highsmith, "The Myth of the Great Principal: Questions of School Management and Instructional Leadership," *Phi Delta Kappan,* 68 (December 1986): 300–304.

[15]Ibid., 300.

[16]Ibid., 303.

[17]Leo Klagholz, *The Preparation and Certification of School Principals in New Jersey* (Trenton, NJ: New Jersey State Department of Education, 1986).

[18]Ibid., 58–61.

[19]E. P. Cubberley, *The Portland Survey* (Yonkers-on-Hudson, NY: World Book Co., 1918).

[20]Ibid., 25.

[21]Ibid., 51.

[22]Michael B. Katz, *Class, Bureaucracy, and Schools* (New York: Praeger Publishers, 1975).

[23]Ibid., 59.

[24]Ibid., 66–67.

[25]Ibid., 103.

[26]P. R. Lawrence and J. W. Lorsch, *Organization and Environment* (Homewood, IL: Richard D. Irwin, 1969).

[27]Roald F. Campbell et al., *A History of Thought and Practice in Educational Administration* (New York: Teachers College Press, 1987).

[28]Thomas J. Peters and Robert H. Waterman, Jr., *In Search of Excellence* (New York: Harper & Row, 1982).

[29]Ibid., 96.

[30]For instance see Arthur E. Wise, "Legislated Learning Revisited," *Phi Delta Kappan* (January 1988): 328–333.

[31]Peter M. Blau and W. Richard Scott, *Formal Organizations* (San Francisco: Chandler, 1962), 60–74.

[32]For a historical treatment see Willard S. Elsbree, *The American Teacher* (New York: American Book, 1939).

[33]Task Force on Teaching as a Profession, *A Nation Prepared,* 55.

[34]Gary Sykes, *Teacher Preparation and Teacher Workforce: Problems and Prospects for the Eighties* (Washington, DC: National Institute of Education, 1981).

[35]National Commission on Excellence in Educational Administration, *Leaders for America's Schools* (Tempe, AZ: University Council for Educational Administration, 1987).

[36]Ibid., xiii.

[37]J. K. Hemphill, D. E. Griffiths, and N. Fredricksen, *Administrative Performance and Personality* (New York: Bureau of Publications, Teachers College, Columbia University, 1962).

[38]The Holmes Group, *Tomorrow's Teachers* (East Lansing, MI: The Holmes Group, 1986).

[39]Egon G. Guba, "Research in Internal Administration—What Do We Know?" in *Administrative Theory as a Guide to Action,* ed. Roald F. Campbell and J. M. Lipham (Chicago: Midwest Administration Center, University of Chicago, 1960), ch. 7.

[40]The work from which the model emerged is more completely explicated in Jacob W. Getzels, James M. Lipham, and Roald F. Campbell, *Educational Administration As a Social Process* (New York: Harper & Row, 1968).

[41]Norman J. Boyan, "Follow the Leader: Commentary on Research in Educational Administration," *Educational Researcher* 10 (February 1981): 13.

[42]Paul W. Hersey, "Validation: New Developments, Assessment Center Project," (Reston, VA: National Association of Secondary School Principals, 1982).

[43]For instance see John E. Coons and Stephen D. Sugarman, *Education by Choice* (Berkeley, CA: University of California Press, 1978).

12
The Teachers

As recent widely publicized national reports on American schools have stressed, the quality of education in any nation is related to the quality of men and women who serve as teachers and administrators in its school systems.[1] The professionals themselves exercise subtle controls over education—what it is and what it can become—through their training, experience, and aspiration. Teachers exercise further control over schools through their behavior as members of formal and informal groups. Both of these forms of control, that reflected in what teachers are and that manifest in formal and informal behaviors, will be explored in this chapter, which discusses the dramatic changes that have come about through the more active role many teachers now play in the governance of education.

THE TEACHER IN AMERICA: PAST AND PRESENT

Statistics show that about 2,150,000 classroom teachers were employed in the public schools in 1985[2] and another estimated 343,000 were teaching in nonpublic schools. The number of K–12 teachers in public and nonpublic schools rose from 1,354,000 in the fall of 1956 to 2,019,000 in the fall of 1966.[3] Then, for the first time in decades, demand for teachers declined perceptibly in the early 1970s. This slackening in teacher demand was attributed largely to enrollment decreases and financial constraints. The declining demand for new teachers continued into the early 1980s but demand rose again in the latter part of the decade as enrollments increased, particularly in elementary schools.

The periodic slackening in teacher demand in both public and nonpublic schools has had a dramatic impact on not only the schools themselves, but also on enrollment in teacher training programs on campuses throughout the nation. For years it had been assumed that additional teachers would be required to meet growth needs, cover retirements, and replace dropouts from the profession. Declining pupil enrollments and the fiscal restraints confronting numerous school systems, however, compelled a reassessment of teacher supply and demand and a reconsideration of education's long-prevalent growth syndrome. This development surfaced in the early 1970s and continued to have a profound impact on teachers and their organizations through the early 1980s. For example, the cumulative demand for additional teachers declined from 896,000 in 1971–1975 to 749,000 in 1976–1980.[4] For the five-year period ending in 1985, only 741,000 additional teacher openings were expected.[5] As enrollments increased in the late 1980s, however, it was expected that 863,000 teachers would be hired for the period from 1986 to 1990.[6] These changes in teacher demand in recent years, not surprisingly, have precipitated marked shifts in the numbers of graduates completing teacher preparation programs. The number of newly qualified graduates of teacher preparatory programs declined from 314,000 in 1971 to 144,000 in 1980. Of the people receiving bachelor's degrees, 37 percent received degrees in education in 1971 but in 1980 this percentage dropped to 17 percent.[7] In response both to increasing elementary enrollments and possibly the attention focused upon education and the importance of teaching by the national reports, the supply of new teacher graduates then began to increase slightly, reaching 146,000 in 1984.[8] Despite these somewhat encouraging developments, many analysts continue to have grave concerns about teacher supply and demand. With approximately half of the nation's teaching force expected to leave or retire within the next decade or so, there are widespread apprehensions about maintaining—much less improving—both the quantity and quality of the country's classroom teachers. Teacher supply remains least adequate in areas such as mathematics, the natural and physical sciences, special and bilingual education, vocational-technical subjects, and agriculture. The greatest oversupply of teachers is found in the social sciences, physical and health education, art, music, and foreign languages. We will return to the issue of teacher supply and demand in some detail later in this chapter.

Teachers, like the schools in which they serve, are a heterogeneous group. There are wealthy ones and poor ones, old ones and young ones, special ones and regular ones, and good ones and poor ones. The latter distinction of course is the most controversial. No one would deny the power of the great teacher in molding the minds of students. Nor would anyone deny the social significance of a nation's teaching force. Almost all children have contact with several teachers during their school experiences. Nearly every child develops a strong bond with one or more of them, based on respect, admiration, or love. Whether experiences were positive or negative, most citizens of this nation have had a more intimate acquaintance with teachers than they have with doctors, dentists, lawyers, engineers, and even clergy.

Teachers in America reflect the spirit of America. Their origins are humble, and through time they have elevated their status to one of social significance, if not yet one of genuine public respect and appreciation. As far back as the first months of colonization in North America, certain individuals set themselves up as teachers and even organized their own private schools. Other persons, such as ministers and even shipbuilders, were sometimes prevailed upon to teach and to share whatever knowledge they possessed with children from the farms and villages. The principal credential for many of these early schoolmasters was the ability to read and write; in some cases charlatans who possessed only the most rudimentary skills passed themselves off as schoolmasters.

The colonists of Virginia, imbued with missionary spirit, established schools for Indians and orphans in the very first years of settlement in the New World and sometimes imported their schoolmasters from Europe. The Puritans of New England, moving early for a system of publicly supported schools, sought university-trained teachers when they could find them. Many were ministers, and some, like Ezekiel Cheever, head of the famed Boston Latin School for a third of a century, achieved a highly revered status. The Dutch settlers were interested in education too, but their capacity to find and support schoolmasters did not match that of the New Englanders.

Professional Criteria

Progress in the selection and training of teachers likewise advanced rapidly in New England, but the first record of the establishment of "certification" for teaching appeared in New Amsterdam.[9] There the privilege of teaching had to be sanctioned by civil and ecclesiastical authorities, and one Jacob von Corler, who failed to seek and gain such approval, was prohibited from conducting his own private school until he had gained a license to pursue his calling. Thus, inadvertently, the practice of having lay citizens certify teachers was introduced—a practice that leaders among teachers have been seeking to overturn ever since. The practice of empowering committees of citizens to examine teachers was adopted by the colonies and eventually by the states of the United States under their plenary power over education. Despite the vehement objections of men like John Swett, State Superintendent of California, lay control over licensing has continued. Swett argued that lawyers would not submit to licensing on the basis of an examination by a citizens committee any more than blacksmiths would stand for postmasters sanctioning the practice of blacksmithing. In a celebrated appearance before the NEA in 1872, Swett attacked the existing systems of certification and cited conditions that perpetuated the status quo in teaching: teachers as a group were made up of a procession of young girls anticipating marriage, young men working their way through college, and traveling Ichabod Cranes *keeping* school rather than *teaching* school.[10]

The certification of teachers continues to be a function of government. In most states the legislatures have delegated the task of determining specific qualifications for teaching to state boards of education or to special committees on teacher certification. The administration of certification and the decisions relative to qualifications in individual cases are now for the most part in the hands of certification divisions within state departments of education. Despite the fact that legislatures are now mostly out of the certification business, they still impose some restrictions on teaching and the right to teach. Loyalty oaths that many states imposed as a condition of employment shortly after World War II constituted a restriction on the freedom to teach not unlike the provision for certification. The oath became a condition of employment much like the license itself. The requirement of the loyalty oath, imposed by legislatures and not state boards of education, is an excellent example of the reluctance of the states to relinquish completely their control over those who teach in the nation's classrooms. More recently, legislatures have required that teachers demonstrate proficiencies in standardized tests and serve internships before becoming fully certified.

As a group, an occupational group if not a professional group, teachers are a much improved lot over those who were teaching a century or more ago. And so are doctors, dentists, and lawyers. The right to practice teaching, medicine, dentistry, or law is still guarded—maybe even safeguarded—through government or some instrument of government. None has achieved complete control, nor is it likely that any professional group ever will achieve complete control. Each profession is going through its own evolution; some are further along than others, but none has "arrived," so to speak. Because most teachers in America are public employees, they experience quite a different client relationship than do the doctors, dentists, and lawyers. Admission to practice for most doctors, dentists, and lawyers is a matter of licensure, and then they either "hang up a shingle" or join some private organization that has use for their professional services. Not so with teachers—the alternatives are few. Either they identify with a nonpublic school where licensing by the state may or may not be required or they become licensed by the state and seek employment in a public school system. Thus, in the latter case admission to the profession comes through licensing, but admission to practice depends on some public employer of teachers—a school district—admitting the licensed teacher to practice.

Among the criteria used to judge whether an occupation is or is not a profession is a body of specialized or esoteric knowledge upon which the occupation is based. Becker argues that an occupation must possess a monopoly on such knowledge and must assume responsibility for protecting and extending its knowledge.[11] Furthermore, Becker asserts, that which is esoteric does not consist of technical skills and the fruits of practical experience, but of abstract principles arrived at by scientific research and refined analysis. Such knowledge can only be applied by those who are privileged to possess it, and then its application must be wise and judicious.

Still another symbol of a profession is the confidence with which its clients receive its professionals' services. The client must trust the professionals completely and feel assured that the professionals put no other interests ahead of their professional activities.

Considered against the single criterion of custodianship over an identifiable body of knowledge, teaching does not yet begin to constitute a profession. Teachers, if they genuinely aspire to become professionals, must concern themselves as a group with what knowledge is exclusive to teaching. Careful analysis of the teaching profession probably will lead to the conclusion that there really is not a teaching or an education profession, but rather professions of teaching or of education. Controversy over issues like the length of teacher education programs reflects the divisions even within the ranks of the educators themselves as to how teachers should be trained and certified. If the "professionals" within a field have such basic philosophical and substantive differences about not only the content but the control of teacher preparation, is it any wonder that the general public is skeptical about teaching's status as a professional field? Indeed, the recent widely heralded Carnegie Forum report, which we will discuss in some detail, is predicated upon the assumption that teachers will not earn professional status until there is a fundamental restructuring of their roles and the way in which schools are organized.[12]

CHARACTERISTICS OF THE TEACHER GROUP

During the period 1945–1970 employment opportunities for college-trained men and women were unprecedented. With few exceptions, the economy was expanding; the nation was preoccupied with growth and growth-related problems. One of the disquieting features of much of this period was the high demand for talented youth and the realization that the supply, at least of trained or developed talent, in the nation was far short of demand. For the most part, increasing demand for highly trained men and women, coupled with an awareness of the talent shortage, stimulated vigorous competition and increased salaries in many fields. The result was that occupations such as nursing, teaching, and some religious vocations found it difficult to compete. Although there has been improvement in teachers' salaries, teaching is still running far behind in terms of lifetime earnings.

What is the teacher like? The National Education Association attempts to answer this question every five years by publishing a monograph on the status of the public school teacher in America.[13] The report that summarized data collected during the 1985–1986 school year is the source for most of the information in the paragraphs to follow. The large majority of the nation's public school teachers are women—more than two-thirds. Female teachers have a median age of forty-one years and 76 percent are married. Male teachers have a median age of forty-two years and 83 percent are married.[14]

Today's teachers come from the families of farmers, managers, the self-employed, professional, and semiprofessional workers in larger proportions than is true of adult Americans in general. Fewer teachers than might be expected come from families of the unskilled, clerical, and sales worker groups. Many teachers are from families where one or more other members have been teachers at one time. About 73 percent have children of their own. Many of the married women who have children are beyond the age of thirty-five and have returned to the classroom following one or more absences for child rearing.

The level of teacher preparation is improving. More than 99 percent of our teachers now have a bachelor's degree or higher college degrees. About half have master's degrees, and many others have completed a year or more of work beyond the master's degree. Teachers employed in urban districts have higher levels of preparation than teachers employed in rural and small-town districts. Teachers have been trained for the most part in publicly supported colleges and universities. Approximately 80 percent of all bachelor's and master's degrees held by teachers in 1986 were earned in public institutions. Teachers continue to attend colleges and universities after earning degrees and initial teaching certificates. Most advanced work is taken at summer schools or through evening and Saturday classes during the school year.

The income levels of teachers continue to improve, although inflation has seriously eroded these increases. Indeed, in the period from 1970–1971 to 1980–1981 teachers, unlike in the previous decade, actually lost buying power since consumer prices went up more than teacher salaries during this period. For the decade ending 1980–81, for example, the Consumer Price Index increased 57 percent while teacher salaries increased only 43 percent.[15] Between the school years of 1980–1981 and 1985–86, however, teacher salaries rose more rapidly than the CPI, increasing 42 percent while prices climbed only 24 percent. The result of all these fluctuations has been positive for teachers, who in 1986 were better off economically than their counterparts had been twenty-five years before. Since 1961, the CPI has increased 266 percent while average teacher salaries have risen 365 percent.[16] This recent improvement in salaries probably can be attributed largely to the influence of the reform movement, which has focused on the importance of recruiting and retaining able classroom teachers. Although the base salaries of teachers are being raised almost everywhere, more than one-half of all American teachers earn additional income. Nearly three-fourths of all male teachers have one or more part-time outside jobs. According to the NEA, teachers rely on three sources of supplemental earnings: (1) a second school job, such as evening or summer school teaching or summer maintenance work; (2) earnings from salaries or wages outside the school system; and (3) dividends, rents, royalties, or any other type of nonsalary income. In addition to the individual incomes of teachers, the family incomes of married teachers are frequently increased through the earnings of the spouse. Almost 90 percent of the husbands of married female teachers are employed full-time, and 59 percent of the married men in teaching have wives who are employed full or part time.[17]

Kershaw and McKean noted years ago that salaries motivate persons to enter occupations or jobs and that the nation can attain an appropriate allocation of its work force through its compensation systems.[18] Since most teachers must rely on their teaching salaries as their basic source of support, these figures are very important. Teaching cannot continue to be viewed by some as a part-time occupation if it is to achieve the status it deserves.

In the 1980s, as wrenching economic changes and recession beset the country, great public attention was focused upon the long-neglected issue of the status of teachers in American society. It became clearer to the nation's political, business, and civic leadership that our survival as an international competitor in an increasingly technical world would depend on improving the quality of our schools and teachers. As we will discuss later, numerous recommendations for improving the status and salaries of teachers emerged at every governmental level and the very directly related and long-neglected issue of quality education became a major national issue. Salaries and salary schedules are often complex matters. School boards confronted with mounting pressures for strengthening the quality of public education encounter forceful teacher groups who argue for sharply increased levels of compensation without giving assurance that eduction will be better. To date most teachers are paid on the basis of salary schedules linked principally to preparation and experience. The merit pay concept has been for years flatly rejected by teacher groups in the face of growing public interest in professional accountability.[19] Growing political pressure, however, may well override these objections and some prominent teacher leaders, perhaps sensing the mounting tide of public opinion in favor of eliminating the almost exclusive dependence on the single salary schedule, have begun to be more flexible on this as well as other sensitive issues.[20] Teachers maintain that there should be a respectable base salary for all teachers before the quality performance argument is even introduced. They point out that the average teacher salary (about $24,500 in 1986) is not comparable to that of engineers, pharmacists, accountants, and business executives. There has been improvement in salary levels in most of the nation's school districts but these gains have not kept pace with increases in other occupations requiring college degrees that are not locked into fixed salary schedules.

TEACHERS ORGANIZATIONS

While organizations and associations are numerous in American society, the largest single organization is the National Education Association. For more than a hundred years this association has seen itself as representing the teachers of the country; at present its membership numbers approximately 1.9 million teachers, most of whom are teaching in public schools. There are fifty-nine state and territory affiliates and thousands of units at the local level. The American Federation of Teachers claims 660,000 members and has state federations in approximately half the states. Many teachers are members of both the NEA and the AFT, where these organizations exist side by side at the local district level. Other significant national organizations of teachers are The National Catholic Educational Association, the Jewish Education Association, and the Lutheran Education Association, though this by no means exhausts the list.

National Groups

Within the past two decades the NEA and AFT have dramatically altered their *modus operandi* and in the process have reshaped the governance of American education. Teacher activism, a national phenomenon that surfaced in the 1960s, has sharply altered traditional organizational alliances and educational decision making. Competition for membership between the NEA and AFT has affected profoundly the organization and control of schools. Both of these influential teacher groups have undergone major internal transformations in recent years as they have attempted to serve more aggressive and more dynamic constituents.

The NEA celebrated its centennial in 1957. Never an influential organization politically in the same way as the National Association of Manufacturers or the AFL-CIO, the NEA is nonetheless an organization to be reckoned with. The NEA through its extensive nationwide network of organizational affiliates and associates has a pervasive support base that reaches from the grassroots to the pinnacle of power in Washington, DC.

In the late 1960s the NEA was compelled to make significant internal changes as the result of escalating teacher activism, which estranged teacher organizations from administrators as well as school board groups. Until this time more than thirty autonomous national education associations were "departments" of the NEA, which attempted to serve the entire education profession. NEA departments focused on the special interests of groups representing the several levels of education (kindergarten-primary, higher education, adult education); the responsibilities of specific positions (school superintendents, principals, supervisors); and various instructional specializations (science, mathematics, social studies). These diverse departments for many years made up a relatively unified education family and held considerable autonomy under the NEA banner, enjoying its financial and logistical support. NEA's departments had their own executive secretaries and budgets, elected their own officers, and had the freedom to establish their own policies, programs, and qualifications for membership.

Rising teacher activism generated teacher-administrator rifts and the old NEA umbrella collapsed as major members of the educational family found themselves in adversary positions. In the late 1960s the NEA dropped its affiliate unification efforts and reorganized into departments, national affiliates, and associated organizations. The few organizations that chose to remain departments—including the Association of Classroom Teachers, which constituted more than 90 percent of the NEA's membership—committed themselves to support the NEA policies and programs and to adhere to the requirement that all their members belong to NEA. More than fifteen former NEA departments opted to become national affiliates, which subjected them to the same requirements as the departments except for having to pay for their office space and assuming the responsibility of raising their own funds.

The ten or so departments that chose the status of associates were those most incompatible with NEA's new militant tactics. Associated organizations are independent and tied to the NEA only through their common professional goals and orientations. Not surprisingly, powerful administrator groups such as the American Association of School Administrators and the National Association of Secondary School Principals opted to become independent organizations. In the course of a few years, then, all remnants of a unified education profession were shattered.

Not all American teachers had been satisfied to let the teachers associations (NEA and affiliates) act as their representatives. At the turn of the century and shortly thereafter, small groups of teachers, principally in larger cities, began building alliances with organized labor. They were disenchanted with existing teachers organizations, dissatisfied with the economic conditions under which teachers were working, and discouraged by the status granted to teachers as individuals. Local teachers unions organized into the American Federation of Teachers in 1916. From modest beginnings in a few cities the AFT grew until it could claim by 1976 a membership of nearly 450,000 teachers; in the early 1960s its membership had numbered barely 50,000.

What were some of the conditions in the 1960s that precipitated the growing activism of the AFT and NEA? Of central importance, of course, were the pressures emanating from the nation's troubled city school systems. Racial conflicts, discipline problems, overcrowding, antiquated facilities, citizen pressures, and inadequate administration all contributed to rising teacher dissatisfaction in the large cities. Teachers were unhappiest in these districts and thus were particularly amenable to supporting organizations that would vigorously attempt to better their salaries and working conditions.

The AFT was traditionally strongest in these urban centers of discontent and unrest, and the union breakthrough occurred in New York City, the country's largest school system. One of the early controversies in which an AFT local was involved arose in New York City. In June of 1961, the 49,000 New York City teachers had voted overwhelmingly (3–1) in favor of collective bargaining. Lieberman, a strong proponent for a single, powerful national teacher organization, described the vote by the New York teachers as a landmark in the history of American education.[21] Then the teachers, in December of 1961, selected the United Federation of Teachers to be their bargaining agent with the New York Board of Education. The United Federation of Teachers, acting as bargaining agent, entered into negotiations with the New York City Board of Education early in 1962. A breakdown in bargaining led to a teacher strike on April 12, 1962—which violated New York State law as well as the bargaining agreement between the union and the board.

The strike in New York City was indeed a landmark because not only did teachers discover that they could strike successfully without suffering dire consequences, but they also found that militancy yielded dividends at the bargaining table. In just one contract, for example, the United Federation of Teachers was able to achieve for its constituents a sizable salary increase, guaranteed duty-free lunch periods, a reduction in teaching load, forty-five-minute preparation periods for elementary teachers, a reduction in class size, a liberalization of sick leave policies, reimbursement for service-incurred injuries, and the provision of teacher aides to relieve many teachers from nonteaching responsibilities.

Other factors also encouraged teacher militancy in the 1960s. Organized labor recognized how crucial teachers were to efforts to organize white-collar workers. Membership in the AFL-CIO had remained stable at a time of general population growth. Blue-collar jobs were disappearing in an age of growing automation and labor's political viability and future rested on the success of efforts to unionize the white-collar segments of the work force. School teachers, long frustrated by low salaries and minimal professional recognition, were an obvious wedge to the organization of other white-collar workers. Thus, during the AFT's struggles to survive, organized labor kept the teachers union afloat with both financial and staff resources. The expertise of experienced AFL-CIO organizers was a significant factor in many of the numerous run-off elections against NEA affiliates as interorganizational rivalry intensified in the 1960s.

The number of governmental employees continued to increase in the decades following World War II. The public work force contained more lawyers, doctors, accountants, and other professionals who were employed by local, state, and federal governments. These better-educated employees wanted a voice in determining their working conditions and salaries and were less than tolerant of paternalistic personnel practices. A few cities and states in the late 1950s and early 1960s had sanctioned collective bargaining or negotiations for governmental employees, but the significant breakthrough occurred in 1962 when President John F. Kennedy issued Executive Order #10988. This order established the right of federal employees to organize and negotiate with their employing units regarding personnel policies and working conditions. Federal workers, however, were not permitted to strike. This executive order facilitated the growth of collective action by public employees at the state and local level as the federal example was emulated by a number of state and local governments. President Kennedy's action was thought by some to represent a Magna Carta for governmental employees, accomplishing for them what the National Labor Relations Act of 1935 had done for workers in private industry.

Other developments also converged in the late 1960s to help teachers organizations develop more aggressive tactics. The continuing growth of urbanization and the necessities of urban life facilitated the acceptance of collective action in all segments of an increasingly interdependent economy. Romantic notions concerning the virtues of rugged and unbridled individualism, the hallmark of America's early pioneering frontier days, were vanishing as three-quarters of the population was now living in urban areas. More teachers were better educated and thus less tolerant of paternalistic school boards and administrators. Educational requirements had increased and by 1965, 92 percent of the nation's teachers held degrees while only one-third possessed them only two decades earlier.

After World War II more males entered teaching. Traditionally, men were more career-oriented and concerned with salaries and related benefits than were their female colleagues. Men accounted for less than one-fifth of the teaching force in the early twentieth century. In only a ten-year period (1954–1964), however, the number of male teachers increased by 93 percent. The number of women in the profession increased only 38 percent during this same decade.[22] The male-female ratio has stabilized within the past decade or two with men constituting about one-third of the teaching force. The overwhelming majority of elementary teachers are women and slightly more than half the secondary school teachers are men.

As federal programs for the disadvantaged were implemented in the mid-1960s and pressures mounted from civil rights groups, teachers were placed on the defensive and had to share decision making, to a greater extent than before, with parents, community leaders, and state and federal officials. This broadened base of participation in educational decision making and the resulting erosion of what many deemed to be professional prerogatives made teachers feel vulnerable. The resentment felt by growing numbers of teachers about being made defenseless scapegoats for societal problems like racial prejudice and poverty strengthened both the AFT and NEA in their organizing efforts. As their schools became focal points of criticism and controversy, teachers felt more and more acutely the need for powerful organizations to protect their interests.

The early 1960s were years of struggle between the AFT and the NEA. The 1961 vote in favor of the United Federation of Teachers to serve as bargaining agent for all New York City teachers precipitated national interest among lay people as well as teachers. The New York teachers strike in April 1962 fanned the flames of unrest. Boycotts and sanctions, as well as strikes, were used by the NEA and its affiliates in response. The 1968 statewide teachers strike in Florida, led and supported by NEA, was evidence that the NEA was matching the AFT stride for stride.[23]

The NEA and AFT battles of the 1960s were viewed from several different perspectives. School boards were anxious about the rapid spread of collective bargaining and professional negotiations across the country. The competition between aggressive national organizations accelerated the adoption of these practices. Other public employee groups took heart from teacher group successes, applauded those achievements, and launched boldly into their own bargaining encounters with public bodies. Citizens were oblivious to the distinctions between the NEA and AFT by and large; strikes, sanctions, and boycotts all looked alike to taxpayers. Lieberman predicted in 1968 that a merger of the NEA and AFT was inevitable.[24]

The conflict continued into the 1970s and 1980s; energies were consumed in minor skirmishes as well as major strikes that attracted national attention. As the tactics of the competing organizations grew more belligerent, the purported ideological differences between the AFT's "unionism" and the NEA's "professionalism" have become blurred. The issue of administrator membership, for example, was often cited as one of the significant differences between the AFT and the NEA. The AFT argued that administrators were a separate breed with responsibilities for selecting, directing, assigning, appraising, suspending, and terminating teachers. Because of these differences in duties, administrators could never be expected to represent teachers in collective bargaining or work with teachers in the same professional body. The NEA position was that because teachers and administrators work together even though they perform different functions, they needed to hold membership in the same professional organization. This argument has been blunted. The militancy of the NEA has forced the reexamination of the membership of administrators within the NEA at all levels. New tensions arose within the professional community, causing associations of principals as well as superintendent groups to reappraise and restructure their relationships with teachers associations. Indeed, the traditional organizational linkages between teachers groups and administrators organizations have been severed in almost every state.

As the differences between the NEA and AFT narrowed, extensive efforts were made for a time to merge the two groups. Although teachers have demonstrated considerable political muscle in recent years, financial constraints, shifting enrollment patterns and the concomitant changes in employment opportunities, and mounting public criticism of both the schools and teachers organizations have made both the NEA and AFT somewhat uneasy. These apprehensions have been exacerbated by the powerful public and political support that proponents of educational alternatives like tuition tax credits and vouchers have been able to muster. Support for these widely discussed alternatives to traditional schooling, along with escalating public criticism and demands for accountability, has caused considerable consternation among teachers at a time of reduced demand for their services. The more aggressive political tactics pursued in recent years by both NEA and AFT affiliates, while undeniably effective in securing improvements in salaries and working conditions, have triggered a backlash among many citizens and politicians who want to see cost-quality justifications for increased educational expenditures. Numerous teachers see public disenchantment both with their performance and the quality of public schools as an ominous sign. These concerns were exacerbated, particularly in the early years of the Reagan presidency, when budget cuts prevailed and educational groups like the NEA were very much on the defensive. Education Secretary Bennett's strident criticisms of teachers organizations and the quality of the schools during Reagan's second term, as discussed in Chapter 3, engendered considerable public support and hardly allayed the apprehensions of the NEA, AFT, or other groups of professional educators.

Thus we have an apparent paradox concerning the recent manifestations of teacher power. While the teachers organizations have exerted unprecedented political muscle in achieving their objectives at the local, state, and federal levels, they are becoming apprehensive about public criticism. Job security frequently replaced salaries and fringe benefits as their major area of interest in the 1970s and early 1980s, at a time of declining enrollments and fiscal retrenchment. Teachers and administrators are also concerned that their political position has been eroded by the fragmentation of their once unified profession. Cleavages between teachers and administrators over negotiations at the local and state levels have weakened efforts to close ranks on issues on which there is agreement. Many statewide coalitions, for example, which once articulated a unified position for educators on the paramount question of state aid, have either disappeared or lost leverage because of bitter divisiveness on other issues.

NEA and AFT leaders, despite their competition for members and ideological differences, a number of years ago discussed merger possibilities. Prior to the 1960s such merger talks would have been virtually inconceivable because of the groups' divergent philosophies and tactics. The first tangible steps toward merger were modest.[25] In 1969 the teacher organizations in Flint, Michigan, merged. A year later in Los Angeles the Association of Classroom Teachers (ACTLA) combined with AFT local 1021 to create the United Teachers of Los Angeles.[26] Numerous merger efforts were made in the early 1970s at local and state levels. Illinois, Massachusetts, and Rhode Island were three of the states where merger possibilities seemed particularly viable.

It was in New York, however, that one of the very few major breakthroughs occurred. On June 5, 1972, the NEA-affiliated New York State Teachers Association approved merger with the AFT-affiliated United Teachers of New York. Lieberman, in discussing the implications of this historic merger, described it as a development that was "likely to have the most profound of effects, not only in teacher organizations and education but in labor relations and politics as well."[27]

The merger, however, was short-lived. In the spring of 1976 the shaky four-year alliance ended when the New York State United Teachers severed its dual affiliation and remained affiliated only with the AFT. The teacher leaders in New York as elsewhere were unable to resolve the seemingly intractable issues that for so long had precluded mergers between NEA and AFT affiliates. The major deterrent was and still is, as we shall see, the issue of ties to organized labor. The AFT insists on maintaining close ties with organized labor or the AFL/CIO, while the NEA and its state and local affiliates have been adamant about preserving the independence of teachers from other organized groups. The NEA posture no doubt reflects the sentiments of many teachers who fear that extra-educational ties will weaken the unique status of the teaching profession. Links with the labor movement are also opposed by many educators who are apprehensive lest their already shaky professional status be further diminished by association with blue-collar workers. Leaders of the AFT, on the other hand, believe with equal conviction that only through building coalitions with millions of working people can the teachers generate a broad enough political base to accomplish not only their specific professional goals but their objectives for improving society at large.

AFT teachers are heavily concentrated in the bigger cities such as Chicago, Philadelphia, Pittsburgh, and Detroit. Without the cities and without New York State—which accounts for a rather substantial proportion of the AFT's current membership—the union would be crippled. The NEA, of course, is very much aware of its still highly significant numerical advantage and sees little need to compromise, particularly when its relatively new militancy is virtually indistinguishable from union tactics. The NEA affiliates at the state and local levels can represent their membership not only as effective bargainers who produce at the table but also as maintainers of professional identity untainted by union affiliation.

These differences persist and the failure of merger talks has caused the open rivalry between the two teachers organizations to continue. Numerous and imminent mergers at the state and local levels, projected earlier, have not materialized. Although hopes for organizational unity at the national level seemed rather unlikely at the time of this writing, economic and political conditions and demographic trends such as the ones discussed in Chapter 2 adverse to teachers and education could revive merger efforts. Reportedly, state associations in California, Minnesota, and Wisconsin recently have been discussing merger possibilities[28] and some observers believe that political, economic, and demographic realities will compel in the not-too-distant future an intensification of unification efforts both at the state and national levels. Indeed, merger talks between the NEA-affiliated California Teachers' Association and the AFT-affiliated California Federation of Teachers were reported to be taking an important "new turn" late in 1987.[29] Later reports, however, were less optimistic and the deterrents to merger appeared too formidable once again as the California Federation of Teachers refused to phase out its ties with the AFT.[30] Some feel, however, that the organizations are now so similar in their goals and tactics that national or state mergers would not significantly alter the status quo in education. Meanwhile, competition between the two organizations persists despite their agreement on issues like opposing tuition tax credits, supporting improvement of public education, and strengthening positions of teachers in the bargaining process. Indeed, the organizations continue to challenge each other throughout the country.

As the conflict continues, the question of its impact on pupils enrolled in schools must be raised. What are the immediate as well as the long-range effects of such rivalry? The pupils enrolled in schools centrally involved in teacher strife may be affected negatively, but no one really knows. On the other hand, if the end result is the hammering out and shaping of an occupational group that is aggressive about improving its own performance, then the results may be salutary.

State Teacher Organizations

Thus far we have focused our attention on recent developments in the two major national teacher organizations. We will focus here mainly on the NEA state affiliates, which are far less visible than their parent, the NEA, but which have had very influential roles in shaping educational policy within their own jurisdictions.

It is extraordinarily difficult to measure the effect of a group or an organization on one of society's institutions. Few would deny, however, that state education associations have had in most cases substantial impact on the course of educational history in the fifty states. The state associations have exhibited many of the altruistic, humanistic characteristics of the parent organization, and like the NEA, have not been totally unmindful of the personal needs of the teachers themselves. In recent years they have become exceedingly aggressive, matching union groups in strategy and toughness, and are perceived by legislators to be as effective as almost any other interest group in having their way.

Although AFT state affiliates exist in a number of state capitals, their relatively small membership and big-city focus have minimized the unions' political influence in rural- and suburban-dominated legislatures. Elected officials as well as state agency personnel understandably have to be more responsive to the much larger NEA-affiliated teacher associations. These associations represent the great majority of school districts in which most of the children of the constituents of elected officials are educated. There have been a few exceptions, notably in industrialized states like Rhode Island and Michigan, where the AFT state affiliates have wielded considerable political influence. Even in a heavily unionized state like Michigan, however, the teacher union is outnumbered heavily by its NEA counterpart.

Several of the state associations, such as the one in Illinois, antedate the NEA. The Illinois Education Association was called the Illinois State Teachers' Institute when it was organized on December 26, 1853.[31] From very humble beginnings the association went through periods of vigorous activity and periods of decline. Early in its history the association helped create the office of Superintendent of Public Instruction, establish a state normal school, and support the movement for a state university. In more recent years the Illinois Education Association has been the prime mover on much of the important education legislation in the state. The Illinois General Assembly and other policymakers have relied on the association for information to help members make up their minds on educational questions. Similar case histories for teachers associations exist in other states.

While associations have supported better educational opportunities in the form of special programs, pupil transportation, higher standards of instruction, curriculum reforms, certification improvements and the like, they have not ignored the need for higher salaries, retirement benefits, sick leave provisions, and other welfare benefits. The fight for teacher tenure legislation, of interest also to the American Federation of Teachers, has been led frequently by state education associations. For example, the twenty-year fight for a tenure law in Ohio was waged primarily by the Ohio Education Association.[32]

The state associations communicate with their memberships through state education association journals, in most cases long established. In Illinois, the *Illinois Teacher* is the official publication; in Nebraska a weekly newspaper serves this purpose. The character of these periodicals has changed sharply. A few years ago their focus was on broad educational issues; now it is on teacher actions—strikes, boycotts, and negotiations—as well as other items relative to teacher welfare. The writing is pointed, the headlines are harsher; the content is oriented toward the organization.

The policies of the state associations are made at state conventions or at special delegate assembly meetings of representatives chosen by local associations to represent them. Some state associations have created state-level educational policies commissions patterned after the former national commission of the same name. Prominent educators as well as a few noneducators usually are named to these bodies; the purpose of the policy commissions is to create a deliberative group and charge it with responsibility for examining the problems of education within the state and articulating long-range directions for the teachers of the state to follow.

The executive secretaries of state associations are key figures in most state-level educational developments. The history of any state association is linked closely to the kind and quality of leadership provided by the occupant of this office. Almost every state can point to one or more vigorous executive secretaries who were responsible for certain kinds of progress within the state. This office sustains the continuity of the state associations, and through the efforts of the executive secretary the internal structure of the association is kept intact. Now in the larger states at least, the state education offices are big, quite bureaucratized, and often populated with young, aggressive former teachers. The political activities of the association are maintained through the full-time staff of the associations. These persons are intimately familiar with the political life of the states; they are called on to testify before legislatures, committees of legislatures, special commissions, state boards of education, and other policy groups. In the American system of state government, association representatives perform an essential information-giving role for government officials. Inherent in this function is the exercise of considerable influence on American schools.

Local Teacher Organizations

An individual American teacher can belong to the NEA or to the state education association in his or her state without holding membership in a local association. But the person who belongs to the NEA without either state or local membership is disfranchised; likewise, the teacher who holds membership in a state association and not in a local affiliate is denied the privilege of participation and representation in policy matters of the association within the state. Nearly all NEA and state association members therefore are also members of local associations. The NEA approved its present representative assembly plan of organization in 1921 after a bitter struggle within the top echelons of the association. The adoption of the delegate assembly scheme was successful immediately—all states but four, with a total of 463 local associations, became affiliated in 1921 with the NEA.[33] Members of local and state associations are represented at the NEA annual conventions by delegates elected locally.

The local associations may draw their membership from a single school district, a combination of school districts, or an entire county. The affairs of the locals are completely in the hands of the local membership and the officers they elect. Locals traditionally have been weak organizations; this seems to stem from an absence of strong, committed leadership, and more basically, from the absence of a vigorous *raison d'être*. The locals usually worked through committees, the most active of which was the salary committee. The associations met several times a year; at these meetings they listened to speakers, heard committee reports, selected delegates to the representative assemblies, planned subsequent programs, heard minutes of previous meetings, and adjourned. It was rare that local association meetings were stimulating or well attended. The business of the local usually fell back on a hard core of long-time believers in the association and a cadre of new recruits who were asked to do some of the more onerous chores of the organization.

Increasingly, however, more locals have been influenced by the escalating teacher militancy of recent years and have begun to recognize the power they possess. Among those local association leaders who realize that they have extraordinary power, increasing numbers are using their capacity to influence local policy decisions. Less frequently does the do-good nature of many teachers and administrators interfere with their assuming a more active political role in the affairs of educational policy in their own communities. Such reluctance in the past has caused education to suffer in many places and has worked against the personal interest of teachers as well. Unlike the historical NEA pattern in which locals usually displayed low political profiles, AFT locals traditionally have been more active politically.

A strong local teachers organization can, of course, affect local policy in several ways. Through voicing positions on crucial educational issues, the group can guide the local board in making up its mind. Second, the local group through its committees can study local problems and report to the community and the school board on its findings. Frequently these reports have been on salary and welfare matters. Third, the local can exercise unusual strength for or against issues brought before the voting public. In school districts with small turnouts at the polls for educational referendums sometimes the issue is decided by the teacher vote itself. Fourth, the local teachers group, possibly with the help of state organizations, can intervene in the political affairs of the local school district. Some locals have instituted recall elections of school board members and succeeded in unseating an entire school board or certain members of the board. This active involvement in politics, of course, has become more common as local as well as state teacher groups mobilize to support particular candidates for public office.[34] Fifth, the local group can support vigorously its own local members for leadership posts within the state or national organization. The prestige of national and state leaders residing in a local may improve the posture of the local in the home district, including its political position with local school officials. Further implications of the political role of local organizations will be outlined in the discussion of collective bargaining.

ASSOCIATIONS, UNIONS, AND CONTROL

Political Activism

Quite logically, teacher groups have become more active politically at the federal as well as at the state and local levels. Both the NEA and AFT have maintained for some years active lobbies in the nation's capital and have tried to maintain a constant liaison with leading legislators and administrative officials. Staff members have developed considerable political sophistication as a consequence of being on the Washington scene over a period of years. Despite this presence and the political potential inherent particularly in the vast NEA membership network, educators historically have had minimal impact on policy planning at the federal level.[35] In recent presidential elections, however, both the NEA and the AFT have become deeply involved. The NEA and its state and local affiliates spent millions on various campaigns during these elections. Much of the power of both unions came from the sheer number of registered voting members. The AFT with concentrated voter registration efforts in major electoral states such as Michigan, New York, Illinois, Ohio, and Pennsylvania says 85 percent of its members registered to vote. The NEA projects that more than 90 percent of its members voted.

Both the NEA and AFT participated extensively in the 1986 congressional elections. The NEA's Political Action Committee contributed $10,000—the maximum generally allowed—to more than 100 congressional candidates while the AFT amassed a campaign chest of well over $1 million. [36] In the first eighteen months of the 1985–86 election cycle, the NEA and AFT ranked second and forty-eighth respectively in campaign contributions among national political action committees.[37] In the 1986 off-year election about 30 to 35 percent of NEA members contributed about $3 million to 375 candidates while the AFT's political arm gave financial support to 200 candidates.[38]

The NEA and AFT were both actively involved in the 1988 presidential and congressional elections and many candidates were anxious to garner their support. The NEA-PAC contributed $3.3 million to federal candidates while the AFT expended a political-action war chest of $1.2 million. [39]

The political record of teacher groups, however, is hardly unblemished. In 1980 and 1984, despite the NEA's strong organizational endorsement of Carter and Mondale, approximately 40 percent of the rank-and-file membership voted for Ronald Reagan. Teachers constituted by far the largest single bloc of delegates at the Democratic nominating conventions in 1980 and 1984. Teachers learned quickly that such active engagement in partisan politics exacts a price when their candidates lose.[40] Reagan, of course, after his landslide victory over Carter in 1980 had no political obligations or debts to the NEA and proceeded to cut a host of educational programs that the teachers and other organizations had supported vigorously for years. Indeed, the Reagan administration initially sought elimination of the Department of Education, which had been created by President Carter reportedly as an act of gratitude to the NEA for its political support of the Carter-Mondale ticket.

Educators at the federal level have also been attempting to remedy a major long-standing political weakness—their failure to present a unified front. In the past there have been few agreements among the widespread segments of educators. The NEA and its affiliates, the Council of Chief State School Officers, the National School Boards Association, the American Association of University Professors, the American Council on Education, and many, many others speak out for education but the chorus of voices not only has lacked harmony but frequently has been caught singing quite different tunes. Those who fear "professional" control of education could gain some reassurance from the knowledge that frequently the "profession" has been so fragmented that it poses little real threat to lay control of education. In recent years, however, greater efforts have been made by the major national educational organizations to act consensually on issues where there is agreement. The Forum for Educational Organization Leaders, for example, was created recently. This group—consisting of the NEA, AFT, American Association of School Administrators, National School Boards Association, Council of Chief State School Officers, National Association of State Boards of Education, and other national education associations—meets regularly to discuss issues of mutual concern and has begun the tedious process of attempting to gain consensus on complex issues among the diverse groups. Many of these same organizations, including the NEA and AFT, formed the Coalition for Public Education to oppose the tuition tax credit proposals promulgated by the Reagan administration.

At the state level the picture is somewhat clearer. Although most states still have a welter of professional organizations speaking out for teachers and education, there is evidence that teacher organizations in many states have increasing influence on educational legislation. Aufderheide found in a sampling of twelve broadly representative states (California, Colorado, Florida, Georgia, Massachusetts, Michigan, Minnesota, New York, Nebraska, Tennessee, Texas, and Wisconsin) that teachers groups because of their large memberships and staffs, financial resources, informational bases, and growing political activism wielded considerable political power.[41] Indeed, among educational interest groups Aufderheide's data showed clearly a pattern of teacher domination in influencing governors and legislators; legislators unanimously assessed the teacher associations as being the most influential educational organizations in the twelve states.[42]

Legislators and the other elected officials are even more apprehensive about the direct and large-scale interventions of teacher groups in elections at the local and state levels. In California, for example, the California Teachers Association created a Political Education Department in 1971 to increase the political influence of teachers. The CTA affirmed its goals in a statement of purpose which still reflects the philosophy of large numbers of teachers organizations in states throughout the country:

> We call for the change we need in the highest traditions of citizenship. We accept the challenge of honest and open participation in politics. As teachers we welcome the responsibility of being a profession in service to the communities of California, and we intend to be involved in the legitimate process of law making, both in Sacramento and the electoral districts. We believe that it is in the best interests of California and California's children that we do so.[43]

The implications of this direct political activity of teacher groups have been indeed profound. Statewide teacher groups with ample resources provided by large numbers of dues-paying members organized in the grassroots of virtually every community have tremendous political potential. At this time of fiscal crisis and special consciousness of job security, teacher groups in many states have become more active in elections.

The Bargaining Role

For years it had been customary for the representatives of the teachers organizations to meet with school boards to discuss salary and teacher welfare matters. In thousands of school districts the superintendent had been the spokesperson for teachers in the presentation of teacher requests to the board. The superintendent frequently worked with salary and welfare committees of teacher groups as they prepared their cases for higher salaries or improved fringe benefits. Most superintendents worked conscientiously at this most difficult assignment; they knew that teachers trusted the superintendent to represent their interests adequately, and they knew that the board of education expected the superintendent to keep the teacher requests within bounds. The practice of collective bargaining as described above is of long standing. It stands in sharp contrast to practices that emerged in the 1960s.

As early as 1950, the West Suburban Teachers' Union, Local 571, made a bargaining agreement with the Proviso Township High School board of Maywood, Illinois. Features of this agreement included the expressed recognition by the school board of the union as the collective bargaining agent for all teachers in the district, no discrimination against teachers who were members of the union, the right of the union to meet in the school building after school hours, and the right for disputes between the union and the board to be considered and decided between representatives of the union and the board. Union members agreed to not enter into union activities during school hours, to adhere to the policies articulated in the agreement, and to give their best efforts to their teaching duties. There was no statute in Illinois prohibiting this kind of agreement.

Edwards pointed out that the law governing the right of teachers to strike or the authority of school boards to negotiate was still in the process of development.[44] Sharp acceleration in this process began with the passage of the 1961 Wisconsin statute that recognized and protected the right of public employees to organize and insisted that school boards negotiate with teachers organizations. The same Wisconsin law denied public employees the right to strike. This legislation signaled the rapid examination of bargaining in the public sector in many other states.

The arrival of bargaining in the public sector has forced changes in attitudes toward negotiations on the part of citizens, board members, administrators, and teachers. There have been concomitant rearrangements in the locations of power. Roles of administrators have been altered. Principals have in many cases been threatened by the arrival of negotiations; they accuse superintendents and teachers of leaving them out of the process.[45] An extensive glossary of fresh terms, for the educator at least, has appeared. New careers have been spawned, such as arbitration specialist and professional negotiator. A new coterie of consultants has been marshaled from the fields of education, law, and labor relations. Some consultants have profited substantially from the negotiations movement as they have worked both sides of the bargaining street. The confusion about negotiations that was widespread in its early history has been somewhat clarified in recent years.[46] The rules of the game are more specific and the players have become more proficient with experience. By the mid-1970s, almost 90 percent of the teachers in school districts with more than 1,000 students were represented by a bargaining agent.[47]

INFORMAL ORGANIZATION

Many teacher influences on learning can be traced to the informal relationships among teachers that exist in every school system. Informal associations within schools become patterned over time, and identifiable structures of these relationships emerge. The existence of informal organizations within formal organizations has been known for some time. Attention was focused on the importance of understanding informal organization in the Hawthorne studies of the 1920s and 1930s. Later, Chester I. Barnard described and defined informal organization in his landmark volume *The Functions of the Executive.*[48]

Since these beginnings, interest has grown rapidly in understanding more clearly the nature of informal organization and its relationship to how workers within a formal organization behave. One focus of observation has been on the relationship between informal organizational structures and decision making. In early writing on informal organizations, there was a tendency to classify organizational behavior as being either strictly formal or strictly informal. Subsequent investigation suggests that such polar separations do not describe what really occurs; rather it is more useful to think of organizational behavior as existing along a continuum with formal behavior at one extreme and informal behavior—probably friendship groupings—at the other.[49]

Still another example of teacher impact on the formal structures of the school is presented by Lortie.[50] Over a period of months Lortie interviewed in depth a large population of elementary teachers, seeking to ascertain what makes them tick as professionals. He wanted to understand more clearly teacher perceptions of teaching in relation to school organization. He posited a control system of three parts—hierarchical, collegial, and teacher autonomy—that coexist in all school systems. Lortie contends that the strength of the autonomy impulse within the teaching occupation has been undervalued, especially as it affects what happens in schools. He argues that teachers protect their autonomy through whatever means they can devise. They are especially wary of attempts to differentiate among teachers either in rewards or specializations. They strive to retain equality of treatment in salary as well as status. Merit pay and teaching teams are often opposed because teachers believe that each of these diminishes their own freedom and transfers more control to superordinates.

Much remains to be learned in this area.[51] School administrators can profit most by keeping an open mind on the nature of organization itself and the relationships of formal and informal structures. They will detect many informal groupings within their own school systems. These groupings may be based on similarities in values, locations of teaching stations, age, experience and tenure, car pools, grade levels, subject fields, and so on. Some staff members may be active in many informal groupings; some staff members may be part of no informal group. Informal group leaders are important opinion leaders, and the promotion or change in assignment of informal leaders can affect markedly the informal structure of a school system. Moving an informal leader into a formal position of leadership is one clear-cut example of the formal organization affecting the informal structure.

Teachers' Influence

Teachers are finding themselves in a somewhat ambiguous position in regard to their role in the organization and control of the educational enterprise. There is little doubt that their power within school systems has increased vis-à-vis administrators and school boards. Collective bargaining has given teachers greater influence over the educational program as well as their own working conditions. Teachers also have become much more visible and influential participants in the political process at every level of the governmental system: their human and financial resources and organizational base cannot be ignored by elected officials. Despite these gains, however, teachers are uneasy and apprehensive about their power and future status because of the larger demographic, political, and economic factors that have so forceful an impact on schools. Periodic economic crises, inflation, declining enrollments, and public demands for accountability represent an imposing configuration of concerns for teachers as they consider the influence they can exert upon the organization and control of American schools in the years ahead.[52]

The quality and status of teachers, because of their visibility and pervasive importance in the educational enterprise, have become matters of major public concern and debate as the result of recent national reports and efforts in many states to create career leaders and/or categories of master teachers.[53]

The need to improve the caliber of the nation's teaching force has been an issue in recent presidential campaigns. Despite this escalating public attention and recognition of the importance of teaching, tensions between teachers and citizens apparently persist as public disaffection and demand for accountability erode both the credibility and influence of teachers in a number of communities. Indeed, even some supporters of Walter Mondale in the 1984 election were somewhat ambivalent when he received endorsement from the NEA. They were concerned that the backing of this major national teachers organization, despite all the resulting advantages of money and cohorts of workers that would accrue to the Mondale campaign, would boomerang with the general public and even hurt the former vice president's bid to become president.

Clashes between teachers and citizens on issues such as professional competence and control, retrenchment policies, accountability legislation, teacher involvement in school board elections, and tax increases going largely to raise teacher salaries are generating considerable tension in communities throughout the nation. The outcome of these struggles will influence profoundly not only the organization and control of American education but also the ultimate power and role of organized teachers.

American teachers may be on the threshold of a new and in many ways both promising and troubling period. The current visibility and criticism of schools and restlessness within the teaching ranks may lead to a change in teachers' conceptions of themselves and their professional status. This may require that administrators, school board members, and the public in general modify their traditional views of teachers and teaching. The militancy of teachers unions and associations has in many cases led to improved compensation for teachers and better conditions for teaching. At the same time, teachers are becoming much more visible as a significant occupational group in our society and public expectations for their performance are being elevated accordingly. The recent militancy and political activism of teachers has created a strong backlash among more quality-oriented taxpayers in an uncertain economy. The public is understandably upset as the number of teacher strikes soared from 5 in 1965 to 218 in 1975 and the number of teachers involved in such activities burgeoned from 1,720 in 1965 to a high of 182,300 in 1975.[54] At the beginning of the 1978 school year there were some 120 public school teacher strikes in twenty-one states; 1,898,394 students had breaks in their education as a result. [55] By the fall of 1987, however, there were only 51 strikes.[56] This dramatic reduction in the number of strikes in recent years not only reflects a more constrained economy but also an understandable reluctance on the part of teacher groups to engage in shutdowns of schools at a time when they are politically as well as fiscally vulnerable.

A persuasive argument can be made that despite their recent political gains, teacher groups are running scared in the light of growing indications that there is genuine public concern about the quality of their members. Many teachers have mixed emotions about this outpouring of concern. While the rekindled public interest certainly is viewed positively in the sense that the central importance of education and teaching to the society is being stressed as it has not been since the Sputnik era more than three decades ago, changes are being proposed and implemented that have caused considerable unrest and apprehension within the ranks of the nation's teachers. The national reports have provided concepts such as career ladders with unexpected momentum and political leverage. Teacher organizations historically have been reluctant to support merit pay or other types of financial reward plans that deviate from the traditional salary criteria based on years of academic training and/or years of experience.

Such proposals for career ladders or differential pay have been discussed and debated with little action being taken for more than fifty years.[57] A few school districts are exceptions to the generalization; systems such as Houston, Texas; Ladue, Missouri; Seiling, Oklahoma; Lower Dauphin, Pennsylvania; and some others have operated on merit or similar pay systems for some time. What is unique in the current environment, however, is the speed with which comprehensive changes are being promulgated and in a number of cases implemented. Congress in 1983 created a Task Force on Merit Pay and countless school systems and many states have initiated studies or actually acted on a volatile issue that only a short time before would have been considered too politically sensitive and perhaps "untouchable" in many jurisdictions because of the opposition of powerful teacher groups. California, Florida, and Tennessee are three important examples of states that have either enacted, proposed, or retracted major programs of merit pay or differentiated compensation for teachers.[58]

Teachers groups understandably have somewhat mixed feelings about these developments. They are certainly grateful for the new visibility given their enterprise and for the prospect of increased financial support to the schools to pay for changes like differential salary schedules and extended school days and years. In California, for example, $800 million was raised to pay for reforms. But other facets are less appealing. The major initiative for the extensive legislative changes in both Florida and California was provided by government officials and business leaders, not by the teachers. In California, chief state school officer William Honig was elected on a reform platform that criticized the educational status quo and a powerful business group (the California Business Roundtable, which consisted of the state's largest and most influential corporations) played a critical role in the passage of the comprehensive legislation. In Florida, reform-minded former governor Robert Graham and a change-oriented legislature provided the necessary clout for passage of the Raise Bill. Even in Tennessee, where teachers were successful in modifying the Master Teacher Proposal (although they were unable to block it entirely), there was extensive support for the governor's initiative.

The type of legislation proposed in California, Florida, and Tennessee in the early 1980s was replicated throughout the country and teacher groups in other states were dealing with new and powerful coalitions that pushed for changes similar to the ones proposed in these three states. In other words, state politics of education substantially changed. Teachers and their organizations, with their rather deep and widespread apprehensions about merit pay, differential salaries, the subjectivity and dangers of abuse inherent in teacher evaluation plans, and other concerns related to these issues, feel uncertain and insecure. The combined influence of civic, business, and governmental elites who have coalesced recently around the need to promote educational reforms is rather formidable, to say the least. These influential groups are buttressed, as we noted earlier, by fairly broad public support for change in the schools. Teacher groups, despite their entrenched and undeniable political strength in many states, have found it difficult to oppose changes with such widespread and powerful backing.

RECENT DEVELOPMENTS

By the late 1980s, however, some of the apprehensions of teachers were somewhat allayed by the growing acceptance of the notion that many of the top-down state-imposed reforms were dysfunctional. In other words, heavy-handed, bureaucratic prescriptions were considered to be antithetical to the flexibility and autonomy that are the hallmarks of true professionalism. The state-imposed Tennessee and Florida career-ladder plans, for example, floundered and were changed substantially because of the widespread opposition of teachers and other groups, who were far more receptive to the local district-based plans now being tried in Utah and elsewhere.[59]

As the reform movement evolved, more attention was focused on the classroom environment and teacher working conditions.[60] Educational policymakers were encouraged not to seek to control teachers but to perform their most important function of "guaranteeing that schools are structured and managed so as to enable and allow teachers to perform their responsibility effectively."[61] Concerned business and political leaders began to pay attention to the urgent need to develop greater motivation and pride in the teaching profession by addressing not only the essential matter of compensation but also issues like higher standards and differential reward systems, improved working conditions such as private offices and phones, and fewer bureaucratic constraints.[62] The concept of teacher empowerment gained credence as the need to expand the status, knowledge, and decision-making prerogatives of teachers became more widely acknowledged.[63]

The increased attention being focused on concepts like school site management will influence not only the role and decision-making prerogatives of teachers and principals, but also the relationships between and among building level personnel and board members, superintendents, and central office staff. Indeed, recent developments establishing school site management approaches in school districts like Jefferson County, Kentucky, and Dade County, Florida, may dramatically alter the entire governance structure as well as the professional role and influence of classroom teachers.

Perhaps the most significant and visible national effort to enhance the professional status of teachers in the next decade will be the work of the recently created National Board for Professional Teaching Standards. The creation of this board was a direct result of recommendations made in the Carnegie Forum on Education and the Economy report, *A Nation Prepared: Teachers for the 21st Century.*[64] Chaired by former North Carolina governor James B. Hunt, Jr. and composed of an impressive and diverse array of nationally prominent business, political, and educational leaders, the board is certain to exercise major influence in the years ahead as a private body with a majority of teacher members as well as public representation.

The board's major objective is to enhance the status of the teaching profession through a system of assessments based on high standards. Certification attesting to the achievement of these standards will signify which teachers meet these requirements. It is anticipated that such board-certified teachers will be in great demand and elevate the prestige of the entire profession. Proponents of this system point out that other established professions like medicine, law, architecture, dentistry, and accounting have professional certification mechanisms that are widely accepted, independent, and make decisions on the basis of a common, accepted body of knowledge and the welfare of the client.

The National Board started operating late in 1987 and at this writing was only in its earliest stages of development.[65] Its agenda and activities, however, will be of increasing importance. The board, which appointed James Kelly as its first president, has the support of the two major teacher organizations, a long-term financial commitment from the prestigious Carnegie Corporation of New York, and a broad base of support among business, political, and media influentials. Indeed, it is quite likely that the board will play a consequential role not only in developing national standards for the teaching profession but also in the larger policy arena of helping to determine the course of the education reform movement in areas such as restructuring schools and changes in the roles of teachers.[66]

A somewhat similar effort has been undertaken by the NEA, which is striving to establish professional standards boards in the states. This is a top priority of a number of powerful state affiliates of the NEA and several states probably will establish such teacher-control boards in the immediate future.

The transcendent issue that will continue to drive the demand for reform is the deep public concern about the quality of the teaching force. The widely publicized recommendations of the Carnegie report, the NEA's efforts to establish professional standards boards in the states, and other national study groups focused on the central importance of improving the quality of teachers is the *sine qua non* of efforts to improve the schools. This emphasis on attracting and retaining better teachers has been endorsed by prominent political leaders, notably numerous governors,[67] as well as by highly influential business and civic leaders. There has been general consensus among these influentials as well as the public at large that any efforts to strengthen education would have to be predicated upon improving the socioeconomic status and intellectual caliber of the classroom teachers who are at the core of the educational enterprise. In recent years because of the constraints on governmental spending there has been a continuing drain of talent from the public sector and service fields in general. Teaching without question is not attracting or retaining the "best and brightest" young people.[68] Attempts to replenish and strengthen the ranks of educators will have to be made to ensure the development of our nation's future intellectual capital.[69] Recent increases in teacher salaries in many parts of the country offer some encouragement.

New bargaining agreements between teachers and boards of education like the ones in Fairfax County, Virginia, and Rochester, New York, will be watched with great interest. In Fairfax County, teachers are to receive an almost 40 percent salary increase over three years in return for a tighter system of assessment that will channel extra money to highly evaluated instructors. In Rochester, a recent collective bargaining contract will raise average annual teacher salaries to $45,000 by 1990 (with a high of $70,000 for those at the very top of the scale) in return for higher standards and expectations, differentiated responsibilities, and extended work assignments from teachers.

The problem of teacher quality is most acute, of course, in areas like math and science, where the economic and status rewards of teaching cannot begin to compete with the salaries and recognition available to talented individuals in business and industry. It is widely recognized that we have a crisis of national proportions because only approximately half of our math and science teachers are appropriately certified. Throughout the country, as we have noted, numerous proposals are being made to differentiate roles and salaries, develop career ladder systems, and recruit part-time instructors from the private sector as efforts intensify to attract and retain talented teachers. The particularly acute problems in the math and science fields and the natural relationship of these realms to economic development may become a major lever for change.

The quality issue has been exacerbated by the fact that women, who still constitute approximately two-thirds of the nation's classroom teachers, now have expanded career options. Talented and intellectually able women who in the past entered teaching because it was one of the few occupational fields open to them are now entering other professional fields. Within the past decade or so, a "perverse form of indentured servitude" has been clearly weakened as our most talented women select from a much broader range of career options. For example, in 1965 only 6.5 percent of medical school graduates were female while in 1980 the percentage soared to 23.4 percent; comparable figures for law school graduates were 3.2 percent in 1965 and 30.2 percent in 1980. In 1950, only an infinitesimal .3 percent of the engineering graduates were women, by 1980, 8.8 percent were female.[70] It is reasonable to assume that many of these women doctors, lawyers, and engineers would have been school teachers in prior years. Losing women to other fields because of the continuing expansion of career opportunities for women, historically the largest pool of prospective teachers, further compounds the problem of attracting adequate numbers of our most intellectually able young people to the teaching profession.

Another major issue that will continue to grow in significance is the decline in the percentage of minority teachers. At a time when minority student enrollment is growing dramatically and already constitutes almost one-third of public school enrollment, the percentage of minority teachers has dropped from 12.5 percent of the teaching force in 1974 to 11 percent in 1983. It is predicted to sink to only 5 percent in 1990.[71] With academically talented minorities pursuing expanded opportunities in other more lucrative and attractive fields and declining numbers of blacks and Hispanics attending college, it will be very difficult to reverse this trend and increase the number of minority school teachers. Newly required competency tests for entering teachers may well further compound the problem and reduce the already limited supply of minority teachers.

Some estimate that an average of 200,000 new teachers will be employed annually for the next few years. Only about 100,000 minority students now graduate from college each year and fully one-half of them, or 50,000, would have to enter the teaching field if parity were to be achieved with the ever-growing minority student population. Thus, it is likely that many students will have no experience with or exposure to role models from their own group. The Carnegie report discusses how children's perceptions of the larger society and their own futures are formed by their school experience:

> The race and background of their teachers tells them something about authority and power in contemporary America. These messages influence children's attitudes toward school, their academic accomplishments, and their views of their own and others' intrinsic worth.[72]

SUMMARY AND FUTURE PROSPECTS

The prospect of a redefinition of or changes in teacher labor relations lies ahead. Many teachers as well as others concerned with school improvement view the more strident unionism of recent decades with great ambivalence. They contend that recent educational labor policy has alienated large segments of the public, divided the education profession, and failed to enhance the status of teaching. A number of policy analysts as well as teacher leaders such as president Albert Shanker of the AFT have begun to call for a reconfiguration or restructuring of unionism if teaching practice is to be aligned with the public's needs in the challenging years ahead.[73] Kerchner and Mitchell call for a shift from industrial to professional unionism and from collective bargaining contracts to trust agreements, in which each side holds "in trust" the judgments and wishes of the other:

> The educational policies that constitute a trust are explicitly negotiated agreements between organized teachers and management, in this sense being similar to labor contracts. The agreements would have legal standing and could be adjudicated either through court review or through procedures developed by the parties.[74]

Such trust agreements are predicated on more collegial and less adversarial modes of reconciling differences.

Whether this concept of trust agreements or other similar ideas gain support, it appears that existing collective bargaining patterns may have to change if teachers are to achieve true professional status and become meaningfully engaged as major participants in the education reform movement. In other words, teachers will have to share responsibility for educational outcomes and standards. Such changes in labor-management relations might empower the public schools "to begin to join the set of experiments that is reshaping work and work lives in other sectors."[75] Kerchner and Mitchell summarize the situation and the need for change in the following way:

> . . . professional unionism offers a means for us to approach the critically important problem of reshaping teaching work as an appealing and productive occupation, one capable of attracting the work force that the nation's educational reform agenda requires.[76]

As the bargaining process evolves, the existing system of local lay control of education may also change. Teachers organizations may need to reconsider the nature and extent of the political activity in which they engage. Some critics of the recent political activism of teachers point to the drawback of the NEA's role in the creation of the Department of Education. The NEA, these critics contend, was so enmeshed with Carter and Mondale and their campaigns in 1980 and 1984 that it had no credibility with the Reagan administration. Some teachers favor a much more aggressive political posture, while other teachers cling to the thesis that the people must continue to make the important decisions about our schools. The truth of the matter is that "the people," broadly conceived, have seldom made decisions about schools by themselves. The opinions of the teacher and administrator have either been sought out or freely offered, with the result that most educational decisions at all levels reflect both lay and professional judgment. The point at issue is whether this balance is to be maintained. There is little doubt that given present conditions teachers organizations will attempt to exert more influence over the future of education.[77] Administrators, those with managerial responsibilities, will need to recognize that as teachers take on more characteristics of professional associations, the role of administrators will change. Close-knit professionalism will introduce a type of collegial self-government and empowerment within teaching that has not been present to date.[78] The appearance of such self-government will increase sharply the need for new and more refined leadership skills.

Teachers, like members of other professions, will be challenged vigorously on the validity of licensing and tenure provisions in the near future. General public, student, and parent unrest will force external reviews of these matters if the profession does not itself lead in their reexamination. Recent events, especially in large cities, have caused school authorities to employ new types of personnel such as teacher aides without reference to formal qualifications. Past teacher shortages, often affecting rural areas more than others, have led to the employment and assignment of persons as teachers who are not licensed[79] or appropriately certified or trained for their specific assignment. The success of many such individuals brings into question not only licensing procedures but also teaching's rather tenuous professional status. Our need for better-qualified math and science teachers will provide perhaps the most significant test of the validity of teacher licensing practices.

A concerted effort needs to be made to consolidate and integrate the many organizational segments within the broad institution of education. It is important that this be done quite apart from any consideration related to making the profession a more potent political force. Such consolidation would contribute to more uniform opinion about the essential problems of teaching and learning and dispel the current image of an undecided and internally divided profession. The achievement of unity within education will not come about easily. There are forces at work that fractionate the profession, such as the trend toward specialization in administration and guidance services and the elevated status of certain groups such as science and mathematics teachers as a consequence of economic and security needs and National Science Foundation programs. The objective of the profession must be to achieve consensus on important questions confronting the profession as a whole and at the same time to maintain an internal governing structure that can tolerate the emergence of powerful subdivisions within itself.

NOTES

[1]National Commission on Excellence in Education, *A Nation at Risk: The Imperative for Educational Reform* (Washington, DC: U.S. Department of Education, 1983), 30–32, Task Force on Education for Economic Growth, *Action for Excellence* (Denver, CO: Education Commission of the States, 1983), 10–11, and Carnegie Forum on Education and the Economy, *A Nation Prepared: Teachers for the 21st Century* (Washington, DC: Carnegie Corp., 1986).

[2]National Center for Education Statistics, *Digest of Education Statistics, 1985–86* (Washington, DC: U.S. Government Printing Office, 1986), 10.

[3]National Center for Education Statistics. U.S. Department of Health, Education, and Welfare, *Statistics of Public Elementary and Secondary Day Schools, Fall 1972* (Washington, DC: U.S. Government Printing Office, 1973), 270.

[4]National Center for Education Statistics, *The Condition of Education* (Washington, DC: U.S. Government Printing Office, 1983), 172.

[5]Center for Education Statistics, *The Condition of Education* (Washington, DC: U.S. Government Printing Office, 1986), 62.

[6]Ibid.

[7]National Center for Education Statistics, *The Condition of Education,* 177.

[8]Center for Education Statistics, *The Condition of Education,* 64.

[9]Edwin Grant Dexter, *History of Education in the United States* (New York: Macmillan, 1922), 15–16.

[10]For an account of Swett's view on certification see R. Freeman Butts and Lawrence A. Cremin, *A History of Education in American Culture* (New York: Holt, Rinehart and Winston, 1953), 398–99. Swett's presentation to the NEA appears in John Swett, "The Examination of Teachers," Transcript of NEA Proceedings, 1972, 76–82.

[11]Howard S. Becker, "The Nature of a Profession," in *Education for the Professions,* ed. Nelson B. Henry, Sixty-first Yearbook of the National Society for the Study of Education (Chicago: University of Chicago Press, 1962), 35–37.

[12]Carnegie Forum, *A Nation Prepared.*

[13]Research Division, National Education Association, *Status of the American Public School Teacher, 1985–86* (Washington, DC: National Education Association, 1987).

[14]Ibid., 14.

[15]Ibid., 65.

[16]Ibid.

[17]Ibid., 78.

[18]Joseph A. Kershaw and Roland N. McKean, *Teacher Shortage and Salary Schedules* (New York: McGraw-Hill, 1962), 6–7.

[19]Dan C. Lortie, "The Balance of Control and Autonomy in Elementary School Teaching" in *The Semi-Professions and Their Organization,* ed. Amitai Etzioni (New York: Free Press, 1969), 40–41.

[20]Albert Shanker, "The Revolution That's Overdue," *Phi Delta Kappan* 66 (January 1985): 311–315.

[21]Myron Lieberman, "The Battle for New York City's Teachers," *Phi Delta Kappan* 43 (October 1961): 8.

[22]James W. Guthrie and Patricia A. Craig, *Teachers and Politics* (Bloomington, IN: Phi Delta Kappa Educational Foundation, 1973), 15.

[23]For a discussion of the AFT-NEA power struggle see Alan Rosenthal, "Pedagogues and Power," *Urban Affairs Quarterly* 2 (September 1966): 83–102.

[24]Myron Lieberman, "Implications of the Coming NEA-AFT Merger," *Phi Delta Kappan* 50 (November 1968): 139–44.

[25]For a succinct review of the history and implications of the merger movement see Myron Lieberman, "The Union Merger Movement: Will 3,500,000 Teachers Put It All Together?" *Saturday Review* 24 (June 1972): 50–56.

[26]Ibid., 52.

[27]Myron Lieberman, "NEA-AFT Merger: Breakthrough in New York," *Phi Delta Kappan* 54 (June 1972): 622.

[28]Blake Rodman, "Quest for Single Voice Spurs Teacher Unions to Discuss Merger," *Education Week* VI (13 May 1987): 1, 18.

[29]"California Unions Talk Merger," *Education USA* 30 (14 December 1987): 121.

[30]"Little Progress Seen in Discussions on Merger of California's 2 Largest Teachers' Unions," *The Chronicle of Higher Education* XXXIV (3 February 1988): A-13, 19.

[31]George Propeck and Irving F. Pearson, *The History of the Illinois Education Association* (Springfield, IL: Illinois Education Association, September, 1961), 32.

[32]La Vern Rasmussen, "Development, Operation, and Evaluation of the Ohio Continuing Contract Law" (Ph.D. diss. University of Chicago, 1961).

[33]Edgar B. Wesley, *NEA: The First Hundred Years* (New York: Harper & Row, 1957), 44.

[34]James Browne, "Power Politics for Teachers, Modern Style," *Phi Delta Kappan* 58 (October 1976): 158–64.

[35]James E. Russell, "Realities of Policy Making for Education at State and Federal Levels of Government," in *Government of Public Education for Adequate Policy Making,* ed. William P. McLure and Van Miller (Urbana, IL: University of Illinois Press, 1960), 77–89.

[36]James Crawford, "Teachers' Unions Raising Millions for Candidates," *Education Week* VI (5 November 1986): 1.

[37]Ibid.

[38]Ibid., 20.

[39]Nancey Mathis, "Fewer Republicans Get N.E.A. Endorsement, PAC Funds," *Education Week* VIII (26 October 1988): 8.

[40]Stanley E. Elam, "The National Education Association: Political Powerhouse or Paper Tiger?" *Phi Delta Kappan* 62 (November 1981): 169–74.

[41]J. Alan Aufderheide, "Educational Interest Groups and the State Legislature," in *State Policy Making for the Public Schools,* ed. Roald F. Campbell and Tim L. Mazzoni, Jr. (Berkeley: McCutchan, 1976), 176–216.

[42]Ibid.

[43]*Statement of Purpose,* CTA Political Education and Action Committee, December 1971.

[44]Newton Edwards, *The Courts and the Public Schools* (Chicago: University of Chicago Press, 1955), 473–74.

[45]For a review of principals' concerns see Bernard C. Watson, "Role of the Principal in Collective Negotiations," *North Central Association Quarterly* 42 (Winter 1968): 233–43.

[46]For a history of the teacher negotiations movement see Anthony Cresswell and Michael Murphy, *Teachers, Unions, and Collective Bargaining in Public Education* (Berkeley: McCutchan, 1980).

[47]Ibid., 32.

[48]Chester I. Barnard, *The Functions of the Executive* (Cambridge, MA: Harvard University Press, 1938).

[49]For a recent analysis of workers in a group setting see Wayne Hoy and Cecil Miskel, *Educational Administration: Theory, Research, Practice,* 3rd edition, (New York: Random House, 1987), ch. 8.

[50]Lortie, "The Balance of Control," 1–53.

[51]For valuable sociological insights into the profession of teaching and dynamics of schools as organizations see Dan C. Lortie, *School-Teacher* (Chicago: University of Chicago Press, 1975).

[52]Myron Lieberman, one of the earliest and most influential advocates of increasing the power of teachers organizations, has dramatically altered his position. See Myron Lieberman, "Eggs That I Have Laid: Teacher Bargaining Reconsidered," *Phi Delta Kappan* 60 (February 1979): 415–19.

[53]See, for example, Kern Alexander and D. Mark, editors, *Attracting and Compensating America's Teachers,* Eighth Yearbook, American Education Finance Association, (Cambridge, MA: Ballinger Publishing Company, 1988).

[54]National Center for Education Statistics, *The Condition of Education,* 182.

[55]Richard G. Neal, "Newsnotes," *Phi Delta Kappan* 60 (December 1978): 327.

[56]"Strike Serving: Hot and Rare," *The American School Board Journal* 175 (12 January 1988).

[57]For an excellent historical review and analysis of these issues, see K. Forbis Jordan and Nancy B. Borkow, *Merit Pay for Elementary and Secondary Teachers: Background Discussion and Analysis of Issue,* Congressional Research Service, Library of Congress, 33–541 S (July 1983) Mimeographed.

[58]Much of this discussion is derived from K. Forbis Jordan, *Comparison of the California Mentor Teacher Law, The Florida Merit Compensation Program, and the Tennessee Master Teacher Proposal,* Congressional Research Service, Library of Congress (August 1983) Mimeographed.

[59]Albert Benderson, "Teaching: the Struggle for Professionalism," *Focus* (1986): 17.

[60]Recently, more attention is being paid to working conditions that harm both the morale and effectiveness of teachers. Many schools, particularly in large urban areas, suffer from antiquated facilities and woefully inadequate supplies. For documentation of these conditions in thirty-one schools in five large city systems, see Thomas B. Corcoran, Lisa J. Walker, and J. Lynne White, *Working in Urban Schools* (Washington, DC: The Institute for Educational Leadership, 1988).

[61]Samuel B. Bacharach, Scott C. Bauer, and Joseph B. Shedd, "The Work Environment and School Reform," *Teachers College Record* 87 (Summer 1986): 255.

[62]Alan K. Campbell, "Restoring Teachers' Dignity," *New York Times,* 28 August 1985, 25.

[63]Gene L. Maeroff, "A Blueprint for Empowering Teachers," *Phi Delta Kappan* 69 (March 1988): 472–477.

[64]Carnegie Forum, *A Nation Prepared.*

[65]Lynn Olson, "Carnegie Unveils Makeup of National Teacher Board," *Education Week* VI (20 May 1987): 1, 14–15.

[66]Lynn Olson, "With Board in Place, Broader Agenda Looms," *Education Week* VI (27 May 1987): 1, 16.

[67]Illustrative of the types of changes being suggested that are less than enthusiastically supported by teachers or their organizations is the recommendation of New Jersey Governor Thomas Kean that persons with college degrees without education courses be permitted to teach. See "New Jersey Governor Would Open Door for Teachers Without Teacher Ed," *Education Times* 4 (26 September 1983): 3.

[68]Phillip C. Schlechty and Victor S. Vance, "Institutional Responses to the Quality/Quantity Issue in Teacher Training," *Phi Delta Kappan* 65 (October 1983): 94–101.

[69]Linda Darling-Hammond, *Beyond the Commission Reports: The Coming Crisis in Teaching* (The Rand Corporation, 1984) and *Attracting, Keeping and Enabling Excellent Teachers,* Findings and Recommendations from the Commission on Excellence in Teaching to the Board of Education of Montgomery County, Maryland, 1987.

[70]Feistritzer Associates, *The American Teacher* (Washington DC: Feistritzer Publications, 1983), 31.

[71]Carnegie Forum, *A Nation Prepared,* 79.

[72]Ibid. For further analysis of the implications of this very important and troubling issue see Dennis Gray, "Help Wanted," *Basic Education* 31 (December 1986): 3–5.

[73]Charles T. Kerchner and Douglas E. Mitchell, "Teaching Reform and Union Reform," *The Elementary School Journal* 86 (1986): 449–469.

[74]Ibid., 464.

[75]Ibid., 469.

[76]Ibid.

[77]For a recent examination of the role of organized teachers in the educational reform movement, see Lorraine M. McDonnell and Anthony Pascal, *Teachers Unions and Educational Reform* (Santa Monica, CA: Rand Corporation, 1988).

[78]Samuel B. Bacharach, Sharon Conley, and Joseph Shedd, "Beyond Career Ladders: Structuring Teacher Career Development Systems," *Teachers College Record* 87 (Summer 1986): 563–574.

[79]Council for Basic Education and the American Federation of Teachers, *Making Do in the Classroom: A Report on the Misassignment of Teachers* (The Council, 1985).

13
School-Oriented Groups

The pluralistic nature of American Society is clearly manifest in the variety of organizations that have an interest in educational matters. Some of these organizations exist only because of their interest in the schools while others are civic associations that only occasionally focus their attention on education. In this chapter we shall consider the former type of organization and the influences it may wield. We'll look first at some representative organizations that have state and national affiliations and then turn our attention to a more general discussion of locally based groups. In Chapter 14 we will examine the education-oriented activities of some organizations whose principal *raison d'etre* is in other areas.

ORGANIZATIONS WITH STATE AND NATIONAL AFFILIATIONS

The National Congress of Parents and Teachers

The PTA remains the largest volunteer organization in the United States with approximately 6.1 million members in 1988 and with overseas branches in Puerto Rico, Guam, and on other military bases around the world. The headquarters of the National PTA is in Chicago, Illinois, and there are fifty-two branches, including a District of Columbia branch, a branch associated with the Dependent Overseas Schools, and a branch in each of the states.

The objectives, policies, and practices of the PTA at the local, state, and national level are closely related to its origins and its development over more than 90 years. Founded in 1897 as the National Congress of Mothers, the organization changed its name in 1908 to the National Congress of Mothers and Parent-Teacher Associations, and changed again in 1924 to the National Congress of Parents and Teachers.[1] The obvious reason for the last change was to encourage male membership and the total membership today includes many men, but there is little doubt that the organization is still dominated by women. Some local units have opened their memberships to high school students, extending to them all privileges and responsibilities but dues, and have changed the organization's name to Parent-Teacher-Student Association.

To assess more accurately its impact on the operation of American schools, let us consider the organizational structure of the PTA and the policies by which it operates. The PTA is a network with more than 26,000 local units concerned primarily with specific problems facing a specific school and concerned secondarily with problems facing the community; fifty-two branch units to provide guidance and services to the local units; and the national office, which attempts to strengthen and unite the efforts of the entire membership on problems affecting children throughout the nation.

The common goals of the national PTA and all of its constituent units are called the Objects and are found in the bylaws of every affiliated group. These are:

- □ to promote the welfare of children and youth in home, school, community, and place of worship.
- □ to raise the standards of home life.
- □ to secure adequate laws for the care and protection of children and youth.
- □ to bring into closer relation the home and the school, that parents and teachers may cooperate intelligently in the education of children and youth.
- □ to develop between educators and the general public such united efforts as will secure for all children and youth physical, mental, social, and spiritual education.

The affairs of the national PTA are governed by a board of directors. This body includes the officers of the national PTA, the immediate past president, the president of each state PTA, and members of the three commissions on education, health and welfare, and individual development. Commissions are established by the board to promote the Objects and carry on the program of the PTA. They are designed to establish both short- and long-term objectives and to develop guidelines for achieving them. Much of the work of the PTA is done through the local units, which are connected to the national organization through the fifty-two state branches.

The national PTA works to influence educational policies at all levels. One publication refers to PTAs as "shareholders in education" and asserts: "We are now exercising our rights and demanding the opportunity to participate in the decisions that shape the educational experience. Through our children's use of the public schools, we are also a consumer organization, seeking to protect our youngsters' well-being by making certain the quality of the educational 'product' is all it should be."[2] Issues the PTA has indicated are of current concern include opposition to tuition tax credits and other types of public subsidies to private schools, violence on television, the impact of federal legislation and public policies on children and families, drug and alcohol abuse, child safety, bilingual education, health education, AIDS education, and opposition to federal standardized testing.[3] In the summer of 1988, the PTA outlined its priorities for the new administration in a memorandum entitled, "Because Children are the Future."

A sign of the PTA's intention to become an aggressive policy advocate was the opening of a Washington office for the organization in September of 1977. The national PTA legislative program is formulated through a process that provides for the submission of program proposals at local, state and national levels; consideration by the national legislative committee; approval by the National Board of Directors; and ratification by at least thirty-one state PTAs or PTSAs. The program is implemented through the Washington office. An important part of this work involves coordinating a network that calls on local PTA members to contact their congressional representatives regarding pending and proposed legislation. A legislative newsletter is sent to all local presidents six times a year.

The PTA has a long record of supporting legislation at the state and national levels designed to help children; such legislation has concerned increased financing for education, school lunch programs, dental clinics and other health measures, juvenile courts, and school safety patrols. National PTA initiatives were evident during the national energy crisis in 1974. The organization contacted the president and other government officials to urge that schools be given a high priority in the allocation of fuel. It also urged its members to get involved on the issue. In a similar vein and at about the same time, the national PTA was among the first organizations to announce opposition to year-round daylight savings time. Calling for repeal of this measure, the national PTA president, Lillie E. Herndon, cited members' "concern for the safety of children."[4] She added that the coordinator of legislative activity had been directed to make this position known to congressional leaders and that PTA members had been asked to urge congressional repeal locally.

More recently the national PTA claimed that a call to action to state and local PTAs was instrumental in persuading Congress to amend the School Lunch Act to provide for increased federal subsidies.[5] In 1977 the new Washington office led the formation of the National Coalition for Public Education, a group of forty organizations that has worked successfully against tax credits to parents of elementary and secondary education students. In 1988, the PTA helped to lobby successfully for an expanded role for parents in developing local Chapter 1 programs for parent involvement. These provisions were incorporated in Public Law 100–297, the Hawkins-Stafford Elementary and Secondary Education Improvement Amendments.[6] Thus the national PTA has become both aggressive and effective in influencing policy at the national level.

At the state level, PTAs rely heavily on volunteers to remain abreast of and speak to state and local policy developments. While PTA representatives often testify about pending state legislation, some observers believe that they have little impact on state policymaking.[7] On the other hand, the PTA has often been a part of coalitions of education interest groups at the state level.

At the local level, the PTA has traditionally been viewed as being supportive of existing policies at the district and building levels. Jennings even referred to local PTAs as "kept organizations" and noted that school boards often lead and influence the interest groups rather than vice versa.[8] The PTA's view of the ideal relationship with the school board is that of a partnership—"For this partnership to work, . . . both parties should have a systematic program for exchanging information and for involving parents in school policy making processes."[9]

In recent years, the PTA has become more assertive at local as well as state and national levels. A 1972 bylaws change altered an article that read, "The organization shall cooperate with schools to support the improvement of education in ways that will not interfere with administration of the schools and shall not seek to control their policies." The revised version states, "The organization shall work with the schools to provide quality education for all children and youth and shall seek to participate in the decision-making process establishing school policy, recognizing that the legal responsibility to make decisions has been delegated by the people to boards of education." In 1982, the PTA published a revision of its workbook, *Looking in on Your School,* stating " . . . parents must become more involved in their children's education. That is why the National PTA is calling upon parents this year to look in on their local school—to study its operation; to determine its strengths and weaknesses; to join with administrators, teachers, and community members to improve their schools in order to better the lives and futures of their children."[10] A major campaign entitled "School is What *We* Make It" was undertaken in 1987–88 to encourage parent involvement in schools.

The local PTA has long been a training ground for prospective board of education members.[11] It provides an opportunity for individuals to take part in school events, become knowledgeable about school issues, and gain public identification as a person who is interested in and supportive of schools. Although the national PTA points out that locals are to support issues and principles and not support or oppose particular candidates,[12] it appears that the informal contacts established by working in PTA have been helpful to school board candidates in many communities.

A comprehensive examination of PTA efforts to influence school board policy was part of a national study by Ziegler and Jennings.[13] Like earlier observers, they noted the tendency of the PTA to support established school policy and to be on good terms with school officials. However, they also found that the PTA was the group most frequently named by board of education members as seeking to influence school policy and concluded that in comparison to teachers the PTA is "a more potent force."[14] While this may continue to be the case in some areas, it should be noted that local teachers associations have become more assertive about a range of policy issues since Ziegler and Jennings conducted their research.

PTA documents, as we have noted, indicate that the organization seeks a stronger and more independent voice in local policymaking. The national PTA has encouraged local units to urge their boards of education to oppose federal- or state-prescribed competency testing in favor of locally developed criterion-referenced tests, to campaign for local teacher in-service training in reading instruction, and to seek a voice in local curriculum development and collective bargaining processes. If local PTA units are assertive about such sensitive matters, however, the bridging relationships between teachers and parents traditionally fostered by the organization may be jeopardized.

The future of the PTA as a policy force at local, state, and national levels is clouded by at least two other factors. The first is the growing tendency of mothers to return to the work force. Working mothers (and fathers) in two-income families often have less time to participate in organizations such as the PTA, which rely primarily upon volunteer activity. Recognizing this, the National PTA created the "Big City PTA Project" to develop ways of increasing the involvement of such parents in local PTAs. Central to this project are demonstration sites in Milwaukee and San Diego and leadership training for other local district leaders. The second factor is the trend in some areas to reject membership in the PTA in favor of a local Parent-Teacher Organization. Advocates of PTOs point out that the organizations are entirely local and therefore pay neither dues nor allegiance to state and national organizations. The national PTA has recognized this challenge and responded to it by pointing to the benefits of affiliation.[15]

The National School Boards Association

The organizational structure of American education places heavy responsibility upon the local school board member. Because these board members are usually lay people rather than professionals in the field of education and because of the importance of the decisions they make, it was only natural for them to create organizations that could serve as clearinghouses and exchange centers for many experiences and activities in which boards are involved. The first state association of school boards was formed in Pennsylvania in 1896. By 1920 there were seven state associations; by 1940, twenty-seven; and by 1957, all states had organized.[16]

At the national level, organization came more slowly. The National Council of State School Board Associations was organized in February 1940, in St. Louis at a meeting held in conjunction with the annual convention of the American Association of School Administrators.[17] World War II slowed the growth of the organization but it was revived in 1945. It was at the 1949 meeting that action was taken that would put the organization on its feet permanently. Edward M. Tuttle, about to retire as editor-in-chief of Row, Peterson, and Company, a textbook publisher, was selected to serve as the full-time executive secretary. By the fall of that year Tuttle had established a headquarters office, had incorporated the NSBA under the "Not for Profit" laws of the state of Illinois, and had distributed the first directory of the presidents and secretaries then in office.

The founders of the NSBA wrestled for some time over the type of organization needed. The early conflict was waged over whether or not the association should work directly with local boards in matters of membership, finance, and service, or whether it should work primarily with state associations of school boards. The original name of the organization, National Council of State School Board Associations, suggests that the founders had the latter alternative in mind. Nevertheless, the question of direct board membership versus the federation of state associations was an issue in all of the early meetings. Tuttle commented:

> Not until the 1950 Convention in Atlantic City was the issue apparently settled by a unanimous vote of delegates from 28 states in support of a motion that: The National School Boards Association be a federation of state school boards associations, and that the National Association serve the state associations, and indirectly local boards through the state associations. A constitution was adopted embodying this principle and eliminating the sustaining membership.[18]

The decision made by the NSBA in 1950 held for twenty years. At its 1970 convention the association amended its constitution to provide for direct affiliation by "any school board that is a member of an Active Member" (i.e., a member state association) on an additional fee basis.[19] The primary advantage of direct affiliation has been in the area of legislative information services. Recently the association expanded policy and information services to direct affiliates, and by 1988, nearly 2,000 school boards had gained this status. The concept of a federation has been sustained as the organization has developed and was reaffirmed in a 1982 governance study of the association. One provision of NSBA Beliefs and Policies states:

> The National School Boards Association recognizes that it is the right and duty of each individual state school boards association and local school board to express to its representatives in the Congress of the United States the positions of the National School Board Association and its own position, with regard to educational issues, even if the two positions are different. However, it is the obligation of the state school boards association and local school districts to keep the National Association informed when they actively pursue a position which differs from the position of the National Association.[20]

While retaining its federated character, the association has changed its policy-making procedures to give proportionately greater representation to state associations that represent school districts with relatively large aggregate enrollments. It has also spoken out increasingly on national policy issues and taken a more aggressive lobbying posture. The organization appears to have grown stronger through these efforts both in membership size and perceived influence. Through its member organizations, NSBA includes 95,000 members in more than 15,300 local school districts who oversee the education of 97 percent of the nation's public school children.

The NSBA has overcome its early reluctance to become involved with national policymaking for education and is now perhaps the most aggressive of existing lay groups in this regard. It provides relevant information for its members and direct affiliates. The association has also established a Federal Relations Network that has up to three school board members from each congressional district serving as liaisons with congressional representatives. In addition, NSBA is active in coalitions with other national education groups regarding federal education issues.

By 1976 the organization had moved its headquarters to Washington, DC, a step symbolic of its intent to influence national policy. In 1984 NSBA moved to new permanent headquarters to house its staff of 100 in the Washington area.

In 1987, the NSBA board adopted a strategic plan with eleven objectives. Among them are: (1) strengthening relations with and services to Federation members in the area of state legislation, school law, and public policy; (2) advocacy for high quality education through school board leadership; (3) expanded research activities; (4) more effective federal advocacy; (5) emphasis on transferring technology to education; (6) specialized programs for unique NSBA constituencies such as urban and rural districts; (7) continued financial health for the association; (8) establishment of a planning council to take the lead in annual revisions of NSBA plans and initiatives.[21] NSBA has also established internal councils through which members with particular interests can share specialized information and activities. These include the Council of School Attorneys, the Council of Urban Boards of Education, the Conference of School Board Negotiators, the Large District Forum, and the Forum of Federal Program Coordinators.

As the influence of the NSBA has increased in recent years, there is some evidence that the impact of the group on federal policy has been substantial. Granted, federal policymakers and certainly the Reagan administration have not been greatly influenced by traditional educational interest groups in recent years but recent legislative successes for NSBA have included working with other education groups to limit cutbacks in federal spending for education, retaining the Department of Education, opposing tuition tax credits, and achieving simplification in the guidelines for certain federal programs. State associations also develop and advocate positions on certain legislative issues. Their officers and staff members testify frequently before legislatures and state boards of education and are often key actors in the formulation of state education policy.[22]

The NSBA and the state associations have been very effective in providing a clearinghouse to facilitate an exchange of ideas and information. For example, the *American School Board Journal,* the *Executive Educator,* and *School Board News* are widely read by board of education members and others interested in education.

The National Citizens Commission for the Public Schools

Although this organization no longer exists, its influence in the first half of this century was extensive. Its meteoric rise to prominence brought thousands of citizens into school improvement work, and its almost as rapid disappearance from the national scene left a legacy of progress and citizen interest that is still proliferating in many areas. Indeed, the recent manifestations of interest in public education by many of the nation's most prominent political, civic, and business leaders have generated some discussion about creating a contemporary analogue to the National Citizens Commission for the Public Schools.

James B. Conant[23] has been credited with founding the commission. In 1943 while president of Harvard University, he suggested that the Educational Policies Commission of the National Educational Association should explore the idea of a citizen-led, citizen-serving group to foster solutions to some of the problems facing education. A year later the EPC formally approached the American Council on Education to explore jointly the establishment of a "national commission of largely lay membership to build a public relations program for education."[24] A committee of nine educators finally recommended the formation of a commission of prominent citizens unconnected with education who could study the schools and seek the public's support in improving them.

In October of 1946 these educators met with nine carefully selected people who had indicated an interest in at least considering the next step. Two particularly relevant facts soon became apparent as this group studied the educational scene. The first was that many efforts to inform the public about the schools were already underway, but these efforts were primarily local, and there was little if any communication or coordination between groups. In addition, except for a lay group that provided advice on policies to the United States Commissioner of Education, all of the national organizations concerned with education were composed either solely or primarily of educators.

As these people studied the problems, they recruited additional members who had a similar commitment to the public schools. The mechanics of organization took time, but by May of 1949 the National Citizens Commission for the Public Schools was incorporated. The initial financial support came from the Carnegie Corporation and the Rockefeller-endowed General Education Board.

The original commission had twenty-five members, none of whom was professionally identified with politics, religion, or education. An advisory panel of six educators was established to serve in a strictly consultative role on many of the technical problems of education. One theme dominated everything the commission did: there is no school problem a citizens committee cannot help solve if the committee is broadly representative of all interests and viewpoints, if it makes an objective continuing study of the facts, and if it is independent but works cooperatively with school officials.

To spread this gospel, the commission undertook a number of activities. Regional offices were established to provide consultative help to the many local and state groups which were organizing. Regional and national workshops, twenty-eight in all, were held to discuss ways of implementing the Better Schools campaigns. The commission published a monthly bulletin and distributed fifteen "Working Guides" in great numbers. These Working Guides were pocket-sized pamphlets that served as how-to source books.[25]

The impact of the commission was immediate and almost startling. When the NCCPS was organized in 1949, it knew of only seventeen communities with citizen committees. In 1957 Henry Toy, Jr., executive director of the commission, estimated that about 15,000 local committees were working actively for school improvement, and approximately 40 committees were operating at the state level.[26]

In 1956 the National Citizens Commission for the Public Schools ceased to operate, but a successor organization was soon in operation. This group, known as the National Citizens Council for Better Schools, which lasted until 1959, began with the same staff, many of the same citizen members, and much the same task. The accomplishments of the NCCPS and its successor were many.[27] They made the public aware of its right to participate in school affairs and of its obligations to make such participation constructive. They convinced educators that public interest in education could be exceedingly useful and need not be either destructive or meddlesome.

The National Committee for Support of the Public Schools

Three years after the demise of the National Citizen Council for Better Schools in 1959, another organization involving prominent lay persons at the national level in education was created. The National Committee for Support of the Public Schools was formed in 1962 by thirty-nine individuals, many of whom had played an active role in the National Citizens Commission for the Public Schools and its successor organization. Like its predecessors this organization has dissolved, but it has left an important legacy.

Chairing the new group was Agnes Meyer, author, lecturer, and former trustee of the National Citizens Commission. Among the nationally prominent founders were novelist John Hersey, a former chairperson of the National Citizens Council; James B. Conant; educator Harold Taylor; President Harry S. Truman; poet Carl Sandburg; and General Omar Bradley.

The original objectives of the National Committee were more specific than those of its predecessors. Whereas the earlier organizations sought "to arouse broad citizen interest and action" for the schools, this committee formed for one purpose— to stimulate more adequate financial support for public education. The committee subsequently broadened its concerns to include the allocation of resources within and among schools and accountability for achieving educational objectives. Thus, while the committee continued to urge higher levels of funding for education, it also sought ways of assuring that these funds would be used to the greatest public advantage.

In announcing the formation of the committee, Meyer said it would not be a lobbying committee and would not propose legislation. It would, Meyer said, "rely on the intelligence of the American people first to make the maximum effort locally, then to demand whatever help may be needed from their state governments, and from the federal government to supplement the resources of local school districts."[28] She added that this would not be just another paper committee, that members were "determined to get results."

The basic strategy of the committee was one of "fostering change through public education and information."[29] One technique was to serve as a clearinghouse for information on school needs, school finance, and the activities of state education groups. One member in each state served as a representative of the committee and was the agent for answering questions about educational matters in that state. State representatives also worked with members and other citizens to increase support for education in their representative states. In addition, the small central staff, headquartered in Washington, DC, often responded directly to citizen requests for information or referred questioners to an appropriate source of information. The central staff gathered considerable information on its own in addition to urging action by state representatives and disseminating information to its members and interested citizens.

In its brief life the committee gained a national audience. In 1970 there were approximately 1,700 active members in all fifty states. The group published a regular newsletter as well as periodic fact sheets and special reports. An early set of fact sheets was designed to help members evaluate the ability of their state in relation to others to finance public education. Special reports were published on topics such as "The Need to Build a New Sense of Community" and "Quality Education, Some Clues for the Citizen." A book sponsored by the committee, *Changing Demands on Education and Their Fiscal Implications,* was distributed to more than 30,000 persons.

Another effective means of dissemination employed by the group was its series of annual conferences. These conferences were regularly attended by more than 500 persons, and the proceedings were widely distributed. The group became an important force at state and national levels by calling attention of policymakers and influential citizens to financial and program needs in education. Meyer's death in 1971, however, precipitated an important change of direction. Meyer had provided much of the voluntary financial support that sustained the committee. The loss of her leadership and the lack of sufficient funds from other sources led the committee to reduce its program efforts for a time. Then, in 1973, a proposal to revitalize the organization was presented to the Ford Foundation. This proposal was approved and in November 1973 the Committee Board of Directors reconstituted the organization as the National Committee for Citizens in Education.

The National Committee for Citizens in Education

The National Committee for Citizens in Education seeks to establish a much broader membership base and agenda than its predecessor. The organization strives to improve the quality of education in public schools and proceeds from the premise that "constructive involvement of parents and citizens in public education is essential." The goals of the organization are to: (1) provide its membership, and as many parent-citizens as it can reach, with intelligible, jargon-free information about current issues in public education through brochures, handbooks, filmstrips, and its newspaper, *Network,* (2) provide direct services to its more than 300 affiliated parent-citizen groups and other groups that request its help, and to assist individual parents and newly organizing groups through direct technical assistance and through its network of education and noneducation groups around the country, and (3) serve as spokespersons for parent-citizen concerns at the national and state levels and to assist parents and their organizations in monitoring education legislation that directly affects them and their children. A unique form of joint leadership for the committee has been provided by Carl L. Marburger, former commissioner of education in New Jersey; J. William Rioux, former president of the Merrill Palmer Institute in Detroit; and Stanley Salett, former director of education, Community Action Programs, Office of Economic Opportunity.

The committee issued its first newsletter in January 1974. Its initial efforts were directed at building a mass membership, and it was assisted by considerable publicity in the national news media. The committee's intention to take an aggressive advocacy position at state and federal levels was indicated when it became the first education-related organization to join in a suit against the secretary of the U.S. Treasury and the commissioner of the Internal Revenue Service that would allow tax-exempt charitable and educational groups to lobby for legislative proposals in the same way that other tax-exempt agencies do.

During its early years, the committee was instrumental in providing information that helped secure passage of the Family Educational Rights and Privacy Act of 1974. The committee also testified before Congress regarding the low level of parent participation in Title I programs and along with other national organizations convened a National Conference of Title I Parents. The committee has conducted hearings on public school governance across the country and has put forth a number of publications suggesting ways in which parents and citizens can become more knowledgeable about school issues, their rights in relation to schools, and how they can become more involved in school affairs. Further assistance in this regard is provided through the Parents Network and through a toll-free telephone hot line parents can use to seek information and help.

Recent activities included a twelve-state review of parent participation in developing individual education plans mandated by Public Law 94–142, research on school-based management, urging educational agencies to comply with public requests for information that fall under the Freedom of Information Act, calling for enforcement of public participation provisions in federal education programs and studies of the relationship between parent participation and student achievement, the special educational needs and problems of children in single-parent families, and the legal rights of handicapped children and their parents. Another example of influence at the federal level was NCCE success in urging the establishment of the Office of Public Participation and Special Concerns in the Department of Education. However, a follow-up study by NCCE in 1982 determined that the office had done little to improve parental or public involvement in education.[30] More recently, NCCE has worked with the Child Advocates Coalition on behalf of stronger requirements for parental participation in Chapter 1 and Chapter 2 programs.[31] In its almost two decades of existence, the committee has demonstrated the ability both to work with citizens at the grassroots level and to influence policy at the national level.

The Council for Basic Education

The Council for Basic Education is an independent, nationwide group of educators, policymakers, parents, and concerned citizens committed to improving elementary and secondary education. The group advocates a curriculum in the liberal arts for all students; promotes challenging and thoughtful approaches to instruction; and speaks as a critical voice on schools and school reform. Founded in 1956 by Mortimer Smith and Arthur Bestor, the council's charter members included Malcolm Cowley, Alfred A. Knopf, and Richard Hofstader. Since its inception, the council has advocated a rigorous education in the liberal arts for all students, regardless of family background or career aspirations.

Although membership in the organization has never been large and currently stands at about 4,500, its independent status has made its publications attractive to policymakers and opinion leaders. The council's former executive director, Mortimer Smith, noted the special character of council membership: "We aim deliberately at key people, teachers and administrators, and lay leaders in the community who are in a position to influence the educational program. It is reassuring to know that many of those responsible for what goes on in the classroom find our publications appealing."[32] Indeed, the influence of the council appears to have expanded significantly since Smith offered this statement.

The council's fundamental principles are simply stated. CBE advocates:

> That a sound education in the basic subjects of the liberal arts—English (including reading, writing, speaking, and listening), mathematics, science, history, geography, government, foreign languages, and the arts—is the single best preparation for work, responsible citizenship, and lifelong learning.
>
> That all elementary and secondary students, regardless of family circumstances or vocational goals, can and should master these basic subjects and are empowered by them.
>
> That strengthening the teaching and learning of basic subjects requires that curricula be focused and coherent; that teachers be knowledgeable in their fields and rigorously educated; that they be recruited, renewed, and retained as professionals; and that administrators understand their roles as educational leaders.[33]

The council emphasizes the intellectual purposes of the schools and criticizes what it considers challenges to these purposes. It takes some credit for reducing the national emphasis placed on "life adjustment" education in the 1960s.[34] During the late 1970s the views of the organization became popular with many citizens as the public showed support for the "back to basics" movement. While recognizing potential in this trend, the council expressed concern about its relatively narrow focus. A. Graham Down, Smith's successor as executive director, set forth these views in the 1976 annual report of the organization:

> The phrase "back to basics" suggests reaction. The old-fashioned school room, the paddle, and political reaction come to mind. Further some proponents of this movement tend to suggest that basic skills and basic education are the same. They are not. . . . While admitting that some subjects are more important than others, we must yet insist that the three R's are not enough and that only those who are conversant with the whole sense of a liberal curriculum can possibly possess the flexibility and imagination to deal with the demands of a world changing at an unprecedented rate of speed.[35]

CBE communicates these views through a series of publications. *Basic Education,* the council's mainstay, is a pocket-size monthly journal that provides a forum for guest writers including Mortimer Adler, James Rutherford, and Elliott Eisner, as well as members of the CBE staff, most notably Dennis Gray and David Lynn. In addition, the council publishes the quarterly *Basic Education: Issues, Answers, and Facts.* Recent issues have included "Television and the Schools—But Not What You Think" by Jacques Barzun, "The Arts, Language, and the Schools" by Ernest Boyer, "Attacking Illiteracy at the Source" by Dennis Gray, and "The Essence of Geography" by C. L. Salter.

The council also publishes reports and books. In February 1988, for instance, CBE published *New Teachers, Better Teachers,* a study of New Jersey's alternate certification route and professional development academy. Other recent publications include *Reforming Science Education: The Search for a New Vision* by Paul DeHart Hurd (1984), *Charting A Course: A Guide to the Excellence Movement in Education* by Ian McNett (1984), and *The Anatomy of Teacher Institutes: A Design for Professional Development,* edited by James M. Banner, Jr. (1985). In 1988, CBE published a major study of textbook adoption policies, *A Conspiracy of Good Intentions* by Harriet Tyson-Bernstein, and a book on what all sixth-graders should know and be able to do by the time they finish elementary school in order to succeed in further education.

Compared to the view that says the public schools are so ineffectual they should be abandoned, the basic reform orientation of CBE seems moderate and perhaps even comforting to some educators. For example, in an article entitled "Are the Schools Worth Saving?" CBE cited several specific characteristics of the structure and procedures of the public school it considered "valid":

> [It offered] a system of public education; formal organization of the curriculum; the authority of the teachers; large group instruction; and some form of segregation by ability. These ideas seem to us to be sound ones that can be pointed to as a part of "what's right with the schools." Within an organizational structure incorporating such ideas, it is possible, we believe, to effect reform that will vastly improve the quality of education offered by the schools to all students.[36]

The council maintains both an "information-service" program and an "educational studies" program.[37] In addition to publishing *Basic Education* and other materials, the council provides informal consulting assistance in response to requests from educators, the media, and citizens. Workshops and conferences are also part of the information service. The educational studies program involves conducting and publishing studies related to basic education. Some of these appear as occasional papers and others are published in book form. Since 1983, the council has received support from the National Endowment for the Humanities to administer a program of independent summer study for high school humanities teachers. In 1983, the council began Project ABCs—Action for Better City Schools. Supported by several major foundations, the project helps administrators improve their instructional leadership and provides teachers with opportunities to increase their subject knowledge, strengthen their teaching skills, and renew their dedication to teaching. Examples of ABCs programs include Mathematics and Science Institutes, which train teachers from other subject areas to teach these subjects, and Writing to Learn, a program that helps teachers of all subjects use writing in their classrooms.[38] CBE is also closely connected with the Paideia Program, because Dennis Gray, the council's deputy director, is a member of the original Paideia group.[39] Through him, the council is involved in training teachers in Paideia-style instruction.

There can be little doubt that the basic concerns of the CBE have become central concerns of American education in recent years. The increased attention to intellectual tasks in the schools is a case in point. It is difficult, however, to find a direct cause-and-effect relationship between the activities of the council and some of these changes. Sputnik, the NDEA, increasing pressure to attend college, tax-conscious consumerism, and concern for economic competitiveness are just a few of the factors that may have had greater influence than the council on the public's basic educational concerns. Nevertheless, in the past twenty-five years the values of the general public have grown closer to the council's values. Indeed, the national studies that have focused on improving the quality of education reinforce some of the major themes propounded by the council for some time.

LOCALLY BASED GROUPS

Many communities have one or more groups that are not officially affiliated with broader organizations and are oriented to school programs. Well-known examples include committees of business executives and industrialists who advise on the development of vocational educational programs and booster clubs that support school athletic programs. These groups are sometimes quite influential in determining school policies at the local level.

The past twenty-five years witnessed an increase in the number of such local ad hoc groups, especially in urban school systems. In some cases, these groups have been created by school officials in much the same way that earlier citizen committees were formed. In other cases, they were formed independently of school sanctions and sometimes in opposition to school policies. This section will focus on these forms of citizen participation in local school affairs.

Most citizens do not become actively involved in attempting to change school policies directly. Notwithstanding the rhetoric of school reform, most tend to regard the performance of schools as satisfactory.[40] Most citizen participation is short-lived and oriented to a particular issue. It is most common in metropolitan area school districts, and persons who espouse liberal rather than conservative views tend to be more active as well as more successful.[41] Recently, however, a new wave of conservative groups has confronted school officials over issues such as sex education, school prayer, and the teaching of scientific creationism.

Background of the New Participation

The traditional belief is that education is a profession in which policy decisions are made by a representative board of lay persons and implemented by professionals. This ideology has been challenged on two grounds which, taken together, provide the rationale for new efforts in citizen involvement. The public has challenged (1) the effectiveness of schools and (2) the representativeness of school policymakers.[42]

Despite records of improved student achievement in some cities, few institutions have received more criticism in recent years than urban school systems. This has been manifest in the press and the popular literature as well as in academic reports and journals.[43] While it has been said many ways and attributed to various factors, the basic conclusion is that schools have not been sufficiently effective. Widespread acceptance of this conclusion has made the public more willing to consider alternatives to present arrangements for schooling.

Citizens have also questioned the representativeness of those who make policies for schools, particularly in large urban districts. To many, the five, seven, or eleven persons elected or appointed to positions on the board of education seem remote and very much unlike themselves. As the vignette in Chapter 1 illustrated, they may even believe that this body has interests and attitudes that are inimical to their own. At another level, they may be suspicious of the principal and teachers at the school attended by their children. Convinced that education is important to their children's future and dissatisfied with the results they see, angry citizens and their advocates may seek to intervene in school policymaking.

Citizen activists have mobilized city residents to confront the institutions close to their lives. These activists have been visible especially in poor and minority group neighborhoods. Their emphasis has been on community determination and achievement of goals in contrast to the traditionally docile acceptance of the benefits offered by established institutions. In short, they have encouraged citizens to participate in decisions concerning their own destiny.[44]

A historical force supporting citizen assertiveness has been the activity of certain foundations and government agencies. Most notable among these have been the Ford Foundation and the Office of Economic Opportunity. The Ford Foundation was instrumental in stimulating citizen participation in the New York City Schools in 1967–69. First by supporting Ocean Hill-Brownsville and other experimental districts during their earliest stages and then by contributing to plans for decentralizing the entire system, foundation officials attempted to influence school policy in that city. Ford Foundation encouragement of citizen involvement, however, predates the saga of Ocean Hill-Brownsville. Earlier efforts (although they emphasized the coordination of services more than participation) included the "grey areas" project that established new community agencies in Boston, New Haven, Oakland, Philadephia, Washington, DC, and several locales in North Carolina and the partial support of the Mobilization for Youth project in New York City.[45] Moynihan has written of Ford intentions in these activities that "it purposed nothing less than institutional change in the operation and control of American cities. To this object it came forth with a social invention of enormous power: the independent community agency. In effect, the Public Affairs Program of the Ford Foundation invented a new level of American government, the inner city community action agency."[46]

The notion of community action was central to the "war on poverty" financed by the Economic Opportunity Act of 1964. Indeed, Community Action Programs were designed initially as the biggest weapons in the antipoverty arsenal. According to the statute, such programs were to be locally based, to mobilize and coordinate sufficient resources "to give promise of progress toward elimination of poverty or causes of poverty," and perhaps most notably to be "developed, conducted, and administered with the maximum feasible participation of residents of the area and members of the groups served."[47]

The history of CAP agencies was tumultuous in many respects. Our purpose here is not to evaluate their product nor their processes but to note their legacy. First, participation in CAP programs provided a type of training in citizen involvement and group leadership for thousands of poor and minority group citizens. In some instances, this training included "field experiences" with instruction in the tactics of conflict and confrontation. Second, and perhaps more important, such participation helped to raise the expectations citizens have for institutions such as schools. Although CAP programs have been discontinued, in many cases a leadership cadre of citizens survived and taught others in the neighborhood to press for improved services.

The early impetus for local CAP agencies and boards to intervene in school affairs was augmented by guidelines for the Elementary and Secondary Education Act, which required evidence of cooperation with CAP agencies in the development of Title I programs. Subsequent federal guidelines for programs such as Head Start, Follow Through, and Title I of the Elementary and Secondary Education Act have also contained various provisions calling for citizen involvement in program advisory roles.

An important factor in the growing demand for citizen involvement has been the development of a participatory ideology. In part, this ideology was a product of frustration adopted by persons tired of waiting for either integration or compensatory education strategies to be employed on a scale large enough to have some possible effect.[48] Thus some citizens castigate the system, charging that its structure or the biases of those who run it make it unresponsive to neighborhood needs. The answer they say is to divide it into smaller parts, each of them being accountable to local constituencies.

The forces discussed thus far in this section have been those urging poor and minority group citizens to seek an expanded role for themselves in school affairs. It should be noted also that many school people have recognized that some citizens are alienated from the schools and have sought to draw them closer to their programs. Hoping to increase their sense of trust in the schools and to direct their energies toward constructive support of their children, some teachers and principals have visited parents in their homes and invited them to school for various activities. Thus, in some instances school people have taken the initiative toward increasing citizen involvement in school matters. Similarly, concerned middle- and upper-class citizens sometimes have recognized the myriad of problems confronting the schools and have organized themselves to help resolve them. In other instances groups have organized to counter conflicting demands set forth by other citizen bodies.

Two developments in the 1970s fostered further expansion of local citizen involvement. The first was the increased pressure, including court orders, to desegregate many school systems. Efforts to implement or even develop desegregation plans were often met by the formation of hostile citizen groups. These groups frequently attracted a broad following and sometimes were successful in delaying further desegregation. In some instances their efforts led to the removal of local superintendents or board of education members.

A second development that led to expanded involvement was the growing emphasis on accountability. In an effort to respond to such pressures, school officials in all kinds of districts have sometimes established citizen advisory committees. Similar steps have been taken at the state level.

In 1973 the Florida legislature mandated an accountability program that required every school district to establish citizen advisory committees. This and subsequent legislation in Florida pointed toward development of a school-based management system that has been advocated as a strategy to increase accountability at the building level.[49] Similar legislation has been passed in other states, including South Carolina and California. School-based or school-site management is a reform strategy that emphasizes professional as well as lay responsibility at the local school level. In this sense, it is consistent with the proposals that empower teachers espoused by the Carnegie Forum and others. The critical question, however, is what balance should exist in terms of decision-making participation between teachers, administrators, and lay persons.[50] Administrators have traditionally resisted the involvement of parents and other citizens in shared governance at the school building level.[51]

Objectives of Citizen Participation

Many objectives have been noted for citizen participation. Burke holds that it is useful to view citizen participation as a strategy, or "basis for various strategies," for achieving various goals rather than as a goal in itself.[52] In keeping with this view, six general objectives for citizen participation in school affairs can be stated.

The first of these is to increase public understanding and general support for the schools. Fantini has argued for this purpose as follows:

> When people have a part in their institutions, they share responsibility for them and are more likely to pay close attention to the stated mission and actual performance of the institution . . . Participatory democracy in education should also give parents and community a tangible respect for the intricacy and complexity of the professional problem in urban education. It is not likely that parents who have gained admission as true partners in the process will oversimplify and lay the blame for educational failures solely on the professional.[53]

During the late 1970s and 1980s corporate and civic leaders became increasingly aware of the strategic importance of public education to the economic and social fabric of the nation. They sought greater involvement with the schools and were welcomed by school officials as advisors on technical aspects of management and as partners in the operation of some schools. For example, the New York Alliance for the Public Schools was founded in 1979 under the auspices of New York University. It is a voluntary civic organization that joins business and civic leaders with educators to support projects on behalf of the New York Public Schools. Similar groups can be found in a number of other cities, including Atlanta, Boston, Dallas, Hartford, Memphis, Pittsburgh, and San Francisco.

A second objective is to provide instruction or assistance of some type for the participants. Burke calls this an "education-therapy" strategy.[54] Examples in the world of education include parent advisory committees to preschool programs, in which an implicit if not stated function is to help parents learn about school programs and ways in which they can assist their own children. The significance of such activities is found in the clear relationship between parental involvement in student learning and student achievement.[55] Thus programs that help parents assist their children with homework and reinforce school priorities can boost student achievement.

A third objective of some citizen participation mechanisms is to co-opt potential opponents of the institutions sponsoring the mechanism.[56] The notion of coopting has been developed by Selznick, who defines it as "the process of absorbing new elements into the leadership or policy determining structure of an organization as a means of averting threats to its stability or existence."[57] For example, a school principal might invite community leaders who are dissatisfied with the school to serve on an advisory committee in the hope that this position would dissuade them from mobilizing opposition to the school program.

A fourth objective is to provide advice and counsel regarding program goals and practices. The extent to which school people feel obligated to accept this advice varies widely and has provoked controversy in many settings. Nevertheless, this is probably the most frequently stated objective for citizen involvement. It was implicit, for example, in the guidelines for Elementary and Secondary Education Act Title I programs which required that "the priority needs of educationally deprived children in the eligible attendance areas (target populations) were determined in consultation with teachers, parents, private school authorities, and representatives of other agencies which have a genuine and continuing interest in such children."[58]

A fifth objective is to increase the amount of human and material resources available to carry out educational programs and to coordinate the application of these resources. For example, a local social club may volunteer the services of its members to serve as library aides, or a group of parents may organize to watch over their young children as they walk to and from school in a busy neighborhood. There are currently more than 4.6 million Americans who provide a broad range of volunteer services to public schools. Since 1968, an increasing number of them have been associated with National School Volunteer Program, Inc., a nonprofit association based in the Washington, DC, area that provides technical assistance and information services. A more recent example of potentially far-reaching significance have been programs organized by business leaders in a number of major cities to assure "at-risk" students of jobs if they complete high school. Initiated in Boston by the Boston

Compact, programs of "education and employment partnership" have been repli-cated in several cities across the country.

In the early 1980s, a new social institution was invented to collect and distribute voluntary contributions to schools. Local education foundations were established in many school districts to receive financial contributions that local corporations and citizens wished to be used for the benefit of local schools. The foundation board is generally apprised of school district priorities and makes its funding decisions and allocations accordingly. In some districts, these foundations now pose formidable competition to the fund-raising efforts of local colleges and universities.

The Public Education Fund, a national nonprofit organization established with support from Ford and several other major foundations, provided seed grants to fifty local education foundations in the 1980s. The fund assisted in forming local founda-tions that linked business, labor, and civic leadership with public schools to raise additional resources in support of improved schools and increased public confi-dence. Requests from urban school districts were given priority, and no support was available to supplant diminished public funds for basic school services. A successor to the fund, the Public Education Fund Network, is now in place to provide technical assistance to the original fifty grantees and other local organizations that operate similar foundations.

The sixth objective, the most threatening to established institutions, is to mon-itor the performance of the institutions and to force changes if that performance is viewed as unsatisfactory. It is within the context of this objective that the words "accountability" and "community control" have significance.

Any given citizen group may have more than one purpose. Moreover, groups of all types may be formed at the initiative of either school officials or citizens themselves. Often those who formed groups and those invited to participate in them have had different views of the purpose of the group. For example, the solicitation of advice by school people has sometimes been interpreted as an invitation to com-munity control.

SUMMARY AND FUTURE PROSPECTS

Citizens have demonstrated increasing interest in organizing to effect changes in school policy at national, state, and local levels. Recognizing this citizen interest, federal and state officials have mandated citizen involvement in many programs. Local use of advisory committees has also expanded.

It is an irony of the past decade or so that the organizations with state and national affiliations described in this chapter have increased in strength but without concomitant effects on state and national policy for education. There are two major reasons for this. The first is a shift in national priorities away from aid to education, a trend that may be reversed in the near future as a result of the recent national reports on education and increased interest in educational reform by prominent business and political leaders. The second is the demise of coalitions that had so effectively influenced legislation in many states.

The nature and effectiveness of such coalitions was described by Bailey and by Masters, Salisbury, and Eliot.[59] The coalitions included the major educational associations and interest groups in a particular state, who came together to develop legislative programs they all would support. Such groups included the Education Council in Michigan, the New York State Educational Conference Board, the Joint Committee on Education in Wisconsin, and the Princeton Group in New Jersey. A 1966 survey revealed that twenty-seven states had some kind of "cooperating council of organization for the purpose of advancing educational legislative aims."[60] In addition, informal cooperative efforts were organized in many states.

The cohesiveness of educational coalitions has been shattered in most states. This is due primarily to teacher militancy, which resulted in splits between teachers associations and other participating groups. Other factors viewed as threatening to coalition structures include the demise of rurally dominated legislatures, to which many coalitions have geared their strategies, and demands from urban officials that their systems receive special state subsidies to cope with pressing city school problems.

The demise of the coalitions made clear the fact that unity as well as a large membership is important for citizen groups that wish to influence educational policy at any level. Such groups are much more likely to gain favorable responses from elected officials if other groups with similar interests are not plying them with counteracting information and opinions.

Information is an important control resource for citizen groups. Policymakers, particularly at state and national levels, are generally interested in knowing how proposed legislation will affect constituents in their home districts. Groups that have the capacity to marshal such information and make it available to policymakers can be influential.

Initiative is also important for such groups. Groups that initiate action without impetus from school people and sometimes even in opposition to them can often affect school policies. For example, publications of the Council for Basic Education have probably influenced leaders in some states and communities to deemphasize nonacademic aspects of the curriculum. Even in cases where educators themselves are not supportive of the council position, they have responded to influential citizens who advocate basic education. Likewise, local groups sometimes form without school encouragement and become influential in school affairs. Thus, pressure for change often comes from outside of school systems.

In contrast to recent years when the efforts of education advocates focused primarily on avoiding budget cutbacks at local, state, and national levels, it appears that the present time may be a time of increased investment in public education, particularly at the state level. The report of the National Commission on Excellence in Education and similar documents have directed public attention to the significance of education at a time of economic change. The time is reminiscent of the post-Sputnik era as the nation once again rediscovers the relationship between education and economic development. Indeed, a few national business leaders recently have been among the most outspoken advocates of increased support for schools.

Despite the growing consensus that education is important and schools should be improved, there are strong voices urging that solution of this problem "does not require throwing money at it." Moreover, public school advocates must still overcome the indifference, if not hostility, of the growing numbers of citizens who no longer have children of school age or who regard public support of nonpublic schools as the *sine qua non* of any change in the level of expenditure for public schools. Thus, new money will not come easily to the schools and a condition of its arrival may be fundamental change in how schools are organized. For example, there appears to be substantial support among citizens and politicians to compensate teachers on the basis of performance as well as experience or education. Likewise, there is widespread agreement about the desirability of higher standards for student performance.

This changing public view of education poses two kinds of challenges to the kinds of groups discussed in this chapter. The first is to achieve sufficient unity among themselves and/or with others who share common interests to achieve changes through the legislative process. The second has to do with adjusting to what appears to be a change in public values. For the past twenty years, equity has been a fundamental concern in educational policy. Many of the groups discussed here have been strong advocates of equity. Progress toward this value has been apparent and substantial. In the current scheme of things, excellence is now of higher priority with the public than equity. Excellence and equity are not necessarily contradictory. An important challenge to advocacy groups at all levels will be to preserve the gains made in the name of equity as they and others seek progress in the name of excellence.

At state and local levels in particular, professionals and lay citizens need to reexamine their mutual obligations and techniques for working together. Hostility has developed among citizen, teacher, and administrator groups in some areas over who will control the schools. The spread of such hostility would be unfortunate. Neither lay citizens nor professionals can make their full contribution to education unless they are sensitive to and trusting of each others' desires and capabilities. An important step in this direction is for professionals to acknowledge both the boundaries of their own expertise and their ultimate accountability to their public as well as to their profession. By the same token, citizens must find the most appropriate and responsible means to participate in the policymaking process. Such cooperative approaches will be even more vital to schools in the future as their traditional constituency of young people shrinks numerically in many sectors of the country.

NOTES

[1] *A Teacher's Guide to the PTA* (Chicago: National Congress of Parents and Teachers, 1957), 15–27.

[2] *PTA Directions, 1978–79* (Chicago: National PTA, 1978), 1.

[3] *The National PTA Legislative Program 1988–89* (Chicago: National PTA, n.d.).

[4] PTA News Release, n.d.

[5] *Why PTA—Instead of PTO?* (Chicago: National PTA, n.d.).

[6]*What's Happening in Washington* 17 (June and July 1988): 2.

[7]See John T. Thompson, *Policymaking in American Education* (Englewood Cliffs, NJ: Prentice-Hall, 1976), 109.

[8]M. Kent Jennings, "Patterns of School Board Responsiveness," in *Understanding School Boards,* ed. Peter J. Cistone (Lexington, MA: Lexington, 1975), 244.

[9]*The School Board and the PTA, Partners in Education* (Chicago: National PTA, n.d.).

[10]National PTA, *Looking in on Your School: A Workbook for Improving Public Education* (Chicago: National PTA, 1982), 5.

[11]See Robert A. Dahl, *Who Governs* (New Haven, CT: Yale University Press, 1961), 155–59, and Harmon Ziegler and M. Kent Jennings, *Governing American Schools* (North Scituate, MA: Duxbury, 1974), 31–32.

[12]*The School Board and the PTA, Partners in Education.*

[13]Ziegler and Jennings, *Governing American Schools.*

[14]Ibid., 99.

[15]See, for example, *A Leaders Guide to Membership* (Chicago: National PTA, 1987).

[16]Edward M. Tuttle, *School Board Leadership in America,* rev. ed. (Danville, IL: Interstate 1963), 169. For a history of the NSBA, see Thomas A. Shannon, *The Story of the National School Boards Association* (Alexandria, VA: The Association, 1987).

[17]Ibid., 211–12.

[18]Ibid., 214.

[19]Constitution and By-Laws of the National School Board Association, Article III, Section 3, as adopted 14 April 1970 and amended 18 April 1972 and 10 April 1973.

[20]Beliefs and Policies of the National School Boards Association as adopted by the Delegate Assembly, 7–10 April 1973, Anaheim, CA.

[21]Shannon, *The Story of the NSBA,* 75–80.

[22]For example, see Susan Fuhrman and Alan Rosenthal, *Shaping Education Policy in the States* (Washington, DC: The Institute for Educational Leadership, 1981).

[23]David B. Dreiman, *How to Get Better Schools: A Tested Program* (New York: Harper & Row, 1956), 68.

[24]For much of this historical detail we are indebted to Dreiman, *How to Get Better Schools,* 63–82.

[25]Condensations of the Working Guides are found in Dreiman, *How to Get Better Schools.*

[26]Roderick F. McPhee, "The Administrator and Lay-Advisory Committees," *Administrator's Notebook* 5 (May 1957).

[27]For specific accounts of local activity see Dreiman, *How to Get Better Schools,* 6–59.

[28]National School Public Relations Association, *Education U.S.A.,* 5 April 1962.

[29]Gerald E. Sroufe, Executive Director of the Committee, to Nystrand, 13 August 1969.

[30]Anne Henderson, *Public Involvement in Education: Is Education on the Right Track?* (Columbia, MD: National Committee for Citizens in Education, 1982, Mimeographed), 15.

[31]National Committee for Citizens in Education, *Annual Report to the Public* (Columbia, MD: NCCE, 1987), 6.

[32]Excerpts from the annual report of the executive director, *Council for Basic Education Bulletin* 18 (November 1973): 3.

[33]*About CBE* (Washington, DC: The Council, n.d.)

[34]"Reflections after Fifteen Years," *Council for Basic Education Bulletin* 15 (June 1971): 2.

[35]*Annual Report of the Council for Basic Education, 1976,* 6.

[36]"Are the Schools Worth Saving?" *Council for Basic Education Bulletin* 13 (January 1969): 5.

[37]"Council for Basic Education," descriptive leaflet (Washington, DC, n.d.), 2–3.

[38]See James Howard, *Writing to Learn* (Washington, DC: Council for Basic Education, 1983).

[39]See Mortimer Jerome Adler, *The Paideia Proposal* (New York: Macmillan, 1982).

[40]See, for example, Alec M. Gallup and David L. Clark, "Nineteenth Annual Gallup Poll on Public Attitudes Toward Education," *Phi Delta Kappan* 69 (September 1987): 17–30.

[41]M. Kent Jennings and Harmon Ziegler, "Interest Representation in School Governance" in *People and Politics in Urban Society,* ed. Harlan Hahn (Beverly Hills, CA: Sage, 1972), 201–30.

[42]A thoughtful treatment of the relationship of these factors is found in Leonard J. Fein, "Community Schools and Social Theory: The Limits of Universalism" in *Community Control of Schools,* ed. Henry M. Levin (Washington, DC: Brookings Institute, 1970), 76–99.

[43]See, for example, the article in a banking trade journal by the chairman of Xerox, David T. Kearns, "U.S. Education Flunks: New Standards Must Be Set," *Financier* (March 1988): 39–44.

[44]Probably the best known community organizer was Saul Alinsky; see Saul D. Alinsky, *Reveille for Radicals* (Chicago: University of Chicago Press, 1946). For a description of Alinsky's tactics and the development of one community organization, see the discussion of the Woodlawn Organization in Charles E. Silberman, *Crisis in Black and White* (New York: Vintage, 1964), 308–58.

[45]For discussion of these projects see Peter Marris and Martin Rein, *Dilemmas of Social Reform* (New York: Atherton, 1967).

[46]Daniel P. Moynihan, *Maximum Feasible Misunderstanding* (New York: Free Press, 1969), 42.

[47]Economic Opportunity Act of 1964, 78 Stat, 508, Title II. Sec 202 (a).

[48]David K. Cohen, "The Price of Community Control," *Commentary* (July 1969): 23–32. See also Diane Ravitch, *The Troubled Crusade* (New York: Basic, 1983).

[49]For a discussion of school-based management, see Lawrence C. Pierce, *School Site Management,* An Occasional Paper (Cambridge, MA: Aspen Institute for Humanistic Studies, 1977). Developments in Florida are discussed in Luvern L. Cunningham et al., *Improving Education in Florida* (Tallahassee, FL: Select Joint Committee of the Florida Legislature, 1978).

[50]Michael W. Kirst, "Who Should Control Our Schools?" *NEA Today* (January 1988): 74–79.

[51]For a six-state survey that compared parental and superintendents' attitudes on such issues, see Nancy Feyl Chavkin and David L. Williams, "Enhancing Parent Involvement," *Education and Urban Society* 19 (February 1987): 164–184.

[52]Edmund M. Burke, "Citizen Participation Strategies" *Journal of American Institute of Planners* 34 (September 1968): 287–94. Burke discusses five strategies of citizen participation that he calls "educational-therapy, behavioral change, staff supplement, cooptation and community power." Also see Don Davies, ed., *Communities and Their Schools* (New York: McGraw-Hill, 1981).

[53]Mario D. Fantini, *Alternatives for Urban School Reform* (New York: Ford Foundation, 1968), 14.

[54]Burke, "Citizen Participation Strategies."

[55]Herbert J. Walberg, "Families as Partners in Educational Productivity," *Phi Delta Kappan* 65 (February 1984): 397–400.

[56]Burke, "Citizen Participation Strategies."

[57]Philip Selznick, "Foundations of the Theory of Organization," *American Sociological Review* 13 (February 1948): 31. As cited in Burke, "Citizen Participation Strategies."

[58]ESEA Title I Program Guide 46, 2 July 1968.

[59]Stephen K. Bailey et al., *Schoolmen and Politics: A Study of State Aid to Education in the Northeast* (Syracuse, NY: Syracuse University Press, 1962) and Nicholas A. Masters, Robert H. Salisbury, and Thomas H. Eliot, *State Politics and the Public Schools* (New York: Knopf, 1964).

[60]National Council of State Education Associations Information Service Report, *Promotion of State Legislation by Cooperating Organizations* 2 (November 1966).

14
Other Interest Groups

In Chapter 13 we looked at organizations that have education as a primary concern. We'll now look at a sampling of groups which have as their primary interest something other than education but which do influence educational policy. Indeed, some of these groups seem perfectly willing to submerge the schools in deep social conflict if that is necessary to further their own goals. Such activities illustrate the fact that the school as a public institution has increasingly become the focal point for the resolution of social or economic problems.

Support and opposition to the schools as demonstrated by these groups take a variety of forms. Some efforts are aimed at textbooks, some at curriculum, some at expenditures, some at educators, and some at the schools as a public institution. Some of the criticism is rational and well deserved, but some of it is not justifiable and is focused on the schools because of their accessibility and resultant vulnerability. In either case, these groups do influence educational decisions and policy in a variety of ways.

Our analysis is not concerned with attempting to refute or answer the charges of groups that criticize the schools. Indeed, informed criticism of education should be encouraged; it can help educators to make those changes that are necessary for improving the schools. Some of the criticism in the past decade or so, however, has been neither informed nor helpful. Rather, at times it has been destructive—destructive to people, to ideas, and to the concept of public education.

In more recent years interest groups representing the nation's influential business community have become increasingly concerned with schools. Groups such as the Committee for Economic Development, whose recent reports on education were discussed in Chapter 2, the U.S. Chamber of Commerce, the National Alliance of Business, and other business organizations at every governmental level have shown growing interest in schools because of their growing cognizance of how vital education is in providing the quality work force essential to maintaining the nation's competitive position in a changing international economy.

GROUPS CONCERNED WITH IDEOLOGY

Education is of increasing interest to the nation's major political parties. Both Republicans and Democrats have shown more interest as pressures on schools have mounted and educational institutions have been drawn into complex social, political, and economic controversies. In addition, a number of interest groups have expressed continuing concern with how schools treat a range of ideological issues. In this section we will discuss briefly a few of the groups that have expressed concerns about American education.

Curriculum issues have deep roots in our history. Nelson and Roberts have discussed the furor caused by textbooks since the Civil War.[1] So bitter were the feelings over texts dealing with that war that in 1897 publishers approached the problem by publishing regional versions, one textbook for distribution in the North and another for the South.

Following World War I a similar problem arose, sparked in large measure by Hearst newspaper attacks on histories the newspaper considered too friendly to our wartime ally, Great Britain. Such attacks led the members of the American Historical Association in 1923 to adopt a resolution stating that "the clearly implied charges that many of our leading scholars are engaged in treasonable propaganda . . . is inherently and obviously absurd." Although it is rare to hear a scholar charged with treason today, school textbooks continue to be very controversial.

The textbook controversies have involved a variety of organizations and individuals. Among the well-known national organizations that have played an active role are the Daughters of the American Revolution and the American Legion, organizations whose patriotic activities have been based on a vigorous defense of the American way of life as they interpret it. Among the more active but perhaps less well-known groups involved in attacks on education and textbooks in recent years have been America's Future, the Minutemen, the Minutewomen, the Circuit Riders, Pro America, the Sons of the American Revolution, and various state groups such as the Texans for America and the Parents for Better Education of California. The John Birch Society, of course, attracted nationwide attention a decade or so ago for its attacks on schools.

Book banning has been effective in a variety of ways. Books have been withdrawn from school libraries, not purchased by library officials because they appeared on the suspect list of one of the alarmist groups, or altered by publishers to become as unobjectionable as possible. A California publisher, for example, once deleted from an eighth-grade civics book an entire chapter on the United Nations.[2] Opposition to specific texts has on occasion reached ludicrous heights. In the mid-1950s a member of the Indiana State Textbook Commission suggested banning Robin Hood on the premise that his philosophy of taking from the rich to give to the poor was the pure Communist line. A healthy wave of laughter managed to dissipate this charge, however.

There have been recurrent examples of conflict concerning how the schools teach the origins of man. Vocal groups of citizens and diverse organizations throughout the country have argued, for example, the respective pros and cons in the seemingly perpetual and vigorous dispute between religionists and scientists. Indeed, in recent years the creation movement has become a consequential national force in articulating its demands to local boards of education that equal time be provided for teaching both creationism and evolution. Several states have enacted laws calling for balance between "creation science" and "evolution science" in the public schools. Similar legislation has been proposed in numerous states, and the courts have been involved as well.[3]

More recently, the Hawkins County case in Tennessee vividly illustrated the recurrent ideological clashes over curriculum content. In this case, a group of fundamentalist parents objected to the school system's use of a series of textbooks that they complained violated their beliefs by including discussions of "secular humanism, one-world government, pacifism, situation ethics, feminism and witchcraft."[4] Several other instances can be cited of more recent ideological conflict over the curriculum and textbooks used in schools. A national furor ignited in 1987 when a federal judge in Alabama upheld fundamentalist parents in their charge that more than forty state-approved home economics and history texts represented "secular humanism," which was avowed to be a religion, as were "vegetarianism," "socialism," "environmentalism," and "feminism."[5] Although this Alabama decision was ultimately reversed, it illustrates, as does the Hawkins County example, how deeply ideological and religious cleavages in a democratic society invariably affect the public schools. Teachers, administrators, and school board members, it is safe to predict, will constantly be confronted with the difficult challenge of providing a comprehensive curriculum that deals equitably with the diverse academic expectations, religious beliefs, and traditional values found in such a pluralistic country.[6]

In a Pennsylvania system, *Huckleberry Finn* is no longer required reading because of the objection of black parents who resented alleged racial stereotyping. The rather variegated works of prominent authors such as Studs Terkel, Kurt Vonnegut, Isaac Asimov, Bernard Malamud, Nathaniel Hawthorne, Ernest Hemingway, Aldous Huxley, and George Orwell continue to be assailed by some critics as being inappropriate for school children.

A 1987 analysis by People for the America Way, a Washington-based interest group devoted to maintaining the separation of church and state and constitutional freedoms, reported that censorship was on the increase with 153 attempts at censorship in forty-one states; this represented a 20 percent increase over the preceding year and a 168 percent rise since 1982, when there were only 57 attempts.[7] Among the most-challenged books were John Steinbeck's *Of Mice and Men* because of its profanities, Mark Twain's *The Adventures of Huckleberry Finn* because of fears of offending blacks, and J. D. Salinger's *The Catcher in the Rye* for alleged promiscuity.[8] At least 43 percent of these efforts to censor books were organized by such watchdog groups as Citizens for Excellence in Education, the Rev. Pat Robertson's National Legal Foundation, Phyllis Schlafly's Eagle Forum, Concerned Women for America, and the relatively new National Association of Christian Educators.[9]

This struggle quite predictably will persist throughout such a diverse nation. On one side are alleged "liberal educationists" who resent encroachments of "doctrinaire conservative lay persons." On the other side are conservatives who seek to halt alleged permissive teaching methodologies they believe erode basic academic standards and undermine fundamental American values. Underlying this ideological clash, of course, is the question of academic freedom: the freedom of teachers to use their own independent professional judgment and not to be shackled by political constraints.[10]

Conservative elements commonly feel that the schools are the origin of much liberal bias, and conservative opposition to the schools is concentrated on the programs of the schools, what is or is not being practiced, rather than on expenditures for education.[11] It is often focused narrowly on the failure of the schools to support adequately the free enterprise system.

These controversies are likely to continue as our schools remain enmeshed in the political, religious, ideological, social and economic controversies that divide our pluralistic society on certain complex issues.[12]

RACIAL MINORITIES

In May 1954 the Supreme Court ruled against school segregation in its famous decision against the doctrine of "separate but equal" schools. In the years immediately following that decision blacks and civil rights sympathizers concentrated on breaking down the legal barriers in the South that contributed to segregation. Among their demands were the reorganization of schools without regard to race and the elimination of racial classifications.

In the early 1960s and after the civil rights movement shifted to the North and West, civil rights advocates concentrated on *de facto* segregation. Such segregation results not from formal, legal classifications based on race but from residential distribution that has the effect of creating separate black and white schools. By the late 1960s some of the enthusiasm for fighting *de facto* school segregation had waned. New black groups and leaders were calling instead for "community control" of neighborhood schools.

Black activism in the 1960s was paralleled by a drive for equality on the part of other minority groups. Chicanos in the Southwest, Puerto Ricans in the Northeast, and American Indians all began to assert themselves more vigorously and, like blacks, strove for greater control over the institutions that served them. These once relatively invisible minorities have become visible as they attempt to improve their lives and the educational opportunities available to their children. Let us now see how these several minority groups have tried to achieve their goals and how these efforts will have even a more significant effect on the schools as minorities constitute an ever-growing proportion of the youngsters enrolled.

Black Americans

The drive for equality by blacks has had considerable impact on the development of black organizations. Until the late 1950s nearly all black efforts were channeled through one of two prominent black civic associations, the National Association for the Advancement of Colored People and the Urban League. Both organizations received much of their financial support from whites, and they operated largely through the conventional procedures of litigation and negotiation. While it is true that cases they took to court contributed greatly to the gains made by blacks, it is also true that their patience and conventional tactics became intolerable to the blacks of the postwar generation.

Handlin pointed out some years ago that improvement leads to increased hope for more improvement among the oppressed, and this rising level of expectations makes intolerable conditions previously accepted by the utterly hopeless. "The proximity to equality only increases the hunger for it. The black man is less willing to wait than before, because his goal has never before been so clearly visible."[13]

Events in recent decades have underscored the validity of Handlin's comment. Rising expectations and dissatisfaction with the rate of progress have led to the development of diverse black organizations, each with increasingly narrow claims as to what it can do for its members. A major factor in the changing nature of these organizations has been the organizational rivalry brought about by the rise of many black civic associations. These associations, dominated by young and aggressive leaders, openly competed with the older groups in a variety of areas: finance, membership, strategy, and tactics. Such competition often resulted in claims and counterclaims as to which group could be most effective.

Active national organizations in the 1960s included the Congress of Racial Equality, the Student Nonviolent Coordinating Committee, and the Southern Christian Leadership Conference. The SCLC was founded by the late Rev. Martin Luther King, Jr., the symbolic leader of many aspects of the black revolution. These organizations were originally active in southern cities, but their activities soon became national, and they played a major role in changing the nature of the battle for black equality. Because of their more aggressive image and their strength, the old agencies had to make major changes to keep pace.

The most visible of the new militants were those who advocated "black power," a slogan that summed up the determination of blacks to control their own destiny. This militant, almost separatist attitude, though far less prevalent now, was the dynamic force behind the efforts of blacks to build unity and strength outside of, and often in opposition to, white organizations. To Carmichael and Hamilton, black power was

> a call for black people in this country to unite, to recognize their heritage, to build a sense of community. It is a call for black people to begin to define their own goals, to lead their organizations and to support those organizations. It is a call to reject the racist institutions and values of this society.[14]

This militancy contrasted with the traditional early civil rights movement in several important respects. The guiding theme was liberation or complete freedom from white society rather than acceptance of it. The emphasis was on self-help, solidarity, and independent action: relatively little help was expected from the government.

The remarkably strong showing made by the charismatic Rev. Jesse L. Jackson in 1988 in seeking the Democratic presidential nomination reflected to a surprised nation how the continuing belief in self-help, solidarity, and independent political action had matured within the black community. Leadership in the civil rights movement up to the 1970s came from a handful of national organizations; by the 1980s it had become a much more diffuse social movement in which numerous local groups addressed local concerns. The Jackson presidential candidacy served to coalesce black groups as well as a considerable number of whites on his behalf.

The black movement, like any other mass movement, is not monolithic. Leaders have differences of opinion with respect to tactics and both short- and long-range goals. While very few leaders actually advocate a permanent separation of the races, a number of others continue to see separation as an interim strategy to be employed in building sufficient strength to achieve "viable coalitions between blacks and whites who accept each other as co-equal partners and who identify their goals as politically and economically similar."[15] Demographic trends have lent credence to the separatist point of view as proponents stress the great difficulties in desegregating a society that more and more is segregated residentially. Indeed, the withdrawal or pulling back in recent years of many liberal whites as well as blacks from the integration push of a decade or two ago has undeniably eroded the influence of the once very visible and influential multiracial civil rights coalition of the 1960s and early 1970s. The courts currently are virtually the only major force in our society actively supporting desegregated schools.

As the civil rights thrust lost much of its momentum in the late 1970s and 1980s, the major black groups underwent considerable financial strain and organizational stress. The leadership turned over in both the NAACP and Urban League during a period when the civil rights struggle was shifting from the more targetable legal area to the less focused and definable realms of economic equality and social policy. The landslide election victories of Ronald Reagan in 1980 and 1984 were viewed by the great majority of blacks as well as other minority group members as a manifestation of national retrenchment in the area of civil rights and affirmative action.[16] To many minorities it was tantamount to a repudiation of the Brown decision of 1954.[17]

Despite the impressive academic gains made by many black youngsters in public schools and the doubling of black college enrollment in the 1970s, blacks in the 1980s continued to lag in income, were increasingly pessimistic about the future, and were trying to protect their recent gains in vital realms like education and employment.[18] In addition to their limited educational and employment opportunities, studies continued to show that black children remained seriously disadvantaged in critical areas like health, nutrition, and family economic status, and were often exposed to more crime in their neighborhoods than their white counterparts.[19]

Cutbacks in human service and education programs in the 1980s plus growing apprehensions about the commitment of the Reagan administration and the nation at large to equity and affirmative action issues helped to force new unity among minority organizations. The political and economic assaults on longstanding programs aiding the poor catalyzed the NAACP and others to coalesce more frequently with organized labor and other civil rights advocates to generate stronger political opposition to what was widely conceived to be a national retreat on efforts to equalize opportunities for minorities.

The power of the Jesse Jackson bid for the Democratic presidential nomination surprised whites as well as minority group members and was thought by some to represent a possible national renaissance and major progress in interracial relations.

Other Minority Groups

Other minority groups have joined in the drive for greater equality. Mexican Americans, Puerto Ricans, and American Indians became more active in the 1960s and 1970s and, like blacks, continued in the 1980s to demand more forcefully greater social justice and participation in the political process.

Hispanics are the nation's most rapidly growing population group and their political influence certainly will continue to expand in the decades ahead as they are projected to become the largest racial ethnic group by the end of the century. The Hispanic population, while constituting only 6.4 percent of the total population in 1980, has increased five times as fast as the rest of the population since the 1980 census.[20] Overall, the Hispanic population increased 30 percent from 1980 to early 1987 and now makes up almost 8 percent of the total U.S. population.[21] Population statistics pertaining to Hispanics, of course, are inexact because of the millions of undocumented workers and their families.

The Spanish-speaking population in the country is a diverse and not an easily identifiable ethnic group. Of the nation's estimated 18.8 million Hispanics, 63 percent are Mexican-Americans, 12 percent are Puerto Ricans, 5 percent are Cubans, and approximately 11 percent are of other Spanish groups, primarily from South and Central America.[22] This population has a roster of common grievances such as police brutality, unilingual education, inferior housing, and job discrimination. Recent efforts have been undertaken to establish *unidos,* or unity among the Spanish-speaking groups. Efforts to create a political coalition, however, have been hampered by the substantial socioeconomic differences among these groups. For example, census data indicate that in the Cuban-American population, the typical family earns almost 90 percent of the typical white family income. But among the Mexican-American and Puerto Rican populations the comparable figures were only 70 and 60 percent, respectively.

Many remain unaware of the full implications of the dramatic population growth of Hispanics because the Hispanic population is clustered in a small number of states. For example, two-thirds of American Hispanics are concentrated in only three states: California, Texas, and New York. Indeed, one-fifth of the residents of California, the most populous state, and Texas, the third most populous state, are of Hispanic origin. When the Hispanic population of Colorado, Florida, Illinois, New Jersey, New

Mexico, and Arizona are added to these three states, the great majority of the nation's Spanish-speaking population is included. In other words, approximately 90 percent of Hispanics reside in only nine states.

This great increase in the number of Hispanics has particular significance for schools because for the most part the Spanish-speaking population is much younger. The median age of Hispanics is twenty-two years while the median age for all Americans is thirty. More than 30 percent of the Hispanic population is between the school-going ages of five and seventeen while less than 25 percent of the total population is of school age.[23] In addition, the Hispanic birth rate is 75 percent higher than the remainder of the population, according to the National Center for Health Statistics. These demographic data, as we discussed in Chapter 2, already are influencing the composition of public school enrollments.

As the number of Hispanics (whose poverty rate is nearly three times that of non-Hispanics) continues to grow and their youngsters become an ever-increasing proportion of the school population, the severe educational problems of this population will become more prominent. Although there is tremendous socioeconomic diversity among Hispanics and group generalizations must be qualified, the following data reflect the educational plight of Hispanics:

- Among 3-to-4 year-olds, only about 27% of the Hispanics, 39% of the Whites, and 43% of the Blacks were enrolled in nursery school in 1985.
- Forty percent of all Hispanic students who leave school do so before reaching the 10th grade, and 25% of the Hispanics who enter high school are over-age.
- Forty-five percent of Mexican American and Puerto Rican students who enter high school never finish, compared to 17% of Anglo students.
- Hispanics were 23% of all persons who dropped out of high school in the 1985-86 school year, but only 6% of all those who graduated that year.
- About 10% of Hispanic youths between the ages of 14 and 24 in 1980 reported that they spoke English poorly or not at all.
- Only 22% of 18-24-year-old Mexican immigrants in 1980 had completed high school.
- The rate for Hispanic high school graduates enrolling in college fell from 36% in 1976 to 27% in 1985.[24]

Puerto Ricans, in particular, lag behind other Hispanic groups in education as well as in other social and economic indices of progress. There are approximately 2 million mainland Puerto Ricans, the large majority of whom live in the Northeast and are caught up in a pattern of "devastating circular migration" between their home island and the mainland.[25] Indeed, 49 percent live in New York State, with the vast majority residing in New York City with appallingly high unemployment rates and low incomes. The median family income of Puerto Ricans fell 18 percent in real terms between 1979 and 1984 (from $14,998 to $12,282) compared with 14 percent for blacks and 9 percent for Mexican-Americans. Between 1969 and 1984 the use of public assistance soared 115 percent among Puerto Rican families headed by couples and 291 percent among families headed by single women; comparable figures for the same period were 2.3 percent and 25 percent increases for black families while the number of traditional Mexican-American families on the welfare roles actually declined 12 percent.[26]

Almost 300,000 Puerto Rican youngsters are enrolled in New York City schools; at least one-third of the enrollment of the nation's largest school system is of Hispanic origin. The historical complaints of Puerto Ricans against school systems have a familiar ring with a devastatingly high dropout rate of well over 50 percent in the metropolitan New York City area. Like comparable statistics for other minorities, these figures are disastrous for a recently migrated group striving for a socioeconomic toehold.

In New York City and elsewhere, the educational plight of Puerto Rican and other Hispanic schoolchildren has galvanized their elders into political action. In recent years Hispanic groups have pushed more aggressively in legal and political arenas for the dramatic expansion of bilingual offerings and other program changes that would improve the quality of education offered their youth.

A concrete example of this growing concern and involvement was the formation late in 1983 of the National Commission on Secondary Schooling for Hispanics. Under the aegis of the Hispanic Policy Development Project, a foundation- and corporate-sponsored nonprofit organization that focuses on public policy issues affecting Hispanics, a prestigious eighteen-member group conducted a study of the condition of Hispanic urban secondary school education in light of the recommendations of the various national reports, which many felt ignored the unique problems of Hispanics. This National Commission on Secondary Schooling for Hispanics conducted widely publicized meetings in Los Angeles, San Antonio, Miami, New York City, and Chicago.

The commission's findings confirmed that a shocking number of Hispanic youngsters were dropping out and that among those staying in school the achievement levels were appallingly low. It found, for example, that 76 percent of the Hispanics who took the "High School and Beyond" achievement tests scored in the bottom half of the national test results and that 75 percent of Hispanic students were in non-academic programs, with 40 percent in the general education track and 35 percent in the vocational track.[27] Of note among the other major findings were that more than 40 percent of all Hispanic students drop out of school before entering high school and 41 percent of Hispanic males and 23 percent of Hispanic females leave secondary school for financial reasons.[28]

Among the commission's recommendations were:

☐ Hispanic students must have more sustained personal attention and more daily contact with adults. Their families must be welcome in their schools.
☐ Parents, students, and school officials must work together to define critical student and family needs. The programs they develop must work both through the schools and through the community to reach students and families who need help.
☐ Greater emphasis must be placed on academic content and student achievement.

□ Work and school should be linked as early as junior high school.
□ English must be taught more effectively to Hispanics.
□ Students, the community, and the nation must learn to appreciate the value of the Spanish language.
□ The federal government must maintain ongoing support of and involvement in programs that have significant impact on inner-city youth.[29]

Illustrative of Hispanic groups with growing interest and influence in education are organizations like the League of United Latin American Citizens, the Mexican-American Legal Defense and Education Fund, the National Council of La Raza, the National Puerto Rican Forum, and the Congressional Hispanic Caucus.[30] These Hispanic organizations, buttressed by the marked growth of their constituency, are in the forefront of efforts to improve the economic, political, social, and educational opportunities available to America's burgeoning Hispanic population.[31]

Yet another ignored minority group has spoken up in recent years. The unique difficulties confronting the American Indian have begun to attract greater attention. Growing national interest in minority groups generally in the 1960s as well as substantial increases in Indian attendance both in their own schools and in public schools rather than in Bureau of Indian Affairs institutions have dramatized the need for comprehensive examination of the status of Indian education. The U.S. Office of Education funded the National Study of American Indian Education. Professors Robert J. Havighurst and Estelle Fuchs directed this study, which was concluded in 1971 and reported their understandings and conclusions in *To Live on This Earth: American Indian Education.*[32]

The failures of Indian education, according to Fuchs and Havighurst's analysis two decades ago, are quite similar to those articulated today by other minority groups:

> With minor exceptions the history of Indian education had been primarily the transmission of white American education, little altered, to the Indian child as a one-way process. The institution of the school is one that was imposed by and controlled by the non-Indian society, its pedagogy and curriculum little changed for the Indian children, its goals primarily aimed at removing the child from his aboriginal culture and assimilating him into the dominant white culture. Whether coercive or persuasive, this assimilationist goal of schooling has been minimally effective with Indian children, as indicated by their record of absenteeism, retardation, and high dropout rates.[33]

Like other minority groups, American Indians in recent years have become much more forceful in stating their belief in the central significance of education:

> We conceive education not only in terms of classroom teaching, but a process which begins at birth and continues through a life span. Of all the studies, surveys, and research made of Indians, the inevitable conclusions and recommendations are that education is the key to salvation of whatever ills may be, wherever Indians reside.[34]

In the last two decades or so the American Indian population has tripled, from a half million to a million and a half. Indians are participating in the dominant non-

Indian society more extensively than ever before. The number of young Indians attending colleges and graduate schools grew dramatically for a period, as did pride in their identity and heritage.[35] American Indians, like other minority groups, will be exerting continuous pressure to ensure that their children receive equal educational opportunities in the years ahead.[36]

THE ISSUE: EQUAL EDUCATIONAL OPPORTUNITY

For many years American educators have considered the problems involved in providing equal educational opportunity to all children. Before the 1954 Supreme Court decision, however, the problems involved in achieving equality were largely problems of equal financial support. Witness, for example, the persistent concern of the proponents of federal aid to education with achieving equal opportunities. Proponents of federal aid pointed to disparities in financing across the nation and used *equal opportunity* to mean *equal expenditures*. In recent years, however, the phrase has been identified with the drive for equal treatment of minority groups.

A major factor that has contributed to increased militancy is the increase in population distribution of nonwhites in America. There are about 50 million nonwhites, which represents more than 20 percent of the American population. Blacks still represent more than half of this nonwhite group. The migration of this segment of the population has been astonishing. In 1900 nearly 90 percent of the nonwhite population was concentrated in the South, largely on farms. A more recent pattern, of course, has been the immigration and growth of the Hispanic population, 90 percent of whom live in urban areas.

These population patterns began to shift somewhat in the late 1960s, and by the 1980s the movement from rural and small-town areas into metropolitan areas had slowed down perceptibly. Whites, however, continued to move out of the cities in substantial numbers. The 1980 census indicated, for example, that most of the central cities were continuing to lose their white residents as well as decreasing in overall population. Alan Campbell noted the demographic watershed reached in the mid-1960s when the suburban population became larger than that of the central cities, saying that "this change does not bode well for the political strength of cities in either state legislatures or Congress."[37]

Despite some improvement in the condition of central cities because of the decline in population density in poor areas and the slow gentrification of a few neighborhoods,[38] the educational problems in the major core cities remain acute. Although blacks and other minority groups are moving into the suburbs in growing numbers, the core cities increasingly are populated by poor nonwhites. It is largely middle-income minority people who are following their white counterparts into the suburbs, leaving poorer people behind.[39] These demographic patterns have concentrated disadvantaged minority groups in urban centers and have thus increased their organizational strength and political potential. Their awareness of the problems created by unequal educational opportunities has also increased.

Equality of educational opportunity is a very complex, subtle, and elusive goal. It is achieved "when each child of school age residing within a school district has equal access to the educative resources of the district essential to his needs."[40] When the educational problem is compounded by social problems based on housing patterns, employment opportunities, population mobility, and community feelings, to name just a few, the problem of determining educational policies becomes even more difficult.

The root cause of *de facto* segregated schools is the extensive racial segregation in housing. Blacks and other minority groups have held that educational segregation, whether deliberate or not, has harmful effects on the children involved, and therefore should be corrected immediately. In northern communities, minorities accuse educators of attempting to shirk their responsibilities by taking the attitude that no one within the school system helped to create the situation and that the responsibility for change should not fall on the school system, or at least not on the school system alone.

One point of attack has been the neighborhood school concept, which has been interpreted by some civil rights leaders as a way to maintain segregated schools that must be eliminated. Historically, children have been assigned to elementary schools in urban areas on a geographic basis, with a child being assigned to the school nearest, or near, his or her residence. Transfers are frequently permitted but not encouraged. At the secondary level more options are usually possible because of the specialized schools available; plus, because high schools have more students, they draw from a broader geographic area. The neighborhood school, however, will inevitably reflect the racial, social, economic, and cultural features of the area it serves. Since most urban minorities live in racially segregated areas, the schools their children attend are largely or entirely segregated.

Such schools have traditionally had a unique set of educational problems. Among these problems are overcrowding, fantastic student mobility (in some classrooms more than 100 percent for the year, meaning that the teacher has none of the students at the end of the year who were enrolled at the beginning of the year or that the number of transfers in and out was greater than the number of students enrolled at the beginning of the year), a high dropout rate, poor physical facilities, and the crucial problem of getting competent teachers to work in these schools. Despite efforts to improve programs in most city schools since the early 1960s, there is little evidence that their effectiveness has increased significantly although there have been encouraging improvements in test results in a number of cities.

Neighborhood schools, however, even though they tend to be segregated, are not always opposed by minorities. The reaction of Los Angeles Chicanos to the city's busing program some years ago is an example. Chicanos were apprehensive lest the integration plan dilute the city's bilingual education efforts and cripple efforts to provide additional teaching jobs for Mexican-Americans. Raul P. Arreola, administrative secretary of the Mexican-American Education Commission, which advised the Los Angeles schools on matters pertaining to Chicanos, was quoted as stating that "very few Mexican-American parents are interested in busing their children into white schools. We feel that we have much to lose if our children are bused out of the neighborhood."[41]

THE APPROACH: DUE PROCESS AND DIRECT ACTION

Minority groups and leaders have disagreed on the next steps for achieving equal educational opportunity. Some have emphasized school desegregation while others have stressed the need to increase accountability to the community. Advocates of equal educational opportunity, however, have generally agreed on a number of ancillary goals. These include more minority group faculty members, greater attention to minority group culture and contributions in the curriculum, increased sensitivity to minority group student needs and interests by teachers and administrators, smaller classes, and more remedial and special instructional services. In recent years, for example, minority groups, particularly Spanish-speaking ones, have pushed vigorously and with some success to expand federal and state bilingual programs (Title VII of the Elementary and Secondary Education Act of 1965).[42]

The bilingual issue provides an excellent example of an issue that is ostensibly educational in nature but has deep symbolic and political meaning that transcends school programs per se. There has been recurring debate, litigation, and direct action on this issue, which has great significance to the nation's rapidly growing Hispanic population anxious to hold on to its linguistic roots. California and numerous other states have been engaged in persistent political struggles on the language issue as an "English Only" backlash has occurred in many parts of the country.[43] The Hispanic groups also were engaged in a running debate with former Secretary of Education William Bennett, fearing that the department's proposals for more flexibility in bilingual education would dilute the attention paid to Spanish.[44]

Traditionally those seeking equal educational opportunities for minorities have held the view that progress can be achieved best by providing information to the public, negotiating directly with school officials, and invoking legal sanctions when necessary and possible. These are strategies of due process. The NAACP, in particular, has maintained steady pressure on the courts for action against segregation. They have opposed *de jure* and *de facto* segregation with equal vigor, holding that regardless of intent there is a constitutional obligation for school officials to take whatever actions may be required and are educationally sound to achieve maximum desegregation.

Other due process approaches include support of state and federal legislation that provides (1) financial assistance to schools attended by poor and minority group children, (2) incentives to desegregate schools or penalties for failing to do so, and (3) bases for reorganizing school districts to achieve greater community control. Legislation of all three types has been passed by various states, and Congress has enacted measures of the first two types (The Elementary and Secondary Education Act of 1965 and the Civil Rights Act of 1964, respectively). The efforts of black groups have influenced the passage of such measures.

It is difficult to gauge how effective minority groups have been in shaping educational policies. Surely progress has been made toward some of their goals, as we will see, but there have been no bold or significant breakthroughs, and urban schools continue to be a pressing national problem. While sympathy for improved educational opportunities for minority group children continues, the tactics used by some groups have alienated some of those who previously gave support. Indeed, many believe that the backlash generated by the militant tactics of black power some years ago seriously eroded white liberal support and thus weakened the political influence of the once-powerful interracial civil rights coalition.

There can be no doubt that minority striving has had impact on American education in recent years. Educators have become aware that schools need to play a major role in bringing poor and minority group children into the mainstream of American life. Considerable legislation has been enacted to this end. In addition to such federal programs as Head Start and the Elementary and Secondary Education Act, numerous states have passed compensatory education legislation.

Minority efforts also have had considerable impact on local school districts. Many school systems have established integration of staff members and students as a policy goal. In general, staff integration has been achieved more easily than student integration. Even so, strong teacher organizations and traditions of internal transfer and promotion within the system through examinations have impeded staff integration in some large cities. The desegregation of students has also been most problematic in our largest cities. However, noteworthy desegregation plans have been implemented in many small and medium-size cities. Desegregation measures have included boundary changes, open enrollment plans, educational parks, new organizational arrangements (e.g., changing from junior high schools to middle schools so students from a broader attendance area will attend school together at an earlier age), pairing two or more schools of differing racial composition and reassigning students on an integrated basis, and "magnet schools" (schools with special programs designed to appeal to students from a broad geographical area).

Other areas in which minority demands have had an impact relate to the school programs. Within the last few years most city school systems have taken steps to offer more realistic learning materials to urban children. Textbooks that emphasize white, middle-class views of society have been supplanted by materials designed to have greater relevance to poorer children of the city. Bilingual instruction and courses in minority history and cultures have been added to many curricula. Many special and remedial programs and services, often funded by federal or special state legislation, are now in operation. Paraprofessionals who serve as valuable links between school people and neighborhood residents as well as help teachers with particular tasks are now found in many inner-city schools.

Finally, minority demands have stimulated the increased accountability of school personnel to parents and other citizens. Parents in the poorer city districts especially ask how well the schools are doing, and they are demanding a response. One form of response has been to grant a measure of community control or establish advisory committees and other mechanisms for citizen participation. Another type of response has been to provide more information about the schools. A pioneering effort in this direction has been the publication of school profiles in many districts. These documents present median aptitude and achievement scores for students in all elementary and junior high schools as well as data describing the student body and staff, including racial composition, turnover, training, and experience.

The cumulative effect of changes resulting from due process and direct action has been the creation of an atmosphere of uncertainty. Confronted with a growing range of demands and expectations for schools, society finds it difficult to agree on a definition of equal educational opportunity in legal or educational terms. The problem is also a political one. The demands of minority groups challenge the status quo in terms of how resources are allocated for educational purposes. Some white, middle-class parents whose children have difficulty reading cannot understand why inner-city schools should have priority in the assignment of remedial reading instructors. Similarly, teachers and administrators who have grown accustomed to making unilateral educational judgments with the security afforded by tenure may resent citizen demands for more accountability and community control. Moreover, it is difficult to tell whether the demands of the future will resemble those of today, and it is hard to predict the tactics that will be used to advance them.

Within the past few years growing numbers of minority group members, largely blacks, have assumed leadership positions in major urban school systems. Minority group members now constitute an increasing percentage of the school superintendents, key central office personnel, and school board members in large, predominantly minority urban school systems. There are great opportunities in this development. The movement of more minority group members into leadership positions in education has many positive by-products. Black superintendents, for example, frequently have credibility in interacting with many minority parents and students and can ease tensions in many situations more effectively than their white counterparts. The image of success the minority leader represents and the sense of group pride he or she inspires are additional positive by-products of this movement. This movement of minority group members into educational leadership positions (with the exception of Spanish-speaking minorities, who remain grossly underrepresented at the top levels) is long overdue. However, educational leaders in the cities continue to face overwhelming problems, and the recent decline in overt conflict and tension cannot be viewed with equanimity by the majority population nestled in comfortable suburbs. The threat of educational apartheid is growing in many sections of the country and the consequences of such a split in a racially pluralistic nation would be drastic.

THE FEMINIST MOVEMENT AND WOMEN'S ORGANIZATIONS

Women's organizations constitute another category of groups that sometimes become involved in school matters. In recent years the feminist movement has brought a growing awareness of the role and influence of women in the organization and control of American schools. Indeed, the feminist movement, especially as it has been bolstered by Title IX of the Education Amendments of 1972 (which prohibited sex discrimination in any education program or activity), has certainly affected the entire educational enterprise.

The feminist movement began to burgeon in the early 1970s as the issue of sexism, or the inferior status of women, surfaced with increasing frequency both in education and in society at large. A rapidly expanding literature of women's rights began to develop, and education quite logically became a focal point of criticism for advocates of equal opportunities for females. For example, Phi Delta Kappa, historically an exclusive male honorary educational fraternity, was pressured late in 1973 to change its constitution and admit women members. Phi Delta Kappa's well-known journal, *Phi Delta Kappan,* devoted an entire issue to the feminist movement's wide-ranging implications for education.[45]

Almost two decades ago Howe cited some of the far-reaching and still relevant aims of those striving to give women improved status in the male-dominated social order:

> Recently something new has occurred, something new not only for women's education but also for the education of minorities, female or male. The hegemony of white, male middle-class control over the education of diverse racial and ethnic groups of women and men continues to be challenged. The voices of women may be the last to be heard, but they are the most numerous "minority" in history. Like the blacks, Chicanos, and other ethnic groups before them, women are saying we must build a curriculum that 1) compensates for prior deprivation; 2) allows us to raise the consciousness of many women; 3) encourages the production of useful research; 4) aims to restore the lost culture and history of women; and 5) actively works towards social change.[46]

Howe also stressed the central importance of education in the efforts of the women's rights movement to equalize opportunity for females:

> What do we need? A parallel movement of elementary and high school teachers to change the sexism of texts and classrooms. Such a movement should grow out of the practice of teachers as they begin to analyze their own behavior, the attitudes they and their students bring to school, and the curriculum materials they have used unthinkingly.
>
> We need nonsexist texts on all levels. We need to revise all social science and literature and language curricula, and much that passes for health, science, physical education, biology, or sex education. We need to become alert to the sexist and non-sexist behavior of teachers in the classroom. We need to develop special strategies to reverse the procedures that turn some boys into nonreaders and most girls into non-mathematicians and nonscientists. We need special efforts to encourage girls also to enter vocational schools long denied them or to learn sports they have only been allowed to observe.[47]

Many women in recent decades have changed their political attitudes and behavior substantially. Growing numbers of women recognized that they were " 'locked out' of the political process, that their brains and talents were not only unused but unwanted. And they began to realize that any society that ignores the ability of more than half its adult population cannot be functioning intelligently. Simultaneously, women's organizations realized that if they wanted political clout (and they do), they would have to go after it."[48]

The feminist movement, of course, has moved with persistent vigor to increase the political potency of women. Although the vigorous national effort by more than fifty women's organizations to secure passage of the Equal Rights Amendment has not succeeded, women have made considerable progress in increasing their political power. the National Women's Political Caucus has worked to increase the number of female delegates at recent national conventions and in 1980 the Republican party for the first time wrote a women's plank into its platform. The number of female delegates at national conventions has increased substantially, and the nomination of Geraldine Ferraro as the Democratic vice presidential candidate in 1984 is dramatic evidence of the growing political influence of women. By 1988, 18,000 women nationally held elected office. This included 15.5 percent of all seats in state legislatures (it was only 4.5 percent in 1971), 3 governors, 23 (out of 435) seats in the U.S. House of Representatives, 2 (out of 100) senators, one Supreme Court Justice, and one cabinet member. This represents a modicum of progress for women but, in a society in which 53 percent of the population is female, also reflects the difficulties still confronting women and how far they still have to go in seeking fuller participation in the American political process.[49]

Feminists have made educational institutions major targets of reform. Lyon and Saario some years ago documented the gross underrepresentation of women in educational leadership positions; in public education, for example, while 67 percent of the teachers were women only 15 percent of the principals and 0.6 percent of the superintendents were female.[50] This problem still persists and confirms the history of sexual discrimination in education that is paralleled in other major spheres of American life.[51] Educational institutions of all kinds were compelled to comply with Title IX of the Education Amendments of 1972, which states that "no person in the United States shall, on the basis of sex, be excluded from participation in, denied benefits of, or be subjected to discrimination under any education program or activity receiving federal financial assistance."

Education policymakers at local, state, and federal levels have become far more cognizant of women's rights and concerns than they were in the past.[52] Specific examples of the greater political leverage of women's groups show that the feminist movement is maturing into a force capable of shaping public policy. For instance, the changes made in public school athletics and physical education programs have been dramatic. When the Title IX regulations went into effect in July 1975, secondary and postsecondary institutions were given a three-year transition period to comply fully. This transition period ended on July 21, 1978, but even with minimum enforcement very significant changes occurred. In 1971, for example, only 7 percent of high school athletes were girls; by 1976, 29 percent were female.[53] Girls' teams in a variety of sports are on the rise as school systems are compelled to provide the necessary facilities and equipment after years of neglect. On national television and in communities throughout the country, women's sports are rapidly capturing enthusiastic public support. In the future, school systems will continue to be under public and legal pressure to provide equal athletic opportunities to women.

There can be no doubt that the multifaceted feminist movement has made a major contribution to expanding the roles and diversifying the aspirations of American women. A national survey of female college freshmen sponsored by the American Council on Education and the University of California at Los Angeles indicated that one in four female college freshmen in the fall of 1980 planned careers in traditionally male fields such as law and engineering. This percentage represented more than a 400 percent increase since 1966.[54] Indeed, women have made notable increases in entering professional fields. A report by the Potomac Institute on the results of affirmative action programs indicated that the biggest increases in women's shares of the private job market in the 1970s were in the top three white-collar categories: officials and managers, up from 10.2 percent to 18.5 percent; professionals, from 24.6 percent to 37.7 percent, and technicians, 26.4 percent to 40.2 percent.[55] Indeed, early in 1986 a watershed was reached when the U.S. Labor Department reported that women for the first time held the majority of professional jobs (defined as knowledge-based occupations) in the country. Although men continued their traditional dominance in fields like engineering, medicine, and law, females constituted the majority in fields like psychology, statistics, and editing and reporting.[56] Even in the traditional male bastions of medicine and law the professional barriers were falling. In 1986, for example, 17.2 percent of the nation's doctors and 18.1 percent of its lawyers were females with the increase projected to continue, as 32 percent of the students enrolled in the country's medical and law schools were women.[57]

A number of nationally significant projects on women in education have kept Title IX and affirmative action issues very much in the limelight. The Equal Rights for Women in Education Project, for example, was initiated by the Education Commission of the States, with support from the Ford Foundation, to help states ensure equal rights for women in education. Materials designed to promote sexual equity in schools were developed for state legislators, state education departments, and state boards of education. The Legal Defense and Education Fund of the National Organization for Women, with the assistance of the Ford Foundation, operated a Project on Equal Education Rights, which focused primarily on the enforcement of Title IX in public schools. PEER monitored and publicized efforts aimed at ensuring compliance with federal laws barring sex discrimination in education. These and other national, state, and local activities have kept the issue of equal rights for women in the forefront of public discourse, and school systems are under constant scrutiny in this regard.[58] The dramatic growth of women's studies programs also has raised public consciousness of sexism in the schools and in society. The number of scholarly and popular publications on women's issues soared. Interdisciplinary women's studies groups have been organized regionally and in local communities as well as on college campuses. By 1969 there were 100 women's studies courses on forty-eight campuses; by June 1978 there were 276 such programs spread across all but nine of the fifty states.[59]

Despite these impressive gains, the advent of the Reagan administration in 1981 represented serious regression to many in the women's movement. The president's opposition to the Equal Rights Amendment, lack of enthusiasm for affirmative action, endorsement of bans on abortion, and support of budget reductions in programs of particular importance to women such as education and support for the poor and elderly precipitated considerable resentment and opposition to Reagan among women's groups. Policy changes such as cuts in Title IX, women-oriented programs in fields such as nursing, the deletion of a women-in-science program, and retrenchment in or the elimination of other federally supported activities heralded a serious threat to the women's movement.

These reverses and the perceived threat of losing recent gains compelled the women's movement in the 1980s to reassess its goals and strategies. With many basic issues such as access to government jobs, professional schools, and political candidacy and getting equal treatment when applying for credit largely resolved, a set of subtler and in some ways more difficult issues confronted the movement.[60] These challenges galvanized the coalescence of the movement and in March 1981, twenty-four women's groups ranging from the League of Women Voters, the Federation of Business and Professional Women's Clubs, the Young Women's Christian Association, and the Planned Parenthood Federation, to NOW and the Women's Equity Action League issued a joint statement condemning federal budget cuts as inimical to their interests. Women's groups joined other organizations in opposing the Reagan administration's dismantling of the federal government's commitments not only to women but also its commitments to other programs pertaining to the undernourished, the handicapped, the environment, mental health, the aged, and minorities.[61]

These developments catalyzed the women's movement in the 1980s to focus energies on increasing the involvement of its constituencies in the political process. Particular efforts were made to elect pro-feminists to office in both the Congress and state legislatures. As discussed earlier, these strategies seem to be reaping tangible dividends as reflected in the increase in numbers of women elected to public offices in recent years.

The implications of the feminist movement remain of great importance both for American education and the society at large, and we can only briefly address these complex issues here. We will focus briefly at this point on its significant impact on other women's groups that traditionally have been involved with public schools.

Two well-established, multi-issue women's organizations, the League of Women Voters and the American Association of University Women, have long been active on education issues. These organizations, of course, are very much part of the women's movement. Both support ERA and have strong women's rights positions. While their more outspoken allies in the movement may have made more headlines lately, the LWV and AAUW for years have exercised great influence throughout the nation. Both organizations have articulate, influential, and highly educated members and are based strategically in communities throughout the nation. Both organizations have shown a keen interest in educational issues through the years.

A nonpartisan organization of men and women for political action (the 1974 National Convention of the LWV voted to admit men to full membership although the name remains the same), today's League of Women Voters bears little resemblance to its predecessor, the flamboyant National American Woman Suffrage Association, whose members perched on flagpoles and marched through saloons to win for women the right to vote in 1920. But despite the league's more dignified approach and relatively small size (200,000 members and supporters), many politicians think its campaigns on state and local issues constitute an important force in American politics.

Political observers attribute the LWV's influence partly to its following among women, including nonmembers who are playing an increasingly important role in public affairs. They also credit its ability to involve members in detailed studies of complex issues to the point where the group sometimes has more facts at its command than professional politicians. Many politicians view with wonder and a degree of frustration the league's ability to assume a mantle of nonpartisanship (chapters cannot side with parties or candidates) while becoming deeply involved in highly controversial issues.

The LWV has some 1,300 state and local chapters. League stands on issues at all levels are reached through a process the league refers to as "consensus." Local and state chapters attempt to generate such consensus after sustained study and group discussion involving a substantial number of members, representative of the membership as a whole. Consensus does not necessarily imply either a simple majority or unanimity. The league concentrates on only a few issues at a time and after a study of available facts and positions on a given issue, members discuss the issue at small and large meetings. When consensus is reached, the LWV works to implement the position through an intensive action program that includes testifying at public hearings, use of public forums, panel discussions, mass media, league publications, and letters to public officials.

In the mid-1980s, for example, the league studied U.S. fiscal policy, focusing on issues such as the funding of entitlement programs, deficit financing, and finding appropriate revenue sources; like other LWV studies it was designed to position the organization to participate in a major national policy debate.[62] On education issues the league has customarily focused on supporting racial integration "as a necessary condition for equal access to education," support for school finance reform at the state level, and support for federal education programs designed to assist the special needs of the poor and minorities.

The League of Women Voters is active in education at the federal, state, and local levels. Since action by the league is nearly always taken in concert with other groups, it is difficult to isolate actions at these levels that can be directly attributed to the efforts of the league. Officials of the organization are among the first to admit this, although in California and some other states the league has become a very active and visible participant in debates on major finance and governance issues.

At the state level most leagues conduct intensive studies before positions are reached. Such studies often result in publications that receive widespread distribution. The state leagues also lobby actively for bills that support their positions. Communication from the state office to local officers is frequent and informative, providing current information on the status of various pieces of legislation, dates of hearings, and suggestions for writing or telephoning legislators.

Local league projects have included comprehensive studies of local school systems. League chapters also sponsor meetings at which voters can meet candidates for boards of education as well as other offices and publish nonpartisan information about candidates and issues. In many communities the LWV fact sheet provides more information about candidates in board of education elections than any other source.

The influence of the league on educational policymaking seems to be the greatest at the state level, and the least at the national level. At the local level the activity of the league has been sporadic but occasionally quite effective.

The American Association of University Women, founded in 1882 in Boston as the Association of Collegiate Alumnae, took its present name in 1921 when the ACA merged with the Southern Association of College Women.[63] Its members number approximately 193,000 in some 1,900 local branches. All of the members are women who hold baccalaureate or higher degrees from colleges and universities that have met the institutional standards for membership set by the association.

The structure and operating procedures of the AAUW are quite similar to those of the League of Women Voters, although it is not as action-oriented as the league. At the national level there is a study-action program dealing with several interest areas, one of which is education. For many years the legislative program at the national level, which is voted by the national convention, as with the League of Women Voters, has supported federal aid to education. At the local level, where groups are referred to as branches, the programs are worked out according to the interests of members and needs of the community. Many branches work for better public schools—studying local school budgets, analyzing the needs of education, and mobilizing public support to meet them. The state division is expected to provide leadership and coordinate activities necessary to carry out the AAUW program on the state level, including action on state legislation related to education. In addition, the association is organized into ten regions, each headed by a vice president who serves on the national board and helps to coordinate local and national efforts.

To aid in keeping members informed, the association publishes *Graduate Woman,* which is distributed to all members. It often contains articles dealing with elementary, secondary, and higher education, so there is ample opportunity for members to keep up to date on educational issues. In addition, state and branch officers and committee chairwomen receive copies of *Leaders in Action,* a publication aimed at assisting and informing these leaders. Traditionally the AAUW has emphasized study more than action, although the national board of directors in 1968 passed a resolution on "Action for a Unified Society" that encouraged state and branch leaders to increase the emphasis on action, particularly through local projects. While there have been signs that the organization is becoming more action-oriented, it generally does not play a militant role. This does not mean that the AAUW is unimportant, for a pool of college graduates interested and knowledgeable about education is an asset in any community, particularly when these people are accustomed to studying the issues before deciding upon a position. Still, their contribution on educational policymaking is indirect.

AAUW and the League of Women Voters make their major contributions by arousing interest in the study of educational problems. Such interest can help create a political climate favorable to educational progress. The active involvement of these organizations is somewhat sporadic but is generally supportive of the proposals of the professional educators. This is not to suggest that they are rubber stamp groups, but often their lack of cohesion is such that they usually become involved only in a supportive sense where the apparent benefits to the public schools seem quite clear-cut.

The AAUW and LWV are important components of the women's movement. They have held women's rights positions for many years, but they are multi-issue organizations and do not focus all their energies on the feminist movement. The women's rights movement has made women more politically active at all levels, and both the LWV and AAUW have become more action-oriented and politically sophisticated in recent years.

One area in which the women's movement has helped to trigger very consequential changes is volunteering. As we discussed in Chapter 2, factors such as changing family lifestyles, rising divorce rates, soaring inflation, and the growing ideology of self-fulfillment are pushing more and more women into the labor force.

> The changing role of the American woman is making an enormous impact on the world of volunteer service. As more women go back to school and work, the supply of volunteers is shrinking. Competition is keen, recruitment has become sophisticated and some traditional organizations have had to cut back on their services.[64]

The volunteer world has been affected to some extent by the argument used by some feminists that women volunteers are being exploited and by donating their services are helping to sustain historical patterns of economic dependency. Service volunteer jobs such as hospital aides, cancer society walkers, and so forth have been most drastically affected. Many contend that volunteerism is currently undergoing a difficult transition. The attrition of volunteers is particularly pronounced among white, educated middle- and upper-middle-class women who historically have been the backbone of service volunteer jobs in organizations such as the PTA, the LWV, and the AAUW.

Both the LWV and AAUW are adapting to the presence of competing interests, changing expectations, and reduced spare time by training leaders (thereby providing valuable management training to members), by adjusting meeting times to accommodate work schedules, and by joining with other organizations to accomplish mutual goals. It is clear that those women's organizations that do adapt to the changes brought about by the feminist movement will be more viable than those organizations that do not. In any event, the threat to volunteer organizations is serious. Ruth C. Clusen, past president of the LWV, was quoted as saying that her organization, like most of its counterparts, is now "an endangered species"; the league reportedly lost between 5,000 and 6,000 members in 1977–78.[65] Indeed, most women's organizations are losing members.

A likely scenario for the future is the creation of political coalitions among women's groups dealing with women's issues as well as with other major public policy matters such as education.

In New York City, for example, fifteen women's organizations coalesced to raise resources to support programs that had been reduced by federal budget cuts. In addition to the New York chapter of NOW, the coalition included the Women Office Workers, the New York chapter of the Coalition of Labor Union Women, the National

Congress of Neighborhood Women, the Pre-School Association of the West Side, and the Reproductive Rights National Network.[66] The coalition had as one of its major objectives the broadening of the choices of charities available to working women. As one of the leaders stated, "Over the years women have been the main fund-raisers for churches, schools, and community organizations. Now we believe that working women want an opportunity to choose to give to programs that benefit women. That option is not available to us now."[67] More organizations like this New York City group are likely to come into existence and become influential political forces.

This coalition style of politics operated when women's groups united in efforts to eliminate sex discrimination in schools. NOW's PEER program monitored sex bias in city school systems in Chicago, Atlanta, Cleveland, and San Francisco. Groups of women vigorously reviewed each complaint of sex discrimination filed by women employed in or students enrolled in the public schools of these cities. Women from the LWV and the AAUW joined NOW members in constituting these monitoring teams.[68]

BUSINESS ORGANIZATIONS

The recent highly publicized and dramatic growth of school-business collaborations throughout the country certainly reflects a broader concept of the role of schools in society. In the 1980s there was widespread recognition that new perspectives are needed on the relationship between public education and the nation's business community. These critically important sectors of American life are too detached from each other and there is a growing awareness that the entire society as well as business has a profound interest in strengthening the public school enterprise. A scientifically and technically trained work force is essential in today's world, essential not only if we are to compete economically with productive nations like Japan and West Germany but also if we are to maintain an adequate defense establishment. National security is not enhanced if technical, multi-page training tomes on operating and maintaining sophisticated weaponry are presented to semi-literate soldiers and sailors who are unable to comprehend complex, sophisticated materials.

There is greater understanding that the schools must offer quality education to produce the educated, productive work force that is essential to sustain the country in an increasingly competitive world. Obviously, businesses, as well as the society at large, would suffer if our schools did not produce well-educated, adaptable young citizens who are able to operate in an increasingly technological world in which change is the only constant.

Indeed, more leaders acknowledge that the business stake in quality public education really is not distinguishable from the entire society's stake. More corporations recognize that buttressing our schools is not mere philanthropy and "do-goodism" but actually "enlightened selfishness." In other words, the business world can "do well by doing good." Also, corporations are more cognizant of their direct, bottom-line stake in the improvement of public education. It is estimated that the private sector expends some $40 billion annually on training programs for employees.[69] Much of this investment is spent on providing remedial work in the basic skills, such as basic arithmetic and English, which quite logically could be assumed to be the primary responsibility of our public schools. In fact, business is investing in duplicative, costly ways in providing a range of basic programs that should be provided as fundamentals by school systems.

It is estimated, moreover, that employee recruitment, hiring, and turnover expenditures total more than $100 billion annually. General Motors, for example, was compelled to hire 9,000 employees to fill only 1,500 jobs in a single year. A widespread consensus has developed that too many entry-level training programs are not cost-effective because of rapid turnover, and it is openly avowed that improved educational opportunities in our schools must prepare people more adequately in a changing economy to move to their second and third jobs, which frequently are more important barometers of meaningful employability than entry-level jobs that too often have been dead-end in nature.

Thus, it has become more apparent that business has a rather obvious and tangible dollar-and-cents economic stake in strengthening the quality of public education as well as the more intangible but equally important interest it has in our democratic system's need to maximize equity, provide social justice, and preserve domestic tranquility. As changes in the economy continue to trigger profound and rapid alterations in the nature of the work force, the need to invest in human capital becomes more important if the country is to be productive, profitable, and viable. Thus, more members in the corporate world recognize that they have an up-front political, economic, and social stake in improving schools.

The 1990s will be a propitious time for systematic and sustained efforts to strengthen relationships between the business and public school worlds. There is an emerging national consensus that basic skills in areas such as reading, writing, and math must be improved; that both the quality and quantity of our math and science instruction must be strengthened; that the effectiveness of teachers and teacher education must be enhanced; and that education like other sectors in our society must be made more productive with greater attention to using new technologies such as computers, video discs, and robotry as well as educational television.

The various national reports to which we have alluded made education in the 1980s a far more visible and publicized enterprise. Reports such as *A Nation at Risk, High School,* and *Action for Excellence,* as well as the new economic realities, spawned a new saliency for schools by integrating concerns about education into the mainstream of major public policy issues. Presidential and gubernatorial declarations on school issues as well as education's importance in the presidential election of 1988 helped sustain public interest. However, some skeptics fear that the educational balloon might be deflated as quickly as it was inflated once the political rhetoric in the 1988 campaign and the freshness of these highly publicized national reports abate.

The reports, however, did help to interest many of the nation's civic and political elites in school issues. A growing number of the nation's most prestigious business and governmental leaders now espouse the importance of the schools to the nation's economic development, and comprehensive reform legislation was enacted in the early 1980s in states such as Texas, South Carolina, Indiana, Mississippi, California, and Florida. Governors like James Hunt of North Carolina, Pierre Dupont of Delaware, Charles Robb of Virginia, Lamar Alexander of Tennessee, Bill Clinton of Arkansas, Tom Kean of New Jersey, and William Winter of Mississippi were in the forefront of political and economic efforts to strengthen the quality of and support base for education. Business leaders from major corporations such as IBM, Control Data, Hewlett-Packard, the Bank of America, Procter and Gamble, Primerica, and numerous other representatives from the private sector throughout the country became engaged in school issues in unprecedented, varied ways.[70]

Major national business organizations such as the Committee for Economic Development, the Chamber of Commerce, the National Alliance of Business, the Business Roundtable, and their counterparts at the state and local levels are increasing their education-related activities. Education is viewed more commonly not just as a consumer of resources but as a necessary investment in human capital and the nation's economic viability.[71]

There are countless examples of growing school-business interaction throughout the country at the local, regional, state, and national levels. These are direct responses not only to economic needs but also to the recommendations of the major reports on education that the private sector become much more involved in schools:

> "Action for Excellence" very strongly urges the involvement of business people and other leaders outside of education in improving our schools, and "High School," "A Place Called School," "Educating Americans for the 21st Century," "Action for Excellence," and "A Nation at Risk," all issue an invitation to business leaders to become more active, not only in supporting schools financially, but also in developing curricula and programs and in sharing nonfinancial resources.[72]

What was largely obscure rhetoric about the importance of business-school partnerships only a short time ago transformed almost overnight into a "front-burner" public issue. Hundreds of grassroots examples of these partnerships can be cited.[73]

The school-business partnership movement, as we have noted, has profound ramifications for the organization and control of schools. School leaders should recognize the recent attention by business leaders as an opportunity to reemphasize education as the engine of our democratic system. "Invisible politics is poor politics," and a public reawakening to the importance of education spurred by private-sector influentials in reports such as those issued recently by the Committee for Economic Development can buttress the schools politically at a time when competition for scarce resources is keener and the political leverage of education is lessened in many parts of the country. Stated differently, educators (for pragmatic as well as substantive public policy reasons) must build new and broader coalitions including the business community.

But we hasten to add that situations that present opportunities also pose problems; there are dangers inherent in today's environment. In addition to the longstanding fear that business involvement could lead to control of our schools, more subtle dangers merit attention. New or rekindled business concern for schools may be viewed as evanescent, a public relations fad that will go the way of team teaching, programmed instruction, educational television, and other "quick fixes." We believe that such an appraisal would be an unfortunate misreading of the current situation.

Other related dangers are that because of current economic uncertainty schools will be unable to acquire monies from the private sector and get "turned off" to pursuing relationships with business and that businesses will fail to recognize the potential of the more significant long-range, non-monetary stake and self-interest they have in supporting education. Despite these dangers, we believe that school-business partnerships and other forms of multi-sector collaboration represent an excellent opportunity to buttress and solidify public support for education. Many hope that business leaders will become directly involved in lobbying for additional resources for education in Washington, DC, the state capitals, and at the local level. Despite the many positive contributions of partnerships and adopt-a-school programs that have burgeoned in recent years, the success of education in the challenging years ahead will rely largely on the adequacy of the public resources provided by local, state, and national governments. Business leaders can be influential advocates for increased funding for education and should be encouraged to participate in the political process at every governmental level. A watershed event that might be emulated in localities and in state capitals throughout the country took place in Washington, DC, in the spring of 1987 when prominent executives from five of the nation's major corporations testified before a joint congressional hearing in support of the reauthorization of Chapter 1 funds for the education of disadvantaged children.[74]

INTEREST GROUPS AND THE POLITICAL PROCESS

The Function of Interest Groups

Interest groups perform a number of functions in government. To begin with, the interest group provides a rallying point for the individual. The simple division implied by the concept of the state and the individual is not a practical concept in the formation of policy in our society. The interest group is a vehicle through which individuals of like circumstances or convictions can collectively develop a position on an important issue and then bring influence to bear upon governmental policymaking. This emphasis on group action does not rule out individual leadership, but it does stress the fact of life in the world of politics that leaders ordinarily have followers organized into groups.

A second function performed by interest groups has to do with the delineation of issues. Hamilton and Jefferson, as leaders of their respective groups, helped clarify the issues of strong versus weak federal government and executive versus legislative power. An explication of different positions helps clarify the issues involved in proposed legislation. Legislators and citizens alike often depend on the opinions articulated by official groups that favor and oppose a particular program for their understanding of a program.

As a third function, interest groups also provide information relevant to a proposed program. To be sure, this information is often biased or selective according to the group's own position. At the same time, every interest group knows that distorted information may in the end be self-defeating. For instance, proponents of a state aid program for schools are aware of the fact that their own figures will be carefully scrutinized by the opponents of such a measure. Nothing would please the opponents more than to show that the proponents had been careless in their collection of statistics.

The fact that interest groups on both sides of a proposal gather information and check the information gathered by the opposition gives legislators considerable confidence that they have a reliable base from which to argue the issues. Debate then centers not on the facts themselves but on what the facts mean. Some state legislatures have even asked lobbyists in whom they have confidence to present and discuss factual material on the floor of the legislative chamber. The information-giving function of interest groups is well established.

Perhaps the most important function of interest groups in government is the role they perform in the processes of compromise and consensus. In a pluralistic society almost any proposal will have advocates and opponents. The position of any group is clarified through the activities of the opposing interest groups. Frequently the formal governmental body, such as the legislature, becomes the arena in which these positions are drawn. Contrasting positions can be resolved only through compromise.

It is at this point that the politician becomes a decision broker. Ways must be found to achieve some kind of compromise, and as far as possible consensus must be achieved on the compromise. A politician who can report that the contending groups have reached an agreement feels a genuine sense of achievement. Moreover, the compromise can usually become the basis for official governmental action. Thus, interest groups, through their facing off and their final acceptance of compromise, facilitate the governmental process.

The functions served by interest groups in the governmental process can be illustrated in the politics of federal aid for education. Major support for federal aid came historically from the National Education Association, the American Federation of Teachers, and the Council of Chief State School Officers, all education interest groups. These groups have had allies in the National Council of Jewish Women, the National Federation of Business and Professional Women's Clubs, the American Association of University Women, the National Congress of Parents and Teachers, the AFL-CIO, and other groups. Opposition to federal aid likewise while no longer overt has been chiefly an interest group activity. The historical opponents have been the U.S. Chamber of Commerce, the National Association of Manufacturers, the Daughters of the American Revolution, and a number of other groups. Groups for and against federal aid for education were so numerous and so varied that the individual had no trouble finding a platform compatible with his or her views. In fact, as we will note later, interest groups may have done more to provide individuals with their views than the other way around.

Three major issues continue to dominate the long debate on federal aid. These issues are the question of control, aid to nonpublic schools, and the integration of schools. In the passage of the Elementary and Secondary Education Act of 1965 certain compromises on these issues were achieved, seemingly made for the sake of helping children from poor families.[75]

The hearings on federal aid proposals have produced literally tons of documents. These materials provide the information needed by legislators. While proponents and opponents have not always agreed on the figures, the data produced in these hearings provoke individual scholars and groups not prominently identified with the proposed legislation to examine the question and produce more objective information.

The century-long effort to secure federal aid for education that we discussed in Chapter 3 illustrates the various interactions between interest groups and government. Interests groups are an integral part of the political process.

SUMMARY AND FUTURE PROSPECTS

A number of significant controls are imposed on schools by groups whose primary interest is something other than education. Demographic factors, such as a rapidly growing Hispanic population in several sections of the country, will influence both the programs and staffing of educational institutions in such communities. Interest groups representing blacks, American Indians, and other ethnic groups will continue to focus on the schools as a major mechanism for equalizing educational, social, and economic opportunities for their constituencies.

Taxpayer groups, concerned about periodic inflation, recession, and energy shortages in an uncertain economy, will continue to scrutinize school expenditures. These taxpayer groups may occasionally express interest in a program, but in nearly every case such interest is tied directly to the cost of the program. Such taxpayer groups, spurred by the success of California's Proposition 13 and by frequent backlash against public expenditures of any kind, are likely to continue to monitor school spending. Indeed, widespread national support of efforts to limit taxation will continue to serve as a deterrent to public spending in every sector, including education. These financial control factors (e.g. Proposition 13) will have a political and economic impact on every phase of public school operations in the years ahead.

Only a handful of the organizations that have some concern for educational policymaking have been described here. We have not discussed, for example, the influence of environmental, anti-nuclear, and other groups that at times attempt to influence the curriculum of schools. We also have not focused any attention on the influence of the media and related organizations on education. Some of the major types of groups most active in school affairs have been presented, however. Some of the groups are sharply critical of one phase of education rather than others. Moreover, even groups that generally support the schools often do so from the viewpoint that existing good programs must be improved. Criticism of the schools will continue, and educators should not anticipate any decrease in pressure. This pressure need not be dreaded, for education is finally receiving the concentrated public attention that educators have long sought.

Millions of American parents expect the schools to play a major role in preparing their children for future success. When the stakes are this high and definitions of success vary, controversy is to be expected. It is clear, for example, that criticism of the schools by blacks will be present for some time. Even with the current crash programs, so many problems remain that it will take a while to treat the overt symptoms of inner-city schools, to say nothing of dealing with the root problems. Similarly, right-wing criticism will continue from those who fear the schools are undermining the patriotic and moral fiber of young people. A newer and more ominous type of right-wing criticism is the occasional backlash in response to attempts to improve educational opportunities for minority group students. This too seems destined to continue at least until substantial gains in interracial understanding are made.

It would be an error to portray any group as being in complete and constant support or opposition to what the schools are doing. Support or opposition for school policies tends to shift from issue to issue. Likewise, many persons belong to more than one group. Overlapping memberships tend to neutralize individual support or opposition when the groups' positions conflict on a particular issue.

The overriding lesson of this chapter is that many groups have interests in school affairs and that these interests and the means used to pursue them vary considerably. As a consequence, educational questions are becoming increasingly controversial in many locales. School board and administrative decisions that used to be routine have become matters for debate. There often are more than two sides in such controversies, and communities sometimes become fractionalized as a result of them.

The life of the school administrator is increasingly one of attempting to resolve and live with public conflict. This is not necessarily a bad situation, but it does take a special kind of person to deal with it. Progress can often be achieved through conflict. Marks of a successful administrator appear to be the ability to help define progress, to work with local groups to recognize and achieve it, and to live with the conflict engendered by these activities.

Some of the groups we have discussed often do not direct their criticisms through what school people would consider appropriate channels. Designs to take over PTA groups or school boards, publication of unfounded charges, boycotts, threats of violence, and other ill-considered approaches defeat the purpose of channels provided in the administrative structure of a school system to receive and evaluate criticism and suggestions. Interest groups, however, should point out when these channels are inadequate. Ways must be sought to establish and refine legitimate channels for dissent and to direct dissatisfied individuals and groups to their use.

Probably the best effort administrators can make to ensure that most criticisms are constructive and that those that are not gain little public credence is to work hard at informing the community of the strengths and the shortcomings of the local schools. In addition, they must show that they are sensitive to the concerns expressed by citizens. Too often educators assume that because the schools have noble ends, they should be exempt from attack.

Administrators must anticipate issues before they surface and take vigorous steps early, rather than just react to problems when they explode and are much more difficult to handle. For example, public school administrators in the 1990s will continue to be challenged by women and minority groups in their persisting efforts to achieve equal educational opportunity.[76] The issues themselves are predictable and school leaders should prepare themselves for this continuing pressure from minority groups whose influence will continue to grow.[77]

The administrator need not wait helplessly to be impaled on these issues. While there is no easy road to community support and understanding, continued participation in school affairs by the responsible citizens of a community can build understanding that will not be easily destroyed by emotional or irrational attacks. To foster such community participation is one of the major tasks confronting the school administrator. Many school systems have already established community relations specialists to encourage communication and broaden the base of participation in school affairs.

NOTES

[1]For a detailed analysis of attacks on textbooks see Jack Nelson and Gene Roberts, Jr., *The Censors and the Schools* (Boston: Little, Brown, 1963), and Mary Anne Raywid, *Ax-Grinders: Critics of Our Public Schools* (New York: Macmillan, 1962).

[2]Raywid, *Ax-Grinders,* 22.

[3]*Issuegram: Scientific Creationism,* Education Commission of the States, October 1981. See for example, *Epperson v. Arkansas,* 393 (U.S.) 97 (1968).

[4]"School, Fundamentalists Clash Over Books in 'Scopes II Trial,' " *School Board News* (20 August 1986): 7.

[5]Fred M. Hechinger, "A Matter of Censorship," *New York Times,* 10 March 1987, C-11.

[6]Edward B. Jenkinson, "The Significance of the Decision in 'Scopes II,' " *Phi Delta Kappan* 68 (February 1987): 445–455 and Harriett T. Bernstein, "The New Politics of Textbook Adoption," *Phi Delta Kappan* 66 (March 1985): 463–466.

[7]"People for the American Way Says School Censorship Soaring," *The Richmond Times,* 28 August 1987, 5.

[8]Ibid.

[9]Fred M. Hechinger, "Censorship Found on the Increase," *New York Times,* 16 September 1986, C-14.

[10]For a penetrating analysis of how these ideological clashes have diluted the quality of textbooks see Harriet T. Bernstein, *America's Textbook Fiasco: A Conspiracy of Good Intentions* (Washington, DC: Council for Basic Education, 1988).

[11]Joe L. Kincheloe, *Understanding the New Right and Its Impact on Education,* Phi Delta Kappa Fastback Series # 195 (Bloomington, IN: Phi Delta Kappa, 1983), 41.

[12]Michelle Marder Kamhi, "Censorship vs. Selection—Choosing Books for Schools," *American Education* (March 1982): 11–16 and "Censorship and the Public Schools: Who Decides What Students will Read?" *American Education* (December 1982): 8–14.

[13]Oscar Handlin, "Is Integration the Answer?" *Atlantic* (March 1964): 50.

[14]Stokely Carmichael and Charles V. Hamilton, *Black Power: The Politics of Liberation in America* (New York: Random House, 1967), 44.

[15]Carmichael and Hamilton, *Black Power,* 84.

[16]Robert Pear, "Civil Rights and Reagan," *New York Times,* 31 August 1983, A-15 and Felicity Barringer, "Studies Say U.S. Desegregation Support Fell Under Block Grant," *The Washington Post,* 18 September 1983, A-8.

[17]The decline in the saliency of civil rights issues has been documented in polls of school administrators. See Luvern L. Cunningham and Joseph T. Hentges, *The American School Superintendency, 1982* (Washington, DC: American Association of School Administrators, 1982), 62–65.

[18]*The Status of Black America 1987* (National Urban League, The League, 1987). See also, Robert Pear, "U.S. Finds Black Economic Improvement Halted," *New York Times,* 21 August 1983, A-22.

[19]*Portrait of Inequality: Black and White Children in America* (Washington, DC: Children's Defense Fund, 1981).

[20]Robert Pear, "Hispanic Population Growing 5 Times as Fast as Rest of U.S.," *New York Times,* 11 November 1987, A-1.

[21]*Windows of Opportunity: How Business Invests in U.S. Hispanic Markets,* (Washington, DC: Hispanic Policy Development Project, 1987), X.

[22]Ibid.

[23]Rafael Valdivieso, *Must They Wait Another Generation? Hispanics and Secondary Reform* (New York: Clearinghouse on Urban Education, Teachers College, Columbia University, 1986), 5–6.

[24]*Windows of Opportunity,* XI.

[25]Marta Tienda and William A. Diaz, "Puerto Ricans' Special Problems," *New York Times,* 28 August 1987, A-31.

[26]Ibid.

[27]*Make Something Happen: Hispanics and Urban High School Reform,* vol. I (Washington, DC: Hispanic Policy Development Project, 1984), 13–15.

[28]Ibid.

[29]Ibid., 13–15.

[30]*A Guide to Hispanic Organizations,* Philip Morris Incorporated, 1983.

[31]For examples of the growing political and economic importance of Hispanics see Paul Taylor, "Hispanics Give Agenda to Candidates," *Washington Post,* 22 October 1987, A-7 and Jack Kelly, "Advertisers Count Hispanic Market," *USA Today,* 4 April 1985, B-6.

[32]Excerpts from *To Live on This Earth: American Indian Education* by Estelle Fuchs and Robert J. Havighurst. Copyright © 1972 by Estelle Fuchs and Robert J. Havighurst. Reprinted by permission of Doubleday & Company, Inc.

[33]Ibid., 19.

[34]Ibid., 20.

[35]Alvin M. Josephy, Jr., *Now That the Buffalo's Gone: A Study of Today's American Indians* (New York: Knopf, 1982).

[36]*Report on BIA Education: Excellence in Indian Education Through the Effective Schools Process: Final Review Draft* (Washington, DC: U.S. Department of the Interior, 1988).

[37]Alan K. Campbell, "Education in Its Metropolitan Setting," in *Metropolitan School Organization: Basic Problems and Patterns,* vol. 1, ed. Troy V. McKelvey (Berkeley, CA: McCutchan, 1973), 14.

[38]Ibid.

[39]For a recent analysis of how the movement of middle-class minorities has exacerbated the problems in "underclass" ghetto neighborhoods, see William Julius Wilson, *The Truly Disadvantaged: The Inner City, the Underclass and Public Policy* (Chicago: University of Chicago Press, 1987).

[40]Luvern L. Cunningham, "Equality of Opportunity: Is It Possible in Education?" *Administrator's Notebook* 16 (November 1967): 1.

[41]"Los Angeles Chicanos Fear School System's Proposed Busing Integration Plan Will Hurt Bilingual Program," *New York Times,* 6 February 1977, 25.

[42]For a persuasive argument in support of bilingual education see Jeffrey W. Kobrick, "The Compelling Case for Bilingual Education," *Saturday Review* 29 (April 1972): 54–58.

[43]James Crawford, "37 States Consider 'English Only' Bills With Mixed Results," *Education Week* 38 (17 June 1987): 1, 14. For a recent study which contradicts the contention that Hispanic immigrants resist learning English see Calvin Veltman, *The Future of the Spanish Language in the United States* (New York and Washington, DC: Hispanic Policy Development Project, 1988).

[44]See, for example, William J. Bennett, *Address Before the 1987 Texas Education Conference,* San Antonio, TX, 16 January 1987, 6–8. Mimeographed.

[45]Myron Lieberman, ed., "Education and the Feminist Movement," *Phi Delta Kappan* 55 (October 1973).

[46]Florence Howe, "Sexism and the Aspirations of Women," *Phi Delta Kappan* 55 (October 1973): 102.

[47]Ibid., 103.

[48]Suzanne Paizis, "Frustrated Majority: Consciousness-Raising at the Ballot Box," *California Journal* 5 (March 1974): 82.

[49]Ronna Romney and Beppie Harrison, *Momentum: Women in American Politics Now* (New York: Crown Books, 1988).

[50]Catherine Dillon Lyon and Terry N. Saario, "Women in Public Education: Sexual Discrimination in Promotions," *Phi Delta Kappan* 55 (October 1973): 120.

[51]As of the fall of 1987, 96 percent of public school superintendents and 76 percent of principals were men. See Emily Feistritzer, *Profile of School Administrators in the U.S.* (Washington, DC: National Center for Education Information, 1988), 10.

[52]See, for example, "Thought-Provoking Comments on the Status of Women and Girls and Boys and Men in Classrooms," Comment Section, *Education Times* (2 August 1982): 2, and National Advisory Council on Women's Educational Programs, *Women's Education: The Challenge of the 80's,* Sixth Annual Report (Washington, DC: The Council, March 1981).

[53]*Update on Title IX and Sports,* Projects on the Status and Education of Women (Washington, DC: Association of American Colleges, June 1978), 7.

[54]"More College Women Pursue Traditionally Male Careers," *Higher Education and National Affairs* 30 (13 February 1981): 4.

[55]Herbert Hammerman, *A Decade of New Opportunity: Affirmative Action in the 1970s* (Washington, DC: The Potomac Institute, 1985).

[56]William R. Greer, "In Professions Women Now the Majority," *New York Times,* 19 March 1986, C-1.

57Ibid.

58The provision of equal educational opportunities for girls in math and science, for example, has been of major concern. See "Girls' Math Achievement: What We Do and Don't Know," *The Harvard Education Letter* II (January 1986).

59*Women's Studies,* Project on the Status and Education of Women (Washington, DC: Association of American Colleges, June 1978), 5.

60See, for example, Nadine Brozan, "NOW at 20: Reassessment in a New Era," *New York Times,* 1 December 1986, A-18, and "Women's Movement, Its Ideals Accepted, Faces Subtler Issues," *New York Times,* 17 July 1987, A-10.

61Linda Charlton, "Sisterhood is Braced for The Reaganauts," *New York Times,* 10 May 1981, E-20.

62*A Great Idea for Today,* (Washington, DC: League of Women Voters, 1986).

63Marion Talbot and Lois K. M. Rosenberry, *The History of the American Association of University Women 1881–1931* (Boston: Houghton Mifflin, 1931), 61.

64Steven V. Roberts, "Volunteer Services Suffer as Self-Image of Women Changes," *New York Times,* 6 August 1978, 46.

65Efthalia Walsh, "Volunteers Now Are Getting Choosier," *New York Times,* 16 April 1978, 9.

66Nadine Brozan, "Women's Groups Join to Raise Funds," *New York Times,* 17 December 1981, C-5.

67Ibid.

68Nancy Hicks, "Women's Groups in Four Cities Monitor Complaints About Sex Bias in Schools," *New York Times,* 31 August 1976, 30.

69*Education Committee Report: New York City Partnership, Inc. 1987* (New York: The Partnership, 1988), 6.

70Marsha Levine and Roberta Trachtman, eds., *American Business and the Public Schools: Case Studies of Corporate Involvement in Education,* (New York: Teachers College Press, 1988).

71John F. Jennings, "The Sputnik of the Eighties," *Phi Delta Kappan* 69 (October 1987): 104–109.

72*A Summary of Major Reports on Education* (Denver, CO: Education Commission of the States, 1983), 10.

73See, for example, Ian McNett, *Let's Not Reinvent the Wheel: Educational Profiles of School-Business Collaboration* (Washington, DC: Institute for Educational Leadership, 1982).

74*The Challenge to the Business Community: Congressional Testimony on Its Stake in the Education of At-Risk Children* (Washington, DC: The Institute for Educational Leadership, 1987).

75See Committee for Economic Development, *Raising Low Income Through Improved Education,* 1965, and *Innovation in Education,* 1968 (New York: The Committee). Also see Philip Meranto, *The Politics of Federal Aid to Education in 1965* (Syracuse, NY: Syracuse University Press, 1967).

76"Balancing the Scales: 200 Years After the Constitution," *Equity and Choice* IV (Special Issue, February 1988).

77"Special Report: A Changing Black Electorate," *The Ford Foundation Letter* 18 (April 1987): 2–3.

15
Availability of Resources

The availability of financial resources is often a limiting factor in the operation of schools. James and his colleagues, whose study gave impetus to a reform movement in school finance, identified three major clusters of variables that in combination seem to determine educational expenditures.[1] These variables included wealth, or the ability to pay; the decision-making process, or governmental arrangements for permitting school board members and citizens to express their preferences regarding proposed school expenditures; and the aspirations of the people, or demand for educational services. Wealth, governmental access, and aspirations for education vary from district to district and state to state.

DIFFERENTIALS IN WEALTH

Among School Districts

Most school districts must rely on the general property tax as a major source of school revenue, and the assessed valuation of the property within the school district becomes the base upon which the general property tax is levied. When assessed value is expressed in terms of some unit of educational load, such as "per pupil in school attendance," a convenient index for comparing the ability of school districts to support education is derived. These comparisons are more accurate when limited to a single state or to a subdivision of a state where assessment practices are more uniform.

In Cook County, Illinois, there are 116 elementary school districts and 27 high school districts. In Table 15.1 the assessed valuations per pupil in average daily attendance (ADA) for four of these elementary districts—two wealthy, two poor—are shown. Note that the wealthiest district is thirty times more able to support an educational program than the poorest district.

The variation among the high school districts is not as great but it is still noteworthy. The wealthiest district has five times the assessed valuation of the poorest district. In terms of area, most high school districts are appreciably larger than the elementary districts. This condition alone tends to decrease the variability found among the districts.

When assessed valuations per pupil for an entire state are calculated, the spread between districts with the lowest and highest assessed valuation per pupil is generally even greater than those shown for Cook County. The ability of local school districts to raise school revenue varies tremendously. This difference is chiefly a function of the great variability in the assessed valuation of property within the school district, particularly when expressed in terms of educational cost per pupil or per classroom.

Among States

There is also considerable variation in the ability of the states to support an educational program. Since assessment practices among the states differ considerably, assessed values per pupil or per classroom are not the best measures to use in comparing state expenditures. Personal income per capita is a more useful measure. As shown in Table 15.2, personal income per capita varies from $18,089 in Connecticut to $9,187 in Mississippi, and the average for the United States is $13,676. The four top states have about one and one-half times the ability of the four bottom states to support an educational program.

TABLE 15.1
Assessed Valuations Per Pupil in Cook County, Illinois, by Selected Districts, 1985–86

	Assessed Valuation Per Pupil
Elementary Districts	
#78	$711,250
#11C	712,434
#140	32,855
#168	23,988
High School Districts	
#212	427,570
#219	456,821
#227	103,012
#228	83,267

Source: Illinois State Board of Education.

TABLE 15.2
Personal Income Per Capita in Selected States, 1985

State	Income Per Capita
Connecticut	$18,089
Illinois	14,738
New Jersey	17,211
Wyoming	13,223
United States	13,676
Kentucky	10,824
Arkansas	10,476
South Carolina	10,586
Mississippi	9,187

Source: Statistical Abstract of the U.S., 1987, 425.

This table, of course, only roughly indicates the relative ability to pay of various states. Higher average income does not necessarily mean more money is available to support education. New Jersey, New York, Illinois, and other industrial states, for instance, impose many taxes on personal income, perhaps more than is found in states that still have large rural populations, such as Mississippi and Alabama. Moreover, cities everywhere, even in industrial states, are in critical need of more money if they are going to provide quality education.

The Role of Federal Aid

Federal aid for education seems to be a logical way to alleviate the differences among the states in their ability to support schools. We have passed the period when the question of providing federal aid was an issue. There has been some form of federal aid to schools throughout American history, as shown by the land grant acts of 1785 and 1787, the Land Grant College Act of 1862, the Vocational Education Act of 1917, the National Defense Education Act of 1958, and the Elementary and Secondary Education Act of 1965. Nearly all federal aid programs, however, have been categorical in nature. Moreover, these programs have been administered by numerous agencies in the federal government.

Berke and Kirst examined who benefits from federal aid and who governs the allotment process.[2] They assessed the impact of eight federal aid programs (Titles I, II, III of ESEA, Titles III and V-A of NDEA, vocational education, school lunch, and assistance to federally impacted areas) on a sample of school districts across the country. While their findings illustrate the differential effect of federal aid among school districts, they also suggest why federal aid does little to reduce inequities among states. The differential effect is noted in the following:

1. Federal aid to education in the aggregate has only a slight equalizing tendency at best, and that within a number of metropolitan areas it displays distinctly disequalizing characteristics;

2. The degree of equalization, where it does exist, is usually too small to offset pre-existing disparities among school districts, and
3. Although Title I (now Chapter 1) of ESEA does flow in greater proportion to poorer and higher need school districts, a number of other federal programs operate to help the rich districts get richer.[3]

Even though federal aid for education increased during the 1960s and 1970s, it has leveled off at about $15 billion for all educational purposes. In 1984–85 about 6.5 percent of the revenue for public schools came from the federal government. As noted in Chapter 3, this percentage is not likely to increase in the near future.

The percentage of federal aid varies among the states, depending in part on the number of programs for which a state is eligible. This variation is suggested in Table 15.3 where percentages of revenues from local, state, and federal sources are shown for selected states. In Wyoming, for instance, expenditure levels are relatively high and federal aid accounts for only 3.3 percent of total revenues. In Mississippi, on the other hand, expenditure levels are relatively low and federal aid accounts for 16.5 percent of total revenues. Expenditure averages do not reveal the wide variations among districts in each of the states; this variation is likely to be even more pronounced in a state like Nebraska, where little has been done to define a minimum or basic school program the state would support.

In assessing the impact of federal aid on the public schools of the nation, a number of conclusions can be drawn. First, federal aid is rather meager. Second, federal aid does little to equalize revenues among school districts or states. Third,

TABLE 15.3
Current Expenditures Per Pupil (ADA) and Percentage of Revenue by Source for Public Elementary and Secondary Schools in Selected States, 1984–85

State	Expenditure Per Pupil	Percentage of Revenues		
		Local	State	Federal
Nebraska	3346	68.1	25.1	6.8
Connecticut	4180	54.5	41.7	3.8
Vermont	3489	62.6	31.7	5.7
Wyoming	4699	58.8	37.9	3.3
United States	3297	44.7	48.8	6.5
Washington	3600	20.3	74.2	5.5
New Mexico	3042	12.3	75.0	12.7
Kentucky	2401	23.5	63.7	12.8
Mississippi	2332	24.3	59.3	16.5
Hawaii	3464	.1	89.0	10.9

Source: National Center for Educational Statistics, *Digest of Education Statistics, 1985–1986* (Washington, DC: U.S. Government Printing Office, 1986), 113.

the categorical nature of most federal aid has made it a vehicle for changing programs in many school districts. Fourth, federal resources have given local districts leverage to work on important and often emotional issues such as bilingual education, preparations for school desegregation, and citizen participation. Fifth, federal aid may be of minor importance to many school districts, but it is of major importance to an increasing number of districts. For instance, Public Law 874 and Public Law 815, first passed in 1950, to aid federally impacted districts, in time came to provide assistance to some 4,100 school districts in which one-third of the public elementary and secondary school pupils of the nation were enrolled.[4] With so many school districts affected, the impacted aid lobby was very influential in Congress, where the desire of every recent president to eliminate such aid has been thwarted.

What of the future? Is general aid apt to replace categorical aid? Munger and Fenno, after their study of the politics of federal aid, thought general aid unlikely.[5] Since that time there has been some use of block grants to states and the consolidation of some categorical programs. However, the consolidated programs are still categorical in nature, even though the categories have been somewhat broadened. For the most part, Congress will probably continue to identify national needs and insist that federal aid appropriations be directed toward those needs.

Financial Resources and Control

State aid programs in most states do not counteract the differential ability of school districts to support school programs. Nor are federal aid programs able to provide poor school districts with adequate school revenue. Helpful as state and federal aid programs are to many school districts, the differential ability of school districts to support education still persists. Moreover, the categorical nature of federal aid has had limited effect in equalizing the abilities of the states to support education. So differential ability to support education at both local and state levels is still a fact of life.

Variations in ability to pay give rise to two kinds of control. One type of control is a result of limited resources, and a second type is a product of state and federal assistance. These controls, while often not deliberate, do affect what is done to provide school programs.

Let's look first at shortage of money as a limiting factor in education. Inadequate funds often mean larger classes for teachers, meager libraries, few instructional supplies, cheap building construction, poor instructional equipment, few guidance and health services, and poorly trained teachers and administrators. Two school districts, each with limited available funds, however, could make quite different decisions about these matters. For instance, large classes may be less of a handicap with superior teachers than with mediocre teachers, high-quality instructional equipment may make more of a difference than ultramodern buildings, and a live-wire principal can stimulate average teachers to become good ones. The wise allocation of limited resources can make a difference in many poor districts.

Nevertheless, lack of money is a limiting factor in poor school districts. This was clearly documented in a Michigan finance study where it was found that the extent and quality of programs for libraries, gifted pupils, handicapped pupils, art, new mathematics, and other program elements were directly related to money expended.[6] To the extent that lack of money prohibits desirable programs, the control of deprivation is operating.

Poor districts tend to receive a great deal of state and sometimes federal aid, and another type of control is inherent in this situation. Most state aid programs make money available to school districts contingent on certain types of school district performance. Often school districts must establish a certain tax rate in order to be eligible for state aid. Or, if the aid is for a particular purpose such as transportation, certain standards must be met. In other words, the provisions of most state aid programs are designed to guarantee that no district in the state will fall below certain minimum operating standards. When districts strive to meet these standards, the state is exerting control.

The control inherent in federal aid is somewhat different. Since most federal aid is for categorical purposes such as vocational education and education of the children of the poor, the amount and kind of control depends on the definition of the program. For instance, a district must operate a vocational education program, often at considerable local cost, to qualify for the federal aid. Federal assistance for the disadvantaged requires that districts identify the disadvantaged and develop programs to improve their education.

Both school districts and states, then, vary in their ability to support education. Despite substantial state aid programs in most states and a variety of federal aid programs, these differentials are only partially eliminated. There are controls inherent in the shortage of resources and in accepting assistance from a higher level of government, and these controls are more pronounced in poor than in wealthy districts.

DIFFERENTIALS IN GOVERNMENTAL ACCESS

Each of the fifty states has a body of law, often expressed in the constitution and always in the statutes, governing the expenditure of school funds. These provisions, which deal with both operating and capital outlay funds, vary greatly among the states, and these variations determine the ease of access of school funds.

Operating Funds

Some of the governmental arrangements regarding current expenditures for school purposes in selected states are shown in Table 15.4. The table suggests that local access to school revenues may be relatively open or closed. If assessment practices and other governmental procedures keep the assessed value of property at a very small proportion of the market value of the property, then school revenue tends to be hard to obtain, or "closed." Conversely, when assessed values represent a fair proportion of market values, access to school revenue is relatively "open." We've used this and several other factors to score selected states on governmental access.

As can be seen in Table 15.4, states vary greatly in how closely assessed values match market values. The national average is that assessed value is 40 percent of market value, and that figure was used to calculate credit for each of the states on this variable: 0 to 19 percent, no points; 20–39 percent, one point; 40 percent and above, two points.

A second access factor has to do with whether school districts in a state are dependent or independent. A dependent district must have its budget approved by another unit of government, usually a city or a county. An independent district can determine its own budget, even though it often has to conform to certain state limitations. Clearly access is more open in independent districts, so states with independent districts were given two points.

As a third access factor, we have assumed that school districts in states with generous state aid programs have access to more revenue. The median level of state support, 54 percent, was used in this calculation: Illinois at 54 percent was given one point, states below the median were given no points, and states above the median were given two points.

Whether boards of education have the power to determine revenue needed for current expenditures or establish tax rates is another access factor. Boards in seven of the nine states scored have that power, so we gave one point to each of those states. Boards in Illinois and Oregon do not have that power, so they were given no points on this variable.

Still another local access factor is the power people have to vote for additional taxes for operating the schools. In Table 15.4 the people in seven states have this power and one point has been awarded to each of those states. Maryland and South

TABLE 15.4
Local Governmental Access Arangements for Current School Funds in Selected States

State	Percent Assessed Value of Property to Sales Value	Dependent or Independent District	State Aid as Percent of State Local Revenues	Authorization of Local Board to Increase School Levy	Authorization of Local Electorate to Increase School Levy	Ascribed Local Access Score
Alabama	8.5 (0)	D (0)	75 (2)	yes (1)	no (0)	3
Illinois	25.7 (1)	I (2)	54 (1)	no (0)	yes (1)	5
Maryland	32.4 (1)	D (0)	34 (0)	yes (1)	no (0)	2
Michigan	43.2 (2)	I (2)	43 (0)	yes (1)	yes (1)	6
Minnesota	17.7 (0)	I (2)	67 (2)	yes (1)	yes (1)	6
Mississippi	6.7 (0)	D (0)	70 (2)	yes (1)	yes (1)	4
New York	25.1 (1)	I* (2)	41 (0)	yes* (1)	yes (1)	5
Oregon	63.1 (2)	I (2)	30 (0)	no (0)	yes (1)	5
South Carolina	2.3 (0)	D (0)	61 (2)	yes (1)	no (0)	3

*Most districts
Note: Numbers in parentheses indicate points earned toward local access score.
Source: 1982 Census of Governments, *Taxable Property Values and Assessment-Sales Price Ratios,* vol. 2, U.S. Dept. of Commerce, Bureau of the Census (Washington, DC: U.S. Government Printing Office, October, 1984); Ester O. Tron, *Public School Finance Programs, 1978–79,* Office of Education (Washington, DC: U.S. Government Printing Office, 1980). Apparently discontinued after 1980.

Carolina do not grant the people that right and thus no points have been given to those states.

Combining these five access factors, we gave each of the states a local access score. Michigan and Minnesota each have access scores of six, thus they seem to be most open. Maryland, with an access score of two seems most closed, followed closely by Alabama and South Carolina with access scores of three. The other four states fall in between with access scores of four and five.

The analysis presented above is intended to be illustrative and not definitive. We have considered five significant access factors; there are many other access factors, some of which may be as significant as the ones we have employed. Under these circumstances, the access scores we have ascribed to each of the states should also be looked upon as suggestive only.

Governmental Access and Control

The governmental arrangements under which current and capital outlay funds are made available to school districts obviously impose controls or limitations on American schools. The nature and extent of control is a function of the number of decision points required, the prescriptions surrounding each decision, and the levels of government involved in the decisions.

The greater the number of decision points the more complex control becomes. A simple arrangement is represented by a local board of education that has complete freedom to determine the school budget and to certify the tax levy needed to raise the money required. Somewhat more complex is the situation in which the board of education has discretion only up to a certain point, and additional taxes require the approval of the voters of the school district. Still more complex is the arrangement in which the school budget must be justified to some city, county, or state agency. In the first instance, there is one decision point while in the last there may be three or more decision points—and thus that many more opportunities to restrict educational expenditures.

Requiring decisions to be made at more than one level of government may present other problems. For instance, the people of a school district may believe firmly that higher taxes are necessary to support an educational program of high quality. If this decision must be approved by a county or state review board of some kind, other interests may be injected into the picture. A county or state representative may see no point in one district taxing itself far beyond what other districts do. This view might, of course, be encouraged by a few large property holders in the district who recognize that they cannot influence their neighbors but that they can, indeed, influence key officials at the county or state levels.

DIFFERENTIALS IN ASPIRATION

The third major variable affecting expenditures for education is the level of aspiration people hold for their schools. This variable has been conceptualized by James and others as demand for education.[7] Since the actual operation of schools is essentially a local function, evidence of this aspiration level can be noted in the purposes espoused by local superintendents of schools, in the budget adoptions of the local boards of education, and in the responses of local electorates at the polls. At the state level, evidence of aspiration may be noted in state aid provisions, particularly as expressed in the state foundation program. Congressional action on federal assistance may also suggest national aspirations for education. We'll give attention here to the nature or kind of education and the quality of education desired in different school districts.

Kind of Education Desired

Downey, Seager, and Slagle, in a series of older but still relevant studies, examined the tasks of public education as perceived by various subpublics in the United States and Canada.[8] They came up with sixteen tasks or purposes, divided into four major categories (intellectual, social, personal, and productive), and developed an appropriate instrument for respondents to order these tasks according to their perceived importance. Almost 4,000 respondents, including educators and noneducators in four regions of the United States and one in Canada, rated these tasks. All groups of respondents agreed that the intellectual tasks (possession of knowledge, communication of knowledge, creation of knowledge, and desire for knowledge) were the most important tasks of the school.

There were, however, subtle variations in the amount of emphasis placed on intellectual tasks versus other task areas. For instance, there were regional differences. The western region (California) favored more than any other region the socializing aspects of education; the South (Alabama and Georgia) stressed physical education and personal development; the East (Massachusetts) emphasized moral training; and Canada (Alberta) stressed the intellectual and aesthetic tasks. In many respects the Midwest (Illinois and Wisconsin) stood in the middle with respect to its expressed preferences. The study also found that certain social and personal characteristics predicted various educational viewpoints:

> Occupation and amount of schooling were the best predictors of educational belief. Perhaps these are related, but the relationship does not explain the whole phenomenon. These two variables emerged more or less independently as consistent indicators of perception of the task. The higher one's position on the occupational continuum, the greater the importance he assigned to the intellectual, the aesthetic, and the world citizenship aspects of the task; conversely, the less importance he assigned to the physical, the moral, the consumer, and the vocational aspects. Similarly, the more schooling respondents had themselves, the more they tended to emphasize the intellectual aspects and minimize the social, physical, and vocational aspects of education.
>
> Age was a somewhat less reliable predictor, as were race and religion. It was rather surprising to note, however, that the older the respondent, the more he tended to favor the physical, the patriotic, the moral, and the family aspects of education; the younger the respondent, the more he tended to favor the intellectual and related aspects. Catholics, as a group, placed greater emphasis upon the patriotic, the civic, and the moral elements than did Protestants. Negroes, as a group, placed greater emphasis upon the physical, the social, and the moral than did whites.

Community-type, income, sex, and proximity to school did not prove to be variables closely associated with educational viewpoint.[9]

More recent evidence on demand for public education can be found in the Gallup polls on education, conducted annually for the past several years. The following statistics are excerpts from the 1987 report and some references are made to earlier reports for comparative purposes.[10] In 1987, 43 percent of the national sample of respondents gave the public schools an A or a B rating on a five-point scale. In 1983 the comparable figure was 31 percent and in 1974 it was 48 percent. Public confidence appeared to decline from 1974 to 1983 and to have increased since that time. Attempts were made to see what factors might help explain these ratings. In neither 1983 or 1987 was sex a differentiating factor. In 1983 age, community size, and level of education did not appear to explain differences among respondents but in 1987 all of these factors seemed to be significant. For instance, 36 percent of the 18–29-year-olds gave the schools A or B ratings, while 46 percent of those 50 and over gave the schools A or B ratings. Regarding community size, 28 percent of respondents in central cities gave A or B ratings, while 53 percent in communities under 2,500 gave A or B ratings. Level of education also made a difference, with 35 percent of those who did not complete high school giving A and B ratings and 49 percent of those with graduate-level education giving such ratings. Race was a differentiating factor in both 1983 and 1987. In 1987, 35 percent of nonwhites accorded the schools A or B ratings, compared to 43 percent for whites. Region also was a differentiating factor in both 1983 and 1987. In 1987, 36 percent of the respondents from the West gave the public schools A or B ratings while 47 percent of respondents in the South gave them such ratings.

Two other factors may have been even more important in explaining the findings. The first of these has to do with the perceptions respondents had of the public schools nationwide as contrasted with perceptions of schools in their own communities. Public schools in the nation were graded A or B by 19 percent of the respondents, while 69 percent gave schools in their own communities an A or B. The other important factor had to do with whether or not respondents were parents with children in the public schools. 56 percent of the parents gave the public schools A and B ratings, whereas only 39 percent of respondents with no children in school gave the schools A and B ratings. Clearly, factors such as those already noted need to be taken into account as information about schools is made available to the public. In 1987, when those polled were asked how well-informed they were about the public schools, 15 percent said well-informed, 36 percent fairly well-informed, 43 percent not well-informed, and 6 percent don't know.

Both the Gallup Poll and the Downey study suggest that occupation and level of education are generally useful indicators of the kind of education people demand. Citizens in professional or managerial occupations and with college educations want schools to stress the academic tasks and give less attention to vocational or personal tasks. On the other hand, citizens who are blue-collar workers and who are not college graduates place more importance on the vocational and personal tasks of the school. In a sense, both groups stress vocational education, but in one case this means preparation for the professions and in the other case it means preparation for skilled or semiskilled occupations. In terms of the school curriculum, however, the two demands have quite different impacts. Those who stress the academic, for instance, are more concerned with securing teachers with liberal arts backgrounds, having adequate libraries, and diagnosing reading disabilities. Those who stress vocational skills are more supportive of shops, home economics laboratories, gymnasiums, and other facilities that foster personal development and work skills.

Quality of Education Desired

The citizens of different school districts not only have different demands regarding the content of the school program, they also have different demands regarding the quality of the school program. If operating expenditures are used as a rough index of quality, this differential demand is illustrated in Table 15.5.

Even though the socioeconomic rankings are old (the Chicago Association of Commerce has not collected more recent data), they are generally supported by the more recent assessed valuations. Table 15.5 again illustrates the differential capacity of school districts to support school programs. Average assessed valuation per pupil in the five wealthy districts is almost four times what it is in the poor districts. Not only do the residents in the wealthy districts have more to work with, they also demand more education. Indeed, expenditures in the wealthy districts are more than half again as high as they are in the poor districts. Despite the great disparity in wealth, the wealthy districts still levy a substantial tax rate on themselves, an average of 2.49 cents on the dollar.

As suggestive as the data in Table 15.5 are, a more extensive study of this matter is required before one can be confident of a relationship between social class and school expenditures. Plus, the relationship will probably never be a perfect one since the variables of wealth and governmental access also affect expenditure levels.

Early but still useful case studies of two contrasting communities shed further light on this matter. Hills examined the educational expectations held for schools in two diverse communities.[11] Community A was an upper-income, residential suburb of 11,500 people while Community B was a lower-income suburb of 3,400 people. The two communities were compared on a number of characteristics. In terms of income, schooling, home values, and occupational distribution, Community A ranked high and Community B low on the socioeconomic scale. Each community was served by a township high school.

As part of the study, teachers were asked to give their perceptions of community expectations for the school. In Community A, teachers were convinced that school patrons expected the school to provide a highly specialized college preparatory program. One teacher's comment was:

> By and large, the majority of the parents think their children should go on to liberal arts colleges. I teach a low-ability section in my subject field. Parents feel that being placed in a group of this kind precludes going to college. Several have requested that their youngsters be transferred to the regular section even though they know they'll get lower grades there.

TABLE 15.5

Socioeconomic Characteristics of Selected Communities in Cook County, Illinois and Operating Expenditures in Corresponding Elementary School Districts

	Social Economic Rank (1–201)* 1975	Operating Expenditures Per Pupil 1985–86	Assessed Valuation Per Pupil 1984	Total Tax Rates 1984**
Kenilworth	1	$5,686	$186,359	2.96
Glencoe	3	6,037	163,458	2.74
Winnetka	6	6,034	184,280	2.74
Wilmette	11	4,803	142,729	2.96
Northbrook	12	4,722	296,334	1.57
Average		5,456	194,632	2.49
Chicago Heights	176	2,757	54,985	3.24
Blue Island	185	3,582	68,495	2.75
Steger	188	3,187	63,134	2.25
Posen-Robins	193	3,733	29,844	3.54
East Chicago	200	3,982	53,283	5.19
Average		3,448	53,948	3.39

*Based on income and home values
**Cents on the dollar
Source: Chicago Association of Commerce and Industry, "The Socioeconomic Rank of Chicago's Suburban Municipalities in 1975" (Chicago: The Association, 1975) and Illinois State Board of Education reports, 1987.

For many parents, just any college or university will not do. Several of the teachers interviewed said some parents insist that their youngsters be prepared for enrollment in a college in the East considered to have prestige. The following is typical:

> They want a college prep course so they can get into a prestige school—an Eastern school. Occasionally students who are not doing as well as they might are taken out of school here and placed in a military or prep school. When parents contact you, it's because they are upset about grades—they're afraid their kid won't be able to get into the right college.

The following sentiment was shared by several teachers:

> There's a growing emphasis on suburban values—monetary position— social status— are terribly important here. Kids are unbelievably practical-minded; there's far too little idealism, very materialistic. Students here exhibit a strong tendency to examine critically their own motives and attributes. As a father, I question how long I want to stay here. I'm concerned about whether we can shield our children against these pressures. Everything is planned to be emblematic of success and prestige. I can't see bringing up my children in the competitive race for social status.

In light of the above comments it is not surprising that 65 percent of the teachers were aware of a high degree of community interest in school affairs. Nor is it surprising that 35 percent of the teachers in Community A commented specifically on the high degree of community pressure on the school.

The comments of teachers in Community B revealed a very different sort of community interest in the school. One teacher noted:

The great majority of parents don't take a particular interest. They want a high school diploma; they're not concerned about grades or grade averages. When they ask, "How's my boy doing?" they mean, "Is he passing or failing?"

Fifty-two percent of the School B faculty specifically mentioned the absence of community pressure on the school. One teacher reported that:

There's no parental pressure here—Johnny gets what he deserves and the parents stand behind the teacher. We get no pressure to give special privileges—people are willing to let the teachers run the school.

This evaluation is confirmed by the fact that 56 percent of the teachers in School B reported a high degree of professional freedom while only 22 percent of the School A sample gave a similar report. Community B does place certain restrictions on the school. For the most part, these center on what one teacher termed their "fundamentalist religious beliefs." One English teacher reported that he had been criticized severely for using *Macbeth* in a literature class because it was said to be obscene.

There were distinct differences between the two communities. Community A, a high-income, residential suburb, preferred a highly academic, college preparatory high school program. Community B, the low-income suburb, preferred a terminal, vocation-oriented high school program. But these are not the only differences that existed. In addition to preferring a college preparatory program, Community A residents actively demanded that such a program be provided. Community B residents, however, despite their preference for a terminal program, were not especially interested in making their views known to the school.

Aspirations and Control

The aspirations people hold for education form a kind of control over education. First, community expectations influence the nature or kind of education offered. Some people insist that the program be highly academic, and they have little tolerance for courses designed to improve vocational or social skills. Other people feel that training in the vocational and social areas is as important as, if not more important than, preparation for college. The people who favor the academic program usually insist that their demands be met.

Aspiration may also affect the level of education a community is willing to pay for. While not uniformly the case, school districts that support high expenditures per pupil and high teacher salaries tend to be those districts that rank high on the socioeconomic scale. It is not entirely by accident that Winnetka and Glencoe are among the Cook County districts with the highest expenditures. The people in those districts, even though conservative in many respects, are not conservative in their aspirations for schools. Willingness or unwillingness to provide money for schools is a significant form of control that citizens can and do exercise upon schools.

Lower aspirations for schools and even indifference, however, may not result in a drastic reduction in the quality of the schools. Traditionally, citizens with lower socioeconomic status have been more willing than citizens of higher socioeconomic status to leave school matters to the professionals. Thus, the nature and quality of the schools in places like Community B tend to reflect the aspirations of the professionals more than the citizens. The Hills study found that the professionals in the two communities were more alike than different. This may have been chance, but more likely it showed that teachers and administrators agree on many educational purposes and programs.

It appears that in communities of high socioeconomic status citizens exercise more influence on schools while in communities of low socioeconomic status school people exercise more influence. This phenomenon seems to be changing, however, particularly in black and other ethnic communities, and this development is placing new demands on professional school workers.

Somewhat contrary to the generalizations above are the findings by Minar.[12] He found that school boards in lower status districts tend to restrict the authority of the superintendent more than those in higher status districts. He hypothesized that boards in lower status districts were less likely to defer to the superintendent's expertise than were boards in higher status districts where there are a disproportionate number of people with organizational and management skills, who are more likely to understand and respect specialization, expertise, and the delegation of authority. By restriction of the superintendent's authority, Minar meant that boards in lower status districts tend to question and focus on minor policy issues, personnel, and administrative matters; boards in higher status districts deal with these routine matters with dispatch, allowing their superintendents great latitude in these areas and focusing their attention on more substantive concerns such as finances and building plans.

Boyd provides a still more comprehensive view of the matter.[13] After a careful analysis of his own and related data, Boyd suggests that citizens and the school boards, especially in smaller and more homogeneous communities, tend to have more influence over external, redistributive, and strategic policy decisions whereas the professionals, especially in larger and more heterogeneous communities, tend to have more influence on internal and routine policy decisions. Perhaps in view of the findings of these studies, a distinction needs to be made between which professionals, the teachers or the superintendents, are influenced more by citizens in lower and higher status districts.

RECENT TRENDS

Three recent movements, the reform of state school finance programs, tax limitation, and the highly publicized reexamination of American education, have implications for the availability of resources to school districts. Each of these movements will be treated briefly.

Reform of State School Finance Programs

In the past 50 years state aid programs have been developed in most states. These programs have been motivated by a number of objectives, including the following: to stimulate improved programs, to compensate local districts for unusual programs, to guarantee a minimum program to all districts, to provide an incentive for local tax effort, and to broaden the tax base for school support. Paul Mort gave considerable emphasis to the equalization objective, while Harlan Updegraff tended to emphasize the reward-for-effort objective. These programs have been scrutinized by scholars and found inadequate in a number of ways. For instance, Berke and others suggested that the New York equalization program had five shortcomings:

> (1) structural limitations; (2) inadequate measures of educational need; (3) failure to relate educational finance to municipal or noneducational finance; (4) no consideration for cost differentials among districts; (5) too great a reliance on the local property tax.[14]

The courts have also examined state programs for financing elementary and secondary schools and in some instances have found such programs unconstitutional. Court initiatives suffered a setback when the U.S. Supreme Court reversed the lower court ruling on Rodriguez. Since then, state courts in California, New Jersey, and Connecticut have mandated new school funding systems. But these mandates are not automatic or universal, as Callahan and Wilken note, for state courts in Idaho, Washington, and Oregon affirmed the constitutionality of the existing programs.[15] The issue continues to be examined in state courts.

Callahan and Wilken contended that the central features of the new state role in public school finance are as follows:

1. Budget surpluses have been tapped and traditional state taxes have been increased.
2. Local school tax rates on property have often been reduced.
3. The distribution of school aid has taken account of unusual needs and costs.
4. Most revised programs have placed systematic controls on the growth of local school budgets.[16]

Callahan and Wilken compared the state share of state-local expenditures in the last year before reform and the first year after reform in eighteen reform states. The average state share before reform was 39 percent while after reform it was estimated to be 51 percent.[17]

As the state share of support for public education exceeded 50 percent in the early 1980s for the first time, the states increased their regulation of schools correspondingly.[18] In some states, such as California and Florida, this puportedly has resulted in pressures to deprofessionalize and routinize schools. Some critics of recent state initiatives contend that these developments have tended to "level down" program resources and opportunities.

Another characteristic of states that have effected reform programs has been the increasing diversity of actors participating in the process. Frequently, these reforms have been initiated by court actions. In many instances, governors have played leading roles in the support of proposals aimed at such reforms.[19] Since augmented state revenues are nearly always required, legislators who are concerned with overall state tax policy have been involved. In many states new configurations of political power have emerged at the state level as school issues have been sucked into the political mainstream. Governors and legislators have superseded the traditional custodians of educational legislation—the state education agencies, the teachers associations, and the superintendents and school board associations.

Tax Limitation

While the prospects for continued school finance reform are good, another movement that swept the country in recent years, is in many ways an anathema to reform. This is the tax limitation movement, particularly in the form represented by Proposition 13 in California and Proposition 2.5 in Massachusetts. While these states and others may have been ripe for tax revolt, the imposition of arbitrary tax limits, coupled with an economic downturn, have had drastic consequences for school finance. The nationwide interest in these movements suggests that many citizens are fed up with big government and with its insatiable appetite for tax revenues. Thoughtful citizens everywhere will find it difficult to espouse rational tax changes in the face of bold and simplistic tax cutbacks.

Ironically, as Guthrie has noted, the most significant outcome of Proposition 13 in California may be a side effect, the substitution of a state school system for a system built on local school control.[20] As the percentage of school revenues from state sources increases and as local school districts are more and more restricted in both raising and expending funds, such an outcome is not hard to visualize.

When one backs away from the specifics of Proposition 13, some general inferences are possible. As Kelly has observed, the fiscal conflict between special government for education and general government has sharpened over the last decade or so.[21] Because at least some functions of schools and other community agencies overlap, many mayors and city councils question the "separateness" of school district finance. The fiscal conflict between general and special government also intensifies as the proportion of state aid increases. State legislators, much more than local board members, place school demands within the context of total demands for all state services. Many legislators want to see schools get their fair share, but they do not fancy starving other state services in order to feed the schools. These developments will also intensify overt competition between education and other public services.

School Reexamination

Particularly since the 1950s questions regarding the purposes and the performance of the public school have been raised. These questions prompted no less than six substantial examinations and reports on the public school during the past few years. These included *A Nation at Risk, Making the Grade, Action for Excellence, High School Reform: The Need for Engineering, High School: A Report on Secondary Education in America,* and *A Place Called School,* the culminating report of the comprehensive study of schooling directed by Goodlad. While these reports differ in the assumptions they make about schools, in the approaches they followed in examining schools, and in the extravagance of the rhetoric used to depict the plight of schools, they do tend to make a number of common recommendations. For instance, they insist that the schools should establish higher standards for students, including English literacy and more knowledge of science and mathematics. They also stress the need for attracting and holding better talent in the teaching ranks through such means as increased salaries, including merit pay, and improved working conditions.

One prominent theme in these reform reports is education for economic survival in a competitive world. That theme has been given specific attention in "Financing Education Reform" by James A. Kelly.[22] The Carnegie-sponsored Task Force on Teaching as a Profession has proposed a vision of an educational system transformed through reforms in four areas: standards and assessment, teacher education, work force structure, and pay and finance. All of these reforms were seen as necessary if the United States was to compete in the world economy. Kelly was asked to examine the financial feasibility of the proposed reforms. He began by analyzing fifteen years of school financing history. With that as a background, Kelly then projected the financial implications of the Carnegie proposals, focusing on "the three key sets of factors that determine trends in education finance: the demography of students and teachers; the economic and fiscal context of school finance; and public support for public schools."[23]

Kelly believed that the implications of the demographic changes seem manageable and that the economic context was "extremely favorable" for school finance because of "a growing economy, single digit interest rates, and negligible inflation." Although substantial increases in teacher salaries would be necessary, the fiscal and economic context was positive for increasing school revenues. Kelly stressed in his analysis that "money *per se* is not a fundamental obstacle" to the implementation of the Carnegie reforms. Kelly maintained that schools still have strong public support and their "market share" of between 85 percent and 90 percent of all student enrollment.

Contrary to much of the ongoing public discourse, the major issue to Kelly was not whether the schools could muster adequate public support or whether the existing tax base could generate adequate revenues for education. Kelly stated the case for school improvement and the Carnegie reform proposal as follows:

> Major improvement in the performance of public schools cannot be accomplished without improving the quality of the teacher work force and adopting simultaneously reforms to strengthen standards, management and productivity in schools. The rationale for major reform is not that schools lack public support, face imminent collapse, and must be saved.
>
> The reason that schools must be improved is because the overwhelming majority of American citizens—and leaders—of tomorrow will continue to be educated in the public schools. If the nation is to compete successfully in a world economy transformed by science and technology, it is the public schools which must educate the persons who will compete.[24]

For our purpose here, these reports seem to place education once again at or near the top of the national agenda. Not since the 1960s have the president, Congress, governors, state legislators, business executives, and other national leaders seemed as much in agreement that public education can and must make significant contributions to the public weal. If these convictions are, or come to be, shared by citizens generally, the public can raise aspirations for education across the land. We expect at least some movement in this direction. As we've noted, heightened aspirations frequently lead to increased resources for the schools.

SUMMARY AND FUTURE PROSPECTS

Expenditures for schools are influenced by wealth, governmental access, and aspiration. Lack of wealth results in control through deprivation and through stipulations that ordinarily accompany financial aid received from state or federal sources. The increase of governmental structure, particularly the multiplication of decision points, imposes additional controls on schools and school districts. Controls growing out of levels of aspiration are obviously a reflection of the values held by lay citizens or professionals connected with the school. There is some evidence, as Boyd has noted, to suggest that in some communities and on some issues lay values dominate, while in other communities and on other issues professional values dominate. Let us consider now some likely developments and try to discern how these may influence wealth, governmental access, or aspiration for education.

If state aid programs continue to be reformed, and this seems likely, the major variables affecting expenditures for schools will be altered. Many school districts in the low and middle ability-to-pay ranges will have more wealth or at least more potential revenue to spend for schools. Since some controls nearly always go along with state aid programs, it might be that local governmental access would become even more difficult. Moreover, with increased state support, even at the classroom level, more fiscal controls will be placed on local school districts. Improved state aid programs will provide no panacea for rising expectations, but such programs, particularly if they contain a reward-for-effort feature, will at least encourage greater aspirations. Moreover, the aspirations of the state at large tend to be substituted for the very low aspirations found in some districts.

The movement toward tax limitation is clearly an attempt to make governmental access more difficult, particularly for school districts and other units of government largely dependent on the property tax. When citizens vote for such limitations, they may also be expressing something about their aspirations for school programs or their doubts about the necessity of such programs.

Perhaps the most serious problems for the future are the diverse aspirations people have for schools and the fragmentation of public support for school programs. Several conditions contribute to this. To begin with, many citizens are disenchanted with government and with governmental agencies, including the schools. The schools have their own special problems. For instance, greatly increased federal aid, particularly for the children of the poor, has brought modest and often disappointing results. Moreover, beginning in the mid-1960s and lasting for more than a decade there was a decline in achievement test scores, particularly the SAT scores of high school students. While one can find extenuating circumstances to explain both of these developments, in the minds of many people they suggest that the school is not doing its job, and providing more money to an inept institution does not make sense to them.

A second condition contributing to differential aspirations and fragmented support is the fact that a smaller percentage of parents now have children in the public schools. Consistently, the polls show that parents with children in the public schools give higher approval ratings to the schools than do adults with no children in the public schools.

A third factor affecting aspirations and support for the public schools is the advocacy of alternatives to the public schools. The alternative movement is described in a book by Coons and Sugarman, *Education by Choice.*[25] The subtitle, *The Case for Family Control,* and the following excerpt make their position clear.

> We . . . argue that the interests of children are best served in a decentralized polity giving maximum scope to free, chosen, communal relationships that are generally organized on a small scale. Systematic domination of education by large enterprises (public or private) ought, therefore, to be disfavored. This suggests to us the strengthening of the family's role in education and the growth of a teaching fraternity which is related to the family as professional to client rather than as master to servant.[26]

In their treatment of school finance Guthrie, Garms, and Pierce, while not going as far as Coons and Sugarman, also advocate an alternative to the present system.[27] They would like to see a basic education, through full state funding, guaranteed to every child. Basic education would include reading, writing, arithmetic, and some knowledge of our democratic government and would ordinarily be completed by the end of the eighth grade. For the rest of elementary schooling parents might purchase "educational coupons" at differential rates, perhaps ten cents on the dollar for poor parents and ninety cents on the dollar for wealthy parents, to be spent on such subjects as music, art, language instruction, remedial reading, or vocational education offered by either public or private schools. In addition, each student would receive a "portable grant" that would entitle him or her to a maximum of six additional years of schooling at any public or private school at any time during a person's lifetime.

A fourth factor in this complex arena of aspirations and support is the growing concern and support for segments of the school program as opposed to the total school program. This is perhaps most pronounced in federal support given to vocational education and to education of the handicapped, both of which are discussed in Chapter 3. One aspect of the law on the handicapped illustrates the selective nature of provisions in special education: each student is to receive an individually prescribed program. Regardless of cost and regardless of the impact of such cost on the total school budget, each student is to receive such service. One can hardly deny the desirability of an individually prescribed program for a handicapped person, but what about an individually prescribed program for other students? Aspirations and support for certain types of special education have grown tremendously, sometimes at the expense of education for all.

Some of the conditions related to public aspirations and support have been affected by actions of the Reagan administration. As noted in Chapter 3, expenditures for equity programs were sharply reduced under the Educational Consolidation and Improvement Act. Moreover, the overall decrease in federal expenditures for education has shifted an even greater part of the total financial burden to state and local sources. These financial strains are being exacerbated by growing minority group populations and their increasing political pressure that government attend to equity problems. These conditions are forcing states to consider ways of increasing resources for education and some states, notably California and Florida, have enacted major financial reforms. It seems likely that these pressures and the widespread reexamination of schools, now under way, will help build a consensus in most states favoring more adequate resources for the operation of the public schools. The growing recognition by political and business leaders that education is essential to economic growth gives added assurance that this consensus will be realized, although the sources of substantial new revenues remain unclear because of the nation's unprecedented budget and trade deficits and wrenching economic transitions.

NOTES

[1] H. Thomas James, J. Alan Thomas, and Harold J. Dyck, "Wealth, Expenditure, and Decision-Making for Education," Cooperative Research Project no. 1241 (Washington, DC: U.S. Office of Education, 30 June 1963).

[2] Joel S. Berke and Michael W. Kirst, *Federal Aid to Education—Who Benefits? Who Governs?* (Lexington, MA: D.C. Heath, 1972).

[3] Ibid., 22.

[4] Committee on Education and Labor, *The Federal Government and Education* (Washington, DC: U.S. Government Printing Office, 1963), 63.

[5] Frank J. Munger and Richard F. Fenno, Jr., *National Politics of Federal Aid to Education* (Syracuse, NY: Syracuse University Press, 1962), 184.

[6] J. Alan Thomas, *School Finance and Educational Opportunity in Michigan* (Lansing: Michigan Department of Education, 1968), ch. 2.

[7] James et al., "Wealth, Expenditure and Decision-Making," ch. 7.

[8] These studies are summarized in Lawrence W. Downey, *The Task of Public Education* (Chicago: Midwest Administration Center, University of Chicago, 1960).

[9] Ibid., 65.

[10] Alex M. Gallup and David M. Clark, "The 19th Annual Poll of the Public's Attitude Toward the Public Schools," *Phi Delta Kappan* 69 (September 1987): 17–30.

[11] R. Jean Hills, "The Relationship Between Educational Expectations of Social Class Groups and the Role Expectations Within the Public High School" (Ph.D. diss., University of Chicago, 1961).

[12] David W. Minar, *Educational Decision-Making in Suburban Communities,* Cooperative Research Project No. 2440 (Evanston, IL: Northwestern University, 1966).

[13]William L. Boyd, "The Public, the Professionals, and Educational Policy Making: Who Governs?" *Teacher's College Record* 77 (May 1976): 573.

[14]Joel S. Berke et al., *Financing Equal Educational Opportunity* (Berkeley, CA: McCutchan, 1972), 23.

[15]John J. Callahan and William H. Wilken, eds., *School Finance Reform: A Legislator's Handbook* (Washington, DC: National Conference of State Legislatures, 1976), 10.

[16]Ibid., 1.

[17]Ibid., 8.

[18]Denis Doyle and Terry Hartle, *The States Take Charge* (Washington, DC: The American Enterprise Institute, 1985).

[19]Roald F. Campbell and Tim L. Mazzoni, Jr., *State Policy Making for the Public Schools* (Berkeley, CA: McCutchan, 1976), ch. 4.

[20]James W. Guthrie, "Proposition 13 and the Future of California's Schools," *Phi Delta Kappan* 60 (September 1978): 12–15.

[21]James A. Kelly, "The Public Context of Education Finance," in *Dilemmas in School Finance.* J. Alan Thomas and R. K. Wimpleberg, eds. (Chicago: Midwest Administration Center, 1978), 45–51.

[22]James A. Kelly, "Financing Education Reform," Prepared for the Task Force on Teaching as a Profession, Carnegie Forum on Education and the Economy (New York: Carnegie Corporation, 1986).

[23]Ibid., 17–18.

[24]Ibid.

[25]John E. Coons and Stephen D. Sugarman, *Education by Choice* (Berkeley, CA: University of California Press, 1978).

[26]Ibid., 2.

[27]James W. Guthrie, Walter I. Garmes, and Lawrence C. Pierce, *School Finance and Educational Policy: Enhancing Educational Efficiency, Equality, and Choice.* 2nd edition (Englewood Cliffs, NJ: Prentice Hall, 1988), 341–343.

16
College Influences

Colleges and universities have always exerted influence on the policies and programs of American schools, but the nature of this influence has varied considerably; some of it has been direct, some indirect; some of it has been purposeful, some accidental. The colleges' greatest influence obviously has been on that segment of the secondary school program to which such high status has been attached—the college preparatory program. For a time, this influence appeared to be lessening. However, the national concern for educational reform that emerged in the 1980s has been accompanied by a resurgence of college interest in and influence on secondary school programs. Much of this interest and influence stems from a new spirit of cooperation between schools and colleges that is rooted in their recognition of common concerns.

In speaking of college influences, *college* in this chapter will refer to colleges as individual institutions, groups of collegiate institutions in concert (as in the College Entrance Examination Board), and college administrators and faculty members, both in the field of education and in other disciplines.

THE HISTORICAL RELATIONSHIP

The Latin School

College influence was the most direct in the early days of American society when the sole function of the secondary school was preparation for college. An interesting but often forgotten fact is that the first secondary school in America was, in a sense, a vocational school with the exclusive function of preparing boys for the ministry. This school, the Boston Latin School, was funded in 1635, a mere five years after the city of Boston was settled. It was created to provide the same classical training that Latin Grammar schools in England had offered.

This school, like other grammar schools found primarily in the northern colonies in the seventeenth and eighteenth centuries, was established to provide the necessary background in Latin, Greek, and mathematics for admission to the colleges. The most influential early secondary schools were in Massachusetts for the Massachusetts Act of 1647 demanded that every town of 100 families maintain a Latin grammar school. As in Boston, these schools were supported by local taxation and were largely locally controlled. Despite considerable variety in these schools, they did have one thing in common: a strict and narrow classical curriculum, totally focused on knowledge. Justified primarily by long use in European nations, this curriculum was designed to provide a direct and essential road to higher education. Some towns with this type of school never sent a boy to college, but the curriculum remained the same until early in the eighteenth century when emphasis on the classical curriculum began to decline.

The influence of this early school is still with us. Spears has pointed out that the Latin grammar school bequeathed two major patterns to American secondary education: (1) the tendency of the college to dictate to the school below and (2) the concept of public support and control.[1]

Strange though it may seem, the preparatory school was created one year before the college that was to receive its students. Harvard was founded in 1636 and was the only college in New England until Yale was established sixty-five years later. Thus, for an extended period one institution set the scholastic standards and thus the curriculum for all Latin grammar schools, with this entrance requirement:

> When scholars had so far profited in the grammar schools, that they could read any classical author in English, and readily make and speak true Latin, and write it in verse as well as prose; and perfectly decline the paradigms of nouns and verbs in the Greek tongue, they were judged capable of admission in Harvard college.[2]

The Growth of Colleges

The growth of colleges in America was quite slow until the early nineteenth century, at which time many institutions of varying quality were established across the country. Regardless of the quality of the institutions, however, they all had an effect on secondary education: by requiring certain subjects as prerequisites for admission, they set the curriculum for the lower schools.[3]

Of course this influence worked in a variety of ways. If a certain standard of Latin and Greek was demanded by a college, schools with students interested in attending that institution developed curricula to meet this standard. If a college admitted students without much attention to their prior scholarly achievements, secondary schools in the area languished and the college itself was in effect the secondary school. Other colleges developed their own "preparatory departments," which trained boys just out of the common schools, a practice that stifled the public or independent secondary school. Thus, the school that trained students for college had "a course of study. . . fashioned by the influence of the college to suit the purposes of the college."[4]

The Academies and the Common High Schools

With the rise of the middle class in the early eighteenth century, the Latin grammar school and the curriculum it offered began to lose favor with large sections of society. Other types of secondary schools began to emerge. The proposals put forth by Benjamin Franklin in 1743 for the education of youth in Pennsylvania stimulated the development of the Public Academy in the city of Philadelphia in 1751. The diversified or differentiated programs of the modern high school have their roots in this academy as Franklin's liberal views on education were reflected in this school.[5] Franklin's recommended curriculum was far broader than that of the Latin grammar school, with emphasis on English, geography, history, even ancient and modern languages, but only as they were thought useful to the individual. Included as electives were such previously ignored subjects as surveying, merchants' accounts, gauging, navigation, and drawing perspective.

The concept of the academy as a publicly supported institution spread quickly, particularly among those people to whom the Latin school did not appeal. Academies grew rapidly in all parts of the country after the Revolutionary War until about 1850. They were established most often by private or local initiative, chartered by the state, and financed by taxes, endowments, state grants, and fees. There was a great variety of institutions. Some academies—Phillips Andover was one of the first—were hardly distinguishable from Latin schools. Others provided secondary schooling for girls for the first time. Some emphasized commercial work, others teacher training.

Despite this diversity, a basic assumption of most of the academies was that many of their students would go on to college, and thus the curriculum for college entrance remained very important, if not predominant, and continued to be controlled by college entrance requirements. The academy, however, introduced "practical" studies, provided education for children from many different social groups, and broadened the aims and content of education.[6]

In the latter half of the nineteenth century, the influence of the academy declined. With the fight for free primary education won by 1850 and with the public high school the dominant form of secondary education by 1890, the role of the academy underwent an ironic shift. In 1885 the NEA Commission on Secondary Education commended the academy for its important works and pointed out there was still room for the academy but stated that the high school was taking over many of its important functions. In considering the task of the academy in American education, the commission stated, "This work will be largely, though not exclusively, in preparing youth for college." Thus the institution that was created because of dissatisfaction with the college preparatory character of the Latin school was destined to evolve into the kind of school against which it had made its original protest. In recent times the nation's independent secondary schools, directly descended from the early academy, have sent nearly all of their graduates to college.

Although there were many other types of schools and many variations within these types, the Latin grammar schools on the one hand and the academies and common schools on the other illustrate the two distinct traditions in American secondary education, one classical and linguistic and the other practical and vocational. The colleges and hence the Latin schools equated education with mastery of Greek, Latin, and mathematics in the tradition of Western education since the Renaissance. The academies and the common schools saw education more in terms of direct application and provided training in subjects that appear to be immediately useful to the students of the day. The public high school drew on both of these approaches. As an extension of the common school it reflected the practical demands of its sponsors on local school boards and therefore provided training in English, commercial subjects, and history; as a school preparing students for college and as an institution aspiring to the social status of the Latin school, it provided course work in the classical languages and mathematics. Thus the public high schools that emerged contained elements of both of the traditions of secondary education.[7]

New Disciplines

In the late nineteenth century industrialization and the rapid growth of cities led to major changes in the nature of American society. The growing importance of science as an intellectual movement also was affecting society, albeit in a different manner. Darwin's *On the Origin of Species,* published in 1859, and other works that followed, particularly those of Herbert Spencer, had significant impact on education as well as on American life.[8] The work of Spencer in linking evolutionary theory to social institutions, G. Stanley Hall in child development, William James in psychology and philosophy, among others, provided the theoretical underpinnings for the subsequent progressive education movement. At the same time the scientific approach was gaining acceptance and other scholars were producing new knowledge in the physical, natural, and social sciences. Even seminars on "scientific history" were being given by Herbert Baxter Evans at Johns Hopkins University. These developments caused problems for the schools. The scholars in many of these new disciplines sought time for their subjects to be offered in the lower schools—time that had to be taken from the old and time-honored subjects.[9] The ultimate question then, as now, was: what should the school teach?

One way to answer this question was simply to expand the number of subjects offered, and this is indeed what happened in the public high schools between 1865 and 1900.[10] As new subjects were added to the curriculum and new course organizations were devised to cope with the needs of an increasingly diverse high school population, the program of the high school became chaotic. With no model to provide order to the work of the high school, each community selected features that seemed best in the local situation, some operating a high school with a four-year program and others providing for three or even two years of study. As Edwards and Richey point out, the entrance requirements of the college served to bring some degree of uniformity to high school programs,[11] although there was a growing need for a more highly standardized institution.

The Committee of Ten

This state of disorganization prompted the National Education Association to appoint the Committee of Ten in 1892 to consider problems confronting secondary education. Once again Harvard was to play an important role through the efforts of its president, Charles W. Eliot. He spoke at the NEA convention in St. Paul in 1890, calling for major reforms in the high school, including strict supervision by state inspectors and the adoption of a uniform system of examinations in college preparatory courses. Eliot said that "the schools need to be brought to common and higher standards, so that the colleges may find in the school courses a firm, broad, and reasonably homogeneous foundation for their higher work."[12]

Eliot, easily the most powerful voice in higher education of the day, was selected as chairman of the Committee of Ten. The charge given the committee was to consider the problems of secondary education. The composition of the committee suggests the dimensions of the problem seen in 1892 for five of the ten were college presidents, one was a college professor, and two others were headmasters of eastern preparatory schools.

Not surprisingly, their report concentrated on the problems of preparing students for college entrance. They stated that the committee recognized that the secondary schools, taken as a group, do not exist solely for the purpose of preparing students for college and that, indeed, only an insignificant percentage of the graduates would go to college. However, the recommendations made no distinction between the college-bound and the terminal student. The report declared that "every subject which is taught at all in a secondary school should be taught in the same way and to the same extent to every pupil so long as he pursues it, no matter what the probable destination of the pupil may be, or at what point his education is to cease."

The Committee of Ten suggested the following subjects were appropriate for the high schools: (1) languages—Latin, Greek, English, German, and French (and locally Spanish); (2) mathematics—algebra, geometry, and trigonometry; (3) general history and intensive study of special epochs; (4) natural history—including descriptive astronomy, meteorology, botany, zoology, physiology, geology, and ethnology; and (5) physics and chemistry. The committee also made three recommendations with respect to the organization of the secondary school curriculum: (1) organize a number of different curricula, such as classical, Latin-scientific, modern languages, and English; (2) introduce the elective system; and (3) define a unit of instruction in terms of the number of hours of instruction given per week in the subject.

The publication of the report caused a considerable stir in educational circles. Numerous articles assessed the findings. The British government even sought the advice of the committee on comparable British problems. Schools throughout the United States changed their courses to conform wholly or in part with the committee's recommendations.

For better or for worse, the report had great influence, influence that has persisted to the present day.[13] In transmitting the report to the secretary of the interior for government publication, Commissioner of Education William T. Harris called it "the most important document ever published in this country." Many others of the time agreed.

Some, however, were dubious and even caustically critical of the report, believing that the committee, in using armchair methods, had served only to increase the traditionalist viewpoint in secondary education and had overlooked the fact that American society was undergoing radical changes.[14] Writing in 1950, Spears admitted the far-reaching influence of the report with these bitter words: "National education bodies, the Commissioner of Education, College presidents, and complacent school administrators were apparently willing, at the turn of the century, to sell the birthright of the American public high school for a pot of college-preparatory pottage."[15]

Sizer observed more recently,

> The fractional curriculum that the high schools have inherited from the 1890s serves us poorly. To reconstruct it will infuriate many academic scholars, scare many teachers who have been trained by those scholars, and send shivers of apprehension down the spines of parents. The core academic structure of high school, legitimized by the Committee of Ten in 1893 maintains a ferocious hold on our thinking.[16]

This college-dominated committee thus had a profound and long-lasting effect on the secondary schools, the most influential outcome perhaps being the standardization imposed upon the high school. Its influence is still apparent in the curriculum recommendations of national study groups and institutions of higher education. Whatever the merit of Sizer's lament, it and his suggestions for reform are less likely to be heeded by state and local boards of education than the recommendations of college officials for additional academic units.

The Cardinal Principles

The Commission on the Reorganization of Secondary Education shifted emphasis to reflect broader social concern when it presented the famous "Cardinal Principles of Secondary Education" in 1918. This commission set the following as the main goals of education: (1) health, (2) command of fundamental processes, (3) worthy home membership, (4) vocation, (5) citizenship, (6) worthy use of leisure, and (7) ethical character.

The composition of this commission indicated that the influence of the colleges had diminished. Eleven members made up the commission, which was chaired by Clarence D. Kingsley, Massachusetts State High School Supervisor. The U.S. Commissioner of Education, P. P. Claxton, was a member. One college president was included, Edward O. Sisson of Montana, but he had spent most of his professional life in the public schools. Three men were professors of education, and the rest were involved in the administration of secondary schools. Spears, who was so caustic in his criticism of the college-dominated Committee of Ten, spoke of the commission in the following manner: "The work of this group came from the active field of secondary education itself, not from the easy chairs in a college conference room far removed from the give-and-take of a public secondary school."[17] Although the "Cardinal Principles" have been criticized for being too general, they have been very influential in the development of curricula at the elementary and secondary level down to the present day.

COLLEGE INFLUENCES ON SCHOOL PROGRAMS

The College Entrance Examination Board

Many of the people who had been influential in the report of the Committee of Ten were also to play a major role in the formation in 1900 of the College Entrance Examination Board. This board was "in its origins an attempt to introduce law and order into an educational anarchy which towards the close of the nineteenth century had become exasperating, indeed almost intolerable, to schoolmasters. The basic trouble lay in a lack of cooperation among colleges as a group and between colleges and secondary schools on the matter of college admissions."[18]

In 1877 Harvard President Eliot had suggested, with no apparent effect, that the colleges should cooperate to standardize admission practices. In 1894, speaking to the New England Association, he made the specific suggestion that the colleges organize a board of examiners to conduct admissions examinations all over the country.

The most scathing indictment of the general disorder in education, however, was made by a secondary school administrator, William Farrand of Newark Academy, in his 1895 inaugural address as president of the Schoolmasters Association of New York and vicinity. In a speech titled "The Reform of College Entrance Requirements" he ridiculed the inconsistencies in the entrance requirements of Harvard, Yale, Princeton, and Columbia, and he illustrated how influential these requirements were on the curriculum of his school. Fuess has abstracted his remarks as follows:

> The more closely we examine the details, the more marked are the differences. For instance, Princeton and Columbia call for six books of the *Aeneid:* Yale requires, in addition, the *Eclogues.* These do not count for maximum standing at Princeton unless combined with the *Georgics.* The elementary Algebra requirement at Harvard is less than is exacted of students at Princeton and Yale; her advanced requirement is greater. . . .
>
> When we come to the Scientific Schools, the discrepancies are even greater. Princeton requires Latin of candidates for one course, but not for the others. Yale demands it of all, Columbia of none. Princeton names five books of Caesar and four orations of Cicero; Yale names four books of Caesar and three books of Virgil. . . . Yale calls for Botany, Columbia for Physics and Chemistry, Princeton for no science. Princeton and Columbia demand both German and French, while Yale is satisfied with either. On the other hand, while Princeton and Columbia demand only American History, Yale calls also for that of England. . . .
>
> For our Princeton boys we must include a review of Arithmetic and carry Algebra farther than is required by Harvard or Columbia; for Yale we must read the Bucolics and study Logarithms and their applications to geometrical problems; for Harvard we must supply a thorough course in Physics. . . . Look again for a moment at the requirements in science. Harvard puts on a stiff requirement in Physics and Chemistry, Yale calls for Botany, Cornell for Physiology.[19]

Farrand was named as one of the original secondary school representatives of the CEEB in 1900 and was actively involved with the board until his death in 1942. According to Fuess, the original idea for the board came from Eliot, but translation of it into action was largely due to the spirit and work of Nicholas Murray Butler. In 1960 the president of the CEEB pointed out that the original board system was based on the concept of college control of the curriculum.[20]

The first examinations, prepared by representatives of both colleges and the secondary schools, were given in June of 1901 to 973 candidates who wrote 7,889 papers. At that time twelve institutions of higher learning were members. By 1977 there were more than 2,400 members of the CEEB.[21] Secondary schools have been eligible for full membership since 1959. The board's membership and services have grown to include meetings and conferences throughout the year; the development of an extensive program of tests and examinations; the supervision and sponsorship of numerous research projects in the field of measurements, testing, and psychology; the support of the College Scholarship Service; and the publication of informational and interpretive guidance materials. Since 1947 the operational phases of the college board's testing have been conducted by Educational Testing Service.

The best known activity of the college board is probably the various college entrance and guidance examinations it administers to secondary school students. In 1986–87 the board gave approximately 1,800,000 admissions tests through its Scholastic Aptitude Test (SAT) Program to prospective college students. An important addition to the program in 1971–72 was the Student Descriptive Questionnaire (SDQ), which enabled prospective students to share information about their interests, experiences, and future plans with colleges to which they applied. This addition reflects the college board's understanding that institutions are increasingly concerned with personal factors in addition to test scores in making selection decisions.[22] In 1980, the college board began its Educational Equality Project, a ten-year effort that has provided materials designed to strengthen secondary school offerings. The initial publication of the project, *Academic Preparation for College,* identified the academic skills required for college success in six basic subject areas. Subsequent publications have provided suggestions to teachers for strengthening the curriculum in each of those areas.

Thousands of students take other tests each year in addition to or instead of the SAT. For example, nearly a million high school seniors are examined by the American College Testing Program (ACT) every year. Schurdson notes that the ACT's examination measures similar skills as the college board aptitude tests and that scores from it are utilized most often by colleges and universities located in the Middle West and parts of the South and West.[23]

Although the number of high school students who take these tests continues to increase, questions are being raised about their effectiveness in helping colleges make admissions decisions.[24] Indeed, some highly selective institutions have reduced their reliance on the tests. Nonetheless, use of the tests continues to be important in college and university decision making. In addition, the selection patterns established by colleges provide a record that can be useful to students in determining the particular colleges to which they will apply.

Testing Programs

One facet of the tendency toward national standardization is the desire to have students do well on the various tests and therefore to attempt to "teach to the test." Early evidence on this point was provided by Brickell's study of change in New York State. Serving as a Consultant on Educational Experimentation to the Commissioner of Education he reported the following observations:

> The Regents Examinations, beyond any question whatsoever, inhibit change in the State of New York. Serious students of the matter could hardly debate the point.
>
> During May and June of 1961, the Consultant visited hundreds of high school classrooms, heard what was being discussed by teachers and students, saw what was written on the blackboards, looked at the books being used in the class, noted the other books students were carrying under their arms to other classes, talked briefly with many teachers and at length with many administrators. He offers this observation based on those visits: *Copies of previous Regents Examinations constitute at least ten percent of the curriculum* in the typical high school course (the old examinations are the material studied for approximately four weeks out of forty). The hesitancy of many schools to break this successful pattern of preparing for Regents Examinations tends to dampen their enthusiasm for innovations which are distinctive in content or in approach.[25]

Thus we have in effect a double indictment of the influence of examinations. Not only do the schools explicitly teach on the basis of previous examinations, but they tend to avoid experimentation with new materials or methods because such innovations might involve knowledge not covered by the examination and conceivably could result in a poor record for the school on the tests. Others assert that tests are not sufficiently valid and reliable to be used as readily as they are in making decisions of great significance to both individuals and society.[26]

A study by La Vigne on the impact of the National Merit Scholarship Program on the public high school revealed that this impact has assumed several expressions.[27] One of the most well-known results of participation is the rating of high schools by patrons in the district. Such a rating turns the program into an external measuring device to determine the relative quality of the high schools. Partially because of the impact of such ratings, a second result has been the use of a variety of coaching methods designed to "produce" scholars.

Another reaction of school personnel is the recognition of the National Merit Scholarship Program as a part of the multitest approach to college admissions and scholarships. High school staff members questioned the wisdom of so many tests. However, because community expectations required them to participate in this program, they felt the freedom to withdraw had been curtailed.

The program was accepted as a key to other scholarship possibilities and as an aid to college admission. The value of the National Merit Scholarship Qualifying Test as a guidance tool, however, was quite limited, apparently because of the variety and numbers of tests already available for such purposes, but it was considered valuable for raising the academic incentive of some students. Finally, La Vigne discovered that respondents disagree with some of the program's policies and procedures, particularly with respect to the selection process, which removes the selection of scholarship winners from the control of local school personnel. We know of no follow-up to La Vigne's study, which was completed nearly thirty years ago. Our impression, however, is that her findings continue to be applicable. The National Merit Scholarship Program is firmly established: in 1986–87, nearly 1,600,000 students took the qualifying examination.

Scores on the SAT declined on a national basis in recent years until 1982. Public notice of this decline has resulted in considerable pressure on public school systems. College and university personnel in particular decry the alleged low ability levels of entering freshmen and the resulting growth in demand for remedial courses at the college level. While a comprehensive study of this phenomenon found that the causes for test score decline were complex and rooted in the general society,[28] many persons and national study groups nevertheless continue to point to these scores as evidence of school failure. By 1986, the average combined score (verbal and mathematics) had risen to 906 from a low of 890 in 1980 and 1981. This matched the average score in 1975 but was substantially below the averages for the 1960s, all of which exceeded 950.

Decline in SAT scores has also fueled the argument for statewide competency testing. More than thirty states have enacted legislation dealing with competency testing. Perhaps the most far-reaching legislation of this type exists in Florida, where all students must now pass a state-designed test to receive a high school diploma. In the first year the test was given, many students failed and criticisms were levied at the test as well as at the schools.[29]

The idea of using standardized achievement tests in the nation's high schools has long been favored by a large majority of the American public according to a survey conducted by the American Institute of Public Opinion. According to one early proposal, tests would be given to all freshmen and seniors to measure their degree of achievement and to compare this with achievement levels of other high schools throughout the country. Proponents of the plan said it would stimulate greater effort in communities whose scores fell below the national average. Those opposed feared it would control the local school curriculum by creating widespread conformity and would put schools that deviate from the subject matter of the tests at a disadvantage, according to institute director George Gallup. The proposal was favored by 77 percent of a representative cross section of the public, opposed by 13 percent, and 10 percent had no opinion.[30] More recent evidence suggests that the public continues to believe that such testing is a good idea. A 1986 Gallup survey found that 77 percent of the population favored national tests of educational achievement, 16 percent opposed such tests, and 7 percent had no opinion.[31]

Whether the influence of tests on curriculum is a trend to be applauded or deplored, it is a force that cannot be ignored. Those responsible for the construction and administration of such tests are among the most vocal critics of those practices whereby teachers "teach for the tests" and are constantly seeking ways to construct examinations to minimize this possibility.

Nevertheless, the pressure to consider test results is always on the schools. Increased opportunities to attend community colleges and the freedom to consider options to university attendance may have decreased the visibility of this pressure somewhat in recent years. A more recent development that may offset this, however, is renewed college and university interest in awarding scholarships on the basis of merit rather than need. Insofar as institutions of higher education employ test scores as indicators of merit, secondary schools may experience increased pressure from parents to prepare students who do well on the tests.

Yet another pressure on secondary schools and their students to do well on standardized tests came from a 1986 decision by the National Collegiate Athletic Association. Beginning in the fall of 1987, college athletes have been required to score at least 700 on the SAT or 15 on the ACT to be eligible for NCAA competition as freshmen. As a result, several outstanding athletes have lost a year of college eligibility. While some assert that this rule has been unfair to university athletes, there is evidence that it has led many high school students to place greater emphasis on academic success. Without question, it has introduced a new set of pressures for students to perform on standardized tests.

The Advanced Placement Program

Another activity of the college board that has had considerable influence on the lower schools is the Advanced Placement Program, which provides examinations for gifted students who have completed college level work in high school. Students who pass these examinations enter college at the sophomore level in the appropriate subject areas. The number of students who take this test has increased from 1,229 from 104 secondary schools in 1955 to 319,224 students from 7,201 schools in 1986.[32] The tests are offered to students in one-third of the nation's high schools, and nearly two-thirds of American colleges and universities offer some kind of advanced placement credit. Participation in the Advanced Placement Program has increased dramatically in recent years; for example, the increase was more than 13 percent from 1985 to 1986. These facts bear out Howe's observation that the Advanced Placement Program has more potential for a permanent effect on secondary education than any of the other activities of the college board.[33] He saw three major advantages to the program: the secondary schools involved have a new grasp of what colleges want; colleges have a new respect for what can be accomplished in secondary school; and many able students have new opportunities for a more stimulating education. He went on to point out that the Advanced Placement Program is a graphic demonstration of the influence of the college on the secondary school. However, because the ends are worthy and the means have involved cooperation rather than dictation, he says that the issue of undesirable control by the colleges has never been a major problem. The tests are offered in a broad range of subjects and are taken most often in English literature and composition, American history, calculus, biology, European history, and chemistry.

Changing Admissions Standards

During the 1960s and 1970s, a number of colleges and universities relaxed their admission standards. Other state institutions have traditionally maintained a policy of open admissions toward graduates of high schools in their respective states.

Societal pressures and incentives to attend college have led increasing numbers of high school graduates with lackluster academic backgrounds to enter these colleges and universities. Some took academic courses in high school and did poorly. Others focused their high school preparation in vocational subjects or "soft" electives either because they made a late decision to attend college, or knowing that a high school diploma would assure them of admission to college, they sought an easier curriculum that would enable them to get better grades and have more time for a part-time job or extracurricular activities. One consequence of these developments has been an increase in the number of students who require remedial instruction at colleges and universities. At some state institutions, more than 50 percent of the freshman class enrolls in pre-college level English or mathematics classes.

Faculty members, administrators, and boards of trustees have expressed growing concern at the number of students who enter college with insufficient preparation and the corresponding need to offer pre-college course work to these students. The result has been sweeping changes in admission requirements to state colleges and universities. A 1982 survey by the National Association of Secondary School Principals found that the state universities in twenty-seven states had recently increased their admissions requirements or were reviewing the possibility of doing so.[34] Some of these changes reflect increased test score, class rank, or class average requirements. However, most of them focus on course requirements and call for students to take additional credits in mathematics, science, English, and social science. For example, the new pre-college curriculum in Kentucky requires students to complete four years of English rather than three, three years of mathematics rather than two, two years of science, and world history in addition to American history.

Such changes have implications for the budgets as well as the curricula of secondary schools. Increasing requirements for science and mathematics will require some small schools to add courses they do not presently teach; to teach them they may have to add faculty members. Virtually all schools will find their response to these changes complicated by the shortage of science and mathematics teachers.

These changes, though expensive initially, should have long-range benefits, according to experts. Thomson points out that the changes may have a "salutary effect upon student attitudes" and he encourages parents to be more vigorous advocates for improved academic standards.[35]

New Developments in Curriculum

Another arena within which the college influence is significant is the development of new curricula in many areas. An important catalytic agent in creating organizations to stimulate and support new curriculum developments has been the National Science Foundation. Though a relatively recent force (established in 1950), the resources of the NSF have had a profound impact. Its budget for educational purposes grew from $1.5 million in 1952 to approximately $116 million in 1981 but had been reduced to $85 million by 1986. By the early 1960s the foundation was supporting extensive programs in the following areas: (1) financial aid for graduate students, advanced scholars, and teachers in seven basic fellowship programs; (2) supplemental training of teachers of science, mathematics, and engineering through an institute program; (3) improvement in the subject matter of science and mathematics, particularly in the high schools, through financing major curriculum studies; and (4) identification and motivation of talented high school and undergraduate science students through a variety of special programs.

The foundation's policy lends support to university scholars and professional scientists and has thereby greatly strengthened the role of these groups in effecting educational change. The foundation also provides support for the continuing education of elementary and secondary school teachers. For example, more than 12,000 science and math teachers took part in NSF training programs during 1981.[36] More recent concern about science and mathematics teaching resulted in NSF funding additional teacher institutes beginning in the summer of 1984. In addition, NSF provided $5 million of increased support for research on teaching, learning, and cognition beginning in 1983–84. This allocation was a direct response to congressional and public concern about mathematics and science education. In 1983, NSF published the report of the National Science Board's Commission on Precollege Education in Mathematics, Science and Technology. The report called for a "series of major strategic actions" and heavy federal involvement in responding to the nation's mathematics, science, and technology problems. Recent projects supported by NSF include development of a new high school chemistry course, CHEMCOM, through the American Chemical Society; an early elementary curriculum project stressing experiments and computers in cooperation with the Technical Education Research Centers group in Cambridge, Massachusetts, several public school systems, and the National Geographic Society; and a series of traveling museum exhibits for school children.[37]

The National Endowment for the Humanities was established in 1965. While it has had much less money than NSF, the endowment has awarded grants to strengthen teaching and curricula in the humanities for elementary and secondary schools as well as colleges and universities. Grants are available to provide teacher institutes, develop new curricula, and support demonstration projects for a limited time. In 1985, NEH allocated nearly $10 million to such activities.[38] For example, NEH has supported a number of summer institutes on college and university campuses where elementary and secondary teachers study advanced topics in the universities with leading scholars.

Most of the developmental work in these new approaches has been done by or in collaboration with college scholars from the appropriate disciplines. Teachers in the secondary and elementary schools were involved in a variety of ways both in the development and try-out of materials, but the major thrust undeniably came from college personnel. These new programs have exerted strong and direct influence particularly in the sciences.

Accrediting Agencies

Another source of rather direct college influence on the secondary school is the accrediting agency, which over the years has been motivated by the desire to create more uniformity and standardization in the kinds of programs provided by the public schools. Accreditation simply means that a given school meets the criteria for a "good" school as determined by a particular agency. Historically, three dominant groups, through accrediting, have had a direct influence on the educational programs of the schools. These groups are universities, national and regional accrediting associations, and state departments of education.

The growth of the high school and the corresponding increase in the number of applicants to colleges created a need for the colleges to standardize the subject requirements for entrance as well as to measure the qualifications of the teachers offering these subjects. Thus in 1871 the University of Michigan introduced a system of admitting without examination the graduates of high schools that had been inspected and approved. Soon after this, regional and national accreditation grew as a voluntary movement because universities could not visit out-of-state schools from which graduates were seeking admission. State universities have provided leadership in this process of voluntary accrediting and have continued to play a dominant role.[39]

At present there are six regional associations. These associations, and the year of their creation, are as follows: The New England Association of Colleges and Secondary Schools (1885), the Middle States Association of Colleges and Secondary Schools (1892), the North Central Association of Colleges and Secondary Schools (1895), the Southern Association of Secondary Schools and Colleges (1895), the Northwest Association of Secondary and Higher Schools (1918), and the Western Association of Secondary Schools and Colleges (1930).

Clearly, accrediting agencies have had a visible impact on the program of the secondary school, particularly in their early years. At first, accreditation focused solely on the college preparatory program, and the universities exercised inordinate control by specifying entrance requirements so detailed there was no room for local initiative. This university influence was so pervasive and indeed oppressive that the state departments of education joined the high schools in a resistance movement. In midwestern states resistance took the form of admission provisions to state universities, which were under the control of state departments of education. In a study of state standardization, Henry H. Hill identified two main issues that he said have been fought out among the universities, high schools, and state departments of education.[40] First, who shall accredit, or standardize, the university or the state department? Second, who shall determine the high school curriculum, the university or the high school?

On the first issue, the movement at the state level has been almost entirely in the direction of the state department. On the second issue, there is still no final answer. The accrediting associations today, while still strongly influenced by collegiate personnel, have granted extensive participation in policy decisions to representatives of the secondary schools.

In addition, the original purpose of accreditation has undergone a significant change. No longer is college preparation the sole, or even major, concern. Rather, standards are set for total school operations to meet the needs of all pupils. Among the areas in which standards are considered are: housing, libraries, length of class period and school year, graduation requirements, teacher qualifications, equipment, guidance, administration, teaching load, and records. Through these standards, agencies seek to ensure overall program quality rather than specific college entrance requirements.[41] The standards are not goals to be sought but really represent floors to be maintained. The determination of these floors is not a matter of local initiative but a matter of outside authority. The local educator is perfectly free to rise as far above this foundation as is possible.

James B. Conant noted the influence of accrediting standards in the enforcement of teacher certification standards and regulations.[42] After examining state department action, he reported that Ohio has revoked high school charters because schools have poorly prepared faculties, Missouri will restudy a school's classification if too many teachers are not adequately trained, and Illinois will threaten loss of accreditation if too many faculty members have been granted temporary approvals. He also specifically cited the Commission on Secondary Schools of the North Central Association; he said this group, with its authority to accredit schools in nineteen states, wielded tremendous power and has its own certification requirements.

Preparation of Teachers and Administrators

Schools depend on colleges and universities to supply them with their professional employees. This practice is legitimated across the fifty states by professional certification requirements embodied in state codes. As noted in Chapter 4, the enforcement of certification standards is an important responsibility of state education officials. Certification standards generally require prospective educators to hold college or university degrees and to have credit for particular courses in professional education. In one state, for example, a prospective elementary teacher must have a bachelor's degree and credit for at least twenty-nine semester hours in course work dealing with (1) the learner and the learning process, (2) the school in relation to society, (3) elementary school curriculum methods including the teaching of reading, and (4) laboratory experiences including student teaching. The same requirements specify particular general education areas (e.g., visual art, English and communication arts) in which candidates must amass at least sixty semester hours.

Such requirements ensure that teacher education institutions have considerable impact upon professional employment in schools. School systems share in teacher preparation to a limited extent through the supervision of practice teaching and other field-based components in preparation programs. For the most part, however, teacher preparation tends to be campus based. Indeed, some critics have charged that the way teachers are educated in colleges and universities is one of the most fundamental problems in American education. Among the most influential recent critics are the Holmes Group and the Carnegie task force, which both called for discontinuing undergraduate programs in teacher education.[43] They would require that all prospective teachers complete an undergraduate degree in liberal arts followed by a professional degree in teaching. Members of the Holmes Group, a consortium of approximately 100 research universities, and some other institutions are revising their programs accordingly.

In addition to providing education for prospective teachers and administrators, colleges and universities also serve as screening or selection agents for the profession. This screening function was not very prominent in the case of teachers for many years. As long as there was a teacher shortage, institutions of higher education were relatively open in allowing students to acquire teaching credentials. More recently, and sometimes in response to state mandates, many institutions have become more selective in their admission policies. Such action naturally raises the question of criteria for entry to preparation programs and the effect of such screening on the choices available to school districts as they select teachers. Programs to prepare administrators are graduate programs and, as such, have traditionally been more selective than teacher preparation programs. The impact of such selection procedures is largely unknown, but they determine the pool from which school districts select their leaders.

The influence of teacher education institutions upon the selection and preparation of prospective educational leaders has been strongly criticized from two different perspectives. Some charge that certification requirements and college education courses are unduly parochial and serve primarily to prevent persons whose education and experience may be in fields outside education from holding positions for which they may have the abilities. The basic argument is that teaching or administration involves skills that can be learned apart from colleges of education and that those who possess such skills should be allowed to use them. Persons who hold this view are often more critical of state certification arrangements than college preparation efforts and seek to have them changed.

A second kind of criticism comes primarily from teachers themselves, who, often through their professional associations, claim that control over preparation of educators should shift from the campuses and state certification departments to the profession itself. To this end, some now advocate the establishment of professional practice boards made up primarily if not entirely of teachers to oversee preparation programs in the respective states. They have also been strong supporters of federally supported teacher education centers to provide in-service preparation for teachers under the aegis of teacher-dominated policy boards.

Criticism of teacher education reached a new crescendo following the 1983 reports of the National Commission on Excellence in Education and other commissions. These reports noted that students entering teacher education programs during the past decade had low ACT and SAT scores in comparison to students entering other fields, and that the most able graduates of teacher education programs do not remain classroom teachers.[44] They also noted that the nation faces a serious shortage of qualified science and mathematics teachers. Officials in some states, including New Jersey and Texas, have responded to this situation by enacting legislation that provides that liberal arts graduates who pass certain examinations and complete internships or similar experiences be certified to teach despite their lack of formal teacher education. A total of forty-four states have mandated competency examinations for prospective teachers, and at least two (Alabama and Florida) require the closing of any teacher education program that graduates substantial numbers of students who fail these examinations.[45] It is too early to assess the implications of those policies already in place or to determine what other changes are likely in teacher education. However, there is little doubt that the capacity of schools to respond to particular demands or curriculum opportunities is dependent on the presence of able teachers. Whatever changes occur in teacher education, colleges and universities will probably continue to be involved in this process.

Colleges and universities also have an impact on teachers already in service as well as on persons preparing for the role. Many take courses at night during the school year or attend special workshops or summer sessions. Attendance at such sessions is often stimulated by salary schedules that reward teachers for extra course work, but many attend primarily to improve their teaching skills and understandings. In recent years, colleges and universities have redirected substantial resources to in-service programs for existing teachers. At the same time, teacher associations have lobbied successfully for changes in certification requirements and salary schedules that reward teachers for district or teacher center in-service activities as well as for university credits. One consequence of this may be to help redirect college and university resources to reflect greater concern with the day-to-day problems of the schools.

Further impetus for university attention to public school problems is the growing recognition by university presidents that colleges and universities have an important stake in helping to strengthen public schools. For example, the presidents of Stanford, Harvard, the University of Chicago, Columbia University, the University of Wisconsin, and the University of Michigan showed their concern for and commitment to public schools by meeting in the summer of 1983 and issuing a joint statement, which said:

> . . . universities must play an active role if we are to ensure excellence in a full system of primary and secondary schools. As university educators, we have a special concern for the centrality of academic objectives in the schools, and for the importance of teaching as an activity. We therefore welcome a role as partner and advocate for our colleagues in the public schools.[46]

SUMMARY AND FUTURE PROSPECTS

The controls colleges and universities have exercised in the past over public schools have been of three basic kinds. They have established expectations, developed curriculum materials, and prepared personnel to work in the schools. College and university expectations for schools have often been formalized through admission requirements. College admission controls are in a state of flux. As more and more students sought higher education, colleges and universities became more selective in their admissions policies. For example, some state universities that formerly admitted any graduate of an accredited high school in their state began to limit enrollment in the 1960s to students who achieved a particular class rank or certain scores on standardized examinations. Many private schools also became more selective. However, the end of the postwar baby boom, escalating college costs, and the pursuit of other alternatives by students have lessened the competition for admission to many institutions. Indeed, some have been forced to close for lack of students. At the same time, some institutions continue to be selective, and the competition for scholarship assistance is mounting as merit again becomes a criterion for such aid. These developments suggest that standardized admissions tests will continue to be important.

One response to the growing public interest in and growing cost of higher education has been the expansion of community and junior colleges. By making higher education available to virtually all high school graduates who wish it, these institutions are now fulfilling one of the original purposes of the land grant colleges, which in many instances have become more selective in admissions policies. The presence of two-year colleges and the pressure for open admissions in some public institutions are evidence of American unwillingness to have a system of higher education that serves only an elite. Financial factors as well as demands to expand enrollment possibilities will probably increase the prominence of these institutions. The rising costs of colleges and universities have led to an upward spiral in tuition rates in public and even more so in private colleges and universities. As further increases are likely, students will probably try to economize by attending nearby public institutions.

Many public as well as private institutions of higher education are presently experiencing financial difficulty. Like some elementary and secondary school districts, these four-year institutions of higher education are confronted with rising costs but declining enrollments. Particularly as opportunities to obtain federal and foundation support dwindle, these institutions will place more pressure on state legislatures for financial support. This may bring them into greater and more open competition with elementary and secondary schools for state tax dollars. Thus the need for improved interlevel cooperation will become more apparent.[47]

Part of the competition for state resources between institutions of higher education and public schools involves college and university claims for money to support developmental or basic education. In making this claim, institutions of higher education point to the deficiencies in basic skills that characterize large numbers of incoming freshmen. By calling attention to declining SAT scores and low scores on local placement tests, colleges and universities help structure public expectations for schools. To a considerable extent, it has been college and university personnel who have made the public aware of the problems in teaching basic skills. The public response has been to demand improved performance by the schools.

Despite the increased competition for state resources, an increase in programmatic cooperation is likely between schools and universities. Such cooperation will focus on improving teaching and learning to alleviate the basic skills deficiencies of entering college freshmen and to provide enrichment opportunities for especially able students. A number of schools and universities have already established cooperative relationships to foster curriculum development, teacher preparation, part-time jobs for high school students, and high school courses for college credit.[48]

One promising strategy for school-university collaboration is the establishment of academic alliances in which secondary and postsecondary teachers of a particular discipline in a common geographical area meet regularly to consider topics of common interest. The American Association for Higher Education received a grant in 1988 from the MacArthur Foundation to expand academic alliances across the nation. The project intends to increase the number of alliances in the country from approximately 250 in 1988 to 750 by 1992.[49]

The final kind of control colleges and universities have exercised over public schools has been in the preparation of teachers and other school personnel. For many years higher education has had a virtual monopoly over both preservice and in-service preparation of educators. There are signs that this may be changing. One response of public school personnel to criticisms of their efforts has been to blame colleges of education for inadequate preparation. Thus tension has developed between school and university personnel over questions of how teachers should be educated and by whom.[50] Another response of teachers and administrators, however, has been a growing tendency to look away from the university and toward their peers for in-service education. The establishment of teacher education centers has been an important development in this area.

As we look to the future, it is tempting to predict that competition for scarce resources and the continuation of educational problems that are more readily criticized than remedied will produce further strain on school-university relationships. To be sure, the university dominance that characterized early twentieth-century relationships has deservedly been put to rest. What remains to be firmly established, however, is the kind of balanced relationship in which school and university personnel recognize that they have common concerns and that both parties can contribute to their resolution. Some important steps have been taken in this direction in recent years. Continued progress should be a matter of high priority for all educators.

NOTES

[1]Harold Spears, *The High School for Today* (New York: American Book, 1950), 289.

[2]Elmer E. Brown, *Secondary Education,* Education in the United States, monograph no. 4, ed. Nicholas Murray Butler (Albany, NY: J. B. Lyon, 1900), 147.

[3]Theodore R. Sizer, *Secondary Schools at the Turn of the Century* (New Haven, CT: Yale University Press, 1964), 55.

[4]A. F. Bechdolt, "The High School as a Fitting-School," Addresses and Proceedings of the National Education Association (1890), 622.

[5]Newton Edwards and Herman G. Richey, *The School in the American Social Order,* rev. ed. (Boston: Houghton Mifflin, 1963), 174.

[6]Sizer, *Secondary Schools,* 3–4.

[7]Ibid., 5.

[8]For discussion of these developments particularly as they pertained to the rise of progressive education, see Lawrence A. Cremin, *The Transformation of the School* (New York: Random House, 1961, ch. 4.

[9]Sizer, *Secondary Schools,* 13.

[10]See Edwards and Richey, *The School,* 546–52.

[11]Ibid., 547.

[12]Charles W. Eliot, "The Gap Between the Elementary Schools and the Colleges," Addresses and Proceedings of the National Education Association (Washington, DC: The Association, 1890), 525.

[13]For a discussion of this report and its effect, see Sizer, *Secondary Schools.*

[14]E. P. Cubberley, *Public Education in the United States,* rev. ed. (Boston: Houghton Mifflin, 1934), 543–44.

[15]Spears, *The High School for Today,* 306.

[16]Theodore R. Sizer, "High School Reform: The Need for Engineering," *Phi Delta Kappan* 64 (June 1983): 682.

[17]Spears, *The High School for Today,* 314.

[18]Claude M. Fuess, *The College Board: Its First Fifty Years* (New York: Columbia University Press, 1950), 3.

[19]Ibid., 17–18.

[20]Frank H. Bowles, *Admission to College: A Perspective for the 1960's* (Princeton, NJ: College Entrance Examination Board, 1960), 24.

[21]*College Board News* (April 1977): 7.

[22]*Individuals and Their Options* (Princeton, NJ: Educational Testing Service, 1973), 19.

[23]Michael S. Schurdson, "Organizing the Meritocracy: A History of the College Entrance Board," *Harvard Educational Review* 42 (February 1972): 62.

[24]For example, see James Crouse, "Does the SAT Help Colleges Make Better Selection Decisions" *Harvard Educational Review* 55 (May 1985): 195–219.

[25]Henry M. Brickell, *Organizing New York State for Educational Change* (Albany, NY: State Education Department, 1961), 40. Italics in original.

[26]See Andrew J. Strenio, Jr., *The Testing Trap* (New York: Rawson, Wade, 1981).

[27]Lorraine La Vigne, "Impact of the National Merit Scholarship Program on the Public High School" (Ph.D. diss., University of Chicago, 1962), as reported in *Nationalizing Influences on Secondary Education,* ed. Roald F. Campbell and Robert A. Bunnell (Chicago: Midwest Administration Center, University of Chicago, 1963), 41–56.

[28]*On Further Examination: Report of the Advisory Board on the Scholastic Aptitude Test Decline* (New York: College Entrance Examination Board, 1977). Among the factors noted by the panel in addition to those related to school curriculum were changes in the population taking the test, the impact of television on learning styles, changes in the family, and a decline in younger people's motivation to learn.

[29]For discussion of the Florida program, see Thomas H. Fisher, "Florida's Approach to Competency Testing" and Gene V. Glass, "Minimum Competence and Incompetence in Florida," *Phi Delta Kappan* 59 (May 1978): 599–605. Also see Arthur E. Wise, *Legislated Learning* (Berkeley, CA: University of California Press, 1979).

[30]*School Boards* 6 (January 1963): 3.

[31]Alec M. Gallup, "The Extended Annual Gallup Poll of the Public's Attitudes Toward the Public Schools," *Phi Delta Kappan* 68 (September 1986): 53.

[32]Jay Mathews, "Tests Help Ordinary Schools Leap Ahead," *Washington Post* 14 May 1987, A1, 21. Also see, Sheppard Ranbom, "Schools' Interest in Advanced-Placement Classes Increases" *Education Week* II (13 April 1983): 14–15.

[33]*College Board News* (April 1977): 7, and Harold Howe II, "Educational Controls Exhibited by the Colleges," *The American Secondary School* (Princeton, NJ: College Entrance Examination Board, 1959), 39.

[34]Scott D. Thomson, *College Admissions: New Requirements by the State Universities* (Reston, VA: National Association of Secondary School Principals, 1982).

[35]Ibid., 7–8.

[36]*National Science Foundation Annual Report: 1981* (Washington, DC: U.S. Government Printing Office, 1982), 86.

[37]*National Science Foundation Annual Report, 1986* (Washington, DC: U.S. Government Printing Office, 1986), 39–40. Also see Michael S. Knapp et al, "Prospects for Improving K–12 Science Education from the Federal Level," *Phi Delta Kappan* 69 (May 1988): 677–683.

[38]*National Endowment for the Humanities Annual Report: 1985* (Washington, DC: U.S. Government Printing Office, 1985), 160.

[39]Lee M. Thurston and William H. Roe, *State School Administration* (New York: Harper & Row, 1957), 310.

[40]*State High School Standardization,* Bulletin of the Bureau of School Service, vol. 2, no. 3 (Lexington, KY: University of Kentucky, College of Education, March 1930).

[41]Thurston and Roe, *State School Administration,* 312.

[42]James B. Conant, *The Education of American Teachers* (New York: McGraw-Hill, 1963), 246.

[43]*Tomorrow's Teachers: A Report of the Holmes Group* (East Lansing, MI: The Holmes Group, 1986) and Carnegie Forum on Education and the Economy, *A Nation Prepared: Teachers for the 21st Century* (New York: Carnegie Corporation, 1986).

[44]See Victor S. Vance and Philip C. Schlechty, "The Distribution of Academic Ability in the Teaching Force," *Phi Delta Kappan* 64 (September 1982): 22–27.

[45]Hope Aldriels, "Few Blacks Passing Georgia Teacher Test, Study Finds," *Education Week,* 9 November 1983, 6.

[46]"University, School Links Urged," *Education Week,* 24 August 1983, 17.

[47]Michael D. Usdan, David W. Minar, and Emanual Hurwitz, Jr., *Education and State Politics* (New York: Teachers College Press, Columbia University, 1969).

[48]See Gene I. Maeroff, *School and College: Partnerships in Education* (Washington, DC: Carnegie Foundation, 1983).

[49]For discussion of academic alliances, see Claire L. Gaudiani and David G. Burnett, *Academic Alliances: A New Approach to School/College Collaboration* (Washington, DC: American Association for Higher Education, 1986).

[50]An example of school district dissatisfaction with teacher education programs and state certification standards has been the introduction of school district testing of potential teachers. See Richard Mitchell, "Testing the Teachers: The Dallas Experiment," *Atlantic* (December 1978): 66–70.

17

Nonpublic Schools and Other Alternatives

In this chapter, we will examine educational alternatives, some public, some private, some traditional, and some nontraditional. We will use the terms *private* and *nonpublic* to refer to elementary and secondary schools not supported by taxes. The term *alternative* is applied to both institutions not supported by taxes and to various forms of schooling within public school systems.

The post-World War II period was marked by the extension of conventional forms of public and private schooling as well as new alternative schools that developed in the 1960s and 1970s. On initial inspection, these alternative institutions seem to have much in common with conventional schools. Structural characteristics of both, such as length of school year and school day, class size, professional staffing, and organizational structures, are much the same. What is new are the forms and varieties of educational alternatives available to persons of all ages. Moreover, parents in several states have acquired legal rights to educate their children at home and private home tutorial programs have been developed to augment instruction received in the public schools. Opportunities to participate in formal and informal learning programs abound for everyone from the age of two through the advancing years. The rhetoric of lifelong learning has moved closer to reality.

In the mid-1960s the public schools, as well as the society's other major institutions, were subjected to a torrent of criticism. Reactions against the war in Vietnam and racism triggered demonstrations against the status quo. Basic questions were asked about the efficacy of public education, particularly in larger cities where the schools were proving to be inadequate in meeting the needs of minority and low-income youngsters.

The civil rights movement, in particular, precipitated growing criticism of American public schools as education, like other fundamental institutions of the society, was accused of suppressing the poor and disadvantaged in order to perpetuate a military-centered and exploitative economic system. The dissatisfaction of the disadvantaged was politically buttressed, if not ideologically supported, by criticism of the schools from another socioeconomic stratum of the society. The nation's most privileged students were accusing the schools of stifling creativity and self-expression. Numerous "alienated" middle- and upper-middle class youngsters protested what they considered to be sterile, uninspiring, and rigidly designed secondary school programs. This chorus of dissatisfaction reached full volume in the late 1960s, continuing though somewhat muted through the 1970s, only to burst forth again in the 1980s. Educational alternatives burgeoned throughout the United States partly in response to parent and other citizen unhappiness with traditional public schools but also because strong political coalitions were formed leading to legislation in fifteen states that encourages family choice and the development of alternatives.[1]

For the most part the spotlight in American education has been on public education. There has existed throughout our history, however, a companion group of nonpublic schools making up a substantial segment of our total educational system. Not as much is known about these schools because the focus has been on public schools and because the collection of data about nonpublic schools has been sporadic, poorly coordinated, and even ignored. Public school educators are not well informed about how nonpublic schools are financed or controlled, nor are they always interested. Nonpublic school educators are, in turn, not well informed about the public schools.

NONPUBLIC SCHOOLS YESTERDAY AND TODAY

Despite the early colonial interest in public schools, especially in New England, considerable support existed for the establishment of nongovernmentally related schools. Butts and Cremin point out that private efforts by individuals and groups of like-minded people appeared early on the American scene and came to be the dominant method of promoting schools in many of the colonies.[2] A U.S. Office of Education survey indicates that 2.6 percent of the nonpublic secondary schools now operating were founded before 1850 and another 16 percent between 1850 and 1900.[3] Most of the older schools are located on the eastern seaboard.

In our early history the lines of demarcation between the management of nonpublic and public schools were often difficult to distinguish. This was particularly true in colonies where the church and the state were allied. Frequently individuals gave private donations to town schools or to public authorities for the use of public schools. In other instances, public funds and other forms of public aid were turned over to private agencies and religious groups for the support of nonpublic education. Early nonpublic schools were endowed by individuals, established as denominational schools by churches and religious societies, developed by individual teachers as their own, or were created as private academies by corporations that served as their governing boards.

Nonpublic schools enjoy the protection of the law in the United States.[4] The states in the exercise of their plenary power over education require all children to attend school and compulsory attendance laws have been enacted in all of the states, but the power of the state does not include the right to determine which schools, public or nonpublic, children must attend. The courts have upheld the right of parents to make this determination. The celebrated case of *Pierce* v. *Society of the Sisters* removed all doubt about the right of parents to send their children to nonpublic schools.[5] In this case, the United States Supreme Court held that an Oregon statute, the Compulsory Education Act of 1922 requiring all children to attend public schools, violated the Fourteenth Amendment. A private military school joined the Society of the Sisters in bringing the suit, and thus the Supreme Court's declaration upheld the existence of not only sectarian or religious schools but nonsectarian private schools as well.

A democracy does not need a single system of public schools to survive. On the contrary, alternatives are desirable, and parents should have the opportunity to survey a range of educational opportunities for their children and the right to select the type of school that in their view offers the best education. Competition, to the extent that it exists, is desirable and contributes to the dynamism we have grown to cherish. A public school system is obligated to be responsive to the society that sponsors it, and a nonpublic school is prized precisely because it need not be responsive to the total society but chiefly to the constituency that supports it. It can innovate, define goals that may not be the same as other schools, specialize, and discriminate within legal limits in its choice of clients.[6]

Controls on Nonpublic Schools

Nonpublic schools for a time operated in a relatively free environment in this country. There was only limited competition from public schools and few controls were imposed by public authorities. Now, however, nonpublic schools function within a body of constitutional, statutory, and case law, both federal and state, which to some extent limits them. Some states regulate or govern nonpublic schools much more rigorously than do others, as we will see.

Several state and local public agencies "regulate" nonpublic schools. Nonpublic schools must abide by public controls that apply to buildings, safety, zoning, and public health. In those instances where the states exercise little or no jurisdiction over nonpublic schools, county or municipal officials have actually closed down nonpublic schools that have failed to meet fire safety codes or health standards.

The most far-reaching constraints are applied by the states. It is generally accepted that the states have the right, within reason, to regulate nonpublic education. These regulatory rights include inspection for the purpose of determining the adequacy of the curriculum and teaching staffs, the enforcement of compulsory attendance laws, and the requirement that students fulfill certain state expectations, especially those for good citizenship. Although there is agreement on the regulatory rights of the states on these matters, there are widespread differences among the states in the stipulation and enforcement of those rights.

To some these restrictions are unnecessarily severe. Erickson, a strong advocate of nonpublic educational alternatives argues, "Perhaps educational reform would come more quickly if public and private agencies were encouraged to specialize on particular aspects of education, unburdened by the total welter of often contradictory custodial, instructional, and 'character building' goals that most schools are asked to achieve simultaneously."[7]

Nonpublic School Statistics

Complete, accurate data on private schools are nonexistent. Enrollment figures are at best rough approximations because not all of the states compile private school enrollment statistics. Enrollment trends of private schools are provided in Table 17.1.

The enrollment growth patterns, in both public and private schools, that marked the twentieth century shifted to decline during the 1970s. There were more than 7 million fewer public school students in 1985 than there were in 1971. Private enrollments decreased 583,000 for the same period but the nature of private school

TABLE 17.1
Private School Enrollment Trends: 1970 to 1985

October of Year	K–12 Enrollment (in thousands)			Private School Enrollment as a Percentage of Total K–12 Enrollment
	Total	Public	Private	
1970	51,848	46,193	5,655	10.9
1971	51,953	46,575	5,378	10.4
1972	50,546	45,343	5,203	10.3
1973	49,890	44,945	4,945	9.9
1974	49,825	44,958	4,867	9.8
1975	49,522	44,521	5,001	10.1
1976	49,006	44,202	4,804	9.8
1977	48,178	43,153	5,025	10.4
1978	46,954	41,976	4,978	10.6
1979	46,006	41,343	4,663	10.1
1980	45,181	—	—	—
1981	45,598	40,897	4,701	10.3
1982	44,834	40,132	4,702	10.5
1983	44,569	39,701	4,868	10.9
1984	44,099	39,793	4,306	9.8
1985	44,660	39,788	4,872	10.9

—Not available.
Source: U.S. Department of Commerce, Bureau of the Census, *School Enrollment—Social and Economic Characteristics of Students: October 1984* (Current Population Reports, Series P–20, No. 404), 1985 and unpublished tabulations.

enrollment experience was different from the public schools. Although the overall trend for private schools over the fifteen-year period was downward, there were slight increases in the first half of the 1980s. Public schools did not experience this enrollment increase.

It is evident from Table 17.2 that large numbers of private school students are found in the Northeast and North Central regions. They are concentrated in central cities and suburbs. Between 1979 and 1985, the proportion of church-related students declined in the Northeast and increased in the North Central region. Ninety-five percent of the private school students in the North Central region attended church-related schools in 1985. The national average in that year was 77 percent.

Table 17.3 contains considerable data about the characteristics of nonpublic schools. Length of the school year, hours per day in session, and years of operation are included, as well as mean enrollment per school. Of importance too are figures on minority enrollments and tuition charges. It is interesting to note that nearly 36 percent have school years of fewer than 180 days. On the other hand nearly 43 percent conduct school between six and seven hours per day. Most public schools have at least 180-day school years but are open for instruction only five or six hours per day. Fifty percent of the nonpublic schools have been operating for twenty-five years or more; 84 percent of the Catholic schools have been open at least a quarter century. In 1985 12.1 percent of the nonpublic schools had no minorities enrolled and 26.8 had less than five percent. More than 8 percent of the schools enrolled 90 percent or more minorities. Schools with high concentrations of minority students, 11.9 percent,

TABLE 17.2

Proportion of All Students Attending Private Schools, By Region and Metropolitan Status

Metropolitan Status and Region	*Proportion of October Enrollment, Grades 1–12, Attending Private Schools*			
	1970	1979	1982	1985
U.S.	10.5	9.8	10.0	10.5
Region:				
Northeast	17.1	12.5	13.3	14.2
North Central	13.4	11.5	11.7	12.4
South	5.7	7.8	7.4	8.2
West	6.0	7.9	8.4	8.2
Metropolitan status:				
Central city	16.4	16.0	13.7	13.8
Suburb	11.6	10.0	11.0	11.9
Nonmetropolitan	5.5	5.0	5.9	6.2

Source: U.S. Department of Commerce, Bureau of the Census, *Private School Enrollment, Tuition, and Enrollment Trends: October 1979* (Current Population Reports, Series P–23, No. 121), 1982 and unpublished tabulations and S. Bianchi, Private School Enrollment: Trends and Debates, *Research in Sociology of Education and Socialization, 3,* 1982.

were Catholic elementary schools. Since 1979, the number and proportion of non-public school students who are black have declined. The low tuition schools were Catholic; the high tuition schools were in the non-religiously affiliated category where 64.3 percent charged more than $2,500 per year. The vast majority of private school students are from low- and middle-income families, thus tuition increases have an immediate impact on families and their decisions to enroll their children in non-public schools.

In 1985–86, there were 25,616 nonpublic schools in operation (see Table 17.3).[8] Of these 20,682 were church-related; 4,934 had no religious affiliation. The largest number of church-related secondary schools were affiliated with the Roman Catholic Church. Catholic high schools range from small single-purpose schools to large multicurricular institutions. The second largest group of church-related secondary schools was Lutheran, followed by the schools of the Seventh Day Adventists.[9] The distributions of church-related schools by denomination and their enrollments are included in Table 17.4 (page 436).

The slight increase in enrollments in nonpublic schools has been paralleled by an increase in the number of nonpublic school teachers. During the 1970–71 school year there were 216,825 nonpublic school teachers. By 1980–81 that number was 281,000.[10] The plateau and decline in nonpublic enrollments that began in 1967 will be reflected naturally in the numbers and distribution of persons teaching in non-public schools in the future. The changing enrollment patterns within the several types of nonpublic schools described in the following section have implications for many public school districts.

TYPES OF NONPUBLIC SCHOOLS

To avoid arguments over definitions of nonpublic schools, we will use the definition of the U.S. Office of Education.

> *Non-public schools* are schools supported by means other than public taxation or pub-lic grants. They include parochial schools, privately operated non-sectarian schools (profit-making or nonprofit); privately operated schools for the deaf, blind, mentally retarded, or students with other types of physical or mental exceptionality, for whom education equivalent to that of the public elementary or secondary schools is pro-vided; private college preparatory schools or military academies; secondary level "fin-ishing" schools; laboratory schools of private colleges and universities; and evening schools offering the equivalent of a high school education.[11]

The principal distinction is one of support and, with support, operational control.[12] The examples of nonpublic schools above are full-time day schools. Not included are the many schools that offer part-time special training in such areas as reading, foreign language, business, vocations, charm, art, and music. Many American youngsters, particularly from middle-class families, who are enrolled during the day in full-time public or nonpublic schools, supplement their day school work with evening and Saturday instruction in these other private schools. No one knows exactly how much part-time, nonpublic education is available in the nation. Nonpublic schools are most

TABLE 17.3

Characteristics of Private Schools, By Level and Affiliation of School: U.S., 1985–86 (Percentage Distribution)

Characteristics	All Private Schools	Level of School				Religious Affiliation of School[1]		
		Elementary	Secondary	Combined	Other	Catholic	Other Religiously Affiliated	Not Religiously Affiliated
Number of Schools	25,616	15,303	2,438	4,949	2,926	9,911	10,771	4,934
Number of days attended in 1984–85								
Total	100.0	100.0	100.0	100.0	100.0	100.0	100.0	100.0
Less than 180 days	35.7	37.4	33.1	43.5	15.5	32.8	42.4	26.7
180 days	49.8	50.0	57.3	47.8	46.4	57.3	48.8	37.2
More than 180 days	14.5	12.6	9.7	8.8	38.2	9.9	8.8	36.2
Number of hours in session each day, 1985–86								
Total	100.0	100.0	100.0	100.0	100.0	100.0	100.0	100.0
5 hours or less	5.6	4.0	16.0	2.3	10.7	8.5	1.4	8.7
More than 5 hours to 6 hours	46.2	51.6	41.5	27.3	53.5	62.1	32.0	45.0
More than 6 hours to 7 hours	42.4	41.5	37.2	53.0	33.9	27.5	57.1	40.3
More than 7 hours	5.8	2.9	5.4	17.4	2.0	1.8	9.4	6.0
Years in operation								
Total	100.0	100.0	100.0	100.0	100.0	100.0	100.0	100.0
10 years or less	25.5	20.2	9.9	41.4	39.2	1.7	45.2	30.2
11 to 24 years	24.2	16.5	27.5	36.7	40.8	14.2	25.5	41.6
25 years or more	50.3	63.8	62.6	21.9	20.0	84.1	29.3	28.2
Mean enrollment per school	234	218	541	211	94	363	142	174

Minority enrollment, 1985–86

Total	100.0	100.0	100.0	100.0	100.0	100.0	100.0	100.0
None	12.1	13.9	2.5	16.2	3.3	7.2	21.8	0.6
Less than 5 percent	26.8	31.2	25.3	20.9	15.4	38.6	18.7	21.0
5 to 14 percent	22.4	19.8	36.1	23.4	22.9	20.4	20.9	29.4
15 to 24 percent	10.6	7.7	14.4	11.6	21.1	8.9	12.7	9.8
25 to 49 percent	10.0	7.8	11.8	5.1	28.6	7.2	8.4	19.3
50 to 74 percent	8.1	7.1	3.7	17.2	2.1	3.8	10.9	11.0
75 to 89 percent	1.8	2.1	0.7	1.0	2.5	2.5	1.2	1.7
90 percent or more	8.1	10.4	5.4	4.6	4.1	11.5	5.4	7.1
Tuition group								
Total	100.0	100.0	100.0	100.0	100.0	100.0	100.0	100.0
Less than $500	13.0	18.8	4.8	5.4	1.1	25.6	6.3	1.1
$500 to $1,000	27.9	35.1	4.4	29.6	5.0	37.1	30.8	1.0
$1,001 to $1,500	26.4	29.1	34.4	22.7	9.3	25.7	30.7	17.6
$1,501 to $2,500	14.6	8.3	28.7	18.0	31.8	7.7	20.4	16.0
More than $2,500	18.2	8.8	27.8	24.4	52.9	3.9	11.9	64.3

¹Includes schools with a religious orientation or religious affiliation.
Note: Data are based on a sample survey and may not be strictly comparable with data reported elsewhere. Elementary schools have no grade higher than 8. Secondary schools have no grade lower than 7. Combined schools have any other grade spans. Other schools include special education, alternative, and vocational schools. Includes only schools which offer first grade or above. Because of rounding, details may not add to totals.
Source: U.S. Department of Education, Center for Educational Statistics, *1985–86 Private School Survey.* (This table was prepared October 1986.)

TABLE 17.4
Private School Statistics by Affiliation with Selected Church Denomination: U.S., 1978–79

	Enrollment	Percent Change Since 1977
1. Roman Catholic Schools	3,269,761	− 3.3
2. Lutheran Schools	217,406	2.3
3. Seventh Day Adventist Schools	148,157	34.1
4. Calvinist Schools (National Union of Christian Schools)	47,269	8.0
5. Jewish Day Schools	101,758	5.2
6. Episcopal	76,452	2.9
7. Friends (Quaker) Schools	14,611	1.3
8. Eastern Orthodox Schools	2,682	0.9
9. Other affiliations*	231,317	5.4
10. Non-affiliated	746,730	− 1.5

*Includes schools affiliated with Amish, Christian, Mennonite, and other denominations
Source: *Private Schools in American Education* (Washington, DC: National Center for Educational Statistics, 1981), 17.

often divided into two groups—sectarian and nonsectarian—and these classifications are sometimes further divided.

Sectarian Schools

Among the array of sectarian schools, systems of school control vary. Data are quite unreliable on the numbers of schools that are maintained and controlled by local churches that have no denominational or other central organizational connection. Thus we know practically nothing about how these schools are governed. A distinction is frequently made between the parochial type and the parent-society type of school. The parochial group outnumbers the parent-society group. In the parochial school, control is tied directly to the local church, parish, or diocese, whereas the control of parent-society schools remains in the hands of a group of parents who may be affiliated with one or more churches.

Many Roman Catholic elementary and secondary schools and most elementary Lutheran schools are of the parochial type. Others in this classification are most of the schools maintained by the Seventh-day Adventists, Jewish schools, all the Los Angeles Baptist City Mission Society schools, and a large number of the schools affiliated with the National Association of Christian Schools. Parent-society schools include schools in the National Union of Christian Schools of the Christian Reformed Church, New England Association of Christian Schools, and many Mennonite schools.

The precise patterns of church-related school control are difficult to discern. The two classifications above are crude for within each class there are variations. Roman Catholic schools, classed as parochial above, are themselves mixed in terms of control because of their close links to local parishes or orders. Catholic schools are all, theoretically, under the direction of the Ordinary (cardinal, arch-bishop, or bishop) of the diocese, according to the limits set by canon law.[13] But within dioceses there are private Catholic schools operated by religious orders, and the lines of authority between order and diocesan school officials frequently are not clear.[14] The distribution of power and control within sectarian schools is extremely varied. Historically, headmasters and headmistresses were powerful, controlled their schools, and seldom sought advice and counsel from boards, faculties, students, or parents. More recently, the patterns of control have shifted somewhat. In some cases, boards are powerful and faculties influential. Parents and students are involved in governance and decision making is a shared responsibility, which is a distinct break with the past.[15] We now turn to a brief examination of three systems of sectarian schools.

Catholic Schools

A majority, 57 percent, of all nonpublic school students were enrolled in Catholic schools in 1985–86, a decrease from the 1975–76 figure of 75.9 percent.[16] The numbers of students enrolled, schools, and teachers increased steadily through 1964. In 1965–66, 80.7 percent of all secondary school students in nonpublic schools were in Catholic high schools; an even higher percentage (88.6) of the total nonpublic elementary school population attended Catholic elementary schools. Catholic elementary school enrollment increased 171 percent during the decade of the 1950s, making it necessary for Catholics to nearly double the number of teachers and classrooms to keep pace. Catholic enrollments continued to increase through 1964 when total Catholic school enrollment reached more than 5,600,000. The 1964 total represented 12 percent of all school enrollments in the United States but after that year Catholic school enrollments began to decline. By 1967 there were 5,250,000 pupils enrolled in Catholic schools, representing 10.7 percent of all enrollments.[17] By the 1985–86 school year, the number of students had declined to 2,841,000.

The current state of the Catholic schools can be placed in sharper perspective by taking a look at their past. The number of Catholics in America prior to 1776 was small and rather insignificant, and the status of the teaching orders was precarious.[18] Catholic schools in the colonial period did not form a "system" of schools, and they persisted primarily through the zeal of the orders that sponsored them. No centralized support or even interest existed at this time; Catholic immigration later spurred the development of a system of Catholic schools. In 1884 the bishops and archbishops of the Third Plenary Council of Baltimore ordered that by 1886 parochial schools were to be constructed and maintained near all the Catholic churches of the United States.[19] The bishops stipulated clearly the duty of every pastor to erect and develop a school and to apprise parents of the obligations to send their children to Catholic schools. The duties of Catholic parents were dramatically reiterated in the 1929 Encyclical of Pope Pius XI, which stated that the only acceptable education was "Catholic education in Catholic schools for all Catholic youth."[20]

The prospect for reversing the downward trend in Catholic schools depends on a number of factors, not the least of which may be the availability of public support. The costs of Catholic schools have grown enormously, and considerable debate has been generated among Catholic leaders as to the future of Catholic schools in America. Obviously policy decisions about Catholic schools made within the Roman Catholic Church have rather sharp implications for public schools. Some of these are explored later.

The diocese is an important unit in Catholic educational control, and in some respects the diocese resembles the local school district. A bishop of a diocese is the chief teacher of the diocese, and he is ultimately responsible for all diocesan schools in his jurisdiction and has, to some extent, control of the Catholic order schools in his diocese. At the parish level the local pastor has traditionally been the responsible administrator of the parochial school in his parish.

The growing problems of school administration within the dioceses have led to the structural changes within many diocesan school administrations, including the creation of a diocesan superintendent of schools and a diocesan school board. In a 1981 survey of 167 dioceses conducted by the National Catholic Educational Association, 130 diocesan boards of education were reported. All those boards function in accord with the canonical structure with authority coming from the bishop.[21] As McCoy points out, each of these boards is the creation of the diocesan bishop and they are no more or less than what he chooses to make of them.[22] Another change is the expansion of lay involvement in parochial education, which McCluskey describes as revolutionary.[23]

In contrast to public schools, where the duties and responsibilities of school boards, and to a lesser extent school superintendents, are prescribed by law, canon law makes no mention of such administrative creations. The influence of both the diocesan superintendents and diocesan boards has mushroomed as Catholic schools struggle with enormous problems. Administrative problems have been magnified because roles and responsibilities are not clearly defined and differentiated. However, the roles of the diocesan school officials are being clarified as the dioceses gain more experience with the new administrative and policy structures.

Beyond the problems associated with ambiguous roles, finances present another difficult issue confronting diocesan school officials. Diocesan superintendents have little or no control over school finances. In fact, they often have had little knowledge of local parish school budgets and very limited resources for the operation of the diocesan school offices. Support of the diocesan superintendent's activities comes from levies on parish elementary schools, special collections, and in some cases, income from the sale of textbooks, courses of study, or workbooks.

Roman Catholic schools have encountered teacher problems that are not easily solved. The supply of religious teachers—nuns, priests, and brothers—has not been adequate, forcing Catholic administrators to employ lay teachers. In 1979 there were about 18,500 more elementary lay teachers than in 1969, and approximately 11,500 more secondary lay teachers; the elementary staff was approximately one-third religious and two-thirds lay. This shift from religious to lay teachers seemingly has not affected the essential character of the Catholic school. School boards, parents, and lay teachers continue to maintain the same conscientious concern exemplified by the religious community members who led the way and still hold key administrative positions.[24]

Lutheran Church, Missouri Synod

Several Lutheran denominations in addition to the Missouri Synod sponsor nonpublic schools. Among these are the American Lutheran Church, Augustana Lutheran Church,

Evangelical Lutheran Church, United Lutheran Church, Lutheran Joint Synod of Wisconsin and Other States, and the Norwegian Synod of the American Evangelical Lutheran Church. We have selected the Missouri Synod Schools for elaboration because they are the second largest group of sectarian schools in the nation.

The Missouri Synod stems from the religious family that predominated in northern Europe, the Lutheran Church. The synod was organized in 1874 and had twelve parishes in five states. By 1959 the synod had grown to more than 6,000 congregations and a membership of over 2.5 million.[25] When the synod was organized all of its parishes had schools, but this is not true today. In 1970–71 the synod enrolled 163,386 students; by 1982–83 the enrollment had increased to 181,568. The total 1982 enrollment for all Lutheran schools (Missouri Synod, Wisconsin Evangelical Lutheran Synod, American Lutheran, Lutheran Church in America, Association of Evangelical Lutheran Church) in junior high, elementary, and preschool was 258,405 and, for high schools, 22,681.[26]

The synod is organized into some thirty-four districts in the United States, with a Synod Parish Board of Education overseeing education in the districts. Each of the districts has its own officers, boards, commissions, and committees to administer the work within the district. One of the district boards is the Board or Committee of Parish Education, and the synod's role in education is to advise and serve the district board. The district boards of parish education promote and supervise the various agencies of Christian education such as day schools, Sunday schools, vacation bible schools, and other educational activities for children and adults. The Synod Board of Parish Education serves the district boards, the district boards serve the congregations within their geographical boundaries, and in most cases the congregations have parish boards of education.

The Missouri Synod historically has placed considerable power in its local congregations and allowed them considerable autonomy in local affairs. Thus the services of boards, counselors, and district superintendents, with respect to the schools, have been advisory and service-oriented for the most part. Beyond this function, the district boards and superintendents have been concerned with advancing, improving, and promoting Lutheran parochial schools. They have helped their schools meet the requirements imposed by the states on nonpublic schools and at the same time have watched for legislation that would be inimical to Lutheran schools.

The Missouri Synod enrollments have grown in recent decades; the elementary enrollment in fact has doubled since World War II. The greatest growth has been in the eastern, southeastern, and western parts of the United States. The enrollment in Lutheran high schools has also increased appreciably. Administrative roles appear to be more clearly delineated in the Missouri Synod districts than in the Catholic dioceses. Pressures exist, however, for more centralization of school control and supervision.

Jewish Schools

Jewish day schools have grown rapidly in the United States since World War II. In 1935 there were 4,600 students enrolled in sixteen Jewish day schools in New York

City and one in Baltimore. Nearly 102,000 students were attending such schools in 1978–79 and most of these students were from orthodox congregations.

Among the reasons cited for this phenomenal growth is the intense interest within the Jewish community in the perpetuation of Jewish values.[27] Jews generally have not expressed the dissatisfaction with the public schools that members of other religious groups often have. Considerable emphasis is placed on Jewish studies in most Jewish day schools. Three or four hours per day are given to the Hebrew language and Jewish law and literature. The usual curriculum sometimes runs until 5 P.M., and in some instances students attend on Saturdays too.

Most schools have been operated on a community basis with supervision and support a local responsibility. There is no central agency in charge of coordinating, organizing, or supervising Jewish day schools. In New York City some cooperation among schools is effected through the Jewish Education Committee of New York; outside of New York the National Society for Hebrew Day Schools has been instrumental in the founding of some schools.

Financial problems have plagued these schools as they have all schools. The shortage of dedicated Jewish teachers has been a problem as well. Because of money difficulties, few schools have been established away from urban centers. A very small percentage of eligible Jewish children attend these schools and future enrollment trends are unclear. On the basis of post-World War II growth, however, and assuming the solid support of leaders in the Jewish community, there may well be continuing increases in the number of Jewish day schools and in enrollments as well.

Nonsectarian Schools

Several types of schools are included in this group—privately owned and operated kindergartens, elementary and secondary schools, academies, special schools for students with physical or mental deficiencies, laboratory schools associated with private colleges and universities, and evening schools that provide the equivalent of high school education.

Independent Schools

Many of the prominent, long-established independent schools are located in New England. Many of these have superb records of performance and are in fact national in terms of their drawing power, prestige, and influence. The headmasters and their faculties, like their schools, frequently are national leaders, giving expression to the values these select schools perpetuate. Larmee found many independent school staff members to be influential in the College Entrance Examination Board program as well as in national curriculum developments.[28] Andover, Punahou, St. Paul's, Groton, Lawrence, Choate, and Francis Parker are prominent private schools. Their contributions to the education of national leaders are well known. For instance, James B. Conant attended Roxbury Latin, Franklin D. Roosevelt attended Groton, and John F. Kennedy graduated from Choate.

The problems of finance, which plague most American schools, are present in the nonsectarian sector as well. Inflation and uncertainty regarding enrollments haunt trustees and headmasters annually. Costs of attending such schools increase each year, causing parents to consider carefully their decisions to send children to nonpublic schools. In 1978 Senator Daniel P. Moynihan of New York cosponsored a bill that would have allowed taxpayers to take tax credits equal to 50 percent of their tuition and fee expenditures up to a maximum of $500. Other tax credit proposals were advanced by members of Congress as well as by President Reagan. Strong objections have been made to tax credits on constitutional grounds, specifically the First Amendment. Others have argued that the legislation would undermine public education and lead to further segregation of schools.[29]

The high costs of attending nonsectarian schools have produced an image of snobbishness that may or may not be accurate. Independent school leaders argue that their student bodies are much more democratic than they were in the past. Even where only top students are admitted, they come from all income groups, races, religions, and parts of the country. High priorities are placed on academic achievement, but not to the complete exclusion of training in the social graces, physical education, the arts, and citizenship.

Despite the faculty resources available to many good independent schools, there is little evidence that they are demonstrably superior to those in good public schools. In general, the quality of independent school education is sufficiently high that states need not be concerned unduly about supervising them.

Preschools

The 1990s is likely to be a period of intense controversy over infant and early childhood education. Day-care was a prominent issue in the 1988 presidential election with both parties developing proposals for public support of custodial forms of day-care for parents in need of such services. Similarly, the number of private preschools, nursery schools, and other educational and developmentally oriented institutions grew. Some public school districts too began offering publicly supported preschools and day-care services. The National Governors Association in 1986 took a strong stand on providing educational programs for preschoolers, especially those that can be identified as "at risk."[30] James S. Coleman added a new dimension to the issue in 1987, arguing that the nation should invest in "social capital" and the invention of new institutions to fill the gaps left by deficiencies in the family and the school. Coleman writes:

> The loss of social capital, inside and outside the family, has extensive implications for the structure of American childrearing. In effect, raising children once took place informally, as a by-product of other activities, in social institutions—the household, the extended family, and neighborhood-based organizations—that were held in place by these other activities. As the locus of the other activities has changed, the institutions have crumbled, and the by-product, childrearing, has crumbled along with them. The institutions that have replaced them (the offices and factories that have replaced households or neighborhoods as workplaces, the shopping malls and catalogs that have replaced neighborhood stores as places to shop, the cocktail parties and rock concerts that have replaced gatherings of extended families as leisure settings) are inhospitable to the relations between adults and children that constitute social capital for the children's growth.[31]

The concentration of public interest in the first five years of life may lead to unanticipated changes in public policy at all levels affecting nonpublic and public schools alike.

Kindergartens and Primary Schools

Nonpublic kindergartens are numerous in sections of the country where public kindergartens are not provided. Even more universal are the nonpublic nursery school and preschools that deal with three-, four-, and sometimes five-year-olds. Supervision of such schools and the growing number of day-care centers is almost nonexistent in many cases. State departments of public instruction exercise only minimal supervision if any. State health agencies that oversee health and safety regulations are more prominent as are departments of welfare in looking after some aspects of preschool, day-care center, and nursery school operations. Such supervision is exercised under the police power of the state.

Some nonpublic school kindergartens have grown into full-blown private elementary schools. Teacher-entrepreneurs, having experienced success with kindergarten programs, have gradually added grades until their schools have become at least primary schools (K–3) and in some instances complete elementary schools. Parental satisfactions with kindergarten training apparently have led to pressures for extending the scope of these schools. Little data are available on the numbers of such schools and their enrollments.

Laboratory Schools

Several private colleges and universities have laboratory schools designed originally as first-rate experimental schools. Schools such as those associated at one time with Teachers College, Columbia University, and currently with the University of Chicago, have been looked upon as leading centers for educational research and experimentation. Laboratory schools in public and private university settings are not the potent forces they used to be. Innovations and research in other educational settings, public and nonpublic, have surpassed the contributions of most laboratory schools.

The laboratory schools' research and development function has been impaired in some cases because they have been expected to serve as student teaching centers; their effectiveness as laboratory schools also has been limited sometimes by parental resistance to experimentation. Many laboratory schools are much more like good prep schools than experimental centers. Despite attempts to be selective in clientele and to enroll a heterogeneous student body, some laboratory schools have acquiesced to pressures to admit children of university faculty members and children of their friends. The student bodies then are often homogeneous, high-ability groups.

THE ALTERNATIVE SCHOOL MOVEMENT

The late 1960s saw a variety of alternative schools come into being. Some were openly nonsectarian protest schools; they were the product of adult and sometimes student frustrations. They carried many labels: freedom schools, storefront schools, black power schools, free schools, and street academies.[32] Their sponsorship was sometimes vague, feeble, and temporary. In other cases, where groups such as the Urban League sponsored street academies, the backing was clear, strong, and continuing.

Although the overt catalysts that triggered the harsh criticism of public schools were proximate political and social issues like the Vietnam war and racial injustice, the seeds of disaffection with American education had been sown some time prior to the protests of the mid and late 1960s. Postman and Weingartner trace the genesis of one stream of indictments back to the attacks launched for decades against John Dewey's progressive education for its alleged "gooey, precious, romantic philosophy which stressed permissiveness and life adjustment."[33] These long-standing attacks on the schools for their alleged failure to stress intellectual development and rigorous thinking crested in the late 1950s and 1960s after the Russian launching of Sputnik I. Much of this criticism centered on the need to eliminate "frills" from the curriculum; it was argued that disciplined scientists and highly trained technicians were needed to meet the Soviet challenge.

By the mid-1960s a much larger number of critics entered the fray with a different set of criticisms. Social critics like Paul Goodman, Edgar Friedenberg, and Jules Henry pointed out that, despite the much-heralded curriculum reform movement, the schools were in deep trouble with dropout rates rising among all social classes. They noted the gap between "the official rhetoric about the purposes of school (for example, to widen the horizons of students) and the real purposes of school, and they found it enormous."[34]

A few early critics, including teacher-writers such as John Holt, triggered between 1965 and 1970 a deluge of assaults against the schools as repressive institutions that destroyed children's spontaneity and natural love of learning. Hundreds of books and articles quickly appeared. These critics included practicing teachers like Jonathan Kozol, Herbert Kohl, and James Hernton; writers and journalists like Charles Silberman, George Leonard, Nat Hentoff, and George Dennison; and social scientists like Marilyn Gittell, David Rogers, and Frank Reissman.[35] Within a very few years a large network of organizations and publications sprouted up that assaulted the conventions of traditional schooling in the United States.

In 1971 the New Schools Directory Project listed 346 non-tax supported alternative schools. By 1980 that number had increased to 504, with enrollments of approximately 40,000 students. Forty-seven states had at least one such school.[36]

Postman and Weingartner contend that sometime around 1970 the "romantic phase" of criticism of the public schools came to an end.[37] Some of the critics, who protested against the processes of schooling more than its basic structure, became frustrated with the system's incapacity to change. Others who were not basically educators moved into other activities. The remaining "romantics," who believed that schools and the potential to function humanely if governance procedures were restructured and democratized, faced a new wave of critics who were almost totally disillusioned with the schools. This development, called "Panic Phase II" by Postman and Weingartner, represented "the second coming of the idea that our schools are a betrayal and an abomination."[38] Interestingly, this assault came from not the political right, which had launched earlier attacks on education, but from the political left.

Ivan Illich was the prime exponent of the view that the schools were not salvageable. The "romantic" critics, although harsh in their indictments of education, at least believed that there was some hope for reform. Illich, however, in his *Deschooling Society* called for the total elimination of schools and urged "replacing them with an informal, noncompulsory network of educational resources."[39]

The ferment concerning schools continued through the 1970s and early 1980s. Marilyn Ferguson, a newcomer to the ranks of educational critics, noted in 1980 that "innovations in education have crisscrossed the sky like Roman candles, and most sputtered quickly out, leaving only the smell of enchantment in the air."[40] The cacophany of strident voices was joined by some of the nation's most respected educational leaders who called for improvements in the system that in many cases they had helped to shape. Ralph Tyler wrote of reconstructing the total educational system, specifying the responsibilities of the school as well as those of other partners in the educational process.[41] He noted too, however, that a revolution in the total educational system was not possible nor even desirable given the destructive side effects of revolution and the tremendous redirection of energy required.[42] Lawrence Cremin called for fresh debate of the means and ends of education as a step toward restoring public confidence and commitment.[43] Cremin, while urging reconsideration of the specific aims and content of education, emphasized the contribution of American education to the advancement of liberty, equality, and fraternity.[44]

Status of Alternatives Within Public Schools

What, then, is the status of alternatives within the public schools? What have been the reactions of the professional educators whose work has been subjected to such scathing criticisms?

Cities like Berkeley, Philadelphia, and Minneapolis were pioneers in alternative education by developing fifty alternative learning environments at the secondary school level. These options were directed at the unique educational needs of individual students and offered a wide range of alternatives such as open classrooms, mini-schools, and work-study programs.[45] The Berkeley and Minneapolis public schools developed alternatives on a systemwide basis. Both school districts received substantial support from the federally funded Experimental Schools Program.

The Berkeley Unified School District created some twenty-three alternative schools that fell into the four broad patterns of multiculture schools, community schools, structured skills training schools, and schools without walls.[46] Thirty percent of Berkeley's parents selected alternative schools for their children. The Minneapolis Public Schools implemented a regional Southeast Alternatives Program that enabled elementary students to attend either a contemporary school, a continuous progress school, an open school, or a free school.

The swing of the political pendulum away from the social activism and institutional experimentation of the 1960s, however, has been of great concern to advocates of alternative education. Change inevitably engenders conflict, which in turn produces political confrontation. Fantini enumerates some basic ground rules he feels are not only good politics but also maximize the chances for institutionalizing the philosophy and concepts of the alternative school movement:

1. Alternatives are not superimposed, but are a matter of choice for all participants— teachers, parents, and students.
2. Alternatives are viewed as another way of providing education alongside the existing pattern, which continues to be legitimate. They are different from special programs for dropouts, unwed mothers, and so forth.
3. They do not practice exclusivity.
4. They do not make exaggerated claims of accomplishments that may be deceptive in the long run.
5. They are aimed at a broad, common set of unlimited educational objectives. Alternative public schools are responsible to the public for comprehensive, cognitive, and affective goals that cannot be compromised; these include basic skills, learning-to-learn skills, talent development, socialization of basic societal roles (citizen, consumer, worker), and self-concept development.
6. They do not cost more money than existing per student expenditures.[47]

Despite some growth in the alternative school movement in the 1970s, it was not without its casualties. Ravitch reported that the Experimental Schools Program of the Nixon administration, which cost $55 million, essentially failed. She cited the Berkeley experience as partial evidence. Only one of the twenty-four alternative schools in the Berkeley district survived even with a $5 million infusion of federal dollars.[48]

Alternative schools, however, were given a boost early in 1974 when the influential North Central Association of College and Secondary Schools after three years of discussion adopted standards for formally accrediting them. The Southern Association of Colleges and Schools, another major regional agency, has also adopted procedures, but not standards, for accrediting alternative schools.[49]

Alternative schools have often played a role in school desegregation. Survey data in the early 1980s from the U.S. Department of Education confirmed the value of magnet schools for school desegregation.[50] Early in 1984 desegregation plans constructed around magnet school concepts were approved in courts in Ohio and California. Milwaukee, Houston, St. Louis, Dallas, Buffalo, Cincinnati, and Boston are among the cities that have emphasized educational options as a primary mechanism for achieving school desegregation. The Dallas Independent School District developed several magnet high schools, early childhood education centers, academies, and vanguard schools as part of their court-ordered remedy plan. The names of some of the Dallas schools tell the story: Health Professions High School, Transportation Institute, Sidney Lanier Center for Expressive Arts, Mark Twain Fundamental School, and the Business and Management Center. The Dallas citizens were extensively involved in the development of options, and many patrons of the school district were dismayed when the court of appeals in the summer of 1978 found the remedy plan inadequate and directed the Dallas Independent School District to prepare a more comprehensive approach to school desegregation.

Raywid surveyed public secondary alternative schools in 1982. Her work was a part of the Project on Alternatives in Education, supported in part by the National Institute of Education. She identified more than 2,500 alternative public secondary schools, but estimated that there may be two to four times that many in existence. Two-thirds of them have 200 students or less. Most such schools are in cities with some population growth in suburban districts.[51]

The PAE-sponsored survey yielded interesting findings including the fact that per student costs in 62 percent of the responding schools were the same or less than those at other schools. Morale was found to be extremely high and the quality of teacher/student interaction to be unusually fine. Attendance was excellent and faculty worked hard in meeting high expectations students had for them. Graduates succeeded as well or better in college than those who attended traditional public secondary schools.[52]

Raywid believes that schools of choice are gaining ground and that the movement that began in the 1960s is alive and well. Furthermore, the trend toward tougher standards that developed in the early 1980s has not diminished respect for alternative programs.[53] Erickson, who studied climates of private schools and the two types of public schools, traditional and alternative, found substantial differences between the social climates of private schools and traditional public schools, but fewer differences between private schools and public alternative schools.[54] Erickson urged that more attention be given to alternative program development within public systems. He described the movement as the "privatization" of the public schools. Central Park East, located in District 4 in East Harlem, fits Erickson's description. It is an integrated school of choice that struggled to establish itself in a New York City elementary district, doing so successfully, and becoming the model for other schools of choice in District 4.[55]

National Calls for Reform

Prestigious groups began to call for reform in the early 1970s. As noted earlier, reports of such bodies were joined by a spate of critical documents in 1983, including *A Nation at Risk: The Imperative for Educational Reform,* the work of the National Commission on Excellence in Education.[56] Most of these documents had implications for alternative schools.

In 1973 a report of national significance called for reducing age segregation and for eliminating the insulation of young people from adults and the world of work.[57] The National Commission on the Reform of Secondary Education, established by the Charles F. Kettering Foundation and chaired by B. Frank Brown, made a series of recommendations that encouraged alternative routes to high school graduation and the funding by local school boards of acceptable alternatives to the comprehensive high school:

> A wide variety of paths leading to completion of requirements for graduation from high school should be made available to all students. Individual students must be

encouraged to assume major responsibility for the determination of their educational goals, the development of the learning activities needed to achieve those goals, and the appraisal of their progress.[58]

The commission even made the rather radical recommendation that because contemporary adolescents mature earlier the states should reduce the formal age to leave school to fourteen.[59]

The report of the Panel on Youth of the President's Science Advisory Committee appeared in 1974.[60] It called for the design of educational environments and opportunities that would permit youth to become adults in all ways, not just intellectually:

> Our basic premise is that the school system, as now constituted, offers an incomplete context for the accomplishment of many important facets of maturation. The school has been well-designed to provide some kinds of training but, by virtue of that fact, is inherently ill-suited to fulfill other tasks essential to the creation of adults. Indeed, it would be unreasonable to expect any institution to suffice as the exclusive environment for youth. Signs of dissatisfaction abound, from parents and taxpayers who have an inarticulate sense that something is amiss, from school administrators and teachers who are experimenting with methods and objectives and forms that differ from those of the established system, and from youth themselves, many of whom are showing individual initiative in the search for extra-curricular experiences.[61]

The panel was critical of American secondary education and noted rising problems with the existing institutional arrangements whereby most students attend large neighborhood comprehensive schools. Some of these problems were: "little consumer choice, the heavy weight of bureaucracy and professional controls; the large size of single-grade students strata; segregation by class, race, and ethnicity; overloading of institutional capacity by an excess of expectations and functions; and the institutional blandness that can follow from ambiguous purpose and amorphous structure."[62]

Willard Wirtz, chairman of the National Institute for Work and Learning and former U.S. Secretary of Labor, became one of the nation's most vocal spokespersons for improving employment-oriented education.[63] He deplored that growing numbers of young persons were unemployable or underemployed. Wirtz urged closer cooperation between schools and their communities, especially local business and industry. Community Education-Work Councils were established in several cities and were devoted to solving the problems of education and unemployment. Wirtz offered several important proposals, including the establishment of more Community Education-Work Councils, increased career-work counseling, a break in the sequence of education to allow for one or two years of work experience, integration of education and work policy at state and federal levels, encouragement of adults who had not completed high school to do so at public expense.

The Paideia Proposal, by Mortimor Adler, appeared in 1982.[64] It was forerunner to more than twenty major analyses of American education, most of which included recommendations for change. *The Paideia Proposal* emphasized an academic education for everyone constructed on the belief that all children can learn, there are no unteachable children, education is lifelong, and schooling is only part of education. The proposed curriculum closely parallels the offerings of many private schools.

A *Nation at Risk* attracted considerable publicity when released in April, 1983.[65] This report was the product of a commission named by Terrel H. Bell, then U.S. Secretary of Education. Weaknesses were identified in education at all levels and recommendations were made regarding curriculum, teachers, teaching, school organization, and school management. Suggestions were offered regarding specific steps to be taken to achieve improvements. John Goodlad published *A Place Called School* in 1983; his book contained a summary of nearly eight years of research.[66] *High School,* authored by former U.S. Commissioner of Education Ernest Boyer, appeared at about the same time.[67] Boyer and Goodlad prepared their work from considerable data acquired from extensive observations in schools. Their reports, like many to follow, contained recommendations for reform including basic policy revisions such as school entering and leaving ages, length of school year, and larger blocks of time for instruction in specific subjects.

The parade of national reports continued through the 1980s. Former governor Lamar Alexander of Tennessee chaired a study group that addressed the assessment of student achievement. H. Thomas James, vice chairman and study director, is president emeritus of the Spencer Foundation and former dean of the School of Education at Stanford. This leadership team, a politician and an academic and philanthropic administrator, produced *The Nation's Report Card,* a document filled with recommendations to strengthen how America's learners and schools are assessed. One of the principal proposals was to create an Educational Assessment Council to serve as national steward of assessment accountable to the public.[68]

Harold Howe II, former U.S. Commissioner of Education chaired an equally prestigious group, the William T. Grant Foundation Commission on Work, Family, and Citizenship, which focused on the educational needs and futures of "the forgotten half," the 20 million Americans between sixteen and twenty-four who are not likely to embark on a college education.[69] This commission's recommendations are far-reaching and join others that emphasize lifelong learning for the noncollege-bound and closer links between schools and employers. Contrary to other findings the Grant Commission reported that today's noncollege-bound were ambitious, wanting to work, and hopeful rather than lazy, chemical dependent, and despair-ridden. Each report has significance for nonpublic schools. The former because it recommends including the testing of private school students in national assessments of student learning and the latter because it describes an incredibly large market for continuing education that may be met by private entrepreneurs.

Private schools may, in the short run, pick up additional students as parents' awareness of public school deficiencies increases. In the long run, the impact on private schools will depend on improvements made in public schools. If, as a result of reforms at all levels of public education, public schools in fact become better institutions, they will be competitive with private schools. In time enrollments in nonpublic schools may dwindle. Many of the reports contained recommendations that teachers be better paid and public school salaries are improving. Should this continue, private schools will be in a more difficult competitive position, especially in regard to employing science and mathematics teachers. Many private schools have reputations for academic excellence; such schools may be challenged seriously by more and more public schools in the years to come.

Vouchers and Tuition Tax Credits

For two decades, the voucher concept has been debated within Congress and at the local school district level. Tuition tax credits for parents of children enrolled in nonpublic schools, although equally controversial, have been prominent since the mid-1970s.[70]

As the 1970s gave way to the 1980s, discussions of educational options intensified. In Michigan voters rejected voucher proposals. In so doing, they reaffirmed, for the time being at least, belief in the traditional concept of public education. Had the voucher proposals been accepted, parents would have had several options for the education of their children. Public monies could have been expended for educational options other than those available through traditional public schools.

Several scholars at the University of California at Berkeley led the reexamination of the voucher concept. Some proposals regarding educational finance were developed essentially within the Childhood and Government Project supported by Ford Foundation and Carnegie Corporation grants. Sugarman advocated that more responsibility should be placed with parents and teachers for determining how significant portions of the school budget would be spent.[71] One of his proposals would establish a teacher-trustee plan. A teacher participating in the plan would be responsible for a trust account that would be available to enrich the educational experiences in her or his classroom.

A nontraditional approach to school desegregation, with some voucher overtone, was advanced by the Berkeley group. Apprehensive about the effectiveness of court-ordered school desegregation, Abrams, Coons, and Sugerman developed a financial incentives program to stimulate voluntary desegregation plans.[72] Basically, the incentives approach would involve paying financial bonuses to school districts that are able to develop high-quality integrated educational opportunities. The idea is similar to Wisconsin school desegregation legislation, which provides incentives for urban students to attend school in suburban districts and for suburban youngsters to enroll in city schools. Families would be involved in the choices, which would include nonpublic schools if they met the criterion of effective integrated education.

In 1978 Coons and Sugarman published a widely discussed book, *Education by Choice*.[73] The volume stimulated discussions of the voucher concept among educators and lay people. The debate intensified regarding issuing vouchers to parents to purchase educational services in either the public or private marketplace. The basic voucher philosophy remains essentially the same as that first voiced by economist Milton Friedman in the 1950s. However, Coons and Sugarman added considerable detail to Friedman's initial concept, particularly by dispelling many of the operational and procedural uncertainties that characterized early proposals.

Wise and Darling-Hammond argued that the sponsors of voucher proposals must demonstrate how public and private schools will achieve the state's goals efficiently and effectively when they said, "They must be prepared to explain how we will achieve public and private purposes in private settings with public money."[74] They note that private control over the public interest has been avoided throughout our nation's history. Public funding of the private sector without public accountability is not likely.[75] Tuition tax credits are quite another matter. This proposal has been before Congress for a decade or more. Opponents of tax credits breathed easier when the Packwood-Moynihan tuition tax credit bill was defeated in August, 1978.[76] The matter is far from resolved, however. The matter came before the Senate again in 1983 in the form of an amendment to other legislation but was defeated once more. Senator Daniel Moynihan doubts that it will go far in Congress but it is likely to be debated again in the 1990s. Moynihan forecasts reduced opposition during national election periods with an improved prospect for passage. Public school advocates see the measure as a substantial threat as do its opponents in Congress.[77]

In 1983 the U.S. Supreme Court approved a Minnesota tuition tax deduction law in a 5–4 decision. The Minnesota case, *Mueller* v. *Allen,* allows parents to subtract from their taxable income up to $500 for grades K through 6, and $700 for grades 7 through 12, for tuition, textbooks, and transportation. It is important to note that the deduction is available to parents of public school children as well as those who have children attending private school.

Tax credit legislation was introduced in Illinois, Wyoming, and Minnesota in 1981.[78] A tax credit referendum was defeated in Washington, DC in November of that year. In 1985, Minnesota enacted legislation authorizing use of state aid monies to pay for courses that eleventh- and twelfth-graders may take at four-year liberal arts colleges when such courses are not available at their own high schools. Although the legislation is aimed at academic acceleration for good students, it is a form of voucher that can be spent at private liberal arts colleges. Other states have voucher-type legislation in place. Alaska and Vermont provide tuition vouchers to private schools where no public high school is available. South Carolina and Virginia offer loans on a competitive basis to students attending nonsectarian, private high schools.[79] Similar initiatives are likely to take place at the federal and state levels where, if successful, they may lead to litigation on several points of constitutionality.[80]

Home Schooling

To this point, our attention has been directed to institutions—schools both public and private. Education, however, takes place in many contexts, including the home. In recent years, many people have converted to the practice of home schooling. Reliable estimates of the numbers of such parents do not exist, although the figure of 10,000 is cited.[81] Teaching children at home, under a variety of conditions, was a prominent part of early American educational history. Distance and remoteness often forced parents to teach at home even if they would have preferred to have their children attend school.

Compulsory education laws were enacted to ensure the state's interest in an educated citizenry. The state's interest is now clashing with parent rights to determine the form and substance of their children's learning. In recent years both local school districts and states have searched for ways to accommodate both interests.[82] Divoky has indicated that many home schoolers are religious fundamentalists disappointed with the failure of public schools to teach moral and spiritual tenets.[83] Where state law or local district policy prohibits home schooling, parents are using various subterfuges to teach their children at home. Some enroll their youngsters in private schools that will then allow the children to stay home. Others hire state certificated tutors or acquire state teacher certification themselves.[84]

Attitudes of educators toward home schooling are mixed. Some local districts have adopted a friendly, facilitative posture toward the phenomenon; others are hostile. Of major concern to public school administrators is loss of state aid when students fail to enroll and/or attend their schools. John Holt, a strong advocate for home schooling, urges school superintendents to abandon their opposition and develop local policies that will permit both home schooling parents and school districts to benefit.[85] This can be achieved by redefining attendance to include attendance at home.

Home schooling may grow moderately in the immediate future although few observers believe it will become widespread or become a parental option that will threaten public or private schools. Home tutoring programs, on the other hand, may assume more acceptance since they are supplements to the offerings of public and private schools.[86]

Entrepreneurial Schools

Myron Lieberman, a critic of education over three decades, argues for "entrepreneurial schools," a curious blend of private and public, which he believes will bring genuine educational reform. Lieberman defines an entrepreneur as one who arranges the factors of production in ways that add economic value to them. An educational entrepreneur is one that arranges the factors of educational production in ways that generate educational value. Entrepreneurial schools could take many forms:

☐ Individual schools operated as an independent business.
☐ Franchised schools, perhaps specializing by grade level or program.
☐ Schools operated by private enterprise under contract with school boards or state educational agencies.
☐ A mixed mode in which schools may be neither wholly public nor wholly private and entrepreneurial but a mixture of both.[87]

Lieberman maintains that the concept is not a private enterprise model although competition is central to its implementation. Competition exists in attracting and retaining students whether the school is embedded in a public school setting or outside. Key to an entrepreneurial school's success is arranging the factors of educational production to meet the individual learner's needs and doing so efficiently so as to make the school profitable in an economic sense. Success also depends on the clarity of the learner's goals, enabling the factors of educational production to be organized specifically to meet those goals. His ideas are a blend of nonsectarian private school experience, performance contracting of fifteen years ago, and proprietary school philosophy.

SUMMARY AND FUTURE PROSPECTS

The future of alternative schools is less distinct than in the recent past. Many of the traditional issues will persist, especially the scope of public control over private schools.[88]

An expansion of private schools sponsored by fundamentalist religious groups has occurred in recent years. The growth has been rapid, so rapid in fact that the precise number of such schools is not known. These schools have produced problems in some states where their existence has run afoul of state regulations. In 1981 a fundamentalist school in Nebraska for example challenged the state's regulatory authority over personnel certification and curriculum materials. The Nebraska state supreme court upheld the authority of the state to regulate private schools and the U.S. Supreme Court refused to review the case on appeal.

Earlier it was pointed out that the states vary widely in the extent to which they control various areas of instruction. Few states have comprehensive statutory provisions governing nonpublic schools while in others there are many regulatory requirements established by state departments or state boards. In some instances, even where statutes or regulations exist, enforcement is weak. Should states' rights to regulate be challenged more frequently, states may respond by increasing the scope of their regulatory powers.

If nonpublic schools should receive more direct public support regardless of the forms in which it is available, it seems clear that there may be increased controls on nonpublic schools. The same standards that are expected of public schools may be extended to nonpublic schools that receive public support. If the states provide the same services to nonpublic schools that are offered to public schools, the programs of state visitation, school reporting, and inspections logically should be uniform for all schools.

The extension of public control has advantages, especially in insuring uniform levels of performance, but there are costs too; nonpublic schools will necessarily forego many of the freedoms that they have cherished. Carried to extremes, controls could lead to the disappearance of nonpublic schools and the substitution of quasi-public schools. Nonpublic schools might retain only the privileges of determining the constituency they would serve and deciding whether to include religious teachings in their curricula. Increased communication between leaders in public and nonpublic schools, including the new alternative institutions, is both necessary and inevitable. Within the American culture the acceptance of public and nonpublic education is well established. Therefore, more is to be gained than lost as a consequence of cooperation and collaboration. There appears to be increased receptivity to dialogue on the part of leaders on both sides.

A final issue of control concerns the expansion of learning opportunities outside and beyond the traditional public and private educational institutions at the elementary, secondary, and higher levels. These institutions serve persons of all ages in contrast to the K–12 institutions that serve essentially the age range of five through sixteen. The control issue involved is subtle. Historically, public school leaders presided over a monopoly. Today they still control the school systems that enroll almost 90 percent of the K–12 group. What has gone relatively unnoticed is the emergence of a vast and highly differentiated body of learning opportunities about which public school officials are not well informed and over which they have no control. The presence of these options implicitly reduces the power and significance of traditional educational institutions.

The intense interest in education on the part of the American public may take several directions. In the late 1980s it appeared that the momentum of public judgment favored the continuation of public education as historically conceived. The concept of public education is consistent with the American commitment to small "d" democracy but that commitment has been and will continue to be subjected to reexamination. Should public schooling slip into further decline, Americans may shift their loyalties to a new balance between public and nonpublic schools. The challenge is real for leaders of public and nonpublic institutions. Expectations will remain high and continued public confidence and the resulting economic and political support cannot be taken for granted.

NOTES

[1] For an overview of state efforts to expand choice and create alternatives see, Joe Nathan, "Results and Future Prospects of State Efforts to Increase Choice Among Schools," *Phi Delta Kappan* 68 (June 1987): 746–52.

[2] R. Freeman Butts and Lawrence A. Cremin, *A History of Education in American Culture* (New York: Holt, Rinehart & Winston, 1953), 108–13. For a more recent and comprehensive overview of nonpublic schools including their origins see Otto F. Kraushaar, *American Nonpublic Schools: Patterns of Diversity* (Baltimore, MD: Johns Hopkins University Press, 1972).

[3] Diane B. Gertler, "Statistics of Nonpublic Schools," *School Life* 46 (October 1963): 31.

[4] Martha M. McCarthy, *A Delicate Balance: Church, State, and the Schools* (Bloomington, IN: Phi Delta Kappan Educational Foundation, 1983), ch. 7.

[5] *Pierce* v. *Society of the Sisters,* 268 U.S. 510 (1925).

[6] For a summary of recent issues in regulation see, Tyll van Geel, "The Constitution and State Regulation of Private Schooling," in *The Church, the State and the Schools,* Charles B. Vergon, ed. (Ann Arbor, MI: The University of Michigan School of Education, 1986), 103–120.

[7] Donald A. Erickson, "Legal Impediments to Private Educational Options" in *The Courts and Education,* Seventy-seventh Yearbook of the National Society for the Study of Educa-

tion, part 1, ed. Clifford P. Hooker (Chicago: University of Chicago Press, 1978), 116–39. See also Helen M. Jellison, ed., *State and Federal Laws Relating to Non Public Schools* (Washington, DC: U.S. Department of Health, Education, and Welfare, 1975).

[8]National Center for Education Statistics, *The Condition of Education, 1987 Edition* (Washington, DC: U.S. Department of Education, Office of Educational Research & Improvement, 1987), 186.

[9]*Digest of Education Statistics 1982* (Washington, DC: National Center for Education Statistics, 1982), 48.

[10]Ibid., 48.

[11]Diane B. Gertler and Leah W. Ramsey, *Non-public Secondary Schools: A Directory, 1960–61* (Washington, DC: U.S. Government Printing Office, 1963), 1.

[12]Ibid.

[13]Raymond F. McCoy, *American School Administration* (New York: McGraw-Hill, 1961), 112–13.

[14]Edward B. Smith, S. J., "Policy Making in Jesuit High Schools" (Ph.D. diss., University of Chicago, 1962).

[15]Otto F. Kraushaar, *American Nonpublic Schools* (Baltimore, MD: Johns Hopkins University Press, 1972).

[16]*Digest of Education Statistics,* 56.

[17]Ibid.

[18]James A. Burns, *The Catholic School System in the United States* (New York: Benziger Brothers, 1908), 109.

[19]Neil G. McCluskey, S. J., *Catholic Viewpoint on Education* (Garden City, NY: Doubleday, 1962), 18.

[20]*Christian Education of Youth,* 1929, Official text published by the National Catholic Welfare Council (Washington, DC, 1930).

[21]The National Association of Boards of Education/NCEA, *The Flowering of Catholic Boardsmanship* 9 (June 1981): 14.

[22]McCoy, *American School Administration,* 113.

[23] McCluskey, *Catholic Education Faces the Future* (Garden City, NY: Doubleday and Co., 1969), 115.

[24]*Catholic Schools in America 1978–1979* (Washington, DC: National Catholic Education Association, 1979), 18. ERIC ED 168 215.

[25]William A. Kranier, *Lutheran Schools* (St. Louis, MO: Board of Parish Education, The Lutheran Church, Missouri Synod, 1961), 5.

[26]*Information Bulletin* (1982–83), No. 33982, (St. Louis, MO: Board for Parish Services, 1983), 7.

[27]One measure of the effect of Jewish education is the greater religious involvement of adults who have attended Jewish schools. For an important analysis of such effects see Harold S. Himmelfarb, "The Non-Linear Impact of Schooling: Comparing Different Types and Amounts of Jewish Education," *Sociology of Education* 42 (April 1977): 114–29.

[28]Roy A. Larmee, "The Relationship Between Certain National Movements in Education and Selected Independent Secondary Schools" (Ph.D. diss., University of Chicago, 1962).

[29]Diane Ravitch, *The Schools We Deserve* (New York: Basic Books, Inc., 1985), 171.

[30]*Time for Results* (Washington, DC: National Governors Association, 1986), 171.

[31]James S. Coleman, "Families and Schools," *Educational Researcher* 26 (August–September 1987): 37.

[32]Mario D. Fantini, "Alternatives for Urban School Systems," *Harvard Educational Review* 38 (Winter 1968): 160–75.

[33]Neil Postman and Charles Weingartner, *How to Recognize a Good School* (Bloomington, IN: Phi Delta Kappa Educational Foundation, 1973), 7.

[34]Ibid., 11.

[35]Ibid., 12–13.

[36]These data provided directly by the National Center for Education Statistics, 400 Maryland Avenue, S.W., Washington, DC, 20202, December 1983.

[37]Postman and Weingartner, *How to Recognize a Good School,* 14.

[38]Ibid.

[39]Ivan Illich, *Deschooling Society* (New York: Harper & Row, 1971).

[40]Marilyn Ferguson, *The Aquarian Conspiracy* (Los Angeles: J. P. Tarcher, 1980), 286.

[41]Ralph W. Tyler, "The Total Educational Environment," in *Education for Responsible Citizenship,* ed. Louis Rubin (New York: McGraw-Hill, 1977), 15–25.

[42]Ralph W. Tyler, "Dynamic Response in a Time of Decline," *Phi Delta Kappan* 63 (June 1982): 655–58.

[43]Lawrence A. Cremin, *Public Education* (New York: Basic, 1976), 96.

[44]Lawrence A. Cremin, *Traditions in American Education* (New York: Basic, 1977), 127–28.

[45]See *Secondary School Alternative Programs: January 1973* (Philadelphia, PA: Board of Education, Alternative Programs Office, 1973).

[46]For an analysis of the Berkeley program see Sherwood Davidson Kohn, "Getting Attention in California," *National Elementary Principal* 52 (April 1973): 90–93. Further evaluation of the Berkeley experimental schools appears in *Education R & D and the Case of Berkeley's Experimental Schools* (Washington, DC: National Institute of Education, 1976).

[47]Mario Fantini, "The What, Why, and Where of the Alternatives Movement," *The National Elementary Principal* 52 (April 1973): 17.

[48]Diane Ravitch, *The Troubled Crusade* (New York: Basic, 1983), 258–59.

[49]"North Central Decides to Accredit Optional Schools," *Education U.S.A.,* (Washington, DC: National School Public Relations Association, 8 April 1974): 177.

[50]For a description of the Dallas options see Daniel U. Levine and Nolan Estes, "Desegregation and Educational Reconstruction in the Dallas Public Schools," *Phi Delta Kappan* 59 (November 1977): 163–67, 221.

[51]Mary Anne Raywid, "Schools of Choice: Their Current Nature and Prospects," *Phi Delta Kappan* 64 (June 1983): 684–88.

[52]Ibid., 686–87.

[53]Ibid., 688.

[54]Donald A. Erickson et al., *The British Columbia Story: Antecedents and Consequences of Aid to Private Schools* (Los Angeles: Institute for the Study of Private Schools, 1982), ch. 15.

[55]Deborah Meier, "Central Park East: An Alternative Story," *Phi Delta Kappan* 68 (June 1987): 753–57.

[56]See National Commission on Excellence in Education, *A Nation at Risk: The Imperative for Educational Reform* (Washington, DC: Government Printing Office, 1983).

[57]*The Reform of Secondary Education: A Report to the Public and the Profession,* National Commission on the Reform of Secondary Education (New York: McGraw-Hill, 1973).

[58]Ibid., 16–17.

[59]Ibid., 21.

[60]*Youth Transition to Adulthood,* Report of the Panel on Youth of the President's Science Advisory Committee (Chicago: University of Chicago Press, 1974).

[61]Ibid., 2.

[62]Ibid., 151–52.

[63]Willard Wirtz, *The Boundless Resource* (Washington, DC: New Republic, 1975).

[64]Mortimer Jerome Adler, *The Paideia Proposal* (New York: Macmillan, 1982).

[65]National Commission on Excellence in Education, *A Nation at Risk.*

[66]John I. Goodlad, *A Place Called School: Prospects for the Future* (St. Louis, MO: McGraw-Hill, 1983).

[67]Ernest L. Boyer, *High School: A Report on Secondary Education in America* (New York: Harper & Row, 1983).

[68]*The Nation's Report Card* (Washington, DC: U.S. Department of Education, Report of the Study Group, 1987), 76.

[69]*The Forgotten Half: Non-College Bound Young in America* (Washington, DC: The William T. Grant Foundation Commission on Work, Family and Citizenship, 1988).

[70]For a comprehensive review of the literature on vouchers (and tax credits) see "Vouchers and Tax Credits—A Special Issue," *Private School Monitor* 4 (Fall 1981).

[71]Stephen D. Sugarman, "Education Reform at the Margins: Two Ideas," *Phi Delta Kappan* 59 (November 1977): 154–57.

[72]Carol Abrams, John E. Coons, and Stephen D. Sugarman, "School Integration Through Carrots, Not Sticks," *Theory Into Practice* 17 (February 1978): 23–31.

[73]John E. Coons and Stephen D. Sugarman, *Education by Choice* (Berkeley, CA: University of California Press, 1978).

[74]Arthur E. Wise and Linda Darling-Hammond, "Educational Vouchers: Regulating Their Efficiency and Effectiveness," *Educational Researcher* 12 (November 1983): 9–18.

[75]Ibid., 18.

[76]Daniel Patrick Moynihan, "The Case for Tuition Tax Credits," *Phi Delta Kappan* 60 (December 1978): 274–76.

[77]Ernest F. Hollings, "The Case Against Tuition Tax Credits," *Phi Delta Kappan* 60 (December 1978): 277–79.

[78]"Vouchers and Tax Credits," Private School Monitor.

[79]For a more detailed review of family choice proposals see Myron Lieberman, *Beyond Public Education* (New York: Praeger, 1986), 179–208.

[80]Donald N. Jensen, "Tuition Tax Credits: Has the Supreme Court Cleared the Way?" *IFG Policy Perspectives* (Stanford, CA: School of Education, Stanford University, June 1983), 12.

[81]McCarthy, *A Delicate Balance,* 149.

[82]Ibid., 52–54.

[83]Diane Divoky, "The New Pioneers of the Home-Schooling Movement," *Phi Delta Kappan* 64 (February 1983): 395–98.

[84]Ibid., 398.

[85]For a comprehensive overview of home schooling see John Holt, *Teach Your Own* (New York: Delacorte/Seymour Lawrence, 1981): 369.

[86]Edward E. Gordon, "Home Tutoring Programs Gain Respectability," *Phi Delta Kappan* 64 (February 1983): 398–99. For an important review of family roles in education read Hope Jensen Leichter, "Families as Educators," *Education in School and Nonschool Settings,* Mario D. Fantini and Robert L. Sinclair, eds., Eighty-Fourth Yearbook of the National Society for the Study of Education (Chicago: The Society, 1985), 81–101.

[87]Lieberman, *Beyond Public Education,* 15, 209–37.

[88]Two sources for the analyses of governmental role and responsibility in regard to private or nonpublic schools are Donald A. Erickson, *Public Controls for Nonpublic Schools* (Chicago: University of Chicago Press, 1969) and Otto F. Kraushaar, *American Nonpublic Schools* (Baltimore, MD: Johns Hopkins University Press, 1972), ch. 11, 12, and 13.

18
Control Elements: Summary and Conclusions

W e began in Chapter 1 by declaring our intention of placing the control variables that appear to affect schools in an open systems context. We defined open systems in terms of interaction between an organization and its environment, largely following Easton, and in terms of loose coupling within the organization itself, largely following Weick. We discovered that a large number of institutions, conditions, and persons control in one way or another what schools are, what they do, and how as organizations they behave. Throughout the book we have used the word *control* in a broad sense to encompass the various expectations, constraints, and influences that affect schools. We have also used the term *schools* in a broad sense. Ordinarily, we have used it to mean a single public school or a public school district but at times we also considered nonpublic or alternative schools. From the previous discussion of the various types of school control, seven general categories can be derived.

THE CONTROL CATEGORIES

The control categories that follow have been developed inductively from the descriptions and analyses of the institutions, conditions, and persons that affect the schools. The open systems approach to administration has informed our analyses and in a sense this book represents an empirical test of the open systems concept in the area of education.

The establishment of these categories was a difficult task. First, there was the problem of terminology. The term *control constraints,* considered because some of these controls do constrain, was rejected because on balance *constraints* seems to emphasize the negative and leave little room for the positive. *Control influences* seemed redundant for we used *control* and *influence* as synonyms throughout this work. *Control determinants* suggested a tightness of relationship that hardly fits the notion of loosely coupled organizations. From the more neutral terms remaining, such as *control factors, control components,* and *control elements,* we have chosen to use the term *control elements.*

A second problem in developing categories was deciding what level of abstraction should be employed. At the highest level of abstraction one might simply say that organizations are affected by internal and external factors. But such a statement is too general to be useful. Therefore, we have categorized internal and external factors that affect schools into seven control elements—demographic, legal, structural, ideational, knowledge, financial, and network—each of which we will examine.

Demographic Control Elements

Demographic control elements include the number and character of adults in a particular school or school district, the number and character of students in a particular school, and the cultural traditions and values of these adults and students. In most areas of control, demography (Chapter 2) appears to make a difference. Federal aid (Chapter 3), for instance, is frequently related to the nature of the people residing in certain school districts or school attendance areas. Federal aid is channeled to areas where the people are poor, to areas where minorities are in need, and to areas where segregation is a problem. Acceptance of the notion of equal opportunity means that the institutions can no longer be racially, economically, or culturally blind; that people do differ; and that these differences often indicate where financial assistance is needed. To some extent, these same considerations are found to affect state support of schools and school districts (Chapter 4), particularly where states have been called on to implement federal provisions for the handicapped and sex equality.

Even where school districts, intermediate units, and attendance areas are concerned (Chapters 5, 6, and 7), demographic considerations form the basis for certain controls. School districts, for instance, may include a great many people or very few people. In large districts the population tends to be heterogeneous economically and culturally while in small districts the population tends to be more homogeneous. These demographic (or socioeconomic) factors explain many of the differences among subgroups within school districts in their aspirations for schools, their ability to support schools, and their level of interest in school programs and policy. Attendance areas, since they represent subunits of school districts, may vary even more economically and culturally than school districts. For this reason, increasing attention is being given to channeling federal and state assistance directly to school sites rather than to school districts. Again, demographic characteristics prompt these efforts to control allocations of resources. Intermediate units represent response to demography. Through them, resources from several school districts or from the state itself are used to meet the special needs of students in schools and school districts where the cost of services would be prohibitive if only local resources were available.

Controls exerted by colleges and universities (Chapter 16) are also affected by demographic factors. Small school districts and attendance areas where a large proportion of the adults are college graduates have different expectations of the schools than do school districts and attendance areas where college graduates are few in number. In the first instance, college preparatory curricula are demanded and college entrance requirements are given serious consideration. In the second, more demand often exists for vocational curricula.

The characteristics of students, as well as adults, are important. Students who are college-bound respond to one type of curriculum while those who have other objectives favor other offerings. Students with special needs due to economic deprivation or physical and mental handicaps require special instructional programs. Some of these program requirements, such as individually prescribed programs and mainstreaming for the handicapped, affect in many ways the curriculum, personnel, and organization of the schools.

A somewhat different order of control has resulted from the decline of student enrollments found in many schools. Where enrollment has declined, teaching staffs have been reduced. Because few teachers are hired and mobility among the current staff is limited, the entire organization becomes less dynamic. These conditions may also give rise to teacher activism. Enrollment decline may prompt the community to demand a reduction in the school budget. Such reductions may be difficult to achieve because of inflation and because some overhead costs are not geared closely to enrollment decreases. An even greater problem stemming from enrollment decline has been the need in many communities to close some schools. In some instances, schools are community centers or at least community symbols. Closing schools portends loss of identity and prestige and frequently means some inconvenience for students and parents. Little wonder that superintendents have lost their jobs and board members have been replaced because of school closings. Thus a demographic condition, enrollment decline, can influence many aspects of school operation.

The control exercised by the superintendent of schools varies greatly in different communities (Chapter 10). Depending on the demographic characteristics of its citizens, a community may encourage the superintendent to employ rational problem-solving procedures, to rely on political skills, or merely to take orders. Indeed, demography can also influence the nature of the board of education with whom the superintendent works and can indirectly influence the kind of person who will be attracted to the superintendency itself. In short, the context within which the school operates is in large part demographic in nature.

Demographic control elements are also found in interest groups (Chapters 13 and 14). In some school districts and school attendance areas, strong school-related interest groups are active in supporting school programs. School board members may actually be recruited from these interest groups. The school board, the superintendent, school principals, and teachers inevitably hear from such groups and are generally aware of their positions on school issues. These groups also may take the initiative in generating proposals for new or improved programs. In other school districts and attendance areas there may be few if any of these school-related interest groups. The absence of such groups reflects on one hand the nature of the community and on the other hand may reinforce community apathy toward school programs. Of interest groups not related to schools, the most vocal are often those interested in tax reductions. Communities with very few school-related interest groups may be influenced much more easily by the groups representing fiscal restraint.

Finally, demographic control elements will influence the extension of the educational program (Chapter 2). That extension will be determined, in large part, by the increasing number of adults in the population and by their demand that programs be designed to meet their needs and/or the needs of their preschool-age children.

In this consideration of demographic control elements the interrelatedness of controls becomes very clear. For instance, the demographic characteristics of a school district or attendance area are in large part a result of the structural arrangements that establish those units. Are they large or small? Does their size contribute to their heterogeneity or their homogeneity? This interrelatedness of controls is apparent in fiscal allocations too. The nature of communities and their student populations determine, in some measure, the amount and kind of monies received from state and national governments. Finally, the influence of school personnel—administrators, teachers, even students—is determined, in part, by the nature of the communities in which the schools are located.

Legal Control Elements

Legal control elements have to do with state and federal constitutions, state and federal statutes, state and federal regulations, and state and federal case law. The role of the courts (Chapter 8) has grown in large part because many educational issues are also social issues. In particular the courts have endorsed the civil rights of minorities, women, teachers, and students, and such endorsements have frequently enhanced the control these groups exercise over certain aspects of school operation.

During the 1970s federal intrusion into school operation reached a new high (Chapter 3). Using recent enactments by Congress to illustrate, we noted that these controls reside in the increasing specificity of the language found in the statutes and also in the regulations; in the mandates of such legislation to establish state and national advisory committees, frequently made up chiefly of persons from lay and professional interest groups in a particular field; and in the powerful sanction of placing the enforcement of many of these provisions within the civil rights context. The Reagan administration attempted to deregulate some programs but the basic statutes remain in place.

Many of the legal controls noted at the national level pertain also at the state level (Chapter 4). There are, however, some interesting differences at the state level. Whereas the federal Constitution affects education by implication, state constitutions deal with it explicitly. Moreover, each state has an extended body of statutory and case law devoted to education. While state education agencies until recently have been loathe to exercise their full regulatory powers over school districts, three conditions have shifted control to state agencies and to governors and legislatures as well: (1) the increasing proportion of funding at the state level; (2) the demand by legislatures that the state agency exercise its control functions over school districts, often expressed in the form of accountability and competency-testing legislation; and (3) the provisions found in much federal legislation that the state agency, with persons paid from federal funds, act as the enforcement agency for federal provisions. In some states, state legislatures appear to be disenchanted with state education agencies and these legislatures have attached legislative oversight provisions to some of the laws they have enacted.

Legal controls are exercised by school districts and boards of education (Chapters 5 and 9). In each state, school districts are the legal entities created by the legislature for the purpose of operating schools, and the legislatures have delegated considerable jurisdiction to the districts. In each district a board of education has been established to exercise the powers given to school districts. While boards of education lament the loss of local control (and indeed there are increasing impingements on local board control), boards still have the legal responsibility to establish schools, to draw attendance boundary lines, to determine curricula, to employ personnel, and to set school budgets. To be sure, all of these prerogatives are exercised within a state framework, and interest groups peer over the shoulders of the boards as they take action, but the board does have broad grants of power. Some boards are coming to recognize the place of the school district in a federal system, where on many issues each partner, ideally, can influence but none can dominate. Many boards also now differentiate more clearly their role and the roles of the professionals they employ to assist them.

Affecting the operation of schools in school districts is the legally constituted intermediate unit (Chapter 6). These intermediate units are found in states with many small districts and are usually designed to provide services that aren't available or feasible in small districts. The degree of legal control residing in these intermediate units varies appreciably among the states. In some states specialized services are an option available to school districts while in others such services are mandated. More and more, states are establishing legal requirements for intermediate units.

While intermediate units tend to place school districts in clusters for the delivery of specialized services, a move in the opposite direction is also in evidence. More attention than ever before is being given to individual school attendance areas or school sites (Chapter 7). Part of this change is discretionary on the part of boards of education and part of it, particularly in California and Florida, is mandatory. In the first case, the board decides basically how much autonomy should be granted to a principal, the staff, and the citizens residing in the attendance area. This type of decentralization has come, in part, from demands of citizens who want a greater voice in the operation of their own schools. In California and Florida, the legislatures acted to establish greater legal control at school sites.

Legal controls have taken another interesting turn. Already noted are federal requirements that state and national advisory committees, made up largely of lay citizens, be established for a number of federal programs. But some states, here too, are in the mandating business. Florida, for instance, requires as part of its school site management program that advisory committees of citizens be established at the local level (Chapter 13). Clearly, lawmakers at both state and national levels are convinced that citizens should exercise a more direct role in the governance of schools and school districts.

Considerable legal attention is being given to alternative schools (Chapter 17). The legal right for such schools to exist was established long ago, but legal provisions to encourage their development and even to provide some public support for them continue to receive attention at both national and state levels. This move is based partly on the argument that parents should have a greater voice in decisions concerning the schooling of their children. This kind of emphasis pertaining to alternative schools tends to carry over, in the minds of many parents, to the control of public schools. Should the public schools be required to take over at least part of the responsibility for preschool education (Chapter 2), additional legal stipulations will be necessary.

All forms of legal control depend ultimately on the respect that most Americans have for the law. While certain laws and regulations may incur the displeasure of some, most people know that redress for unwise or unfair provisions is possible. Regulations may be changed at the agency level, laws may be rescinded at the legislative level, and the courts are available as a last resort. The courts, particularly at the appellate level, are seen by most people as sustaining basic legal rights and American values.

Structural Control Elements

Structural control elements include governmental arrangements, official organizational arrangements, and unofficial organizational arrangements in employee organizations. While there are limits to the controls derived from structure alone, frequently structure may permit or prohibit, encourage or discourage, facilitate or complicate actions desired by those concerned with schools. The controls exerted by state education agencies (Chapters 3 and 4), for example, derive from the fact that federal money is used to staff state agencies with persons committed to implementing certain federal programs. In many states one-half or more of the staff in the state agency is supported through federal subventions. Obviously, this is a form of financial control, as we shall note later, but it also constitutes structural control. Schools must confront and deal with a state agency that is structured in large part around federal programs. For years, this condition has been prevalent in the divisions of vocational education. More recently divisions have been established to deal with sex equity, the education of the handicapped, and other federal interests.

Closely related to the structuring of state agencies is the establishment of new regional resource centers across the country. In the area of the education of the handicapped, for instance, seventeen centers were established under federal auspices. Each center (there are now only six) is staffed with persons committed to the program for the handicapped and with expertise in that area. An obvious purpose of these structures is to provide resource people and materials to schools and school districts. If schools do not solicit that help readily, the center must find ways to make its resources appealing.

Structural controls are at work within school districts, intermediate units, and attendance areas (Chapters 5, 6, and 7). In a small district, for instance, organizational structure may be simple, and face-to-face relationships among professionals and lay citizens encouraged; in a large district organizational structure can be formidable, and communication among professionals and lay citizens extremely difficult. In some states intermediate units are set up to be controlled largely by school board members or others from the component school districts. In other states, the intermediate units are allowed much more autonomy. The autonomy granted by school districts or by state mandate to single schools or school sites also represents structural control. A school district may set up a highly centralized structure or it may operate with a much more decentralized arrangement.

Territorial structures, whether school districts, intermediate units, or attendance areas, affect the actors who operate within them. Of primary importance are the structural relationships, formal and informal, between the board and the superintendent (Chapters 9 and 10). While this relationship is affected by demographic factors, structural arrangements are also significant. Some superintendents dominate their boards, some boards dominate their superintendents, and in some situations a sensitive partnership has been established between the board and the superintendent. In such partnerships control may go beyond legal definitions; the board may delegate to the superintendent the responsibility for program development. When recommendations growing out of program considerations are approved by the board, the board then holds the superintendent responsible for their implementation. In such a situation the superintendent enjoys considerable power of office not only with the board but with the professional staff as well.

Teachers organizations (Chapter 12) are relatively new structures, particularly in the form they have now assumed and in the role they now play. A few decades ago school administrators belonged to teachers organizations and such membership seemed quite acceptable to both groups. Indeed, some administrators became representatives for teacher groups at both local and state levels. That day has virtually disappeared. Teachers organizations are now led by teachers. They see a major function of those organizations as the protection of the economic well-being of teachers, and they insist that decisions affecting teachers, economic or otherwise, be made only with the participation of teacher representatives. Moreover, teachers organizations have learned that most policy decisions affecting schools are made at the state level, chiefly in the state legislature. Thus the teacher lobby, an unofficial structure, exercises considerable influence at the state level in policy formation and considerable influence, chiefly through the bargaining process, at the local level in policy implementation. Few principals, superintendents, or school boards can now ignore this new structure.

Controls exercised by school-related groups (Chapter 13) are frequently benign, but as more citizens raise questions about the school enterprise, that picture is changing. Even the Parent Teacher Association, long under the domination of school administrators, has decided to be more aggressive in its review of school policy. Its current organizational emphasis, particularly at the state and national levels, is on a number of issues, such as alcohol, drugs, and pornography, which the PTA is convinced affect learning outcomes of children and youth in and out of school. Another item of interest is the extent to which schools and school districts structure their organizations to permit or encourage interaction with school-related groups. Where such structures are not fostered by the school, these groups may speak for the community at large and demand such participation.

Governmental access is generally a function of the number and levels of decision points (Chapter 15). The multiplicity of decision points may discourage and even deter citizens trying to affect the school. For school or school district officials the multiplication of decision points may also prove burdensome. For instance, some boards of education can by themselves adopt a school budget. Other boards of education are required to have their budget proposals approved by a town meeting, or a city council, or a county board of some kind, even by a state agency. As decision points increase, governing bodies must devote more and more of their time to procedural details. This point is well documented in state and national programs where citizen participation is mandated.

Clearly, schools are affected by a wide range of structural controls, both horizontal and vertical in nature. Horizontal arrangements frequently include impingements by city or county government. Vertical arrangements always include the demands of state and federal agencies. Nongovernmental structures, particularly teacher organizations, have both horizontal and vertical expressions.

Ideational Control Elements

Ideational control elements go beyond the more obvious controls imposed by legal provisions and structural arrangements and arise from the concepts and values people hold. People inside and outside the schools and school district organizations have concepts concerning government, organizations, and schools themselves. These same people also favor or explicitly espouse certain ideas and values that influence school operation. For instance, long-standing federal programs, notably vocational education, contain provisions for the preservice and in-service training of teachers (Chapter 3). Such teacher education programs are clearly an attempt to socialize teachers into a certain way of thinking about their teaching area; they instill in those teachers certain concepts and values. In the military this process is called indoctrination. By whatever name, the purpose is to shape a person's way of viewing the world.

In school districts, intermediate units, and attendance areas, the perceptions and aspirations of people inside and outside the schools make a difference (Chapters 5, 6, and 7). In school districts, for instance, when there is a proposal to close a school, the strength of these perceptions becomes readily apparent. Frequently, when intermediate units are established that combine several small districts for certain purposes, persons in a small unit who have certain perceptions and values must deal with the perceptions and values of other persons in a larger context. Where this kind of interaction produces a new level of ideational agreement, the new structure generally succeeds. If a new consensus does not emerge, the new structure probably can do little to enhance school programs. In some cases persons in a particular attendance area may want to become or remain more homogeneous than is possible in the larger school district. They wish their particular perceptions and values about education to be given greater recognition and even to control their particular school.

Legal controls (Chapter 8) are effective only to the extent that such provisions embody concepts and values acceptable to most people. In periods of social change, certain legal provisions may become irrelevant to many people. Under these circumstances the provisions will tend to be ignored or they will be changed. New legal status accorded minority groups, women, and now students reflects changes in attitudes that brought further changes in legal arrangements themselves.

The controls exerted by school boards and superintendents (Chapters 9 and 10) are also, in part, ideational in nature. Board members have certain concepts and values regarding schools, and superintendents also have a set of concepts and values that influences their thinking about school operation. The superintendent has been subjected to professional training, through which certain concepts and values are taught. When the superintendent's professional viewpoint differs appreciably from that of board members, conflict will ensue. Or, when board members and superintendent espouse one set of beliefs and major groups in the community operate from another, conflict will also ensue. There is no way of escaping the old proverb: as a man thinketh in his heart, so is he.

Controls exercised by teachers (Chapter 12) came about primarily through a change in thinking about teachers. Teachers see themselves in a new light. Legislative enactments and court decisions have established the right of teachers to organize and to bargain. People generally have accepted teachers in their new role, and teachers exercise greater control because people's perceptions of teachers have undergone a change. To some extent, the same is true for students. The courts, in particular, have developed the doctrine that students are people too and as people they have certain rights. For instance, due process is to be followed when students are disciplined.

The influence of school-related groups (Chapter 13) and other interest groups (Chapter 14) is also, in part, ideational. Two developments are pertinent here. The first is a growing concern, even doubt, about the capacity of the school to achieve its purposes or at least the purposes traditionally ascribed to the school. The second development is a rejection of big government, which must necessarily be representative in nature, and a resurgence of direct participation in government. Many different interest groups espouse these positions and are determined to influence decisions affecting schools and other institutions in our society. In many cases these groups become preoccupied with single issues, such as the selection of textbooks, and give little attention to other policy issues. When several interest groups speak out on different issues, those who must operate public institutions find it nearly impossible to respond to all of them. The inability of a school to respond to conflicting demands tend to reinforce, in the minds of many, the perception of school failure and governmental inadequacy.

The aspirations people have for the school often influence the financial support they will give the school. If people believe that schooling is important, that schools are offering relevant programs to their children, they tend to support schools both morally and financially. On the other hand, if schooling itself seems irrelevant or if school procedures seem misdirected, moral and financial support will be withheld.

College influences (Chapter 16) are, in large part, a matter of expectations. Admission requirements are one vehicle that permits colleges to exercise some control over the schools. Through admission requirements, colleges express their expectations for entering students. Schools, students, and parents may accept such requirements as useful and conform to them, or they may question such requirements and join in efforts to change them. In either case, the response is essentially an ideational one. Over the past few decades, some prestigious colleges maintained rigorous admission requirements but many colleges, particularly public institutions, relaxed their requirements. Most of the recent studies on education have urged more demanding admission requirements and many colleges, public and private, have responded to these recommendations.

Controls concerning alternative schools (Chapter 17) again are largely a matter of ideation. Those who believe that public schools are too large, too impersonal, too godless, too integrated, or whatever, frequently support the move to establish alternative schools. The establishment of these schools, their support by many people, and increasing efforts by government to provide some financial support to such schools pose ideational problems for the public schools. Indeed, the whole idea of public education, once accepted by many as almost a secular religion, is brought into question. At best, however, alternative schools do provide competition for the public schools and can be seen as a way of accommodating the diverse values and interests of a pluralistic society. If this understanding comes to be shared by more people, both public and private schools may flourish.

The extension of the educational program (Chapters 2 and 17) is in large part an ideational matter. The idea that public schools are for children in grades K–12 is deeply entrenched in our society. Education and schooling have been equated. Now social conditions are bringing both of these assumptions into question. Clearly, schools can serve preschoolers, adults generally, and older people in particular if people want them to. Indeed, highly innovative learning arrangements can be established if the extended educational program finds widespread support.

This nation is in a period when the ideational landscape surrounding schools and school governance is changing. While not all of the basic concepts and values of the Reagan administration have been implemented, they have made a difference (Chapter 3). One has only to consider such terms as federal-state, public-private, regulation, desegregation, tuition tax credits, or school prayer to recognize that values, once largely taken for granted, have been challenged.

To some, we have reached a point where our pluralism has produced so diverse an array of concepts and values that we can no longer find a common ground. If that were true, governance would be impossible. Our diversity does pose new challenges. Indeed, there are probably places where governance has been quite hopeless, but there are many instances where people have taken account of new conditions and where they have increased their efforts to make the system work.

Knowledge Control Elements

There is some truth in the adage that knowledge is power. Knowledge control elements include general knowledge and special knowledge, or expertise. In either case, those who know are usually in a position to exercise some control.

Knowledge controls are in evidence at both federal and state levels (Chapters 3 and 4). For instance, federally funded resource centers are established, in part, for the purpose of extending knowledge about particular programs in education and for bringing together a group of persons with expertise in that area. In similar manner, state education agencies frequently have research, evaluation, and development divisions for the purpose of learning more about the educational needs of the state and of ascertaining how certain programs are affecting schools and the students who attend them. The state agency can and does determine what knowledge should be uncovered, what methods should be used, and what use should be made of the knowledge, including its availability to others. State agencies also exercise another kind of knowledge control. They usually determine what kinds of knowledge, at least as expressed in college courses, teachers and administrators should possess in order to secure certificates permitting them to work in a school system. In both state and federal agencies those who work constantly in a particular area tend to develop an expertise in that area few others possess. These experts or technicians are frequently called upon, not only in their own organizations but in the world beyond, to offer informed opinions and to recommend courses of action.

Information is also generated, or at least organized, in other agencies. Most school districts must generate information about their own operation (Chapter 5). Intermediate units (Chapter 6), now found in many states, were formed, in part, to bring more information and expertise to the operation of small school districts. For instance, such intermediate units frequently provide health and psychological services, both requiring some expertise, to their component districts. Colleges and universities (Chapter 16) are also in the business of generating knowledge and provide a base of operation for persons with specialized knowledge and interests. Schools, school districts, and related agencies often see the experts in colleges and universities as somewhat more objective than the experts in their own organizations. This perception tends to extend the influence of college people.

A rather dramatic example of the control exercised by experts is found in recent court procedures. Judges often seek the knowledge and recommendations of persons in specialized areas—including the areas of teaching and learning, organizational arrangements, and environmental influences—as part of the background needed to make legal determinations. Thus, the increasing control of the courts is, in part, based on the expert testimony of knowledgeable people (Chapter 8).

Knowledge control in school districts is exercised to some extent by the school board (Chapter 9), the superintendent (Chapter 10), the other administrators (Chapter 11), and the teachers (Chapter 12). Board members obviously come to possess some knowledge about school operation. Presumably they also have some knowledge of the world beyond the school and how that world and the school are related. But most boards feel the need to employ one or more persons, reputedly with some specialized knowledge, to help them understand the institution over which they preside and to give them additional advice on the decisions they have to make. For many boards the superintendent of schools is their chief or only expert. In a less complicated world that arrangement may have worked fairly well. In today's world with its many complex problems, the expertise of the superintendent alone is simply not adequate. Superintendents need to be analysts, but as such they need to call on many others with special expertise.

This need for both special and general knowledge is frequently recognized in the organization of the superintendent's office. While in larger districts the superintendent may need to assign line officers major divisions of the district program, the superintendent also needs staff specialists whose major function is to generate information and advise the superintendent, the board, and others concerned. Often staff advice is the most important ingredient in board and administrative decisions. Thus, the roles of decision makers and decision advisers have sometimes been reversed—dramatic proof that knowledge is indeed a control element. In addition, the more specialized knowledge becomes, the greater the need for competent generalists. The superintendent and board members, as generalists, need to rely on the unique contributions of specialists.

In many ways, the real experts on school operation are the teachers. Only the teachers have a day-to-day knowledge of student behavior, including student reaction to procedures and instructional materials. This argument is used by teachers organizations as they press for greater teacher participation in decisions made by schools and school districts. While these organizations frequently seem to be more interested in the well-being of teachers than in the well-being of students, the fact remains that competent teachers have a reservoir of knowledge that can and does make a difference in many school systems. Much of the conflict between teachers and administrators is based on the issue of professional versus bureaucratic control. Bureaucratic control has been too pervasive in most school districts, but there is no way for it to be eliminated, particularly the hierarchical arrangements found in school districts. At the same time, the professional knowledge of teachers ought to be given a more prominent place in school decision making.

School-related and other interest groups (Chapters 13 and 14) exercise considerable control in an open system, and their control depends on what they know about the schools. For instance, more and more groups outside the school are insisting that the school release information about its operation. Movements for accountability and for competency testing are attempts by persons and organizations outside the school to force the school to study itself in order to tell the community how well it is achieving its purposes.

Citizens generally are better educated than ever before and are capable of raising more relevant questions about school operation. In a sense, this condition reflects the success of the schools as an institution over the last several decades. Schools must now deal with well-informed citizens, some of whom possess specialized knowledge in relevant fields. Schools can no longer claim that they have a monopoly on knowledge about learning, evaluation, organization, and finance. Experts in all these areas among parents and other school patrons are using that expertise to affect the direction of the schools.

Many of our conclusions about knowledge control are based on the assumption that people are rational beings. Rational people would obviously be interested in generating information and in using information in decisions affecting their lives, but non-rational considerations often affect people's decisions. Schools, have, as a part of their mission, the extension of rational or problem-solving behavior.

Financial Control Elements

As other control elements have been discussed, financial controls have been mentioned. In this category are included financial resources or money made available at the local, state, and federal levels; categorical aids at state and federal levels; and the use of money to foster the development of lay and professional interest groups. Wealth has been identified as one of three major clusters of variables determining the level of expenditures in school districts (Chapter 15). Obviously, there must be, in addition to the possession of wealth, a willingness to use it for school purposes. While there is not a one-to-one relationship between money and the quality of a school program, money does make a difference.

Both federal and state levels of government exert a number of financial controls over schools and school districts (Chapters 3 and 4). For instance, nearly all money at the national level is for categorical assistance, thereby determining that specific aspects of the educational program will be supported. While federal financial assistance covers only about 6 percent of the total cost of public education, the percentage of support for certain programs, such as those for the poor, is much higher; hence the inducement to many school districts to accept federal assistance is enhanced. Even so, few federal programs are supported entirely from federal funds, meaning that states and school districts must support such programs with additional revenues. The need for state and local contributions is dramatically illustrated in the law for the education of the handicapped. Categorical assistance at the federal level, then, means categorical assistance at state and local levels as well. While categorical programs may be entirely desirable, pressure to fund them may prevent a balanced look at other programs supported by the school budget.

In addition to allocating federal monies and providing additional monies to match federal programs, state agencies may also sponsor certain categorical programs of their own. When that is done, budget control is again imposed upon school districts. State agencies also exercise another financial control over school districts: they interpret and implement the general state aid program. While most of the details of that program are ordinarily spelled out in the statutes, there is frequently some room for discretion at the state level. Moreover, state agencies are often given the power to cut off funds to local districts when such districts are found to be in noncompliance with the law or state regulation. These controls may appear to be completely justified and the categorical assistance at state and federal levels may be for worthy purposes, but the fact remains that substantial control is imposed upon schools and school districts.

Financial controls operate in school districts, intermediate units, and attendance areas (Chapters 5, 6, and 7). School districts vary greatly in assessed valuation per child, the most common way of expressing their wealth or capacity to support schools. While state aid programs tend to alleviate these disparities, much variation remains. In poor districts lack of money may result in what might be called the control of deprivation. Intermediate units are often able to provide certain services, in such areas as health and transportation, on a more cost-effective basis than would be possible in small school districts. Where that is so, school districts ordinarily give up some control in return for the added benefits. These trade-off provisions vary greatly among the states. Attendance areas depend almost entirely on school districts for financial support. Nearly all fiscal arrangements at the local level are made by school districts, and the districts also channel most state and federal money to attendance areas. While some attempt has been made to modify this situation, attendance areas have little control over financial matters. Since attendance areas may vary even more widely than school districts in assessed value per student, district discretion in finances may be a desirable condition.

The basic control instrument in the hands of the board of education and the superintendent (Chapters 9 and 10) is the annual school budget. Ordinarily the superintendent, with the help of staff, formulates the budget and recommends its adoption to the board. To be sure, many constraints other than program requirements are present in the development of the budget: the wealth of the district, the tax limits imposed by state statute, the nature and amounts of state and federal funds anticipated, the demands of employees for salary increases and for other benefits, and the perceived willingness of citizens to vote for a tax override. Even so, most boards and superintendents exercise some discretion in arriving at a total figure for expenditures and in allocating monies within that figure to various programs. Once the budget is adopted, allocations for various functions and for individual schools are ordinarily set for the year.

Teachers, whose salaries often represent 75–85 percent of the total budget, have considerable influence on the budget (Chapter 12). In recent years teachers organizations have insisted on recognition and the right to bargain with school boards on pay levels and other provisions. In many instances, where agreements were not reached, teachers have gone out on strike until boards were ready to resume bargaining. Increasingly, the local teachers organization, often with the help of staff from the state or the national organization, makes careful analyses of both proposed budget expenditures and budget revenues. As a result, the budget process in most school districts has become a more open process with information made available to both teachers and the public.

School-related and other interest groups (Chapters 13 and 14) exert considerable financial control. When these groups concur with budget proposals their support becomes a positive element in budget adoption and in passing a tax override, if that is necessary. When some or all of these groups find budget proposals unacceptable, the budget proposal is frequently adjusted. Such budget adjustments usually require that total expenditures be reduced, but specific budget provisions may also be altered. Tax limitation proposals, now popular with certain interest groups, get at budget reductions by limiting revenues that can be made available to school districts. In any case, citizens and citizen groups do exercise great control over the local school budget.

Financial support for alternative schools (Chapter 17), at least those outside the public school system, may present a challenge or even a threat to the support of public schools. More money for alternative schools may mean that less money is available for public schools. Perhaps more significant, in the process of establishing alternative schools, the role and performance of public schools may become devalued in many people's opinion. If that happens, the desire to support public schools will undoubtedly be reduced.

In many ways, financial controls are the means whereby other controls are imposed on the schools. For instance, when states and school districts do not respond adequately to certain educational needs, as perceived by congressional representatives, categorical aid for those specific programs may be established. Or, at the local level when citizens become disenchanted with some aspects of the school program, their chief recourse is to deny money to the school district, often through defeat of a tax override.

Network Control Elements

No school or school district is an island. Schools as institutions are related to many other institutions. The conditions affecting schools are often pervasive in the society and affect other institutions as well. The people, lay and professional, who make the schools what they are, are connected with many other persons and organizations who have special interests. Network controls also include the relationships of schools and school districts to state and federal agencies, to state and national nongovernmental organizations, and to other local governmental and nongovernmental agencies and organizations. These relationships may be both vertical and horizontal, they may involve both governmental and nongovernmental organizations, and they may evolve into countless combinations and variations. In all of these relationships the potential for influence is present and in many of them that potential is realized.

Governmental networks exist at state and national levels (Chapters 3 and 4). Most of the federal programs are channeled through state education agencies and then to local education agencies. Frequently these programs require that advisory committees be established at state and federal levels and take part in approving and monitoring the programs. These advisory committees are often composed primarily of persons who represent interest groups concerned with the particular program.

The use of such persons on advisory committees extends the governmental network to nongovernmental interest groups and, in a sense, provides a sanction for those groups and for the viewpoints they espouse.

Another type of nongovernmental network is found in the relationships among schools, colleges, accrediting associations, and testing agencies. Colleges and agencies dominated by college personnel, have traditionally exercised great influence over the high school curriculum (Chapter 16). That influence, while modified somewhat in recent decades by standards established by state departments of education, has been reaffirmed in the recent studies of education.

Still another set of network relationships is found in the school districts (Chapter 5), intermediate units (Chapter 6), and attendance areas (Chapter 7). While school districts, as such, may have many or few network relationships, frequently school district officials will select a number of other districts of comparable size, location, wealth, or demographic characteristics to develop comparative data on tax levies, teachers' salaries, expenditures per student, and so on. In many instances, these comparative data become most persuasive to school board members and the citizens of the community. Those concerned with the operation of schools in attendance areas also may make use of comparative data about schools in the same school district or in nearby or similiar districts. The intermediate unit is deliberately established to encourage network relationships, first among a group of school districts, second with state and federal education agencies. Frequently the intermediate unit acts as agent to see that its component districts get "their share" of available resources from state and federal sources.

School personnel (Chapters 9, 10, 11, and 12) have a wide range of network relationships. For instance, nearly every state has an active state school boards association and generally membership is extended to the board and not to individual board members. The National School Boards Association is essentially a federation of state school board associations but individual memberships are also permitted. Regardless of how official membership status is arranged, board members attend the state and national meetings of these associations by the tens of thousands. Board members also make use of the publications of these organizations. Frequently, attendance at such meetings and the materials acquired there influence board behavior back home. On some issues, board members have also arrived at a common position and communicated that position to state and local government. Again, network influence may involve governmental and nongovernmental actors. Superintendents, like board members, have both state and national organizations and these affiliations also make some difference in the thinking and action of many superintendents. Those who serve in the administrative hierarchy also belong to many state and national organizations. These memberships may be quite diverse and each organization may represent a specialization in the field of education, such as school law, curriculum and instruction, or evaluation; any number of subject specialities, such as reading, mathematics, or science; or even some of the more recent emphases such as special education. In each case, members and organization materials provide justifications for particular views and concerns in education and thus influence those who operate school systems.

Teachers, like other school personnel, are tied into many networks. At the local level most teachers belong to a local association or a local union, with unions being most prominent in large cities (Chapter 12). Most states have strong professional associations and some have strong union organizations. At the national level are the National Education Association and the American Federation of Teachers. These organizations at local, state, and national levels tend to emphasize teacher welfare issues. Teachers may also belong to organizations that focus chiefly on teaching and learning or on some specialty in the field of education. Teacher influence at all levels of government has grown in recent years. Many state legislators, for instance, assert that the teacher lobby is much more powerful than the school administrator lobby and generally more powerful than the school board lobby in influencing state legislation. Indeed, the teachers organization is considered to be among the most powerful of all lobbying groups in many states.

But teachers are not alone in their efforts to influence legislation and other aspects of policy formation. School-related and other interest groups (Chapters 13 and 14) also have a network nature. The PTA, for example, has strong organizations at local, state, and national levels. In like manner, the U.S. Chamber of Commerce has local, state, and national expressions and a network linking all three levels. Similar network arrangements can be found in labor organizations, agricultural organizations, and other special interest fields. Most local school issues are not merely local issues. Whether the issue is textbook selection in West Virginia or the teaching of evolution in Arkansas, local groups are soon joined by their state and national counterparts. What began as a school or school district problem can become the basis for a state and even a national confrontation. Frequently many actors, governmental and nongovernmental, at all levels of our society become involved and their influence is felt in the local arena and beyond.

The network controls noted above are, in part, a result of our federal system of government. Major policy issues in education can seldom be confined to one level of government. Local concerns often get bucked up to the state or even the national level. National concerns must be bucked down to state and local levels for their implementation. These networks are also a product of interest group activity and the need of such groups to form coalitions to augment their influence. While most coalitions of teachers and school administrators came apart over the bargaining issue, in many states and school districts these groups are now considering ways of collaborating, at least on some issues.

GENERAL NATURE OF CONTROLS

What can we conclude about the general nature of controls? In part, the wide range of controls on schools and school districts is a consequence of our federal system of government. In the beginning federalism represented a rough division of powers between national and state governments. Experience over nearly two centuries has brought a number of developments in federalism. First, there has been a move from dual to national federalism (Chapter 3). Second, for many practical purposes not only two but three levels of government are involved. Indeed, with the new emphasis on school site management, there are in effect four levels of government. Third, despite the Reagan reversion, each level of government must be involved on many important policy questions. This inevitably means that government is more extensive, more complex, and more time-consuming.

The wide range of controls on schools and school districts is also a consequence of the extensive development of interest groups and the role they play in the governmental process. Interest groups have proliferated more in America than in any other nation. In many ways interest groups have undercut and even replaced the political parties in taking positions on policy issues and exerting pressure on local, state, and national governmental officials. While these pressures are sometimes lamented, the activities of interest groups are generally praised. Whether lamented or praised, attempted influence by interest groups is considered a normal part of governance even though it adds to the array of controls exerted on schools.

In some cases individuals and interest groups have resisted all governmental controls, to the point of making governance almost meaningless. For instance, some court orders to desegregate schools have been met with foot-dragging that has stalled implementation for years. And in some states where laws make strikes illegal, teachers have nevertheless gone out on strike. While some state laws and court directives may be ill-considered and even unfair, deliberate disobedience of such provisions is a serious matter. Some choose disobedience to dramatize the need to change the law and willingly accept the consequences; others simply ignore the law and expect to suffer no consequences, and their actions cannot be condoned, for in that way lies anarchy.

Controls over schools and school districts are complex. Some of those who write treatises on school operation do us a disservice when they ascribe control to a single person or group of persons. As this book and the summary of control categories demonstrate, controls emanate from many institutions, conditions, and persons. To be sure, in some situations a single person or group of persons may exert considerable influence but even in these cases institutions and conditions cannot be ignored.

Controls are also interrelated. Legal and structural arrangements are obviously shaped and reshaped by people's perceptions. Demographic characteristics of people in particular jurisdictions determine, in large part, the knowledge they possess, the values they hold, and frequently the financial resources at their command. Financial controls, while fateful in their own right, are usually symbolic of the perceptions and values of those who impose financial conditions, be they penurious or generous. Network controls emphasize the fact that institutions, conditions, and persons do not stand in isolation; what others think and what other institutions do become very important.

Those who would influence schools and school districts need to take account of the complexity and interrelatedness of controls. This means that such persons need to be knowledgeable, politically astute, and personally persistent.

Controls and Open Systems

Throughout this work we have tried to show that controls reside both in the institution—a school or school district—and in the environment in which the institution exists. The many interactions between institution and environment make the open systems concept a useful one. Easton suggests that the relationship between a political system (i.e., an institution) and its environment is characterized by both inputs and outputs. The inputs are expressed in terms of demands and support. The outputs are expressed in terms of decisions and policies. This model is helpful but it is extremely general. Lawrence and Lorsch have defined environment more specifically for business organizations to include technological development and market changes.[1] In education we also need to think more specifically about the environment that surrounds educational institutions. The seven control elements explicated in this chapter may serve as a start in this direction.

A second limitation in applying the open systems view to schools and school districts is that it is often difficult to distinguish sharply between what is outside (environmental) and what is inside (organizational). For instance, the board of education is, in one sense, outside the organization. Yet as board members become socialized to organization norms and as they place greater reliance on the "expertise" of the superintendent, they tend to become more a part of the organization and less a part of the environment. Or, take students. In one sense they are inside the organization. But students live at home, they participate in many nonschool community functions, and they obviously absorb many of the values of home and community, and are thus also outside the organization. Or, consider teachers. As individuals they are clearly inside the organization. Even the local teachers association, while not a formal part of the school or school district, might be considered to be inside the organization. But the local association is intimately tied to the state and even to the national association, both of which are outside the organization. This makes classifying the local associations even more difficult.

The difficulty of determining what is inside and what is outside the organization is alleviated by combining Weick's concept of loose coupling with Easton's model of political systems. As noted earlier, according to Weick, "coupled events are responsive, but each event also preserves its own identity. . . ." In other words, a decision at the top level in the school hierarchy may or may not affect behavior at the bottom level in hierarchy. This kind of loose coupling or independence in a school organization brings to light vulnerable points in the organization on which forces in the environment may focus. For example, a teachers organization might choose to approach the school district through teachers who are most disaffected from the organization and least inclined to accept organization directives. Linking the concepts of loose coupling and political systems makes for a comprehensive and useful model for understanding the organization and control of American schools.

NOTES

[1] P. R. Lawrence and J. W. Lorsch, *Organization and Environment* (Homewood, IL: Irwin, 1961).

Index

Abrams, Carol, 449
"Academic bankruptcy" laws, 82
Academic Preparation for College, 414
Academic success, social class and, 29
Academy, influence of, 409
Accrediting agencies
   influence of, 419–21
   listing of, 420
Achievement, school decentralization and, 165–66
Act of Massachusetts General Court of 1647, 110
Adams, John, 181
Adler, Mortimer, 341, 447
Administration
   differing views of, 282–83
   power and
     administrative relationships, 289
     early model, 288–89
     open systems approach, 289–90
     superintendent versus subordinate hierarchy, 291
   views of
     bureaucratic view, 282
     human relations approach, 282
     open systems approach, 282, 284
     scientific management view, 282
Administrative Behavior (Simon), 246
Administrators, recommendations for. *See also*
     specific types of administrators
   instructional factors, 291
   political skills, improvement of, 294
   role clarification of administrators, 292–93
   selection/preparation procedures, 293–94
   specialization of administrators, 291–92
Advanced Placement Program, impact on
     secondary schools, 417
Advisory Commission on Intergovernmental
     Relationships, 106, 108, 114
Alexander, Lamar, 2
Alioto, Joseph, 219
Alioto, Robert, 251
Allen, Hollis P., 50
Alternative schools, 163, 174, 442–46
   casualties of, 445
   characteristics of, 445

Alternative schools, *continued*
  desegregation and, 445
  growth of, 443–44
  within public schools, 444–46
American Association of School Administrators,
      45, 58, 68, 121, 123, 239, 304
American Association of University Women, 373–74
American College Testing Program (ACT), 414
American Federation of Teachers, 30, 303, 305, 307
  opposition to NEA, 307, 309
  political activism, 313–14
  state affiliates, 310
American School Board Journal, 216, 335
American schools
  college influences, 407–25
  development of, 10–11
  educational purpose and social problems, 16–17
  federal government and, 42–69
  finance issue, 17–18
  judicial influence, 186–200
  lay–professional relationships, 18
  legal mile stones, 11–15
  needs/interests of students, 22
  as open systems, 4–9
  school districts, 105–29
  socioeconomic trends, 23–39
  state government and, 76–102
  statistical information, 4–5
  tasks of schools, 15–16
Amiot, Mary Ann, 61
*Anatomy of Teacher Institutes: A Design for
      Professional Development, The* (Banner), 341
Anderson, James G., 246
Anglican Church, 77
Appellate court, 186
Area Redevelopment and the Manpower Training
      acts, 53
Armor, David, 162
Asian-Americans, 23
Aspiration levels, financial resources and, 393–99
Association of Classroom Teachers, 304, 308
Astuto, Terry A., 65–66
"At risk" children, family structure, 26
Attendance areas. *See also* Decentralization;
      Desegregation
  compared to school district, 154
  controversy related to, 153, 155–57

decision-making, case examples, 168–72
definitional problems, 154
determination of, 154–55
geographic-organizational problems, 157–59
  enrollment decline, 157–58
  school level, 158
  transportation, 158
parental involvement, 166–67
political-social problems
  decentralization, 164–68
  desegregation issue, 156–57, 159–63
recommendations for change, 173–75
Attendance requirements, 92
Aufderheide, J. Alan, 83, 86

Bailey, Stephen K., 54, 348
Bainbridge, William L., 124
Banfield, Edward C., 124
Bankhead-Jones Act of 1935, 47
Barnard, Chester I., 316
Barnard, Henry, 10, 78
Barry, Marion, 219
Barzun, Jacques, 341
Basic Education: Issues, Answers, and Facts, 341
Becker, Howard S., 300
Bell, Derrick, 156
Bell, Terrell H., 58, 63, 167
Bell v. *School of Gary*, 193
Bennett, William J., 66–67, 365
Bensman, Joseph, 220, 221
Berger, Peter L., 32
Berke, Joel S., 54, 400
Berkeley Unified School District, 444
Bestor, Arthur, 340
Bettelheim, Bruno, 159
Better Schools Act of 1973, 56
Better Schools Program, 2
Bilingual issue, 365
"A Bill for the More General Diffusion of
      Knowledge, " 77–78
Black, Hugo, 13, 181, 182
Blackmun, James, 182
Blacks, 23, 24 *See also Desegregation*
  black activist groups, 356–59
Blau, Peter M., 283
Board of Cooperative Educational Services, 135
Board of Inquiry, recommendations, 35

Board of Regents of the State of New York, 80
Boards of education
    collective bargaining and, 223, 226
    control function, 205–8
    discretionary power and obligations, 208–9
    effectiveness, indicators of, 229
    ethical responsibilities, 209–11
    future view, 230
    historical view, 206–7
    local control issue, 224–26
    mandatory powers and obligations, 208
    members
        appointment, 87, 211–12
        characteristics of, 217–18, 219
        community ties, 218–19
        elections, 213–14
        governor-appointed, 91
        male vs. female membership, 215–17
        reasons for membership, 214–15
    powers of, 207–8
    recommendations, 227–29
    research on, 219–24
    role of, 87–88, 204
    school district, state delegation to, 89–90
    superintendent, influence of, 255–57
Bobbitt, Franklin, 244
Bork, Robert, 182
Bossert, Stephen T., 275
Boston Compact, 344–47
Boston Latin School, 408
Boulding, Elise, 230
Boyan, Norman J., 291
Boyd, William L., 228, 248, 256, 399
Boyer, Ernest, 341, 448
Bradley, Omar, 337
Bradley v. *Milliken*, 161
Bradley v. *School Board of the City of Richmond, Virginia*, 161
Brickell, Henry M., 415
Bronscomb, Lewis M., 277
Brown, B. Frank, 446
Brown v. *Board of Education of Topeka*, 14, 155–56, 187, 191–92, 193
Building-level committees, 166, 167, 174
Bureaucracy
    administration approaches to, 282
    influence of superintendency, 246–47

    versus open system perspective, 6
    versus professionalism, 283–84
    Weber's view, 245–46
Bureau of Indian Affairs, 362
Burger, Warren E., 42, 181, 182
Burke, Edmund M., 345, 346
Burns, James MacGregor, 228
Bush, George, 182
Business–school partnerships, 375–78
    impact on schools, 377–78
    reasons for, 376–77
Busing
    attendance areas, 158
    Reagan opposition to, 156
Butler, Nicholas Murray, 414
Butts, R. Freeman, 429

Cahill decision, 82
Callahan, John J., 400
Callahan, Raymond E., 225, 244
Campbell, Roald F., 90–91, 108
"Cardinal Principles," 412–13
Carlson, Richard O., 250, 256
Carmichael, Stokely, 357
Carnegie Forum on Education and the Economy, 16, 167, 277, 283, 301, 321–23, 344, 402
Carswell, Harold, 181
Carter, Jimmy, 1, 156, 182, 314, 324
Catholic schools, 433, 437–38
Centralized executive model of state governance, 90
Central office staff, 279–80
    conformity to environment, 281
    issues related to, 281–82
    line and staff issue, 281
    permanent versus temporary appointments 281–82
Certification
    state regulations, 93
    teachers, 299–300
Changing Demands on Education and Their Fiscal Implications, 338
Charters, W. W., Jr., 219, 220
Charting a Course: A Guide to the Excellence Movement in Education (McNett), 341
Cheever, Ezekiel, 299
Chief state school officer, 236
    role of, 80

Child benefit theory, 13
Children's Defense Fund, family study, 26, 27
Church-related schools. *See* Nonpublic schools
Citizen participation
    objectives of, 345–47
    rise in, 342–43
Citizens Commission on Civil Rights, 156
Civil case, 186
Civilian Conservation Corps, 48
Civil Rights Act of 1964, 55, 190, 365
Civil rights movement, 356, 429
Civil Works Administration, 48
Clark, David L., 61, 65–66
Claxton, P. P., 412
Cleveland, Harlan, 128
Clune, William, 196
Clusen, Ruth C., 374
Coalitions
    decline of, 347–48
    state, 84, 100
Cohen, Michael, 260
Coleman, James S., 55, 161, 441
Coleman report, 161–62
Collective bargaining
    boards of education and, 223, 226
    teachers' organizations, 305, 315–16
College Entrance Examination Board, impact on
        secondary schools, 413–14
College influences on education
    accrediting agencies, 419–21
    admission standards, changes, 417–18
    Advanced Placement Program, 417
    College Entrance Examination Board, 413–14
    curriculum development, 418–19
    future view, 424–25
    historical view, 407–13
        academy, 409
        "Cardinal Principles," 412–13
        Committee of Ten, 411–12
        Latin School, 407–8
        preparatory departments, 408–9
        science, influence of, 410–11
    teacher preparation, 421–23
    testing programs, 415–17
Colonial era
    academy, 409
    boards of education, 206–7
    compulsory education laws, 76

establishment of schools, 111
    Latin School, 407–8
    states and education, 76–78
    teachers, 299
Commission on Excellence in Educational
        Administration, 263
Commission on School District Reorganization,
        121, 123
Commission on the Role of Women in Education
        Governance, 216
Committee for Economic Development (CED),
        report/recommendations, 33–37
Committee for Support of the Public Schools,
        organization/activities of, 337–38
Committee for the Advancement of School
        Administration, 248
Committee of Ten, 411–12
Common law, 179
Common school districts, 124
Common School Journal, 78
Common schools, 12, 124
Community
    community districts, 123–24
    superintendent, influence of, 259–60
Community Action Agencies, 187
Community Action Programs, 343–44
Community control
    attendance areas and, 166–67
    compared to decentralization, 164
    historical view, 109
    recommendations, 166
Community Education–Work Councils, 447
Compensation issue, teachers, 303, 319–20
Competency issue, teachers, 318–19, 321, 322
Compulsory education laws, 92
    colonial era, 76
    legal milestones, 11
Conant, James B., 336, 337, 421
Connecticut Laws of 1650, 206
Conspiracy of Good Intentions, A
        (Tyson-Bernstein), 341
Constitution, lack of educational provisions,
        42–43
Constitutional Convention, 179
Controls
    demographic elements, 459–61
    extralegal control, 9
    fiscal elements, 470–72

Controls, *continued*
   ideation elements, 465–68
   knowledge elements, 468–70
   legal control, 8–9, 461–63
   nature of, 474
   network elements, 472–74
   open systems and, 476–77
   structural elements, 463–65
   terms related to, 458–59
   use of term, 8–9
Coons, John E., 196, 404, 449
Cooperative Research Program, role of, 52–53
Cooper, Shirley, 135
Cooper v. *Aaron*, 192
Corler, Jacob von, 299
Council for Basic Education,
      organization/activities of, 339–42
Counts, George S., 217
County district, 133
Court of Appeals, 180. *See also* Judicial influence
   federal court system, 179–82
   historical view, 179
   judicial policymaking, 185–86
   state court system, 182–85
Cowley, Malcolm, 340
Crain, Robert L., 221
Craton Liddell et al. v. *The Board of Education of the City of St. Louis*, 163
Creative Experiences (Follett), 244
Cremin, Lawrence A., 429, 444
Crowson, Robert L., 247
Cubberley, Elwood P., 12, 279
Cunningham, Luvern L., 239, 241, 252
Curriculum development by colleges, 418–19

Darling-Hammond, Linda, 450
Darwin, Charles, 410
Daycare, increasing need, 27
Decentralization
   achievement and, 165–66
   compared to community control, 164
   district studies, 165–66
   legislation, 164–65
   public participation efforts, 166
"Decision seminar, " 228
Declaration of Independence, 179
Democracy in School Administration
      (Kooperman, Miel, Misner), 245

Demographic trends, intermediate units and, 144–46
Dennison, George, 443
Departments of education, state, 88–89, 96–99
Depression legislation, 48–49
Deputy superintendent, 134
Deschooling Society (Illich), 444
Desegregation
   alternative schools and, 445
   attendance areas and, 156–57
   Coleman report, 161–62
   court decisions, 160–61
   de facto segregation, 160, 193–94
   de jure segregation, 193
   federal courts and, 156–57
   freedom of choice plan, 192
   future options, 162
   implementation, 192–95
   incremental segregative effect, 161
   judicial decisions, 191–96
   legal milestones, 14–15
   magnet schools, 163
   northern cases, 193–94, 195
   pupil assignment, 193
   purpose/intent in, 194–95
   racial imbalance, definition, 160
   remedial measures, 366
   research on, 161–62
   school district reorganization, 117
   settlement plan, St. Louis, 163
   voluntary approaches, 162–63
Detroit Central Board of Education, 210
Dewey, John, 129, 245, 443
Dickson, William J., 245
Disadvantaged youth, 25
Districts. *See* School districts
"Divided school, " 110
Divoky, Diane, 451
Dolbeare, Kenneth M., 190
Doughty, James J., 215
Down, A. Graham, 340
Downey, Lawrence W., 394, 395
Doyle, Dennis P., 65, 83
Dror, Yehezkel, 131
Dual federalism, 43–44
Due process
   clause, 188
   equal educational opportunity and, 365
Duignan, Patrick, 252

Easton, David, 4, 246–47
Economic Opportunity Act of 1964, 187, 343
Edelman, Marvin Wright, 35
Educational Administration Abstracts, 248
Educational Administration Quarterly, 248
Educational Consolidation and Improvement Act, 62
Educational Equality Project, 414
Educational Professions Development Act of 1967, 53
Educational Testing Service, 57
Education Amendments of 1972, 367, 369
Education by Choice (Coons and Sugarman), 404, 449
Education Commission of the States, 101
Education for a Competitive America Act, 68
Education for All Handicapped. See Public Law 94–142
Education, U.S. Department of, creation of, 1, 58, 61, 63
Eisner, Elliott, 341
Elderly Americans, population growth, 24
Elected-chief model of state governance, 90
Elementary and Secondary Education Act of 1965, 29, 46, 53, 365, 380
Elementary and Secondary Education Improvement Amendments, 331
Eliot, Charles W., 411
Elliott, John, 227
Empowerment of teachers, 174
Enrollment
    effects on teachers, 297–98
    nonpublic schools, 431–33
    statistical information, 4, 27
Entrepreneurial schools, 451–52
Environment
    environmental influences on administration, 284–85
    open system approach, 6–7
Equal educational opportunity issue, 363–67
    causes of, 364
    changes related to, 366–67
    due process approaches, 365
Equalization programs, 82
Equal protection clause, 188
Equal Rights for Women in Education Project, 370
Erickson, Donald A., 446
Evans, Herbert Baxter, 410

Excellence in the Making, 118
Executive Educator, 335
Executive Order #10988, 306
Expenditures, statistical information, 4. *See also* Financial resources
Experimental Schools Program, 444
Extended aid, legal milestones, 13
Extralegal control, 9

Family Educational Rights and Privacy Act of 1974, 339
Family structure
    "at risk" children, 26
    changes, 25–27
    major trends, 26
    women's roles, 26–27
Fantini, Mario D., 345, 444
Farrand, William, 413
Fast-track program, 2
Federal aid, 388–90
    control element, 390–91
    differential effect, 388–89
    early laws, 46
    impact of, 389–90
Federal court system, 179–82
Federal government
    dual federalism, 43–44
    national federalism, 44–45
Federal government and education, 42–49, 55, 70–72
Federal offices, 69
Federal Security Agency, 48, 49
Feedback, in open system perspective, 5
Feilders, John F., 251, 252
Feldman, Sandra, 227
Feminist groups, 367–75
Ferguson, Marilyn, 444
Ferraro, Geraldine, 369
Fifth Amendment, 187
Finance reform
    judicial decisions, 196–98
    state, 399–401
Financial resources
    access arrangements, 391–93
    aspiration levels and, 393–99
        control factors, 398–99
        quality of desired education, 396–98
        type of desired education, 394–96
    control and, 390–91, 393, 470–72

Financial resources, *continued*
  educational limitations and, 390–91
  federal aid, 388–90
  future view, 403–5
  reforms highlighted in major reports, 401–3
  state, role of, 81–82, 84, 94–95
  tax limitation movement, 401
  wealth differentials
    among districts, 386–87
    among states, 387–88
First Amendment, 187
Fiscal independence, school districts, 114–15
Fitzwater, Charles O., 135
Fleishmann Report, 166
Fleming, Thomas, 245
Follett, Mary Parker, 244
Follow Through, 166, 344
Ford Foundation, 343
Ford, Gerald, 156, 182
Fortas, Abe, 182
Forum for Educational Organization Leaders, 314
Fourteenth Amendment, 44, 155, 180, 188, 196
Franklin, Benjamin, 77, 409
Fraser, Hugh W., 253
Friedenberg, Edgar, 443
Friedman, Milton, 449
Fuchs, Estelle, 362
Fuhrman, Susan, 84
Functions of the Executive, The, (Barnard), 316

Gallup, George, 416
Gardner, David P., 63
Gender differences
  among superintendents of schools, 242–43
  among teachers, 306
  school board membership, 215–17
George-Barden Act of 1946, 48
George-Deen Act of 1937, 48
George-Ellzey Act of 1934, 48
George-Reed Act of 1929, 48
Getzels, J. W., 247
GI bills, 50–51
Gifted children, segregation, 159
Gittell, Marilyn, 165, 443
Goldhammer, Keith, 221
Goodlad, John, 401, 448
Goodman, Paul, 443
Governance Project, 84

Governors
  appointment of state board, 91
  influence of, 86
Graduate Woman, 373
Graham, Robert, 319
Grant Commission, 448
Gray, Dennis, 341, 342
Gray power, 24
"Great Law" of 1682, 77
Greeley, Andrew, 162
Greenfield, Meg, 64
Griffiths, Daniel, 241, 285
Grodzins, Morton, 44
Gross, Neal, 214
Guba, Egon G., 288, 289
Guthrie, James W., 401

Haberman, Martin, 93
Hall, G. Stanley, 410
Halpin, Andrew W., 247
Hamilton, Alexander, 44, 77
Hamilton, Charles V., 357
Hammond, Phillip E., 190
Hamphill, John, 253
Handicapped children, Public Law 94–142, 59–60
Hansen, Carl, 253
Hansot, Elizabeth, 264
Hanus, Paul H., 279
Harris, William T., 412
Hartle, Terry W., 65, 83
Harvard University, 408, 411
Hatch Act of 1887, 47
Havighurst, Robert J., 362
Hawthorn studies, 244–45, 316
Haynsworth, Clement, 181
Head Start, 166, 344, 366
Health, Education and Welfare, U.S. Department
  of, 49, 57–58
Heath, Shirley Brice, 35–36, 37
Helvering v. *Davis*, 43
Henry, Jules, 443
Hentges, Joseph T., 239, 241, 257
Hentoff, Nat, 443
Herndon, Lillie E., 331
Hernton, James, 443
High School (Boyer), 448
Highsmith, Martha C., 277
Hills, R. Jean, 396, 399

Hispanics
    activist groups, 359–62
    population growth, 24
Hodgkinson, Harold L., 23, 26
Hofstader, Richard, 340
Hogan, John C., 186
Hold, John, 443
Holmes Group, 167, 286, 421
Holt, John, 451
Home schooling, 428, 450–51
Honig, William, 319
Hooker, Clifford P., 209
Houle, Cyril O., 251
Howe, Florence, 368
Howe, Harold, II, 35, 64, 417, 448
Hufstedler, Shirley, 58
Human relations approach, 244–45, 282
Hummel, Judythe A., 242–43
Hunt, James B., Jr., 321

Ideology-oriented groups, 354–56
Illich, Ivan, 444
Immegart, Glenn L., 248
Imposed segregation, 159
Incremental segregative effect, 161
Indian Affairs, Bureau of, 49
Informal organization, teachers', 316–17
In Search of Excellence (Peters and Waterman), 282
Institute for Educational Leadership, Inc., 211, 224,
    229
Instructional Management Program, 275
Instructional program
    improving outcomes, 291
    state decisions, 91–93
Interest groups
    black activist groups, 356–59
    business–school partnerships, 375–78
    equal educational opportunity issue, 363–67
    feminist groups, 367–75
    function of, 378–80
    future view, 381–82
    Hispanic activist groups, 359–62
    ideology-oriented groups, 354–56
    Native American groups, 362–63
    professional, 70
    special, 70
    state, influence of, 86
Interim Certification Commission, 2

Intermediate superintendent, 134
Intermediate unit
    alternatives to, 137–38
    board members, selection, 142
    developmental trends, 135
    financial support of, 142
    future view, 148–51
    historical view, 133–36
    recommendations, 146–48
    socioeconomic forces
        demographic trends, 144–46
        school district reorganization, 144
        technological growth, 143, 151
    status of, 136–42
        function issue, 138–41
        leadership issue, 141
        need issue, 137–38
        structure issue, 141–42
    use of term, 132
Isaacs, Harold R., 160

Jackson, Jesse L., 358, 359
James, H. Thomas, 448
James, William, 410
Jefferson, Thomas, 10, 43, 44, 77, 78
Jenkins v. *Missouri*, 117
Jennings, Jack, 65
Jennings, M. Kent, 332
Jewish day schools, 439–40
Johns, Roe L., 221
Judicial influence
    compliance with judicial decisions, 189–90
    examples
        school desegregation, 191–96
        school finance reform, 196–98
    federal involvement, basis of, 186–89
    future view, 199–200
    trends in, 186
Judicial policymaking, 185–86
Judiciary Act of 1789, 179
Judiciary Act of 1875, 180
Junior college legislation, 91

Kalamazoo case, 238
Kammeyer, Kenneth C. W., 119
Katz, Michael B., 78, 280
Kellogg Foundation, 248
Kelly, James A., 401, 402

Kelly v. *Guinn*, 194
Kennedy, Anthony, 182
Kennedy, John F., 306
Keppel, Francis, 56, 57
Kerchner, Charles T., 323
Kershaw, Joseph A., 302
Keyes v. School District No. 1, Denver, Colorado, 161, 194
Kimbrough, Ralph B., 221
Kindergartens, nonpublic, 442
King, Martin Luther King, Jr., 357
Kingsley, Clarence D., 412
Kirp, David L., 162
Kirst, Michael W., 190
Knapp, Michael, 54
Knopf, Alfred A., 340
Kohl, Herbert, 443
Koopman, G. Robert, 266
Kozol, Jonathan, 443
Krist, Michael W., 54
Kurland, Philip B., 188

Laboratory schools, 442
Land grants, 46–47
Lanham Act of 1941, 49
Latch-key children, 23
Latin School, influence of, 407–8
La Vigne, Lorraine, 415
Lawrence, P. R., 281
Leaders for America's Schools, 294
Leaders in Action, 373
League of Women Voters, 371–72, 373–74
Least restrictive environment, use of term, 60
Legal control, 8–9, 461–63
Legal Services Corporation, 187
Legislative Education Leadership in the States, 84
Leonard, George, 443
Levin, Henry M., 25
Lewis, Anne, 68
Lieberman, Myron, 309, 451
Literature, controversy related to, 355–56
Local government
    limitations, 108
    recommendations for operation, 125–27
    views of, 106
Local organizations
    citizen participation
        objectives of, 345–47

rise in, 342–43
Community Action Programs, 343–44
future view, 349
for teachers, 312–13
Looking in on Your School, 332
Lorsch, J. W., 281
Lortioe, Dan C., 317
Loyalty oaths, 300
Lugar, Richard, 219
Lutheran schools, 438–39
Lynn, David, 341

MacArthur Foundation, 425
McCarthy, Martha M., 95
McCarty, Donald J., 214, 215, 256
McCloud, Barbara, 252
McCollum v. *Board of Education*, 13
McGraw, Onalee, 63
McKean, Roland N., 302
McLaughlin, Milbrey Wallin, 35–36, 37
McLennan, Kenneth, 226
McMurrin, Lee, 252
McPherson, R. Bruce, 247
Magnet schools, 163, 174
Mann, Horace, 10, 78, 80, 110
Marburger, Carl L., 339
Marbury v. *Madison*, 188
March, James C., 249
March, James G., 246, 249, 260, 263–64
Marshall, John, 181, 188, 190
Massachusetts Act of 1647, 408
Massachusetts Act of 1989, 110
Massachusetts School Ordinance of 1642, 206
Massachusetts School Ordinance of 1647, 206
Master Teacher Program, 2
Master Teacher Proposal, 319
Mayo, Elton, 244–45
Mazzoni, Tim L., Jr., 90–91
Mediation
    principals, 291
    superintendent of schools, 261
Merit pay, 317, 320
Merrimack Education Center Technology
        Lighthouse Project, 151
Meyer, Agnes, 337, 338
Michaelson, Jacob B., 7
Miel, Alice, 266
Miles, Rufus, 58

Mills, Caleb, 78
Minar, David W., 222
Minority populations, 23–25
    achievement, 55
    birth rates, 23
    demands on schools, 23–24
    "majority-minority" populations, 24
Minority teachers, decline of, 322–23
Mintzberg, Henry, 252
Misner, Paul J., 266
Missouri Synod schools, 438–39
Mitchell, Douglas E., 323
Model cities, 166
Mondale, Walter, 314, 318, 324
Moore, Hollis A., Jr., 249
Morrill Act of 1862, 46, 47
Morrill Act of 1890, 47
Morrill, Justin, 47
Mort, Paul, 400
Mosher, Edith K., 54, 248
Moskow, Michael H., 226
"Moving school," 110
Moynihan, Daniel P., 343, 441, 450
Mueller v. *Allen*, 450
Municipalities, school districts and, 113

Naisbitt, John, 166
National Academy for School Executives, 249
National Assessment of Educational Progress
        (NAEP), 26
    role of, 56–57
National Association for the Advancement of
        Colored People (NAACP), 187, 357, 358
National Association of Elementary School
        Principals, 270
National Association of Secondary School
        Principals, 270, 272, 293, 304
National Board for Professional Teaching
        Standards, 320–21
National Center for Vocational Education, 70
National Citizens Commission for the Public
        Schools, organization/activities of, 335–37
National Citizens Council for Better Schools, 337
National Coalition for Public Education, 331
National Coalition of Advocates for Students, 35
National Collegiate Athletic Association, 417
National Commission of School District
        Reorganization, 116

National Commission on Excellence in Education,
        63–64, 173, 230, 446
National Commission on Secondary Schooling for
        Hispanics, 361
National Committee for Citizens in Education,
        organization/activities of, 338–39
National Congress of Parents and Teachers,
        organization/activities of, 327–33
National Council for the Accreditation of Teacher
        Education, 93
National Council of State School Board
        Associations, 333, 334
National Council on Educational Research, 57, 62–63
National Defense Education Act of 1958, 46, 53
National Education Association, 58, 304–5
    local affiliates, 312
    new structure, 304
    opposition to AFT, 307, 309
    organization/activities of, 303–9, 313–14
    political activism, 313–14
    teacher status report, 301
National Endowment for the Humanities, 419
National federalism, 44–46
National Governors Association, 83
National Institute of Education, role of, 57, 63
National Merit Scholarship Program, 415–16
National Opinion Research Center, 221
National School Boards Association, 211, 215
    organization/activities of, 333–35
National School Volunteer Program, Inc., 344
National Science Board, 52
National Science Foundation
    curriculum development, 418–19
    role of, 51–52
National Women's Political Caucus, 369
National Youth Administration, 48
Nation at Risk, A, 57, 64–65, 68, 167, 230, 264, 446, 448
Nation Prepared: Teachers for the 21st Century, A,
        277, 321
Nation's Report Card, The, 448
Native Americans, 23
    activist groups, 362–63
    federally aided schools, 49
Natural community approach to school district
        reorganization, 121, 123
Neighborhood school, use of term, 159
Nelson Amendment of 1907, 47
Neuhaus, Richard John, 32

New Deal, 181
New Schools Directory Project, 443
New Teachers, Better Teachers, 341
New York City Board of Education, 209
New York Governance in the 21st Century—A Public-Private Partnership, 129
Nicholls, David A., 138
Nixon, Richard, 156, 181, 188, 190
Non-operation district, 123
Nonpublic schools
  alternative schools, 442–46
  Catholic schools, 433, 437–38
  characteristics, statistical information, 434–35
  competition with public schools, 448–49
  controls on, 430–31
  definition of, 433
  development of, 428–29
  enrollment patterns, 431–33
  entrepreneurial schools, 451–52
  home schooling, 428, 450–51
  independent schools, 440–41
  Jewish day schools, 439–40
  kindergartens, 442
  laboratory schools, 442
  legal protection, 429
  Missouri Synod schools, 438–39
  preschools, 441–42
  primary schools, 442
  state regulations, 95
  tuition tax credit, 199, 441, 450
  voucher concept, 449–50
Northwest Territory, 46

Ocean Hill-Brownsville, 165, 343
O'Connor, Sandra Day, 182
Office of Public Participation and Special Concerns in the Department of Education, 339
Open system approach, 4–7
  administration, 282, 284
  administrative power, 289–90
  versus bureaucratic model, 6
  controls and, 476–77
  environment, 6–7
  influence on superintendency, 246–47
  key concepts in, 5
  loose coupling, 6, 247, 289, 291
  political systems, 247
Operation Exodus, 149

Ordinance of 1785, 46
Ordinance of 1787, 47
Organization, use of term, 7–8
Organizational problems
  administration
    differing views of, 282–83
    selection and evaluation, 285–87
  bureaucracy/professionalism reconciliation, 283–84
  environmental influences, 284–85
  professional development, 287–88
Organization of schools
  Board of Inquiry recommendations, 35
  Committee for Economic Development recommendations, 34–35
  open system perspective, 4–7
Organizations (March and Simon), 246

Paideia Program, 342
Paideia Proposal, 447
Paige, Glen D., 228
Parent Advisory Committees, 166
Parent Teacher Association, 84
Peters, Thomas J., 282
Peterson, Paul E., 108
Pettigrew, Thomas, 162
Pierce, John D., 78
Pierce, Paul P., 270
Pierce v. *Society of the Sisters*, 430
Pitner, Nancy J., 247, 252
Place Called School, A (Goodlad), 448
Planning, specialists, 290
Plymouth Colony, 206
Political activism
  black activists, 356–59
  Hispanic activists, 359–62
  Native American activists, 362–63
  teachers' organizations, 305, 313–15, 318
Population shifts, 28
  school district reorganization, 120
Portland Survey, The, 279
Postman, Neil, 443
Powell, Lewis, 182
Preparation programs
  superintendent of schools, 248–49
  teacher preparation, 241–43
Preschool programs
  human-services approach, 30

Preschool programs, *continued*
  needs for, 31
  nonpublic, 441–42
  public schools, 30–31
President and Directors of the Literary Fund, 80
President's Task Force on Private Sector
        Initiatives, 167
Primary schools, nonpublic, 442
Principals
  historical view, 10–11, 269–71
  management behavior, variables in, 290
  as middle managers, 271–27
  role, debate on, 275–79
  scope of activities, 272–75
Principal Selection Guide, 272
Principal teacher, 270
Principles of Scientific Management, The (Taylor),
        243
Private schools. *See* Nonpublic schools
Profession
  characteristics of, 247–48
  criteria for, 300
Professional Administrators for America's Schools,
        249
Professional development
  continuing, needs for, 287–88
  as organizational issue, 287–88
    superintendent of schools, 247–50
Professional groups
  interest groups, 70
  practices boards, 83
Professionalism, versus bureaucracy, 283–84
Program for Economic Recovery, A, 61
Project ABCs, 341
Project on Equal Education Rights, 370
Project Wingspread, 149
Public Academy, 409
Public Education Fund, 347
Public Education Fund Network, 347
Public Law 16, 50
Public Law 85–864, 53
Public Law 92–540, 51
Public Law 94–142, 59–60, 339
Public Law 94–482, 62
Public Law 96–88, 1
Public Law 100–297, 331
Public Law 346, 50–51
Public Law 531, 52

Public Law 550, 51
Public Law 815, 46, 390
Public Law 874, 46, 390
Public School Act of 1732, 77
Public schools, decline in number, 154–55, 157
Public Works Administration, 48
Puerto Ricans, status of, 360–61

Quattlebaum, Charles A., 50
Quincy School of Boston, 10, 270

Racial imbalance, definition, 160
Raise Bill, 319
Rallis, Sharon E., 277
Ramsey, Charles E., 256
Ravitch, Diane, 445
Raywid, Mary Ann, 167, 446
Reagan, Ronald, 1, 14, 17, 156, 167, 182, 314, 358
  educational policy, 61–67
*Reforming Science Education: The Search for a
        New Vision* (Hur), 341
Regional service centers, 69, 139–41
  benefits of, 140–41
  elements of, 147
Rehabilitation Act of 1973, 55
Rehnquist, William, 161, 182
Reissman, Frank, 443
Related services, to handicapped, use of term, 59
Religious practices, legal milestones, 13, 14
Reports on education
  major reports, 401
  reform recommendations, 446–49
Response, in open system perspective, 5
Results in Education, 83–84
Rhodes, James, 219
Rioux, J. William, 339
Roche, George, 63
Rodriguez decision, 82
Roethlisberger, F. J., 245
Roe, William H., 77
Rogers, David, 443
Rosenthal, Alan, 84
Rudner, Lawrence M., 93
Rural areas
  intermediate units, role of, 147–48
  population changes, 143
  school district reorganization, 119
  technology, effect of, 143

Rural Electrification Administration, 143
Rutherford, James, 341

Salett, Stanley, 339
Salter, C. L., 341
San Antonio Independent School District v.
    Rodriguez, 197–98
Sandburg, Carl, 337
San Francisco Unified School District, 113, 124
Scalia, Antonin, 182
Schmandt, Henry J., 185, 188
Scholastic Aptitude Test (SAT), 414
    decline in scores, 416
School Advisory Councils, 166
School Board News, 335
School closings, 153
    attendance areas and, 157–58
"School committee, " 207
School day, state regulation, 92
School districts
    boards of education, state delegation to,
        89–90
    categories of
        common school districts, 124
        community districts, 123–24
        county districts, 124
        non-operation district, 123
        schemes used, 121–22
        town districts, 124
        unified school districts, 123
    federal government and, 107
    fiscal independence, 114–15
    future view, 128–29
    historical view, 110–11
    legal basis, 111–12
    local control, myth of, 108–9
    municipalities and, 113
    population characteristics and, 120–21, 124
    public opinion of, 109
    as quasi-corporations, 112–13
    reorganization of, 115–20
        criteria, definitional difficulties, 121
        desegregation and, 117
        historical view, 115–18
        intermediate units and, 144
        legal action, 115–17
        natural community approach, 121
        population changes and, 120

    rural areas, 119
    urban areas, 119–20, 121
    socioeconomic factors, 120–21
        wealth differentials, 386–87
    structure/function of, 106–8
School Efficiency Series, 279
School facilities, state regulations, 93–94
School Lunch Act, 331
School management, historical view, 10
Schools, use of term, 9
Schools of emphasis, 163, 174
School term, state regulation, 92
Science, influence on education, 410–11
Scientific management
    administration, 282
    influence on superintendency, 243–44
Scott, W. Richard, 283
Segregation, 159. *See also* Desegregation
Select Committee on Education, 2
Senior High School Principalship, 272
Separate agency model of state governance, 90
Serrano v. *Priest*, 82, 196–97, 198
Servicemen's Readjustment Act of 1944, 50
Settlement plan, St. Louis, desegregation, 163
Sex discrimination, law against (Title IX), 58–59,
        367–69
Shanker, Albert, 30, 323
Shannon, Thomas A., 187
Siegel, Peggy M., 82
Silberman, Charles, 443
Simon, Herbert A., 246, 258
Single-parent families, 25
Sisson, Edward O., 412
Sizer, Theodore R., 412
Smith-Hughes Act of 1917, 46, 47
Smith, Mortimer, 340
Social class, academic success and, 29
Social problems
    educational purpose and, 16–17
    support systems, 32
Society for the Propagation of the Gospel in
        Foreign Parts, 77
Socioeconomic trends, 23–39
    family structure, changes, 25–27
    future and, 37–39
    implications for schools, 30–36
    minority populations, 23–25
    student characteristics, 27–30

Socioeconomic trends, *continued*
  distribution, 28
  numbers, 27
  socioeconomic composition, 29–30
Something to Steer By, 248
Sonedecker, John, 251
Southeast Alternatives Program, 444
Southern Christian Leadership Conference, 357
Sowell, Thomas, 156
Spears, Harold, 253, 412
Special education, use of term, 59
Special interest groups. *See* Interest groups
Specialists, administrative staff, 291–92
Special service personnel, 284
Spencer, Herbert, 410
Sroufe, Gerald E., 58, 88
Staff of school, superintendent's influence on, 257–58
Stare decisis, 185
State court system, 182–85
  educational issues and, 183–84
  judges, selection of, 161
  procedures, 183
  set-up of, 182–83
State finance reform, 399–401
State government and schools
  accountability in education, 82–83
  boards of education, 80–81, 87
  chief state school officers, 80
  controls, types of, 99–101
  decision-making areas
    certification of personnel, 93
    funds, 94–95
    instructional programs, 91–93
    nonpublic schools, 95
    school facilities, 93–94
  delegation to local agencies, 89–90
  departments of education, 88–89, 96–99
  educational coalitions, decline of, 84
  executive influence, 86–89
  finance, 81–82, 84
  future view, 101–2
  growth of role, 83–85
  historical view, 76–81
  legislatures
    committees, 86
    oversight function, 86, 100
    role of, 85–86
  models for governance of education, 90–91

state as federal proxy, 101
  teacher power, 83
State organizations, teachers, 310–12
Stinnett, T. M., 93
Strategic planning by superintendent of schools, 261
Structuralism, 246
Stuart v. *School District No. 1 of Village of Kalamazoo*, 12, 238
Student characteristics, 27–30
Student Descriptive Questionnaire (SDQ), 414
Studies in School Administration, 248
Sugarman, Stephen D., 196, 404, 449
Superintendents of schools
  characteristics of, 241–43
  historical view, 237–38
  influence of
    on board of education, 255–57
    on larger community, 260
    on local community, 259–60
    on school staff, 257–58
  influences on position
    bureaucracy, 245–46
    human relations movement, 244–45
    open systems, 246–47
    scientific management, 243–44
  legal definition and status, 239–41
  power, superintendent versus subordinate hierarchy, 291
  professional development, 247–50
    preparation programs, 248–49
    superintendent as career, 249–50
  recommendations for, 261–64
    fewer superintendents, 261–62
    improved preparation, 263
    improved role definition, 263–64
    selection procedures, 262
  role of
    administrative role, 253–54
    in larger environment, 254–55
    organization role, 250–51
    political role, 255
    range of activities, 251–52
  use of term, 236
Supervising principal, 239
Supervisory unions, 133–34
Supreme Court, 179–82
  judges, appointments, 181–82
  major work of, 180

Survey of Public Education in the Nation's Big City School Districts, 216
Swann et al. v. *Charlotte-Mecklenburg Board of Education et al.*, 14, 161, 192–93
Swett, John, 299
System, in open system perspective, 5

Tasks of schools, issue of, 15–16
Taxes and schools
  historical view, 10
  issues related to, 17–18
  legal milestones, 11–12
Tax limitation movement, 401
Taylor, Frederick W., 243
Taylor, Harold, 337
Teacher preparation, 301–2
  criticism of, 421–22
  federal role, 70
  in-service programs, 423
  requirements, 421
Teachers
  career ladders, 319
  certification, 299–300
  characteristics of, 301–3
  compensation issue, 303, 319–20
  competency issue, 318–19, 321, 322
  control and, 283–84
  empowerment of, 174
  enrollment effects, 297–98
  future view, 324–25
  historical view, 298–99
  influence in school system, 317–18
  informal organization, 316–17
  minority teachers, decline of, 322–23
  professional criteria, 300–301
  professionalism, 283–84
  professional status, enhancement of, 321
  recommendations, 323–24
  salaries and supplemental earnings, 302
  socioeconomic preferences, 29
  statistical information, 4
  teacher empowerment, 320
Teachers organizations
  collective bargaining, 305, 315–16
  influence of, 83, 86
  local organizations, 312–13
  mergers of, 308–10
  national organizations, 303–10

  political activism, 305, 313–15, 318
  professional practices boards, 83
  state organizations, 310–12
Technical services, state, 99
Technological growth, intermediate units and, 143, 151
Tennessee Education Association (TEA), 2
Tenth Amendment, 42
Testing programs, impact on secondary schools, 415–17
Textbooks
  controversy related to, 354–55
  state regulation, 92
Thurston, Lee M., 77
Time for Results: The Governors' 1991 Report on Education, 166, 285
Title I programs, 344, 346
Title IX, 58–59
To Live on This Earth: American Indian Education, 362
Town commission, 134
Town districts, 124
Toy, Henry, Jr., 336
Truman, Harry S., 337
Tuition tax credit, nonpublic schools, 199, 441, 450
Tuttle, Edward M., 333, 334
Tyack, David B., 264
Tyler, Ralph W., 56, 444

Underwood, Kenneth, 219
Unified school districts, 123
United Federation of Teachers, 305, 307
University Council of Educational Administration, 248, 249
Updegraff, Harlan, 400
Urban areas
  intermediate units, role of, 150
  problems of, 145
  school district reorganization, 119–20, 121
Urban League, 357, 358
Urban sprawl, 120, 145
Usdan, Michael D., 225
U.S. District Court, 180

Vidich, Arthur J., 220, 221
Vocational education
  as American priority, 16
  early legislation, 47–48

Vocational Education Act of 1963, 53
Vocational Rehabilitation Act of 1943, 50
Vouchers, 167, 449–50

Wagoner, Jennings L., Jr., 248
Ward v. *Scott*, 89
Warren, Earl, 182
Washington, George, 77
Waterman, Robert H., Jr., 282
Weber, Max, 245–46
Weick, Karl E., 6, 247, 258
Weingartner, Charles, 443
White, Alpheus L., 217
Wiley, Calvin H., 78
Wilken, William H., 400
William T. Grant Foundation Commission on
    Work, Family, and Citizenship, 448
Willis, Benjamin, 253
Willower, Donald J., 253
Wirt, Frederick M., 190

Wirtz, Willard, 447
Wise, Arthur E., 196, 450
Wolcott, Harry F., 273–74
Women
    American Association of University Women,
        373–74
    career options, 322, 369–70
    feminist groups, 367–75
    in teacher career, 306, 322
    League of Women Voters, 371–72, 373
    projects on women in education, 370
    role changes, 26–27
    school board membership, 216–17
    superintendent of schools, 242–43

Yale University, 408
Yankelovich, Daniel, 228

Zeigler, L. Harmon, 218, 222–23, 256, 332
Zorach v. *Clauson*, 21